SUPERCHARGED

C GRAPHICS

A Programmer's Source Code Toolbox

Lee Adams

About the Cover

The images on the front cover were created using the program listings from the book. No special computer equipment or camera equipment was used. Each display was photographed with Kodak Ektachrome 100 Daylight color slide film using a standard 35mm camera with 1/4 second exposure at f2.8. The monitor was an IBM Enhanced Color Display. The programs were running in the 640 × 350 × 16-color mode on an IBM PC equipped with a third-party EGA graphics adapter. The program listings in the book will run on VGA, EGA, MCGA, CGA, and Hercules adapters.

Notice

Lee Adams is a trademark of Lee Adams

FIRST EDITION
FIRST PRINTING

Library of Congress Cataloging in Publication Data

Adams, Lee.
   Supercharged C graphics \ a programmer's source code toolbook / by Lee Adams.
     p. cm.
   ISBN 0-8306-9289-4 :   ISBN 0-8306-3289-1 (pbk.) :
   1. Computer graphics. 2. C (Computer program language)
I. Title.
T385.A334 1990   89-29131
006.6'6—dc20   CIP

TAB BOOKS offers software for sale. For information and a catalog, please contact TAB Software Department, Blue Ridge Summit, PA 17294-0850.

Questions regarding the content of this book should be addressed to:

     Reader Inquiry Branch
     TAB BOOKS
     Blue Ridge Summit, PA 17294-0214

Acquisitions Editor: Ron Powers
Technical Editor: David Harter
Production: Katherine Brown

Contents

_____ PART ONE _____
The Programming Environment

_____ **PART TWO** _____

2D Software Skills

_____ **PART THREE** _____

3D Software Skills

APPENDICES

Acknowledgments

Thanks again to Ron Powers for recognizing a good thing when he saw it and for having the courage to give a new author a chance to prove himself—six books ago.

Thanks to Stephen Moore for gracefully enduring repeated delays during the research and the preparation of the manuscript—while still having the foresight to negotiate future manuscripts.

And a special thanks to my partner in this great game of life, Victoria, for always being there when I needed her, and for discretely keeping out of my way when I didn't. Other men should be so fortunate.

Appreciation is extended to Quadram Corporation for providing a QuadVGA Spectra graphics adapter for my use during preparation of the program listings.

Thanks is also due to Hercules Computer Technology, Inc. for providing a Hercules VGA for testing and evaluation.

Kurta Corporation generously provided an IS/ONE digitizing tablet, complete with corded four-button cursor and corded pen.

WACOM Co., Ltd. kindly provided an SD-420L digitizing tablet, complete with cordless four-button cursor and cordless, pressure-sensitive pen.

GTCO Corporation provided their GT Mouse and mouse driver software for my use.

Media Cybernetics, Inc. graciously provided the Microsoft C version of their fine graphics toolkit, HALO 88 1.00.04.

Metagraphics Software Corporation kindly provided the Microsoft C version of their graphics toolkit, MetaWINDOW 3.4b, in addition to QuickWINDOW/C 3.4b and TurboWINDOW/C 3.4b.

Lattice, Incorporated generously provided versions 3.4 and 6.0 of their superb compiler, Lattice C, which includes the versatile GFX graphics library.

South Mountain Software Inc. provided versions 2.0 and 3.0 of their graphics toolkit, Essential Graphics.

Custom Real-Time Software, Inc. generously provided a copy of their program performance analyzing tool, STOPWATCH.

Paradigm Systems Incorporated provided the QuickC and Turbo C versions of their fine performance analyzer, INSIDE!.

Software Security Inc. provided an evaluation unit of their hardware-based copy-protection unit, The Activator.

Rainbow Technologies provided evaluation units of their hardware-based copy-protection products, SentinelPro and SentinelShell.

Notices

How to Get the Most from This Book

This book provides you with many of the programming skills you need to write high-performance, interactive 2D and 3D graphics programs on your IBM-compatible personal computer. The graphics features you have admired in commercial software products are now within your grasp as a C programmer using the powerful, interactive compilers made popular by Microsoft and Borland: QuickC and Turbo C.

This book contains over 7,000 lines of invaluable source code, supported by explanatory illustrations and easy-to-follow text. The book follows the same here-is-how-it-is-done approach established by previous texts in Windcrest's high-performance graphics series. You will learn many of the legendary techniques used by master programmers. Using the ready-to-run program listings, you will see how to manage and control the keyboard, mouse, tablet, and disk. You will learn how your programs can automatically detect and support the highest graphics available on any IBM-compatible system, including VGA, EGA, MCGA, CGA, and Hercules graphics. You will discover how to use an interactive menu system to act as a front end for any graphics program you write. And—best of all—you get complete C source code for two major programs: a full-color paint/draw program and a full-featured 3D CAD modeling and shading program. The book's clear writing style ensures that you understand all the concepts involved in making your programs full-featured and powerful, so they can compete successfully in the worldwide software marketplace.

WHO SHOULD USE THE BOOK?

If you use a personal computer and you are interested in computer graphics, then you will want to read this book. If you are new to C programming, the challenging and rewarding world of computer-generated graphics is waiting for you to discover. If you are a corporate programmer creating in-house software programs, or a professional developer creating applications for the retail market, the book will provide information that can make your software more efficient, effective, and competitive. If you are an experienced amateur programmer interested in writing shareware, freeware, or even commercial software, this book will show you some high-performance graphics techniques that you might have thought impossible with an ordinary personal computer.

Simply stated, this book is an easy-to-read, advanced text that starts where other graphics texts stop. It provides the information you need to speed you on your way to becoming a world-class graphics programmer—and it is suitable for beginner, intermediate, and advanced programmers.

ABOUT THE BOOK

This book has been designed as a learning tool. Throughout the production process—from my manuscript, to the editor's revisions, to the art director's layout, and through the finished printing—each member of the production team was keenly aware of the book's fundamental purpose: to teach. The book you now hold in your hands reflects that unshakable determination.

Although C has been called a write-only language, the program listings in this book are surprisingly easy to read, easy to understand, and easy to experiment with. The source code is optimized for clarity—ready for you to optimize for performance.

If you want to turn back corners of pages which interest you so you can quickly find them again, go right ahead. You might find it helpful to highlight portions of the text with a marker pen. Writing your own insights and observations into the margins can be helpful, too.

SPECIAL FEATURES OF THE BOOK

The book is organized in an easy-to-follow format. Important fundamentals introduced early in the text become the foundation and cornerstones for the more advanced programs that appear later in the text. Yet, unlike other texts, this book does not force any particular style of learning upon you—each chapter and demonstration program has been carefully designed as an independent packet of information. This means you can arbitrarily jump from topic to topic in the book if you prefer to learn that way. It also means that if you prefer to study the material in the order in which it is presented, you will benefit from the easily absorbed modules of information.

The book lays flat. This is an important feature if you are typing in the program listings or perhaps adding a routine you have found in the book to one of your own original programs.

Each program listing is presented in a stand-alone form. You will appreciate this approach if you have struggled through other C books whose programs make reference to separate pieces of code scattered throughout the book. Each plug'n'play program is ready to run. Simply load it in and the program is ready to compile in the integrated programming environment of Microsoft QuickC and Borland Turbo C on your IBM PC, XT, AT, PS/2 or compatible—no matter whether you are using a VGA, EGA, MCGA, CGA, or Hercules graphics adapter.

The innovative use of the #if, #elif, and #endif preprocessor directives in each demonstration program ensures that the source code is fully compatible with both QuickC and Turbo C, in spite of the syntax differences between the two compilers. (See Chapter 1 for discussion of how this approach can benefit your own software projects.)

A special autodetect module in each program listing enables the demonstration program to adapt itself at start-up to produce the best graphics possible on your particular system—or, more important, on the end user's system. If a VGA is present, the 640x480x16-color mode is displayed. If an EGA and enhanced monitor are present, the 640x350x16-color mode is used. If an EGA and standard monitor are found, the 640x200x16-color mode is activated. If an MCGA is present, the 640x480x2-color mode is used. If a CGA is found, the 640x200x2-color mode is set up. If a Hercules Graphics Card, Hercules Graphics Card Plus, or Hercules Incolor are present, the 720x348x2-color mode is invoked.

⸺ REMINDER ⸺

In today's competitive software marketplace, your graphics programs must be able to recognize and support a wide range of incompatible graphics adapters. The day is long gone when a programmer could simply support the lowest common denominator, the CGA. All five major graphics standards must be supported: VGA, EGA, MCGA, CGA, and Hercules.

In this book, each major demonstration program uses a graphics syntax that is graphics library independent. This means that both QuickC's and Turbo C's built-in graphics libraries can be seamlessly used to run the programs without any changes to the source code, in spite of incompatibilities between the two libraries. It also means that it is a straightforward task to quickly adapt the programs to work with your favorite third-party graphics toolkit, like MetaWIN-DOW, QuickWINDOW/C, TurboWINDOW/C, HALO 88, Essential Graphics, or even Lattice C's GFX graphics.

In addition to keyboard input, many of the program listings also accept input from any Microsoft-compatible mouse or any Kurta-compatible digitizing tablet. Accepting input from coordinate devices like a mouse or tablet can give your original graphics programs a professional touch.

┌─────────────────── **WHERE TO LOOK** ───────────────────┐

    See Appendix B for more information about converting to third-party graphics libraries.

└──┘

HOW THE BOOK IS ORGANIZED

The material in this book is organized into three topical sections for your ready reference.

PART ONE introduces you to the graphics programming environment.

Chapter 1 explains how to get the most from the prototyping capabilities of QuickC and Turbo C, including how to organize your programming efforts to yield maximum results with minimum downtime.

Chapter 2 shows you how to use the powerful command-line options of QuickC and Turbo C to fine-tune your finished program. Chapter 3 discusses keyboard management techniques, including how to detect professional key-strokes such as Ctrl+ combinations, the function keys, and others. A demonstration program provides keyboard routines that can be plugged into any of your own programs.

Chapter 4 introduces powerful techniques for detecting and controlling a mouse or tablet on a VGA, EGA, MCGA, CGA, or Hercules screen. A powerful program listing demonstrates the portable low-level routines in action.

Chapter 5 provides a thorough discussion of the different image file formats in use today, as well as a demonstration program listing that can save any VGA, EGA, MCGA, CGA, or Hercules image to disk—and then retrieve and display the image from disk.

Chapter 6 deals with the front end: the menu system that gives your end-user access to the core functions in your program. Graphics routines that are both hardware-independent and library-independent are introduced and explained. A program listing for a shell menu system that can be readily adapted for any interactive graphics program is provided. Chapter 6 also introduces the powerful technique of multi-module C programming, paving the way for you to master large, complex, commercial-quality software projects.

PART TWO presents the programming skills needed to write interactive 2D graphics software such as paint programs, draw programs, illustration programs, and drafting programs.

Chapter 7 discusses the many features found in today's programs. You can use this information to make your own programs more competitive in the world software marketplace. In addition, two program listings show you how to use the 256-color color modes and how to use exciting bitmapped fonts and vector fonts ·to display text in any graphics mode.

Chapter 8 provides the full source code for Your Microcomputer SketchPad™, a powerful, full-color paint program for VGA, EGA, MCGA, CGA, and Hercules graphics. The versatile routines that you'll find in this full-length program will most likely become useful additions to your own programming toolkit.

Chapter 9 is the User's Guide for the paint program, including a section on sample sessions and tutorial. You will see first-hand how to create realistic illustrations in black and white or color, and how to create special effects like color transparency.

Chapter 10 is a Programmer's Reference. It is here where you learn how the demonstration program works its magic. Suggested enhancements are described and known bugs and workarounds are discussed.

PART THREE provides you with the programming skills you need to write competitive 3D graphics programs, including those that manipulate fully-shaded 3D models with hidden surfaces removed.

Chapter 11 describes the impressive features of the powerful 3D CAD programs in today's marketplace. Fundamental concepts of 3D programming are introduced.

Chapter 12 takes a careful look at the exciting concepts of 3D models, touching upon algorithms for hidden surface removal, computer-controlled shading, moving the light source, rotating a 3D model inside a 3D world environment, and more.

Chapter 13 provides the full source code for Your Microcomputer 3D CAD Designer™, a full-length modeling and shading program for VGA, EGA, MCGA, CGA, and Hercules graphics. The powerful routines in this program expose many of the heretofore top-secret algorithms used in many commercial 3D CAD software packages.

Chapter 14 is the User's Guide for Your Microcomputer 3D CAD Designer. The Guide shows you how to use the program to create 3D models from cubes and cylinders. A section of sample sessions provides hands-on experience with a typical 3D industrial widget, a typical 3D business chart, and some 3D text.

Chapter 15 is a Programmer's Reference for the 3D CAD program listing. A step-by-step, here-is-how-it-works analysis gives you a solid understanding of vital routines and algorithms that you can adapt for your own programs. Suggested program enhancements and known bugs are thoroughly discussed.

REMINDER

Don't overlook the useful information in the appendices of the book.

The appendices provide important background material for your graphics programming endeavors. If you are a raw beginner to C programming, you will appreciate Appendix A, which describes in a no-nonsense fashion how to get the demonstration programs up and running. If you are using a third-party graphics library, Appendix B shows you how to quickly adapt the major demonstration programs for MetaWINDOW, HALO 88, Essential Graphics, and Latice C's GFX graphics. Appendix C provides guidance on graceful recovery from runtime errors like open disk drive doors. Appendix D discusses the important role that third-party performance analyzer software can play in your programming project. Appendix E provides some important insights into professional copy protection techniques for your original C graphics programs. An extensive glossary explains the often cryptic parlance used by programmers, and a useful index can help you quickly find a particular topic in the main body of the book.

WHAT YOU NEED TO USE THE BOOK

You likely already have everything you need to get the most out of this book.

Software Requirements

If you have Microsoft QuickC 2.00 or newer, or Borland Turbo C 2.0 or newer, or Microsoft C 5.10 or newer, then you have everything you need. See FIG. 1. Both QuickC and Turbo C have powerful and versatile built-in graphics libraries. If you are still using QuickC 1.00, now is a good time to upgrade to a newer version because version 1.00 does not support different memory models, or 43-line text in the 640x350x16-color mode, or fonts, or the Hercules graphics adapters. If you are still using Turbo C 1.5, now is a good time to upgrade to a newer version to take advantage of undocumented bug fixes.

___ CAUTION ___

Some important changes have been made to the new versions of QuickC and Turbo C. Prudent programmers like to keep current.

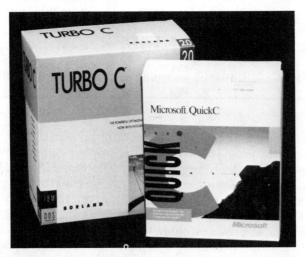

Fig. 1. Everything you need to create world-class, professional-caliber graphics programs can be found in these two cartons. Which one you use is a matter of personal preference and programming style.

You can also use any ANSI-compatible C compiler, although you might need to make a few minor adjustments to the source code to accommodate features unique to your compiler.

In addition, you can use a third-party graphics library like MetaWINDOW, HALO 88, Essential Graphics, or Lattice C's GFX. See Appendix B if you are adopting this approach.

Hardware Requirements

If you have access to an IBM PC, XT, AT, PS/2 or strict compatible, then you have the hardware you need. The program listings support any IBM-compatible VGA, EGA, MCGA, CGA, and Hercules graphics adapters.

Although it is optional, if you have a Microsoft-compatible mouse, you can explore the mouse routines in many of the demonstration programs. Likewise, if you have a Kurta-compatible digitizing tablet, or any tablet with a mouse emulation mode, you can use the tablet with the programs.

If you are using QuickC, a fixed disk is strongly recommended, although Microsoft claims the compiler will run on a two-floppy disk system. If you are using Turbo C, either a fixed disk system or a floppy disk system is workable.

The Companion Disk

The companion disks to this book contain the high-energy source code for all the demonstration programs in the book. Nothing is missing. The code is compatible with both QuickC and Turbo C. Using the companion disks, you can begin immediately to dig into the high-performance graphics discussed in the text. There is no need to spend your time keying in the program listings when the keyboard work has been done for you. Instead, you can concentrate on learning.

To get the most out of the companion disks, set the tab value to 2 on your QuickC or Turbo C editor, and be sure to name the approriate .MAK or .PRJ file for the multi-module program files. (See Chapter 2 for more information about using .MAK and .PRJ files with QuickC and Turbo C.)

The disks are not copy-protected and you have the royalty-free right to use and distribute the routines in your own programs, as described in the License Agreement. You get over 7,000 lines of valuable source code. Refer to the order coupon at the back of the book.

COMPATIBILITY AND INTEGRITY OF THE DEMO PROGRAMS

The demonstration programs in this book were created on an IBM PC using IBM DOS 3.20, QuickC 2.00, Turbo C 2.0, an NEC MultiSync monitor, and a Quadram QuadVGA Spectra graphics adapter. Each program was further tested on a Samsung XT clone using a QuadEGA+ graphics adapter and an IBM Enhanced Color Display.

A Microsoft Mouse and a GT Mouse were used to test the mouse routines. A Kurta IS/ONE digitizing tablet and four-button cursor were also used to test the programs.

The graphics print which accompanies each program listing was produced on a Hewlett Packard Laser Jet series II printer by using the Pizazz™ screen print program.

Although each program was tested in VGA, EGA, MCGA, CGA, and Hercules modes, a small number of anomolies persist in the programs, primarily due to ethereal incompatibilities between specific hardware and software. You might experience occasional problems when using programs created with Turbo C running on a Hercules clone, and when using mouse programs created with either Turbo C or QuickC running on a Hercules screen.

FACT

As an aspiring C graphics programmer, you must accept the unfortunate fact that hardware and software do not always work as expected, or as described in the documentation. The personal ability to adapt to unexpected and changing conditions is a valuable programming skill.

Although this book supports six different graphics modes and two different C compilers, the book does not—indeed, it cannot—support bugs in the QuickC and Turbo C compilers, nor does it support workalike hardware that strays from the IBM standard. The source code in the book occasionally provides a workaround solution to common problems, however. These workarounds are described where appropriate in the text.

IF YOU INTEND TO ADAPT MATERIAL FROM THIS BOOK

If you have aspirations of writing professional-quality software, you are reading the right book, and you are not alone in your programming dreams. Other readers have taken material from previous books by the author and they have used that information to help write successful—often profitable—software. Commercial software shops and corporate programming departments often maintain in-house libraries that contain copies of the author's books.

The book you are holding will give you a headstart, but it is important that you read the following paragraphs and the Limited Warranty if you intend to adapt any material from this book for your own purposes, or if you intend to use the information or program listings to write commercial software, corporate software, shareware, or freeware.

License Agreement

As purchaser of this book, you are granted a non-exclusive royalty-free license to reproduce and distribute the program routines, whether found in the book or on the companion disks, in executable form as part of your software product, subject to any trademark or patent rights of others, and subject to the Limited Warranty described here. The programs in the book and on the companion disks are Copyright 1990 Lee Adams. All other rights are reserved.

My best efforts have been used to prepare the information and program listings contained in the book. These efforts include research, development, and testing of the information and the program listings to determine their effectiveness and accuracy. In spite of this care, however, I cannot make any guarantees that the information and program listings will solve your specific programming needs.

You will find many powerful techniques in this book, but you should thoroughly test the information and program listings before you rely upon their accuracy. I make no express or implied warranty and will not be liable for incidental or consequential damages arising from use of the information and program listings. I am not rendering legal, accounting, marketing, or management counselling service. If legal advice or other expert assistance is required, you should acquire the services of a professional. In particular, it is important that you understand that you are responsible for ensuring that your use or adaptation of the materials or programs in the book or on the companion disk does not infringe upon any copyright, patent, or trademark rights of others.

Limited Warranty

The programs contained in this book and on the companion disks are provided "as is" without warranty of any kind, either express or implied, including, but not limited to, the implied warranties of merchantability and fitness for a particular purpose. The entire risk related to the quality and performance of the programs is on you. In the event there is any defect, you assume the entire cost of all necessary servicing, repair, or correction. Some states do not allow the exclusion of implied warranties, so the above exclusion might not apply to you. This warranty gives you specific legal rights and you might also have other rights which vary from state to state.

I do not warrant that the functions contained in the programs will meet your requirements or that the operation of the programs will be uninterrupted or error-free.

In no event will I be liable to you for any damages (including any lost profits, savings, or other incidental or consequential damages arising out of the use of or inability to use such programs even if the author has been advised of the possibility of such damages) or for any claim by any other party. Some states do not allow the limitation or exclusion of liability for incidental or consequential damages so the above limitation or exclusion might not apply to you.

If you purchase the companion disks, the publisher warrants the disks on which the programs are furnished to be free from defects in the materials and workmanship under normal use for a period of thirty (30) days from the date of delivery to you as evidenced by a copy of your receipt, and the entire liability of the publisher and your exclusive remedy shall be replacement of any disk which does not meet the Limited Warranty and which is returned to the publisher.

This agreement constitutes the complete and exclusive statement of the terms of the agreement between you and the author. It supersedes and replaces any previous written or oral agreements and communications relating to the programs. No oral or written information or advice given by me, my dealers, distributors, agents, or employees create any warranty or in any way increase the scope of the warranty provided in this agreement, and you may not rely on any such information or advice.

Questions concerning this license may be directed to TAB BOOKS, Blue Ridge Summit, PA, USA 17294-0850.

COMMENTS AND DISCUSSION

Your comments—whether complimentary or critical—are valued by the author and the publisher. If you enjoy this book, please tell your associates, coworkers, and friends. If you find fault—or even worse, bugs—then please feel welcome to write.

Correspondence concerning the contents of the book may be directed to the author in care of TAB BOOKS, Reader Inquiry Branch, Blue Ridge Summit, PA, USA 17294-0214. Please allow three weeks for your correspondence to reach the author. Include your area code and telephone number if you wish a spoken reply.

ADDITIONAL MATERIAL

If you enjoy the material in this book, further information can be found in other books in Windcrest's high-performance graphics series, available wherever fine computer books are sold, or order direct from Windcrest Books. See the back of the book for a complete listing.

About the Illustrations in the Book

The 52-line drawings in the book were created by the author using the two major interactive graphics programs whose complete source code appears in this text. The images were printed on a standard dot matrix printer using a third-party graphics print utility.

List of Programs

The program listings in this book are presented in their entirety, with nothing missing. Improving upon the format made popular by other books in the Windcrest graphics programming series, each program in *Supercharged C Graphics* is ready to type in and run on your VGA, EGA, MCGA, CGA, and Hercules graphics adapter. In addition, each program listing uses #if and #elif directives to ensure that you can use your favorite C compiler—either Microsoft QuickC or Borland Turbo C—to compile and link the program. Even the graphics instructions have been made library-independent to support the built-in graphics syntax of both QuickC and Turbo C. If you are using a third-party graphics toolkit, see Appendix B for easy conversion guidelines for MetaWINDOW, HALO, Essential Graphics, and Lattice C's GFX graphics.

DETECT.C	autodetect of graphics hardware at start-up
MEMORY.C	determine amount of free RAM at runtime
KEYBOARD.C	capture normal and special keystrokes at runtime
MOUSEMGR.C	detect and control a mouse or mouse-compatible tablet
IMAGES.C	save a VGA, EGA, MCGA, CGA, Hercules image to disk
MENUMGR1.C	manage a pull-down menu system
MENUMGR2.C	module 2 for the pull-down menu system manager
HUES.C*	select and display 256 simultaneous colors
FONTS.C	display bitmapped fonts and vector (stroked) fonts
SKETCH1.C	Your Microcomputer SketchPad™, module 1
SKETCH2.C	Your Microcomputer SketchPad, module 2
SKETCH3.C	Your Microcomputer SketchPad, module 3
DESIGN1.C	Your Microcomputer 3D CAD Designer™, module 1
DESIGN2.C	Your Microcomputer 3D CAD Designer, module 2
DESIGN3.C	Your Microcomputer 3D CAD Designer, module 3

---

* HUES.C requires QuickC and a VGA or MCGA graphics adapter. Turbo C 2.0 does not support the 320x200x256-colon mode.

Part One

The Programming Environment

1

Getting Started:
Prototyping With QuickC and Turbo C

THE WORLD is full of good ideas. As any entrepreneur will tell you, good ideas are a dime a dozen. In fact, there is simply no shortage of exciting ideas.

What is in short supply, however, is the ability to develop an idea into a project and then bring that project to completion. In programming jargon, that means serious software development.

SERIOUS SOFTWARE DEVELOPMENT

Serious software development means bringing your ideas to completion in the form of a software product—and if you are interested in writing marketable graphics programs in C, you are in the right place at the right time. There are three important factors working in your favor.

First, the programming tools that you need to bring a project to completion have never been more accessible and available. Second, the hardware needed to display graphics images has never been more widely installed on standard personal computers; and, third, the marketing potential for new graphics software—whether retail, corporate, shareware, or otherwise—has never been more exciting . . . and the market is still growing.

These three factors, combined with the strong trend towards more graphics in personal computer applications, translate into increased opportunities for graphics programmers who use C.

3

THE TREND TOWARDS GRAPHICS

The long-term trend in computer application programs is clearly towards increased use of graphics. Because humans tend to think in terms of images—and not in terms of text—a *graphical user interface* (GUI) makes it easier for the end-user to interact with the operating system and with the application program, especially when the core functions of the program are graphics-oriented.

_____ **FACT** _____

The long-term trend in computer programs is towards increased use of graphics.

Consider, for example, three specialized applications: paint/draw programs, 2D CADD drafting programs, and 3D CAD modeling/rendering programs.

The GUI and the drawing capabilities of paint programs make it easier for the end-user to create illustrations for use in newsletters, manuals, reports, sales literature, and business presentation graphics. The GUI and the drafting capabilities of CADD programs make it easier for the end-user to plan, develop, and organize a wide range of projects. The GUI and the modeling capabilities of 3D CAD programs make it easier for the end-user to conceptualize, design, and manufacture new products.

The graphics trend in these specialized applications—and also general applications like operating systems, word processing programs, spreadsheet programs, and others—is well under way and is endorsed by major hardware manufacturers and software developers.

NEW OPPORTUNITIES
FOR PROGRAMMERS

What this trend towards graphics means is increased opportunities for programmers, especially C programmers. The powerful, easy-to-use, interactive features of the QuickC and Turbo C compilers make those opportunities immediately available to you, no matter whether you work as a corporate programmer, or if you tinker on your personal computer at home.

QuickC and Turbo C provide a rapid prototyping environment. *Prototyping* means the development and testing of ideas in a programming environment. In graphics programming this means the ability to quickly edit and run a program over and over again during development. It is this immediate interactive feedback during your programming session that can supercharge your work by allowing you to improve your project incrementally. By continually running and changing your program, you can produce a finished product that would have been impossible to create on the first attempt.

A STRATEGY
FOR PROGRAM DEVELOPMENT

Both QuickC and Turbo C provide a programming environment that fits seamlessly into an overall strategy for efficient and productive program development.

When using QuickC on a 640K computer, you have approximately 275K bytes of memory free for actual program development. When using Turbo C with a 640K computer, about 145K bytes are free (see FIG. 1-1). Because all of this free memory can be used by any executable (EXE) program running under the control of QuickC or Turbo C, you can develop and test large programs while enjoying the interactive advantages of the integrated programming environment offered by these two compilers. Even the 64,605 byte limit imposed by Turbo C on your source file is unimportant, because you can easily instruct the compiler to collect a group of source files (modules) together to create the finished EXE program. Provided that the EXE program's runtime requirements do not exceed 145K, it can be executed under the control of the Turbo C editor. QuickC offers the same ability to assemble groups of source files into a single executable program. This practice is called multi-module programming, and it is a vital component of C graphics programming.

A BULLETPROOF 5-STEP PROCESS

A good development strategy for programmers using QuickC or Turbo C fits into a five-step process.

TIP

Increase your productivity by using a five-step strategy for program development with Quick C or Turbo C.

Step One—First, you use QuickC or Turbo C to create and test small, independent programs that provide specific features or functions. The demon-

Fig. 1-1. Comparison of typical memory conditions during a programming session with QuickC or Turbo C. Refer to Chapter 2 for a program listing to determine the amount of free memory in your particular system at runtime.

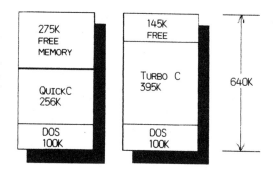

stration program in Chapter 5 is a good example of this approach. The program, IMAGES.C, saves a VGA, EGA, MCGA, CGA, or Hercules full-screen image to disk and then reads the binary file from disk and restores the image to the screen. It is easy to test and debug a program function like image save/load when it is in a stand-alone program—there are no unknown variables to complicate your debugging efforts. The same advantages apply to building and testing other functions.

Step Two—Next, you can combine the core functions from your stand-alone programs into the source code for your master project. This is easy to do because of the powerful editing features provided by both QuickC and Turbo C. You simply load a stand-alone program into the editor, mark the portion of the text which you want to move, copy it into the scratchpad buffer, then load your master source file into the editor and copy the text from the buffer into the appropriate location in the master source file. Because the new section of source code has already been tested and debugged, your only task now is to fit it smoothly into the functions which already exist in the source file. This is sometimes called the black box approach, because you no longer need to concern yourself with how the newly-added functions work—you know they work correctly and you can treat them like a black box where you cannot see the contents.

A CLOSER LOOK: Debugging Techniques

A good C graphics programmer possesses strong debugging skills. The ability to debug a program under development is simply an extension of the same problem-solving skills you used to build the program code in the first place. Like any other skill, you can acquire debugging skills by careful study, practice, and observation. Because of their on-screen visible output, C graphics programs are often easy to debug.

The most important programming habit you can develop is to change only one section of code at a time—and then run the program to exercise that function. If the program produces unexpected on-screen results, you immediately know where to start your debugging efforts: in the section of code you just edited. This one-change/one-run principle is the single most important tool in your bag of debugging tricks.

Rather than rely upon third-party software or contrived debugging aids, you can hone your debugging skills by following a simple, yet powerful, three-step process during program development.

First, check your source code for syntax. Use the compile and link processes of QuickC and Turbo C to catch and correct language syntax errors like spelling, punctuation, and correct usage. The QuickC and Turbo C editors will also flag variable declaration errors for you. Your first goal, after all, is to get your source code to compile and link.

Second, check your program for exception-based errors. Run your program under the control of QuickC or Turbo C and let the built-in error-trapping features of the integrated programming environment catch runtime errors like stack overflow, invalid far pointers, math overflow or underflow, and so on. By systematically exercising every possible function of your program you can discover which portions of your source code have the potential for exception-based runtime errors. You can then use the tips provided in Appendix C to write an error-handler routine to protect against specific conditions during program execution.

It is important that you take the time to thoroughly exercise each function under as many different conditions as you can think of. Be brutal. Test the extreme limits of each function. Push it as far as it will go. Find out where it starts to break down because, if you don't, you can rest assured that your end-user most certainly will.

Third, check the conceptual algorithms used in your program. Run the program and carefully observe the on-screen performance while you rigorously exercise each function of your program. At this stage, you should assume that any erratic behavior is your fault: a programming oversight—simply telling the computer to do the wrong thing. After all, no debugger can tell you to use cosine when you have inadvertently used sine. No debugger can tell you that the reason you are not seeing any graphics on the screen is because you are drawing in the same color as the background color. On rare occasions you will find that the problem resides in some undocumented feature or idiosyncracy of the compiler or graphics library; but if you have used the one-change/one-run principle, you can test for this condition by writing a workaround: code that compensates for a library shortcoming.

Step Three—Now you can incrementally build up the many features and core functions of your program by using the powerful interactive features of QuickC and Turbo C. This means making a few changes to your source code, running the program, then returning to the editor to make corrections or add new features. Be sure to keep a pen and scratchpad handy so you can write down the changes you want to make while you are watching your program run. This systematic approach ensures that you won't forget what you wanted to change when you return to the editor—especially if you have identified five or six changes you want to make.

Building a program in this manner is sometimes called the *white box* approach, because you must be able to tinker with the innards of each new function you write. However, on any occasion where you need to write a substantive, complex, new function, you simply revert to Step One to build and test a stand-alone program, and then copy the tested source code into your master program.

Step Four—As the size of your command program (the EXE file) grows, and as the size of your source file (the C file) grows, you can begin to work with a second or even a third module of source code. Both QuickC and Turbo C offer powerful tools for managing multiple modules of source code. Functions (sometimes called *routines* or *subroutines*) in any module can call functions in any other module, and your variables can be global (visible to all functions in all modules) or local (visible only inside one module), depending on your programming style and on the requirements of your project. The multi-module programming approach forces you to keep your project well-organized and makes it easier to edit one part of your source code without producing unexpected changes in another part. Chapter 6 will introduce you to a two-module program which manages a menu system in the graphics mode.

Step Five—Finally, when you have tested and debugged your program to the point where you are ready to release it for distribution, you can use the powerful optimizing features of the command-line versions of QuickC and Turbo C to produce a lean and mean EXE program. At this stage, if you are really serious, you might even use third-party performance analyzing software to further identify bottlenecks and chokepoints in your program. See Appendix D for more on this.

OVERCOMING THE EDITOR'S MEMORY LIMITATIONS

The five-step programming strategy makes it easy to overcome the 275K QuickC limit and the 145K Turbo C limit that these compilers impose on the size of your master EXE program. Don't be misled into thinking that these limits are a serious problem, however. Even the powerful 3D CAD modeling and rendering program listing provided in Chapter 13 can run under the Turbo C editor. Using QuickC, there are still a whopping 100K bytes free when running the 3D CAD program. Most of the C graphics programs you write will easily fit into the programming environment of QuickC and Turbo C, but it is comforting to know that you can readily create executable programs of 400K or more if you want to.

─────────── **SUGGESTION** ───────────

The five-step programming strategy makes it easy to overcome the memory limitations of the QuickC and Turbo C editors.

By using the algorithm provided in Chapter 2, you can dynamically monitor the size of available RAM at runtime (when your program is actually executing). When memory becomes scarce, you can adopt one of three strategies.

Out of Memory Tactic #1—First, you can turn off the debugging code produced by the compiler. This results in a smaller EXE file, although it means the editor cannot tell you where an error occurs. Use the Debug menu in Turbo C or the Options menu in QuickC to disable the debugging tokens. See Appendix A for more on this.

Out of Memory Tactic #2—Second, you can disable one or more source modules. By only compiling and linking the front-end modules and the module on which you are currently working, you can keep the size of the resulting EXE program small during development. The main advantage of this strategy is that you still have access to the time-saving interactive debugging and error-reporting features provided by the QuickC and Turbo C integrated programming environment. The primary disadvantage is that you must spend time disabling each call to any function which is located inside a module that you are omitting during the compilation and linking of your program.

Out of Memory Tactic #3—Third, you can continue to use QuickC or Turbo C to write your source code, but you will begin to use the command-line version of each compiler to create the EXE program. The advantage is that you free up an additional 265K (QuickC) or 395K (Turbo C) of RAM for your program to run in. The disadvantage is the loss of each compiler's interactive debugging features— but if you have been using the five-step strategy described earlier you should be encountering only simple, easily-repaired bugs.

You can also revert to stand-alone debugging tools like CodeView, but it is my belief that, when you use either QuickC or Turbo C with a well-organized programming plan, you do not need to involve extraneous debugging tools which divert your attention from the task at hand, and which dilute the powerful capabilities of the QuickC and Turbo C editors.

PLANNING AHEAD
AND DEFENSIVE PROGRAMMING

Before you start your programming project, you must plan ahead. You should be sure that your finished program will be marketable. You should make sure that your computer equipment will not let you down. You should ensure that your programming tools are up to the task. You should practice defensive programming, and you should implement a backup plan.

Planning ahead in each of these five areas can save you a lot of grief later in your project.

Make Your Software Marketable

Although there are many marketing factors to be considered (see the next book in the Windcrest series on C graphics), a prime consideration for your graphics project is the graphics modes which you support. Simply stated, the more graphics modes supported by your program, the wider its potential market. Contrary to what you may have read in the popular computer magazines and in other books, it is not an insurmountable task to make your graphics source code compatible with a wide range of different graphics modes and graphics adapters. This feature is called device-independence and it is a powerful marketing tool.

CAUTION

Planning ahead and defensive programming can save you from having to rewrite large sections of code later.

The demonstration programs in this book endorse that important marketing principle by supporting all six major graphics modes which are used on today's personal computers (see FIG. 1-2). Each program uses an auto-detect algorithm to determine which graphics adapter and monitor are present at start-up. Depending upon the results of the algorithm, the program configures itself to support one of six modes. You can add more modes for your own original programs.

ADAPTER	RESOLUTION	COLORS	TEXT	PAGES
VGA	640x480	16	80x60	1
EGA	640x350	16	80x43	2
EGA	640x200	16	80x25	4
MCGA	640x480	2	80x60	1
CGA	640x200	2	80x25	1
HERC	720x348	2	80x25	2

Fig. 1-2. The six graphics modes used by the major demonstration programs in this book.

If a VGA is present, the software executes in the 640x480x16-color graphics mode using 60 rows of 80 alphanumeric characters each. If an EGA and enhanced monitor are present, the software uses the 640x350x16-color graphics mode using 43 rows of 80 alphanumeric characters each. If an EGA and standard monitor are found, the software runs in the 640x200x16-color graphics mode using 25 rows of 80 alphanumeric characters each. If an MCGA is present, the software executes in the 640x480x2-color graphics mode using 60 rows of 80 alphanumeric characters each. If a CGA is found, the software uses the 640x200x2-color graphics mode using 25 rows of 80 alphanumeric characters each. Finally, if a Hercules graphics adapter is present, the software runs in the 720x348x2-color graphics mode using 25 rows of 80 alphanumeric characters each.

Although the bitmaps for each of these modes occupies a different location in the 256K bytes of potential display memory on IBM-compatible personal computers (see FIG. 1-3), the powerful graphics libraries of QuickC and Turbo C take care of the low-level graphics calls. Your task is simply to ensure that the correct parameters are provided to the QuickC and Turbo C graphics routines.

You must also be familiar with the location and length of each bitmap in order to write C code that moves graphics pages or saves images to disk. The table in FIG. 1-4 summarizes these details. A more detailed discussion of graphics adapter idiosyncracies, bitplanes, and bitmaps is provided in Chapter 5.

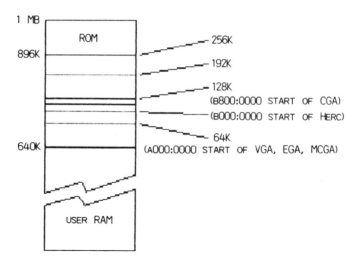

Fig. 1-3. Memory map of 256K display memory which begins where user-RAM ends at 640K.

RELATED MATERIAL

Important information about graphics adapters may also be found in one of the author's previous books, High-Performance CAD Graphics In C, Windcrest book #3059, ISBN 0-8306-9359-9, published March 1989, available direct from the publisher or order through your favorite bookstore.

The page-copying algorithm provided in this book which supports the Undo function found in many graphics programs takes into account the different

ADAPTER	MODE	DISPLAYED BITMAP	HIDDEN BITMAP	BITMAP LENGTH	BITPLANES
VGA	640x480x16	A000:0000	RAM	38400 x 4	4
EGA	640x350x16	A000:0000	A800:0000	28000 x 4	4
EGA	640x200x16	A000:0000	A400:0000	16000 x 4	4
MCGA	640x480x2	A000:0000	RAM	38400 x 1	1
CGA	640x200x2	B800:0000	RAM	16384 x 1	1
HERC	720x348x2	B000:0000	B800:0000	32406 x 1	1

Fig. 1-4. Bitmap information for the major IBM-compatible graphics modes.

requirements of the VGA, EGA, MCGA, CGA, and Hercules graphics adapters. Likewise, the image save/load functions found in the program listings in Chapters 5, 8, and 13 provide you with ready-to-use tools for managing different graphics modes.

Pretest Your Hardware

Many programmers make the mistake of assuming that their hardware adheres unflinchingly to the IBM standard. This is a serious oversight. By way of example, a mouse tested by this author during development of the demonstration programs did not display its cursor correctly in the 640x200x16-color mode of the EGA. An unwary C graphics programmer could easily fritter away days—perhaps weeks trying to track down a suspected programming error, when in fact the real culprit was the hardware.

Before you start to write your master program, use the stand-alone programs that you are developing to exercise every graphics mode and every hardware peripheral. See which modes are supported on your hardware, and make arrangements to get access to another computer system for the purpose of testing your programs in modes not available on your system.

Be particularly wary of graphics adapters. It is essential that you regularly test your project on different graphics cards. It is an unpleasant fact of life that not all computer hardware performs according to published specifications—and not all computer hardware is explicitly supported by the QuickC and Turbo C graphics libraries. See Appendix B for a discussion of enhanced graphics modes and graphics adapters supported by some third-party graphics libraries.

Pretest Your Software Tools

It is the wise programmer who carefully tests his/her programming tools before beginning a large project. Discovering late in a project that a particular function in your C graphics library does not work as described in the documentation can mean rewriting huge sections of code in an effort to work around the problem. Surprisingly, even a major programming project will use only a handful of graphics functions, so it is not an unduly time-consuming task to write a short program which explicitly tests each important graphics routine.

_____ **FACT** _____

It is a fact of life that both hardware and software products often exhibit undocumented features or idiosyncracies which must be taken into account by a serious programmer.

By way of example, the version of QuickC used by this author during preparation of the demonstration programs exhibited the following quirk. An attempt to clear the 640x350x16-color screen with the _clearscreen( ) function would leave the final six scan lines on the screen untouched if 80x43 alphanumerics had been activated. The edition of Turbo C used during preparation of the program listings forces the current position to revert to 0,0 each time the setviewport( ) function is called, making it difficult to recursively set up and disable a window on the screen during a complicated graphics procedure.

Both of these idiosyncracies are easy to work around if you know about them in advance, as the program listings in this book demonstrate; but suppose, for example, that you had been developing your master program with QuickC in the 640x480x16-color mode and did not test it in the 640x350x16-color mode until you had invested a lot of time and effort in the code. No one enjoys rewriting code to create workarounds for undocumented software idiosyncracies.

QuickC and Turbo C are powerful, versatile programming tools, but it makes sense to become familiar with each tool's strengths and weaknesses before you burn any bridges behind you. Protect yourself by pretesting.

Even more important is ensuring that the graphics library you intend to use offers the features you need. This book will give you the experience you need to make a wise decision if you decide you need even more power than the robust built-in graphics libraries of QuickC and Turbo C. See Appendix B for more on this. For 99% of your graphics programming requirements, however, QuickC and Turbo C will serve you well.

Defensive Programming

Defensive programming is the process of attempting to protect yourself from unexpected shortcomings or changes in hardware, software, or the marketplace itself.

The major program listings in this book, for example, will compile under both QuickC and Turbo C, even though the graphics library of each compiler is incompatible with the other. By careful use of directives embedded in the source code, the compiler will compile only certain sections of code, depending upon which compiler is being used. You simply change one line of code at the beginning of the program to alert the compiler to which set of graphics routines is to be used. Most of this coding takes place in a separate module which actually performs the drawing on the screen, so once the code has been created it need not be done again, no matter how large or complicated your project becomes.

This little extra coding is a prime example of defensive programming. Suppose, for example, that either Microsoft or Borland releases a vastly improved version of their compiler which far surpasses the capabilities of their competitor. Because you have crafted your source code to compile under either compiler, it is an easy task to upgrade to this hypothetical new supercharged compiler. If, however, you had written your source code explicitly for one or the other, it may require weeks or months of recoding to make it possible to compile your program under the new compiler.

Keeping the graphics routines separate from the rest of the source code and keeping them library-independent also makes it easy to switch to a different graphics library at a later date. The same principles can be used to make it possible to quickly adapt your program to non-IBM computer systems.

In a nutshell, defensive programming means not limiting yourself to one particular software or hardware product. Large corporations are often leary of single-sourcing arrangements—you should be too. Defensive programming means being device-independent. After all, today's faster microprocessors easily overcome the decrease in runtime performance incurred when you attempt to make your source code as independent as possible.

Defensive programming also means speculating about features that you might (or might not) want to add later. Suppose you change your mind and decide you wish to incorporate copy protection into your code after your program is nearly complete.

A CLOSER LOOK

Do not fall into the trap of dismissing copy protection out of hand. A lot of high-end, expensive graphics software priced above the $1000 mark uses some form of copy protection to protect the investment of the software developer. Even some large software publishers self-righteously applaud themselves for abandoning copy protection on their mass-market U.S. products—while they continue to use copy protection on versions of their products distributed in foreign countries.

If you employ a copy protection product that requires changes to your source code (see Appendix E for a discussion of copy protection products), you might be in for some serious rewriting. By investigating copy protection software requirements first, however, you can structure your code to easily accept these software hooks or entry points.

Proper Backup Methods

If you do not back up your work, you are eventually going to lose it; and the only viable strategy for foolproof backups involves two important principles: serial backups and remote storage.

TRAP

If you do not practise safe backup techniques, then you are eventually going to lose an important piece of source code.

Serial Backups

Serial backups are backed-up disks that you never overwrite. Suppose, for example, that you back up your work on an hourly basis. Clearly, you will be overwriting previously saved source code each hour; but at the end of the day, you might wish to make a daily backup, or even a weekly backup. If something goes horribly wrong with your disk drive and garbage is written to disk during this backup session, you might have overwritten all your backups. If, however, you do not overwrite last week's weekly backup disks, you still have a fallback position. You might even wish to maintain seven sets of daily backup disks, using a different set for each day of the week.

Remote Storage

Remote storage means exactly what is says: remote. By keeping a set of backup disks at some other physical location, you reduce the possibility of a total loss caused by burglary, fire, or flood. I keep a regularly updated set of backups in two bank safety deposit boxes. Corporate programmers often keep backups on other floors of the building, or even at other branches.

Remote storage backups also reduce the possibility of you accidentally overwriting previously-saved code and later discovering that you need that code to undo some serious errors in programming.

GETTING UP AND RUNNING: The First Sample Program

The demonstration program listing in this chapter provides an opportunity for you to get your programming environment up and running. The program, DETECT.C, uses an auto-detect algorithm to start up in the highest graphics mode supported by your computer system.

This program listing provides a number of opportunities for you. First, you can easily force the program to start up in a specific graphics mode other than the highest mode supported by your system, thereby testing all the graphics modes supported on your hardware. An EGA graphics adapter, for example, will support all EGA and CGA modes. A VGA adapter will support all VGA, EGA, MCGA, and CGA modes. Hercules supports, well... Hercules.

Second, you can easily add a few simple graphics routines to the program to tinker around with the graphics library of QuickC or Turbo C, depending on which compiler you are using. By running the program in different graphics modes, you can see how your graphics routines are affected by different screen resolutions. The chart in FIG. 1-5 illustrates the program variables which make it possible to run in six different graphics modes. These variables will be used for the remainder of the program listings in the book.

⎯⎯⎯⎯⎯⎯ WHERE TO LOOK ⎯⎯⎯⎯⎯⎯

See Appendix A for step-by-step instructions on getting the demonstration programs up and running.

Third, the program listing gives you an opportunity to make certain that you are able to correctly compile, link, and run the demonstration programs in the

MODE_FLAG	X_RES	Y_RES	ALPHA_X	ALPHA_Y	PLANE_LENGTH	ASPECT RATIO
1	640	480	8	8	38400	1
2	640	350	8	8	28000	.7291666
3	640	200	8	8	16000	.4166666
4	640	480	8	8	38400	1
5	640	200	8	8	16384	.4166666
6	720	348	9	14	32406	.6444444

Fig. 1-5. Device-dependent global variables which are used at start-up to detect and support six major graphics modes.

book. See Appendix A if you are a beginner, or if you want to be sure your compiler is set up exactly the same as the compilers which were used to create the programs. Don't forget to use QuickC's Utility menu to set the runtime stack size to 4K. If you are using Turbo C, the _stklen variable in the source code takes care of this minor housekeeping chore for you.

A sample image produced by DETECT.C is shown in FIG. 1-6. The complete source code for DETECT.C is provided in FIG. 1-7. If you are using the companion disk, load DETECT.C into the editor. You might have to copy the source file from the companion disk to your fixed disk first if you are running QuickC or Turbo C from a hard disk. If you experience any problems with loading, compiling, linking, or running the program, refer to Appendix A for step-by-step instructions.

HOW THE PROGRAM WORKS

The program listing is organized and optimized for easy readability. C code has a reputation for being write-only—for being difficult to read.

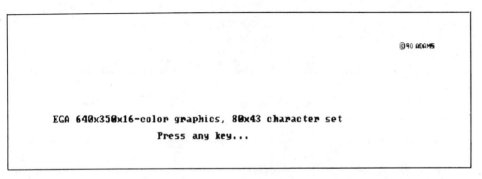

Fig. 1-6. Print of the image generated by the demonstration program, DETECT.C.

Fig. 1-7. Source code for DETECT.C, designed to detect and support six major graphics adapter modes. Ready to compile under QuickC or Turbo C.

```
/*
Graphics Hardware Autodetect            Source file:  DETECT.C

Purpose:  demonstrates how to write C graphics programs which
detect and support different graphics hardware.

Compiler:  QuickC or Turbo C.  Default is QuickC.  To use
Turbo C, change one line in COMPILER DIRECTIVES below.

Memory model:  medium memory model.

Marketability:  will detect and support these platforms...
VGA        640x480x16 colors     80x60 characters
EGA        640x350x16 colors     80x43 characters
EGA        640x200x16 colors     80x25 characters
MCGA       640x480x2 colors      80x60 characters
CGA        640x200x2 colors      80x25 characters
Hercules   720x348x2 colors      80x25 characters

(c) Copyright 1990 Lee Adams.  As purchaser of the book in which
this program is published, you are granted a non-exclusive
royalty-free license to reproduce and distribute these routines in
executable form as part of your software product, subject to any
trademark or patent rights of others, and subject to the limited
warranty described in the Introduction of the book.  All other
rights reserved.
_____

COMPILER DIRECTIVES
These are instructions to your C compiler. */

#define QuickC    1
#define TurboC    2
#define Compiler QuickC    /* NOTE: Change to TurboC if required */
#define FAIL      0
#define EMPTY     0

#include <bios.h>               /* supports the keyboard functions */
#include <stdio.h>              /* supports the printf function */
#if Compiler==QuickC
   #include <graph.h>              /* supports QuickC's graphics */
#elif Compiler==TurboC
   #include <graphics.h>          /* supports Turbo C's graphics */
#endif
#include <process.h>            /* supports the exit function
_____

FUNCTION PROTOTYPES
These ANSI C function declarations allow your C compiler to check
each function for correct arguments and return value. */

void Keyboard();                     /* checks for a keystroke */
void Quit_Pgm();                     /* terminates the program */
void Graphics_Setup();        /* autodetect of graphics hardware */
void GetTextCoords();              /* converts QC to TC text */
void Notice(int,int);              /* displays copyright notice */
/*_____

DECLARATION OF GLOBAL VARIABLES
These variables are declared and initialized outside of any
function and are visible to all functions in this source file.   */

#if Compiler==QuickC
  struct videoconfig vc;           /* QuickC's video data table */
```

Fig. 1-7.
Continued.

```
#endif
int C0=0,C1=1,C2=2,C3=3,C4=4,C5=5,C6=6,C7=7,C8=8,C9=9,C10=10,
C11=11,C12=12,C13=13,C14=14,C15=15;           /* color codes */
int mode_flag=0;                        /* indicates graphics mode */
float x_res,y_res;        /* screen resolution for mapping routine */
float sx,sy;              /* device-independent screen coordinates */
int t1=1;                                        /* loop counter */
int TextRow=1,TextColumn=1;           /* text position for QuickC */
int TextX=0,TextY=0;                  /* text position for Turbo C
```

```
FUNCTION DEFINITIONS */

main(){                              /* this is the master routine */
Graphics_Setup();                      /* establish graphics mode */
#if Compiler==QuickC
  _getvideoconfig(&vc);        /* initialize QuickC's video table */
  _setcolor(C7);
#elif Compiler==TurboC
  setcolor(C7);
#endif
Notice(589,2);
for (t1=1;t1!=2; ) Keyboard();         /* press any key to stop */
Quit_Pgm();}}                          /* end the program gracefully
                                                                  */
```

```
void Keyboard(){                     /* checks the keyboard buffer */
#if Compiler==QuickC
  if (_bios_keybrd(_KEYBRD_READY)==EMPTY) return;
  else (_bios_keybrd(_KEYBRD_READ);Quit_Pgm();}
#elif Compiler==TurboC
  if (bioskey(1)==EMPTY) return;else {bioskey(0);Quit_Pgm();}
#endif
}
/*_____*/
```

```
void Quit_Pgm(){                       /* terminates the program */
#if Compiler==QuickC                       /* if using QuickC */
  _clearscreen(_GCLEARSCREEN);            /* clear the screen */
  _setvideomode(_DEFAULTMODE);        /* restore the original mode */
#elif Compiler==TurboC                     /* if using Turbo C */
  cleardevice();                          /* clear the screen */
  closegraph();     /* shut down graphics, restore original mode */
#endif
exit(0);}}                               /* terminate the program
                                                                  */
```

```
void Graphics_Setup(){        /* autodetect of graphics hardware */
#if Compiler==QuickC
  if (_setvideomoderows(_VRES16COLOR,60)!=FAIL) goto VGA_mode;
  if (_setvideomoderows(_ERESCOLOR,43)!=FAIL) goto EGA_ECD_mode;
  if (_setvideomoderows(_HRES16COLOR,25)!=FAIL) goto EGA_SCD_mode;
  if (_setvideomoderows(_VRES2COLOR,60)!=FAIL) goto MCGA_mode;
  if (_setvideomoderows(_HRESBW,25)!=FAIL) goto CGA_mode;
  if (_setvideomoderows(_HERCMONO,25)!=FAIL) goto Hercules_mode;
#elif Compiler==TurboC
  int graphics_adapter,graphics_mode;
  detectgraph(&graphics_adapter,&graphics_mode);
  if (graphics_adapter==VGA) goto VGA_mode;
  if (graphics_mode==EGAHI) goto EGA_ECD_mode;
  if (graphics_mode==EGALO) goto EGA_SCD_mode;
  if (graphics_adapter==MCGA) goto MCGA_mode;
  if (graphics_adapter==CGA) goto CGA_mode;
  if (graphics_adapter==HERCMONO) goto Hercules_mode;
#endif
goto abort_pgm;                  /* if no graphics hardware found */

VGA_mode:       /* VGA 640x480x16-color mode, 8x8 character matrix */
x_res=640;y_res=480;mode_flag=1;
```

Fig. 1-7.
Continued.

```
#if Compiler==QuickC
  _settextcolor(C7);
  _settextposition(10,15);
  _outtext("VGA 640x480x16-color graphics, 80x60 character set");
  _settextposition(12,33);
  _outtext("Press any key...");
#elif Compiler==TurboC
  graphics_adapter=VGA;graphics_mode=VGAHI;
  initgraph(&graphics_adapter,&graphics_mode,"");
  settextstyle(0,0,1);setcolor(C7);
  TextRow=10;TextColumn=15;GetTextCoords();
  outtextxy(TextX,TextY,"VGA 640x480x16-color graphics,"
                        " 80x60 character set");
  TextRow=12;TextColumn=33;GetTextCoords();
  outtextxy(TextX,TextY,"Press any key...");
#endif
return;

EGA_ECD_mode: /* EGA 640x350x16-color mode, 8x8 character matrix */
x_res=640;y_res=350;mode_flag=2;
#if Compiler==QuickC
  _settextcolor(C7);
  _settextposition(10,15);
  _outtext("EGA 640x350x16-color graphics, 80x43 character set");
  _settextposition(12,33);
  _outtext("Press any key...");
#elif Compiler==TurboC
  graphics_adapter=EGA;graphics_mode=EGAHI;
  initgraph(&graphics_adapter,&graphics_mode,"");
  settextstyle(0,0,1);setcolor(C7);
  TextRow=10;TextColumn=15;GetTextCoords();
  outtextxy(TextX,TextY,"EGA 640x350x16-color graphics,"
                        " 80x43 character set");
  TextRow=12;TextColumn=33;GetTextCoords();
  outtextxy(TextX,TextY,"Press any key...");
#endif
return;

EGA_SCD_mode: /* EGA 640x200x16-color mode, 8x8 character matrix */
x_res=640;y_res=200;mode_flag=3;
#if Compiler==QuickC
  _settextcolor(C7);
  _settextposition(10,15);
  _outtext("EGA 640x200x16-color graphics, 80x25 character set");
  _settextposition(12,33);
  _outtext("Press any key...");
#elif Compiler==TurboC
  graphics_adapter=EGA;graphics_mode=EGALO;
  initgraph(&graphics_adapter,&graphics_mode,"");
  settextstyle(0,0,1);setcolor(C7);
  TextRow=10;TextColumn=15;GetTextCoords();
  outtextxy(TextX,TextY,"EGA 640x200x16-color graphics,"
                        " 80x25 character set");
  TextRow=12;TextColumn=33;GetTextCoords();
  outtextxy(TextX,TextY,"Press any key...");
#endif
return;

MCGA_mode:    /* MCGA 640x480x2-color mode, 8x8 character matrix */
x_res=640;y_res=480;C0=0;C1=1;C2=1;C3=1;C4=1;C5=1;C6=1;C7=1;
C8=1;C9=1;C10=1;C11=1;C12=1;C13=1;C14=1;C15=1;mode_flag=4;
#if Compiler==QuickC
  _settextcolor(C7);
  _settextposition(10,15);
  _outtext("MCGA 640x480x2-color graphics, 80x60 character set");
  _settextposition(12,33);
  _outtext("Press any key...");
#elif Compiler==TurboC
  graphics_adapter=MCGA;graphics_mode=MCGAHI;
```

Fig. 1-7.
Continued.

```
      initgraph(&graphics_adapter,&graphics_mode,"");
      settextstyle(0,0,1);setcolor(C7);
      TextRow=10;TextColumn=15;GetTextCoords();
      outtextxy(TextX,TextY,"MCGA 640x480x2-color graphics,"
                            " 80x60 character set");
      TextRow=12;TextColumn=33;GetTextCoords();
      outtextxy(TextX,TextY,"Press any key...");
#endif
return;

CGA_mode:         /* CGA 640x200x2-color mode, 8x8 character matrix */
x_res=640;y_res=200;C0=0;C1=1;C2=1;C3=1;C4=1;C5=1;C6=1;C7=1;
C8=1;C9=1;C10=1;C11=1;C12=1;C13=1;C14=1;C15=1;mode_flag=5;
#if Compiler==QuickC
   _settextcolor(C7);
   _settextposition(10,15);
   _outtext("CGA 640x200x2-color graphics, 80x25 character set");
   _settextposition(12,33);
   _outtext("Press any key...");
#elif Compiler==TurboC
      graphics_adapter=CGA;graphics_mode=CGAHI;
      initgraph(&graphics_adapter,&graphics_mode,"");
      settextstyle(0,0,1);setcolor(C7);
      TextRow=10;TextColumn=15;GetTextCoords();
      outtextxy(TextX,TextY,"CGA 640x200x2-color graphics,"
                            " 80x25 character set");
      TextRow=12;TextColumn=33;GetTextCoords();
      outtextxy(TextX,TextY,"Press any key...");
#endif
return;

Hercules_mode: /* Hercules 720x348x2-color mode,
                      9x14 character matrix */
x_res=720;y_res=348;C0=0;C1=1;C2=1;C3=1;C4=1;C5=1;C6=1;C7=1;
C8=1;C9=1;C10=1;C11=1;C12=1;C13=1;C14=1;C15=1;mode_flag=6;
#if Compiler==QuickC
   _settextcolor(C7);
   _settextposition(10,15);
   _outtext("Hercules 720x348x2-color graphics,"
                      " 80x25 character set");
   _settextposition(12,33);
   _outtext("Press any key...");
#elif Compiler==TurboC
      graphics_adapter=HERCMONO;graphics_mode=HERCMONOHI;
      initgraph(&graphics_adapter,&graphics_mode,"");
      setcolor(C7);
      TextRow=10;TextColumn=15;GetTextCoords();
      outtextxy(TextX,TextY,"Hercules 720x348x2-color graphics,"
                            " 80x25 character set");
      TextRow=12;TextColumn=33;GetTextCoords();
      outtextxy(TextX,TextY,"Press any key...");
#endif
return;

abort_pgm:        /* jump to here if no supported graphics hardware */
printf("\n\nUnable to proceed.\n\r");
printf("Requires VGA, EGA, CGA, MCGA, or\n\r");
printf("Hercules adapter and appropriate monitor.\n\n\r");
exit(0);
}
/*_____*/

void GetTextCoords(){       /* convert QuickC text to Turbo C text */
TextX=(TextColumn*8)-8;TextY=(TextRow*8)-8;return;}
/*_____*/

void Notice(int x, int y){       /* displays the copyright notice */
int copyright[][3]={0x7c00,0x0000,0x0000, /* array of bit styles */
```

Fig. 1-7.
Continued.

```
                          0x8279,0x819c,0x645e,
                          0xba4a,0x4252,0x96d0,
                          0xa27a,0x4252,0x955e,
                          0xba0a,0x43d2,0xf442,
                          0x8219,0x825c,0x945e,
                          0x7c00,0x0000,0x0000};
   int a,b,c; int t1=0;                              /* local variables */
   #if Compiler==QuickC
      for (t1=0;t1<=6;t1++){                         /* draw 7 styled lines */
         a=copyright[t1][0];b=copyright[t1][1];c=copyright[t1][2];
         _setlinestyle(a);_moveto(x,y);_lineto(x+15,y);
         _setlinestyle(b);_moveto(x+16,y);_lineto(x+31,y);
         _setlinestyle(c);_moveto(x+32,y);_lineto(x+47,y);y=y+1;};
      _setlinestyle(0xFFFF);return;
   #elif Compiler==TurboC
      for (t1=0;t1<=6;t1++){                         /* draw 7 styled lines */
         a=copyright[t1][0];b=copyright[t1][1];c=copyright[t1][2];
         setlinestyle(USERBIT_LINE,a,NORM_WIDTH);
         moveto(x,y);lineto(x+15,y);
         setlinestyle(USERBIT_LINE,b,NORM_WIDTH);
         moveto(x+16,y);lineto(x+31,y);
         setlinestyle(USERBIT_LINE,c,NORM_WIDTH);
         moveto(x+32,y);lineto(x+47,y);y=y+1;};
      setlinestyle(USERBIT_LINE,0xFFFF,NORM_WIDTH);return;
   #endif
   }
   /*_____

End of source file. */
```

Compiler Directives

The section of code labelled COMPILER DIRECTIVES contains the definitions for the constants which make this program able to be compiled under either QuickC or Turbo C. If you are using QuickC, the program is ready to run. If you are using Turbo C, change the line:

#define Compiler QuickC

to read:

#define Compiler TurboC

Just a few lines later in the source code, you can see how the #if preprocessor directive is used to instruct the compiler to make a decision based on the value of the variable named Compiler. Both QuickC and Turbo C require a comprehensive set of variables to be initialized and functions to be declared before their graphics library will function correctly. Because each compiler uses a different filename for the file which contains these initializations, the #if directive ensures that the correct file is included at this point in the source code, regardless of which compiler is being used.

Further examples of the #if directive appear elsewhere throughout DETECT.C.

Function Prototypes

The next section in the source code is labelled FUNCTION PROTOTYPES. This is simply a listing of the functions used in the program. By telling the compiler what values each function expects to receive or return, the compiler can perform sophisticated error checking during compilation to catch improper calling syntax. A function prefaced by void means that it does not return any value to the caller. The items inside the trailing parentheses indicate what arguments, if any, the function expects to receive when it is called.

Function Definitions

The next section in the source code is called FUNCTION DEFINITIONS. This section contains the executable code for all the functions in the program.

First comes the main( ) function, or the master routine. This is the point at which the operating system begins execution of the program. Notice how the #if and #elif directives have been used to ensure that only compatible code is compiled for each compiler.

The main( ) routine calls a function named Graphics_Setup( ) to invoke the highest graphics mode supported by the hardware. Next, notice how an endless loop is used to keep calling the Keyboard( ) function, waiting for you to press any key to stop the program. Refer to your compiler user's guide if you are not familiar with this type of loop.

After the main( ) function comes a function named Keyboard( ). This function is responsible for checking to see if any key has been pressed. If it cannot find a keystroke, it simply returns to the caller. If it does find a keystroke, it calls a function named Quit_Pgm( ) to terminate the program. The QuickC version of the program uses the built-in _bios_keybrd( ) function of the compiler to check the keyboard buffer. The Turbo C version of the program uses the built-in bioskey( ) function to check the keyboard buffer.

The Quit_Pgm( ) function gracefully shuts down the program and returns the screen to the default mode. Clearly, it would not be good programming practise to leave the screen in a graphics mode if a text mode had been in effect before the program was started. To clear the screen, QuickC uses the _clearscreen (_GCLEARSCREEN) instruction. Turbo C uses the cleardevice( ) instruction. To restore the previously existing screen mode, QuickC uses the _setvideomode (_DEFAULTMODE) instruction. Turbo C uses the closegraph( ) instruction.

The most important section of code in DETECT.C is the function named Graphics_Setup( ). This function sets up the highest graphics mode supported by your computer system and displays a simple message alerting you which mode has been invoked.

Depending on which compiler you are using, one of two different algorithms are used.

The QuickC Auto-detect Algorithm

QuickC checks the value returned by the _setvideomoderows( ) instruction to see if the function was successful or not. The constant named FAIL was defined in the section named COMPILER DIRECTIVES. If the call failed, the program next attempts to invoke a graphics mode slightly less demanding. The logic keeps cascading downward until the function is successful and returns a value other than zero. You can see how the program then jumps to a label to continue initializing the graphics mode before returning to the main( ) routine.

The Turbo C Auto-detect Algorithm

Turbo C uses the detectgraph( ) function to check which graphics hardware is present. The pertinent information is automatically stored in two global variables named graphics_adapter and graphics_mode. By checking the contents of these variables after a call to detectgraph( ) you can tell which graphics mode can be invoked. The program then jumps to a label to continue initializing the graphics mode before returning to the main( ) routine.

Note how the variables shown in Fig. 1-5 are initialized by this section of source code. Some of these global variables will be very helpful in later program listings.

The next section of source code is a function named GetTextCoords( ). This function compensates for the incompatible text-plotting algorithms used by QuickC and Turbo C. QuickC uses rows and columns to position text in the graphics mode. Turbo C uses pixel coordinates to position text in the graphics mode. The function named GetTextCoords( ) assumes an 8x8 alphanumeric character size. This is not technically correct in the case of the Hercules graphics adapter's 9x14 text matrix, but is used here for simplicity.

The final section of source code is a function named Notice( ). This is a graphics-based copyright notice which is displayed on the screen at runtime. If you are so inclined, you can tinker with the array named copyright[ ][ ] to develop a copyright notice for use on your own original C graphics programs.

WHAT IS MISSING
IN THE PROGRAM

Remember, this program listing has been optimized for legibility. It has been made easy to read and easy to learn. It should not be taken as code which produces optimum performance. Neither does the coding style take full advantage of syntax offered by C.

Most noteworthy about the trade-off between readability and optimization is the use of global variables in the program listings in this book. Global variables are declared outside of any executable function. They can be used and altered by any function in the program. This strategy makes it easy to keep track of variables, especially when you are adding new functions incrementally by trial and error to your master program. However, global variables also introduce the possibility of one function inadvertently changing a variable that is to be used later by another function.

In many cases, it makes more sense to use local variables, which can be used only by the function in which they are declared and initialized. The library-independent graphics routines used by the two major program listings in this book use local variables—each routine expects to receive on the stack the parameters it needs when it is called.

The final function in DETECT.C, named Notice( ), expects to receive two integers on the stack when it is called. It assigns these two parameters to two local variables and uses those variables to plot the starting location of the graphic which it is expected to display. Of course, the graphic is drawn in a color which has been assigned to a global variable used by the QuickC or Turbo C graphics library. This global variable is the current drawing color maintained by the graphics library. See Appendix B for a discussion of how other graphics libraries handle this situation, often called the graphics state.

Also missing from the program listing is any serious effort at runtime error trapping. Although this omission is not so important in DETECT.C, it becomes critical in later demonstration programs—and it is vital for programs which you might wish to distribute. See Appendix C for a discussion of error-trapping techniques to handle open diskdrive doors, insufficient disk space, math overflow, and other conditions.

Missing also from the program listing is serious graphical output. Using the existing code as a guide, you can easily write your own function to draw on the screen. Try adding the following instruction just before the instruction, Notice(589,2), in the main( ) routine. If you are using QuickC, add:

```
_rectangle(_GBORDER,0,0,x_res-1,y_res-1);
```

If you are using Turbo C, add:

```
rectangle(0,0,x_res-1,y_res-1);
```

These instructions will draw a rectangle around the outermost edge of the display screen. They will work in any graphics mode supported by the program because 0,0 is always the upper left corner in any mode, and because x_res and y_res have been defined appropriately in the Graphics_Setup( ) function.

THE RIGHT WAY
TO SHUT DOWN

When you are finished programming, it is important that you end the session in a consistent fashion. You should always take care to tidy up your fixed disk. Both QuickC and Turbo C generate files during the compile/link process that are of no particular use to you. These files can, in fact, cause some problems under certain conditions. With both QuickC and Turbo C it is possible to fool the compiler into running a previous version of your EXE program even after you have made changes to the source file with the editor. However, if the EXE program from a previous programming session is not on disk, QuickC and Turbo C are forced into recompiling and linking your source file from scratch.

In addition, a lot of disk space can be used up by the extraneous files created by QuickC and Turbo C during the compilation of your programs. Both compilers generate OBJ object files and EXE files. QuickC also generates a plethora of specialized debugging files, including MDT, ILK, and SYB. Turbo C automatically generates BAK backup source files when you make edits. These files will rapidly accummulate on your fixed disk as you compile different source files.

──────── TRAP ────────

Both QuickC and Turbo C can be fooled into running an outdated version of an EXE file. You can reduce the chances of this happening by deleting unnecessary output files after each programming session.

After you have run DETECT.C a few times, exit to DOS and check the contents of the QuickC or Turbo C output subdirectory. It is simply good programming practise to delete these interim files before you shut down for the day. Be careful not to delete your C source files (which you have, of course, already also backed up!). Good shutdown habits give you the peace of mind of knowing that each time you start a fresh session you are starting in a consistent environment. Working programmers are like bank auditors: they do not like unexpected surprises.

2

Turning Professional:
Command-Line Options for Compiling
Your Finished Programs

ALTHOUGH BOTH QuickC and Turbo C offer a powerful interactive programming environment for the development of full-featured C graphics programs, each compiler also offers a command-line version of its functions.

A *command-line* compiler is a program which you call directly from the operating system prompt. By passing arguments on the command line you can specify how the command-line compiler preprocesses, compiles, and links your C source module(s).

———— FACT ————

A command-line compiler is a program which you call directly from the operating system prompt.

Because the interactive menu system of QuickC and Turbo C offers such a rich array of options, it seems redundant to even consider using the command-line version of the compiler, but there are significant advantages to using the command line.

If all this seems a bit too technical for you, don't worry. Every demonstration program in this book can be compiled and run under the QuickC and Turbo C editors. You can safely skip this chapter if you are a beginner, or if you are in a hurry to get to the flashier demo programs.

ADVANTAGES OF COMMAND-LINE COMPILATION

The most important advantage of using command-line compilation is one of availability. Simply stated, many of the compile/link options available in the command-line version of the compiler are not available through the menu system of the interactive version of the compiler. These command-line options can offer powerful increases in performance for your program.

This means you can use the versatile prototyping features of QuickC and Turbo C to build and test your program—and then use the powerful options of the command-line version of the compiler to optimize your program for distribution.

Another significant advantage to using command-line compilation is the elimination of dead RAM. When your program is running under the control of either QuickC or Turbo C, the interactive editor/compiler remains in memory while your program executes. In the case of QuickC this means 265K is sitting idle; in the case of Turbo C 395K is sitting unused. On a computer with 640K user RAM available, this is not an insignificant chunk of memory. (See FIG. 1-1 in Chapter 1.)

By using the command-line version of QuickC or Turbo C to preprocess, compile, link, and run your program, you can gain access to the full 640K of user RAM during execution of your program, minus any memory normally used by the operating system, of course.

If you are using Turbo C, you should begin to switch over to command-line compilation when your EXE program approaches 145K bytes in length. When using QuickC, you should consider using the command line when your EXE program nears 250K. By using the program development strategies discussed in Chapter 1 you can continue to avail yourself of the powerful debugging and error-reporting capabilities of the QuickC and Turbo C integrated programming environments.

COMMAND-LINE OPTIONS

Command-line options are mnemonic codes which you type directly onto the command line as you invoke the compiler. If you are using QuickC, each option is preceded by a slash "/". If you are using Turbo C, each option is preceded by a dash "-". QuickC users can also use the dash, but the QuickC manual employs the slash, and that typographic convention is retained in this book for consistency.

Figure 2-1 illustrates the QuickC command-line options which will be used to compile and link the demonstration program provided later in this chapter. Figure 2-2 shows the corresponding options for Turbo C command-line compilation.

USING THE COMMAND LINE

If you were running QuickC 2.00 from a fixed disk, your command-line session might look something like this: First, from the operating system prompt, you set the default drive to the directory where your C source files are located, called \SOURCE in this instance.

CD C:\QC2\SOURCE

SWITCH	EFFECT
/Ox	INSTRUCTS COMPILER TO USE ALL OPTIMIZATION POSSIBLE
/AM	INSTRUCTS COMPILER TO USE THE MEDIUM MEMORY MODEL
/F 1000	SETS SIZE OF RUNTIME STACK (IN THIS EXAMPLE 1000H BYTES)
/W1	INSTRUCTS COMPILER TO ALERT YOU TO ONLY SERIOUS WARNINGS, BUT ALL ERRORS
/LINK	THE OBJ FILES WILL BE LINKED INTO AN EXE FILE WHEN THE COMPILER IS FINISHED
/INF	INSTRUCTS THE LINKER TO DISPLAY THE VARIOUS FILES IT IS LINKING FOR YOUR INFORMATION

Fig. 2-1. The effects of major options available with the command-line version of QuickC.

SWITCH	EFFECT
-MM	INSTRUCTS COMPILER TO USE THE MEDIUM MEMORY MODEL
-G	INSTRUCTS COMPILER TO USE ALL OPTIMIZATIONS POSSIBLE
-I	WHERE THE FIND #INCLUDE FILES
-L	WHERE TO FIND LIB FILES
-N	WHERE TO WRITE THE RESULTING OBJ AND EXE FILES

Fig. 2-2. The effects of major options available with the command-line version of Turbo C.

Next, you invoke the command-line compiler, named QCL.EXE on the QuickC distribution disks, by using the following syntax.

```
C:\QC2\BIN\QCL /Ox /AM /F 1000 /FeMEMORY /W1 MEMORY.C /link /INF
```

In this example, QCL.EXE is located in the directory named C:\QC2\BIN.

Note how the command-line options after each slash correspond to the tokens in FIG. 2-1. The /Fe option tells the command-line compiler what to name the resulting EXE program.

If you were running Turbo C 2.0 from a fixed disk, your command-line session might look something like this: First, from the operating system prompt, you set the default drive to the directory where the command-line compiler, TCC.EXE, is located. The command-line linker, TLINK.EXE, should also be in this directory.

```
CD C:\TC2\BIN
```

Next, you invoke the command-line compiler by using the following syntax.

```
TCC -mm -G -IC:\TC2\INCLUDE -LC:\TC2\LIB -nC:\TC2\SOURCE MEMORY
    GRAPHICS.LIB
```

Note how the command-line options after each dash correspond to the tokens in FIG. 2-2. The C source file is named MEMORY.C and it should be in the same directory as TCC.EXE.

It is important to note that if you are using the command-line version of Turbo C, you must explicitly name the graphics library GRAPHICS.LIB on the command line—otherwise the compiler will be unable to the find the graphics routines it needs.

Whether you are using QuickC or Turbo C in the command-line mode, it is important to type in the command line exactly as shown here. In all cases, the spacing and punctuation is critical. In most cases, the case—whether upper- or lower- —is important.

In the examples given here, only a single C source file (module) is being compiled and linked into an executuable EXE program. The C source file is called MEMORY.C. If you were working on a program composed of more than one C source file, you would simply list all the source files to be collected together. A hands-on example of multi-module command-line compilation will be provided in Chapter 6 (although the two-module program listing can just as easily be compiled under the control of the integrated programming environment of either QuickC or Turbo C).

OPTIONS USEFUL FOR C GRAPHICS PROGRAMMING

The QuickC and Turbo C manuals contain an extensive listing of the command-line options available. Many options are highly specialized and not likely to be used during your normal programming efforts. A few, however, are deserving of mention here.

Overlays

An *overlay* is an executable module of code which is loaded in from disk only when it is explicitly needed during execution of your program. See FIG. 2-3. The overlay is loaded directly over other executable code in RAM, thereby conserving memory. When the operation finishes, the previously-existing code can be reloaded from disk or the overlay can remain in RAM, whichever is more convenient for your program. Figure 2-4 depicts a memory map after an overlay has been loaded into RAM from disk. Compare the map with the illustration in FIG. 2-3.

Clearly, using overlays has significant advantages if your project is going to result in a very large EXE program. By swapping overlays in and out of memory at runtime, you can run programs much larger than 640K in only 640K of memory. You can also use overlays to keep other portions of memory free for graphics databases, hidden graphics pages, temporary image buffers, and so on.

If you are using QuickC, you can use the command-line compilation/link environment to set up overlays. Microsoft's linker handles all the necessary

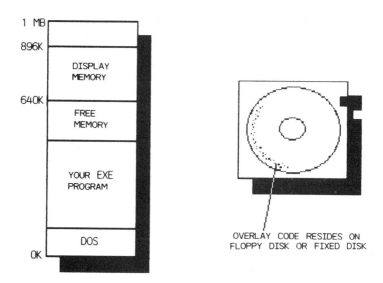

Fig. 2-3. Runtime memory map on a 640K DOS system. Overlay code, if any, resides in file(s) on disk, waiting to be invoked.

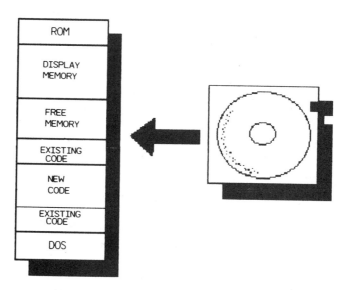

Fig. 2-4. Overlay code is written directly over existing executable code in memory. Previously-existing code is either already waiting on disk or explicitly written to disk, ready to be restored to RAM when required.

spadework for you. This overlay feature is not available through the menu system of the integrated programming environment, however.

If you are using Turbo C, you must use third-party software such as .RTLink or Overlay Toolkit if you wish to activate runtime overlays, because neither the integrated programming environment nor the command-line version of Turbo C supports overlays.

You can also use .RTLink and Overlay Toolkit with QuickC, of course, but the built-in overlay capabilities of QuickC's linker are more than up to the task.

Obviously, overlays will work only with multi-module programs. By careful planning, you can place seldom-used C routines into a separate C source file. Then, when you name the file(s) to be compiled and linked on the command line, you simply use parentheses to tell the linker which files are to be designated as overlay modules.

For example, if you were compiling and linking five source files named MEMORY1.C, MEMORY2.C, MEMORY3.C, MEMORY4.C, and MEMORY5.C, you could set up MEMORY3.C as an overlay by typing the names in their appropriate place in the command line thus:

MEMORY1.C MEMORY2.C (MEMORY3.C) MEMORY4.C MEMORY5.C

The resulting EXE program would be MEMORY1.EXE and would contain all the code from MEMORY1.C, MEMORY2.C, MEMORY4.C, and MEMORY5.C, but not MEMORY3.C. During program execution, if any function calls a function that is in MEMORY3, the overlay manager in the built-in runtime library will automatically load the overlay code into memory. The overlay code will reside in memory until the called function executes a return to the caller, at which time the original code (called the root, or resident part of the program) is loaded back into memory.

If you want two or more C source modules to be grouped together into a single overlay, you simply enclose them in a single set of parentheses. You can have more than one overlay by simply using parentheses around each C source module(s) you wish to set up as an overlay.

Microsoft has done a fine job in making the difficult task of managing overlays at runtime virtually transparent to you, the programmer. If your master project ever reaches a critical point in memory use, or if you need to free up large chunks of memory for a database or a backup page, then you should investigate QuickC's ability to manage overlays at runtime. If you are using Turbo C, you might find it useful to secure a copy of .RT Link or Overlay Toolkit, available through computer programming specialty stores, or direct from the manufacturers listed earlier in this chapter.

Assembly Language Listings

If you are an experienced programmer, an assembly language listing of the output of the compiler is often useful. By studying the listing, you can often rewrite slow portions of code in your own assembly language style.

If you are using Turbo C, use the -S command-line option to force the command-line compiler to generate an ASM listing. Note that your C source file is not actually assembled into an object file, so no EXE program is produced, only an ASM listing.

If you are using QuickC, you will need to use the Microsoft C Optimizing Compiler version 5.10 or later, if you wish to create an assembly language output using the /Fa command-line option. QuickC does not support the /Fa option, although it is in all other respects fully compatible with the full-blown Microsoft C compiler. It is interesting to note that QuickC supports a substantive variety of undocumented command-line options which are present in Microsoft C, but alas the /Fa option is not one of them—at least not in the sub-version of QuickC I tested.

Compiling Without Linking

The compiler produces OBJ object files. These files are collected together by the linker, along with the required routines from the libraries, to produce the finished EXE executable program.

If you are writing routines for a programming toolkit that you intend to distribute to other C programmers, you can provide your routines to your customers in OBJ form if you do not want to reveal your C source code. Your programming customers would simply link in your OBJ files to create their own programs, of course.

If you are using the QuickC command-line version, use the /c option to instruct the compiler to produce the object file(s), but not to invoke the linker. If you are using the Turbo C command-line version, use the -c option.

Ensuring Portability for Your Programs

If you intend to convert your original C graphics program to a non-IBM environment, you will likely need to create code which strictly conforms to the ANSI C standard. Both QuickC and Turbo C use syntax which enhances the C standard, but which might not be supported in a different environment.

Use QuickC's /Za option to catch all non-ANSI syntax in your program. Use Turbo C's -A option to keep your code strictly ANSI compatible.

Using 80286/80386 Instructions

If you wish to take advantage of the improved performance available on personal computers equipped with either the 80286 or 80386 microprocessor, you can use QuickC's /G2 command-line option. The resulting EXE program will not run on 8086 or 8088 microprocessors, however.

The Turbo C command-line compiler supports the 80286 instruction set by the -1 options. Note that the option mnemonic is a numeric digit, not a lower case L.

Using Math Coprocessors

If you wish to take advantage of the incredible speed improvements provided by the 8087, 80287, and 80387 math coprocessors—and if you are certain that your program will never run on a computer without a math coprocessor—you can use QuickC's /FPi87 or Turbo C's -f87 command-line option.

QuickC by default will produce EXE programs that use built-in software routines which emulate (simulate) the performance of a math coprocessor if no coprocessor is detected at program start-up. If a coprocessor is present, the runtime code will use it, however, and the unused emulation routines will simply take up memory without performing any useful purpose.

TRAP

Don't use QuickC's /FP-i87 option or Turbo C's -f87 option if there is any possibilty of your finished EXE program being run on a computer without a math coprocessor.

Turbo C will likewise produce EXE programs which attempt to detect the presence of a math coprocessor at start-up. Turbo C's emulation routines are used if no math coprocessor is present, otherwise all math functions are routed directly through the coprocessor. By using the -f87 command-line option, you can remove these space-wasting math emulation routines from your code if you are confident your EXE program will be used only on computers equipped with math coprocessors.

A SAMPLE COMMAND-LINE PROGRAM

The image in FIG. 2-5 was generated by the program listing provided in FIG. 2-6. This demonstration program reports how much RAM is still available while your program is running. By including the core functions from this example in

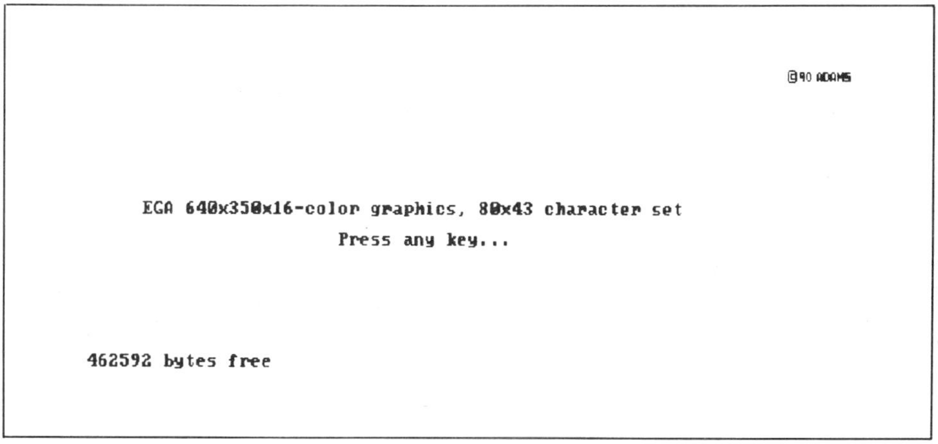

Fig. 2-5. Print of the image generated by the demonstration program, MEMORY.C.

Fig. 2-6. Source code for MEMORY.C, designed to determine the amount of free memory available at runtime. Ready to compile under QuickC or Turbo C.

```
/*
Report amount of free memory              Source file:  MEMORY.C

Purpose:  demonstrates how to write C graphics programs which
can detect the amount of free memory available at run-time.

Compiler:  QuickC or Turbo C.  Default is QuickC.  To use
Turbo C, change one line in COMPILER DIRECTIVES below.

Memory model:  medium memory model.

(c) Copyright 1990 Lee Adams.  As purchaser of the book in which
this program is published, you are granted a non-exclusive
royalty-free license to reproduce and distribute these routines in
executable form as part of your software product, subject to any
trademark or patent rights of others, and subject to the limited
warranty described in the Introduction of the book.  All other
rights reserved.
_____

COMPILER DIRECTIVES
These are instructions to your C compiler. */

#define QuickC     1
#define TurboC     2
#define Compiler   QuickC   /* NOTE: Change to TurboC if required */
#define FAIL       0
#define EMPTY      0
#define CHUNK      32768  /* size of block to attempt to allocate */
#define REMAINDER 255                       /* accuracy limit */
#define ATTEMPTS  40                /* max number of attempts... */
            /* increase this constant by 40 for each megabyte... */
               /* of extended memory in your system beyond 640K. */

#include <bios.h>              /* supports the keyboard functions */
#include <stdio.h>               /* supports the printf function */
```

Fig. 2-6.
Continued.

```
#if Compiler==QuickC
  #include <graph.h>              /* supports QuickC's graphics */
  #include <malloc.h>             /* supports memory allocation */
#elif Compiler==TurboC
  #include <graphics.h>           /* supports Turbo C's graphics */
  #include <alloc.h>              /* supports memory allocation */
#endif
#include <process.h>              /* supports the exit function
```

```
FUNCTION PROTOTYPES
These ANSI C function declarations allow your C compiler to check
each function for correct arguments and return value. */

void Keyboard(void);             /* checks for a keystroke */
void Quit_Pgm(void);             /* terminates the program */
void Graphics_Setup(void);    /* autodetect of graphics hardware */
void GetTextCoords(void);        /* converts QC to TC text */
void Notice(int,int);         /* displays copyright notice */
long GetFreeMemory(void);        /* calculate size of free RAM */
/*
```

```
DECLARATION OF GLOBAL VARIABLES
These variables are declared and initialized outside of any
function and are visible to all functions in this source file.    */

#if Compiler==QuickC
  struct videoconfig vc;         /* QuickC's video data table */
#endif
int C0=0,C1=1,C2=2,C3=3,C4=4,C5=5,C6=6,C7=7,C8=8,C9=9,C10=10,
C11=11,C12=12,C13=13,C14=14,C15=15;            /* color codes */
int mode_flag=0;                 /* indicates graphics mode */
float x_res,y_res;       /* screen resolution for mapping routine */
float sx,sy;          /* device-independent screen coordinates */
int t1=1;                             /* loop counter */
int TextRow=1,TextColumn=1;      /* text position for QuickC */
int TextX=0,TextY=0;             /* text position for Turbo C */
long freemem=0;                  /* size of free RAM available
```

```
FUNCTION DEFINITIONS */

main(){                          /* this is the master routine */
Graphics_Setup();                /* establish graphics mode */
#if Compiler==QuickC
  _getvideoconfig(&vc);      /* initialize QuickC's video table */
  _setcolor(C7);
  _settextposition(20,10);       /* set the text position */
  freemem=GetFreeMemory();     /* determine size of free RAM... */
  printf("%lu bytes free",freemem);     /* ...and display it */
#elif Compiler==TurboC
  setcolor(C7);
  TextRow=20;TextColumn=10;GetTextCoords();
  moveto(TextX,TextY);           /* set the text position */
  freemem=GetFreeMemory();     /* determine size of free RAM... */
  printf("%lu bytes free",freemem);     /* ...and display it */
#endif
Notice(589,2);
for (t1=1;t1!=2; ) Keyboard();          /* press any key to stop */
Quit_Pgm();}                    /* end the program gracefully
                                                                */
```

```
long GetFreeMemory(void){        /* determine size of free RAM */
  int c1=0;                          /* counter */
  unsigned block=0;             /* size of block to allocate */
  long totalmem=0;                 /* accumulated total */
  char far * vptr;                 /* temporary pointer */
  char far * vptrarray[ATTEMPTS];  /* storage of pointers */
c1=0;                               /* reset counter */
```

Fig. 2-6.
Continued.

```
totalmem=0;                             /* initialize accumulated total */
block=CHUNK;                          /* reset size of allocation request */
#if Compiler==QuickC                      /* QuickC memory allocation */
  while (block>REMAINDER){        /* while allocation > 255 bytes... */
    if((vptr=(char far *)_fmalloc(block))!=NULL){ /* if not NULL */
      vptrarray[c1]=vptr;                  /* store current pointer */
      totalmem=totalmem+block;           /* increase running total */
      c1++;}                              /* increment counter */
    else                             /* else if malloc failed... */
      block=block/2;}            /* ...halve the request and retry */
  for ( ;c1;c1--){                      /* for all saved pointers... */
    _ffree(vptrarray[c1-1]);}   /* ...de-allocate memory block... */
#elif Compiler==TurboC                     /* Turbo C memory allocation */
  while (block>REMAINDER){        /* while allocation > 255 bytes... */
    if((vptr=(char far *)farmalloc(block))!=NULL){/* if not NULL */
      vptrarray[c1]=vptr;                  /* store current pointer */
      totalmem=totalmem+block;           /* increase running total */
      c1++;}                              /* increment counter */
    else                             /* else if malloc failed... */
      block=block/2;}            /* ...halve the request and retry */
  for ( ;c1;c1--){                      /* for all saved pointers... */
    farfree(vptrarray[c1-1]);}} /* ...de-allocate memory block... */
#endif
return totalmem;}              /* ... and return the size of free RAM */
/*_____*/

void Keyboard(){                      /* checks the keyboard buffer */
#if Compiler==QuickC
  if (_bios_keybrd(_KEYBRD_READY)==EMPTY) return;
  else {_bios_keybrd(_KEYBRD_READ);Quit_Pgm();}
#elif Compiler==TurboC
  if (bioskey(1)==EMPTY) return;else {bioskey(0);Quit_Pgm();}
#endif
}
/*_____*/

void Quit_Pgm(){                          /* terminates the program */
#if Compiler==QuickC                          /* if using QuickC */
  _clearscreen(_GCLEARSCREEN);                  /* clear the screen */
  _setvideomode(_DEFAULTMODE);        /* restore the original mode */
#elif Compiler==TurboC                        /* if using Turbo C */
  cleardevice();                                /* clear the screen */
  closegraph();       /* shut down graphics, restore original mode */
#endif
exit(0);}                                    /* terminate the program
_____*/

void Graphics_Setup(){       /* autodetect of graphics hardware */
#if Compiler==QuickC
  if (_setvideomoderows(_VRES16COLOR,60)!=FAIL) goto VGA_mode;
  if (_setvideomoderows(_ERESCOLOR,43)!=FAIL) goto EGA_ECD_mode;
  if (_setvideomoderows(_HRES16COLOR,25)!=FAIL) goto EGA_SCD_mode;
  if (_setvideomoderows(_VRES2COLOR,60)!=FAIL) goto MCGA_mode;
  if (_setvideomoderows(_HRESBW,25)!=FAIL) goto CGA_mode;
  if (_setvideomoderows(_HERCMONO,25)!=FAIL) goto Hercules_mode;
#elif Compiler==TurboC
  int graphics_adapter,graphics_mode;
  detectgraph(&graphics_adapter,&graphics_mode);
  if (graphics_adapter==VGA) goto VGA_mode;
  if (graphics_mode==EGAHI) goto EGA_ECD_mode;
  if (graphics_mode==EGALO) goto EGA_SCD_mode;
  if (graphics_adapter==MCGA) goto MCGA_mode;
  if (graphics_adapter==CGA) goto CGA_mode;
  if (graphics_adapter==HERCMONO) goto Hercules_mode;
#endif
goto abort_pgm;                       /* if no graphics hardware found */

VGA_mode:       /* VGA 640x480x16-color mode, 8x8 character matrix */
x_res=640;y_res=480;mode_flag=1;
```

Fig. 2-6.
Continued.

```
#if Compiler==QuickC
  _settextcolor(C7);
  _settextposition(10,15);
  _outtext("VGA 640x480x16-color graphics, 80x60 character set");
  _settextposition(12,33);
  _outtext("Press any key...");
#elif Compiler==TurboC
  graphics_adapter=VGA;graphics_mode=VGAHI;
  initgraph(&graphics_adapter,&graphics_mode,"");
  settextstyle(0,0,1);setcolor(C7);
  TextRow=10;TextColumn=15;GetTextCoords();
  outtextxy(TextX,TextY,"VGA 640x480x16-color graphics,"
                        " 80x60 character set");
  TextRow=12;TextColumn=33;GetTextCoords();
  outtextxy(TextX,TextY,"Press any key...");
#endif
return;

EGA_ECD_mode: /* EGA 640x350x16-color mode, 8x8 character matrix */
x_res=640;y_res=350;mode_flag=2;
#if Compiler==QuickC
  _settextcolor(C7);
  _settextposition(10,15);
  _outtext("EGA 640x350x16-color graphics, 80x43 character set");
  _settextposition(12,33);
  _outtext("Press any key...");
#elif Compiler==TurboC
  graphics_adapter=EGA;graphics_mode=EGAHI;
  initgraph(&graphics_adapter,&graphics_mode,"");
  settextstyle(0,0,1);setcolor(C7);
  TextRow=10;TextColumn=15;GetTextCoords();
  outtextxy(TextX,TextY,"EGA 640x350x16-color graphics,"
                        " 80x43 character set");
  TextRow=12;TextColumn=33;GetTextCoords();
  outtextxy(TextX,TextY,"Press any key...");
#endif
return;

EGA_SCD_mode: /* EGA 640x200x16-color mode, 8x8 character matrix */
x_res=640;y_res=200;mode_flag=3;
#if Compiler==QuickC
  _settextcolor(C7);
  _settextposition(10,15);
  _outtext("EGA 640x200x16-color graphics, 80x25 character set");
  _settextposition(12,33);
  _outtext("Press any key...");
#elif Compiler==TurboC
  graphics_adapter=EGA;graphics_mode=EGALO;
  initgraph(&graphics_adapter,&graphics_mode,"");
  settextstyle(0,0,1);setcolor(C7);
  TextRow=10;TextColumn=15;GetTextCoords();
  outtextxy(TextX,TextY,"EGA 640x200x16-color graphics,"
                        " 80x25 character set");
  TextRow=12;TextColumn=33;GetTextCoords();
  outtextxy(TextX,TextY,"Press any key...");
#endif
return;

MCGA_mode:    /* MCGA 640x480x2-color mode, 8x8 character matrix */
x_res=640;y_res=480;C0=0;C1=1;C2=1;C3=1;C4=1;C5=1;C6=1;C7=1;
C8=1;C9=1;C10=1;C11=1;C12=1;C13=1;C14=1;C15=1;mode_flag=4;
#if Compiler==QuickC
  _settextcolor(C7);
  _settextposition(10,15);
  _outtext("MCGA 640x480x2-color graphics, 80x60 character set");
  _settextposition(12,33);
  _outtext("Press any key...");
#elif Compiler==TurboC
  graphics_adapter=MCGA;graphics_mode=MCGAHI;
```

Fig. 2-6.
Continued.

```
    initgraph(&graphics_adapter,&graphics_mode,"");
    settextstyle(0,0,1);setcolor(C7);
    TextRow=10;TextColumn=15;GetTextCoords();
    outtextxy(TextX,TextY,"MCGA 640x480x2-color graphics,"
                               " 80x60 character set");
  TextRow=12;TextColumn=33;GetTextCoords();
  outtextxy(TextX,TextY,"Press any key...");
#endif
return;

CGA_mode:        /* CGA 640x200x2-color mode, 8x8 character matrix */
x_res=640;y_res=200;C0=0;C1=1;C2=1;C3=1;C4=1;C5=1;C6=1;C7=1;
C8=1;C9=1;C10=1;C11=1;C12=1;C13=1;C14=1;C15=1;mode_flag=5;
#if Compiler==QuickC
  _settextcolor(C7);
  _settextposition(10,15);
  _outtext("CGA 640x200x2-color graphics, 80x25 character set");
  _settextposition(12,33);
  _outtext("Press any key...");
#elif Compiler==TurboC
  graphics_adapter=CGA;graphics_mode=CGAHI;
  initgraph(&graphics_adapter,&graphics_mode,"");
  settextstyle(0,0,1);setcolor(C7);
  TextRow=10;TextColumn=15;GetTextCoords();
  outtextxy(TextX,TextY,"CGA 640x200x2-color graphics,"
                                " 80x25 character set");
  TextRow=12;TextColumn=33;GetTextCoords();
  outtextxy(TextX,TextY,"Press any key...");
#endif
return;

Hercules_mode: /* Hercules 720x348x2-color mode,
                       9x14 character matrix */
x_res=720;y_res=348;C0=0;C1=1;C2=1;C3=1;C4=1;C5=1;C6=1;C7=1;
C8=1;C9=1;C10=1;C11=1;C12=1;C13=1;C14=1;C15=1;mode_flag=6;
#if Compiler==QuickC
  _settextcolor(C7);
  _settextposition(10,15);
  _outtext("Hercules 720x348x2-color graphics,"
                       " 80x25 character set");
  _settextposition(12,33);
  _outtext("Press any key...");
#elif Compiler==TurboC
  graphics_adapter=HERCMONO;graphics_mode=HERCMONOHI;
  initgraph(&graphics_adapter,&graphics_mode,"");
  setcolor(C7);
  TextRow=10;TextColumn=15;GetTextCoords();
  outtextxy(TextX,TextY,"Hercules 720x348x2-color graphics,"
                                " 80x25 character set");
  TextRow=12;TextColumn=33;GetTextCoords();
  outtextxy(TextX,TextY,"Press any key...");
#endif
return;

abort_pgm:       /* jump to here if no supported graphics hardware */
printf("\n\n\rUnable to proceed.\n\r");
printf("Requires VGA, EGA, CGA, MCGA, or\n\r");
printf("Hercules adapter and appropriate monitor.\n\n");
exit(0);
}
/*_____*/

void GetTextCoords(){       /* convert QuickC text to Turbo C text */
TextX=(TextColumn*8)-8;TextY=(TextRow*8)-8;return;}
/*_____*/

void Notice(int x, int y){        /* displays the copyright notice */
int copyright[][3]={0x7c00,0x0000,0x0000, /* array of bit styles */
```

Fig. 2-6.
Continued.

```
              0x8279,0x819c,0x645e,
              0xba4a,0x4252,0x96d0,
              0xa27a,0x4252,0x955e,
              0xba0a,0x43d2,0xf442,
              0x8219,0x825c,0x945e,
              0x7c00,0x0000,0x0000);
int a,b,c; int t1=0;                              /* local variables */
#if Compiler==QuickC
  for (t1=0;t1<=6;t1++){                          /* draw 7 styled lines */
    a=copyright[t1][0];b=copyright[t1][1];c=copyright[t1][2];
    _setlinestyle(a);_moveto(x,y);_lineto(x+15,y);
    _setlinestyle(b);_moveto(x+16,y);_lineto(x+31,y);
    _setlinestyle(c);_moveto(x+32,y);_lineto(x+47,y);y=y+1;};
  _setlinestyle(0xFFFF);return;
#elif Compiler==TurboC
  for (t1=0;t1<=6;t1++){                          /* draw 7 styled lines */
    a=copyright[t1][0];b=copyright[t1][1];c=copyright[t1][2];
    setlinestyle(USERBIT_LINE,a,NORM_WIDTH);
    moveto(x,y);lineto(x+15,y);
    setlinestyle(USERBIT_LINE,b,NORM_WIDTH);
    moveto(x+16,y);lineto(x+31,y);
    setlinestyle(USERBIT_LINE,c,NORM_WIDTH);
    moveto(x+32,y);lineto(x+47,y);y=y+1;};
  setlinestyle(USERBIT_LINE,0xFFFF,NORM_WIDTH);return;
#endif
}
/*_____

End of source file. */
```

any program you are developing, you can monitor your memory usage and take appropriate steps if RAM becomes scarce.

———— REMINDER ————

If you are using Turbo C, be certain to change the variable named Compiler in the directives section of the source code before compiling the program.

Although you can run this program from within the integrated programming environment of either QuickC or Turbo C, you might find it illustrative to use command-line compilation and linking. If you test your command-line capabilities now, you will know that—if the need arises—you can easily port your master project over to the command-line when necessary. It is a prudent C graphics programmer who pre-tests the software.

NO-NONSENSE GUIDE TO RUNNING THE PROGRAM

Here is a straightforward, step-by-step guide to compiling and linking the demonstration program from the command line. For additional help, you can turn to Appendix A.

Guide for QuickC

If you are using QuickC, the following command-line assumes that the QCL.EXE compiler and LINK.EXE linker are located in the C:\QC2\BIN directory, the C source file to be compiled is located in the C:\QC2\SOURCE directory, and the output of the compilation/link process (OBJ and EXE files) is to be written to the C:\QC2\SOURCE directory. If you are using different directories, or if you are using a dual disk drive system, change the directory names to accommodate your system's arrangement.

First, set the default drive and directory to the directory which holds the C source file (and which will receive the output of the compilation/link process).

CD C:\QC2\SOURCE

Next, invoke the command-line compiler and linker with the following line:

C:\QC2\BIN\QCL /Ox /AM /F 1000 /FeMEMORY /W1 MEMORY.C /link /INF

Be sure to type the command line exactly as shown, except for any directory names which you might change to match your particular system. Be especially careful to include the blank space between the /F option and the 1000 entry, which defines a stack frame of 1000 hex bytes, or 4K.

Refer back to FIG. 2-1 for a description of the option mnemonics used on the command line.

As the compilation/link process is carried out, the /INF option ensures that the linker will provide an ongoing display of all the various routines which are being linked into your program.

After the session is finished, the resulting EXE file will be found in the directory C:\QC2\SOURCE. To run the program from the operating system prompt, type:

C:\QC2\SOURCE MEMORY

The program will display a message similar to that depicted in FIG. 2-5. The amount of free memory will vary, depending upon the version of DOS you are using, the way you have configured DOS, the number of memory-resident programs you have loaded (if any), and the amount of user RAM in your system (usually 640K). Now try compiling and running the program under the control of the QuickC editor and note the drastic difference in the size of free memory.

Guide for Turbo C

If you are using Turbo C, the following command-line assumes that the TCC.EXE compiler and TLINK.EXE linker are located in the C:\TC2\BIN directory, the C source file to be compiled is located in the C:\TC2\BIN directory, the Turbo C include files are located in the C:\TC2\INCLUDE directory, the Turbo C runtime library files are located in the C:\TC2\LIB directory, and the output of the compilation/link process (OBJ and EXE files) is to be written to the C:\TC2\SOURCE directory. If you are using different directories, or if you are using a dual disk drive system, change the directory names to accommodate your system's arrangement.

First, set the default drive and directory to the directory which holds the C source file (and which will receive the output of the compilation/link process).

CD C:\TC2\BIN

Next, invoke the command-line compiler and linker with the following instruction typed on a single line:

TCC -mm -G -IC:\TC2\INCLUDE -LC:\TC2\LIB -nC:\TC2\SOURCE MEMORY
    GRAPHICS.LIB

Be sure to type the command line exactly as shown, except for any directory names which you might change to match your particular system.

Note that Turbo C's graphics library, GRAPHICS.LIB, must be explicitly mentioned on the command line, otherwise Turbo C will not know where to find the graphics routines used by your program. The -L option on the command line tells Turbo C where to locate any LIB files, of course.

Refer back to Fig. 2-2 for a description of the mnemonics used on the command line.

After the session is finished, the resulting EXE file will be found in the directory C:\TC2\SOURCE. To run the program from the operating system prompt, type:

C:\TC2\SOURCE\MEMORY

The appropriate graphics driver, called a .BGI file by Borland, must be in the current drive and directory when you run the EXE program. If you are using an EGA, for example, EGAVGA.BGI must be present in the C:\TC2\SOURCE directory when you attempt to run MEMORY.EXE. To be safe, you might wish to copy all the BGI graphics drivers to the directory from which you will be executing this and future EXE programs.

TRAP

If you are using Turbo C, your graphics program will refuse to run unless the appropriate .BGI graphics driver file is in the current drive and directory.

The program will display a message similar to that depicted in Fig. 2-5. The amount of free memory will vary, depending upon the version of DOS you are using, the way you have configured DOS, the number of memory-resident programs you have loaded (if any), and the amount of user RAM in your system (usually 640K). Now try compiling and running the program under the control of the Turbo C editor and note the drastic difference in the size of free memory.

HOW THE PROGRAM WORKS

The program determines how much memory is free by repeatedly attempting to allocate memory for a 32K block. When the attempt eventually fails, the size of the request is halved until almost all memory has been utilized. A running total provides the number of bytes allocated. Before returning to the caller, the core function de-allocates the memory in the reverse order, thereby restoring RAM to its previous state.

Compiler Directives

The section of source code named COMPILER DIRECTIVES initializes the constants used by the program and declares the #include files. Be certain to change the compiler definition in this section if you are using Turbo C.

The constant named CHUNK defines the size of the block which will be attempted during the first allocation. You can make this larger or smaller, of course, but it makes sense to keep it a power of two. Values of 16K or 64K are useful.

The constant named REMAINDER specifies the smallest size that will be attempted during the allocation loop. This means the result returned by the program will be accurate to only plus-or-minus 255 bytes.

The constant named ATTEMPTS is used later in the core function to set the size of a numeric array used to hold pointers which manage each successful memory allocation. A value of 40 is always enough for a computer with 640K or even 1MB of user RAM.

The main( ) Routine

The most important role of main( ) is to call the function named GetFreeMemory( ). Note how the printf( ) function is then used to display the amount of free memory returned by GetFreeMemory( ) in the variable named freemem.

The GetFreeMemory( ) Routine

The first act of GetFreeMemory( ) is to create and initialize five local variables. These variables are visible only within this function and cannot be used (or changed) by any other function in the program. The comments in the source code describe the purpose of each local variable, but a few further remarks about the points might be useful.

The pointer named vptr will be used to point to the beginning of a block of memory which has just been allocated by the GetFreeMemory( ) function. In other words, the pointer holds the memory address of the block. As the allocation loop continues, the value of this interim pointer will be stored in an array of pointers named vptrarray. Note how the constant ATTEMPTS is used to set the size of this array. The array is needed so that the routine can de-allocate the memory in reverse before it returns to the caller. Otherwise, all available memory would have been allocated during the memory check and would thereafter be unavailable for use.

The essence of the GetFreeMemory( ) routine resides in the while/else loop. In plain english, here is what is happening:

While the size of the block to be requested in less than 255 bytes, try to allocate another block. If successful, store the address of the block in an array, add the number of bytes allocated to the running total, increment the loop counter, and loop back. Otherwise, if the attempt to allocate fails, halve the size of the request and try again. When no more memory can be allocated, de-allocate the blocks in reverse order by using the addresses stored in the array.

A CLOSER LOOK: Near Heap vs. Far Heap

The *near heap* is actually the default data segment, which is the same as the DS register. The *far heap* is unused memory. In the medium memory model, the default data segment never exceeds 64K, although the code segment can be as large as available memory permits. QuickC accesses the near heap with _malloc( ), while Turbo C uses malloc( ). Quick allocates memory on the far heap via _fmalloc( ), while Turbo C uses farmalloc( ). Using the so-called compact memory model provides only 64K for code, but as many 64K segments for data as memory will allow. Using the large memory model allows both data and code to occupy as much memory as is available.

It is important to note that the program always uses the far heap for its allocations and de-allocations. The far heap is unused memory. It is important to distinguish this from what some C programmers call the near heap, which is the default data segment (the value of the DS register). QuickC uses _fmalloc( ) to allocate blocks of memory in the far heap and uses _ffree( ) to de-allocate memory in the far heap. Turbo C uses farmalloc( ) to allocate blocks of memory in the far heap and uses farfree( ) to de-allocate memory in the far heap. In either instance, when all the far heap has been exhausted, both QuickC and Turbo C will attempt to use any free memory in the default data segment in order to meet any allocation request. So, all available memory is eventually used.

If you were to use QuickC's _malloc( ) or Turbo C's malloc( ), however, the compiler would first look in the default data segment for free memory. When that memory is exhausted, neither QuickC nore Turbo C will look outside the near heap, and the reported amount of free memory will only represent the default data segment, not all of RAM.

SPECIAL COMMAND-LINE BENEFITS

Using command-line compilation and linking provides a few special benefits unique to Turbo C, but of interest also to QuickC users.

Graphics Driver Files

As an added bonus for Turbo C users, the command-line version of the compiler makes it possible to link in the BGI graphics drivers. This means the graphics drivers are actually a part of your EXE program, just like they are in QuickC-generated EXE programs. You can link in as many or as few drivers as you wish, but if you are going to distribute your program you would likely wish to link in all the drivers. The advantage of this single-file approach is that your end-user will not be confused by any requirement to have the graphics drivers in a particular drive or directory when your EXE program is started.

Font Files

In addition, you can use the Turbo C command-line to incorporate Turbo C's font files right into your EXE program. Using font files to create vector and bitmapped alphanumeric characters in the graphics mode is discussed in detail in Chapter 7. QuickC provides no easy method for incorporating its font files into the resulting EXE file, and the licensing agreement for version 2.00 seems to remain silent on the issue of distribution. Turbo C's manual makes it clear that your license includes the right to distribute the font files with your finished EXE program.

3

User Input:

Managing the Keyboard

ONE OF THE MOST important functions of any interactive C graphics program is the ability to detect a wide range of keystrokes. Both QuickC and Turbo C offer built-in library functions which test to see if a keystroke has been pressed and which test for the identity of the keystroke.

If you are using QuickC, the _bios_keybrd(_KEYBRD_READY) function can be used to check if a keystroke is present in the keyboard buffer. If you are using Turbo C, the bioskey(1) function performs the check. Each function returns a value of 0 if no keystroke is found, a value of anything else means a keystroke is in the buffer waiting to be read.

FACT

Both QuickC and Turbo C contain built-in library functions to detect and fetch keystroke values from the keyboard buffer.

Whenever a key is pressed on the keyboard, the low-level BIOS routines place the ASCII code for that keystroke in a buffer, waiting to be used by your program. When you test for the presence of a keystroke in the buffer, neither QuickC nor Turbo C alters the buffer if a keystroke is found. It is still there, waiting to be fetched.

If you are using QuickC, the _bios_keybrd(_KEYBRD_READ) function can be used to fetch the ASCII value of the keystroke from the keyboard buffer. If you are using Turbo C, the bioskey(0) function can be used. In either instance, the keystroke value is actually removed from the buffer.

NORMAL KEYSTROKES AND EXTENDED KEYSTROKES

If the keystroke being detected is a normal alphanumeric keystroke such as A to Z, a to z, 0 to 9, and so on, the low-order byte of the word returned by the function contains the ASCII code of the keystroke. Some useful normal keystrokes are depicted in FIG. 3-1.

If the keystroke being detected is a specialized keystroke such as a function key, or a combination keystroke using the Ctrl, Alt, and Shift key, then the low order byte of the word returned by the function will be zero, while the high order byte will contain the ASCII code of the keystroke. Some useful specialized keystrokes are depicted in FIG. 3-2. Note that there is some overlap of ASCII values between FIG. 3-1 and FIG. 3-2.

Fig. 3-1. Code numbers for useful regular keystrokes, as returned by QuickC's bioskeybrd( ) instruction and Turbo C's bioskey( ) instruction.

ASCII CODE	KEYSTROKE
13	ENTER
32	SPACEBAR
27	ESC
8	BACKSPACE
9	TAB
42	PRTSC
97 TO 122	A TO Z
65 TO 90	A TO Z
48 TO 57	0 TO 9

WRITING A KEYBOARD INPUT MANAGER

Both QuickC and Turbo C make it a relatively easy chore to write a powerful and versatile keyboard input manager. The keyboard routine would work as follows.

First, a data structure would be created to receive the word returned by the function. This structure would allow your program to access the returned value either as a word (an integer value) or as a byte (a char value). Clearly, the library's built-in function returns a word, but your program must check the low-order byte and the high-order byte separately in order to make an intelligent decision concerning whether the captured keystroke was a normal key or a specialized keystroke.

EXTENDED ASCII CODE (0 + CODE)	KEYSTROKES
59 TO 68	F1 TO F10
84 TO 93	SHIFT+F1 TO SHIFT+F10
94 TO 103	CTRL+F1 TO CTRL+F10
104 TO 113	ALT+F1 TO ALT+F10
83	DEL
82	INS
71	HOME
79	END
73	PGUP
81	PGDN
75	LEFT ARROW
77	RIGHT ARROW
72	UP ARROW
80	DOWN ARROW
119	CTRL+HOME
117	CTRL+END

Fig. 3-2. Code numbers for useful extended keystrokes (where the first byte returned is 0 and the second byte holds the code shown in this table).

Next, the routine would use QuickC's and Turbo C's built-in function to test if a keystroke is waiting to be read. If no keystroke is present, the routine would return control to the caller rather than sitting idle waiting for the user to enter a keystroke. On the other hand, if a keystroke was detected, the routine would then use QuickC's and Turbo C's built-in function to read the value into the structure defined at the beginning of the routine.

Now the routine checks the low-order byte of the word which was fetched from the keyboard buffer. If the byte is non-zero, then the value is the ASCII value of a normal keystroke. C's powerful switch( ) instruction can be used to perform a program control branch based upon the value. If, however, the low-order byte is zero, then the routine proceeds to check the value of the high-order byte, which contains the ASCII value of a specialized or combination keystroke as depicted in FIG. 3-2. Again, the switch( ) statement can be used to effect a branch.

Typical source code to retrieve a keystroke from the buffer might be written for QuickC thus:

```
union u_type{int a;char b[3];}keystroke;
char inkey = 0;
if (_bios_keybrd(_KEYBRD_READY) = = 0) {keycode = 0;return;}
keystroke.a = _bios_keybrd(_KEYBRD_READ);
```

Typical source code to retrieve a keystroke from the buffer might be written for Turbo C thus:

```
union u_type{int a;char b[3];}keystroke;
char inkey = 0;
if (bioskey(1) = = 0) {keycode = 0;return;}
keystroke.a = bioskey(0);
```

In both examples, the first line of code initializes a structure named keystroke, which can be manipulated either as an integer (a word) or as a char (either of the bytes within the structure).

The second line of code declares and initializes a char variable named inkey. A char is a one-byte variable.

The third line of code uses QuickC's and Turbo C's built-in library function to determine if any keystroke is waiting in the buffer. If the value returned by this call is zero, then no keystroke is waiting, and the routine sets a global variable before returning to the caller. The global variable is simply a method to advise your calling routine that no keystroke is present.

If program execution falls through to the fourth line of code, then some sort of keystroke is in the buffer. QuickC's and Turbo C's built-in routine is used to fetch the integer value from the buffer and store it in the structure named keystroke. Note how the keystroke.a syntax is used to access the structure as an integer (a two-byte word).

It is important to realize that the code fragments provided here can be written smaller and faster, but the goal in this chapter is to make the code as understandable as possible.

WRITING A KEYSTROKE CATEGORIZING ROUTINE

Now that your program has captured a keystroke value, your source code must be smart enough to discover whether the keystroke is a normal keystroke such as A to Z, or some exotic combination keystroke such as Ctrl+F1 or PgUp. An appropriate piece of C source code might look something like this:

```
inkey = keystroke.b[0];
if (inkey! = 0){
    keycode = 1;keynum = inkey;return;}
if (inkey = = 0){
    keycode = 2;keynum = keystroke.b[1];return;}
```

In this example, the first line of code uses the keystroke.b syntax to assign the value of the first byte (the low-order byte) in the structure to a variable named inkey. Remember, the structure contains the word (integer) which was fetched from the keystroke buffer.

The second line of code tests to see if the variable named inkey is non-zero. If this is the case, then a global variable named keycode is set to a value of 1, another global variable named keynum is set to the ASCII value of the normal keystroke, and the routine returns to the caller. The two global variables named keycode and keynum are simply your way of telling the caller that the key is a normal keystroke and the ASCII value of the key.

TRAP

Your program must be smart enough to know if the inbound keystroke is a normal key or an extended key, otherwise it will be subject to erratic and unpredictable behavior caused by the same ASCII code being shared by some normal and some extended keystrokes. For example, ASCII 71 can be either G or Home.

If, however, program control falls through to the fourth line of code, then the example tests to be certain the low-order byte stored in inkey is equal to zero. If it is, the global variable named keycode is set to 2 in order to advise the caller that the keystroke was a specialized or combination keystroke. The ASCII value of the keystroke is then fetched from the HIGH-ORDER BYTE of the structure and stored in a global variable named keynum. Control is then returned to the caller.

Your calling routine now has all the information it needs to decide what to do next. It knows whether the keystroke was a normal keystroke or a specialized—perhaps a combination—keystroke. It also knows the ASCII value of the keystroke.

It must have all this information because there is some redundancy in the ASCII codes assigned to various keystrokes. Refer again to FIG. 3-1 and FIG. 3-2. You can see that ASCII value 71 means the G key has been pressed, but it could also mean that the extended keystroke Home (on the numeric keypad) was pressed. Clearly, your program must know whether the ASCII code refers to a normal key or an extended key if it is to correctly handle keyboard input. Erratic and undesirable results could arise if your program mistakenly processed ASCII 65 as the letter A when in fact the end-user had pressed F7.

WRITING A KEYSTROKE SWITCHER

You can use the variable named keycode to decide whether to call a routine which performs branches based upon normal keystrokes, or to call a different routine which performs branches based upon extended keystrokes. You might use a variable of a different name in your own original C graphics programs—or you might use a local variable which is passed back and forth on the stack—but the concept of using a token to define the existing state is a sound one.

Both QuickC and Turbo C support the powerful switch( ) statement. Suppose, for example, that you wish your program to make a decision dependent upon the value of a normal keystroke. Your QuickC or Turbo C source code might look something like this:

```
switch (keynum) {
    case 27: Quit_Pgm( );
    case 13: Enter_Key( ); return;
    case 8:  Bkspc_Key( ); return;
    case 32: Space_Bar( ); return;
    default: MakeSound( ); return; }
```

In the preceding example, program control branches based upon the value of the variable named keynum. Remember, this variable was set to the ASCII value of the keystroke by the earlier source code fragments.

If the value equals 27, then the second line of source code calls a routine which might terminate the program. ASCII value 27 is the escape key, or Esc. Refer back to FIG. 3-1.

If, however, the value equals 8, which is the Backspace key, the program would branch to a different function and then return to the caller after the function finishes executing.

TIP

Always use the default keyword to make your switch( ) routines bulletproof.

Note the final line of the example, which establishes a bulletproof safety vest around the code by telling the compiler that in the event no match is found by the switch( ) statement, then the program should make a noise and return to the caller. You should always write a default condition into all your switch( ) routines. In this example, if the end-user pressed a normal key other than Enter, Backspace, spacebar, or Esc your routine would simply issue a sound (and perhaps loop back to wait for a legal keystroke).

A switcher to handle specialized, combination, or extended keystrokes might look something like this:

```
switch (keynum) {
    case 59:  F1_Key( ); return;
    case 60:  F2_Key( ); return;
    case 84:  ShiftF1_Key( ); return;
    case 94:  CtrlF1_Key( ); return;
    case 118: CtrlPgDn_Key( ); return;
    default: MakeSound( ); return; }
```

Refer back to FIG. 3-2 for a table of ASCII codes for extended keystrokes.

DETECTING 150 DIFFERENT KEYSTROKE COMBINATIONS

The tables in FIG. 3-1 and FIG. 3-2, when combined with the source code examples and demonstration program provided in this chapter, give you the ability to detect and use over 150 different keystrokes and keystroke combinations in your C graphics programs. Using the demonstration program as a toolkit, you can support 71 different normal keystrokes and 84 different specialized or combination keystrokes. Clearly, this is more than enough to make your own programs very professional and robust.

For advanced programmers, however, both the QuickC manual and the Turbo C manual provide further guidance on detecting such esoteric conditions as whether the Ctrl key was pressed, whether Num Lock is on or off, whether Caps Lock is on or off, and which shift key (left or right) was pressed.

WHERE TO LOOK

Check your user's manual for advanced keystroke management techniques for Caps Lock, Num Lock, and others.

Some of the power of keystroke management is exploited in the two major demonstration programs in this book, presented in Chapter 8 and Chapter 13. Both the interactive drawing program and the interactive 3D CAD program contain a keyboard text editor which the end-user can use to create a filename for saving and loading images. The editor works its magic by manipulating a text string in memory.

MANAGING THE KEYBOARD:
A Demonstration Program

The image in FIG. 3-3 is a graphics print of the output produced by the demonstration program listing in FIG. 3-4. This program, KEYBOARD.C., is ready to compile and run under either QuickC or Turbo C. If you are using Turbo C, don't forget to change the variable named Compiler in the COMPILER DIRECTIVES section of the source code before beginning to compile the program.

Use Alt+X or Ctrl+End to stop the program after you have experimented with the keyboard at runtime.

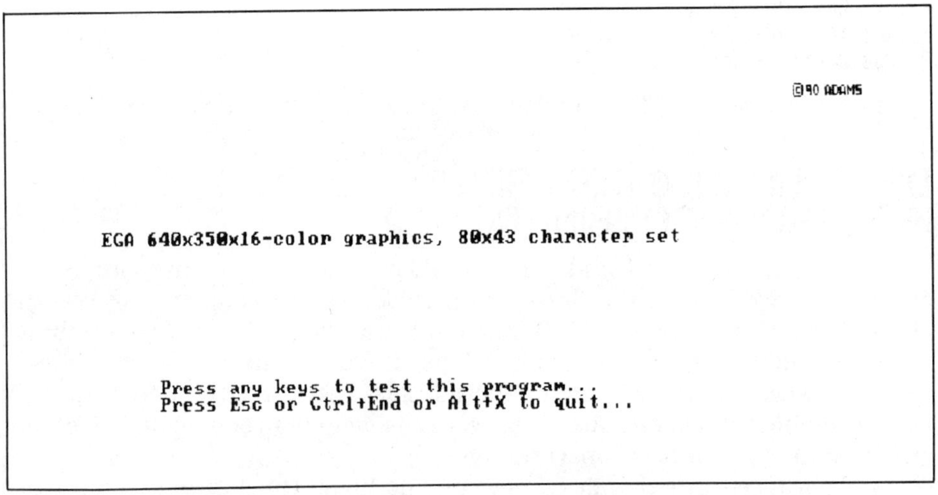

Fig. 3-3. Print of the image generated by the keystroke demonstration program, KEYBOARD.C.

Fig. 3-4. Source code for KEYBOARD.C, designed to poll the keyboard for a wide range of keystrokes, including Ctrl+, Alt+, functions keys, and others. Ready to compile under QuickC or Turbo C.

```
/*
Keyboard Input Manager                      Source file: KEYBOARD.C

Purpose: demonstrates how to write C graphics programs that
use a keyboard for user input.

Compiler: QuickC or Turbo C. Default is QuickC. To use
Turbo C, change one line in COMPILER DIRECTIVES below.

Memory model: medium memory model.

Marketability: will detect and support VGA, EGA, MCGA, CGA, and
Hercules graphics adapters; will detect and trap F1...F10
function keys, Ctrl+ keys, Alt+ keys, Shift+ keys, arrow keys,
PgUp, PgDn, and many others.

(c) Copyright 1990 Lee Adams. As purchaser of the book in which
this program is published, you are granted a non-exclusive
royalty-free license to reproduce and distribute these routines in
executable form as part of your software product, subject to any
trademark or patent rights of others, and subject to the limited
warranty described in the Introduction of the book. All other
rights reserved.
_____

COMPILER DIRECTIVES
These are instructions to your C compiler.  */

#define QuickC    1
#define TurboC    2
#define Compiler QuickC    /* NOTE: Change to TurboC if required. */
#define FAIL      0        /* for graphics auto-detect algorithm */
#define EMPTY     0         /* for checking keyboard buffer */

#include <bios.h>                  /* supports keyboard functions */
#include <stdio.h>                 /* supports the printf function */
#if Compiler==QuickC
  #include <graph.h>                  /* supports QuickC's graphics */
  #include <conio.h>                   /* supports QuickC port IO */
#elif Compiler==TurboC
  #include <graphics.h>             /* supports Turbo C's graphics */
  #include <dos.h>                     /* supports TurboC port IO */
#endif
#include <process.h>                 /* support the exit function
_____

FUNCTION PROTOTYPES
These ANSI C function declarations allow your C compiler to check
each function for correct arguments and return value.  */

void Keyboard();                        /* checks for a keystroke */
void Quit_Pgm();                     /* ends the program gracefully */
void Notice(int,int);              /* displays the copyright notice */
void Graphics_Setup();              /* initializes the graphics mode */
void GetTextCoords();        /* convert QuickC text to Turbo C text */
void NormalKey();                   /* switcher for normal keystrokes */
void ExtendedKey();           /* switcher for extended keystrokes */
void MakeSound(int,int);                  /* generates a sound
_____

DECLARATION OF GLOBAL VARIABLES
These variables are declared and initialized outside of any
function and are visible to all functions in this source file.   */
```

Fig. 3-4.
Continued.

```
#if Compiler==QuickC
   struct videoconfig vc;               /* QuickC's graphics table */
#endif
int C0=0,C1=1,C2=2,C3=3,C4=4,C5=5,C6=6,C7=7,C8=8,C9=9,C10=10,
C11=11,C12=12,C13=13,C14=14,C15=15;              /* color codes */
int x_res=640,y_res=480;                    /* screen resolution */
int mode_flag=0;   /* indicates which graphics mode is being used */
int t1=1;                                        /* loop counter */
int sx=0,sy=0;                        /* xy screen drawing coords */
int TextRow=1,TextColumn=1;             /* text position for QuickC */
int TextX=0,TextY=0;                    /* text position for Turbo C */
char keycode=0;         /* flag for normal or extended keystroke */
char keynum=0;                        /* ASCII number of keystroke


FUNCTION DEFINITIONS   */

main(){                               /* this is the master routine */
Graphics_Setup();                     /* establish graphics mode */
#if Compiler==QuickC
   _getvideoconfig(&vc);                /* initialize video table */
   _setcolor(C14);_rectangle(_GBORDER,0,0,x_res-1,y_res-1);
   _setcolor(C7);Notice(589,2);
   _settextposition(19,20);
   _outtext("Press any keys to test this program...");
   _settextposition(20,20);
   _outtext("Press Esc or Ctrl+End or Alt+X to quit...");
#elif Compiler==TurboC
   setcolor(C14);rectangle(0,0,x_res-1,y_res-1);
   setcolor(C7);Notice(589,2);
   TextRow=19;TextColumn=20;GetTextCoords();
   outtextxy(TextX,TextY,"Press any keys to test this program...");
   TextRow=20;TextColumn=20;GetTextCoords();
   outtextxy(TextX,TextY,"Press Esc or Ctrl+End or"
                         " Alt+X to quit...");
   setfillstyle(SOLID_FILL,C0);
#endif
Label1:                           /* start of keyboard polling loop */
   Keyboard();                              /* poll the keyboard */
   if (keycode==1) NormalKey();          /* if normal keystroke */
   if (keycode==2) ExtendedKey();      /* if extended keystroke */
   goto Label1;                      /* if no keystroke, loop */
Quit_Pgm();                                       /* boilerplate */
}
/*_____*/

void Quit_Pgm(){                      /* terminates the program */
#if Compiler==QuickC                       /* if using QuickC */
   _clearscreen(_GCLEARSCREEN);              /* clear the screen */
   _setvideomode(_DEFAULTMODE);      /* restore the original mode */
#elif Compiler==TurboC                     /* if using Turbo C */
   cleardevice();                            /* clear the screen */
   closegraph();       /* shut down graphics, restore original mode */
#endif
exit(0);}                             /* terminate the program */
/*_____*/

void Keyboard(){                      /* checks for keystrokes */
union u_type{int a;char b[3];}keystroke; /* define the structure */
char inkey=0;
#if Compiler==QuickC
   if (_bios_keybrd(_KEYBRD_READY)==EMPTY){keycode=0;return;}
   keystroke.a=_bios_keybrd(_KEYBRD_READ);   /* fetch ASCII codes */
#elif Compiler==TurboC
   if (bioskey(1)==EMPTY){keycode=0;return;}
   keystroke.a=bioskey(0);              /* fetch ASCII codes */
#endif
inkey=keystroke.b[0];                    /* retrieve first code */
if (inkey!=0){                       /* if a normal keystroke... */
```

Fig. 3-4.
Continued.

```
       keycode=1;                              /* set flag to normal keystroke */
       keynum=inkey;                   /* and load ASCII code into variable */
       return;}
    if (inkey==0){                             /* if an extended keystroke... */
       keycode=2;                       /* set flag to extended keystroke */
       keynum=keystroke.b[1];   /* and load second code into variable */
       return;}
    }
    /*_____*/

    void NormalKey(void){            /* switcher for normal keystrokes */
    #if Compiler==QuickC
       _settextposition(22,20);
    switch (keynum){
       case 27:   _outtext("Esc                ");Quit_Pgm();
       case 13:   _outtext("Enter              ");return;
       case 8:    _outtext("Backspace          ");return;
       case 9:    _outtext("Tab                ");return;
       case 32:   _outtext("Spacebar           ");return;
       case 121:  _outtext("y                  ");return;
       case 89:   _outtext("Y                  ");return;
       case 110:  _outtext("n                  ");return;
       case 78:   _outtext("N                  ");return;
       case 42:   _outtext("PrtSc              ");return;
       case 43:   _outtext("+ (norm or pad)    ");return;
       case 45:   _outtext("- (norm or pad)    ");return;
       case 127:  _outtext("Ctrl+Backspace     ");return;
       default:   _outtext("untrapped key      ");
             MakeSound(400,16000);return;}
    #elif Compiler==TurboC
       TextRow=22;TextColumn=20;GetTextCoords();
       bar(TextX,TextY,TextX+144,TextY+9);

    switch (keynum){
       case 27:   outtextxy(TextX,TextY,"Esc              ");Quit_Pgm();
       case 13:   outtextxy(TextX,TextY,"Enter            ");return;
       case 8:    outtextxy(TextX,TextY,"Backspace        ");return;
       case 9:    outtextxy(TextX,TextY,"Tab              ");return;
       case 32:   outtextxy(TextX,TextY,"Spacebar         ");return;
       case 121:  outtextxy(TextX,TextY,"y                ");return;
       case 89:   outtextxy(TextX,TextY,"Y                ");return;
       case 110:  outtextxy(TextX,TextY,"n                ");return;
       case 78:   outtextxy(TextX,TextY,"N                ");return;
       case 42:   outtextxy(TextX,TextY,"PrtSc            ");return;
       case 43:   outtextxy(TextX,TextY,"+ (norm or pad)  ");return;
       case 45:   outtextxy(TextX,TextY,"- (norm or pad)  ");return;
       case 127:  outtextxy(TextX,TextY,"Ctrl+Backspace   ");return;
       default:   outtextxy(TextX,TextY,"untrapped key    ");
             MakeSound(400,16000);return;}
    #endif
    }
    /*_____*/

    void ExtendedKey(){              /* switcher for extended keystrokes */
    #if Compiler==QuickC
       _settextposition(22,20);
    switch (keynum){
       case 59:   _outtext("F1                 ");return;
       case 60:   _outtext("F2                 ");return;
       case 61:   _outtext("F3                 ");return;
       case 62:   _outtext("F4                 ");return;
       case 63:   _outtext("F5                 ");return;
       case 64:   _outtext("F6                 ");return;
       case 65:   _outtext("F7                 ");return;
       case 66:   _outtext("F8                 ");return;
       case 67:   _outtext("F9                 ");return;
       case 68:   _outtext("F10                ");return;
       case 84:   _outtext("Shift+F1           ");return;
       case 85:   _outtext("Shift+F2           ");return;
       case 86:   _outtext("Shift+F3           ");return;
```

Fig. 3-4.
Continued.

```
case 87:  _outtext("Shift+F4         ");return;
case 88:  _outtext("Shift+F5         ");return;
case 89:  _outtext("Shift+F6         ");return;
case 90:  _outtext("Shift+F7         ");return;
case 91:  _outtext("Shift+F8         ");return;
case 92:  _outtext("Shift+F9         ");return;
case 93:  _outtext("Shift+F10        ");return;
case 15:  _outtext("Shift+Tab        ");return;
case 94:  _outtext("Ctrl+F1          ");return;
case 95:  _outtext("Ctrl+F2          ");return;
case 96:  _outtext("Ctrl+F3          ");return;
case 97:  _outtext("Ctrl+F4          ");return;
case 98:  _outtext("Ctrl+F5          ");return;
case 99:  _outtext("Ctrl+F6          ");return;
case 100: _outtext("Ctrl+F7          ");return;
case 101: _outtext("Ctrl+F8          ");return;
case 102: _outtext("Ctrl+F9          ");return;
case 103: _outtext("Ctrl+F10         ");return;
case 3:   _outtext("Ctrl+@           ");return;
case 104: _outtext("Alt+F1           ");return;
case 105: _outtext("Alt+F2           ");return;
case 106: _outtext("Alt+F3           ");return;
case 107: _outtext("Alt+F4           ");return;
case 108: _outtext("Alt+F5           ");return;
case 109: _outtext("Alt+F6           ");return;
case 110: _outtext("Alt+F7           ");return;
case 111: _outtext("Alt+F8           ");return;
case 112: _outtext("Alt+F9           ");return;
case 113: _outtext("Alt+F10          ");return;
case 119: _outtext("Ctrl+Home        ");return;
case 117: _outtext("Ctrl+End         ");Quit_Pgm();
case -124:_outtext("Ctrl+PgUp        ");return;         /* kludge */
case 118: _outtext("Ctrl+PgDn        ");return;
case 115: _outtext("Ctrl+left arrow ");return;
case 116: _outtext("Ctrl+right arrow");return;
case 83:  _outtext("Del              ");return;
case 82:  _outtext("Ins              ");return;
case 71:  _outtext("Home             ");return;
case 79:  _outtext("End              ");return;
case 73:  _outtext("PgUp             ");return;
case 81:  _outtext("PgDn             ");return;
case 75:  _outtext("left arrow key  ");return;
case 77:  _outtext("right arrow key ");return;
case 72:  _outtext("up arrow key     ");return;
case 80:  _outtext("down arrow key  ");return;
case 30:  _outtext("Alt+A            ");return;
case 48:  _outtext("Alt+B            ");return;
case 46:  _outtext("Alt+C            ");return;
case 32:  _outtext("Alt+D            ");return;
case 18:  _outtext("Alt+E            ");return;
case 33:  _outtext("Alt+F            ");return;
case 34:  _outtext("Alt+G            ");return;
case 35:  _outtext("Alt+H            ");return;
case 23:  _outtext("Alt+I            ");return;
case 36:  _outtext("Alt+J            ");return;
case 37:  _outtext("Alt+K            ");return;
case 38:  _outtext("Alt+L            ");return;
case 50:  _outtext("Alt+M            ");return;
case 49:  _outtext("Alt+N            ");return;
case 24:  _outtext("Alt+O            ");return;
case 25:  _outtext("Alt+P            ");return;
case 16:  _outtext("Alt+Q            ");return;
case 19:  _outtext("Alt+R            ");return;
case 31:  _outtext("Alt+S            ");return;
case 20:  _outtext("Alt+T            ");return;
case 22:  _outtext("Alt+U            ");return;
case 47:  _outtext("Alt+V            ");return;
case 17:  _outtext("Alt+W            ");return;
case 45:  _outtext("Alt+X            ");Quit_Pgm();
```

Fig. 3-4.
Continued.

```
    case 21:  _outtext("Alt+Y            ");return;
    case 44:  _outtext("Alt+Z            ");return;
    default:  _outtext("untrapped key    ");
              MakeSound(400,16000);return;}              /* undefined */
#elif Compiler==TurboC
  TextRow=22;TextColumn=20;GetTextCoords();
  bar(TextX,TextY,TextX+144,TextY+9);
switch (keynum){
    case 59:  outtextxy(TextX,TextY,"F1                ");return;
    case 60:  outtextxy(TextX,TextY,"F2                ");return;
    case 61:  outtextxy(TextX,TextY,"F3                ");return;
    case 62:  outtextxy(TextX,TextY,"F4                ");return;
    case 63:  outtextxy(TextX,TextY,"F5                ");return;
    case 64:  outtextxy(TextX,TextY,"F6                ");return;
    case 65:  outtextxy(TextX,TextY,"F7                ");return;
    case 66:  outtextxy(TextX,TextY,"F8                ");return;
    case 67:  outtextxy(TextX,TextY,"F9                ");return;
    case 68:  outtextxy(TextX,TextY,"F10               ");return;
    case 84:  outtextxy(TextX,TextY,"Shift+F1          ");return;
    case 85:  outtextxy(TextX,TextY,"Shift+F2          ");return;
    case 86:  outtextxy(TextX,TextY,"Shift+F3          ");return;
    case 87:  outtextxy(TextX,TextY,"Shift+F4          ");return;
    case 88:  outtextxy(TextX,TextY,"Shift+F5          ");return;
    case 89:  outtextxy(TextX,TextY,"Shift+F6          ");return;
    case 90:  outtextxy(TextX,TextY,"Shift+F7          ");return;
    case 91:  outtextxy(TextX,TextY,"Shift+F8          ");return;
    case 92:  outtextxy(TextX,TextY,"Shift+F9          ");return;
    case 93:  outtextxy(TextX,TextY,"Shift+F10         ");return;
    case 15:  outtextxy(TextX,TextY,"Shift+Tab         ");return;
    case 94:  outtextxy(TextX,TextY,"Ctrl+F1           ");return;
    case 95:  outtextxy(TextX,TextY,"Ctrl+F2           ");return;
    case 96:  outtextxy(TextX,TextY,"Ctrl+F3           ");return;
    case 97:  outtextxy(TextX,TextY,"Ctrl+F4           ");return;
    case 98:  outtextxy(TextX,TextY,"Ctrl+F5           ");return;
    case 99:  outtextxy(TextX,TextY,"Ctrl+F6           ");return;
    case 100: outtextxy(TextX,TextY,"Ctrl+F7           ");return;
    case 101: outtextxy(TextX,TextY,"Ctrl+F8           ");return;
    case 102: outtextxy(TextX,TextY,"Ctrl+F9           ");return;
    case 103: outtextxy(TextX,TextY,"Ctrl+F10          ");return;
    case 3:   outtextxy(TextX,TextY,"Ctrl+@            ");return;
    case 104: outtextxy(TextX,TextY,"Alt+F1            ");return;
    case 105: outtextxy(TextX,TextY,"Alt+F2            ");return;
    case 106: outtextxy(TextX,TextY,"Alt+F3            ");return;
    case 107: outtextxy(TextX,TextY,"Alt+F4            ");return;
    case 108: outtextxy(TextX,TextY,"Alt+F5            ");return;
    case 109: outtextxy(TextX,TextY,"Alt+F6            ");return;
    case 110: outtextxy(TextX,TextY,"Alt+F7            ");return;
    case 111: outtextxy(TextX,TextY,"Alt+F8            ");return;
    case 112: outtextxy(TextX,TextY,"Alt+F9            ");return;
    case 113: outtextxy(TextX,TextY,"Alt+F10           ");return;
    case 119: outtextxy(TextX,TextY,"Ctrl+Home         ");return;
    case 117: outtextxy(TextX,TextY,"Ctrl+End          ");Quit_Pgm();
    case -124:outtextxy(TextX,TextY,"Ctrl+PgUp         ");return;
    case 118: outtextxy(TextX,TextY,"Ctrl+PgDn         ");return;
    case 115: outtextxy(TextX,TextY,"Ctrl+left arrow   ");return;
    case 116: outtextxy(TextX,TextY,"Ctrl+right arrow  ");return;
    case 83:  outtextxy(TextX,TextY,"Del               ");return;
    case 82:  outtextxy(TextX,TextY,"Ins               ");return;
    case 71:  outtextxy(TextX,TextY,"Home              ");return;
    case 79:  outtextxy(TextX,TextY,"End               ");return;
    case 73:  outtextxy(TextX,TextY,"PgUp              ");return;
    case 81:  outtextxy(TextX,TextY,"PgDn              ");return;
    case 75:  outtextxy(TextX,TextY,"left arrow key    ");return;
    case 77:  outtextxy(TextX,TextY,"right arrow key   ");return;
    case 72:  outtextxy(TextX,TextY,"up arrow key      ");return;
    case 80:  outtextxy(TextX,TextY,"down arrow key    ");return;
    case 30:  outtextxy(TextX,TextY,"Alt+A             ");return;
    case 48:  outtextxy(TextX,TextY,"Alt+B             ");return;
    case 46:  outtextxy(TextX,TextY,"Alt+C             ");return;
```

Fig. 3-4.
Continued.

```
   case 32:   outtextxy(TextX,TextY,"Alt+D               ");return;
   case 18:   outtextxy(TextX,TextY,"Alt+E               ");return;
   case 33:   outtextxy(TextX,TextY,"Alt+F               ");return;
   case 34:   outtextxy(TextX,TextY,"Alt+G               ");return;
   case 35:   outtextxy(TextX,TextY,"Alt+H               ");return;
   case 23:   outtextxy(TextX,TextY,"Alt+I               ");return;
   case 36:   outtextxy(TextX,TextY,"Alt+J               ");return;
   case 37:   outtextxy(TextX,TextY,"Alt+K               ");return;
   case 38:   outtextxy(TextX,TextY,"Alt+L               ");return;
   case 50:   outtextxy(TextX,TextY,"Alt+M               ");return;
   case 49:   outtextxy(TextX,TextY,"Alt+N               ");return;
   case 24:   outtextxy(TextX,TextY,"Alt+O               ");return;
   case 25:   outtextxy(TextX,TextY,"Alt+P               ");return;
   case 16:   outtextxy(TextX,TextY,"Alt+Q               ");return;
   case 19:   outtextxy(TextX,TextY,"Alt+R               ");return;
   case 31:   outtextxy(TextX,TextY,"Alt+S               ");return;
   case 20:   outtextxy(TextX,TextY,"Alt+T               ");return;
   case 22:   outtextxy(TextX,TextY,"Alt+U               ");return;
   case 47:   outtextxy(TextX,TextY,"Alt+V               ");return;
   case 17:   outtextxy(TextX,TextY,"Alt+W               ");return;
   case 45:   outtextxy(TextX,TextY,"Alt+X               ");Quit_Pgm();
   case 21:   outtextxy(TextX,TextY,"Alt+Y               ");return;
   case 44:   outtextxy(TextX,TextY,"Alt+Z               ");return;
   default:   outtextxy(TextX,TextY,"untrapped key       ");
         MakeSound(400,16000);return;}                       /* undefined */
#endif
}
/*_____

FUNCTION: GENERATE A SOUND
Enter with frequency in the range 40 to 4660 hertz.
Comfortable frequency range for the human ear is 40 to 2400.
Enter with duration expressed as an integer to be used in a
for...next delay loop (which is dependent upon CPU speed).    */

void MakeSound(int hertz,int duration){      /* generates a sound */
int t1=1,high_byte=0,low_byte=0;
short count=0;unsigned char old_port=0,new_port=0;
if (hertz<40) return;        /* avoid math overflow for int count */
if (hertz>4660) return;      /* avoid math underflow for low_byte */
count=1193180L/hertz;                   /* determine timer count */
high_byte=count/256;low_byte=count-(high_byte*256);
#if Compiler==QuickC
   outp(0x43,0xB6);                     /* prep the timer register */
   outp(0x42,low_byte);                      /* send the low byte */
   outp(0x42,high_byte);                     /* send the high byte */
   old_port=inp(0x61);          /* store the existing port value */
   new_port=(old_port|0x03);  /* use OR to set bits 0 and 1 to on */
   outp(0x61,new_port);                  /* turn on the speaker */
   for (t1=1;t1<=duration;t1++);                      /* wait */
   outp(0x61,old_port);                 /* turn off the speaker */
#elif Compiler==TurboC
   outportb(0x43,0xB6);
   outportb(0x42,low_byte);
   outportb(0x42,high_byte);
   old_port=inportb(0x61);
   new_port=(old_port | 0x03);
   outportb(0x61,new_port);
   for (t1=1;t1<=duration;t1++);
   outportb(0x61,old_port);
#endif
return;}
/*_____*/

void Graphics_Setup(){          /* autodetect of graphics hardware */
#if Compiler==QuickC
   if (_setvideomoderows(_VRES16COLOR,60)!=FAIL) goto VGA_mode;
   if (_setvideomoderows(_ERESCOLOR,43)!=FAIL) goto EGA_ECD_mode;
   if (_setvideomoderows(_HRES16COLOR,25)!=FAIL) goto EGA_SCD_mode;
```

Fig. 3-4.
Continued.

```
      if (_setvideomoderows(_VRES2COLOR,60)!=FAIL) goto MCGA_mode;
      if (_setvideomoderows(_HRESBW,25)!=FAIL) goto CGA_mode;
      if (_setvideomoderows(_HERCMONO,25)!=FAIL) goto Hercules_mode;
#elif Compiler==TurboC
   int graphics_adapter,graphics_mode;
   detectgraph(&graphics_adapter,&graphics_mode);
   if (graphics_adapter==VGA) goto VGA_mode;
   if (graphics_mode==EGAHI) goto EGA_ECD_mode;
   if (graphics_mode==EGALO) goto EGA_SCD_mode;
   if (graphics_adapter==MCGA) goto MCGA_mode;
   if (graphics_adapter==CGA) goto CGA_mode;
   if (graphics_adapter==HERCMONO) goto Hercules_mode;
#endif
goto abort_pgm;                       /* if no graphics hardware found */

VGA_mode:       /* VGA 640x480x16-color mode, 8x8 character matrix */
x_res=640;y_res=480;mode_flag=1;
#if Compiler==QuickC
   _settextcolor(C7);
   _settextposition(10,15);
   _outtext("VGA 640x480x16-color graphics, 80x60 character set");
#elif Compiler==TurboC
   graphics_adapter=VGA;graphics_mode=VGAHI;
   initgraph(&graphics_adapter,&graphics_mode,"");
   settextstyle(0,0,1);setcolor(C7);
   TextRow=10;TextColumn=15;GetTextCoords();
   outtextxy(TextX,TextY,"VGA 640x480x16-color graphics,"
                          " 80x60 character set");
#endif
return;

EGA_ECD_mode: /* EGA 640x350x16-color mode, 8x8 character matrix */
x_res=640;y_res=350;mode_flag=2;
#if Compiler==QuickC
   _settextcolor(C7);
   _settextposition(10,15);
   _outtext("EGA 640x350x16-color graphics, 80x43 character set");
#elif Compiler==TurboC
   graphics_adapter=EGA;graphics_mode=EGAHI;
   initgraph(&graphics_adapter,&graphics_mode,"");
   settextstyle(0,0,1);setcolor(C7);
   TextRow=10;TextColumn=15;GetTextCoords();
   outtextxy(TextX,TextY,"EGA 640x350x16-color graphics,"
                          " 80x43 character set");
#endif
return;

EGA_SCD_mode: /* EGA 640x200x16-color mode, 8x8 character matrix */
x_res=640;y_res=200;mode_flag=3;
#if Compiler==QuickC
   _settextcolor(C7);
   _settextposition(10,15);
   _outtext("EGA 640x200x16-color graphics, 80x25 character set");
#elif Compiler==TurboC
   graphics_adapter=EGA;graphics_mode=EGALO;
   initgraph(&graphics_adapter,&graphics_mode,"");
   settextstyle(0,0,1);setcolor(C7);
   TextRow=10;TextColumn=15;GetTextCoords();
   outtextxy(TextX,TextY,"EGA 640x200x16-color graphics,"
                          " 80x25 character set");
#endif
return;

MCGA_mode:      /* MCGA 640x480x2-color mode, 8x8 character matrix */
x_res=640;y_res=480;mode_flag=14;
C0=0;C1=1;C2=1;C3=1;C4=1;C5=1;C6=1;C7=1;
C8=1;C9=1;C10=1;C11=1;C12=1;C13=1;C14=1;C15=1;
#if Compiler==QuickC
   _settextcolor(C7);
```

Fig. 3-4.
Continued.

```
  _settextposition(10,15);
  _outtext("MCGA 640x480x2-color graphics, 80x60 character set");
#elif Compiler==TurboC
  graphics_adapter=MCGA;graphics_mode=MCGAHI;
  initgraph(&graphics_adapter,&graphics_mode,"");
  settextstyle(0,0,1);setcolor(C7);
  TextRow=10;TextColumn=15;GetTextCoords();
  outtextxy(TextX,TextY,"MCGA 640x480x2-color graphics,"
                        " 80x60 character set");
#endif
return;

CGA_mode:        /* CGA 640x200x2-color mode, 8x8 character matrix */
x_res=640;y_res=200;mode_flag=5;
C0=0;C1=1;C2=1;C3=1;C4=1;C5=1;C6=1;C7=1;
C8=1;C9=1;C10=1;C11=1;C12=1;C13=1;C14=1;C15=1;
#if Compiler==QuickC
  _settextcolor(C7);
  _settextposition(10,15);
  _outtext("CGA 640x200x2-color graphics, 80x25 character set");
#elif Compiler==TurboC
  graphics_adapter=CGA;graphics_mode=CGAHI;
  initgraph(&graphics_adapter,&graphics_mode,"");
  settextstyle(0,0,1);setcolor(C7);
  TextRow=10;TextColumn=15;GetTextCoords();
  outtextxy(TextX,TextY,"CGA 640x200x2-color graphics,"
                        " 80x25 character set");
#endif
return;

Hercules_mode: /* Hercules 720x348x2-color mode,
                     9x14 character matrix */
x_res=720;y_res=348;mode_flag=6;
C0=0;C1=1;C2=1;C3=1;C4=1;C5=1;C6=1;C7=1;
C8=1;C9=1;C10=1;C11=1;C12=1;C13=1;C14=1;C15=1;
#if Compiler==QuickC
  _settextcolor(C7);
  _settextposition(10,15);
  _outtext("Hercules 720x348x2-color graphics,"
                    " 80x25 character set");
#elif Compiler==TurboC
  graphics_adapter=HERCMONO;graphics_mode=HERCMONOHI;
  initgraph(&graphics_adapter,&graphics_mode,"");
  setcolor(C7);
  TextRow=10;TextColumn=15;GetTextCoords();
  outtextxy(TextX,TextY,"Hercules 720x348x2-color graphics,"
                        " 80x25 character set");
#endif
return;

abort_pgm:      /* jump to here if no supported graphics hardware */
printf("\n\nUnable to proceed.\n\r");
printf("Requires VGA, EGA, CGA, MCGA, or\n\r");
printf("Hercules adapter and appropriate monitor.\n\n\r");
exit(0);
)
/*_____*/

void GetTextCoords(){      /* convert QuickC text to Turbo C text */
TextX=(TextColumn*8)-8;TextY=(TextRow*8)-8;return;}
/*_____*/

void Notice(int x, int y){      /* displays the copyright notice */
int copyright[][3]={0x7c00,0x0000,0x0000, /* array of bit styles */
              0x8279,0x819c,0x645e,
              0xba4a,0x4252,0x96d0,
              0xa27a,0x4252,0x955e,
              0xba0a,0x43d2,0xf442,
              0x8219,0x825c,0x945e,
              0x7c00,0x0000,0x0000};
```

Fig. 3-4.
Continued.

```
int a,b,c; int t1=0;                              /* local variables */
#if Compiler==QuickC
  for (t1=0;t1<=6;t1++){                           /* draw 7 styled lines */
    a=copyright[t1][0];b=copyright[t1][1];c=copyright[t1][2];
    _setlinestyle(a);_moveto(x,y);_lineto(x+15,y);
    _setlinestyle(b);_moveto(x+16,y);_lineto(x+31,y);
    _setlinestyle(c);_moveto(x+32,y);_lineto(x+47,y);y=y+1;};
  _setlinestyle(0xFFFF);return;
#elif Compiler==TurboC
  for (t1=0;t1<=6;t1++){                           /* draw 7 styled lines */
    a=copyright[t1][0];b=copyright[t1][1];c=copyright[t1][2];
    setlinestyle(USERBIT_LINE,a,NORM_WIDTH);
    moveto(x,y);lineto(x+15,y);
    setlinestyle(USERBIT_LINE,b,NORM_WIDTH);
    moveto(x+16,y);lineto(x+31,y);
    setlinestyle(USERBIT_LINE,c,NORM_WIDTH);
    moveto(x+32,y);lineto(x+47,y);y=y+1;};
  setlinestyle(USERBIT_LINE,0xFFFF,NORM_WIDTH);return;
#endif
}
/*_____

End of source code   */
```

HOW THE PROGRAM WORKS

The master loop for this demonstration program resides in the main() routine. Note the loop which begins at Label1:. This loop first calls a function named Keyboard() to test for or fetch a keystroke, and then uses the results returned from Keyboard() to call either Normalkey() or Extendedkey() to make a branching decision based upon the value of the keystroke.

Note, for example, the code which makes up Normalkey(). Depending upon the result of the switch() statement, the program simply displays on the screen the name of the keystroke. Observe how the #if directives are used to instruct the compiler to compile only the section of code which is compatible with the particular compiler being used: either QuickC or Turbo C.

The Turbo C code in Normalkey() is interesting for the way in which it handles the alphanumerics on the screen. Because Turbo C does not overwrite the background, the background must be cleared before the new text is written. Otherwise, the new text will be merely superimposed over the previous text, making for illegible words. Note the use of Turbo C's bar() function to draw a black rectangle on the screen to obliterate the former text. This tactic will be used through the book. QuickC's text functions always overwrite the background, avoiding any need to prepare the background before displaying new text.

Also of interest in this demonstration program is the function named MakeSound(). This routine uses direct manipulation of the hardware ports in order to produce a sound. In its current form the routine produces pleasant sounds on a computer running at 4.77 MHz. If you are using a faster CPU, you might wish to experiment with the values that are passed to this routine when it is called. By altering the variable named hertz you can adjust the pitch of the sound. By changing the variable named duration you can lengthen or shorten the time interval during which the sound is produced.

4

Graphics Input:
Managing the Mouse and Tablet

THE MARKETABILITY of any C graphics program can be enhanced significantly if the programmer adds routines to accept input from a mouse or a digitizing tablet. These two types of peripherals are called *coordinate input devices.* When used in combination with keyboard input, your programs can provide a truly sophisticated level of interaction with the end-user through these highly intuitive, point-and-shoot graphics devices. By supporting both mouse and tablet input, you can turn your original program from a millstone to a maelstrom, making it exciting and fun to use.

SOFTWARE DRIVERS

Most, but not all, mouse units and tablets are provided with bundled software called a *driver.* This software permits the mouse or tablet to communicate with your application program. If the input device is not bundled with a driver, then you must write your own software to control the device and to receive input signals from the device. Kurta and WACOM digitizing tablets, for example, are shipped with a driver, but WACOM assumes the programmer will write code to control the tablet's advanced features like pressure-sensitive stylus.

In most instances, your C graphics program will assume that the necessary mouse driver or tablet driver has already been loaded into memory by the end-user. This resident software is usually accessed through interrupt 33 hex.

The driver must be loaded before you start up either the QuickC or the Turbo C editor if you are developing a graphics program which uses mouse input or tablet input. See FIG. 4-1. A mouse driver is bundled with the QuickC product disks, but not with Turbo C.

Figure 4-2 depicts a typical memory map when an EXE program is using a mouse driver or tablet driver. The end-user first loads the driver software from the operating system prompt, and then loads and runs your EXE program. As will be discussed later in this chapter, your program can easily check for the presence or absence of a driver and can take appropriate subsequent action if no driver is found.

Mouse and tablet input devices normally display a cursor (usually an arrow-head) on the display screen. The driver software ensures that this cursor is displayed correctly on all VGA, EGA, MCGA, CGA, and Hercules graphics modes.

Fig. 4-1. Location of mouse driver or tablet driver software in RAM during a typical programming session with QuickC or Turbo C.

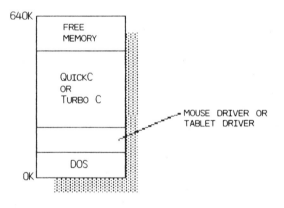

Fig. 4-2. Location of user-installed mouse driver or tablet driver during execution of your finished program.

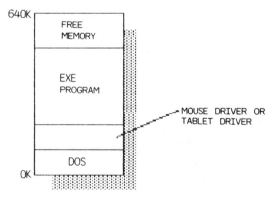

A CLOSER LOOK: Hercules Graphics Adapter

In order to display a mouse cursor or a tablet cursor correctly on a Hercules graphics adapter, you must write a value of 6 hex to address 40:49 hex before initializing the driver. This will ensure that the cursor is displayed on page 0 (the default page) of the adapter. If you wish to display the mouse cursor or tablet cursor on page 1, you should write a value of 5 hex to address 40:49 hex.

TYPICAL HARDWARE

There is a variety of hardware available in the marketplace for end-users who wish to use coordinate input devices. A typical mouse, as illustrated in FIG. 4-3, is meant to sit under the palm of the hand. A small sphere is rotated inside the mouse as the user moves the mouse around on the desktop. The mouse driver software is responsible for moving the cursor on the screen in a manner which corresponds to relative movements of the mouse on the desktop. The mouse hardware unit is connected to the host computer by a cable to a serial port, although specialized add-on cards are also sometimes used. At any point in time your graphics program can ask the mouse where the cursor is located, whether any of the buttons on the mouse have been pressed, and so forth.

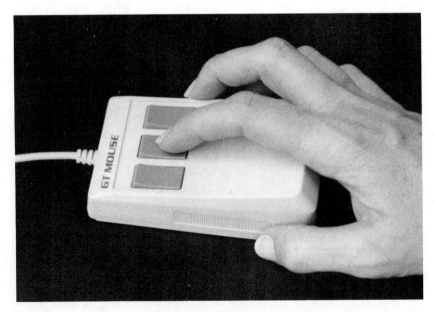

Fig. 4-3. A typical mouse, in this case the GT Mouse from GTCO Corporation.

Most mouse manufacturers provide a driver which is compatible with the Microsoft standard mouse interface. This means that the code you write to control one manufacturer's mouse will also work with almost any other mouse product in the worldwide marketplace.

A digitizing tablet employs a similar principle via the handheld crosshair cursor. A Kurta handheld cursor device is illustrated in FIG. 4-4. The tablet surface is actually a grid of electronic signals. The position of the handheld cursor on the grid is transmitted by the tablet hardware components to the tablet driver software. Handheld cursors are available with a varying number of buttons, but four-button cursors are the most widely available. Some tablet cursors are connected to the tablet by a cord. Some are battery-driven cordless models which transmit their position to the tablet hardware by FM signal. Other, more advanced, units are non-corded, non-battery, non-magnetic devices which passively react to pulses generated by the grid itself, creating a unique electromagnetic field, such as the WACOM cursor shown in FIG. 4-5.

In addition to handheld crosshair cursors, digitizing tablets often offer a stylus, or pen, as depicted in FIG. 4-6. These pens usually operate in the same manner as the handheld cursor, except for a reduced number of buttons and a more intuitive feel. Some manufacturers, such as WACOM, provide a pressure-sensitive stylus which can provide data to your program concerning how hard the end-user is pressing the pen against the tablet.

Most tablet manufacturers bundle a software driver with their product which offers functionality equivalent to the Microsoft mouse driver, although in many cases the tablet driver offers additional enhanced features which take full advantage of the unique features of a tablet design. Kurta and WACOM tablets are an example of this approach. This adherence to the Microsoft standard is a boon

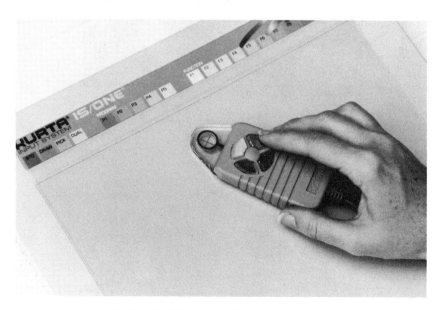

Fig. 4-4. The Kurta crosshair four-button cursor.

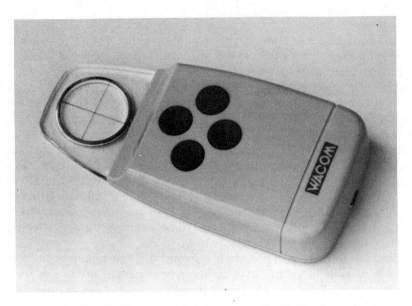

Fig. 4-5. The Wacom crosshair cursor, a cordless battery-free unit.

Fig. 4-6. A typical stylus or pen, often available in both corded and cordless models.

for C graphics programmers. It means that it is very easy indeed to adapt source code to support both a mouse and a digitizing tablet.

PROGRAMMING FUNDAMENTALS

Writing source code to control a mouse or tablet is not a debilitating task if the manufacturer's driver is Microsoft-compatible, as most are. Accessing the driver is a two-step process. First, your C program loads the microprocessor's registers with appropriate values. Second, your C program executes an INT 33H. An optional third step is to read the values returned to the registers by the mouse or tablet. These return values usually contain the x,y coordinates of the on-screen cursor.

Figure 4-7 illustrates a toolkit for managing a coordinate input device like a mouse or tablet. The functions in FIG. 4-7 adhere to the Microsoft standard. Although many more functions are available in the Microsoft mouse interface, the fundamental functions in FIG. 4-7 are suitable for most graphics applications.

If, for example, you wished to display the mouse/tablet cursor on the screen, you would load a value of 1 into the AX register and execute INT 33H. To remove (hide) the mouse/tablet cursor from the screen, you load a value of 2 into the AX register and execute INT 33H. In both instances, the values of the BX, CX, and DX registers are ignored by the driver, although in other functions these registers might be required to pass important values to the driver.

FUNCTION CODE AX	BX	CX	DX	PURPOSE	RETURNS
0				INITIALIZATION	AX = 0 IF NO MOUSE BX = NO. OF BUTTONS
1				DISPLAY CURSOR	
2				REMOVE CURSOR	
3				RETRIEVE BUTTON STATUS AND XY COORDINATES	BX = 1 LEFT OR 2 RT CX = X COORDINATE DX = Y COORDINATE
4		X COORD	Y COORD	RESET CURSOR LOCATION	CX = NEW X DX = NEW Y
7		MIN X	MAX X	SET MINIMUM AND MAXIMUM CURSOR DISPLAY RANGE	
8		MIN Y	MAX Y	SET MINIMUM AND MAXIMUM CURSOR DISPLAY RANGE	

Fig. 4-7. Fundamental function codes for Microsoft-compatible mouse drivers and Kurta-compatible digitizing tablets running in mouse-emulation mode. Features are accessed by loading the appropriate registers and executing interrupt 33 hex.

Showing the Cursor

The C code to turn on the cursor might look something like this for QuickC:

```
inregs.x.ax = 1;
int86(0x33,&inregs,&outregs);
```

If you are using Turbo C, the code to turn on the cursor might look thus:

```
regs.x.ax = 1;
int86(0x33,&regs,&regs);
```

In the two examples above, the first line of code loads the value 1 into the AX register. The variable named inregs (QuickC) or regs (Turbo C) is a data structure that holds values which the compiler will pass to the registers when an interrupt is executed by your program.

The second line of code in the examples executes INT 33H. The syntax 0x33 is C's way of saying 33 hex. The address of a data structure to pass and receive register contents is also included in the calling arguments, designated by the & token.

If you are using QuickC, you access the contents of the AX register by using the inregs.x.ax syntax. Use inregs.x.bx to handle the BX register, inregs.x.cx for the CX register, and inregs.x.dx for the DX register.

If you are using Turbo C, use regs.x.ax to deal with the AX register, regs.x.bx for the BX register, regs.x.cx for the CX register, and regs.x.dx for the DX register.

Determing the Mouse/Tablet Coordinates

To fetch the x,y screen coordinates of the mouse/tablet cursor, you must read the registers to find out which values have been returned to you after your call to the driver. The following code fragment will work with both QuickC and Turbo C:

```
#if Compiler = = QuickC
  inregs.x.ax = 3;
  int86(0x33,&inregs,&outregs);
  mouse_button = outregs.x.bx;
  mouse_x = outregs.x.cx;
  mouse_y = outregs.x.dx;
#elif Compiler = = TurboC
  regs.x.ax = 3; int86(0x33,&regs,&regs);
  mouse_button = regs.x.bx;
  mouse_x = regs.x.cx; mouse_y = regs.x.dx;
#endif
```

You can see how the #if and #elif preprocessor directives have been used to tell your compiler which part of the source code should be compiled and which part should be ignored. Whether you are using QuickC or Turbo C, the first line in the example loads the AX register with a value of 3. If you refer to FIG. 4-7, you can see that mouse/tablet function 3 is used to test if a mouse or tablet button has been pressed, and to determine the current position of the on-screen cursor.

The second line of source code executes an INT 33H.

The third line of code reads the value which was returned in the CX register and assigns the value to a variable named mouse_button. The fourth line fetches the cursor's x coordinate from the CX register. The fifth line reads the y coordinate from the DX register.

After you have retrieved these values from the registers, how your C graphics program manipulates or uses them is entirely up to you, the programmer.

Other Functions

Other functions from FIG. 4-7 provide specialized services. Mouse function 4, for example, will reset the position of the on-screen cursor. This particular function works only with a mouse, however. Because the on-screen cursor is tied to a physical location on the surface of a tablet, the on-screen cursor will immediately jump to the actual crosshair position.

Functions 7 and 8 are used to set up a viewport on the display screen. The boundaries of the viewport are the limits for displaying the mouse/tablet cursor. No matter how far you move the mouse or handheld cursor, the on-screen cursor will not travel past the boundary of the viewport created by function 7 and function 8. These particular functions are used often in Your Microcomputer SketchPad, the full-length drawing program provided in Chapter 8, in order to restrict the screen cursor to the drawing canvas.

An interesting advanced feature for showing and hiding the mouse/tablet cursor is illustrated in FIG. 4-8. Whereas function 1 is an absolute function to display the cursor, function 16 is a conditional function. Using function 16, an on-screen cursor will become automatically hidden if the end-user moves it into a viewport which you have defined. This feature can save you the trouble of always removing the cursor from the screen before performing any graphics.

Other advanced functions include the ability to adjust the movement ratio between the on-screen cursor and the pointing device, the ability to step up the speed of movement of the on-screen cursor, and the capability to change the

AX	BX	CX	DX	PURPOSE
2				REMOVES CURSOR FROM DISPLAY
16			POINTER	CURSOR WILL BECOME HIDDEN ONLY IF IT MOVES INTO VIEWPORT

Fig. 4-8. Comparison of unconditional and conditional removal of the pointing device cursor.

shape of the cursor to one of your own liking. You can also change the hotspot position, which is the single pixel on the on-screen cursor which determines the precise x,y coordinates being transmitted.

MOUSE/TABLET PROGRAMMING TIPS

Because the software and interrupt activities can create very complex runtime situations, the cardinal rule in writing routines for mouse and tablet input is keep it simple. Most C graphics programs will need only four functions: 0 to initialize the driver, 1 to display the screen cursor, 2 to delete the screen cursor, and 3 to fetch the screen coordinates and to see if a button has been pressed. Other functions, if used, will enhance the graphics pizazz of your program, but will also introduce the possibility of buggy incompatibilities between non-Microsoft mouse devices, and between non-Kurta tablet products. Don't take this as an admonition against using these advanced functions, but rather as a gentle reminder that you will need to put a lot more work into your program to ferret out these potential compatibility conflicts.

A CLOSER LOOK: Mouse/Tablet Programming Tips

You can keep your mouse and tablet code manageable during development by adhering to three rules:

1) Keep it simple. Use only functions 0, 1, 2, and 3.
2) Route all mouse and tablet calls through one routine.
3) Do not attempt to change the shape of the screen cursor on an EGA graphics adapter.

Another important principle to keep in mind when writing routines for the mouse or tablet is that of modularity. If possible, use just one routine as the entry point to the driver. This makes it easier to track down any erratic behavior during development of your progrram. Any time that any portion of your program needs to access the mouse or tablet, the program should call the routine you've written to handle the driver. In the major demonstration program listing in Chapter 8, the driver handler is called MouseMgr( ).

If your program is intended to run on an EGA graphics adapter, you would be well advised to avoid using any functions that change the shape of the screen cursor. Program performance will slow considerably because of the software gymnastics required to support the built-in INT 10H BIOS routines that manipulate the EGA's registers. If you wish to change the shape of the cursor, it is far better to use mouse function 3 to determine the x,y coordinates and then use C to draw your own cursor.

CASE STUDY: Kurta Tablet

The Kurta IS/ONE tablet is a good example of a digitizing tablet which comes bundled with a mouse-compatible software driver. Refer back to Fig. 4-4.

Kurta calls its driver the IS Pensmith driver. This software provides a consistent method of manipulating the entire range of Kurta tablet products. In addition to 100% Microsoft mouse compatibility, Kurta's driver provides advanced tablet-specific features like macro key sequences. This means that your program can define one of the areas on the tablet as hot. When the end-user positions the handheld cursor or stylus in this area and presses a button, a series of simulated keystrokes will be sent to your program by the driver. This means your C graphics program can provide complex, macro-like functions which normally might require many inputs from the end-user. It is almost like having your own graphics programming language built into the tablet driver.

WHERE TO LOOK: Kurta Digitizing Tablet

For further information about the Kurta series of digitizing tablets, crosshair cursors, and pens, you can contact Kurta Corporation, P.O. Box 60250, Phoenix, AZ, USA 85082-0250.

Of particular interest is tablet-specific function 81 hex, which can be used to define the actual area on the tablet surface that will correspond to the display screen. Noteworthy also is tablet-specific function 84 hex, which is used to create and to read macro strings.

The Kurta line of tablets can be used with AutoCAD and similar drafting software. Kurta supports the Autodesk Device Interface (ADI) built into AutoCAD.

A typical Kurta driver is K_ISPS.COM, which takes up approximately 15K in RAM, compared to the 14K occupied by the Microsoft driver, MOUSE.COM.

CASE STUDY: WACOM Tablet

The WACOM SD-420L tablet (refer back to FIG. 4-5) is an example of a light-end tablet which is shipped with a bundled software driver. Because only choose emulation is provided, you must go to a bit more work to program the tablet, but it also means you have many more advanced features to choose from, such as pen pressure, for example.

You access the tablet hardware via the serial port of your personal computer using C's read( ) and write( ) statements.

Although the WACOM tablet will send and receive data in a binary mode using bits and bytes, the most manageable method is to use the ASCII mode. WACOM's programming manual provides a comprehensive listing of all the commands recognized by the tablet, as well as the syntax and number of parameters involved. Each ASCII command is communicated in uppercase characters and is terminated by a carriage return line feed combination (0x0d0a).

A typical ASCII transmission to or from the tablet follows a format similar to:

D,x1,x2,x3,x4,x5,y1,y2,y3,y4,y5,D,T

where each token is an ASCII value.

In this example, D refers to the device currently being used with the tablet: either a crosshair cursor, a standard stylus or pen, or WACOM's proprietary pressure-sensitive stylus.

Next come five digits which represent the x coordinate. Leading zeros are required if the value occupies fewer than five characters. Immediately following are five digits which represent the y coordinate.

D refers to button, switch, and pressure data. The programming manual provides tables to explain this data. For example, it is interesting to note that pressure data can range from -30 units to +30 units when a pressure-sensitive pen is being used.

T is the carriage return line feed combination mentioned earlier.

Needless to say, these hieroglyphics sound more complicated than they really are. Consider the following ASCII example, which might typically be sent by the tablet to your program:

*,00319,00174,01CRLF

The * token means the handheld crosshair cursor is being currently used. # means standard stylus mode. ! means pressure-sensitive stylus mode.

The next packet of ASCII values, 00319, means the x coordinate is 319. This would be horizontally centered on the EGA's 640x350x16-color graphics screen. The next digits, 00174, refer to the current y coordinate, which would be vertically halfway in the 640x350x16-color mode of the EGA.

The 01 packet means the top button on the crosshair cursor has been pressed by the end-user. This value would be set to 99 if the pointing device was outside the active area. A value of 30 would indicate maximum pressure if the pen was being used in the pressure-sensitive mode.

The final data on the ASCII transmission is the carriage return line feed combination, of course.

WHERE TO LOOK: WACOM Digitizing Tablet

For further information about the WACOM series of digitizing tablets, crosshair cursors, and pressure-sensitive pens, you can contact WACOM Inc., West 115 Century Road, Paramus NJ, USA 07652.

A major advantage to using a product like the WACOM series of tablets is the advanced features. Clearly, using a pressure-sensitive stylus opens up a new environment for paint and draw programs. And a cordless, batteryless, nonmagnetic handheld crosshair cursor keeps the possibility of hardware problems to an absolute minimum.

DEMONSTRATION PROGRAM: A Mouse/Tablet Manager

The image in FIG. 4-9 shows the start-up display produced by the program listing in FIG. 4-11, MOUSEMGR.C. The image in FIG. 4-10 shows a typical session created using a mouse or a tablet. The program supports VGA, EGA, MCGA, CGA, and Hercules graphics adapters.

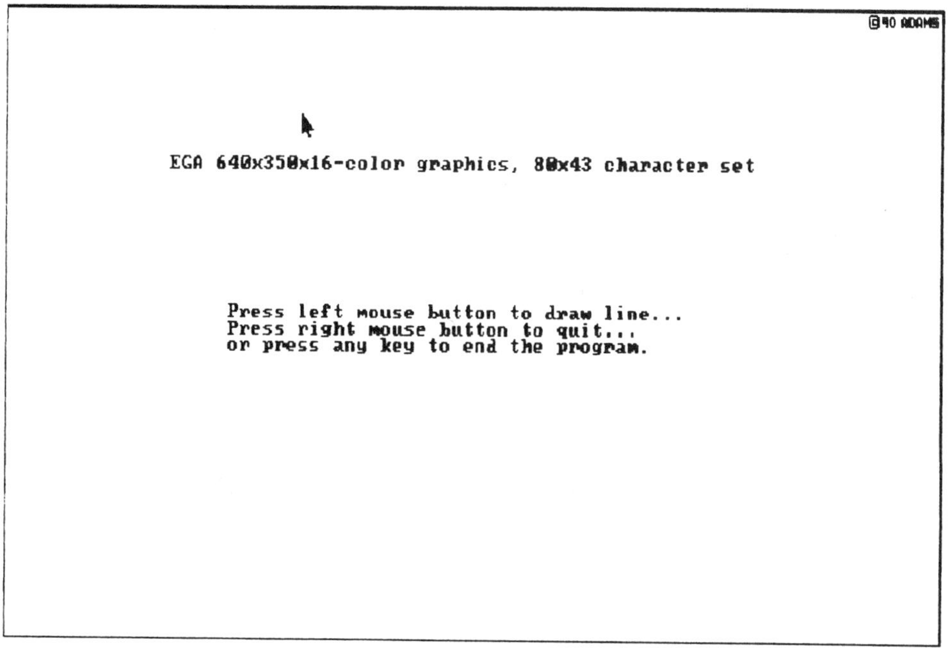

Fig. 4-9. Print of the start-up image generated by the mouse/tablet demonstration program, MOUSE-MGR.C.

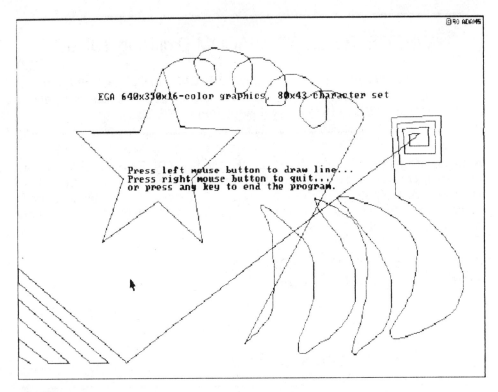

Fig. 4-10. Print of a typical test session provided by the mouse-tablet demonstration program, MOUSEMGR.C.

Fig. 4-11. Source code for MOUSEMGR.C, designed to demonstrate algorithms to accept graphical input from a Microsoft-compatible mouse or a Kurta-compatible digitizing tablet running in mouse-emulation mode. Ready to compile under QuickC or Turbo C.

```
/*
Mouse Input Manager                    Source file: MOUSEMGR.C

Purpose:  demonstrates how to write C graphics programs that
use a mouse for user input and for graphics output.

Compiler:  QuickC or Turbo C.  Default is QuickC.  To use
Turbo C, change one line in COMPILER DIRECTIVES below.

Memory model:  medium memory model.

Marketability:  will detect and support VGA, EGA, MCGA, CGA, and
Hercules graphics adapters.  A Microsoft-compatible mouse must be
connected to your computer and the appropriate mouse driver
software must be already loaded.

(c) Copyright 1990 Lee Adams.  As purchaser of the book in which
this program is published, you are granted a non-exclusive
royalty-free license to reproduce and distribute these routines in
executable form as part of your software product, subject to any
trademark or patent rights of others, and subject to the limited
```

**Fig. 4-11.
Continued.**

COMPILER DIRECTIVES
These are instructions to your C compiler. */

```
#define QuickC    1
#define TurboC    2
#define Compiler QuickC    /* NOTE: Change to TurboC if required. */
#define FAIL      0            /* for graphics auto-detect algorithm */
#define EMPTY     0              /* for checking keyboard buffer */
#define MOUSE     0x33        /* DOS interrupt for mouse driver */

#include <bios.h>                  /* supports keyboard functions */
#include <stdio.h>                 /* supports the printf function */
#if Compiler==QuickC
  #include <graph.h>                  /* supports QuickC's graphics */
  #include <memory.h>             /* supports QuickC memory moves */
#elif Compiler==TurboC
  #include <graphics.h>            /* supports Turbo C's graphics */
  #include <mem.h>              /* supports Turbo C memory moves */
#endif
#include <process.h>               /* support the exit function */
#include <dos.h>              /* supports int 33h for mouse routines
```

FUNCTION PROTOTYPES
These ANSI C function declarations allow your C compiler to check
each function for correct arguments and return value.   */

```
void Keyboard();                        /* checks for a keystroke */
void Quit_Pgm();                     /* ends the program gracefully */
void Notice(int,int);              /* displays the copyright notice */
void Graphics_Setup();             /* initializes the graphics mode */
void GetTextCoords();     /* convert QuickC text to Turbo C text */
void Mouse_Initialize();                /* initializes the mouse */
void Mouse_Show();                    /* displays the mouse cursor */
void Mouse_Hide();                       /* hides the mouse cursor */
void Mouse_Setposition();         /* resets mouse cursor xy coords */
void Mouse_Status();       /* checks mouse location, button status */
void Mouse_Setrangeh();             /* sets mouse horizontal range */
void Mouse_Setrangev();               /* sets mouse vertical range
```

DECLARATION OF GLOBAL VARIABLES
These variables are declared and initialized outside of any
function and are visible to all functions in this source file.   */

```
#if Compiler==QuickC
  struct videoconfig vc;                /* QuickC's graphics table */
  union REGS inregs,outregs;     /* data structure for interrupt */
#elif Compiler==TurboC
  union REGS regs;                   /* data structure for interrupt */
#endif
int mouse_flag=0;                    /* indicates if mouse present */
int mouse_button=0;           /* indicates if mouse button pressed */
int mouse_x=200,mouse_y=50;     /* mouse cursor screen coordinates */
int mouse_minx=1,mouse_maxx=627;         /* mouse horizontal range */
int mouse_miny=1,mouse_maxy=182;           /* mouse vertical range */
int C0=0,C1=1,C2=2,C3=3,C4=4,C5=5,C6=6,C7=7,C8=8,C9=9,C10=10,
C11=11,C12=12,C13=13,C14=14,C15=15;              /* color codes */
int x_res=640,y_res=480;               /* screen resolution */
int mode_flag=0;  /* indicates which graphics mode is being used */
int t1=1;                                      /* loop counter */
int sx=0,sy=0;                         /* xy screen drawing coords */
int TextRow=1,TextColumn=1;            /* text position for QuickC */
int TextX=0,TextY=0;                  /* text position for Turbo C */
```

```
char Herc=6;                          /* preparatory value for Hercules mode */
char far *HPtr;                       /* will point to Herc variable */
/*_____


FUNCTION DEFINITIONS   */

main(){                               /* this is the master routine */
Graphics_Setup();                     /* establish graphics mode */
#if Compiler==QuickC
  _getvideoconfig(&vc);                      /* initialize video table */
  _setcolor(C14);_rectangle(_GBORDER,0,0,x_res-1,y_res-1);
  _setcolor(C7);Notice(589,2);
  _settextposition(19,20);
  _outtext("Press left mouse button to draw line...");
  _settextposition(20,20);
  _outtext("Press right mouse button to quit...");
  _settextposition(21,20);
  _outtext("or press any key to end the program.");
#elif Compiler==TurboC
  setcolor(C14);rectangle(0,0,x_res-1,y_res-1);
  setcolor(C7);Notice(589,2);
  TextRow=19;TextColumn=20;GetTextCoords();
  outtextxy(TextX,TextY,"Press left mouse button to draw line...");
  TextRow=20;TextColumn=20;GetTextCoords();
  outtextxy(TextX,TextY,"Press right mouse button to quit...");
  TextRow=21;TextColumn=20;GetTextCoords();
  outtextxy(TextX,TextY,"or press any key to end the program.");
#endif
if (mode_flag==6){          /* special prep required for Hercules */
  HPtr=&Herc;               /* make HercPtr point to Herc variable */
  movedata(FP_SEG(HPtr),FP_OFF(HPtr),0x40,0x49,1);
  }                         /* move 1 byte (the value 6) to address 40:49 hex */
Mouse_Initialize();                         /* initialize the mouse */
if (mouse_flag==0) {                /* equals 0 if no mouse found */
  #if Compiler==QuickC
  _settextcolor(C14);_settextposition(10,15);
  _outtext("Error: no mouse was found by the demo program.    ");
  _settextcolor(C7);goto label1;
  #elif Compiler==TurboC
  setcolor(C14);
  TextRow=10;TextColumn=15;GetTextCoords();
  outtextxy(TextX,TextY,"Error: no mouse was found by"
                        " the demo program.    ");
  setcolor(C7);goto label1;
  #endif
  }
Mouse_Setrangeh();      /* set minimum, maximum horizontal range */
Mouse_Setrangev();      /* set minimum, maximum vertical range */
Mouse_Setposition();            /* set starting cursor location */
sx=mouse_x;sy=mouse_y;          /* initialize the drawing coords */
#if Compiler==QuickC
  _moveto(sx,sy);           /* initialize C's most-recent coords */
  _setcolor(C12);               /* initialize the drawing color */
#elif Compiler==TurboC
  moveto(sx,sy);setcolor(C12);
#endif
Mouse_Show();                           /* display the mouse cursor */
mouse_manager:                  /* mouse and keyboard polling loop */
  Mouse_Status();                       /* check the mouse's status */
  if (mouse_button==1){    /* if left mouse button pressed... */
    sx=mouse_x;sy=mouse_y;       /* reset hotspot screen coords */
    Mouse_Hide();                       /* remove the mouse cursor */
    #if Compiler==QuickC
      _lineto(sx,sy);                       /* draw a line segment */
    #elif Compiler==TurboC
      lineto(sx,sy);
    #endif
    Mouse_Show();;}                     /* restore the mouse cursor */
```

Fig. 4-11.
Continued.

Fig. 4-11.
Continued.

```
   if (mouse_button==2){         /* if right mouse button pressed... */
     Quit_Pgm();}                         /* end the demonstration */
   Keyboard();                          /* press any key to quit */
   goto mouse_manager;                            /* infinite loop */
label1:
for (t1=1;t1!=2; ) Keyboard();        /* press any key to stop */
Quit_Pgm();                              /* bulletproof barrier */
}
/*_____*/

void Keyboard(){                      /* checks the keyboard buffer */
#if Compiler==QuickC
  if (_bios_keybrd(_KEYBRD_READY)==EMPTY) return;
  else (_bios_keybrd(_KEYBRD_READ);Quit_Pgm();}
#elif Compiler==TurboC
  if (bioskey(1)==EMPTY) return;else (bioskey(0);Quit_Pgm();}
#endif
}
/*_____*/

void Quit_Pgm(){                       /* terminates the program */
if (mouse_flag!=0) Mouse_Hide();       /* remove the mouse cursor */
#if Compiler==QuickC                            /* if using QuickC */
  _clearscreen(_GCLEARSCREEN);              /* clear the screen */
  _setvideomode(_DEFAULTMODE);     /* restore the original mode */
#elif Compiler==TurboC                        /* if using Turbo C */
  cleardevice();                           /* clear the screen */
  closegraph();        /* shut down graphics, restore original mode */
#endif
exit(0);}                                /* terminate the program
_____*/

void Graphics_Setup(){          /* autodetect of graphics hardware */
#if Compiler==QuickC
  if (_setvideomoderows(_VRES16COLOR,60)!=FAIL) goto VGA_mode;
  if (_setvideomoderows(_ERESCOLOR,43)!=FAIL) goto EGA_ECD_mode;
  if (_setvideomoderows(_HRES16COLOR,25)!=FAIL) goto EGA_SCD_mode;
  if (_setvideomoderows(_VRES2COLOR,60)!=FAIL) goto MCGA_mode;
  if (_setvideomoderows(_HRESBW,25)!=FAIL) goto CGA_mode;
  if (_setvideomoderows(_HERCMONO,25)!=FAIL) goto Hercules_mode;
#elif Compiler==TurboC
  int graphics_adapter,graphics_mode;
  detectgraph(&graphics_adapter,&graphics_mode);
  if (graphics_adapter==VGA) goto VGA_mode;
  if (graphics_mode==EGAHI) goto EGA_ECD_mode;
  if (graphics_mode==EGALO) goto EGA_SCD_mode;
  if (graphics_adapter==MCGA) goto MCGA_mode;
  if (graphics_adapter==CGA) goto CGA_mode;
  if (graphics_adapter==HERCMONO) goto Hercules_mode;
#endif
goto abort_pgm;                   /* if no graphics hardware found */


VGA_mode:     /* VGA 640x480x16-color mode, 8x8 character matrix */
x_res=640;y_res=480;mode_flag=1;
mouse_maxx=x_res-13;mouse_maxy=y_res-17;
#if Compiler==QuickC
  _settextcolor(C7);
  _settextposition(10,15);
  _outtext("VGA 640x480x16-color graphics, 80x60 character set");
#elif Compiler==TurboC
  graphics_adapter=VGA;graphics_mode=VGAHI;
  initgraph(&graphics_adapter,&graphics_mode,"");
  settextstyle(0,0,1);setcolor(C7);
  TextRow=10;TextColumn=15;GetTextCoords();
  outtextxy(TextX,TextY,"VGA 640x480x16-color graphics,"
                        " 80x60 character set");
#endif
return;
```

Fig. 4-11.
Continued.

```
EGA_ECD_mode: /* EGA 640x350x16-color mode, 8x8 character matrix */
x_res=640;y_res=350;mode_flag=2;
mouse_maxx=x_res-13;mouse_maxy=y_res-17;
#if Compiler==QuickC
  _settextcolor(C7);
  _settextposition(10,15);
  _outtext("EGA 640x350x16-color graphics, 80x43 character set");
#elif Compiler==TurboC
  graphics_adapter=EGA;graphics_mode=EGAHI;
  initgraph(&graphics_adapter,&graphics_mode,"");
  settextstyle(0,0,1);setcolor(C7);
  TextRow=10;TextColumn=15;GetTextCoords();
  outtextxy(TextX,TextY,"EGA 640x350x16-color graphics,"
                        " 80x43 character set");
#endif
return;

EGA_SCD_mode: /* EGA 640x200x16-color mode, 8x8 character matrix */
x_res=640;y_res=200;mode_flag=3;
mouse_maxx=x_res-13;mouse_maxy=y_res-17;
#if Compiler==QuickC
  _settextcolor(C7);
  _settextposition(10,15);
  _outtext("EGA 640x200x16-color graphics, 80x25 character set");
#elif Compiler==TurboC
  graphics_adapter=EGA;graphics_mode=EGALO;
  initgraph(&graphics_adapter,&graphics_mode,"");
  settextstyle(0,0,1);setcolor(C7);
  TextRow=10;TextColumn=15;GetTextCoords();
  outtextxy(TextX,TextY,"EGA 640x200x16-color graphics,"
                        " 80x25 character set");
#endif
return;

MCGA_mode:     /* MCGA 640x480x2-color mode, 8x8 character matrix */
x_res=640;y_res=480;mode_flag=14;
mouse_maxx=x_res-13;mouse_maxy=y_res-17;
C0=0;C1=1;C2=1;C3=1;C4=1;C5=1;C6=1;C7=1;
C8=1;C9=1;C10=1;C11=1;C12=1;C13=1;C14=1;C15=1;
#if Compiler==QuickC
  _settextcolor(C7);
  _settextposition(10,15);
  _outtext("MCGA 640x480x2-color graphics, 80x60 character set");
#elif Compiler==TurboC
  graphics_adapter=MCGA;graphics_mode=MCGAHI;
  initgraph(&graphics_adapter,&graphics_mode,"");
  settextstyle(0,0,1);setcolor(C7);
  TextRow=10;TextColumn=15;GetTextCoords();
  outtextxy(TextX,TextY,"MCGA 640x480x2-color graphics,"
                        " 80x60 character set");
#endif
return;

CGA_mode:      /* CGA 640x200x2-color mode, 8x8 character matrix */
x_res=640;y_res=200;mode_flag=5;
mouse_maxx=x_res-13;mouse_maxy=y_res-17;
C0=0;C1=1;C2=1;C3=1;C4=1;C5=1;C6=1;C7=1;
C8=1;C9=1;C10=1;C11=1;C12=1;C13=1;C14=1;C15=1;
#if Compiler==QuickC
  _settextcolor(C7);
  _settextposition(10,15);
  _outtext("CGA 640x200x2-color graphics, 80x25 character set");
#elif Compiler==TurboC
  graphics_adapter=CGA;graphics_mode=CGAHI;
  initgraph(&graphics_adapter,&graphics_mode,"");
  settextstyle(0,0,1);setcolor(C7);
  TextRow=10;TextColumn=15;GetTextCoords();
  outtextxy(TextX,TextY,"CGA 640x200x2-color graphics,"
                        " 80x25 character set");
```

Fig. 4-11.
Continued.

```
#endif
return;

Hercules_mode: /* Hercules 720x348x2-color mode,"
                        " 9x14 character matrix */
x_res=720;y_res=348;mode_flag=6;
mouse_maxx=x_res-13;mouse_maxy=y_res-17;
C0=0;C1=1;C2=1;C3=1;C4=1;C5=1;C6=1;C7=1;
C8=1;C9=1;C10=1;C11=1;C12=1;C13=1;C14=1;C15=1;
#if Compiler==QuickC
  _settextcolor(C7);
  _settextposition(10,15);
  _outtext("Hercules 720x348x2-color graphics,"
                        " 80x25 character set");
#elif Compiler==TurboC
  graphics_adapter=HERCMONO;graphics_mode=HERCMONOHI;
  initgraph(&graphics_adapter,&graphics_mode,"");
  setcolor(C7);
  TextRow=10;TextColumn=15;GetTextCoords();
  outtextxy(TextX,TextY,"Hercules 720x348x2-color graphics,"
                        " 80x25 character set");
#endif
return;

abort_pgm:      /* jump to here if no supported graphics hardware */
printf("\n\nUnable to proceed.\n\r");
printf("Requires VGA, EGA, CGA, MCGA, or\n\r");
printf("Hercules adapter and appropriate monitor.\n\n\r");
exit(0);
}
/*_____*/

void GetTextCoords(){      /* convert QuickC text to Turbo C text */
TextX=(TextColumn*8)-8;TextY=(TextRow*8)-8;return;}
/*_____

MOUSE CONTROL FUNCTIONS   */

void Mouse_Initialize(){                   /* initializes the mouse */
#if Compiler==QuickC
  inregs.x.ax=0;                           /* mouse function #0 */
  int86(MOUSE,&inregs,&outregs);       /* call interrupt 33 hex */
  mouse_flag=outregs.x.ax;        /* equals 0 if no mouse present */
#elif Compiler==TurboC
  regs.x.ax=0;int86(MOUSE,&regs,&regs);mouse_flag=regs.x.ax;
#endif
return;}                                   /* return to caller */

void Mouse_Show(){                     /* displays the mouse cursor */
#if Compiler==QuickC
  inregs.x.ax=1;                           /* mouse function #1 */
  int86(MOUSE,&inregs,&outregs);       /* call interrupt 33 hex */
#elif Compiler==TurboC
  regs.x.ax=1;int86(MOUSE,&regs,&regs);
#endif
return;}                                   /* return to caller */

void Mouse_Hide(){                     /* erases the mouse cursor */
#if Compiler==QuickC
  inregs.x.ax=2;                           /* mouse function #2 */
  int86(MOUSE,&inregs,&outregs);       /* call interrupt 33 hex */
#elif Compiler==TurboC
  regs.x.ax=2;int86(MOUSE,&regs,&regs);
#endif
return;}                                   /* return to caller */

void Mouse_Status(){      /* gets cursor location, button status */
#if Compiler==QuickC
  inregs.x.ax=3;                           /* mouse function #3 */
```

Fig. 4-11.
Continued.

```
      int86(MOUSE,&inregs,&outregs);          /* call interrupt 33 hex */
      mouse_button=outregs.x.bx; /* 1 (left) or 2 (right) if pressed */
      mouse_x=outregs.x.cx;                    /* get x coordinate */
      mouse_y=outregs.x.dx;                    /* get y coordinate */
#elif Compiler==TurboC
   regs.x.ax=3;int86(MOUSE,&regs,&regs);
   mouse_button=regs.x.bx;
   mouse_x=regs.x.cx;mouse_y=regs.x.dx;
#endif
return;}                                       /* return to caller */

void Mouse_Setposition(){          /* sets mouse cursor location */
#if Compiler==QuickC
   inregs.x.ax=4;                          /* mouse function #4 */
   inregs.x.cx=mouse_x;                    /* set the x coordinate */
   inregs.x.dx=mouse_y;                    /* set the y coordinate */
   int86(MOUSE,&inregs,&outregs);          /* call interrupt 33 hex */
#elif Compiler==TurboC
   regs.x.ax=4;regs.x.cx=mouse_x;regs.x.dx=mouse_y;
   int86(MOUSE,&regs,&regs);
#endif
return;}                                       /* return to caller */

void Mouse_Setrangeh(){         /* sets min max horizontal range */
#if Compiler==QuickC
   inregs.x.ax=7;                          /* mouse function #7 */
   inregs.x.cx=mouse_minx;                 /* set the minimum x coord */
   inregs.x.dx=mouse_maxx;                 /* set the maximum x coord */
   int86(MOUSE,&inregs,&outregs);          /* call interrupt 33 hex */
#elif Compiler==TurboC
   regs.x.ax=7;regs.x.cx=mouse_minx;regs.x.dx=mouse_maxx;
   int86(MOUSE,&regs,&regs);
#endif
return;}                                       /* return to caller */

void Mouse_Setrangev(){           /* sets min max vertical range */
#if Compiler==QuickC
   inregs.x.ax=8;                          /* mouse function #8 */
   inregs.x.cx=mouse_miny;                 /* set the minimum y coord */
   inregs.x.dx=mouse_maxy;                 /* set the maximum y coord */
   int86(MOUSE,&inregs,&outregs);          /* call interrupt 33 hex */
#elif Compiler==TurboC
   regs.x.ax=8;regs.x.cx=mouse_miny;regs.x.dx=mouse_maxy;
   int86(MOUSE,&regs,&regs);
#endif
return;}                                       /* return to caller */
/*_____*/

void Notice(int x, int y){       /* displays the copyright notice */
int copyright[][3]={0x7c00,0x0000,0x0000, /* array of bit styles */
              0x8279,0x819c,0x645e,
              0xba4a,0x4252,0x96d0,
              0xa27a,0x4252,0x955e,
              0xba0a,0x43d2,0xf442,
              0x8219,0x825c,0x945e,
              0x7c00,0x0000,0x0000};
int a,b,c; int t1=0;                           /* local variables */
#if Compiler==QuickC
   for (t1=0;t1<=6;t1++){                 /* draw 7 styled lines */
     a=copyright[t1][0];b=copyright[t1][2];
     _setlinestyle(a);_moveto(x,y);_lineto(x+15,y);
     _setlinestyle(b);_moveto(x+16,y);_lineto(x+31,y);
     _setlinestyle(c);_moveto(x+32,y);_lineto(x+47,y);y=y+1;};
   _setlinestyle(0xFFFF);return;
#elif Compiler==TurboC
   for (t1=0;t1<=6;t1++){                 /* draw 7 styled lines */
     a=copyright[t1][0];b=copyright[t1][1];c=copyright[t1][2];
     setlinestyle(USERBIT_LINE,a,NORM_WIDTH);
     moveto(x,y);lineto(x+15,y);
```

Fig. 4-11.
Continued.

```
        setlinestyle(USERBIT_LINE,b,NORM_WIDTH);
        moveto(x+16,y);lineto(x+31,y);
        setlinestyle(USERBIT_LINE,c,NORM_WIDTH);
        moveto(x+32,y);lineto(x+47,y);y=y+1;};
    setlinestyle(USERBIT_LINE,0xFFFF,NORM_WIDTH);return;
#endif
}
/*_____

End of source code  */
```

To use the program, press the left button of your mouse or crosshair cursor to draw a line from the most recent xy coordinate. To stop drawing and terminate the program, either press the right button of your pointing device or use Alt + X.

How the Program Works

The core functions for MOUSEMGR.C are contained in the section of source code titled MOUSE CONTROL FUNCTIONS.

The function Mouse_Initialize( ) uses mouse function 0 and INT 33H to initialize the mouse driver or tablet driver. The routine places the returned value from the AX register into a variable named mouse_flag. The caller uses mouse_flag to determine if a driver is actually loaded or not. If mouse_flag is 0, then no driver is present and the program will thereafter support only keyboard input. If mouse_flag is any value other than 0, then all is well and the program proceeds to process graphical input. The mouse driver or tablet driver must be initialized before any calls are made, otherwise unpredictable and erratic results may occur. The initialization sets up the shape of the cursor, the legal xy range, and so on.

The function Mouse_Show( ) uses function 1 and INT 33H to display the screen cursor. For most mouse and tablet products, this cursor is usually an arrowhead which points up and to the left. Example code for this function was provided earlier in this chapter.

The function Mouse_Hide( ) uses function 2 and INT 33H to remove the cursor from the screen. You should use this function before you draw any graphics on the screen. If you draw directly over the cursor, it will leave a spot of trash on the screen when the XOR operator is used by the driver to remove the cursor and redraw it at its next location.

The function Mouse_Status( ) is the real workhorse of this program. Mouse_Status( ) performs two vital services. First, it reports whether or not a button has been pressed by the end-user. This information is returned in the BX register and is stored in a variable arbitrarily named mouse_button. Second, it fetches the current x,y coordinates of the on-screen cursor. These x,y coordinates are called the *hot spot*, and are located at the tip of the default arrowhead cursor.

The function Mouse_Setposition( ) resets the location of the cursor on the screen. The routine uses mouse function 4 and passes the desired x,y coordinates in the CX and DX registers. Remember, this function is not entirely compatible with tablets because the handheld crosshair cursor is physically tied to a specific location on the tablet, unlike the free-roaming mouse on the table top.

The function Mouse_Setrangeh( ) uses mouse function 7 and INT 33H to define the maximum and minimum x coordinates range for the on-screen cursor. If the end-user moves the pointing device outside this range, the screen cursor will act as if it has hit an invisible wall. The minimum x coordinate is passed in the CX register, the maximum x coordinate in the DX register.

The function Mouse_Setrangev( ) sets the minimum and maximum y coordinates range for the on-screen cursor. The minimum y coordinate is passed in the CX register. The maximum y coordinate is passed to the driver in the DX register.

By following the style used in this program listing, you can readily write your own mouse and tablet routines for the advanced features found in your mouse or tablet user's guide.

Important Declarations and Initializations

Note the definition for the constant named MOUSE near the beginning of the program. This is set to 0x33, the number of the interrupt service to be called. Using this convention makes the source code easier to read and maintain, of course.

Also important is the initialization of the data structure which is used to access the microprocessor's registers. Both QuickC and Turbo C use the union syntax to create a structure conforming to a type defined in the compiler's #include file.

The section named DECLARATION OF GLOBAL VARIABLES declares and initializes some important variables. Note how the active viewport for the cursor is defined in terms of minimum and maximum x,y coordinates, for example. You can see how these and other conditions are set up in the main( ) routine when the mouse or tablet is started up.

The Executive Loop

The master loop in this demonstration program is called mouse_manager:. It is simply a line label located in the main( ) routine.

Note how the loop first calls Mouse_Status( ) to see if a button has been pressed and to retrieve the current x,y coordinates. C's if statement is used to perform branches based on the value of mouse_button. For example, if mouse_button equals 2 the program knows that the right button has been pressed and the program should terminate. Note how the routine named Quit_Pgm( ) performs a failsafe check to make sure the mouse or tablet cursor is safely removed from the screen before switching screen modes and ending the program.

The Autodetect Routine

Note the addition of pointing device variable initializations in the autodetect routine, named Graphics_Setup( ). Variables such as mouse_maxx and mouse_ minx, among others, are given the correct values for the particular graphics mode being set up.

THE TIMING DILEMMA

Any loop that is being used to read data from a pointing device like a mouse or tablet contains the potential for a serious bug. In particular, if the loop is fast enough and if the user holds the button down long enough, the x,y coordinates will be read more than once in the time it takes to perform some graphics function and return to the loop. If, for example, all your program is doing is storing coordinates for the eventual creation of a smooth curve, it is all too easy for the program to read three or four sets of the same x,y coordinates into memory when the end-user presses the button just once.

The program listing in this chapter makes no attempt to deal with this problem, although there are two methods for overcoming this timing pitfall. First, you can use a deliberate delay routine in your source code to make certain the user has released the button before you next read the device's x,y coordinates. Second, you can compare the new x,y coordinates with the former coordinates, and if they are identical your program simply ignores the new coordinates. Unfortunately, both methods are fraught with snares for the unwary. The two major demonstration programs in this book use a microprocessor-dependent timing delay approach, which yields satisfactory performance on most personal computers running at less than 12 MHz. See the source code in Chapter 8 for more on this. As a professional developer, you would want to write a delay routine which operates in real time and which functions independent of CPU speed.

5

User Output:
Managing a Disk

WHILE YOUR END-USER interacts with your C graphics program, the natural output is an image on the display screen; but for this fleeting impression to become more permanent, the data which makes up the image must be stored—usually on disk.

The ability to save and reload images gives your end-user the option of editing images at a later date, or exporting images to other programs such as desktop publishing software, or importing images from other devices such as handheld scanners, or printing an image on a laser printer or dot matrix printer.

BITMAP FILES AND VECTOR FILES

There are two fundamental formats for saving and loading images as files. They are bitmap files and vector files.

Bitmap Files

The buffer which is scanned by the computer's hardware and sent to the display monitor is called a *bitmap*. By simply saving the entire contents of the bitmap buffer to disk, you can create a bitmap file. To redisplay the image from a bitmap file, you read the data from disk back into the display buffer.

Although bitmap files are a straightforward and nearly foolproof method of saving and loading images, they suffer from one significant drawback. They consume disk space very quickly. A full-screen image from the 640x350x16-color mode of the EGA takes up 112,000 bytes on disk (4 bitplanes x 28000 bytes each). A VGA image using the 640x480x16-color mode requires a whopping 153,600 bytes.

Run-length Encoding

In order to overcome these massive memory requirements, programmers often resort to run-length encoding, which is a short algorithm that converts long sequences of identical data into a short formula. Rather than storing many rows of a solid color, for example, the algorithm saves only the color and the number of bytes which hold that color number. When the encoded image file is loaded from disk, the algorithm expands these short formulas back into their original raw data condition in the screen buffer.

Some run-length encoded images can require more data than a simple bitmap image, however. The length of the encoded image is dependent upon the complexity of the image. Because run-length encoding algorithms usually encrypt the data in sequence, row by row, an image with many non-horizontal lines or with a strongly patterned background can wreak havoc with the algorithm. File length savings of less than 15% are common in such circumstances.

Vector Files

A more compact method for storing images is the vector file approach. Rather than saving the data from the screen buffer, a vector file contains the drawing instructions necessary to dynamically recreate the image when it is reloaded.

Whereas a bitmap file would save, among other things, the data for each pixel position along the length of a line which has been drawn on the screen, a vector file would save only four data items: the starting coordinates, the ending coordinates, the color of the line, and the fact that the entity is a line. Using C, such a description could take up as few as 7 bytes of storage, no matter how long the line is. Using assembly language, storage requirements could be reduced to 5 bytes.

File Format Usage

Vector files are usually supported by 2D CADD drafting programs, where the geometry used to construct a drawing is as important as the drawing itself. Many 3D CAD programs support vector files.

Bitmap files are usually supported by draw, paint, and illustration programs, where the overall image is often more important than the geometry (or graphical entities) used to create the image.

Many programs support both vector file and bitmap file formats. Bitmap files are often called slides, images, or binary image files. Vector files are often called drawing files, data files, or graphics metafiles.

ACCESSING THE IMAGE BUFFER

In order to write the data contained in the image buffer to disk, you must know the starting address for the data and the length of the data.

Figure 5-1 depicts a display memory map for a VGA running in the 640x480x16-color mode. One graphics page is available in this mode. Four bitplanes are used: blue, green, red, and intensity. The display hardware automatically combines (sandwiches together) these four bitplanes to create the image you see on the monitor. Each bitplane is 38,400 bytes in length. An entire full-screen image requires 153,600 bytes of disk space. Bitplane 0 starts at A000:0000 hex. You must modify the internal latching registers of the VGA to gain access to read or write the other three bitplanes. The program listing later in this chapter will demonstrate the proper technique for achieving this.

RELATED MATERIAL: Graphics Adapters

For a more detailed discussion of the internal operation of graphics adapters, consult some of the author's other books, such as *High-Performance CAD Graphics in C*, Windcrest book #3059, ISBN 0-8306-9395-9, published March 1989. Also see *High-Performance Graphics in C: Animation & Simulation*, Windcrest book #3049, ISBN 0-8306-9394-1, published November 1988. Books can be ordered through your favorite bookstore or direct from Windcrest, a division of TAB BOOKS. See the listings at the end of this book.

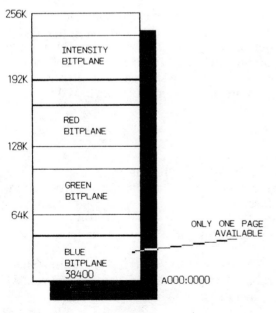

Fig. 5-1. Memory map of the VGA 640x480x16-color mode. Each bitplane is 38,400 bytes in length.

Figure 5-2 illustrates a display memory map for an EGA running in the 640x350x16-color mode. Two graphics pages are available in this mode. Four bitplanes are used: blue, green, red, and intensity. Each bitplane is 28,000 bytes in length. An entire full-screen image requires 112,000 bytes of disk space. Bitplane 0 begins at A000:0000 hex. Page 0 starts at A000:0000. Page 1 starts at A800:0000. The internal latching registers of the EGA must be modified in order to read or write the other three bitplanes. This is demonstrated in the program listing in this chapter.

Figure 5-3 shows a memory map for an EGA board running in the 640x200x16-color mode. Four graphics pages are available in this mode. Four bitplanes are employed: blue, green, red, and intensity. Each bitplane is 16,000 bytes in length. A full-screen image requires 64,000 bytes of disk space. Bitplane 0 commences at A000:0000 hex. Page 0 starts at A000:0000, page 1 at A400:0000, page 2 at A800:0000, and page 3 at AC00:0000. The internal latching registers of the EGA must be adjusted in order to read or write data from bitplanes 1, 2, and 3. The program listing later in this chapter provides an example of this technique.

Figure 5-4 illustrates a memory map for a CGA graphics adapter running in the 640x200x2-color mode. Only 16K of display memory, located at starting address B800:0000, is actually physically present on the graphics adapter. The image data is organized into two banks. Bank 0 contains even scanline rows 0 to 198. Bank 1 contains odd scanline rows 1 to 199. A full-screen image requires 16,000 bytes of data (although in practise an additional 384 bytes is needed if the unused memory areas adjacent to each bank are also stored).

Figure 5-5 depicts a display memory map for a Hercules Graphics Adapter running in the 720x348x2-color mode. 32K of display memory is physically

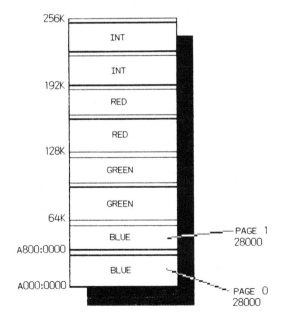

Fig. 5-2. Memory map of the EGA 640x350x16-color mode. Each bitplane is 28,000 bytes in length.

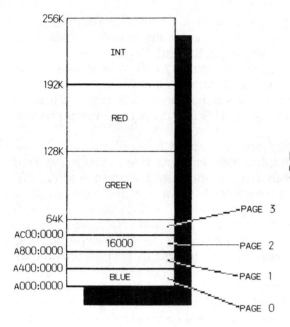

Fig. 5-3. Memory map of the EGA 640x200x16-color mode. Each bitplane is 16,000 bytes in length.

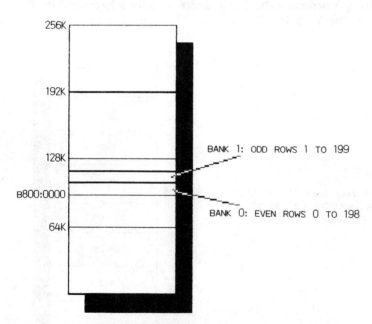

Fig. 5-4. Memory map of the CGA 640x200x2-color mode. Each bank is 8,000 bytes in length, totalling 16,000 bytes—although 16,384 bytes of memory is reserved for CGA display memory.

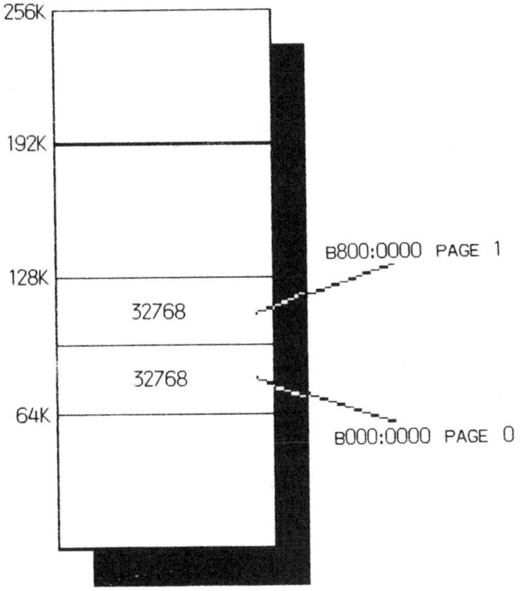

Fig. 5-5. Memory map of the Hercules 720x348x2-color mode. Each page is comprised of four frames of 8K bytes each, providing a quad-interleaving scheme.

256K

192K

128K

64K

32768

32768

B800:0000 PAGE 1

B000:0000 PAGE 0

installed on the adapter, commencing at memory address B000:0000. A full-screen image requires 32,768 bytes of disk space. The image data is organized into four banks of 8,192 bytes each, with 362 bytes of unused memory between each bank. Two pages are available. Page 0 begins at B000:0000. Page 1 begins at B800:0000.

A DEMONSTRATION PROGRAM

The image in FIG. 5-6 shows the graphics that are saved to disk and then reloaded and displayed by the demonstration program listing in FIG. 5-7, IMAGES.C.

The program listing is fully compatible with the 640x480x16-color mode of the VGA, the 640x350x16-color mode of the EGA, the 640x200x16-color mode of the EGA, the 640x480x2-color mode of the MCGA, the 640x200x2-color mode of the CGA, and the 720x348x2-color mode of the Hercules graphics adapters.

CAUTION

Before you compile and run the demonstration program, be sure there is enough space on the default drive and directory to store the image files created by the program.

Before you run the program, ensure that there is sufficient space on the current drive and directory to hold the resulting image files. The program is hard-coded to write to and read from the current drive/directory. You will need at

Fig. 5-6. Print of the image which is saved to disk and then retrieved and redisplayed by the demonstration program, IMAGES.C.

least 160K if you are using a VGA, 120K for an EGA and enhanced monitor, 65K for an EGA and standard monitor, 40K for an MCGA, 16K for a CGA, and 34K for a Hercules.

If you are using QuickC, you can compile and run the program as is. If you are using Turbo C, remember to change the variable named Compiler in the COMPILER DIRECTIVES section of the source code before compiling the program.

Fig. 5-7. Source code for IMAGES.C, designed to save and retrieve graphics images to and from disk using VGA, EGA, MCGA, CGA, and Hercules graphics adapters. Ready to compile under QuickC and Turbo C.

```
/*
Image Saving and Loading                    Source file: IMAGES.C

Purpose:  demonstrates how to write C graphics programs which
save a VGA, EGA, CGA, MCGA, or Hercules screen image to disk, and
which can retrieve a previously-saved image from disk.

Compiler:  QuickC or Turbo C.  Default is QuickC.  To use
Turbo C, change one line in COMPILER DIRECTIVES below.

Memory model:  medium memory model.
```

Fig. 5-7.
Continued.

```
Marketability:  will detect and support these platforms...
VGA          640x480x16 colors   80x60 characters
EGA          640x350x16 colors   80x43 characters
EGA          640x200x16 colors   80x25 characters
MCGA         640x480x2 colors    80x60 characters
CGA          640x200x2 colors    80x25 characters
Hercules     720x348x2 colors    80x25 characters
```

This program uses 640x480 virtual coordinates which are mapped
to the runtime physical screen by GetX() and GetY(). The image
produced by the program is saved to the current working drive
and directory before being retrieved and displayed.

```
COMPILER DIRECTIVES
These are instructions to your C compiler. */

#define QuickC    1
#define TurboC    2
#define Compiler QuickC    /* NOTE: Change to TurboC if required */
#define FAIL      0
#define EMPTY     0

#include <bios.h>              /* supports the keyboard functions */
#include <stdio.h>                /* supports printf and file IO */
#if Compiler==QuickC
  #include <graph.h>                 /* supports QuickC's graphics */
  #include <conio.h>        /* supports QuickC port manipulation */
  #include <memory.h>          /* supports QuickC memory moves */
  #include <dos.h>                 /* supports QuickC segread */
#elif Compiler==TurboC
  #include <graphics.h>             /* supports Turbo C's graphics */
  #include <dos.h>       /* Turbo C port manipulation and segread */
  #include <mem.h>               /* supports Turbo C memory moves */
#endif
#include <process.h>               /* supports the exit function
```

```
FUNCTION PROTOTYPES
These ANSI C function declarations allow your C compiler to check
each function for correct arguments and return value. */

void Keyboard();                        /* checks for a keystroke */
void Quit_Pgm();                        /* terminates the program */
void Graphics_Setup();        /* autodetect of graphics hardware */
void GetTextCoords();                  /* converts QC to TC text */
void Notice(int,int);               /* displays copyright notice */
void SaveImage();                 /* saves VGA or EGA image to disk */
void LoadImage();              /* loads VGA or EGA image from disk */
void SaveCGAimage();                /* saves CGA image to disk */
void LoadCGAimage();             /* loads CGA image from disk */
void SaveHGAimage();            /* saves Hercules image to disk */
void LoadHGAimage();         /* loads Hercules image from disk */
void SaveMCGAimage();               /* saves MCGA image to disk */
void LoadMCGAimage();            /* loads MCGA image from disk */
float GetX(float);  /* converts virtual coord to physical screen */
float GetY(float);  /* converts virtual coord to physical screen */
/*_____
```

```
DECLARATION OF GLOBAL VARIABLES
These variables are declared and initialized outside of any
function and are visible to all functions in this source file.   */
```

Fig. 5-7.
Continued.

```
#if Compiler==QuickC
  struct videoconfig vc;               /* QuickC's video data table */
#endif
struct SREGS segregs;          /* structure of CPU register values */
int C0=0,C1=1,C2=2,C3=3,C4=4,C5=5,C6=6,C7=7,C8=8,C9=9,C10=10,
C11=11,C12=12,C13=13,C14=14,C15=15;                  /* color codes */
int mode_flag=0;                   /* indicates current graphics mode */
float x_res=0,y_res=0;  /* screen resolution for mapping routine */
float sx=0,sy=0;                    /* physical screen coordinates */
float sx1=0,sy1=0,sx2=0,sy2=0;
int t1=1;                                          /* loop counter */
int TextRow=1,TextColumn=1;             /* text position for QuickC */
int TextX=0,TextY=0;                   /* text position for Turbo C */
unsigned int segment=0;           /* value of data segment register */
unsigned int offset=0;         /* destination offset for movedata */
FILE *image_file;                                    /* data stream */
unsigned int plane_length=38400;      /* length of one bit plane */
char image_buffer[38400]; /* temporary buffer to store bit plane
```

```
FUNCTION DEFINITIONS */

main(){                             /* this is the master routine */
Graphics_Setup();                   /* establish graphics mode */
#if Compiler==QuickC
  _getvideoconfig(&vc);       /* initialize QuickC's video table */
  _setcolor(C7);Notice(589,2);
  _setfillmask(NULL);_setcolor(C15);
  sx1=GetX(100);sy1=GetY(280);
  sx2=GetX(560);sy2=GetY(320);
  _rectangle(_GFILLINTERIOR,sx1,sy1,sx2,sy2);    /* white graphic */
  _setcolor(C4);                         /* draw the red graphic */
  sx=GetX(260);sy=GetY(200);_moveto(sx,sy);
  sx=GetX(380);sy=GetY(400);_lineto(sx,sy);
  sx=GetX(140);sy=GetY(400);_lineto(sx,sy);
  sx=GetX(260);sy=GetY(200);_lineto(sx,sy);
  sx=GetX(260);sy=GetY(300);_floodfill(sx,sy,C4);
  _setcolor(C2);                       /* draw the green graphic */
  sx=GetX(320);sy=GetY(200);_moveto(sx,sy);
  sx=GetX(440);sy=GetY(400);_lineto(sx,sy);
  sx=GetX(200);sy=GetY(400);_lineto(sx,sy);
  sx=GetX(320);sy=GetY(200);_lineto(sx,sy);
  sx=GetX(320);sy=GetY(300);_floodfill(sx,sy,C2);
  _setcolor(C1);                        /* draw the blue graphic */
  sx=GetX(380);sy=GetY(200);_moveto(sx,sy);
  sx=GetX(520);sy=GetY(400);_lineto(sx,sy);
  sx=GetX(260);sy=GetY(400);_lineto(sx,sy);
  sx=GetX(380);sy=GetY(200);_lineto(sx,sy);
  sx=GetX(380);sy=GetY(300);_floodfill(sx,sy,C1);
#elif Compiler==TurboC
  setcolor(C7);Notice(589,2);
  setcolor(C15);setfillstyle(SOLID_FILL,C15);/* set clr and fill */
  sx1=GetX(100);sy1=GetY(280);
  sx2=GetX(560);sy2=GetY(320);
  bar(sx1,sy1,sx2,sy2);                          /* white graphic */
  setcolor(C4);setfillstyle(SOLID_FILL,C4);  /* draw red graphic */
  sx=GetX(260);sy=GetY(200);moveto(sx,sy);
  sx=GetX(380);sy=GetY(400);lineto(sx,sy);
  sx=GetX(140);sy=GetY(400);lineto(sx,sy);
  sx=GetX(260);sy=GetY(200);lineto(sx,sy);
  sx=GetX(260);sy=GetY(300);floodfill(sx,sy,C4);
  setcolor(C2);setfillstyle(SOLID_FILL,C2);      /* green graphic */
  sx=GetX(320);sy=GetY(200);moveto(sx,sy);
  sx=GetX(440);sy=GetY(400);lineto(sx,sy);
  sx=GetX(200);sy=GetY(400);lineto(sx,sy);
  sx=GetX(320);sy=GetY(200);lineto(sx,sy);
  sx=GetX(320);sy=GetY(300);floodfill(sx,sy,C2);
  setcolor(C1);setfillstyle(SOLID_FILL,C1);       /* blue graphic */
  sx=GetX(380);sy=GetY(200);moveto(sx,sy);
```

Fig. 5-7.
Continued.

```
      sx=GetX(520);sy=GetY(400);lineto(sx,sy);
      sx=GetX(260);sy=GetY(400);lineto(sx,sy);
      sx=GetX(380);sy=GetY(200);lineto(sx,sy);
      sx=GetX(380);sy=GetY(300);floodfill(sx,sy,C1);
      setcolor(C7);
#endif
switch(mode_flag){          /* call appropriate image save function */
   case 1: SaveImage();break;          /* VGA 640x480x16-color mode */
   case 2: SaveImage();break;          /* EGA 640x350x16-color mode */
   case 3: SaveImage();break;          /* EGA 640x200x16-color mode */
   case 4: SaveMCGAimage();break;      /* MCGA 640x480x2-color mode */
   case 5: SaveCGAimage();break;        /* CGA 640x200x2-color mode */
   case 6: SaveHGAimage();break; /* Hercules 720x348x2-color mode */
   default: break;}
#if Compiler==QuickC
  _clearscreen(_GCLEARSCREEN);
  _settextposition(10,10);
  _outtext("Image successfully saved to disk.");
  _settextposition(11,10);
  _outtext("Loading image from disk.");
#elif Compiler==TurboC
  cleardevice();
  TextRow=10;TextColumn=10;GetTextCoords();
  outtextxy(TextX,TextY,"Image successfully saved to disk.");
  TextRow=11;TextColumn=10;GetTextCoords();
  outtextxy(TextX,TextY,"Loading image from disk.");
#endif
for (t1=1;t1<=30000;t1++);                              /* pause */
for (t1=1;t1<=30000;t1++);
for (t1=1;t1<=30000;t1++);
switch(mode_flag){          /* call appropriate image load function */
   case 1: LoadImage();break;          /* VGA 640x480x16-color mode */
   case 2: LoadImage();break;          /* EGA 640x350x16-color mode */
   case 3: LoadImage();break;          /* EGA 640x200x16-color mode */
   case 4: LoadMCGAimage();break;      /* MCGA 640x480x2-color mode */
   case 5: LoadCGAimage();break;        /* CGA 640x200x2-color mode */
   case 6: LoadHGAimage();break; /* Hercules 720x348x2-color mode */
   default: break;}
#if Compiler==QuickC
  _settextposition(12,33);
  if (mode_flag==3) _settextposition(10,33);
  if (mode_flag==5) _settextposition(10,33);
  _outtext("Press any key to quit...");
#elif Compiler==TurboC
  setfillstyle(SOLID_FILL,C0);
  TextRow=12;TextColumn=33;
  if (mode_flag==3) {TextRow=10;bar(250,72,500,80);goto Line01;}
  if (mode_flag==5) {TextRow=10;bar(250,72,500,80);goto Line01;}
  bar(250,88,500,96);
  Line01:
  GetTextCoords();
  outtextxy(TextX,TextY,"Press any key to quit...");
#endif
for (t1=1;t1!=2; ) Keyboard();             /* press any key to stop */
Quit_Pgm();}                           /* end the program gracefully
                                                                    */


void SaveImage(){       /* saves VGA or EGA screen image to disk */
segread(&segregs);segment=segregs.ds; /* determine segment value */
offset=(unsigned int)image_buffer;     /* determine offset value */
image_file=fopen("IMAGE-01.BLU","wb");          /* open the file */
#if Compiler==QuickC
  outp(0x3ce,4);outp(0x3cf,0);     /* set EGA,VGA to read plane 0 */
#elif Compiler==TurboC
  outportb(0x3ce,4);outportb(0x3cf,0);
#endif
movedata(0xa000,0x0000,segment,offset,plane_length);
fwrite((char *)image_buffer,1,plane_length,image_file);
```

Fig. 5-7.
Continued.

```
fclose(image_file);                                /* close the file */
image_file=fopen("IMAGE-01.GRN","wb");             /* open the file */
#if Compiler==QuickC
  outp(0x3ce,4);outp(0x3cf,1);     /* set EGA,VGA to read plane 1 */
#elif Compiler==TurboC
  outportb(0x3ce,4);outportb(0x3cf,1);
#endif
movedata(0xa000,0x0000,segment,offset,plane_length);
fwrite((char *)image_buffer,1,plane_length,image_file);
fclose(image_file);                                /* close the file */
image_file=fopen("IMAGE-01.RED","wb");             /* open the file */
#if Compiler==QuickC
  outp(0x3ce,4);outp(0x3cf,2);     /* set EGA,VGA to read plane 2 */
#elif Compiler==TurboC
  outportb(0x3ce,4);outportb(0x3cf,2);
#endif
movedata(0xa000,0x0000,segment,offset,plane_length);
fwrite((char *)image_buffer,1,plane_length,image_file);
fclose(image_file);                                /* close the file */
image_file=fopen("IMAGE-01.INT","wb");             /* open the file */
#if Compiler==QuickC
  outp(0x3ce,4);outp(0x3cf,3);     /* set EGA,VGA to read plane 3 */
#elif Compiler==TurboC
  outportb(0x3ce,4);outportb(0x3cf,3);
#endif
movedata(0xa000,0x0000,segment,offset,plane_length);
fwrite((char *)image_buffer,1,plane_length,image_file);
fclose(image_file);                                /* close the file */
#if Compiler==QuickC
  outp(0x3ce,4);outp(0x3cf,0);        /* restore EGA,VGA registers */
#elif Compiler==TurboC
  outportb(0x3ce,4);outportb(0x3cf,0);
#endif
return;}
/*_____*/

void LoadImage(){       /* loads VGA or EGA screen image from disk */
segread(&segregs);segment=segregs.ds; /* determine segment value */
offset=(unsigned int)image_buffer;       /* determine offset value */
image_file=fopen("IMAGE-01.BLU","rb");             /* open the file */
#if Compiler==QuickC
  outp(0x3c4,2);outp(0x3c5,1);     /* set EGA,VGA to write plane 0 */
#elif Compiler==TurboC
  outportb(0x3c4,2);outportb(0x3c5,1);
#endif
fread((char *)image_buffer,1,plane_length,image_file);
movedata(segment,offset,0xa000,0x0000,plane_length);
fclose(image_file);                                /* close the file */
image_file=fopen("IMAGE-01.GRN","rb");             /* open the file */
#if Compiler==QuickC
  outp(0x3c4,2);outp(0x3c5,2);     /* set EGA,VGA to write plane 1 */
#elif Compiler==TurboC
  outportb(0x3c4,2);outportb(0x3c5,2);
#endif
fread((char *)image_buffer,1,plane_length,image_file);
movedata(segment,offset,0xa000,0x0000,plane_length);
fclose(image_file);                                /* close the file */
image_file=fopen("IMAGE-01.RED","rb");             /* open the file */
#if Compiler==QuickC
  outp(0x3c4,2);outp(0x3c5,4);     /* set EGA,VGA to write plane 2 */
#elif Compiler==TurboC
  outportb(0x3c4,2);outportb(0x3c5,4);
#endif
fread((char *)image_buffer,1,plane_length,image_file);
movedata(segment,offset,0xa000,0x0000,plane_length);
fclose(image_file);                                /* close the file */
image_file=fopen("IMAGE-01.INT","rb");             /* open the file */
#if Compiler==QuickC
  outp(0x3c4,2);outp(0x3c5,8);     /* set EGA,VGA to write plane 3 */
```

Fig. 5-7.
Continued.

```
#elif Compiler==TurboC
  outportb(0x3c4,2);outportb(0x3c5,8);
#endif
fread((char *)image_buffer,1,plane_length,image_file);
movedata(segment,offset,0xa000,0x0000,plane_length);
fclose(image_file);                              /* close the file */
#if Compiler==QuickC
  outp(0x3c4,2);outp(0x3c5,0xF);     /* restore EGA,VGA registers */
#elif Compiler==TurboC
  outportb(0x3c4,2);outportb(0x3c5,0xF);
#endif
return;}
/*_____*/

void SaveCGAimage(){           /* saves CGA screen image to disk */
segread(&segregs);segment=segregs.ds; /* determine segment value */
offset=(unsigned int)image_buffer;      /* determine offset value */
image_file=fopen("IMAGE-01.CGA","wb");          /* open the file */
movedata(0xb800,0x0000,segment,offset,plane_length);
fwrite((char *)image_buffer,1,plane_length,image_file);
fclose(image_file);                              /* close the file */
return;}
/*_____*/

void LoadCGAimage(){           /* loads CGA screen image from disk */
segread(&segregs);segment=segregs.ds; /* determine segment value */
offset=(unsigned int)image_buffer;      /* determine offset value */
image_file=fopen("IMAGE-01.CGA","rb");          /* open the file */
fread((char *)image_buffer,1,plane_length,image_file);
movedata(segment,offset,0xB800,0x0000,plane_length);
fclose(image_file);                              /* close the file */
return;}
/*_____*/

void SaveHGAimage(){        /* saves Hercules screen image to disk */
segread(&segregs);segment=segregs.ds; /* determine segment value */
offset=(unsigned int)image_buffer;      /* determine offset value */
image_file=fopen("IMAGE-01.HGA","wb");          /* open the file */
movedata(0xb000,0x0000,segment,offset,plane_length);
fwrite((char *)image_buffer,1,plane_length,image_file);
fclose(image_file);                              /* close the file */
return;}
/*_____*/

void LoadHGAimage(){     /* loads Hercules screen image from disk */
segread(&segregs);segment=segregs.ds; /* determine segment value */
offset=(unsigned int)image_buffer;      /* determine offset value */
image_file=fopen("IMAGE-01.HGA","rb");          /* open the file */
fread((char *)image_buffer,1,plane_length,image_file);
movedata(segment,offset,0xb000,0x0000,plane_length);
fclose(image_file);                              /* close the file */
return;}
/*_____*/

void SaveMCGAimage(){          /* saves MCGA screen image to disk */
segread(&segregs);segment=segregs.ds; /* determine segment value */
offset=(unsigned int)image_buffer;      /* determine offset value */
image_file=fopen("IMAGE-01.MCG","wb");          /* open the file */
movedata(0xa000,0x0000,segment,offset,plane_length);
fwrite((char *)image_buffer,1,plane_length,image_file);
fclose(image_file);                              /* close the file */
return;}
/*_____*/

void LoadMCGAimage(){          /* loads MCGA screen image from disk */
segread(&segregs);segment=segregs.ds; /* determine segment value */
offset=(unsigned int)image_buffer;      /* determine offset value */
image_file=fopen("IMAGE-01.MCG","rb");          /* open the file */
fread((char *)image_buffer,1,plane_length,image_file);
```

Fig. 5-7.
Continued.

```
movedata(segment,offset,0xa000,0x0000,plane_length);
fclose(image_file);                              /* close the file */
return;}
/*_____*/

float GetX(float vx){    /* scales virtual x coord to phys screen */
float sx;
sx=vx*(x_res/640);return sx;}
/*_____*/

float GetY(float vy){    /* scales virtual y coord to phys screen */
float sy;
sy=vy*(y_res/480);return sy;}
/*_____*/

void Keyboard(){                    /* checks the keyboard buffer */
#if Compiler==QuickC
  if (_bios_keybrd(_KEYBRD_READY)==EMPTY) return;
  else (_bios_keybrd(_KEYBRD_READ);Quit_Pgm();}
#elif Compiler==TurboC
  if (bioskey(1)==EMPTY) return;else (bioskey(0);Quit_Pgm();}
#endif
}
/*_____*/

void Quit_Pgm(){                         /* terminates the program */
#if Compiler==QuickC
  _clearscreen(_GCLEARSCREEN);               /* clear the screen */
  _setvideomode(_DEFAULTMODE);      /* restore the original mode */
#elif Compiler==TurboC
  cleardevice();                             /* clear the screen */
  closegraph();     /* shut down graphics, restore original mode */
#endif
exit(0);}    /* flush buffers, close files, terminate the program
_____*/

void Graphics_Setup(){       /* autodetect of graphics hardware */
#if Compiler==QuickC
  if (_setvideomoderows(_VRES16COLOR,60)!=FAIL) goto VGA_mode;
  if (_setvideomoderows(_ERESCOLOR,43)!=FAIL) goto EGA_ECD_mode;
  if (_setvideomoderows(_HRES16COLOR,25)!=FAIL) goto EGA_SCD_mode;
  if (_setvideomoderows(_VRES2COLOR,60)!=FAIL) goto MCGA_mode;
  if (_setvideomoderows(_HRESBW,25)!=FAIL) goto CGA_mode;
  if (_setvideomoderows(_HERCMONO,25)!=FAIL) goto Hercules_mode;
#elif Compiler==TurboC
  int graphics_adapter,graphics_mode;
  detectgraph(&graphics_adapter,&graphics_mode);
  if (graphics_adapter==VGA) goto VGA_mode;
  if (graphics_mode==EGAHI) goto EGA_ECD_mode;
  if (graphics_mode==EGALO) goto EGA_SCD_mode;
  if (graphics_adapter==MCGA) goto MCGA_mode;
  if (graphics_adapter==CGA) goto CGA_mode;
  if (graphics_adapter==HERCMONO) goto Hercules_mode;
#endif
goto abort_pgm;                   /* if no graphics hardware found */

VGA_mode:     /* VGA 640x480x16-color mode, 8x8 character matrix */
x_res=640;y_res=480;plane_length=38400;mode_flag=1;
#if Compiler==QuickC
  _settextcolor(C7);
  _settextposition(10,15);
  _outtext("VGA 640x480x16-color graphics, 80x60 character set");
  _settextposition(12,33);
  _outtext("Saving the screen...");
#elif Compiler==TurboC
  graphics_adapter=VGA;graphics_mode=VGAHI;
  initgraph(&graphics_adapter,&graphics_mode,"");
  settextstyle(0,0,1);setcolor(C7);
  TextRow=10;TextColumn=15;GetTextCoords();
```

Fig. 5-7.
Continued.

```
        outtextxy(TextX,TextY,"VGA 640x480x16-color graphics,"
                             " 80x60 character set");
    TextRow=12;TextColumn=33;GetTextCoords();
    outtextxy(TextX,TextY,"Saving the screen...");
#endif
return;

EGA_ECD_mode: /* EGA 640x350x16-color mode, 8x8 character matrix */
x_res=640;y_res=350;plane_length=28000;mode_flag=2;
#if Compiler==QuickC
  _settextcolor(C7);
  _settextposition(10,15);
  _outtext("EGA 640x350x16-color graphics, 80x43 character set");
  _settextposition(12,33);
  _outtext("Saving the screen...");
#elif Compiler==TurboC
  graphics_adapter=EGA;graphics_mode=EGAHI;
  initgraph(&graphics_adapter,&graphics_mode,"");
  settextstyle(0,0,1);setcolor(C7);
  TextRow=10;TextColumn=15;GetTextCoords();
  outtextxy(TextX,TextY,"EGA 640x350x16-color graphics,"
                        " 80x43 character set");
  TextRow=12;TextColumn=33;GetTextCoords();
  outtextxy(TextX,TextY,"Saving the screen...");
#endif
return;

EGA_SCD_mode: /* EGA 640x200x16-color mode, 8x8 character matrix */
x_res=640;y_res=200;plane_length=16000;mode_flag=3;
#if Compiler==QuickC
  _settextcolor(C7);
  _settextposition(8,15);
  _outtext("EGA 640x200x16-color graphics, 80x25 character set");
  _settextposition(10,33);
  _outtext("Saving the screen...");
#elif Compiler==TurboC
  graphics_adapter=EGA;graphics_mode=EGALO;
  initgraph(&graphics_adapter,&graphics_mode,"");
  settextstyle(0,0,1);setcolor(C7);
  TextRow=8;TextColumn=15;GetTextCoords();
  outtextxy(TextX,TextY,"EGA 640x200x16-color graphics,"
                        " 80x25 character set");
  TextRow=10;TextColumn=33;GetTextCoords();
  outtextxy(TextX,TextY,"Saving the screen...");
#endif
return;

MCGA_mode:     /* MCGA 640x480x2-color mode, 8x8 character matrix */
x_res=640;y_res=480;plane_length=38400;
C0=0;C1=1;C2=1;C3=1;C4=1;C5=1;C6=1;C7=1;
C8=1;C9=1;C10=1;C11=1;C12=1;C13=1;C14=1;C15=1;mode_flag=4;
#if Compiler==QuickC
  _settextcolor(C7);
  _settextposition(10,15);
  _outtext("MCGA 640x480x2-color graphics, 80x60 character set");
  _settextposition(12,33);
  _outtext("Saving the screen...");
#elif Compiler==TurboC
  graphics_adapter=MCGA;graphics_mode=MCGAHI;
  initgraph(&graphics_adapter,&graphics_mode,"");
  settextstyle(0,0,1);setcolor(C7);
  TextRow=10;TextColumn=15;GetTextCoords();
  outtextxy(TextX,TextY,"MCGA 640x480x2-color graphics,"
                        " 80x60 character set");
  TextRow=12;TextColumn=33;GetTextCoords();
  outtextxy(TextX,TextY,"Saving the screen...");
#endif
return;
```

Fig. 5-7.
Continued.

```
CGA_mode:        /* CGA 640x200x2-color mode, 8x8 character matrix */
x_res=640;y_res=200;plane_length=16384;mode_flag=5;
C0=0;C1=1;C2=1;C3=1;C4=1;C5=1;C6=1;C7=1;
C8=1;C9=1;C10=1;C11=1;C12=1;C13=1;C14=1;C15=1;
#if Compiler==QuickC
  _settextcolor(C7);
  _settextposition(8,15);
  _outtext("CGA 640x200x2-color graphics, 80x25 character set");
  _settextposition(10,33);
  _outtext("Saving the screen...");
#elif Compiler==TurboC
  graphics_adapter=CGA;graphics_mode=CGAHI;
  initgraph(&graphics_adapter,&graphics_mode,"");
  settextstyle(0,0,1);setcolor(C7);
  TextRow=8;TextColumn=15;GetTextCoords();
  outtextxy(TextX,TextY,"CGA 640x200x2-color graphics,"
                        " 80x25 character set");
  TextRow=10;TextColumn=33;GetTextCoords();
  outtextxy(TextX,TextY,"Saving the screen...");
#endif
return;

Hercules_mode: /* Hercules 720x348x2-color mode,
                      9x14 character matrix */
x_res=720;y_res=348;plane_length=32406;mode_flag=6;
C0=0;C1=1;C2=1;C3=1;C4=1;C5=1;C6=1;C7=1;
C8=1;C9=1;C10=1;C11=1;C12=1;C13=1;C14=1;C15=1;
#if Compiler==QuickC
  _settextcolor(C7);
  _settextposition(10,15);
  _outtext("Hercules 720x348x2-color graphics,"
                      " 80x25 character set");
  _settextposition(12,33);
  _outtext("Saving the screen...");
#elif Compiler==TurboC
  graphics_adapter=HERCMONO;graphics_mode=HERCMONOHI;
  initgraph(&graphics_adapter,&graphics_mode,"");
  setcolor(C7);
  TextRow=10;TextColumn=15;GetTextCoords();
  outtextxy(TextX,TextY,"Hercules 720x348x2-color graphics,"
                      " 80x25 character set");
  TextRow=12;TextColumn=33;GetTextCoords();
  outtextxy(TextX,TextY,"Saving the screen...");
#endif
return;

abort_pgm:      /* jump to here if no supported graphics hardware */
printf("\n\nUnable to proceed.\n\r");
printf("Requires VGA, EGA, CGA, MCGA, or\n\r");
printf("Hercules adapter and appropriate monitor.\n\n\r");
exit(0);
}
/*_____*/

void GetTextCoords(){      /* convert QuickC text to Turbo C text */
TextX=(TextColumn*8)-8;TextY=(TextRow*8)-8;return;}
/*_____*/

void Notice(int x, int y){      /* displays the copyright notice */
int copyright[][3]={0x7c00,0x0000,0x0000, /* array of bit styles */
            0x8279,0x819c,0x645e,
            0xba4a,0x4252,0x96d0,
            0xa27a,0x4252,0x955e,
            0xba0a,0x43d2,0xf442,
            0x8219,0x825c,0x945e,
            0x7c00,0x0000,0x0000};
int a,b,c; int t1=0;                      /* local variables */
#if Compiler==QuickC
  for (t1=0;t1<=6;t1++){                 /* draw 7 styled lines */
```

Fig. 5-7.
Continued.

```
      a=copyright[t1][0];b=copyright[t1][1];c=copyright[t1][2];
      _setlinestyle(a);_moveto(x,y);_lineto(x+15,y);
      _setlinestyle(b);_moveto(x+16,y);_lineto(x+31,y);
      _setlinestyle(c);_moveto(x+32,y);_lineto(x+47,y);y=y+1;};
   _setlinestyle(0xFFFF);return;
#elif Compiler==TurboC
   for (t1=0;t1<=6;t1++){                    /* draw 7 styled lines */
      a=copyright[t1][0];b=copyright[t1][1];c=copyright[t1][2];
      setlinestyle(USERBIT_LINE,a,NORM_WIDTH);
      moveto(x,y);lineto(x+15,y);
      setlinestyle(USERBIT_LINE,b,NORM_WIDTH);
      moveto(x+16,y);lineto(x+31,y);
      setlinestyle(USERBIT_LINE,c,NORM_WIDTH);
      moveto(x+32,y);lineto(x+47,y);y=y+1;};
   setlinestyle(USERBIT_LINE,0xFFFF,NORM_WIDTH);return;
#endif
}
/*_____

End of source file. */
```

HOW THE PROGRAM WORKS

The program works by using C's movedata( ) function to copy the appropriate data from display memory down into a buffer in RAM. Then, C's fopen( ) and fwrite( ) functions are used to open a file and write the data from the buffer to disk. The tricky part of the program is determining the memory addresses for the particular graphics mode being used and keeping track of how many bitplanes must be saved.

COMPILER DIRECTIVES

Note the #include files in this section. For QuickC, conio.h is required in order to manipulate the registers of the VGA and EGA, and to read the contents of the segment registers of the microprocessor. The #include file memory.h is needed in order to support movement of data from one memory location to another. For Turbo C, dos.h is required in order to manipulate the VGA/EGA registers and to read CPU segment registers. The #include file mem.h supports memory moves.

FUNCTION PROTOTYPES

Note the device-dependent routines declared in this section. SaveImage( ) and LoadImage( ) operate on the three VGA and EGA modes supported by this program. SaveCGAimage( ) and LoadCGAimage( ) work in the CGA mode. SaveMCGAimage( ) and LoadMCGAimage( ) provide support for the MCGA graphics adapter. SaveHGAimage( ) and LoadHGAimage( ) work with the Hercules adapters.

DECLARATION OF GLOBAL VARIABLES

The last three lines of source code in this section serve to set up the capability to write files to disk. First, the data stream is initialized via the appropriate pointer. Then a variable named plane_length is declared and initialized. The value of this variable will be adjusted later in the program to meet the needs of whichever graphics mode is activated at start-up. Finally, an array of 38,400 bytes is established, named image_buffer. This array is large enough to hold a bitplane from the VGA's 640x480x16-color mode, and will easily accommodate any of the other graphics modes supported by the program listing.

A CLOSER LOOK: Temporary Image Buffers

Using a hard-coded, fixed-length array like this demonstration program does is very wasteful. As a serious C graphics programmer, you would prefer instead to use dynamic memory allocation and de-allocation, in order to conserve space in the near heap at run-time. The method used in this demonstration program is employed to make the algorithm as easy to understand as possible.

Note also the struct segregs which is declared in this section of the source code. This variable will be used to read the contents of the microprocessor's segment registers. The contents of DS will be needed when data is moved by movedata( ).

FUNCTION DEFINITIONS

The main( ) routine calls Graphics_Setup( ) to initialize the best graphics mode for the hardware. Then main( ) proceeds to create the image which will be saved to disk. Refer back to FIG. 5-6.

The main( ) routine then uses C's powerful switch( ) statement to decide which routine should be used to save the screen image. Remember, the variable named mode_flag was set by Graphics_Setup( ) to indicate the current graphics mode. After the image has been saved to disk, main( ) clears the screen, pauses, and then again uses switch( ) to call the appropriate routine to load the image back into memory from disk.

SaveImage( )

The SaveImage( ) function works with any of the VGA and EGA modes supported by the program. First, the segread( ) function is used to obtain the contents of the DS data segment register. Note how the segment value is stored in a variable named segment, while the offset value of the temporary buffer is stored into a variable named offset.

Next, fopen( ) is used to open a file.

QuickC's outp( ) or Turbo C's outportb( ) function is then used to tweak the latching registers of the VGA or EGA, as the case may be. This action ensures that the proper bitplane is being accessed.

Next, the movedata( ) function is employed to copy the contents of the bitplane down to the temporary buffer in the near heap. Then C's fwrite( ) function is used to write the contents of the buffer to disk.

Finally, the fclose( ) function closes the file.

This four-step process is repeated for each of the four bitplanes of the VGA and EGA. The hex values used to adjust the internal latching registers are taken from IBM's technical reference documentation.

LoadImage( )

The LoadImage( ) function operates exactly as the SaveImage( ) routine just described, only in reverse. First the image is read into the temporary buffer from the disk file. Then the data is written to the appropriate bitplane in display memory by modifying the latching registers.

SaveCGAimage( )

The SaveCGAimage( ) operates on the CGA graphics adapter. It functions similar to SaveImage( ) described previously, but only a single bitplane is present, of course. The value of plane_length was defined in Graphics_Setup( ) at program start-up. The hex addresses used as arguments to the movedata( ) function are taken from FIG. 5-4.

SaveHGAimage( )

The SaveHGAimage( ) works with the Hercules graphics adapters. It operates just like SaveCGAimage( ), except for the starting address and data length used by movedata( ) and fwrite( ). Refer to FIG. 5-5 for the appropriate memory addresses.

SaveMCGAimage( )

The SaveMCGAimage( ) saves bitplane 0 of the MCGA graphics adapter in the 640x480x2-color mode. It is interesting to note that if a VGA is running in this mode, all four bitplanes are originally written by the internal VGA registers, but only bitplane 0 corresponds to the memory layout used by a genuine MCGA.

MODIFICATIONS

By studying the starting memory addresses in the illustrations you can readily modify the source code in this demonstration program to save hidden pages on VGA, EGA, and Hercules graphics adapters.

In addition, by referring to the major program listings in Chapter 8 and Chapter 13 for guidance, you can easily modify the hard-coded filenames in this demonstration program to accept user-defined filenames at run-time to make the routines more flexible and responsive to the user's needs.

In its current form, the demonstration program contains no error handlers. If the program is unable to write to the current drive and directory, or if there is insufficient space left on the disk, the program makes no effort to inform you of a failure. However, when you attempt to load in the file, only a partial image or only a few of the bitplanes will be loaded and displayed. To add your own error handling routines, refer to the discussion in Appendix C.

Mode Dependence

The binary image format used by the demonstration program is mode-dependent, as are many bitmapped formats such as PCX and others. This means that you should always ensure that a previously-saved image is loaded back into a graphics adapter running in the same mode from which the image was saved. Attempting to criss-cross graphics modes can result in images with unacceptable aspect ratios, or even garbage on the screen.

The algorithm used to grab the raw data from the graphics adapter is very robust. You could easily add your own run-length encoding algorithm and header information to the temporary buffer and thereby create your own proprietary bitmapped file format.

COMMON IMAGE FILE FORMATS

If it weren't already confusing enough having to deal with bitmap files, run-length encoded bitmap files, and vector files, each major software developer seems to have created a proprietary file format. Many of these formats are so close in format as to be ALMOST compatible with other developers' files. Unfortunately, "almost" only counts in hand grenades and horseshoes, and the end-user can be left with an image file that is incompatible with other software.

PCX File Format

The PCX file format is a run-length encoded bitmap format made popular by a major paint program, PC Paint. Refer to FIG. 5-8. The specifications for this format have been published and are available from a number of sources, including third-party programmers' kits such as PCX Programmer's Toolkit from Genus Microprogramming.

If there is a standard for bitmap image files, it is likely the PCX format. There is strong pressure in the marketplace for all graphics software to offer support for PCX format images, whether for exporting or importing such files. PCX files can be exchanged between drawing and paint programs, FAX boards, scanners, desktop publishing programs such as PageMaker™ and Ventura™, and various clip art databases.

PCX files often use the filename extension .PCX.

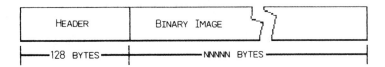

Fig. 5-8. Conceptual representation of a PCX image file. The binary image portion of the file is compressed with a run-length encoding algorithm.

TIFF File Format

TIFF is an acronym for Tagged Image File Format. TIFF is an enhanced bitmap format. Refer to Fig. 5-9. Although the binary image is essentially a run-length encoded image, the header for the file is flexible. It can be as long or as short as it needs to be, containing as much information or as little as the programmer sees fit. Parameters such as resolution, color, number of bitplanes, aspect ratio, and other control fields might or might not be present, depending upon the hardware being used to display the image. This flexibility makes TIFF a device-independent format.

A coarse-resolution graphics adapter simply ignores parameters in the header which do not apply to it. A high-resolution adapter, on the other hand, reads those parameters and uses the information to construct a much richer rendering of the image.

TIFF's flexibility even extends to the run-length encoding algorithm, which is optional, meaning that raw data can be saved in the binary image portion of the file.

TIFF files often use the filename extension .TIF. Microsoft has endorsed the TIFF format and plans to make it standard under Presentation Manager (OS/2) graphics programs.

CGM File format

CGM is an acronym for computer graphics metafile, a vector-based file format. Support for CGM is widespread and it has received ANSI sanction as the industry-wide standard for image interchange between different software and hardware systems.

CGM files often use the filename extension .CGM.

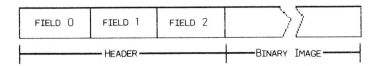

Fig. 5-9. Conceptual representation of a TIFF image file using the tag image file format, whereby a varying number of control fields are stored in the header, as required by the resolution, color, and other qualities of the image. If the binary image is compressed, a number of optional compression schemes are supported by the TIFF standard.

Other File Formats

Other file formats are often easily recognized by their filename extensions on disk.

A .PIF file uses the picture interchange format which is essentially a run-length encoded bitmapped image.

A .PIC file uses the picture file format, as supported by Lotus™, and by IBM's Storyboard ™.

A .DXF file uses AutoCAD's drawing interchange format, which is a vector file format. The .SLD format is used by AutoCAD to save and load bitmapped images.

A .DRW file uses a proprietary format supported by Micrografx Draw™.

.EPS files use the encapsulated postscript format and are compatible with laser printers.

A .WMF file uses the Windows™ metafile format.

.GEM files use the format of, naturally enough, the GEM system.

.MAC and .PICT files are found on Macintosh computers.

Also of interest is the .RIB filename extension, which signifies the RenderMan™ interface bytestream, a photographic-quality rendering standard being promoted by Pixar.

CASE STUDY: PCX Programmer's Toolkit

Noteworthy among the various programming aids available for serious C graphics programmers is the PCX Programmer's Toolkit, available from Genus Microprogramming, 11315 Meadow Lake, Houston TX, USA 77077. The toolkit is a collection of over 60 routines supplied in OBJ file format which you can link into your C programs. The routines provide full PCX save and load capabilities. Full-screens and programmer-defined partial screens can be saved and loaded. Dot matrix printer and laser printer output is also provided.

The user's manual, shown in FIG. 5-10, is a comprehensive listing of the routines, which can be called just like the built-in routines of QuickC and Turbo C. The PCX Programmer's Toolkit supports small, medium, and large memory models. A diversified range of graphics adapters is supported, including all VGA, EGA, MCGA, CGA, and Hercules modes. Expanded memory is also supported.

Genus' comprehensive licensing agreement gives you the right to link the routines right into your own C graphics program, and to distribute the resulting program as you see fit. For C programmers who want to leave nothing to chance, complete ASM source code is available as a separate option from Genus Microprogramming.

During program development, you use the PCX Programmer's Toolkit just like the libraries which come with QuickC and Turbo C. The line,

```
#include pcxLib.H
```

will include the various declarations and initializations for variables and constants used by the PCX graphics routines. Depending upon which memory model you are using, these routines are actually found in the disk files pcx_CS.LIB, pcx_CM.LIB , or pcx_CL.LIB.

Fig. 5-10. Programmers' utilities and toolkits like the PCX Programmer's Toolkit from Genus Microprogramming provide versatile image management routines that can be linked into C programs.

To save an image from the display buffer to a file, you would employ the following syntax:

pcxDisplayFile(*filename,x1,y1,x2,y2,pagenum*);

where *x1,y1,x2,y2* are the four corners of the rectangle to be saved as *filename*. The pcxDisplayFile function returns a value which indicates whether the function was successful or not.

To load a previously-saved PCX image from disk, you would use the following syntax:

pcxFileDisplay(*filename,x,y,pagenum*);

where *x,y* is the upper left location of the target position for the image to be displayed, and *pagenum* is the target page of the graphics adapter.

An important enhanced feature of the PCX Programmer's Toolkit is its ability to place images into image libraries on disk. You can add new image files to a library as you see fit, and you can delete existing image files from a library. Libraries are very useful for creating strips of animation, of course, allowing you to place all the frames for an animation sequence in a single library. A library is also useful for maintaining a visual database of images to help explain a text database. The individual files in a library can be kept hidden from the end-user if you wish.

The source code for PCX Programmer's Toolkit is well worth the investment for any C graphics programmer who seeks inspiration from well-written, well-documented ASM source code. Similar to the program listings in this book, the ASM source code provides support for many different graphics modes by means of tokens which keep track of the current graphics state. A noteworthy enhancement, however, is the different languages supported by the source code's calling syntax—including C, Pascal, BASIC, and assembly language.

Using the toolkit can make your programs capable of exporting image files to desktop publishing software and other graphics programs. You can also load images created by handheld scanners and analog video cameras which support the industry-wide PCX format.

6

The Front End:
Managing a Menu System

THE MOST EFFECTIVE way for your program to interact with the end-user is via the single-screen solution approach. Everything your end-user requires in order to make decisions or to control the program should be available on a single screen. This usually means an on-screen menu system.

Menu systems come in many flavors and with many options, including pull-down menus, pop-up menus, active windows, overlapping windows, nested menus, tagboxes, sliders, and more. The jury is still out on which of these interactive input mechanisms is the most effective, but all these devices rely upon only a few fundamental programming concepts like non-destructive screen overwrites and source code modules that can be nested. An understanding of these two concepts, combined with the ability to create scrolling and panning highlight bars, will give you the tools you need to create powerful menu systems which can act as a front end for virtually any C graphics program that you might build.

MENUS: The Fundamentals

In order to operate a menu system in a graphics mode, you must be able to place a menu on the screen. More important, however, is the ability to remove the menu from the screen after the end-user has made a selection. Removing the menu means restoring the screen to its original condition, including the graphics which you obliterated when you installed the menu in the first place.

The fundamental algorithm for a non-destructive screen overwrite is illustrated in FIG. 6-1. This algorithm is the mainstay of all menuing systems which use graphics modes on personal computers, and will be demonstrated in the program listing later in this chapter.

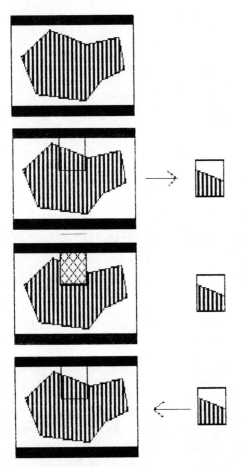

Fig. 6-1. Algorithm for non-destructive screen overwrites by a menu system. From top: 1. Original image. 2. Background where menu will appear is saved in a graphic array in RAM. 3. Menu is drawn on the screen. 4. To remove menu, previously-saved background is written back to the screen.

Non-destructive Overwrite

The most important concept of the non-destructive overwrite algorithm is preparation. Before using a bitblt (or graphic array) technique to install the menu on the screen, a copy of the appropriate background area is saved in a graphic array in RAM. Then the pull-down menu or pop-up menu or exploding menu is placed on the screen using a bitblt procedure.

It is important to understand that the menus are not created dynamically as the program is running. There is simply too much data contained in even the smallest of menus for this to happen in real-time. All the menus at all levels in the user interface must be created in advance and stored in graphic arrays in RAM.

TIP

In order to keep run-time performance at acceptable levels, all menu images should be created in advance and saved as graphic arrays before the menuing system is activated by the end-user, especially when using a graphics mode.

The major demonstration programs in this book create the menus at program start-up and store them in graphic arrays in RAM, ready to be used at run-time. A program intended for distribution, however, would use a dedicated utility program to create the arrays and store them as files on the distribution disk. When the end-user starts up your program, the code would merely read in the files from disk into arrays in RAM, the entire procedure being hidden from the user's view, of course.

After the end-user has finished using a menu, the program must remove it from the screen and restore the background which existed before the menu was installed in the first place. This is usually accomplished in a single step: the graphic array which saved the background is simply written back to the screen, thereby restoring the background graphics and obliterating the menu in one process.

Types of Menu Apparatus

There are as many menu mechanisms as there are C programmers. An understanding of the fundamentals will give you the background you need to be creative in your menu system programming endeavors.

Figure 6-2 depicts the difference between pull-down menus and pop-up menus. Setting aside all the ballyhoo and rhetoric, the only real differences between the two are: first, the location where each is placed on the screen, and, second, the place in the program from which the menu can be called by the end-user.

A pull-down menu is usually placed directly below a main menu bar on the display screen, as if it were pulled down from the menu bar, so to speak. The pull-down menu is usually accessed from the main menu bar. The end-user employs a panning highlight bar to select the appropriate label on the menu bar, and then presses Enter to display the pull-down menu. Alternatively, the end-user might press a left-arrow key or a right-arrow key to directly jump from one pull-down menu to another, bypassing the main menu bar. It is unusual for an end-user to be able to jump directly into a pull-down menu from any other

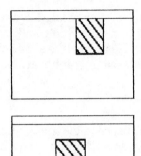

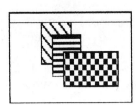

Fig. 6-2. Top: pull-down menu. Center: pop-up menu. Bottom: nested menus.

location in the program. Pull-down menus are conceptually a direct appendage of the menu system itself.

A pop-up menu, on the other hand, can be structured to be accessed from two fundamentally different locations in the running program. First, the pop-up menu can be used as a nested menu. See FIG. 6-2 for an illustration of this approach. After your end-user makes a selection from the main menu bar to jump into a pull-down menu, a scrolling highlight bar can be used to select another choice which installs the next layer of the menu system: usually implemented on the screen as a pop-up menu. Provided that your source code has been written to support this nesting capability—as the program listing in this chapter will demonstrate—you can create as many layers of menus as your graphics program requires.

REMINDER

> A pull-down menu can be accessed either from the main menu bar or from another pull-down menu at the same level. A pop-up menu can be accessed either from its parent pull-down menu or from anywhere in the program via a hot key.

A second implementation of the pop-up menu concept involves the hot key approach. From virtually anywhere in your program, the end-user can simply strike a designated key (often a function key) and a pop-up menu will appear on the screen. This hot key approach is very useful for implementing online help systems, screen save functions, and swapping active viewports. Clearly, this so-called hot key feature is not a direct appendage of the menu system, but rather floats on its own, ready to be accessed by your end-user without having to traverse the other layers of the menu system.

Bells and Whistles

A myriad of interesting twists on the design of menu systems is currently being used in the marketplace.

Dropshadows are often used to make the menu stand out from the background graphics, as depicted in FIG. 6-3. This effect can be readily created by a high-level C graphics library like QuickC's or Turbo C's. The dropshadow—including the portion which cannot be seen because it lies directly beneath the menu—is handled as one graphic array, while the menu itself is handled as a second graphic array.

First, the rectangular background which will receive the dropshadow bitblt is saved to RAM as a graphic array. Then, the XOR or OR boolean operator is used to write the dropshadow array to the screen.

Second, the rectangular background which will receive the pull-down or pop-up menu is saved in a graphic array in RAM. Then, the menu is written to the screen. By experimentation with different logical operators (XOR, PSET, OR, AND), you can control the appearance of the dropshadow on the screen, allowing all or none of the background to be visible where the dropshadow falls.

Although dropshadows can produce very exciting menu systems, they must usually be coded in assembly language to overcome the performance degradation caused by writing two or more graphic arrays to the screen each time your end-user enters a menu.

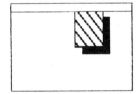

Fig. 6-3. Dropshadow effect.

Tagboxes

Another highly useful adjunct to a graphical menu system is the tagbox. Graphic designers and typesetters call this an election box. Simply put, your end-user selects a single box which corresponds to a group of items. Other boxes might refer to other groups of items. The tagbox concept avoids having to ask your end-user to choose five or six items to activate a certain feature in your program. The end-user selects only one tagbox, and your source code implements all the other required conditions automatically.

Dialog boxes

Dialog boxes are also very helpful, especially when the end-user is being asked to supply a filename or on-screen text. A mini-editor is usually built right into your C source code to allow the end-user to enter characters one at a time, using the backspace key to back up and make corrections. Sample code for such a mini text editor is provided in Your Microcomputer SketchPad in Chapter 8 and Your Microcomputer 3D CAD Designer in Chapter 13.

Pushbuttons and Sliders

Radiobuttons, pushbuttons, sliders, and rangebars are also handy features. Pushbuttons and radiobuttons simply simulate the performance of these mechanisms in real life. By placing the current cursor over the appropriate button, the end-user can activate a desired core function of your program. A graphic-based slider can be used to simulate an analog condition, where your end-user can choose a mixture, much like the sliding control knob on a hi-fi set, of course. A rangebar operates similar to a slider, but sets instead the minimum and maximum ranges to be output by your program.

BUILDING A MENU MANAGER

The manner in which you structure your source code will determine the operating characteristics of your menu system. Source code modules which allow nesting of menus are almost mandatory. Also important is source code which allows the end-user to jump directly from one menu to another without having to return to the main menu bar.

___ FACT ___

Source code for menu systems must be modular and granular in order to support nesting of menus and jumping directly to one menu from another without traversing the main menu bar.

Although clever C programmers can easily write a single source code module which can handle any sized menu at any level in the menu system, such code is virtually impossible to understand and maintain, except by the original programmer. This book, on the other hand, takes the approach that source code must be maintainable—in other words, it must be easy to understand.

This is the same advice this author gives major clients like government departments and statutory agencies when asked for guidance during their recruitment of programmers for in-house software requirements. It matters little how fast the program runs if the client is unable to make simple fixes at a future date simply because the contract programmer is no longer available and no one on staff understands the code. It is not so much a question of not understanding the source code as simply not being able to justify allocating the disproportionate amount of time required to unravel the logic of the code in order to make the desired changes.

Figure 6-4 depicts a robust module useful for controlling the panning highlight bar on the main menu bar. This example of pseudocode permits panning of the highlight bar in either direction, activation of a pull-down menu by the Enter key, trapping of other keys (hot keys or unsupported keys), and a foolproof re-entrant position after program control returns from a pull-down menu or hot key.

The algorithm in FIG. 6-4 can be broken down into four logical steps: a keyboard poll, a left/right arrow key handler, an Enter key handler, and a handler for all other keystrokes. The pseudocode loops until the Enter key is used to jump to a lower level menu or until a hot key (such as Alt + X in the demonstration program) is pressed to terminate the program.

When the Enter key is pressed, a lower-level loop of code is called to manage the menu which has been activated from the main menu bar. Pseudocode which controls such a pull-down menu is illustrated in FIG. 6-5. Note the additon of a backup handler in this loop. This permits the end-user to return to the previous layer in the menu system by pressing the Esc key.

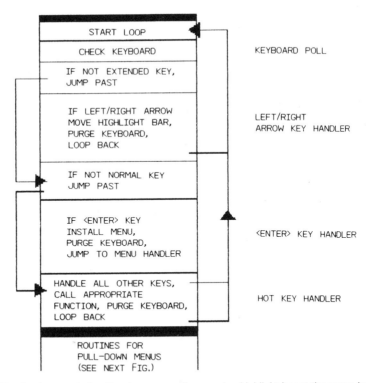

Fig. 6-4. The fundamental algorithm to manage the panning highlight bar at the menu bar level. The algorithm facilitates the use of hot keys for access to online help and other core functions. The loop is perpetual unless Enter is pressed to force processing to proceed to the routines which manage the pull-down menus.

```
┌──────────────────────────────────────┐
│ ████████████████████████████████████ │
│            START LOOP                 │
├──────────────────────────────────────┤
│          CHECK KEYBOARD               │      KEYBOARD POLL
├──────────────────────────────────────┤
│ IF NOT EXTENDED KEY                   │
│ JUMP PAST                             │
│                                       │
│ IF UP/DOWN ARROW                      │
│ SCROLL HIGHLIGHT BAR,                 │
│ PURGE KEYBOARD,                       │
│ LOOP BACK                             │      ARROW KEY HANDLER
│                                       │
│ IF LEFT/RIGHT ARROW                   │
│ INSTALL NEXT MENU,                    │
│ PURGE KEYBOARD,                       │
│ LOOP BACK                             │
├──────────────────────────────────────┤
│ IF NOT NORMAL KEY                     │
│ JUMP PAST                             │
│                                       │
│ IF <ESC> KEY REMOVE                   │
│ MENU, PURGE KEYBOARD,                 │      BACKUP HANDLER
│ LOOP BACK TO MENU                     │
│ BAR ROUTINES                          │
│                                       │
│ IF <ENTER> KEY CALL                   │
│ APPROPRIATE CORE                      │
│ FUNCTION, PURGE KEYBOARD,             │      <ENTER> KEY HANDLER
│ JUMP TO LOOP DECIDER                  │
├──────────────────────────────────────┤
│ HANDLE ALL OTHER KEYS,                │
│ CALL APPROPRIATE CORE                 │
│ FUNCTION, PURGE KEYBOARD,             │
│ LOOP BACK                             │      HOT KEY HANDLER
│                                       │
│ IF NO KEY FOUND                       │
│ LOOP BACK                             │
├──────────────────────────────────────┤
│ ████████████████████████████████████ │
│                                       │
│ DECIDE WHERE TO LOOP                  │
│ BACK AFTER <ENTER> KEY                │
│ ████████████████████████████████████ │
├──────────────────────────────────────┤
│                                       │
│         NEXT LEVEL OF                 │
│         NESTED MENUS                  │
│                                       │
│                                       │
│                                       │
│                                       │
│                                       │
│                                       │
│                                       │
└──────────────────────────────────────┘
```

Fig. 6-5. The fundamental algorithm to manage the first level of pull-down menus. These routines can be chained together to create an unlimited number of nested menus.

The remainder of the loop in FIG. 6-5 adheres to the same format as the loop in FIG. 6-4, except for one important difference. Note the final part of the code in FIG. 6-5, which is a short module to decide where to return after the user has struck some key. This piece of code decides whether to loop back to the beginning of the pull-down menu loop or whether to jump back to the beginning of the main menu bar loop. Here is why this code is important. Some core functions in your program will want to conclude by restoring your end-user to a neutral position in the main menu bar. Other core functions might not even be activated yet and will simply want to beep and leave the end-user in the pull-down menu. Other portions of your source code might need to return to the pull-down loop to do some tidying up, as you will see in the demonstration program.

TIP

Source code modules are chained together to produce what appears to the end-user as nested menus. What the programmer sees as a linear chain the end-user sees as nested levels.

Note also how the code in FIG. 6-5 is structured to call either a core function or yet another level of menus. This pseudocode gives you the ability to chain as many loops together as you want, each giving you access to another nested level of menus—and each giving your end-user access to more program features while retaining the all-important ability to use the Esc key to back up through the system and the Enter key to proceed farther down through the system.

A SAMPLE PROGRAM

The image in FIG. 6-6 shows the menu system interface produced by the demonstration program listings in FIG. 6-7. The scrolling highlight bar is visible on the Settings menu.

When the demonstration program is running, you can use the left-arrow and right-arrow keys to pan the highlight bar on the main menu bar. Pressing the Enter key will activate a pull-down menu. Then you can use the up-arrow and down-arrow keys to scroll the highlight bar through the selections of the pull-down menu. You can use the left-arrow and right-arrow keys to jump directly from one pull-down menu to another.

In addition, the program is designed to be adapted to permit a scrolling cursor to control the pushbuttons along the left side of the display screen. These pushbuttons will form a major component of the draw/paint program demonstrated in Chapter 8.

COMPILING THE PROGRAM

Because this example program is comprised of two modules, you must tell QuickC or Turbo C which source files to collect together during compilation and linking.

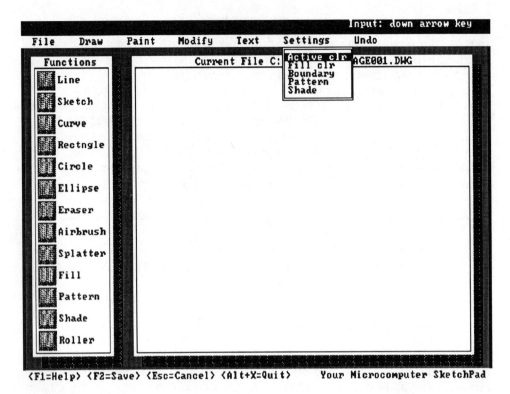

Fig. 6-6. Print of the dynamic image which is produced by the menu manager demonstration program, MENUMGR1.C and MENUMGR2.C.

Fig. 6-7. Source code for MENUMGR1.C and MENUMGR2.C, a two-module program designed to demonstrate a bulletproof menu management shell. Supports VGA, EGA, MCGA, CGA, and Hercules graphics adapters. Ready to compile under QuickC and Turbo C.

```
/*
Interactive menu system              Source file: MENUMGR1.C

By: Lee Adams    Version: 1.00    Revision: n/a.
Notices: (c) Copyright 1990 Lee Adams.  All rights reserved.
Your Microcomputer SketchPad is a trademark of TAB Books
   and is used by permission.
First published: 1990 by Windcrest Books (div. of TAB Books)

Source notes:  module 1 of 2.  The project list should include
MENUMGR1.C and MENUMGR2.C named in QuickC's MAK file or Turbo C's
PRJ file.

Operation:  demonstrates how to create a full-featured, interactive
menu system as a front end to any complex graphics program.

Compiler:  QuickC or Turbo C integrated programming environment.
Default is QuickC. To use Turbo C change the preprocessor directive
in COMPILER DIRECTIVES (see below).  Compile using the medium
memory model.  Refer to the book for instructions on command-line
compiling and linking.
```

Fig. 6-7.
Continued.

Graphics library: QuickC, Turbo C, or third-party add-on library.
Default is QuickC. To use Turbo C graphics library, change the
preprocessor directive in COMPILER DIRECTIVES (see below). To use
a third-party graphics library, refer to the book.

Marketability: will detect and support VGA, EGA, MCGA, CGA, and
Hercules graphics adapters.

```
COMPILER DIRECTIVES  */

#define QuickC    1
#define TurboC    2
#define Compiler QuickC           /* change to TurboC if required */
#define GraphicsLibrary QuickC    /* change to library being used */
#define FAIL      0               /* for graphics auto-detect */

#include <bios.h>                 /* supports keyboard functions */
#include <stdio.h>                  /* supports printf function */
#include <string.h>              /* supports string manipulation */
#if Compiler==QuickC
  #include <conio.h>                 /* supports QuickC port IO */
  #include <malloc.h>   /* supports memory allocation for arrays */
#elif Compiler==TurboC
  #include <dos.h>                   /* supports TurboC port IO */
  #include <alloc.h>    /* supports memory allocation for arrays */
#endif
#if GraphicsLibrary==QuickC
  #include <graph.h>                 /* QuickC graphics library */
#elif GraphicsLibrary==TurboC
  #include <graphics.h>             /* Turbo C graphics library */
#endif
#include <process.h>              /* supports the exit function
```

```
FUNCTION PROTOTYPES  */

/* ROUTINES IN THIS MODULE */
void Quit_Pgm(void);                 /* ends the program gracefully */
void Notice(int,int);            /* displays the copyright notice */
void Graphics_Setup(void);        /* initializes the graphics mode */
void SetParameters(void); /* defines sizes, colors for interface */
void DrawScreen(void);     /* creates the user interface graphics */
void CreateBars(void);                     /* creates menu bars */
void CreateButton(void);              /* creates pushbutton array */
void CreateList(void);                 /* creates button text list */
void CreateMenus(void);           /* creates the pull-down menus */
void CreateHiBars(void);            /* creates the highlight bars */
void FreeBlock(char far *);       /* deallocate far heap memory */

/* ROUTINES IN MODULE 2 CALLED BY THIS MODULE */
void MenuBarLoop(void);    /* manages the menu system at runtime */
void SetHue(int);              /* sets the current drawing color */
void SetLine(int);              /* sets the current line style */
void SetFill(char *, int);          /* sets the area fill style */
void BlankPage(void);        /* blanks the current active page */
void SetPosition(int,int);       /* sets the current xy position */
void DrawLine(int,int);    /* draws line from current xy position */
void DrawBorder(int,int,int,int);           /* draws rectangle */
void DrawPanel(int,int,int,int);       /* draws solid rectangle */
void Fill(int,int,int);                        /* area fill */
```

Fig. 6-7.
Continued.

```
char far * MemBlock(int,int,int,int);     /* allocate array memory */
void GetBlock(int,int,int,int,char far *); /* save graphic array */
void PutXOR(int,int,char far *);          /* show XOR graphic array */
void PutPSET(int,int,char far *);         /* show PSET graphic array */
void PutText(int,int,int,char far *);           /* display text */
void SetTextRowCol(int,int);              /* set text position */
/*_____

DECLARATION OF GLOBAL VARIABLES
Visible to all functions in all source files. */

#if GraphicsLibrary==QuickC
  struct videoconfig vc;              /* QuickC's graphics table */
#endif
#if Compiler==TurboC
    extern unsigned _stklen=4096;         /* set stack to 4096 bytes */
#endif  /* (QuickC uses the Utility/Make menu to set stack size */
int C0=0,C1=1,C2=2,C3=3,C4=4,C5=5,C6=6,C7=7,C8=8,C9=9,C10=10,
C11=11,C12=12,C13=13,C14=14,C15=15;              /* color codes */
int x_res=0,y_res=0;                         /* screen resolution */
int mode_flag=0;  /* indicates which graphics mode is being used */
int alpha_x=0,alpha_y=0;      /* dimensions of character matrix */
int x1=0,y1=0,x2=0,y2=0;       /* coords for graphic array saves */
int t1=1;      /* loop counter & panning bar position indicator */
int sx=0,sy=0;                      /* xy screen drawing coords */
int ty1=0,ty2=0,ty3=0;      /* y coord for text list items */
int TextRow=1,TextColumn=1;       /* text position for QuickC */
int TextX=0,TextY=0;              /* text position for Turbo C */
char keycode=0;  /* flag for NULL, normal, or extended keystroke */
char keynum=0;              /* ASCII number of keystroke */
char far *menubarBitBlt;       /* menu bar graphic array */
char far *helpbarBitBlt;       /* help bar graphic array */
char far *fileBitBlt;          /* file name graphic array */
char far *funcBitBlt;          /* function graphic array */
char far *buttonBitBlt;        /* pushbutton graphic array */
char far *listBitBlt;          /* on-screen list array */
char far *itemBitBlt;          /* single item in list */
char far *FileMenu;               /* File Menu array */
char far *ModifyMenu;           /* Modify Menu array */
char far *TextMenu;               /* Text Menu array */
char far *SettingsMenu;         /* Settings Menu array */
char far *PanBar;             /* panning highlight bar */
char far *ScrollBar;          /* scrolling highlight bar */
int vx1=0,vy1=0,vx2=0,vy2=0;               /* canvas coords */
int clipx1=0,clipy1=0,clipx2=0,clipy2=0;      /* clipping coords */
int ix1=0,iy1=0,ix2=0,iy2=0;             /* icon panel coords */
int shx=0,shy=0;             /* width, depth of dropshadow */
int ox1=0,ox2=0,oy1=0,oy2=0;          /* width, depth of rule */
int bx1=0,by1=0,bx2=0,by2=0;          /* size of pushbutton */
int bxo=0,byo=0;             /* offset to pushbutton top */
int syoffset=0;              /* spacing of pushbuttons */
int numbuttons=0;             /* number of pushbuttons */
int buttoncount=0;         /* calculate button size, position */
int vertspace=0,vertsize=0;  /* calculate button size, position */
int barclr=0,bgclr=0;              /* user interface colors */
int bgtint=0,canvasclr=0;          /* user interface colors */
int shadowclr=0,panelclr=0,ruleclr=0;   /* user interface colors */
int buttonclr=0,buttontint=0;          /* pushbutton colors */
char fill_0[]={0,0,0,0,0,0,0,0};            /*   0% fill */
char fill_3[]={0,32,0,0,0,2,0,0};            /*   3% fill */
char fill_6[]={32,0,2,0,128,0,8,0};          /*   6% fill */
char fill_12[]={32,2,128,8,32,2,128,8};      /*  12% fill */
char fill_25[]={68,17,68,17,68,17,68,17};    /*  25% fill */
char fill_37[]={170,68,170,17,170,68,170,17};  /*  37% fill */
char fill_50[]={85,170,85,170,85,170,85,170};  /*  50% fill */
char fill_62[]={85,187,85,238,85,187,85,238};  /*  62% fill */
char fill_75[]={187,238,187,238,187,238,187,238};  /*  75% fill */
char fill_87[]={223,253,127,247,223,253,127,247};  /*  87% fill */
char fill_93[]={255,223,255,255,255,253,255,255};  /*  93% fill */
```

Fig. 6-7.
Continued.

```
char fill_100[]={255,255,255,255,255,255,255,255};   /* 100% fill */
int p1=0,p2=0;        /* install coords for panning highlight bar */
int px1=0,px2=0,px3=0,px4=0,px5=0,px6=0,px7=0;         /* pan coords */
int py1=0,py2=0,py3=0,py4=0,py5=0,py6=0;            /* scroll coords */
int t2=0;                      /* position of scrolling highlight bar */
int t3=0;                       /* number of choices in active menu */
int p3=0,p4=0;                   /* xy install coords for active menu */
int p5=0,p6=0;            /* xy coords for scrolling highlight bar */
int pbg1=0,pbg2=0;        /* width,depth of bg to save under menu */
int status=0;                       /* status of level 1 menus logic */
int choice=0;      /* flag to indicate user-selected core function */
char * textptr;          /* text to be displayed on graphics screen */
char text1[]="SketchPad ready.";
char text2[]="Input:";
char text3[]="Your Microcomputer SketchPad";
char text4[]="Current File  C:\\SOURCE\\IMAGE001.DWG";
char text5[]="               ";         /* empty string */
char text6[]="Inactive feature. Consult User's Manual.";
char text7[]="SketchPad ready for your next command.";
/*_____

FUNCTION DEFINITIONS  */

main(){                                /* this is the master routine */
Graphics_Setup();              /* establishes the graphics mode */
#if GraphicsLibrary==QuickC
  _getvideoconfig(&vc);                /* initialize QuickC's table */
#endif
SetParameters();            /* defines menu system sizes & colors */
CreateBars();                            /* creates the menu bars */
CreateButton();                         /* creates the pushbutton */
CreateList();                   /* creates text list of functions */
CreateMenus();                 /* creates level 1 pull-down menus */
CreateHiBars();     /* creates panning & scrolling highlight bars */
DrawScreen();                      /* creates the sign-on screen */
MenuBarLoop();                      /* activate the menu system */
Quit_Pgm();                                    /* boilerplate */
}
/*_____*/

void SetParameters(void){  /* define sizes, colors for interface */
vx1=(alpha_x*18)+6;vy1=(alpha_y*2)+18;vx2=x_res-((alpha_x*3)+2);
vy2=y_res-(alpha_y+18);                        /* canvas coords */
ix1=alpha_x+6;iy1=vy1;ix2=vx1-((alpha_x*2)+12);
iy2=vy2;                            /* icon panel coords */
shx=12;shy=10;                /* width, depth of dropshadow */
ox1=4;oy1=alpha_y+3;ox2=4;oy2=3;         /* width, depth of rule */
barclr=C7;bgclr=C1;bgtint=C9;canvasclr=C7;shadowclr=C0;
panelclr=C7;ruleclr=C0;
bx1=100;by1=100;bx2=124;by2=118;          /* coords for pushbutton */
bxo=5;byo=4;                            /* offsets for pushbutton */
buttonclr=C4;buttontint=C12;              /* pushbutton colors */
sx=22;sy=48;                     /* install position for pushbutton */
syoffset=21;                     /* vertical spacing for pushbutton */
ty1=alpha_y;                      /* capture position for text items */
ty2=sy;                          /* install position for text items */
ty3=ty2;                   /* final capture position for text items */
numbuttons=13;buttoncount=13;            /* number of pushbuttons */
  vertspace=(iy2-oy2)-(iy1+oy1)-((buttoncount+1)*3);
  vertsize=vertspace/buttoncount;
  by2=by1+vertsize;     /* device-dependent coord for pushbuttons */
  syoffset=vertsize+3;   /* device-dependent spacing forbuttons */
if (mode_flag==6){                    /* device-dependent pan spacing */
  px1=17;px2=89;px3=161;px4=242;px5=332;px6=405;px7=512;}
else {px1=15;px2=79;px3=143;px4=215;px5=295;px6=359;px7=455;}
p1=px1;p2=15;         /* initialize coords for panning highlight bar */
if (mode_flag==6){                  /* device-dependent scroll spacing */
  py1=38;py2=52;py3=66;py4=80;py5=94;py6=108;}
else {py1=32;py2=40;py3=48;py4=56;py5=64;py6=72;}
```

Fig. 6-7.
Continued.

```
p4=py1-6;                             /* y coord for level 1 pull-down menus */
return;)
/*_____*/

void CreateBars(void){                          /* creates bar arrays */
SetHue(C7);SetFill(fill_100,C7);
BlankPage();
strcpy(text5,"File");PutText(2,3,C7,text5);     /* create menu bar */
strcpy(text5,"Draw");PutText(2,11,C7,text5);
strcpy(text5,"Paint");PutText(2,19,C7,text5);
strcpy(text5,"Modify");PutText(2,28,C7,text5);
strcpy(text5,"Text");PutText(2,38,C7,text5);
strcpy(text5,"Settings");PutText(2,46,C7,text5);
strcpy(text5,"Undo");PutText(2,58,C7,text5);
x1=0;y1=alpha_y-2;                              /* upper left coords */
x2=x_res-1;y2=(alpha_y*2)+1;                    /* lower right coords */
menubarBitBlt=MemBlock(x1,y1,x2,y2);            /* allocate memory */
GetBlock(x1,y1,x2,y2,menubarBitBlt);
DrawPanel(x1,y1,x2,y2);
PutXOR(x1,y1,menubarBitBlt);
GetBlock(x1,y1,x2,y2,menubarBitBlt);     /* store menubar graphic */
BlankPage();
strcpy(text5,"<F1=Help>");PutText(4,2,C7,text5);
strcpy(text5,"<F2=Save>");PutText(4,12,C7,text5);
strcpy(text5,"<Esc=Cancel>");PutText(4,22,C7,text5);
strcpy(text5,"<Alt+X=Quit>");PutText(4,35,C7,text5);
PutText(4,52,C7,text3);            /* Your Microcomputer SketchPad */
x1=0;y1=(alpha_y*3)-2;
x2=x_res-1;y2=(alpha_y*4)+1;
helpbarBitBlt=MemBlock(x1,y1,x2,y2);            /* allocate memory */
GetBlock(x1,y1,x2,y2,helpbarBitBlt);
DrawPanel(x1,y1,x2,y2);
PutXOR(x1,y1,helpbarBitBlt);
GetBlock(x1,y1,x2,y2,helpbarBitBlt);     /* store helpbar graphic */
BlankPage();
PutText(5,1,C7,text4);                          /* filename display */
x1=0;y1=alpha_y*4;
x2=alpha_x*38;y2=alpha_y*5;
fileBitBlt=MemBlock(x1,y1,x2,y2);               /* allocate memory */
GetBlock(x1,y1,x2,y2,fileBitBlt);
DrawPanel(x1,y1,x2,y2);
PutXOR(x1,y1,fileBitBlt);
GetBlock(x1,y1,x2,y2,fileBitBlt);        /* store filename graphic */
BlankPage();
strcpy(text5,"Functions");PutText(7,1,C7,text5);
x1=0;y1=alpha_y*6;
x2=alpha_x*9;y2=alpha_y*7;
funcBitBlt=MemBlock(x1,y1,x2,y2);               /* allocate memory */
GetBlock(x1,y1,x2,y2,funcBitBlt);
DrawPanel(x1,y1,x2,y2);
PutXOR(x1,y1,funcBitBlt);
GetBlock(x1,y1,x2,y2,funcBitBlt);        /* store functions graphic */
BlankPage();
return;)
/*_____*/

void CreateButton(void){              /* creates the button array */
SetHue(buttonclr);SetFill(fill_100,buttonclr);         /* shadow */
DrawPanel(bx1,by1,bx2,by2);
SetHue(shadowclr);SetFill(fill_62,shadowclr);
DrawPanel(bx1,by1,bx2,by2);
SetHue(C6);SetFill(fill_100,C6);                    /* highlight */
SetPosition(bx1,by1);DrawLine(bx2,by1);
DrawLine(bx1,by2);DrawLine(bx1,by1);
Fill(bx1+2,by1+2,C6);
SetHue(buttonclr);SetFill(fill_100,buttonclr);
SetPosition(bx1,by1);DrawLine(bx2,by1);
DrawLine(bx1,by2);DrawLine(bx1,by1);
Fill(bx1+2,by1+2,buttonclr);
```

Fig. 6-7.
Continued.

```
SetHue(buttontint);SetFill(fill_25,buttontint);
SetPosition(bx1,by1);DrawLine(bx2,by1);
DrawLine(bx1,by2);DrawLine(bx1,by1);
Fill(bx1+2,by1+2,buttontint);
SetHue(shadowclr);                                      /* outline */
SetPosition(bx1,by1);DrawLine(bx2,by1);DrawLine(bx1,by2);
DrawLine(bx1,by1);
SetHue(buttonclr);SetFill(fill_100,buttonclr);    /* top surface */
DrawPanel(bx1+bxo,by1+byo,bx2-bxo,by2-byo);
SetHue(buttontint);SetFill(fill_50,buttontint);
DrawPanel(bx1+bxo,by1+byo,bx2-bxo,by2-byo);
buttonBitBlt=MemBlock(bx1,by1,bx2,by2);          /* allocate memory */
GetBlock(bx1,by1,bx2,by2,buttonBitBlt);
BlankPage();
return;}
/*_____*/

void CreateList(void){ /* creates text list of program functions */
SetHue(C7);
strcpy(text5,"Line");PutText(2,4,C7,text5);
strcpy(text5,"Sketch");PutText(3,4,C7,text5);
strcpy(text5,"Curve");PutText(4,4,C7,text5);
strcpy(text5,"Rectngle");PutText(5,4,C7,text5);
strcpy(text5,"Circle");PutText(6,4,C7,text5);
strcpy(text5,"Ellipse");PutText(7,4,C7,text5);
strcpy(text5,"Eraser");PutText(8,4,C7,text5);
strcpy(text5,"Airbrush");PutText(9,4,C7,text5);
strcpy(text5,"Splatter");PutText(10,4,C7,text5);
strcpy(text5,"Fill");PutText(11,4,C7,text5);
strcpy(text5,"Pattern");PutText(12,4,C7,text5);
strcpy(text5,"Shade");PutText(13,4,C7,text5);
strcpy(text5,"Roller");PutText(14,4,C7,text5);
x1=alpha_x*3;y1=alpha_y;
x2=(alpha_x*11)-1;y2=(alpha_y*2)-1;
itemBitBlt=MemBlock(x1,y1,x2,y2);                /* allocate memory */
for (t1=1;t1<=13;t1++){
  GetBlock(x1,ty1,x2,ty1+(alpha_y-1),itemBitBlt);
  PutPSET(x_res/2,ty2,itemBitBlt);
  ty1=ty1+alpha_y;ty2=ty2+syoffset;}
FreeBlock(itemBitBlt);                       /* deallocate memory block */
ty2=ty2-syoffset;ty2=ty2+(alpha_y-1);
x1=x_res/2;x2=x1+((alpha_x*8)-1);
listBitBlt=MemBlock(x1,ty3,x2,ty2);              /* allocate memory */
GetBlock(x1,ty3,x2,ty2,listBitBlt);
BlankPage();
return;}
/*_____*/

void CreateMenus(void){                   /* creates the pull-down menus */
strcpy(text5,"New");PutText(2,4,C7,text5);
strcpy(text5,"Load...");PutText(3,4,C7,text5);
strcpy(text5,"Save");PutText(4,4,C7,text5);
strcpy(text5,"Save as...");PutText(5,4,C7,text5);
strcpy(text5,"Delete...");PutText(6,4,C7,text5);
strcpy(text5,"Shutdown");PutText(7,4,C7,text5);
x1=alpha_x*2;y1=alpha_y-6;
x2=x1+((alpha_x*12)-1);y2=y1+((alpha_y*6)+11);
pbg1=x2-x1;pbg2=y2-y1; /* width, depth of bg to save under menus */
FileMenu=MemBlock(x1,y1,x2,y2);                    /* allocate memory */
GetBlock(x1,y1,x2,y2,FileMenu);          /* temporary store of text */
SetHue(C7);SetFill(fill_100,C7);
DrawPanel(x1,y1,x2,y2);                             /* menu panel */
SetHue(C0);DrawBorder(x1+2,y1+2,x2-2,y2-2);        /* rule trim */
DrawBorder(x1,y1,x2,y2);                            /* border trim */
PutXOR(x1,y1,FileMenu);                    /* xor text onto menu */
GetBlock(x1,y1,x2,y2,FileMenu);            /* File Menu is done */
BlankPage();
strcpy(text5,"Copy...");PutText(2,4,C7,text5);
strcpy(text5,"Move...");PutText(3,4,C7,text5);
```

```
    strcpy(text5,"Cut...");PutText(4,4,C7,text5);
    strcpy(text5,"Paste...");PutText(5,4,C7,text5);
    y2=y2-(alpha_y*2);
    ModifyMenu=MemBlock(x1,y1,x2,y2);                    /* allocate memory */
    GetBlock(x1,y1,x2,y2,ModifyMenu);        /* temporary store of text */
    SetHue(C7);SetFill(fill_100,C7);
    DrawPanel(x1,y1,x2,y2);                                /* menu panel */
    SetHue(C0);DrawBorder(x1+2,y1+2,x2-2,y2-2);             /* rule trim */
    DrawBorder(x1,y1,x2,y2);                              /* border trim */
    PutXOR(x1,y1,ModifyMenu);                     /* xor text onto menu */
    GetBlock(x1,y1,x2,y2,ModifyMenu);          /* Modify Menu is done */
    BlankPage();
    strcpy(text5,"Height...");PutText(2,4,C7,text5);
    strcpy(text5,"Width...");PutText(3,4,C7,text5);
    strcpy(text5,"Sans serif");PutText(4,4,C7,text5);
    strcpy(text5,"Serif");PutText(5,4,C7,text5);
    TextMenu=MemBlock(x1,y1,x2,y2);                      /* allocate memory */
    GetBlock(x1,y1,x2,y2,TextMenu);          /* temporary store of text */
    SetHue(C7);SetFill(fill_100,C7);
    DrawPanel(x1,y1,x2,y2);                                /* menu panel */
    SetHue(C0);DrawBorder(x1+2,y1+2,x2-2,y2-2);             /* rule trim */
    DrawBorder(x1,y1,x2,y2);                              /* border trim */
    PutXOR(x1,y1,TextMenu);                       /* xor text onto menu */
    GetBlock(x1,y1,x2,y2,TextMenu);              /* Text Menu is done */
    BlankPage();
    strcpy(text5,"Active clr");PutText(2,4,C7,text5);
    strcpy(text5,"Fill clr");PutText(3,4,C7,text5);
    strcpy(text5,"Boundary");PutText(4,4,C7,text5);
    strcpy(text5,"Pattern");PutText(5,4,C7,text5);
    strcpy(text5,"Shade");PutText(6,4,C7,text5);
    y2=y2+alpha_y;
    SettingsMenu=MemBlock(x1,y1,x2,y2);                  /* allocate memory */
    GetBlock(x1,y1,x2,y2,SettingsMenu);      /* temporary store of text */
    SetHue(C7);SetFill(fill_100,C7);
    DrawPanel(x1,y1,x2,y2);                                /* menu panel */
    SetHue(C0);DrawBorder(x1+2,y1+2,x2-2,y2-2);             /* rule trim */
    DrawBorder(x1,y1,x2,y2);                              /* border trim */
    PutXOR(x1,y1,SettingsMenu);                   /* xor text onto menu */
    GetBlock(x1,y1,x2,y2,SettingsMenu);        /* Settings Menu is done */
    BlankPage();
    return;}
    /*_____*/

    void CreateHiBars(void){       /* creates the menu highlight bars */
    SetHue(C7);SetFill(fill_100,C7);
    x1=0;y1=0;
    x2=(alpha_x*8)-1;y2=alpha_y+1;
    DrawPanel(x1,y1,x2,y2);
    PanBar=MemBlock(x1,y1,x2,y2);                        /* allocate memory */
    GetBlock(x1,y1,x2,y2,PanBar);         /* store panning highlight bar */
    x1=0;y1=0;
    if (mode_flag==6){x2=(alpha_x*11)+2;}
    else {x2=(alpha_x*11)+1;}
    y2=alpha_y-1;
    DrawPanel(x1,y1,x2,y2);
    ScrollBar=MemBlock(x1,y1,x2,y2);                     /* allocate memory */
    GetBlock(x1,y1,x2,y2,ScrollBar);/* store scrolling highlight bar */
    BlankPage();
    return;}
    /*_____*/

    void DrawScreen(void){            /* creates the sign-on screen */
    SetHue(bgclr);SetFill(fill_100,bgclr);
    DrawPanel(4,14,x_res-5,y_res-1);                        /* bg prep */
    #if GraphicsLibrary==QuickC
      SetHue(bgtint);SetFill(fill_0,bgtint);      /* optional overlay */
      DrawPanel(4,14,x_res-5,y_res-1);            /* finished backgrnd */
    #endif
    if (mode_flag>3){             /* if bw mode on CGA, MCGA, or Herc */
```

Fig. 6-7.
Continued.

Fig. 6-7.
Continued.

```
      SetHue(C0);SetFill(fill_100,C0);
      DrawPanel(4,14,x_res-5,y_res-1);
      SetHue(bgclr);SetFill(fill_50,bgclr);
      DrawPanel(4,14,x_res-5,y_res-1);}
   PutPSET(0,14,menubarBitBlt);                          /* install menu bar */
   FreeBlock(menubarBitBlt);                      /* deallocate memory block */
   if (mode_flag==6){
     PutPSET(0,y_res-18,helpbarBitBlt);}
   else {PutPSET(0,y_res-12,helpbarBitBlt);}        /* install help bar */
   FreeBlock(helpbarBitBlt);                      /* deallocate memory block */
   #if GraphicsLibrary==QuickC
     SetHue(bgclr);SetFill(fill_100,bgclr);          /* icon shadow prep */
     DrawPanel(ix1+shx,iy1+shy,ix2+shx,iy2+shy);
     SetHue(shadowclr);SetFill(fill_75,shadowclr);     /* icon shadow */
     DrawPanel(ix1+shx,iy1+shy,ix2+shx,iy2+shy);
   #elif GraphicsLibrary==TurboC
     SetHue(bgclr);SetFill(fill_25,bgclr);
     DrawPanel(ix1+shx,iy1+shy,ix2+shx,iy2+shy);        /* icon shadow */
   #endif
   SetHue(panelclr);SetFill(fill_100,panelclr);         /* icon panel */
   DrawPanel(ix1,iy1,ix2,iy2);
   SetHue(ruleclr);                                  /* icon panel rule */
   DrawBorder(ix1+ox1,iy1+oy1,ix2-ox2,iy2-oy2);
   #if GraphicsLibrary==QuickC
     SetHue(bgclr);SetFill(fill_100,bgclr);     /* canvas shadow prep */
     DrawPanel(vx1+shx,vy1+shy,vx2+shx,vy2+shy);
     SetHue(shadowclr);SetFill(fill_75,shadowclr); /* canvas shadow */
     DrawPanel(vx1+shx,vy1+shy,vx2+shx,vy2+shy);
   #elif GraphicsLibrary==TurboC
     SetHue(bgclr);SetFill(fill_25,bgclr);
     DrawPanel(vx1+shx,vy1+shy,vx2+shx,vy2+shy);     /* canvas shadow */
   #endif
   SetHue(canvasclr);SetFill(fill_100,canvasclr);          /* canvas */
   DrawPanel(vx1,vy1,vx2,vy2);
   SetHue(ruleclr);                                    /* canvas rule */
   DrawBorder(vx1+ox1,vy1+oy1,vx2-ox2,vy2-oy2);
   PutPSET(32,iy1+2,funcBitBlt);                          /* Function */
   FreeBlock(funcBitBlt);                         /* deallocate memory block */
   PutPSET(238,vy1+2,fileBitBlt);                         /* filename */
   SetHue(C7);Notice(x_res-60,1);                       /* copyright */
   PutText(1,2,C7,text1);                          /* SketchPad ready. */
   PutText(1,57,C7,text2);                                  /* Input: */
   ty1=sy;                                            /* realign ty1 */
   if (mode_flag==6){sy=sy+18;}                   /* if Hercules mode */
   for (t1=1;t1<=numbuttons;t1++){
     PutPSET(sx,sy,buttonBitBlt);                 /* install pushbutton */
     sy=sy+syoffset;}
   sx=sx+((bx2-bx1)+4);                      /* realign list install coord */
   switch (mode_flag){                          /* adjust install coord */
     case 1: ty1=ty1+10;break;                  /* 640x480x16 VGA mode */
     case 2: ty1=ty1+5;break;                   /* 640x350x16 EGA mode */
     case 3: break;                             /* 640x200x16 EGA mode */
     case 4: ty1=ty1+5;break;                   /* 640x480x2 MCGA mode */
     case 5: break;                             /* 640x200x2 CGA mode  */
     case 6: ty1=ty1+20;break;                  /* 720x348x2 Herc mode */
     default: break;}
   PutXOR(sx,ty1,listBitBlt);                          /* install list */
   FreeBlock(listBitBlt);                         /* deallocate memory block */
   return;}

   /*_____*/

   void Quit_Pgm(void){                          /* terminates the program */
   #if GraphicsLibrary==QuickC                          /* if using QuickC */
     _clearscreen(_GCLEARSCREEN);                       /* clear the screen */
     _setvideomode(_DEFAULTMODE);            /* restore the original mode */
   #elif GraphicsLibrary==TurboC                      /* if using Turbo C */
     cleardevice();                                     /* clear the screen */
     closegraph();          /* shut down graphics, restore original mode */
```

```
#endif
exit(0);}                                  /* terminate the program
/*_____*/

void FreeBlock(char far *blk){        /* deallocate far heap block */
#if GraphicsLibrary==QuickC
  _ffree(blk);
#elif GraphicsLibrary==TurboC
  farfree(blk);
#endif
return;}
/*_____*/

void Graphics_Setup(void){     /* autodetect of graphics hardware */
#if GraphicsLibrary==QuickC
   if (_setvideomoderows(_VRES16COLOR,60)!=FAIL) goto VGA_mode;
   if (_setvideomoderows(_ERESCOLOR,43)!=FAIL) goto EGA_ECD_mode;
   if (_setvideomoderows(_HRES16COLOR,25)!=FAIL) goto EGA_SCD_mode;
   if (_setvideomoderows(_VRES2COLOR,60)!=FAIL) goto MCGA_mode;
   if (_setvideomoderows(_HRESBW,25)!=FAIL) goto CGA_mode;
   if (_setvideomoderows(_HERCMONO,25)!=FAIL) goto Hercules_mode;
#elif GraphicsLibrary==TurboC
   int graphics_adapter,graphics_mode;
   detectgraph(&graphics_adapter,&graphics_mode);
   if (graphics_adapter==VGA){
      graphics_adapter=VGA;graphics_mode=VGAHI;
      initgraph(&graphics_adapter,&graphics_mode,"");
      settextstyle(0,0,1);
      goto VGA_mode;}
   if (graphics_mode==EGAHI){
      graphics_adapter=EGA;graphics_mode=EGAHI;
      initgraph(&graphics_adapter,&graphics_mode,"");
      settextstyle(0,0,1);
      goto EGA_ECD_mode;}
   if (graphics_mode==EGALO){
      graphics_adapter=EGA;graphics_mode=EGALO;
      initgraph(&graphics_adapter,&graphics_mode,"");
      settextstyle(0,0,1);
      goto EGA_SCD_mode;}
   if (graphics_adapter==MCGA){
      graphics_adapter=MCGA;graphics_mode=MCGAHI;
      initgraph(&graphics_adapter,&graphics_mode,"");
      settextstyle(0,0,1);
      goto MCGA_mode;}
   if (graphics_adapter==CGA){
      graphics_adapter=CGA;graphics_mode=CGAHI;

      initgraph(&graphics_adapter,&graphics_mode,"");
      settextstyle(0,0,1);
      goto CGA_mode;}
   if (graphics_adapter==HERCMONO){
      graphics_adapter=HERCMONO;graphics_mode=HERCMONOHI;
      initgraph(&graphics_adapter,&graphics_mode,"");
      goto Hercules_mode;}
#endif
goto abort_pgm;                        /* if no graphics hardware found */

/* ASSIGN MODE-DEPENDENT VARIABLES */
VGA_mode:      /* VGA 640x480x16-color mode, 8x8 character matrix */
x_res=640;y_res=480;mode_flag=1;
alpha_x=8;alpha_y=8;return;
EGA_ECD_mode: /* EGA 640x350x16-color mode, 8x8 character matrix */
x_res=640;y_res=350;mode_flag=2;
alpha_x=8;alpha_y=8;return;
EGA_SCD_mode: /* EGA 640x200x16-color mode, 8x8 character matrix */
x_res=640;y_res=200;mode_flag=3;
alpha_x=8;alpha_y=8;return;
MCGA_mode:    /* MCGA 640x480x2-color mode, 8x8 character matrix */
x_res=640;y_res=480;mode_flag=4;
C0=0;C1=1;C2=1;C3=1;C4=1;C5=1;C6=1;C7=1;
```

Fig. 6-7.
Continued.

Fig. 6-7.
Continued.

```
C8=1;C9=1;C10=1;C11=1;C12=1;C13=1;C14=1;C15=1;
alpha_x=8;alpha_y=8;return;
CGA_mode:        /* CGA 640x200x2-color mode, 8x8 character matrix */
x_res=640;y_res=200;mode_flag=5;
C0=0;C1=1;C2=1;C3=1;C4=1;C5=1;C6=1;C7=1;
C8=1;C9=1;C10=1;C11=1;C12=1;C13=1;C14=1;C15=1;
alpha_x=8;alpha_y=8;return;
Hercules_mode:   /* Hercules 720x348x2-color mode, 9x14 character */
x_res=720;y_res=348;mode_flag=6;
C0=0;C1=1;C2=1;C3=1;C4=1;C5=1;C6=1;C7=1;
C8=1;C9=1;C10=1;C11=1;C12=1;C13=1;C14=1;C15=1;
alpha_x=9;alpha_y=14;return;

abort_pgm:       /* jump to here if no supported graphics hardware */
printf("\n\n\rUnable to proceed.\n\r");
printf("Requires VGA, EGA, CGA, MCGA, or\n\r");
printf("Hercules adapter and appropriate monitor.\n\n\r");
exit(0);
}
/*_____*/

void Notice(int x,int y){       /* displays the copyright notice */
int copyright[][3]={0x7c00,0x0000,0x0000, /* array of bit styles */
                    0x8279,0x819c,0x645e,
                    0xba4a,0x4252,0x96d0,
                    0xa27a,0x4252,0x955e,
                    0xba0a,0x43d2,0xf442,
                    0x8219,0x825c,0x945e,
                    0x7c00,0x0000,0x0000};
int a,b,c; int t1=0;                        /* local variables */
for (t1=0;t1<=6;t1++){                  /* draw 7 styled lines */
  a=copyright[t1][0];b=copyright[t1][1];c=copyright[t1][2];
  SetLine(a);SetPosition(x,y);DrawLine(x+15,y);
  SetLine(b);SetPosition(x+16,y);DrawLine(x+31,y);
  SetLine(c);SetPosition(x+32,y);DrawLine(x+47,y);y=y+1;};
SetLine(0xFFFF);return;
}
/*_____*/

End of source code  */
```

```
/*
Interactive menu system                 Source file: MENUMGR2.C
```

By: Lee Adams   Version: 1.00   Revision: n/a.
Notices: (c) Copyright 1990 Lee Adams. All rights reserved.
  Your Microcomputer SketchPad is a trademark of TAB Books Inc.
  and is used by permission.
First published: 1990 by Windcrest Books (div. of TAB Books Inc.)

Source notes: module 2 of 2. The project list should include
MENUMGR1.C and MENUMGR2.C named in QuickC's MAK file or Turbo C's
PRJ file.

Operation: provides menu system management routines and
library-independent low-level graphics routines for the run-time
environment established by module 1.

Compiler: QuickC or Turbo C integrated programming environment.
Default is QuickC. To use Turbo C change the preprocessor directive
in COMPILER DIRECTIVES (see below). Compile using the medium
memory model. Refer to the book for instructions on command-line
compiling and linking.

Graphics library: QuickC, Turbo C, or third-party add-on library.
Default is QuickC. To use Turbo C graphics library, change the
preprocessor directive in COMPILER DIRECTIVES (see below). To use
a third-party graphics library, refer to the book.

Fig. 6-7.
Continued.

```
COMPILER DIRECTIVES   */

#define QuickC     1
#define TurboC     2
#define Compiler QuickC          /* change to TurboC if required */
#define GraphicsLibrary QuickC   /* change to library being used */
#define EMPTY      0             /* for checking keyboard buffer */
#define ACTIVE     1                   /* menu system status */
#define BACKOUT    2                   /* menu system status */
#define STUB       3                   /* menu system status */

#include <bios.h>             /* supports keyboard functions */
#include <stdio.h>                /* supports printf function */
#include <string.h>          /* supports string manipulation */
#if Compiler==QuickC
  #include <conio.h>                 /* supports QuickC port IO */
  #include <malloc.h>   /* supports memory allocation for arrays */
#elif Compiler==TurboC
  #include <dos.h>                   /* supports TurboC port IO */
  #include <alloc.h>    /* supports memory allocation for arrays */
#endif
#if GraphicsLibrary==QuickC
  #include <graph.h>                /* QuickC graphics library */
#elif GraphicsLibrary==TurboC
  #include <graphics.h>            /* Turbo C graphics library */
#endif
#include <process.h>             /* supports the exit function
```

```
FUNCTION PROTOTYPES   */

/* MENU MANAGEMENT ROUTINES IN THIS MODULE */
void MenuBarLoop(void);     /* manages the menu system at runtime */
void CheckForKey(void);             /* checks for user keystrokes */
void KeySwitch1(void);    /* manages keystrokes at menu bar level */
void Panning(void);            /* moves the panning highlight bar */
void Purge(void);              /* empties the keyboard buffer */
void InstallMenu(void); /* installs a level 1 menu on the screen */
void UninstallMenu(void);/* removes level 1 menu from the screen */
void PanMenu(void);        /* manages inter-menu panning */
void Scrolling(void);       /* manages scrolling highlight bar */
void KeySwitch2(void);    /* manages keystrokes for level 1 menus */
void MenuChoices(void); /* calls pgm functions for level 1 menus */
void StubRoutine(void);       /* do-nothing stub for prototyping */
void MenuBarText(void);     /* back-out stub for prototyping */
void ClearTextLine(void);       /* blanks the dialog text line */
void MakeSound(int,int);           /* generates a sound */
void GetTextCoords(void); /* convert QuickC text to Turbo C text */

/* LOW-LEVEL GRAPHICS ROUTINES IN THIS MODULE */
void SetHue(int);           /* sets the current drawing color */
void SetLine(int);              /* sets the current line style */
void SetFill(char *, int);       /* sets the area fill style */
void BlankPage(void);       /* blanks the current active page */
void SetPosition(int,int);      /* sets the current xy position */
void DrawLine(int,int);    /* draws line from current xy position */
void DrawBorder(int,int,int,int);          /* draws rectangle */
void DrawPanel(int,int,int,int);        /* draws solid rectangle */
void Fill(int,int,int);                       /* area fill */
char far * MemBlock(int,int,int,int);    /* allocate array memory */
```

Fig. 6-7.
Continued.

```
void GetBlock(int,int,int,int,char far *); /* save graphic array */
void PutXOR(int,int,char far *);        /* show XOR graphic array */
void PutPSET(int,int,char far *);       /* show PSET graphic array */
void PutText(int,int,int,char *);            /* display text */
void SetTextRowCol(int,int);              /* set text position */

/* ROUTINES IN MODULE 1 CALLED BY THIS MODULE */
void Quit_Pgm(void);              /* ends the program gracefully */
void FreeBlock(char far *);       /* deallocate far heap memory */
/*_____*/

/* DECLARATION OF GLOBAL VARIABLES */
char far *SaveBgd;     /* array to save background under each menu */

/* RE-DECLARATION OF GLOBAL VARIABLES initialized in Module 1,
but also visible to all functions in this source file. */

#if GraphicsLibrary==QuickC
  extern struct vc;
#endif
extern int C0,C1,C2,C3,C4,C5,C6,C7,C8,C9,C10,C11,C12,C13,C14,C15;
/* color codes */
extern int x_res,y_res,mode_flag,alpha_x,alpha_y,x1,y1,x2,y2,t1;
extern int sx,sy,ty1,ty2,ty3,TextRow,TextColumn,TextX,TextY;
extern char keycode,keynum;
extern char far *menubarBitBlt;
extern char far *helpbarBitBlt;
extern char far *fileBitBlt;
extern char far *funcBitBlt;
extern char far *buttonBitBlt;
extern char far *listBitBlt;
extern char far *itemBitBlt;
extern char far *FileMenu;
extern char far *ModifyMenu;
extern char far *TextMenu;
extern char far *SettingsMenu;
extern char far *PanBar;
extern char far *ScrollBar;
extern int vx1,vy1,vx2,vy2,clipx1,clipy1,clipx2,clipy2;
extern int ix1,iy1,ix2,iy2,shx,shy,ox1,ox2,oy1,oy2;
extern int bx1,by1,bx2,by2,bxo,byo;
extern int syoffset,numbuttons,buttoncount;
extern int vertspace,vertsize;
extern int barclr,bgclr,bgtint,canvasclr;
extern int shadowclr,panelclr,ruleclr,buttonclr,buttontint;
extern char fill_0[],fill_3[],fill_6[],fill_12[];
extern char fill_25[],fill_37[],fill_50[],fill_62[];
extern char fill_75[],fill_87[],fill_93[],fill_100[];
extern int p1,p2,px1,px2,px3,px4,px5,px6,px7;
extern int py1,py2,py3,py4,py5,py6;
extern int t2,t3,p3,p4,p5,p6,pbg1,pbg2,status,choice;
extern char * textptr;
extern char text1[],text2[],text3[],text4[],text5[];
extern char text6[],text7[];


/*_____

            M E N U   S Y S T E M   M A N A G E R
_____*/

void MenuBarLoop(void){    /* manages the menu system at runtime */
t1=1;     /* initialize panning highlight bar position indicator */
SaveBgd=MemBlock(16,2,127,61);      /* allocate memory to save bg */
PutXOR(p1,p2,PanBar);              /* install panning hilite bar */
MakeSound(250,10000);                          /* audio cue */
loop0:                                 /* menu bar loop begins */
CheckForKey();                       /* check for user keystroke */
if (keycode!=2) goto Label1;    /* jump if not an extended key */
```

Fig. 6-7.
Continued.

```
switch (keynum){
   case 77: t1=t1+1;Panning();Purge();
            ClearTextLine();goto loop0;              /* right arrow */
   case 75: t1=t1-1;Panning();Purge();
            ClearTextLine();goto loop0;}             /* left arrow */
Label1:
if (keycode!=1) goto Label2;    /* jump past if not a normal key */
if (keynum==13){                           /* if <Enter> key... */
   InstallMenu();Purge();
   switch (t1){
      case 1: goto menuloop;
      case 2: goto loop0;                         /* Draw icons */
      case 3: goto loop0;                         /* Paint icons */
      case 4: goto menuloop;
      case 5: goto menuloop;
      case 6: goto menuloop;
      case 7: goto loop0;}}                             /* Undo */
Label2:
if (keycode!=0){                      /* if a key was retrieved */
   KeySwitch1();                /* switcher for system keystrokes */
   Purge();}                      /* empty the keyboard buffer */
goto loop0;                                        /* loop back */
menuloop:                            /* level 1 menus loop begins */
CheckForKey();                       /* check for user keystroke */
if (keycode!=2) goto Label3;        /* jump if not an extended key */
switch (keynum){
   case 80: t2=t2+1;Scrolling();Purge();          /* down arrow */
            ClearTextLine();goto menuloop;
   case 72: t2=t2-1;Scrolling();Purge();            /* up arrow */
            ClearTextLine();goto menuloop;
   case 77: t1=t1+1;                             /* right arrow */
            if (t1==2) t1=4;                /* bypass position 2 */
            if (t1==3) t1=4;                /* bypass position 3 */
            PanMenu();Purge();
            ClearTextLine();goto menuloop;
   case 75: t1=t1-1;                              /* left arrow */
            if (t1==2) t1=1;                /* bypass position 2 */
            if (t1==3) t1=1;                /* bypass position 3 */
            PanMenu();Purge();
            ClearTextLine();goto menuloop;}
Label3:
if (keycode!=1) goto Label4;    /* jump past if not a normal key */
if (keynum==13){                           /* if <Enter> key... */
   MenuChoices();Purge();goto Label5;} /* call the core function */
if (keynum==27){                             /* if <Esc> key... */
   UninstallMenu();Purge();            /* back out of the menu */
   PutXOR(p1,p2,PanBar);MenuBarText();
   goto loop0;}
Label4:
if (keycode!=0){                      /* if a key was retrieved */
   KeySwitch2();         /* switcher for level 1 menus keystrokes */
   Purge();}                      /* empty the keyboard buffer */
goto menuloop;                                     /* loop back */
Label5:               /* decide re-entrant point after core function */
switch (status){
   case ACTIVE:   status=BACKOUT;PutXOR(p1,p2,PanBar);
                  goto loop0;
   case BACKOUT:  UninstallMenu();goto loop0;
   case STUB:     status=BACKOUT;goto menuloop;}
return;}                                          /* boilerplate */
/*_____*/


void Panning(void){          /* moves the panning highlight bar */
if (t1>7) t1=1;                       /* wraparound past right */
if (t1<1) t1=7;                        /* wraparound past left */
switch (t1){          /* use t1 to determine where to move cursor */
   case 1: PutXOR(p1,p2,PanBar);p1=px1;                 /* File */
           PutXOR(p1,p2,PanBar);break;
```

Fig. 6-7.
Continued.

```
        case 2: PutXOR(p1,p2,PanBar);p1=px2;                  /* Draw */
                PutXOR(p1,p2,PanBar);break;
        case 3: PutXOR(p1,p2,PanBar);p1=px3;                 /* Paint */
                PutXOR(p1,p2,PanBar);break;
        case 4: PutXOR(p1,p2,PanBar);p1=px4;                /* Modify */
                PutXOR(p1,p2,PanBar);break;
        case 5: PutXOR(p1,p2,PanBar);p1=px5;              /* Settings */
                PutXOR(p1,p2,PanBar);break;
        case 6: PutXOR(p1,p2,PanBar);p1=px6;                  /* Text */
                PutXOR(p1,p2,PanBar);break;
        case 7: PutXOR(p1,p2,PanBar);p1=px7;                  /* Undo */
                PutXOR(p1,p2,PanBar);break;
        default: break;}
    return;}
    /*_____*/

    void InstallMenu(void){        /* install level 1 menu on screen */
    t2=1;                          /* reset virtual scroll position */
    p6=py1;                        /* reset y coord scroll position */
    switch (t1){
        case 1: p3=px1-1;      /* reset x install coord for File menu */
                PutXOR(p1,p2,PanBar);            /* remove panning bar */
                GetBlock(p3,p4,(p3+pbg1),(p4+pbg2),SaveBgd);   /*save */
                PutPSET(p3,p4,FileMenu);             /* install menu */
                p5=px1+2;  /* reset x install coord for scrolling bar */
                PutXOR(p5,p6,ScrollBar);            /* install bar */
                t3=6;          /* reset number of choices in menu */
                break;                     /* get out of switch branch */
        case 2: StubRoutine();break;                   /* Draw icons */
        case 3: StubRoutine();break;                  /* Paint icons */
        case 4: p3=px4-1;                              /* Modify menu */
                PutXOR(p1,p2,PanBar);
                GetBlock(p3,p4,(p3+pbg1),(p4+pbg2),SaveBgd);
                PutPSET(p3,p4,ModifyMenu);
                p5=px4+2;PutXOR(p5,p6,ScrollBar);t3=4;break;
        case 5: p3=px5-1;                                /* Text menu */
                PutXOR(p1,p2,PanBar);
                GetBlock(p3,p4,(p3+pbg1),(p4+pbg2),SaveBgd);
                PutPSET(p3,p4,TextMenu);
                p5=px5+2;PutXOR(p5,p6,ScrollBar);t3=4;break;
        case 6: p3=px6-1;                            /* Settings menu */
                PutXOR(p1,p2,PanBar);
                GetBlock(p3,p4,(p3+pbg1),(p4+pbg2),SaveBgd);
                PutPSET(p3,p4,SettingsMenu);
                p5=px6+2;PutXOR(p5,p6,ScrollBar);t3=5;break;
        case 7: StubRoutine();break;                         /* Undo */
        default: break;}
    return;}
    /*_____*/

    void UninstallMenu(void){   /* removes level 1 menu from screen */
    PutPSET(p3,p4,SaveBgd);           /* restore previous background */
    return;}
    /*_____*/

    void PanMenu(void){                  /* manages inter-menu panning */
    if (t1>6) t1=1;                       /* wraparound to skip Undo */
    if (t1<1) t1=6;                                    /* wraparound */
    t2=1;                          /* reset virtual scroll position */
    p6=py1;                        /* reset y coord scroll position */
    UninstallMenu();               /* remove existing level 1 menu */
    switch (t1){
        case 1: p1=px1;              /* reset x coord for panning bar */
                t3=6;          /* reset number of choices on menu */
                p3=px1-1;                  /* reset x coord for menu */
                p5=px1+2;         /* reset x coord for scrolling bar */
                GetBlock(p3,p4,(p3+pbg1),(p4+pbg2),SaveBgd);   /*save */
                PutPSET(p3,p4,FileMenu);             /* install menu */
```

Fig. 6-7.
Continued.

```
            PutXOR(p5,p6,ScrollBar);                    /* install bar */
            break;                          /* get out of switch branch */
  case 4: p1=px4;t3=4;p3=px4-1;p5=px4+2;
            GetBlock(p3,p4,(p3+pbg1),(p4+pbg2),SaveBgd);
            PutPSET(p3,p4,ModifyMenu);
            PutXOR(p5,p6,ScrollBar);
            break;
  case 5: p1=px5;t3=4;p3=px5-1;p5=px5+2;
            GetBlock(p3,p4,(p3+pbg1),(p4+pbg2),SaveBgd);
            PutPSET(p3,p4,TextMenu);
            PutXOR(p5,p6,ScrollBar);
            break;
  case 6: p1=px6;t3=5;p3=px6-1;p5=px6+2;
            GetBlock(p3,p4,(p3+pbg1),(p4+pbg2),SaveBgd);
            PutPSET(p3,p4,SettingsMenu);
            PutXOR(p5,p6,ScrollBar);
            break;}
return;}
/*_____*/

void Scrolling(void){            /* manages scrolling highlight bar */
if (t2>t3) t2=1;  /* handle vertical wraparound of scrolling bar */
if (t2<1) t2=t3;                        /* vertical wraparound */
switch (t2){
  case 1: PutXOR(p5,p6,ScrollBar);                    /* remove former */
            p6=py1;                                   /* reset y coord */
            PutXOR(p5,p6,ScrollBar);                     /* install new */
            break;                        /* get out of switch branch */
  case 2: PutXOR(p5,p6,ScrollBar);p6=py2;

            PutXOR(p5,p6,ScrollBar);break;
  case 3: PutXOR(p5,p6,ScrollBar);p6=py3;
            PutXOR(p5,p6,ScrollBar);break;
  case 4: PutXOR(p5,p6,ScrollBar);p6=py4;
            PutXOR(p5,p6,ScrollBar);break;
  case 5: PutXOR(p5,p6,ScrollBar);p6=py5;
            PutXOR(p5,p6,ScrollBar);break;
  case 6: PutXOR(p5,p6,ScrollBar);p6=py6;
            PutXOR(p5,p6,ScrollBar);break;}
return;}
/*_____*/

void MenuChoices(void){            /* calls level 1 core functions */
switch (t1){                /* determine which menu is being used */
  case 1: goto filechoices;
  case 4: goto modifychoices;
  case 5: goto textchoices;
  case 6: goto settingschoices;}
filechoices:
switch (t2){                    /* determine which scroll choice */
  case 1: choice=1;StubRoutine();break;                    /* New */
  case 2: choice=2;StubRoutine();break;               /* Load... */
  case 3: choice=3;StubRoutine();break;               /* Save */
  case 4: choice=4;StubRoutine();break;          /* Save as... */
  case 5: choice=5;StubRoutine();break;            /* Delete... */
  case 6: choice=6;Quit_Pgm();}                     /* Shutdown */
return;
modifychoices:
switch (t2){                    /* determine which scroll choice */
  case 1: choice=20;StubRoutine();break;             /* Copy... */
  case 2: choice=21;StubRoutine();break;             /* Move... */
  case 3: choice=22;StubRoutine();break;              /* Cut... */
  case 4: choice=23;StubRoutine();break;}            /* Paste... */
return;
textchoices:
switch (t2){                    /* determine which scroll choice */
  case 1: choice=24;StubRoutine();break;           /* Height... */
  case 2: choice=25;StubRoutine();break;            /* Width... */
  case 3: choice=26;StubRoutine();break;         /* Sans serif */
  case 4: choice=27;StubRoutine();break;}              /* Serif */
```

Fig. 6-7.
Continued.

```
        return;
settingschoices:
switch (t2){                           /* determine which scroll choice */
   case 1: choice=28;StubRoutine();break;          /* Active clr */
   case 2: choice=29;StubRoutine();break;            /* Fill clr */
   case 3: choice=30;StubRoutine();break;           /* Boundary */
   case 4: choice=31;StubRoutine();break;            /* Pattern */
   case 5: choice=32;StubRoutine();break;}             /* Shade */
return;}
/*_____*/

void StubRoutine(void){                   /* do-nothing core function */
status=STUB;
ClearTextLine();
PutText(1,2,C14,text6);                      /* Inactive feature. */
MakeSound(250,10000);
return;}
/*_____*/

void MenuBarText(void){              /* back-out status dialog text */
ClearTextLine();
PutText(1,2,C7,text7); /* SketchPad ready for your next command. */
return;}
/*_____*/

void ClearTextLine(void){              /* blanks the dialog text line */
SetHue(C0);SetLine(0xffff);SetFill(fill_100,C0);
#if GraphicsLibrary==TurboC
   setfillstyle(SOLID_FILL,C0);
#endif
if (mode_flag==6){                   /* if Hercules 9x14 characters */
   DrawPanel(0,0,486,13);}
else {DrawPanel(0,0,431,7);}              /* if 8x8 characters */
return;}
/*_____*/

void CheckForKey(void){              /* checks for user keystrokes */
union u_type{int a;char b[3];}keystroke; /* define the structure */
char inkey=0;
#if Compiler==QuickC
   if (_bios_keybrd(_KEYBRD_READY)==EMPTY){keycode=0;return;}
   keystroke.a=_bios_keybrd(_KEYBRD_READ);   /* fetch ASCII codes */
#elif Compiler==TurboC
   if (bioskey(1)==EMPTY){keycode=0;return;}
   keystroke.a=bioskey(0);               /* fetch ASCII codes */
#endif
inkey=keystroke.b[0];                      /* retrieve first code */
if (inkey!=0){                         /* if a normal keystroke... */
   keycode=1;                      /* set flag to normal keystroke */
   keynum=inkey;               /* and load ASCII code into variable */
   return;}
if (inkey==0){                      /* if an extended keystroke... */
   keycode=2;                    /* set flag to extended keystroke */
   keynum=keystroke.b[1];   /* and load second code into variable */
   return;}
}
/*_____*/

void KeySwitch1(void){     /* switcher for keys at menu bar level */
int tempclr=0;
if (keycode==2) goto ExtendedKeys;   /* if extended key, jump... */
NormalKeys:                 /* ...else use switcher for normal keys */
#if Compiler==QuickC
   _settextposition(1,64);_settextcolor(C7);
switch (keynum){
   case 27: _outtext("Esc           ");return;
   case 13: _outtext("Enter         ");return;
   case 8:  _outtext("Backspace     ");return;
   case 9:  _outtext("Tab           ");return;
   case 32: _outtext("Spacebar      ");return;
```

Fig. 6-7.
Continued.

```
          default:  _outtext("inactive key    ");
                    MakeSound(400,16000);return;}
#elif Compiler==TurboC
    tempclr=getcolor();
    setcolor(C0);setlinestyle(USERBIT_LINE,0xffff,NORM_WIDTH);
    setfillstyle(SOLID_FILL,C0);
    TextRow=1;TextColumn=64;GetTextCoords();
    if (mode_flag==6){              /* if Hercules 9x14 characters */
       bar(TextX,TextY,TextX+144,TextY+13);}
    else {bar(TextX,TextY,TextX+128,TextY+7);}/* if 8x8 characters */
    setcolor(C7);
switch (keynum){
    case 27:  outtextxy(TextX,TextY,"Esc             ");break;
    case 13:  outtextxy(TextX,TextY,"Enter           ");break;
    case 8:   outtextxy(TextX,TextY,"Backspace       ");break;
    case 9:   outtextxy(TextX,TextY,"Tab             ");break;
    case 32:  outtextxy(TextX,TextY,"Spacebar        ");break;
    default:  outtextxy(TextX,TextY,"inactive key    ");
              MakeSound(400,16000);break;}
setcolor(tempclr);return;
#endif
ExtendedKeys:                    /* switcher for extended keystrokes */
#if Compiler==QuickC
    _settextposition(1,64);_settextcolor(C7);
switch (keynum){
    case 59:  _outtext("F1              ");return;
    case 60:  _outtext("F2              ");return;
    case 61:  _outtext("F3              ");return;
    case 62:  _outtext("F4              ");return;
    case 63:  _outtext("F5              ");return;
    case 64:  _outtext("F6              ");return;
    case 65:  _outtext("F7              ");return;
    case 66:  _outtext("F8              ");return;
    case 67:  _outtext("F9              ");return;
    case 68:  _outtext("F10             ");return;
    case 119: _outtext("Ctrl+Home       ");return;
    case 117: _outtext("Ctrl+End        ");return;
    case -124:_outtext("Ctrl+PgUp       ");return;
    case 118: _outtext("Ctrl+PgDn       ");return;
    case 83:  _outtext("Del             ");return;
    case 82:  _outtext("Ins             ");return;
    case 71:  _outtext("Home            ");return;
    case 79:  _outtext("End             ");return;
    case 73:  _outtext("PgUp            ");return;
    case 81:  _outtext("PgDn            ");return;
    case 75:  _outtext("left arrow key  ");return;
    case 77:  _outtext("right arrow key ");return;
    case 72:  _outtext("up arrow key    ");return;
    case 80:  _outtext("down arrow key  ");return;
    case 45:  _outtext("Alt+X           ");Quit_Pgm();
    default:  _outtext("inactive key    ");
              MakeSound(400,16000);return;}        /* undefined */
#elif Compiler==TurboC
    tempclr=getcolor();
    setcolor(C0);setlinestyle(USERBIT_LINE,0xffff,NORM_WIDTH);
    setfillstyle(SOLID_FILL,C0);
    TextRow=1;TextColumn=64;GetTextCoords();
    if (mode_flag==6){              /* if Hercules 9x14 characters */
       bar(TextX,TextY,TextX+144,TextY+13);}
    else {bar(TextX,TextY,TextX+128,TextY+7);}/* if 8x8 characters */
    setcolor(C7);
switch (keynum){
    case 59:  outtextxy(TextX,TextY,"F1               ");break;
    case 60:  outtextxy(TextX,TextY,"F2               ");break;
    case 61:  outtextxy(TextX,TextY,"F3               ");break;
    case 62:  outtextxy(TextX,TextY,"F4               ");break;
    case 63:  outtextxy(TextX,TextY,"F5               ");break;
    case 64:  outtextxy(TextX,TextY,"F6               ");break;
    case 65:  outtextxy(TextX,TextY,"F7               ");break;
```

Fig. 6-7.
Continued.

```
  case 66:  outtextxy(TextX,TextY,"F8              ");break;
  case 67:  outtextxy(TextX,TextY,"F9              ");break;
  case 68:  outtextxy(TextX,TextY,"F10             ");break;
  case 119: outtextxy(TextX,TextY,"Ctrl+Home       ");break;
  case 117: outtextxy(TextX,TextY,"Ctrl+End        ");break;
  case -124:outtextxy(TextX,TextY,"Ctrl+PgUp       ");break;
  case 118: outtextxy(TextX,TextY,"Ctrl+PgDn       ");break;
  case 83:  outtextxy(TextX,TextY,"Del             ");break;
  case 82:  outtextxy(TextX,TextY,"Ins             ");break;
  case 71:  outtextxy(TextX,TextY,"Home            ");break;
  case 79:  outtextxy(TextX,TextY,"End             ");break;
  case 73:  outtextxy(TextX,TextY,"PgUp            ");break;
  case 81:  outtextxy(TextX,TextY,"PgDn            ");break;
  case 75:  outtextxy(TextX,TextY,"left arrow key  ");break;
  case 77:  outtextxy(TextX,TextY,"right arrow key ");break;
  case 72:  outtextxy(TextX,TextY,"up arrow key    ");break;
  case 80:  outtextxy(TextX,TextY,"down arrow key  ");break;
  case 45:  outtextxy(TextX,TextY,"Alt+X           ");Quit_Pgm();
  default:  outtextxy(TextX,TextY,"inactive key    ");
            MakeSound(400,16000);break;}              /* undefined */
setcolor(tempclr);return;
#endif
}
/*_____*/

void KeySwitch2(void){      /* switcher for keys at level 1 menus */
int tempclr=0;
if (keycode==2) goto ExtendedKeys2;  /* if extended key, jump... */
NormalKeys2:                    /* ...else use switcher for normal keys */
#if Compiler==QuickC
  _settextposition(1,64);_settextcolor(C7);
switch (keynum){
  case 27:  _outtext("Esc             ");return;
  case 13:  _outtext("Enter           ");return;
  case 8:   _outtext("Backspace       ");return;
  case 9:   _outtext("Tab             ");return;
  case 32:  _outtext("Spacebar        ");return;
  default:  _outtext("inactive key    ");
            MakeSound(400,16000);return;}
#elif Compiler==TurboC
  tempclr=getcolor();
  setcolor(C0);setlinestyle(USERBIT_LINE,0xffff,NORM_WIDTH);
  setfillstyle(SOLID_FILL,C0);
  TextRow=1;TextColumn=64;GetTextCoords();
  if (mode_flag==6){            /* if Hercules 9x14 characters */
    bar(TextX,TextY,TextX+144,TextY+13);}
  else (bar(TextX,TextY,TextX+128,TextY+7);}/* if 8x8 characters */
  setcolor(C7);
switch (keynum){
  case 27:  outtextxy(TextX,TextY,"Esc             ");break;
  case 13:  outtextxy(TextX,TextY,"Enter           ");break;
  case 8:   outtextxy(TextX,TextY,"Backspace       ");break;
  case 9:   outtextxy(TextX,TextY,"Tab             ");break;
  case 32:  outtextxy(TextX,TextY,"Spacebar        ");break;
  default:  outtextxy(TextX,TextY,"inactive key    ");
            MakeSound(400,16000);break;}
setcolor(tempclr);return;
#endif
ExtendedKeys2:                  /* switcher for extended keystrokes */
#if Compiler==QuickC
  _settextposition(1,64);_settextcolor(C7);
switch (keynum){
  case 59:  _outtext("F1              ");return;
  case 60:  _outtext("F2              ");return;
  case 61:  _outtext("F3              ");return;
  case 62:  _outtext("F4              ");return;
  case 63:  _outtext("F5              ");return;
  case 64:  _outtext("F6              ");return;
  case 65:  _outtext("F7              ");return;
```

Fig. 6-7.
Continued.

```
  case 66:  _outtext("F8                ");return;
  case 67:  _outtext("F9                ");return;
  case 68:  _outtext("F10               ");return;
  case 119: _outtext("Ctrl+Home         ");return;
  case 117: _outtext("Ctrl+End          ");return;
  case -124:_outtext("Ctrl+PgUp         ");return;
  case 118: _outtext("Ctrl+PgDn         ");return;
  case 83:  _outtext("Del               ");return;
  case 82:  _outtext("Ins               ");return;
  case 71:  _outtext("Home              ");return;
  case 79:  _outtext("End               ");return;
  case 73:  _outtext("PgUp              ");return;
  case 81:  _outtext("PgDn              ");return;
  case 75:  _outtext("left arrow key    ");return;
  case 77:  _outtext("right arrow key   ");return;
  case 72:  _outtext("up arrow key      ");return;
  case 80:  _outtext("down arrow key    ");return;
  case 45:  _outtext("Alt+X             ");Quit_Pgm();
  default:  _outtext("inactive key      ");
            MakeSound(400,16000);return;}          /* undefined */
#elif Compiler==TurboC
  tempclr=getcolor();
  setcolor(C0);setlinestyle(USERBIT_LINE,0xffff,NORM_WIDTH);
  setfillstyle(SOLID_FILL,C0);
  TextRow=1;TextColumn=64;GetTextCoords();
  if (mode_flag==6){             /* if Hercules 9x14 characters */
    bar(TextX,TextY,TextX+144,TextY+13);}
  else {bar(TextX,TextY,TextX+128,TextY+7);}/* if 8x8 characters */
  setcolor(C7);
switch (keynum){
  case 59:  outtextxy(TextX,TextY,"F1                ");break;
  case 60:  outtextxy(TextX,TextY,"F2                ");break;
  case 61:  outtextxy(TextX,TextY,"F3                ");break;
  case 62:  outtextxy(TextX,TextY,"F4                ");break;
  case 63:  outtextxy(TextX,TextY,"F5                ");break;
  case 64:  outtextxy(TextX,TextY,"F6                ");break;
  case 65:  outtextxy(TextX,TextY,"F7                ");break;
  case 66:  outtextxy(TextX,TextY,"F8                ");break;
  case 67:  outtextxy(TextX,TextY,"F9                ");break;
  case 68:  outtextxy(TextX,TextY,"F10               ");break;
  case 119: outtextxy(TextX,TextY,"Ctrl+Home         ");break;
  case 117: outtextxy(TextX,TextY,"Ctrl+End          ");break;
  case -124:outtextxy(TextX,TextY,"Ctrl+PgUp         ");break;
  case 118: outtextxy(TextX,TextY,"Ctrl+PgDn         ");break;
  case 83:  outtextxy(TextX,TextY,"Del               ");break;
  case 82:  outtextxy(TextX,TextY,"Ins               ");break;
  case 71:  outtextxy(TextX,TextY,"Home              ");break;
  case 79:  outtextxy(TextX,TextY,"End               ");break;
  case 73:  outtextxy(TextX,TextY,"PgUp              ");break;
  case 81:  outtextxy(TextX,TextY,"PgDn              ");break;
  case 75:  outtextxy(TextX,TextY,"left arrow key    ");break;
  case 77:  outtextxy(TextX,TextY,"right arrow key   ");break;
  case 72:  outtextxy(TextX,TextY,"up arrow key      ");break;
  case 80:  outtextxy(TextX,TextY,"down arrow key    ");break;
  case 45:  outtextxy(TextX,TextY,"Alt+X             ");Quit_Pgm();
  default:  outtextxy(TextX,TextY,"inactive key      ");
            MakeSound(400,16000);break;}          /* undefined */
setcolor(tempclr);return;
#endif
return;}
/*_____*/

void Purge(void){  /* empties kybrd buffer, avoids cursor run-on */
do {CheckForKey();}      /* keep fetching keys from the buffer... */
while (keycode!=0);      /* ...while the keystroke is not NULL */
return;}                          /* then return to caller */
/*_____*/

void MakeSound(int hertz,int duration){      /* generates a sound */
```

Fig. 6-7.
Continued.

```
int t1=1,high_byte=0,low_byte=0;
short count=0;unsigned char old_port=0,new_port=0;
if (hertz<40) return;
if (hertz>4660) return;
count=1193180L/hertz;
high_byte=count/256;low_byte=count-(high_byte*256);
#if Compiler==QuickC
  outp(0x43,0xB6);outp(0x42,low_byte);outp(0x42,high_byte);
  old_port=inp(0x61);new_port=(old_port|0x03);outp(0x61,new_port);
  for (t1=1;t1<=duration;t1++);outp(0x61,old_port);
#elif Compiler==TurboC
  outportb(0x43,0xB6);outportb(0x42,low_byte);
  outportb(0x42,high_byte);old_port=inportb(0x61);
  new_port=(old_port | 0x03);outportb(0x61,new_port);
  for (t1=1;t1<=duration;t1++);outportb(0x61,old_port);
#endif
return;}
/*_____*/

void GetTextCoords(void){         /* convert QC row,col to TC xy */
if (mode_flag==6){                /* if Hercules 9x14 characters */
  TextX=(TextColumn*9)-9;TextY=(TextRow*14)-14;}
else {TextX=(TextColumn*8)-8;TextY=(TextRow*8)-8;}      /* if 8x8 */
return;}

/*_____
```

```
                L I B R A R Y - I N D E P E N D E N T
                G R A P H I C S     R O U T I N E S
```

This set of library-independent routines is currently able to
map generic calls to the specific syntax of the QuickC and the
Turbo C graphics libraries. It is a straightforward task to add
code to support the syntax of third-party graphics libraries such
as Essential Graphics, MetaWINDOW, and others. Refer to the book.*/

```
void SetHue(int hueclr){          /* sets the active drawing color */
#if GraphicsLibrary==QuickC
  _setcolor(hueclr);
#elif GraphicsLibrary==TurboC
  setcolor(hueclr);
#endif
return;}
/*_____*/

void BlankPage(void){          /* blanks the current active page */
#if GraphicsLibrary==QuickC
  _clearscreen(_GCLEARSCREEN);
#elif GraphicsLibrary==TurboC
  cleardevice();
#endif
return;}
/*_____*/

void SetLine(int style){          /* sets the current line style */
#if GraphicsLibrary==QuickC
  _setlinestyle(style);
#elif GraphicsLibrary==TurboC
  setlinestyle(USERBIT_LINE,style,NORM_WIDTH);
#endif
return;}
/*_____*/

void SetFill(char *pattern,int hueclr){     /* sets fill pattern */
#if GraphicsLibrary==QuickC
  _setcolor(hueclr);
  _setfillmask(pattern);
```

Fig. 6-7.
Continued.

```
#elif GraphicsLibrary==TurboC
  setfillpattern(pattern,hueclr);
#endif
return;}
/*_____*/

void SetPosition(int x,int y){    /* sets the current xy position */
#if GraphicsLibrary==QuickC
  _moveto(x,y);
#elif GraphicsLibrary==TurboC
  moveto(x,y);
#endif
return;}
/*_____*/

void DrawLine(int x,int y){   /* draws line from current position */
#if GraphicsLibrary==QuickC
  _lineto(x,y);
#elif GraphicsLibrary==TurboC
  lineto(x,y);
#endif
return;}
/*_____*/

void DrawBorder(int x1,int y1,int x2,int y2){ /* draws rectangle */
#if GraphicsLibrary==QuickC
  _rectangle(_GBORDER,x1,y1,x2,y2);
#elif GraphicsLibrary==TurboC
  rectangle(x1,y1,x2,y2);
#endif
return;}
/*_____*/

void DrawPanel(int x1,int y1,int x2,int y2){   /* solid rectangle */
#if GraphicsLibrary==QuickC
  _rectangle(_GFILLINTERIOR,x1,y1,x2,y2);
#elif GraphicsLibrary==TurboC
  bar(x1,y1,x2,y2);
#endif
return;}
/*_____*/

void Fill(int x,int y,int edgeclr){               /* fountain fill */
#if GraphicsLibrary==QuickC
  _floodfill(x,y,edgeclr);
#elif GraphicsLibrary==TurboC
  floodfill(x,y,edgeclr);
#endif
return;}
/*_____*/

char far * MemBlock(int x1,int y1,int x2,int y2){
/* allocate array block in far heap */
char far *blk;
#if GraphicsLibrary==QuickC
  blk=(char far*)_fmalloc((unsigned int)_imagesize(x1,y1,x2,y2));
#elif GraphicsLibrary==TurboC
  blk=(char far*)farmalloc((unsigned long)imagesize(x1,y1,x2,y2));
#endif
return blk;}
/*_____*/

void GetBlock(int x1,int y1,int x2,int y2,char far *blk){
/* save graphic array in pre-allocated memory block */
#if GraphicsLibrary==QuickC
  _getimage(x1,y1,x2,y2,blk);
#elif GraphicsLibrary==TurboC
  getimage(x1,y1,x2,y2,blk);
#endif
```

Fig. 6-7.
Continued.

```
return;}
/*_____*/

void PutXOR(int x,int y,char far *blk){    /* XOR a graphic array */
#if GraphicsLibrary==QuickC
  _putimage(x,y,blk,_GXOR);
#elif GraphicsLibrary==TurboC
  putimage(x,y,blk,XOR_PUT);
#endif
return;}
/*_____*/

void PutPSET(int x,int y,char far *blk){ /* PSET a graphic array */
#if GraphicsLibrary==QuickC
  _putimage(x,y,blk,_GPSET);
#elif GraphicsLibrary==TurboC
  putimage(x,y,blk,COPY_PUT);
#endif
return;}
/*_____*/

void PutText(int row,int col,int clr,char * tptr){ /* write text */
int TCrow,TCcol,tempclr;
#if GraphicsLibrary==QuickC
  _settextposition(row,col);_settextcolor(clr);_outtext(tptr);
#elif GraphicsLibrary==TurboC
  TCcol=(col*alpha_x)-alpha_x;                /* convert col to x */
  TCrow=(row*alpha_y)-alpha_y;                /* convert row to y */
  tempclr=getcolor();setcolor(clr);   /* save, set active color */
  outtextxy(TCcol,TCrow,tptr);                /* display the text */
  setcolor(tempclr);              /* restore previous active color */
#endif
return;}
/*_____*/

void SetTextRowCol(int row,int col){          /* set text position */
int TCrow,TCcol;
#if GraphicsLibrary==QuickC
  _settextposition(row,col);
#elif GraphicsLibrary==TurboC
  TCcol=(col*alpha_x)-alpha_x;TCrow=(row*alpha_y)-alpha_y;
  moveto(TCcol,TCrow);
#endif
return;}
/*_____

End of Module 2 source code.  */
```

REMINDER

The demonstration program consists of two separate C source files. If you are compiling with QuickC, use a .MAK file to tell the compiler which files to collect together. If you are compiling with Turbo C, use a .PRJ file.

Compiling a Two-module Program with QuickC

If you are using QuickC, you must first create an appropriate .MAK file. This MAKE file simply contains a list of the C source files (modules) which make up the entire project.

First, you select the Make menu from the main menu bar in QuickC. Then, you choose Set Program List... from the Make menu.

Type in the name MENUMGR.MAK and press the Enter key. QuickC will respond by telling you that no such file yet exists and will ask you if you wish to create it. Answer yes. QuickC will present a menu that allows you to indicate which files should be in the new MAK file. Choose MENUMGR1.C and MENUMGR2.C.

If you are using the companion disk, you should have copied the .MAK files along with the .C files to to fixed disk and QuickC will load MENUMGR.MAK when you ask for it. There is no need to create it if it is already on your fixed disk.

After you have set MENUMGR.MAK as the current project file, simply press F5 to compile and run the program. QuickC will check the contents of the MAK file and will compile the appropriate C modules to create MENUMGR.EXE.

Compiling a Two-module Program with Turbo C

If you are using Turbo C, you must first create an appropriate .PRJ file. This MAKE file simply contains a list of the C source files (modules) which make up the entire project.

First, you select the Project menu from the main menu bar in Turbo C. Then, you choose Project name from the Project menu.

Type in the name MENUMGR.PRJ and press the Enter key. If MENUMGR .PRJ does not yet exist on your fixed disk, you should create it before naming it in the Project menu. Using the Turbo C editor, type MENUMGR1.C on the first line and MENUMGR2.C on the second line. Then use the editor to save this as MENUMGR.PRJ. If you are using the companion disk, you should copy the .PRJ files along with the source files to your fixed disk.

After you have set MENUMGR.PRJ as the current project file, simply choose Run from the Run menu to compile and run the program. Turbo will check the contents of the PRJ file and will compile the appropriate C modules to create MENUMGR.EXE.

COMMAND-LINE COMPILATION

If you are using command-line compilation with either QuickC or Turbo C, you must name each C source file on the command line. Refer back to Chapter 2 for guidance in setting up the appropriate directories before starting the command line.

Command-line Compilation with QuickC

The following line will produce MENUMGR.EXE:

```
C:\QC2\BIN\QCL /Ox /AM /F 1000 /FeMENUMGR /W1 MENUMGR1.C MENUMGR2.C /link
    /INF ⟨Enter⟩
```

This line assumes that the current drive and directory have already been set to the location of the C source files. Enter the line exactly as shown; the upper- or lowercase quality of each character is important, as are the blank spaces (or lack of blank spaces, as the case may be). ⟨Enter⟩ means to press the Enter key.

Command-line Compilation with Turbo C

The following line will produce MENUMGR.EXE:

```
TCC -mm -G -IC:\TC2\INCLUDE -LC:\TC2\LIB -nC:\TC2\SOURCE MENUMGR1.C
    MENUMGR2.C GRAPHICS.LIB ⟨Enter⟩
```

This line assumes that the current drive and directory have already been set to the location of the TCC.EXE and TLINK.EXE files. Be careful to enter the line exactly as shown, paying particular attention to the upper-/lowercase of each character and the spacing. ⟨Enter⟩ means to press the Enter key.

FEATURES OF THE DEMONSTRATION PROGRAM

The program listings in Fig. 6-7 introduce some important new concepts. Some of these concepts are defensive programming—others are implemented to increase future marketability of your own original software which might be built around this demonstration program.

Graphics Library Independence

If you review the second module, MENUMGR2.C, you can see how all the low-level graphics routines have been collected here in a library-independent form. If you want to change the active color, for example, you call a routine which uses the #if and #elif preprocessor directive to use either the QuickC graphics library or the Turbo C graphics library syntax.

This programming paradigm makes it easy to add support for other third-party graphics libraries like Essential Graphics, MetaWINDOW, HALO, GFX, and others. See Appendix B for more information about this.

Note how the low-level graphics routines in module 2 expect to receive parameters from the caller on the stack, thereby improving the modularity (sometimes called *granularity*) of the source code. Contrast this with the extensive use of global variables in the other parts of the program listings.

Stub Routines for Expandability

This demonstration program also makes extensive use of stub routines. A stub routine is a placeholder for code that has not been written yet. It is often nothing more than a return; statement. This programming approach is ideal for large, complex programs. You can write the skeleton of the code and use stub routines to leave hooks for future routines, just waiting to be fleshed out. It ensures that the foundation of your menu system is sound and that you will not have to rewrite any major sections of code in order to add new features or extensions to your C graphics project.

_____ FACT _____

A stub routine is simply a placeholder for future code.

Device Independence

Noteworthy also is the device-independent nature of these two source code listings. Not only will the graphics routines run in any one of six different graphics modes on five different graphics adapters, but the text output is also mode-independent.

The graphics are made device-independent by using either a virtual 640x480 imaginary screen and then using simple ratio formulas to convert the virtual x,y coordinates to actual physical coordinates, or else by using offsets from 0,0 or x_res,y_res. You will recall x_res and y_res were introduced in previous demonstration programs.

The text output is made device-independent by using offsets from the upper-left corner of the display screen, whether expressed as 1,1 (row-column coordinates) or as 0,0 (pixel coordinates).

Although the device-independence methods used in this menuing demonstration program leave room for optimization and improvement, they go a long way towards making it easy to add support for even more graphics modes.

Heavily Remarked

Note how the source code has been peppered with remarks throughout the listing. Even for the original programmer, this practise makes it easy to understand how the executable portion of the code works, and for what each global or local variable is used. This makes it easy to adapt this menu manager to act as a front end for a wide variety of C graphics programs. The menu interface was used in its present form (the pushbuttons were activated, of course) as a front end for the draw/paint program in Chapter 8. With a few significant modifications, the same menu shell was used as a front end for the full-featured 3D CAD modeling and rendering program presented in Chapter 13.

Segregation of Purpose

Also of importance is the manner in which the overall program has been split into two modules.

Module 1 contains the fundamental preparation and start-up code for the menu manager. The graphic arrays for the menu systems and the graphics for the on-screen interface are drawn in module 1. After all this preparatory work as been accomplished, program control is passed to the master menu loop in module 2.

This clean segregation of purpose makes it easy for you to modify module 1 to become a utility program for creating the various graphics and storing them as binary image files on disk. You could then use module 2 as the start-up code which loads these graphic arrays into RAM from disk before beginning the menu loop. This strategy would keep the details of the graphic arrays hidden from your end-user, of course.

Compiler Independence

In addition to graphics library independence, the source code maintains the compiler-independent nature of the previous demonstration programs. This means that if you wish to use Lattice C as your primary C compiler, you can easily adapt the program by adding additional #elif directives where appropriate.

Further, if either Microsoft or Turbo C should offer a new version with specific features that you determine are of special importance to your project, you can easily change compilers, without any extensive revisions to your source code.

Marketplace Support

The menuing system shell presented here also provides a good level of support for different graphics hardware. The VGA is supported by the

640x480x16-color mode. The EGA is supported in two modes: if an enhanced monitor is present the 640x350x16-color mode is used; if a standard monitor is found the 640x200x16-color mode is used. The MCGA is supported in its 640x480x2-color mode. The CGA is supported by the 640x200x2-color mode; and the Hercules series of graphics adapters is supported in the 720x348x2-color mode.

HOW THE PROGRAM WORKS

A section-by-section discussion of the source code for this menu system shell will provide a working knowledge of how it gets the job done. The following analysis is arranged in the order the routines appear in the source code.

The Module 1 Header

The first section of module 1 is a remark header which provides compilation instructions and programmer's reminder notes.

Compiler Directives and Include Files

The next section of source code is entitled COMPILER DIRECTIVES. This section defines a set of constants, most noteable being the Compiler and Graphics-Library tokens. A set of #include statements makes certain that the necessary declarations and initializations for variables used by the QuickC and Turbo C libraries are ready for use.

Function Prototypes

The next section of source code is entitled FUNCTION PROTOTYPES. First, routines that are actually present in module 1 are declared. This ensures that the compiler will detect any syntax errors in the source code, such as wrong number of arguments, and so on. Next, routines that are actually present in module 2 but which are called from module 1 are declared.

When you are writing code, you can use the powerful text copying functions of the QuickC and Turbo C editors to simply copy these declarations from the beginning of one module to another, of course.

TIP

Use the powerful text-copying features of the QuickC and Turbo C editors to declare global functions at the beginning of multiple C source files.

Declaration of Global Variables

The next section of source code is entitled DECLARATION OF GLOBAL VARIABLES. These are variables that are visible to all functions in both modules.

In particular, note how the _stklen variable is used to set the run-time stack size to 4096 bytes (4K) when Turbo C is being used. QuickC uses a selection in its menu system to allow you to set the run-time stack size. See Appendix A for more on this.

WHERE TO LOOK

See Appendix A for more information about setting the size of the run-time stack with either QuickC or Turbo C.

Note the char far pointers that are used to name the graphic arrays for the menus in this program. These pointers will be re-declared at the beginning of module 2 to ensure that the menu system loops will be able to install and de-install these menus. The highlight bars that are used to pan and scroll through the menus are declared here also.

The final seven lines in this section serve to declare and define a set of text strings that will be used at run-time.

Function Definitions

The next section of source code is entitled FUNCTION DEFINITIONS. The executable code for the functions (routines) is contained in this section.

First, of course, is the main( ) routine. This routine calls the Graphics_Setup( ) function to initialize the best graphics mode for the hardware at program start-up.

The main( ) function then calls eight routines to prepare the various menu arrays and screen image that will be used by module 2 to manage the menu system.

The final function, which is called Quit_Pgm( ), should never execute. It is included in the source code only as a boilerplate: a bulletproof barrier just in case something goes wrong during development and debugging.

Setting Graphics Parameters

The function named SetParameters( ) defines the colors, image sizes, and other variable values used by the other routines that draw the menus and the screen interface.

Note, for example, the line which defines vx1. This value is derived from the text size of the graphics mode, alpha_x by alpha_y, defined when the graphics mode is initialized. The variables defined in this line ensure that the size of the windows on the display screen are linked to the screen resolution which has been invoked at program start-up.

CAUTION

To make your graphics programs device-independent, you must take into account both the horizontal/vertical resolution of the screen, and the size of the alphanumeric character box. VGA, EGA, and MCGA graphics adapters can use either an 8x8 or 8x14 box. The CGA always uses an 8x8 box. Hercules graphics adapters use a 9x14 box.

Observe also how the mode_flag variable is used to decide how to define the spacing variables for the panning and scrolling highlight bars.

Creating the Main Menu Bar

The function named CreateBars( ) creates the main menu bar with its white reverse labels, the help bar at the bottom of the screen, and a few other text labels.

Note how C's strcpy function is used to load a text string into a variable named text5, which is then used to write the text string to the screen. You can tinker with the lines which use this algorithm to change the labels in the main menu bar or the help bar.

The main menu bar is created by first saving the text labels in an array. A filled rectangle is then created on the screen and the text array is XOR'd onto the rectangle. The finished image is then saved in an array, ready for later use when the screen interface is to be created.

Creating a Pushbutton

The function named CreateButton( ) creates a graphic array which holds the image for one of the pushbuttons. This array will be repeatedly written to the screen in different locations to create the vertical set of buttons along the left side of the screen interface.

The coordinates that are used for the drawing functions were defined earlier in the function named SetParameters( ), of course.

Naming the Program's Visible Features

The function named CreateList creates the text contents of the various functions supported by the pushbuttons. By altering the text strings in this function, you can modify this menu shell to act as a front-end for your own original C graphics programs. Note how the graphics mode-dependent variables named alpha_x and alpha_y are used to determine the x,y coordinates necessary to save the resulting text in a graphic array.

Creating the Pull-down Menus

The function named CreateMenus( ) contains the code which actually creates and saves the pull-down menus for the program. Each line which begins with the strcpy instruction can be modified if you want to change the contents of a particular pull-down menu.

To create a menu, the code first saves the text content in a graphic array. Then a bordered rectangle is drawn. The previously saved graphic array containing the text is then XOR'd onto the rectangle. The finished image is then saved in RAM as a graphic array, ready to be used by the menu manager loops in module 2.

Note also how CreateMenus( ) initializes the coordinates for a graphic array that will be used by module 2 to save the underlying background before any new menu is placed on the screen.

Creating the Highlight Bars

The function named CreateHiBars( ) creates the panning and scrolling highlight bars used by the menu system. These are simply filled rectangles that are saved as graphic arrays. The highlight bar which pans across the main menu bar is called PanBar. The highlight bar which scrolls through the different pull-down menus is called ScrollBar.

Creating the Sign-on Screen

The function named DrawScreen( ) draws the user interface. Note how mode _flag is used to differentiate between the 16-color modes and the black-and-white modes. You can see how the graphic arrays which hold the main menu bar and the help bar are written to the screen.

It is interesting also to observe how the dropshadows are drawn for the two viewports which appear on the screen. Refer back to Fig. 6-6. In many graphics modes, these dropshadows use the bit tiling codes initialized in the DECLARATION OF GLOBAL VARIABLES section of the source code.

RELATED MATERIAL: Bit tiling.

Further discussion about bit tiling, halftoning, and line dithering may be found in other books by the author. See *High-Performance CAD Graphics in C*, #3059, published March 1989, ISBN 0-8306-9359-9. Also refer to *High-Performance Graphics in C: Animation and Simulation*, #3049, published November 1988, ISBN 0-8306-9349-1.

Note also the for/next loop that installs the set of pushbuttons along the left side of the screen. The number of buttons and the spacing between the buttons is mode-dependent, as made clear by the switch( ) statement.

When this routine returns control to main( ), the program next jumps to the first menu system loop, called MenuBarLoop( ), which is located in module 2. Control will never again return to module 1, unless the program is terminated by the user.

Terminating the Program

The function named Quit_Pgm( ) will gracefully terminate the program. This is the same function used in previous demonstration programs.

De-allocating Memory in the Far Heap

The function named FreeBlock( ) is called by DrawScreen( ) after some of the single-use graphic arrays have been written to the screen. This function is merely for housekeeping purposes.

Graphics Mode Auto-detect

The function named Graphics_Setup( ) ensures that the highest graphics mode supported by the available hardware is initialized at program start-up. This function and the algorithm were discussed in the first demonstration program in Chapter 1.

Study this section of code to see the assorted run-time variables that are defined after the graphics mode has been determined by the routine. These variables are used mainly to control the location of pull-down menus and the x,y coordinates for the on- screen interface.

Copyright Notice

The function named Notice( ) is the standard copyright notice in graphical form. Whenever you write an original program, you should also ensure that a proper copyright notice appears on the sign-on screen. Placing a notice in the source code and on the disk label are not enough to protect your rights of ownership. If you are creating a program under contract for a client, in most cases the client's copyright notice should be used.

REMINDER

Always place a copyright notice on the sign-on display, on the disk label, and in the source code of any C program you create.

The Module 2 Header

The remarks header to module 2 contains explanatory information useful to the programmer.

Compiler Directives and Include Files

The #define directives placed here are similar in purpose to the directives appearing in module 1. Note the additional constants such as ACTIVE and BACKOUT, which are used at run-time by the menu manager loops.

The #include directives are used to include only the files specifically needed by the function calls in this module.

Function Prototypes

The next section of source code is entitled FUNCTION PROTOTYPES. Note how the source code is organized into different types of function declarations. Most of the functions actually found in module 2 are called by other functions in module 2. Only two functions in module 1 are called from module 2.

Declaration of Variables

The next section of code declares or re-declares variables, as the case may be. Any global variables declared and initialized in module 1 must be re-declared here as extern if the functions in module 2 are to use them.

It is important to note that you should only re-declare the global variables; you cannot re-define them at this stage. Only executable code can be used to re-define a variable after it has been initialized. Attempting a re-definition in this section of the source code will cause the QuickC or Turbo C compiler to generate an error message.

Managing the Main Menu Bar

The next function in the source code is named MenuBarLoop( ). This routine is a loop which is responsible for managing the panning highlight bar on the main menu bar at the top of the display screen. This source code is the working implementation of the pseudocode depicted previously in FIG. 6-4.

The beginning of this loop is named menuloop:. The label loop0: is the beginning of the loop which manages the pull-down menus. This section of code is the semantic implementation of the pseudocode illustrated earlier in FIG. 6-5.

Note the section of code which begins at the label named Label5:. This code uses a switch( ) statement to decide where to loop back after the user has pressed the Enter key.

Panning the Highlight Bar

The function named Panning( ) is responsible for moving the highlight bar left and right along the main menu bar. Because this graphic array is XOR'd onto the screen, the underlying labels on the menu bar can be seen as the highlight bar is positioned over them.

Note the use of the px1,px2,px3... variables to update the horizontal position of the panning bar.

Because the switch( ) function is used along with a t1 token, which describes the logical position of the highlight bar on the menu bar, this function can pan either left or right. Note how if statements are used to handle both left and right wraparounds of the panning highlight bar.

Installing a Pull-down Menu

The function named InstallMenu( ) installs a menu on the screen. Two variables named t2 and p6 are used to control the logical and the coordinate scrolling position of the highlight bar.

The switch( ) statement is used to branch to the installation code for each of the supported menu positions. Note how the StubRoutine( ) function is also used here.

Before any menu is written to the screen, InstallMenu( ) first removes the panning highlight bar from the main menu bar and then saves the appropriate background area.

Removing a Pull-down Menu

The function named UninstallMenu( ) de-installs a pull-down menu from the screen. This function is menu-independent because the same graphic array is used to save the background before any pull-down menu is installed.

Jumping from One Menu to Another

The function named PanMenu( ) allows the user to jump directly from one pull-down menu to another by using the left-arrow and right-arrow keys. This is installed by using C's powerful switch( ) statement. The trick is to carefully upgrade all pertinent variables, of course, and to make sure to tidy up everything on the display screen before installing the next menu.

Scrolling the Menu Highlight Bar

The function named Scrolling( ) is responsible for managing the scrolling highlight bar on the various pull-down menus. This one routine can handle any menu of any size because variables—not hard-coded constants—are used to determine the wraparound limits of the scrolling. Again, C's switch( ) function comes to the rescue.

Activating the Programs' Core Functions

The function named MenuChoices( ) is the switcher that is used to branch to the various core graphics functions supported by the program (none at present, of course). Note how nested switch( ) functions are used to set up this switcher. At present, MenuChoices( ) calls a routine named StubRoutine( ), but you would replace this call with a call to your graphics routine when you implement this demo program, of course. The first major demonstration program in Chapter 8, Your Microcomputer SketchPad, will illustrate this programming paradigm.

Stub Routines

The function named StubRoutine( ) is nothing more than a glorified placeholder. In its current implementation, it displays a line of text on the dialog line of the menu system, telling the user that the desired feature is inactive. In reality, however, all StubRoutine( ) does is execute a return jump to the caller. Despite their conceptual simplicity, stub routines provide a powerful developmental tool for C graphics programmers.

Displaying the Menu System Status

The function named MenuBarText( ) is used to display a line of text on the dialog line which tells the user the system is idling, waiting for the next command. Because this state is so often encountered in the menu system, a separate routine has been set up to handle it.

Clearing the Dialog Line

The function named ClearTextLine( ) blanks the text line at the top of the screen. In both the QuickC version and the Turbo C version, a graphics rectangle is used to clear the text line before the next line of text is used.

Checking for User Keyboard Input

The function named CheckForKey( ) checks to see if the user has pressed any key. If not, the routine simply returns to the caller. If a key is found, the routine categorizes it before returning to the caller. The caller then calls other routines to make branching decisions based upon the value of the keystroke. This algorithm was discussed previously in Chapter 3.

Accepting Keystrokes from the Main Menu Bar

The function named KeySwitch1( ) is a keystroke switcher for all keystrokes received while the program is looping at the main menu bar level. Like the demonstration program in Chapter 3, the code uses C's powerful switch( ) function to make appropriate branching decisions. Note how Alt + X can be used to terminate the program. The appropriate feature in the File pull-down menu is also active.

Accepting Keystrokes from the Pull-down Menus

The function named KeySwitch2( ) is the keystroke switcher for all keystrokes received while the program is looping in any of the pull-down menus. It operates similarly to KeySwitch1( ).

Avoiding Cursor Run-on

The function named Purge( ) is used to empty the keyboard buffer. This function is useful for ensuring that no unwanted keystrokes remain in the buffer after a core function has executed or while the user is panning or scrolling the highlight bar. When the user lifts their finger from the arrow-key, the highlight bar will stop instantly. If the Purge( ) function was not used, the highlight bar would keep panning until all the keystrokes in the buffer were used.

Making Warning Sounds

The function named MakeSound( ) is used to make various audio cues while the menu system is running. This algorithm has been discussed previously.

The use of sound in serious computer programs is somewhat controversial, and some users want the option of being able to disable sound. You should keep this in mind when you are writing your own original C graphics programs.

QuickC and Turbo C Text Ouput

The function named GetTextCoords( ) uses simple math to convert the row-column text coordinates of QuickC to the pixel-based x,y coordinates for Turbo C text. Note how the unique 9x14 text matrix of the Hercules 720x348 mode has been accommodated by this section of source code.

LIBRARY-INDEPENDENT GRAPHICS

The next section of source code contains 15 library-independent graphics routines. Each routine uses #if and #elif preprocessor directives to ensure that only the correct source code is compiled for the particular graphics library being used.

SetHue( ) is used to change the current drawing color. BlankPage( ) is employed to clear the entire graphics screen.

SetLine( ) will alter the current line style. SetFill( ) is used to set the current fill pattern, or bit tiling matrix.

To set the current x,y position (or pen position), the function named SetPosition( ) can be called. DrawLine( ) is used to draw a line in the current color (set by SetHue( )) to the coordinates passed to DrawLine( ). DrawBorder( ) can be used to draw a rectangle outline in the current color. To create a solid rectangle, sometimes called a *bar*, use DrawPanel( ). Note how Turbo C's graphics library offers a specialized function for drawing a filled rectangle, while QuickC's library must first draw a rectangular outline and then explicitly fill it.

Fill( ) is used to implement a floodfill or fountain fill function.

The MemBlock( ) routine can be used to allocate a block of memory in the far heap useful for storage of a graphic array. Then, GetBlock( ) can be used to capture the rectangular image from the screen buffer and copy it into the memory block in the far heap. PutXOR( ) is used to XOR the array back onto the screen. PutPSET is used to overwrite (PSET) the array back onto the screen.

The function named PutText( ) can be employed to write a text string onto the display screen. The QuickC portion of the code is straightforward, but the Turbo C portion must convert the row-column coordinates to pixel coordinates before displaying the text string. Note how the alpha_x and alpha_y variables are used to compensate for the size of the character box in effect. SetTextRowCol( ) can be used to set the starting position for a line of text.

EXERCISING THE PROGRAM

You might find it illustrative to start the program and use the keyboard to work your way through each and every menu position. In its current implementation, the demonstration program is robust. Every menu feature has been carefully tied to a stub routine and a text message is displayed as you try each core function. The File menu contains an active feature which terminates the program, however.

Even pressing unsupported keys will produce an explanatory message in the upper right corner of the dialog line. Some unsupported keys are explicitly identified, such as the spacebar and the function keys, while others are grouped together in a generic dialog output.

Hold down the right-arrow key while you are on the main menu bar. The panning cursor will continue to pan and wraparound until you release the key, whereupon it will instantly stop with no run-on. Now, activate a pull-down menu. Hold down the down-arrow key and the scrolling cursor will fly by, wrapping around when it needs to jump back to the beginning of the menu list.

If you have a VGA or an EGA, try modifying the function named Graphics _Setup( ) in module 1 to force the program to start up in another mode. This will permit you to see how the device-independent graphics routines handle other modes, and how the aspect ratio of these other modes affects the visual appearance of the menu interface. If you have a VGA, try forcing the program into the black-and-white MCGA 640x480x2-color mode. If you have an EGA, try forcing the program into the black-and-white CGA 640x200x2-color mode. In addition, try forcing the program into a mode not supported on your hardware and watch how Graphics_Setup( ) handles the start-up sequence.

Part Two

2D Software Skills

7

Making Your Program Competitive:

Features of Paint, Draw, Illustration, and Drafting Programs

2D GRAPHICS DRAWING programs are generally based upon one of two programming algorithms. Paint programs and draw programs are usually driven by buffer-based algorithms—otherwise known as bitmap graphics. Illustration programs and drafting programs are usually driven by vector-based algorithms—otherwise known as object-based graphics.

BITMAP GRAPHICS AND VECTOR GRAPHICS

Bitmap graphics are represented as the pixel-by-pixel data in a screen buffer, also known as a *bitmap*. When you save your work in a buffer-based program, you save the contents of the bitmap, which is nothing more than a large array of bits indicating which pixel is which color. When you reload previously saved work, you are merely filling the screen buffer with a picture.

On the other hand, vector graphics are represented by the geometric entities or drawing commands which are used to construct the image. The starting coordinates, radii, color, thickness, etcetera of lines, points, circles, ovals, polygons, and so on are saved in a database as these images are drawn on the display screen.

FACT

When you save your drawing using a bitmap-based draw program, you are saving the bitmap image. When you save your drawing using a vector-based draw program, you are saving the commands and parameters necessary to reconstruct the image.

When you save your work using a vector-based program, you save the database of geometric entities, not the bitmap. When you reload previously saved work, you are in essence re-constructing the image from the instructions stored in the database.

Programs that employ bitmap graphics are more concerned with the visual appeal of the overall image than with the specific geometric entities used to construct the image.

Consider, for example, the writer who uses a paint program to create a simple illustration for use in the company newsletter. The user does not care that polylines, ellipses, and halftone shading are the graphical entities arranged in such and such a way to construct the drawing; the user cares only that the illustration is clear, appealing to the eye, and gets the message across to the reader of the newsletter.

Consider, on the other hand, the draftsperson who uses an illustration program or a drafting program to create a scale drawing of an assembly-line widget for use on a specification sheet to accompany a formal request for tender. The draftsperson will be very concerned that an ellipse of radius such and such is centered on a five-sided polygon... etcetera. In this instance, the objects or graphical entities that make up the overall drawing are as important as the drawing itself.

Whether your ambition is to build a bitmap-based 2D drawing program or a vector-based 2D drawing program, you can be confident that the built-in graphics libraries of QuickC and Turbo C are up to the task, as the demonstration program listing in Chapter 8 will clearly demonstrate.

But whether you use QuickC, Turbo C, or a third-party graphics library, you will want to ensure that your program competes effectively against the features of other drawing programs already in the marketplace. A general overview of typical features found in these types of programs will be useful to any serious software developer.

TYPICAL FEATURES OF DRAWING PROGRAMS

Bitmap programs, like draw programs and paint programs, contain a diverse toolbox of drawing commands, ranging from simple features like the ability to draw a line to more advanced features like the ability to create a mirror image of an existing graphic.

Vector programs, like illustration programs, offer advanced features at the geometry level, including angle measurements, scaling routines, and regeneration (regen).

The individual graphic entities that are available to the end-user are called *primitives*. The most fundamental primitive is the point: a single dot.

Line, Polyline, Polygon

Figure 7-1 depicts some rudimentary drawing primitives. A *line* is a single segment connecting two vertices. A *polyline* is a series of connected lines. When a polyline is formed into a closed loop, it becomes a *polygon*. Probably the most used polygon is a four-sided polygon, which can also be a parallelogram, a square, or a rectangle as shown in FIG. 7-1. The built-in graphics libraries of QuickC and Turbo C can easily create these fundamental entitites.

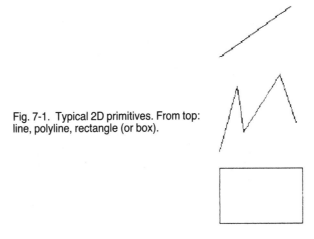

Fig. 7-1. Typical 2D primitives. From top: line, polyline, rectangle (or box).

Ellipse, Arc, Curve

The primitives illustrated in FIG. 7-2 are based upon curved lines, rather than the straight lines shown in FIG. 7-1. Circles are a specialized case of the ellipse entity, where the vertical radius and horizontal radius are equal. An arc is just a segment of a circle or an ellipse. A smooth curve is often based on parametric equations, using two end-points (anchors) and two or more magnetic points (control points) along the way. Ellipses, arcs, and smooth curves are well within the capabilities of QuickC's and Turbo C's graphics libraries.

Line Style and Weight

Many bitmap-based drawing programs—and, indeed, many vector-based drawing programs—are able to draw lines in a variety of different styles. Figure 7-3 depicts a random sampling of linestyles.

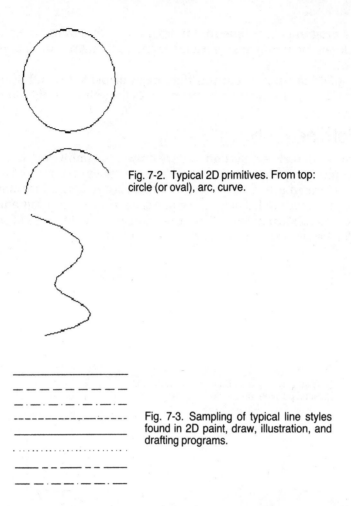

Fig. 7-2. Typical 2D primitives. From top: circle (or oval), arc, curve.

Fig. 7-3. Sampling of typical line styles found in 2D paint, draw, illustration, and drafting programs.

Many styles have special meaning for draftspersons and are used to mean center lines, measurement lines, and so on. Again, both QuickC and Turbo C are capable of drawing a diverse variety of linestyles, as the demonstration program in the next chapter will show.

WHERE TO LOOK

Most of the graphics features discussed here can be found implemented in the full-length program listing in the next chapter.

In addition to different linestyles, drawing programs can offer a choice of different line colors and line thicknesses (called *line weights* by professionals). Even esthetic effects which simulate charcoal, pencil, and crayon effects are offered by some high-end illustration programs.

Undo

An important feature of any drawing program is the ability to undo the most recent drawing command and restore the drawing to its previous condition. If you are using a bitmap-based or buffer-based programming approach, you can achieve this impressive effect by placing a copy of the screen in a hidden buffer before the end-user enters a drawing sequence loop. If the end-user subsequently requests an undo function, your program simply copies the saved image back onto the display screen.

If you are using a vector-based approach to programming, you can still use a hidden page to undo the image, but it is more common to simply redraw the offending commands in the background color (even though this algorithm tends to produce cluttered drawings, especially when lines cross over one another and some lines are subsequently undrawn, so to speak).

Rotate

A useful advanced feature of some bitmap-based programs is the ability to rotate an entity. See Fig. 7-4. This rotation is based upon applying sine and cosine equations to the x,y coordinates of the entity. Although rotation is easier to produce when vector-based graphics are being used, a pixel-by-pixel analysis of the shape being rotated allows bitmap-based programs to produce dramatic rotation effects (usually of a rectangle portion of the screen, however).

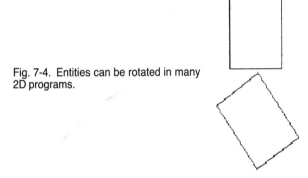

Fig. 7-4. Entities can be rotated in many 2D programs.

Mirror, Flop

Closely related to rotation is the ability to mirror an entity. Both bitmap-based programs and vector-based programs can offer this feature, and it is a question of debate as to which system makes it easier to implement. By allowing the end-user to specify an axis which indicates the plane of the mirror, the software simply copies the various coordinates or pixels over to the other side of the axis, being careful to express all locations as offsets from the axis, of course. Vertical and horizontal axis arrangements are the easiest to deal with. Diagonal axes require sine and cosine calculations.

Simply turning an object over is called *flop*. Using this feature left becomes right, top becomes bottom, and so forth.

Copy, Cut, Paste

Probably the most useful function that any drawing program can offer to the end-user is the ability to make copies of existing entities, as shown in FIG. 7-5. This capability makes it easy for the end-user to quickly create drawings which are comprised of often-repeated components like bolts, wheels, patterns, and so on.

Bitmap programs can offer this function by saving a copy of the object in a graphic array in RAM and then permitting the end-user to specify various locations on the screen where the graphic array is to be placed.

RELATED MATERIAL

A detailed discussion of the algorithm behind placing an irregularly-shaped, colored object onto a multicolored background by using graphic arrays may be found in another of the author's books. See *High-Performance Graphics in C: Animation and Simulation*, #3049, published November 1988, ISBN 0-8306-9349-1.

Vector-based programs can offer the same feature by specifying all coordinates for an entity as offsets from a starting point. By permitting the end-user to declare different starting points, the entity can be reconstructed at differing locations on the display screen.

The act of writing an entity to the screen, whether as a graphic array or as a vector-based object, is often called *paste*. The act of removing or deleting a specific object from the screen is called *cut*. A buffer-based program can cut an entity which has been outlined by the end-user by clever use of XOR, OR, AND,

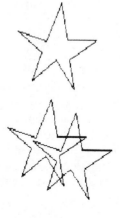

Fig. 7-5. Even complex entities can be moved and/or copied in many 2D programs.

PSET boolean operations and mattes at the graphic array level. A vector-based program can cut an entity in the same manner as a vector-based undo.

Distortion

Another handy function available on many drawing programs is distortion. See FIG. 7-6. This distortion can take the form of stretch or shear. It can be very useful for correcting mistakes in the original entity or for showing a series of entities in a transformation sequence (called *morphing* in high-end animation systems).

The distortion feature is relatively easy to implement on a vector-based program, where all that is needed is to modify the values of sets of coordinates. It can also be implemented in a bitmap-based program, but requires a pixel-by-pixel analysis of the area of the screen being distorted.

Fig. 7-6. Entities can be distorted and modified by stretch and shear functions.

Fillet, Chamfer

The ability to create rounded corners is a feature found in almost all illustration programs and drafting programs. See FIG. 7-7. It can be implemented in vector-based software by using a parametric curve which uses the end-points of the two lines as its own end-points.

A straight line which connects two such lines would be called a *chamfer.*

Measurements

Dimension lines are mandatory in drafting programs. See FIG. 7-8. Although both bitmap-based programs and vector-based programs can create dimension lines by explicit, manual drawing by the end-user, drafting programs often offer automatic routines. The end-user simply indicates the end-points of the entity to be measured, and the software makes the necessary calculations and then draws the leaderlines, arrows, and text.

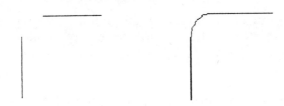

Fig. 7-7. Example of a fillet corner.

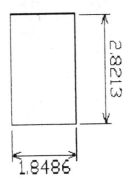

2.8213

1.8486

Fig. 7-8. Dimension lines and leader lines
are used to label an entity.

Fill, Pattern, Hatch

A variety of fill functions are offered by drawing programs. The most straightforward is the filling of a polygon object in a solid color. QuickC's and Turbo C's floodfill routines are easily up to the task. Even advanced features like airbrushing can be simulated by the halftoning and bit tiling capabilities of QuickC and Turbo C, as the full-featured drawing program in the next chapter will show.

By placing different halftoning patterns adjacent to one another, gradient airbrush fills can be created which simulate an almost infinite variety of colors, even in 16-color displays. Some illustration programs and advanced paint programs offer radial gradient and linear gradient fill capabilities. *Linear gradient* is a fill pattern which changes in intensity from top to bottom or from left to right. The fill might get darker, for example, as it works its way down the screen. *Radial gradient* is based on the bullseye effect. The center of a fill area might be very light, for instance, and the fill gradually becomes darker the further it gets from the center of the area being filled.

Seemingly spectacular effects like patterned fill can easily be offered by 2D drawing programs written with the built-in graphics libraries of QuickC and Turbo C. See FIG. 7-9. By careful specification of the bit tiling codes to pass to the

Fig. 7-9. Assorted patterns for area fill are offered by many 2D programs.

library routines, you can readily create anything from striped lines to wallpaper patterns. The powerful floodfill capabilities of QuickC and Turbo C make certain that even odd-shaped polygons can be filled by your pattern. Drafting programs often refer to such patterns as *hatching.*

Rubberband

A drawing aid often present in draw programs is the *rubberband.* This is a temporary line which is XOR'd onto the screen to provide a what-if look at what the final result will appear like if the end-user accepts the entity at its current location. When the end-user moves the cursor, the software quickly removes the rubberband line and draws an updated one. The feature is also available as rubberband boxes and rubberband ellipses.

Although run-time performance is slowed considerably by the necessity to draw an entire object each time the end-user moves the cursor, many end-users demand the ability to foresee what the end result will be if they draw the entity at the current cursor position.

Regen

Vector-based drawing programs need to reconstruct the drawing when a new database is loaded from disk. In addition, during a drawing session, an image can become cluttered by broken lines if the undo function is used often. When the end-user requests a reconstruction of the drawing to clean up these blemishes, it is called *regen*—an abbreviation of regeneration. Because the drawing commands and their arguments have been stored in the database, the software simply re-executes all the commands, thereby re-drawing the image.

Layers

Both bitmap-based programs and vector-based programs can offer a *layering* feature. This function is similar in concept to placing clear sheets of mylar plastic on top of one another. If each sheets contains a different part of the drawing (the plumbing system on one sheet, the electrical wiring on another, for example), they can be sandwiched together to create the entire image. By picking and choosing which layers to use during a regen, the end-user can produce specialized drawings from the same database.

In illustration programs and drafting programs which use vector-based graphics, this means that a number of databases are required: one database for each layer. The software simply queries the end-user at drawing time which database (layer) to store the commands in. Again, at regen time, the software asks the end-user which layers (databases) to reconstruct on the display screen.

When layering is offered in a bitmap-based drawing program, bitblt techniques are often used to XOR, OR, AND, or PSET the contents of one bitmap onto another on the display screen. A type of layering is offered by the full-length drawing program in the next chapter, where different fill patterns can be layered on top of one another to create an almost infinite variety of patterns.

Group, Ungroup

Vector-based programs—most notably drafting software—offer to the end-user the ability to tie together different primitives. The software places a group of primitives together as a cohesive unit in the database.

The circles and lines that make up the rim and spokes of a bicycle wheel, for example, might be grouped together. The software will thereafter manipulate all the individual primitives as a single unit if a request is made to copy the object or to erase it. Clearly, this is a timesaving feature for the end-user, who draws only one bicycle wheel and then copies the grouped object to another location to create the second wheel.

An ungroup feature is also often offered, in order to make it possible to edit previously-created objects.

Scaling, Zoom, Pan, Scroll, Auto-dimension

By drawing on a hidden bitmap in memory, your software can create pan and scroll effects by sending a different rectangular portion of the hidden bitmap to the display buffer. Panning means moving from left to right. Scrolling means moving up and down. The tricky part of this feature is the creation of the hidden bitmap, which must be a lot larger in horizontal and vertical dimension than the display buffer. Neither the graphics library of QuickC nor Turbo C offers the ability to draw on hidden, oversized bitmaps, although these capabilities are found in some of the third-party graphics libraries discussed in Appendix B.

Zooming means scaling: making a drawing larger or smaller. A bitmap-based program can offer this feature by analyzing the portion of the screen which is to be enlarged, and by redrawing each pixel as a four-pixel matrix, for example.

Some of the third-party graphics libraries discussed in Appendix B offer this as a built-in routine. A vector-based program can offer this feature by always using virtual coordinates, which are imaginary coordinates at a scale not linked to any particular graphics mode or screen resolution. Simple ratioing formulas can be used to manipulate the coordinates of primitives, thereby scaling the objects larger or smaller. When the software automatically recalculates the dimensions of objects for text labels, the process is called auto-dimensioning.

Distance, Angle

Some drafting software offers routines that will calculate the angle between two lines on the display screen. Routines are also often provided to calculate distances automatically, based on the scale being used by the end-user.

Color Models

There are a variety of compatible and incompatible color theories in use today. Each color model attempts to make order out of the way nature creates and exhibits color. Color as it is generally known is actually made up of three components. These are *hue, chroma* (intensity, saturation), and *value* (brightness). Red, for example, is a hue. A red with a lot of chroma (pigment or die) in it might be called a rosy red or a fire engine red. By reducing the intensity (chroma: pigment or die) in the red, and by increasing the value (brightness, or amount of black-gray-white scale level), you can produce a pink.

The HSV color model uses hue, saturation, and value to define a color scheme. The HVC color model uses hue, value, and chroma to make its definitions. The RGB color model uses differing intensities of the red, green, and blue electron guns of a display monitor to create a structure for orderly color analysis. The CMYB color model uses the cyna, magenta, yellow, and black hues used by printing plants to define a color scheme.

Each color model has its field of applications. A drawing program which could produce separate CMYB output of a drawing, for example, could be used to create the four separate cyna-magenta-yellow-black images used in color process printing.

The only way to generate a wide choice of colors when you are using a 16-color graphics mode is by using halftoning or bit tiling. Mixing different ratios of different colored pixels together in a small patch can fool the eye into believing that a new color has been created. The eye sees the patch as a whole, not the individual pixels which make up the patch. The full-length paint program listing in the next chapter provides a full range of halftone codes for you to experiment with or to include in your own original C graphics programs.

USING ENHANCED COLOR: 256-COLOR GRAPHICS

In today's marketplace, however, any drawing or paint program worth its salt must provide full support for color selection in the 256-color modes of the VGA and MCGA graphics adapters.

The MCGA supports the 320x200x256-color mode with 40x25 text capabilities. The VGA also supports that mode. The QuickC graphics library provides graphics drivers for this mode. Version 2.0 of Turbo C does not support the 320x200x256-color mode, but instead supports the 640x480x256-color mode of the high-end IBM 8514/A graphics adapter.

So-called enhanced VGA cards which surpass the IBM standard support the 640x480x256-color mode. Some of these VGA adapters are supported by some of the third-party graphics libraries discussed in Appendix B.

ANALOG COLOR

The VGA and MCGA graphics adapters use analog, not digital, technology to electronically create a color. The ability to use C to create a particular hue from the available palette of 256K colors is a powerful tool in any graphics programmer's kit.

The hardware of the VGA and MCGA mixes different percentages of the red, green, and blue guns to create a hue. Each RGB component can range from 0 to 63. 0 is fully off. 63 is fully on. If all three guns are set to 0, the result is black. If all three guns are set to 63, the result is high intensity white. If all three guns are set to 32, the result is a mid-gray. Obviously, a full range of 64 different gray values ranging from black to white can be created by increasing all three guns in equivalent steps from 0 to 63.

_____ **FACT** _____

When running in the VGA or MCGA analog mode, each RGB gun can vary in intensity from 0 to 63. This means that 262,144 different colors are available (64x64x64 = 262,144), of which either 256 or 16 can be simultaneously displayed, depending upon which graphics mode is in effect.

Both QuickC and Turbo C provide built-in routines to let you access these RGB analog controls. Using QuickC, you can write programs for the 320x200x256-color mode of the VGA and MCGA, in addition to the other modes supported in this book. Using Turbo C, you can write programs for the 640x480x256-color mode of the IBM 8514/A graphics adapter, in addition to the other modes supported in this book.

Setting the Color Code

QuickC sets the RGB guns by its _remappalette( ) statement. Two arguments must be passed with _remappalette( ). First, the color index which is being set, which ranges from 0 to 255 in the 256-color mode. Next, the intensity values of the three guns which are being used to set the color for this color index. A long integer four bytes in length is used to convey this information.

Of the four bytes, only the last three carry information. Byte number two carries the blue gun intensity; byte number three holds the green gun intensity; byte number four carries the red gun intensity. The argument is expressed as:

long int code = (*blue**65536) + (*green**256) + (*red**1)

where each *blue, green, red* value is in the range of 0 to 63, of course. The resulting long integer code is used in the library call thusly:

_remappalette(clr,code);

Turbo C's library provides a more straightforward method of setting the guns. The first argument to Turbo C's setrgbpalette( ) function is the color index which is being set. The next three arguments are integers (0 to 63 range) for the red, green, and blue guns. The resulting call looks like this:

setrgbpalette(clr,red,green,blue);

In both cases, the gun-setting scheme can be used to redefine any of the 16 colors in a 16-color mode on a VGA. Each of the 16 color indexes can be redefined to any of the 262,144 colors available (64x64x64 = 262,144 possible colors).

DEMONSTRATION PROGRAM: 256-Color Rainbow

The image in FIG. 7-10 shows the matrix to be filled with rainbow-like hue shifts by the demonstration program in FIG. 7-11. The program runs in the 320x200x256-color mode of the VGA and MCGA. You must use QuickC to

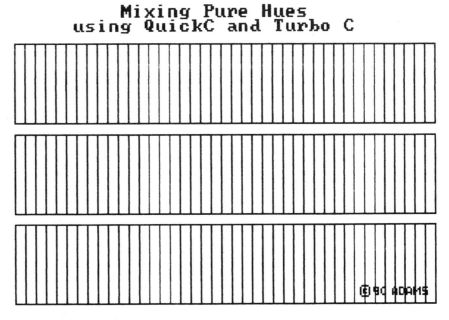

Fig. 7-10. Print of the matrix to be filled by a rainbow shift of colors in the demonstration program, HUES.C, using the 256-color mode of the VGA and MCGA.

compile and run the program, because Turbo C does not support the 320x200x256-color mode. If you have an IBM 8514/A graphics adapter, you can easily use Turbo C to modify the program to run in the 640x480x256-color mode, because the RGB gun-setting algorithm is equally valid in all analog modes.

If you are using an EGA, the program will start up in the 320x200x16-color mode. It will draw the matrix depicted in Fig. 7-10, but will make no attempt to set any colors.

Fig. 7-11. Source code for HUES.C, designed to demonstrate subtle manipulation of the red, green, and blue guns of the cathode ray tube in the 320x200x256-color mode of the VGA and MCGA. Ready to compile under QuickC. (Turbo C 2.0 does not support the 320x200x256-color mode.)

```
/*
Mixing Pure Hues                        Source file:  HUES.C

Purpose:  demonstrates how to use additive color mixing to produce
an infinite selection of different hues from the VGA palette.

Compiler:  QuickC.

Memory model:  medium memory model.

Marketability:  will detect and support these platforms...
VGA          320x200x256 colors    40x25 characters
MCGA         320x200x256 colors    40x25 characters
EGA          320x200x16 colors     40x25 characters (debugging mode)

(c) Copyright 1990 Lee Adams.  As purchaser of the book in which
this program is published, you are granted a non-exclusive
royalty-free license to reproduce and distribute these routines in
executable form as part of your software product, subject to any
trademark or patent rights of others, and subject to the limited
warranty described in the Introduction of the book.  All other
rights reserved.
_____

COMPILER DIRECTIVES
These are instructions to your C compiler. */

#define FAIL    0       /* used in graphics autodetect routine */
#define EMPTY   0           /* used in keyboard fetch routine */

#include <bios.h>         /* supports the keyboard functions */
#include <stdio.h>          /* supports the printf function */
#include <graph.h>          /* supports QuickC's graphics */
#include <process.h>        /* supports the exit function */
/*_____

FUNCTION PROTOTYPES
These ANSI C function declarations allow your C compiler to check
each function for correct arguments and return value. */

void Keyboard();                       /* checks for a keystroke */
void Quit_Pgm();                       /* terminates the program */
void Graphics_Setup();        /* autodetect of graphics hardware */
void Notice(int,int);              /* displays copyright notice */
int GetV(int);                   /* calculate 0-63 gun voltage */
void SetHdwr(int,int,int,int);        /* set the hardware color */
void DrawPatch(int,int,int,int,int);      /* draws a rectangle */
void DrawSwatch(int,int,int,int,int);   /* draws a color swatch */
/*_____
```

Fig. 7-11.
Continued.

```
DECLARATION OF GLOBAL VARIABLES
These variables are declared and initialized outside of any
function and are visible to all functions in this source file.   */

struct videoconfig vc;               /* QuickC's video data table */
int x_res=0,y_res=0;                 /* current screen resolution */
int mode_flag=0;                        /* current graphics mode */
int C0=0,C1=1,C2=2,C3=3,C4=4,C5=5,C6=6,C7=7,C8=8,C9=9,C10=10,
C11=11,C12=12,C13=13,C14=14,C15=15;       /* default color codes */
int t1=1;                                       /* loop counter */
int sx=0,sy=0;                  /* upper left vertex of swatch */
int wsx=0,wsy=0;                    /* width, depth of swatch */
int clr=0;                               /* color of swatch */
int Rlum=0,Glum=0,Blum=0;       /* virtual luminance 0 to 100 */
int Rv=0,Gv=0,Bv=0;                 /* gun voltage 0 to 63 */
/*_____*/


/* FUNCTION DEFINITIONS */

main(){                              /* this is the master routine */
Graphics_Setup();                    /* establish graphics mode */
_getvideoconfig(&vc);         /* initialize QuickC's video table */

            /* draw preparatory rectangles */
sx=15;sy=55;wsx=7;wsy=44;clr=C7;    /* set red swatch parameters */
for (t1=1;t1<=41;t1++){                     /* for 21 iterations... */
  DrawPatch(sx,sy,wsx,wsy,clr);          /* ...draw one swatch... */
  sx=sx+7;}                   /* ...and move to next location... */
sx=15;sy=105;wsx=7;wsy=44;clr=C7; /* set green swatch parameters */
for (t1=1;t1<=41;t1++){                     /* for 21 iterations... */
  DrawPatch(sx,sy,wsx,wsy,clr);          /* ...draw one swatch... */
  sx=sx+7;}                   /* ...and move to next location... */
sx=15;sy=155;wsx=7;wsy=44;clr=C7;       /* set blue parameters */
for (t1=1;t1<=41;t1++){                     /* for 21 iterations... */
  DrawPatch(sx,sy,wsx,wsy,clr);          /* ...draw one swatch... */
  sx=sx+7;}                   /* ...and move to next location... */
Notice(250,189);

            /* draw additive color mixtures as swatches */
if (mode_flag==8) goto Label1;  /* jump if 320x200x16-color mode */
Rlum=100;Glum=0;Blum=0;                  /* set to pure Red hue */
clr=16;                             /* choose hardware color ID */
sx=15;sy=55;wsx=7;wsy=44;        /* set for red/yel/green swatches */
for (t1=1;t1<=41;t1++){                     /* for 21 iterations... */
  Rv=GetV(Rlum);                        /* ...get R gun voltage... */
  Gv=GetV(Glum);                        /* ...get G gun voltage... */
  Bv=GetV(Blum);                        /* ...get B gun voltage... */
  SetHdwr(clr,Rv,Gv,Bv);            /* ...and set the hardware color */
  DrawSwatch(sx,sy,wsx,wsy,clr);          /* ...draw one swatch... */
  sx=sx+7;                           /* ...move to next location... */
  if (t1<21) Glum=Glum+5;           /* ...shift red to yellow or... */
  if (t1>=21) Rlum=Rlum-5;          /* ...shift yellow to green... */
  clr=clr+1;           /* ...choose the next hardware color ID... */
  }                                               /* end of loop */

Rlum=0;Glum=100;Blum=0;                  /* set to pure Green hue */
sx=15;sy=105;wsx=7;wsy=44;       /* set for green/cyan/blue swatches */
for (t1=1;t1<=41;t1++){                     /* for 21 iterations... */
  Rv=GetV(Rlum);                        /* ...get R gun voltage... */
  Gv=GetV(Glum);                        /* ...get G gun voltage... */
  Bv=GetV(Blum);                        /* ...get B gun voltage... */
  SetHdwr(clr,Rv,Gv,Bv);            /* ...and set the hardware color */
  DrawSwatch(sx,sy,wsx,wsy,clr);          /* ...draw one swatch... */
  sx=sx+7;                           /* ...move to next location... */
  if (t1<21) Blum=Blum+5;           /* ...shift green to cyan or... */
  if (t1>=21) Glum=Glum-5;          /* ...shift cyan to blue... */
  clr=clr+1;           /* ...choose the next hardware color ID... */
  }                                               /* end of loop */
```

Fig. 7-11.
Continued.

```
Rlum=0;Glum=0;Blum=100;                    /* set to pure Blue hue */
sx=15;sy=155;wsx=7;wsy=44;        /* set for blue\mag\red swatches */
for (t1=1;t1<=41;t1++){                   /* for 21 iterations... */
  Rv=GetV(Rlum);                         /* ...get R gun voltage... */
  Gv=GetV(Glum);                         /* ...get G gun voltage... */
  Bv=GetV(Blum);                         /* ...get B gun voltage... */
  SetHdwr(clr,Rv,Gv,Bv);         /* ...and set the hardware color */
  DrawSwatch(sx,sy,wsx,wsy,clr);         /* ...draw one swatch... */
  sx=sx+7;                        /* ...move to next location... */
  if (t1<21) Rlum=Rlum+5;        /* ...shift blue to magenta or... */
  if (t1>=21) Blum=Blum-5;        /* ...shift magenta to red... */
  clr=clr+1;           /* ...choose the next hardware color ID... */
  }                                            /* end of loop */
_setcolor(C0);Notice(250,189);

Label1:                  /* jump to here if 320x200x16-color mode */
for (t1=1;t1!=2; ) Keyboard();           /* press any key to stop */
Quit_Pgm();}                          /* end the program gracefully */
/*_____*/

void DrawSwatch(int sx,int sy,int wsx,int wsy,int clr){
_setcolor(clr);_setfillmask(NULL);
_rectangle(_GFILLINTERIOR,sx,sy,(sx+wsx),(sy+wsy));
return;}
/*_____*/

void DrawPatch(int sx,int sy,int wsx,int wsy,int clr){
_setcolor(clr);_setfillmask(NULL);_setlinestyle(0xffff);
_rectangle(_GBORDER,sx,sy,(sx+wsx),(sy+wsy));
return;}
/*_____*/

void SetHdwr(int clr,int Rv,int Gv,int Bv){
  long int VGAcode=0;                         /* local variables */
  long int Rv1=0,Gv1=0,Bv1=0;
Rv1=(long)Rv;Gv1=(long)Gv;Bv1=(long)Bv;   /* convert to long int */
VGAcode=(Bv1*65536)+(Gv1*256)+Rv1;       /* calculate analog code */
_remappalette(clr,VGAcode);            /* change the hardware table */
return;}
/*_____*/

int GetV(int luminance){               /* calculate gun voltage */
  int voltage=0;                             /* local variable */
switch(luminance){ /* set gun voltage based on virtual luminance */
case 0:   voltage=0;break;
case 5:   voltage=17;break;
case 10:  voltage=23;break;
case 15:  voltage=29;break;
case 20:  voltage=33;break;
case 25:  voltage=37;break;
case 30:  voltage=40;break;
case 35:  voltage=42;break;
case 40:  voltage=45;break;
case 45:  voltage=47;break;
case 50:  voltage=48;break;
case 55:  voltage=51;break;
case 60:  voltage=52;break;
case 65:  voltage=54;break;
case 70:  voltage=56;break;
case 75:  voltage=58;break;
case 80:  voltage=59;break;
case 85:  voltage=60;break;
case 90:  voltage=61;break;
case 95:  voltage=62;break;
case 100: voltage=63;break;}
return voltage;}
/*_____*/

void Keyboard(){        /* checks the keyboard buffer for any key */
```

Fig. 7-11.
Continued.

```
if (_bios_keybrd(_KEYBRD_READY)==EMPTY) return;
else {_bios_keybrd(_KEYBRD_READ);Quit_Pgm();}
}
/*_____*/

void Quit_Pgm(){                        /* terminates the program */
_clearscreen(_GCLEARSCREEN);                   /* clear the screen */
_setvideomode(_DEFAULTMODE);          /* restore the original mode */
exit(0);}                                  /* terminate the program
_____*/

void Graphics_Setup(){          /* autodetect of graphics hardware */
if (_setvideomoderows(_MRES256COLOR,25)!=FAIL) goto VGA256_mode;
if (_setvideomoderows(_MRES16COLOR,25)!=FAIL) goto EGA16_mode;
goto abort_pgm;                     /* if no graphics hardware found */

VGA256_mode: /* VGA 320x200x256-color mode, 8x8 character matrix */
x_res=320;y_res=200;mode_flag=7;
_settextcolor(C7);
_settextposition(3,12);
_outtext("Mixing Pure Hues");
_settextposition(4,8);
_outtext("using QuickC and Turbo C");
return;

EGA16_mode:  /* EGA 320x200x16-color mode, 8x8 character matrix */
x_res=320;y_res=200;mode_flag=8;
_settextcolor(C7);
_settextposition(3,12);
_outtext("Mixing Pure Hues");
_settextposition(4,8);
_outtext("using QuickC and Turbo C");
return;

abort_pgm:      /* jump to here if no supported graphics hardware */
printf("\n\nUnable to proceed.\n");
printf("Requires VGA or MCGA adapter\n");
printf("and analog monitor.\n\n");
exit(0);
}
/*_____*/

void Notice(int x, int y){      /* displays the copyright notice */
int copyright[][3]={0x7c00,0x0000,0x0000, /* array of bit styles */
             0x8279,0x819c,0x645e,
             0xba4a,0x4252,0x96d0,
             0xa27a,0x4252,0x955e,
             0xba0a,0x43d2,0xf442,
             0x8219,0x825c,0x945e,
             0x7c00,0x0000,0x0000};
int a,b,c; int t1=0;                        /* local variables */
for (t1=0;t1<=6;t1++){                     /* draw 7 styled lines */
  a=copyright[t1][0];b=copyright[t1][1];c=copyright[t1][2];
  _setlinestyle(a);_moveto(x,y);_lineto(x+15,y);
  _setlinestyle(b);_moveto(x+16,y);_lineto(x+31,y);
  _setlinestyle(c);_moveto(x+32,y);_lineto(x+47,y);y=y+1;};
_setlinestyle(0xFFFF);return;
}
/*_____

End of source file. */
```

HOW THE PROGRAM WORKS

The program works its magic by implementing an adaptation of the HVC (hue-value-chroma) color model. First, the gray scale value is computed. Next, a pure hue is mixed with the gray scale value to compute a color formula within the HVC scale. Then the resulting formula is converted to the QuickC color coding format. Finally, _remappalette is used to set the hardware table to the appropriate RGB mix.

The main( ) Function

After drawing the matrix shown in FIG. 7-10, main( ) creates and displays a red to green color shift composed of 42 increments. At the beginning of the shift, the red gun is set to 63, the green gun is set to 0, and the blue gun is set to 0. At the end of the shift, the red gun has been decremented to 0, the green gun is now set at 63, and the blue gun of course remains steady at 0.

Next, main( ) builds a shift from green to blue, using the algorithm in the preceding paragraph. Finally, main( ) creates and displays the color shift from blue to red, completing the color circle.

DrawSwatch( )

The function named DrawSwatch( ) draws a solid, filled rectangle at a specified location on the display screen. This function is called after the correct hue has been computed, of course.

DrawPatch( )

The function named DrawPatch( ) creates the hollow rectangles which make up the matrix to be filled. See FIG. 7-10.

SetHdwr( )

The function named SetHdwr( ) converts the separate red, green, and blue 0-63 values to the QuickC long integer and then sets the hardware.

GetV( )

The function named GetV( ) calculates gun voltage in the range 0 to 63 from the percentage supplied to it in the 0% to 100% range. Note how C's powerful switch( ) statement is used. Also note how the gun voltages do not correspond directly to the percentage values, which range from 0% to 100% in increments of 5%.

Note how the voltage values quickly approach the high end of the range, and then hover in the 50 to 63 range. This phenomenon is a direct result of the human eye's perception of the luminance of the guns. For example, the perceived difference between a gun set at 0 and a gun set at 17 is almost nothing—less than

5% difference; but at the higher end of the scale, changing a gun's voltage from only 60 to 61 will seem like a whopping 5% change.

USING ENHANCED TEXT: Vector and Bitmapped Fonts

Another useful tool in your programming kit is the ability to use QuickC's and Turbo C's text fonts in the graphics mode. Using fonts with these compilers is surprisingly easy. First, you make sure that the compiler can find the appropriate font files at program start-up. Second, you carefully pick the font style and size to be used.

Both QuickC and Turbo C provide two types of fonts: stroked fonts (vector fonts) and bitmapped fonts. *Vector* fonts are geometrical constructs built by drawing lines as offsets from a user-specified starting point. Vector fonts can be drawn at many different sizes, but tend to look skeletal at larger renderings. *Bitmapped* fonts are similar to the default ROM character fonts. They are matrix-based designs which simply set a checkerboard-like pattern of pixels on or off.

Refer to your QuickC or Turbo C manual for a description of the different font styles offered by each compiler.

DEMONSTRATION PROGRAM: Fonts

The image in FIG. 7-12 shows the output of the demonstration program in FIG. 7-13. This program can be compiled with either QuickC or Turbo C. It will run on a VGA, EGA, MCGA, CGA, or Hercules graphics adapters.

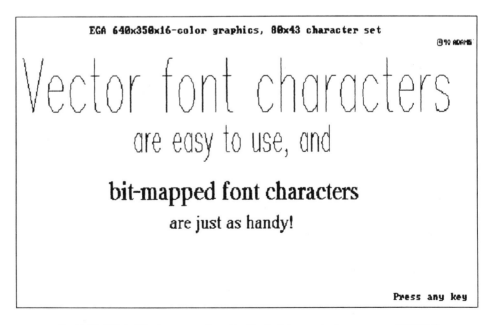

Fig. 7-12. Print of the image produced by the font demonstration program, FONTS.C.

Fig. 7-13. Source code for FONTS.C, designed to demonstrate the use of bitmapped fonts and vector fonts (stroked fonts) on VGA, EGA, MCGA, CGA, and Hercules graphics adapters. Ready to compile under QuickC or Turbo C.

```
/*
Typeface Designs                            Source file:  FONTS.C

Purpose:  demonstrates how to write C graphics programs which
use vector fonts and bit-map fonts for text display.

Compiler:  QuickC or Turbo C.  Default is QuickC.  To use
Turbo C, change one line in COMPILER DIRECTIVES below.  The
appropriate font files must be in the current directory.

Memory model:  medium memory model.

Marketability:  will detect and support these platforms...
VGA          640x480x16 colors    80x60 characters
EGA          640x350x16 colors    80x43 characters
EGA          640x200x16 colors    80x25 characters
MCGA         640x480x2 colors     80x60 characters
CGA          640x200x2 colors     80x25 characters
Hercules     720x348x2 colors     80x25 characters

(c) Copyright 1990 Lee Adams.  As purchaser of the book in which
this program is published, you are granted a non-exclusive
royalty-free license to reproduce and distribute these routines in
executable form as part of your software product, subject to any
trademark or patent rights of others, and subject to the limited
warranty described in the Introduction of the book.  All other
rights reserved.
_____

COMPILER DIRECTIVES
These are instructions to your C compiler. */

#define QuickC    1
#define TurboC    2
#define Compiler QuickC     /* NOTE: Change to TurboC if required */
#define FAIL      0
#define EMPTY     0

#include <bios.h>            /* supports the keyboard functions */
#include <stdio.h>              /* supports the printf function */
#if Compiler==QuickC
  #include <graph.h>              /* supports QuickC's graphics */
#elif Compiler==TurboC
  #include <graphics.h>          /* supports Turbo C's graphics */
#endif
#include <process.h>           /* supports the exit function
_____

FUNCTION PROTOTYPES
These ANSI C function declarations allow your C compiler to check
each function for correct arguments and return value. */

void Keyboard();                      /* checks for a keystroke */
void Quit_Pgm();                      /* terminates the program */
void Graphics_Setup();       /* autodetect of graphics hardware */
void GetTextCoords();             /* converts QC to TC text */
void Notice(int,int);           /* displays copyright notice */
/*_____

DECLARATION OF GLOBAL VARIABLES
These variables are declared and initialized outside of any
function and are visible to all functions in this source file.   */
```

Fig. 7-13.
Continued.

```
#if Compiler==QuickC
  struct videoconfig vc;               /* QuickC's video data table */
#endif
int C0=0,C1=1,C2=2,C3=3,C4=4,C5=5,C6=6,C7=7,C8=8,C9=9,C10=10,
C11=11,C12=12,C13=13,C14=14,C15=15;              /* color codes */
int mode_flag=0;                        /* indicates graphics mode */
float x_res,y_res;              /* screen resolution for mapping routine */
float sx,sy;              /* device-independent screen coordinates */
int t1=1;                                        /* loop counter */
int TextRow=1,TextColumn=1;              /* text position for QuickC */
int TextX=0,TextY=0;                      /* text position for Turbo C


FUNCTION DEFINITIONS */

main(){                                  /* this is the master routine */
Graphics_Setup();                        /* establish graphics mode */
#if Compiler==QuickC
  _getvideoconfig(&vc);            /* initialize QuickC's video table */
  _setcliprgn(0,0,x_res-1,y_res-1);          /* set clipping window */
  _registerfonts("MODERN.FON");           /* initialize font table */
  _registerfonts("TMSRB.FON");            /* initialize font table */
  _setfont("t'modern',h80,w30");          /* pick Modern typeface */
  _setcolor(C7);                                   /* set color */
  _moveto(20,20);_outgtext("Vector font characters");
  _setfont("t'modern',h40,w15");          /* set new type size */
  _moveto(170,90);_outgtext("are easy to use, and");
  _setfont("t'tms rmn',h26,w16");    /* pick Times Roman typeface */
  _moveto(138,148);_outgtext("bit-mapped font characters");
  _setfont("t'tms rmn',h20,w12");
  _moveto(220,180);_outgtext("are just as handy!");
#elif Compiler==TurboC
  setviewport(0,0,x_res-1,y_res-1,1);       /* set clipping window */
  settextstyle(3,HORIZ_DIR,0);               /* vector typeface */
  setusercharsize(4,3,5,2);                   /* set type size */
  setcolor(C7);                               /* set color */
  moveto(90,20);outtext("Vector font characters");
  setusercharsize(1,1,1,1);                   /* set new type size */
  moveto(166,90);outtext("are easy to use, and");
  settextstyle(0,HORIZ_DIR,2);               /* bit-map typeface */
  moveto(124,148);outtext("bit-mapped font characters");
  settextstyle(0,HORIZ_DIR,1);               /* set new type size */
  moveto(245,170);outtext("are just as handy!");
#endif
Notice(589,12);
for (t1=1;t1!=2; ) Keyboard();           /* press any key to stop */
Quit_Pgm();}                             /* end the program gracefully
                                                                      */

void Keyboard(){                       /* checks the keyboard buffer */
#if Compiler==QuickC
  if (_bios_keybrd(_KEYBRD_READY)==EMPTY) return;
  else {_bios_keybrd(_KEYBRD_READ);Quit_Pgm();}
#elif Compiler==TurboC
  if (bioskey(1)==EMPTY) return;else {bioskey(0);Quit_Pgm();}
#endif
}
/*_____*/

void Quit_Pgm(){                         /* terminates the program */
#if Compiler==QuickC                         /* if using QuickC */
  _clearscreen(_GCLEARSCREEN);              /* clear the screen */
  _setvideomode(_DEFAULTMODE);       /* restore the original mode */
#elif Compiler==TurboC                     /* if using Turbo C */
  cleardevice();                          /* clear the screen */
  closegraph();        /* shut down graphics, restore original mode */
#endif
exit(0);}                                /* terminate the program
                                                                      */
```

Fig. 7-13.
Continued.

```
void Graphics_Setup(){          /* autodetect of graphics hardware */
#if Compiler==QuickC
  if (_setvideomoderows(_VRES16COLOR,60)!=FAIL) goto VGA_mode;
  if (_setvideomoderows(_ERESCOLOR,43)!=FAIL) goto EGA_ECD_mode;
  if (_setvideomoderows(_HRES16COLOR,25)!=FAIL) goto EGA_SCD_mode;
  if (_setvideomoderows(_VRES2COLOR,60)!=FAIL) goto MCGA_mode;
  if (_setvideomoderows(_HRESBW,25)!=FAIL) goto CGA_mode;
  if (_setvideomoderows(_HERCMONO,25)!=FAIL) goto Hercules_mode;
#elif Compiler==TurboC
  int graphics_adapter,graphics_mode;
  detectgraph(&graphics_adapter,&graphics_mode);
  if (graphics_adapter==VGA) goto VGA_mode;
  if (graphics_mode==EGAHI) goto EGA_ECD_mode;
  if (graphics_mode==EGALO) goto EGA_SCD_mode;
  if (graphics_adapter==MCGA) goto MCGA_mode;
  if (graphics_adapter==CGA) goto CGA_mode;
  if (graphics_adapter==HERCMONO) goto Hercules_mode;
#endif
goto abort_pgm;                 /* if no graphics hardware found */

VGA_mode:       /* VGA 640x480x16-color mode, 8x8 character matrix */
x_res=640;y_res=480;mode_flag=1;
#if Compiler==QuickC
  _settextcolor(C7);
  _settextposition(1,15);
  _outtext("VGA 640x480x16-color graphics, 80x60 character set");
  _settextposition(59,67);
  _outtext("Press any key");
#elif Compiler==TurboC
  graphics_adapter=VGA;graphics_mode=VGAHI;
  initgraph(&graphics_adapter,&graphics_mode,"");
  settextstyle(0,0,1);setcolor(C7);
  TextRow=1;TextColumn=15;GetTextCoords();
  outtextxy(TextX,TextY,"VGA 640x480x16-color graphics,"
                " 80x60 character set");
  TextRow=59;TextColumn=67;GetTextCoords();
  outtextxy(TextX,TextY,"Press any key");
#endif
return;

EGA_ECD_mode: /* EGA 640x350x16-color mode, 8x8 character matrix */
x_res=640;y_res=350;mode_flag=2;
#if Compiler==QuickC
  _settextcolor(C7);
  _settextposition(1,15);
  _outtext("EGA 640x350x16-color graphics, 80x43 character set");
  _settextposition(43,67);
  _outtext("Press any key");
#elif Compiler==TurboC
  graphics_adapter=EGA;graphics_mode=EGAHI;
  initgraph(&graphics_adapter,&graphics_mode,"");
  settextstyle(0,0,1);setcolor(C7);
  TextRow=1;TextColumn=15;GetTextCoords();
  outtextxy(TextX,TextY,"EGA 640x350x16-color graphics,"
                        " 80x43 character set");
  TextRow=43;TextColumn=67;GetTextCoords();
  outtextxy(TextX,TextY,"Press any key");
#endif
return;

EGA_SCD_mode: /* EGA 640x200x16-color mode, 8x8 character matrix */
x_res=640;y_res=200;mode_flag=3;
#if Compiler==QuickC
  _settextcolor(C7);
  _settextposition(1,15);
  _outtext("EGA 640x200x16-color graphics, 80x25 character set");
  _settextposition(25,67);
  _outtext("Press any key");
#elif Compiler==TurboC
```

Fig. 7-13.
Continued.

```
      graphics_adapter=EGA;graphics_mode=EGALO;
      initgraph(&graphics_adapter,&graphics_mode,"");
      settextstyle(0,0,1);setcolor(C7);
      TextRow=1;TextColumn=15;GetTextCoords();
      outtextxy(TextX,TextY,"EGA 640x200x16-color graphics,"
                            " 80x25 character set");
      TextRow=25;TextColumn=67;GetTextCoords();
      outtextxy(TextX,TextY,"Press any key");
#endif
return;

MCGA_mode:     /* MCGA 640x480x2-color mode, 8x8 character matrix */
x_res=640;y_res=480;C0=0;C1=1;C2=1;C3=1;C4=1;C5=1;C6=1;C7=1;
C8=1;C9=1;C10=1;C11=1;C12=1;C13=1;C14=1;C15=1;mode_flag=4;
#if Compiler==QuickC
  _settextcolor(C7);
  _settextposition(1,15);
  _outtext("MCGA 640x480x2-color graphics, 80x60 character set");
  _settextposition(59,67);
  _outtext("Press any key");
#elif Compiler==TurboC
  graphics_adapter=MCGA;graphics_mode=MCGAHI;
  initgraph(&graphics_adapter,&graphics_mode,"");
  settextstyle(0,0,1);setcolor(C7);
  TextRow=1;TextColumn=15;GetTextCoords();
  outtextxy(TextX,TextY,"MCGA 640x480x2-color graphics,"
                        " 80x60 character set");
  TextRow=59;TextColumn=67;GetTextCoords();
  outtextxy(TextX,TextY,"Press any key");
#endif
return;

CGA_mode:       /* CGA 640x200x2-color mode, 8x8 character matrix */
x_res=640;y_res=200;C0=0;C1=1;C2=1;C3=1;C4=1;C5=1;C6=1;C7=1;
C8=1;C9=1;C10=1;C11=1;C12=1;C13=1;C14=1;C15=1;mode_flag=5;
#if Compiler==QuickC
  _settextcolor(C7);
  _settextposition(1,15);
  _outtext("CGA 640x200x2-color graphics, 80x25 character set");
  _settextposition(25,67);
  _outtext("Press any key");
#elif Compiler==TurboC
  graphics_adapter=CGA;graphics_mode=CGAHI;
  initgraph(&graphics_adapter,&graphics_mode,"");
  settextstyle(0,0,1);setcolor(C7);
  TextRow=1;TextColumn=15;GetTextCoords();
  outtextxy(TextX,TextY,"CGA 640x200x2-color graphics,"
                        " 80x25 character set");
  TextRow=25;TextColumn=67;GetTextCoords();
  outtextxy(TextX,TextY,"Press any key");
#endif
return;

Hercules_mode: /* Hercules 720x348x2-color mode,
                     9x14 character matrix */
x_res=720;y_res=348;C0=0;C1=1;C2=1;C3=1;C4=1;C5=1;C6=1;C7=1;
C8=1;C9=1;C10=1;C11=1;C12=1;C13=1;C14=1;C15=1;mode_flag=6;
#if Compiler==QuickC
  _settextcolor(C7);
  _settextposition(1,15);
  _outtext("Hercules 720x348x2-color graphics,"
                        " 80x25 character set");
  _settextposition(24,67);
  _outtext("Press any key");
#elif Compiler==TurboC
  graphics_adapter=HERCMONO;graphics_mode=HERCMONOHI;
  initgraph(&graphics_adapter,&graphics_mode,"");
  setcolor(C7);
  TextRow=1;TextColumn=15;GetTextCoords();
```

```
      outtextxy(TextX,TextY,"Hercules 720x348x2-color graphics,"
                            " 80x25 character set");
    TextRow=24;TextColumn=67;GetTextCoords();
    outtextxy(TextX,TextY,"Press any key");
#endif
return;

abort_pgm:        /* jump to here if no supported graphics hardware */
printf("\n\nUnable to proceed.\n\r");
printf("Requires VGA, EGA, CGA, MCGA, or\n\r");
printf("Hercules adapter and appropriate monitor.\n\n\r");
exit(0);
}
/*_____*/

void GetTextCoords(){      /* convert QuickC text to Turbo C text */
TextX=(TextColumn*8)-8;TextY=(TextRow*8)-8;return;}
/*_____*/

void Notice(int x, int y){      /* displays the copyright notice */
int copyright[][3]={0x7c00,0x0000,0x0000, /* array of bit styles */
              0x8279,0x819c,0x645e,
              0xba4a,0x4252,0x96d0,
              0xa27a,0x4252,0x955e,
              0xba0a,0x43d2,0xf442,
              0x8219,0x825c,0x945e,
              0x7c00,0x0000,0x0000};
int a,b,c; int t1=0;                         /* local variables */
#if Compiler==QuickC
  for (t1=0;t1<=6;t1++){                    /* draw 7 styled lines */
    a=copyright[t1][0];b=copyright[t1][1];c=copyright[t1][2];
    _setlinestyle(a);_moveto(x,y);_lineto(x+15,y);
    _setlinestyle(b);_moveto(x+16,y);_lineto(x+31,y);
    _setlinestyle(c);_moveto(x+32,y);_lineto(x+47,y);y=y+1;};
  _setlinestyle(0xFFFF);return;
#elif Compiler==TurboC
  for (t1=0;t1<=6;t1++){                    /* draw 7 styled lines */
    a=copyright[t1][0];b=copyright[t1][1];c=copyright[t1][2];
    setlinestyle(USERBIT_LINE,a,NORM_WIDTH);
    moveto(x,y);lineto(x+15,y);
    setlinestyle(USERBIT_LINE,b,NORM_WIDTH);
    moveto(x+16,y);lineto(x+31,y);
    setlinestyle(USERBIT_LINE,c,NORM_WIDTH);
    moveto(x+32,y);lineto(x+47,y);y=y+1;};
  setlinestyle(USERBIT_LINE,0xFFFF,NORM_WIDTH);return;
#endif
}
/*_____

End of source file. */
```

Fig. 7-13.
Continued.

HOW THE PROGRAM WORKS

The main( ) routine contains the important meat of this program. Note how the #if and #elif preprocessor directives are used to separate the font-handling code for QuickC and Turbo C. This paradigm is needed because QuickC and Turbo C use fundamentally different approaches to fonts.

Initializing the Font Table

QuickC uses the _registerfonts( ) function to initialize its internal font-drivers with the filename of the font. This function must be called before any other font

178   2D SOFTWARE SKILLS

functions will work. Next, the _setfont( ) function is called to set the current active font style.

Setting the Current Font

_setfont( ) takes three important arguments: the font style, the vertical height of the font, and the horizontal width. For example, the line:

_setfont("t'fontname',h40,w15");

would activate a font named "fontname," using a height of 40 units and a width of 15 units. Only specific heights and widths are supported. See your manual for permitted values.

Turbo C, on the other hand, combines these two steps into its single settextstyle( ) function. If the font is a vector font, the setusercharsize( ) function is used to set the horizontal and vertical dimensions of the characters. If the font is a bitmapped font, the arguments of the settextstyle( ) function will set the size to one of two supported heights. With a vector font, the size is related as a ratio of the default size. For example, the line:

setusercharsize(4,3,5,2);

sets the horizontal size to 4/3 (or 1.33x) the default width, and sets the vertical size to 5/2 (or 2.5x) the default height.

QuickC employs the outgtext( ) function to write a text string using a font. Turbo C uses the familiar outtext( ).

Sizing Idiosyncracies

It is interesting to note that an infinite range of vertical and horizontal sizes are supported for Turbo C's vector fonts, but only a few sizes are supported for bitmapped fonts. QuickC, on the other hand, offers only half-a-dozen fixed sizes for its vector fonts, but compensates by also offering half-a-dozen sizes for its bitmapped fonts. Clearly, the two compilers are using entirely different algorithms to write their fonts to the screen.

Availability of Font Files

If you are using QuickC to compile and run the demonstration program, be sure that the font files MODERN.FON and TMSRB.FON are in the default drive and directory. If you are using Turbo C to compile and run the demonstration program, be sure that the font files SANS.CHR and TRIP.CHR are in the default drive and directory. As you can see from the main( ) routine in the demonstration program, QuickC explicitly names its font files, while Turbo C uses numbers 0 through 3 to identify a font.

You may find it instructive to tinker with this demonstration program. If you are using QuickC, refer to your user manual to see the various height and width sizes permitted for each font. If you are using Turbo C, try tinkering with the ratios expressed in the setusercharsize( ) function.

8

Program Listing:
Your Microcomputer Sketchpad

THIS CHAPTER contains the complete source code for a full-length, full-featured paint/draw program entitled "Your Microcomputer SketchPad." The program listing is comprised of three C source files: SKETCH1.C, SKETCH2.C, and SKETCH3.C.

The image in FIG. 8-1 shows the sign-on screen for Your Microcomputer SketchPad.

Your Microcomputer SketchPad will run on VGA, EGA, MCGA, CGA, and Hercules graphics adapters. If you are using a VGA, the program will run in the 640x480x16-color graphics mode using 60 rows of text. If you are using an EGA and enhanced monitor, the program will run in the 640x350x16-color graphics mode using 43 rows of text. If you are using an EGA and standard monitor, the program will run in the 640x200x16-color graphics mode using 25 rows of text. If you are using an MCGA, the program will run in the 640x480x2-color graphics mode using 60 rows of text. If you are using a CGA, the program will run in the 640x200x2-color graphics mode using 25 rows of text. If you are using a Hercules graphics adapter, the program will run in the 720x348x2-color graphics mode using 24 rows of text.

The interactive menu system used by the program is controlled by the keyboard. You can load and save images, change various colors, fill patterns, and so on, by using the arrow keys, the Enter key, the Esc key, and the Tab key. To actually draw on the canvas, however, you will need a Microsoft-compatible

180

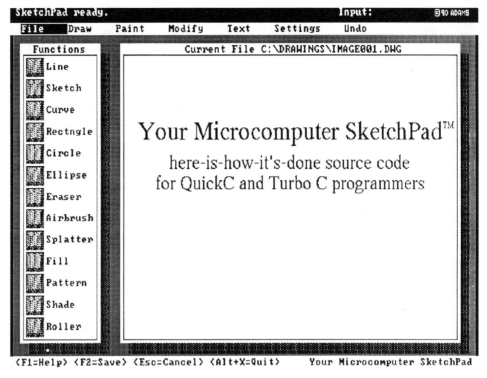

File   Draw   Paint   Modify   Text   Settings   Undo

Functions
Line
Sketch
Curve
Rectngle
Circle
Ellipse
Eraser
Airbrush
Splatter
Fill
Pattern
Shade
Roller

Current File C:\DRAWINGS\IMAGE001.DWG

Your Microcomputer SketchPad™

here-is-how-it's-done source code
for QuickC and Turbo C programmers

<F1=Help> <F2=Save> <Esc=Cancel> <Alt+X=Quit>   Your Microcomputer SketchPad

Fig. 8-1. Print of the start-up image produced by the full-length program listing in this chapter.

mouse or a Kurta-compatible tablet connected to your personal computer. The program will still run without a mouse or tablet present, but the drawing commands cannot be accessed.

The image depicted in FIG. 8-2 is an example of the graphics which can be created by this powerful, full-featured demonstration program. Other examples and tutorial sessions may be found in Chapter 9's mini User's Guide.

The complete source code for Your Microcomputer SketchPad is presented in FIG. 8-3. This program listing is comprised of three separate C source modules, SKETCH1.C, SKETCH2.C, and SKETCH3.C.

HOW TO COMPILE THE PROGRAM

There are four different ways to compile, link, and run this demonstration program. First, you can compile it within the integrated programming environment of QuickC. Second, you can compile it within the integrated programming environment of Turbo C. Third, you can use QuickC's command-line compilation procedure. Fourth, you can use Turbo C's command-line compilation procedure.

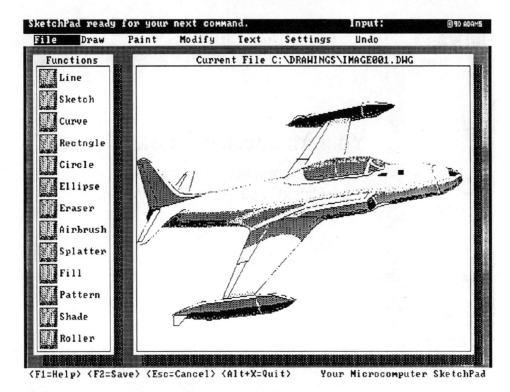

File　　Draw　　Paint　　Modify　　Text　　Settings　　Undo

Functions

Line
Sketch
Curve
Rectngle
Circle
Ellipse
Eraser
Airbrush
Splatter
Fill
Pattern
Shade
Roller

Current File C:\DRAWINGS\IMAGE001.DWG

<F1=Help> <F2=Save> <Esc=Cancel> <Alt+X=Quit>　　　Your Microcomputer SketchPad

Fig. 8-2. Example of graphics which can be produced by the interactive drawing program presented in this chapter.

Fig. 8-3. Source code for Your Microcomputer SketchPad™, a full-featured, interactive paint program which supports VGA, EGA, MCGA, CGA, and Hercules graphics adapters. Refer to Chapter 9 for the user's guide. See Chapter 10 for the programmer's reference. The three modules for this program, SKETCH1.C, SKETCH2.C, and SKETCH3.C, are ready to compile under QuickC or Turbo C.

```
/*                              tm
Your Microcomputer SketchPad              Source file: SKETCH1.C

By: Lee Adams     Version: 1.00     Revision: n/a.
Notices: (c) Copyright 1990 Lee Adams.  All rights reserved.
   Your Microcomputer SketchPad is a trademark of
   TAB Books Inc. and is used by permission.
First published: 1990 by Windcrest Books (div. of TAB Books)

Source notes:  module 1 of 3.  The project list should include
SKETCH1.C, SKETCH2.C, and SKETCH3.C named in QuickC's MAK file
or Turbo C's PRJ file.  At run-time the program expects to find
the appropriate font file in the current directory (TMSRB.FON if
using QuickC, TRIPP.CHR if using Turbo C).

Operation:  demonstrates how to create a full-featured, interactive
draw/paint program with QuickC or Turbo C by using multi-module
programming techniques and device-independent algorithms.
```

Fig. 8-3.
Continued.

Compiler: QuickC or Turbo C integrated programming environment.
Default is QuickC. To use Turbo C change the preprocessor directive
in COMPILER DIRECTIVES (see below). Compile using the medium
memory model. Refer to the book for instructions on command-line
compiling and linking.

Graphics library: QuickC, Turbo C, or third-party add-on library.
Default is QuickC. To use Turbo C graphics library, change the
preprocessor directive in COMPILER DIRECTIVES (see below). To use
a third-party graphics library, refer to the book.

Marketability: will detect and support VGA, EGA, MCGA, CGA, and
Hercules graphics adapters; will detect and support a mouse;
will detect and support a graphics tablet; will save the user's
drawings to disk for export or later editing.

License: As purchaser of the book in which this program is
published, you are granted a non-exclusive royalty-free license
to reproduce and distribute these routines in executable form
as part of your software product, subject to any copyright,
trademark, or patent rights of others, and subject to the limited
warranty described in the introduction of the book. All other
rights reserved.

```
COMPILER DIRECTIVES   */

                        /* compilers and graphics libraries */
#define QuickC      1
#define TurboC      2
#define MicrosoftC 3
#define LatticeC    4
#define HALO        7
#define MetaWINDOW 8
#define Essential   9
#define GSS        10
#define Compiler QuickC          /* change to TurboC if required */
#define GraphicsLibrary QuickC   /* change to library being used */

#define FAIL      0                      /* for graphics auto-detect */
#define CHUNK     32768  /* size of block to attempt to allocate */
#define REMAINDER 255                        /* accuracy limit */
#define ATTEMPTS  40                  /* max number of attempts... */
             /* increase this constant by 40 for each megabyte... */
             /* of extended memory in your system beyond 640K. */

#include <bios.h>                   /* supports keyboard functions */
#include <stdio.h>                     /* supports printf function */
#include <string.h>                 /* supports string manipulation */
#if Compiler==QuickC
  #include <conio.h>                      /* supports QuickC port IO */
  #include <malloc.h>   /* supports memory allocation for arrays */
#elif Compiler==TurboC
  #include <conio.h>                     /* supports text cursor */
  #include <dos.h>                        /* supports TurboC port IO */
  #include <alloc.h>    /* supports memory allocation for arrays */
#endif
#if GraphicsLibrary==QuickC
  #include <graph.h>                      /* QuickC graphics library */
#elif GraphicsLibrary==TurboC
  #include <graphics.h>                  /* Turbo C graphics library */
#endif
#include <process.h>                /* supports the exit function

FUNCTION PROTOTYPES   */

/* ROUTINES IN THIS MODULE */
void Quit_Pgm(void);                 /* ends the program gracefully */
```

```
void Notice(int,int);            /* displays the copyright notice */
void Graphics_Setup(void);       /* initializes the graphics mode */
void SetParameters(void); /* defines sizes, colors for interface */
void DrawScreen(void);     /* creates the user interface graphics */
void CreateBars(void);                   /* creates menu bars */
void CreateButton(void);          /* creates pushbutton array */
void CreateList(void);            /* creates button text list */
void CreateMenus(void);        /* creates the pull-down menus */
void CreateHiBars(void);         /* creates the highlight bars */
void FreeBlock(char far *);    /* deallocate far heap memory */
void InitUndo(void);      /* initializes hidden page for Undo */
void MouseStartUp(void);     /* initializes a mouse, if present */
long GetFreeMemory(void);        /* calculate size of free RAM */


/* ROUTINES IN MODULE 2 CALLED BY THIS MODULE */
void MenuBarLoop(void);    /* manages the menu system at runtime */
void ClearTextLine(void);        /* blanks the dialog text line */


/* ROUTINES IN MODULE 3 CALLED BY THIS MODULE */
void SetHue(int);               /* sets the current drawing color */
void SetLine(int);               /* sets the current line style */
void SetFill(char *, int);       /* sets the area fill style */
void BlankPage(void);          /* blanks the current active page */
void SetPosition(int,int);       /* sets the current xy position */
void DrawLine(int,int);    /* draws line from current xy position */
void DrawBorder(int,int,int,int);            /* draws rectangle */
void DrawPanel(int,int,int,int);       /* draws solid rectangle */
void Fill(int,int,int);                         /* area fill */
char far * MemBlock(int,int,int,int);    /* allocate array memory */
void GetBlock(int,int,int,int,char far *); /* save graphic array */
void PutXOR(int,int,char far *);       /* show XOR graphic array */
void PutPSET(int,int,char far *);     /* show PSET graphic array */
void PutText(int,int,int,char *);               /* display text */
void SetTextRowCol(int,int);            /* set text position */
char far * InitHiddenPage(void);    /* initialize hidden bitmap */
void Mouse_Initialize(void);         /* initializes the mouse */
void Mouse_Show(void);         /* displays the mouse cursor */
void Mouse_Hide(void);            /* hides the mouse cursor */
void Mouse_Setposition(void);    /* resets mouse cursor xy coords */
void Mouse_Status(void); /* checks mouse location, button status */
void Mouse_Setrangeh(void);      /* sets mouse horizontal range */
void Mouse_Setrangev(void);        /* sets mouse vertical range */
void BackUp(void);          /* copies page 0 to hidden page */


/*_____


DECLARATION OF GLOBAL VARIABLES
Visible to all functions in all source files. */

#if GraphicsLibrary==QuickC
  struct videoconfig vc;            /* QuickC's graphics table */
#endif
#if Compiler==TurboC
  struct textsettingstype loadquery;    /* use to test font load */
  extern unsigned _stklen=4096;      /* set stack to 4096 bytes */
#endif   /* (QuickC uses the Utility/Make menu to set stack size */
int C0=0,C1=1,C2=2,C3=3,C4=4,C5=5,C6=6,C7=7,C8=8,C9=9,C10=10,
C11=11,C12=12,C13=13,C14=14,C15=15;             /* color codes */
int x_res=0,y_res=0;                     /* screen resolution */
int mode_flag=0;  /* indicates which graphics mode is being used */
int alpha_x=0,alpha_y=0;      /* dimensions of character matrix */
unsigned int plane_length=0; /* length of bitmap or one bitplane */
int t1x=0,t1y=0,t2x=0,t2y=0,t3x=0,t3y=0,t4x=0,t4y=0;    /* title */
int x1=0,y1=0,x2=0,y2=0;       /* coords for graphic array saves */
int t1=1;      /* loop counter & panning bar position indicator */
int sx=0,sy=0;                          /* current pen position */
int ty1=0,ty2=0,ty3=0;         /* y coord for text list items */
int TextRow=1,TextColumn=1;          /* text position for QuickC */
int TextX=0,TextY=0;               /* text position for Turbo C */
```

Fig. 8-3.
Continued.

Fig. 8-3.
Continued.

```
char keycode=0;    /* flag for NULL, normal, or extended keystroke */
char keynum=0;                        /* ASCII number of keystroke */
char far *menubarBitBlt;               /* menu bar graphic array */
char far *helpbarBitBlt;               /* help bar graphic array */
char far *fileBitBlt;                  /* file name graphic array */
char far *funcBitBlt;                  /* function graphic array */
char far *buttonBitBlt;             /* pushbutton graphic array */
char far *listBitBlt;                 /* on-screen list array */
char far *itemBitBlt;                /* single item in list */
char far *FileMenu;                      /* File Menu array */
char far *ModifyMenu;                  /* Modify Menu array */
char far *TextMenu;                      /* Text Menu array */
char far *SettingsMenu;                /* Settings Menu array */
char far *PanBar;                    /* panning highlight bar */
char far *ScrollBar;               /* scrolling highlight bar */
char far *ButtonBar;        /* scrolling button highlight bar */
char far *swatchprep;       /* preps area for swatch display */
char far *swatchbg;           /* stores area beneath swatch */
int vx1=0,vy1=0,vx2=0,vy2=0;               /* canvas coords */
int clipx1=0,clipy1=0,clipx2=0,clipy2=0;  /* clipping coords */
int ix1=0,iy1=0,ix2=0,iy2=0;            /* icon panel coords */
int shx=0,shy=0;            /* width, depth of dropshadow */
int ox1=0,ox2=0,oy1=0,oy2=0;        /* width, depth of rule */
int bx1=0,by1=0,bx2=0,by2=0;         /* size of pushbutton */
int bxo=0,byo=0;            /* offset to pushbutton top */
int syoffset=0;              /* spacing of pushbuttons */
int numbuttons=0;            /* number of pushbuttons */
int buttoncount=0;      /* calculate button size, position */
int vertspace=0,vertsize=0;  /* calculate button size, position */
int barclr=0,bgclr=0;              /* user interface colors */
int bgtint=0,canvasclr=0;          /* user interface colors */
int shadowclr=0,panelclr=0,ruleclr=0;  /* user interface colors */
int buttonclr=0,buttontint=0;          /* pushbutton colors */
char fill_0[]={0,0,0,0,0,0,0,0};            /*    0% fill */
char fill_3[]={0,32,0,0,0,2,0,0};           /*    3% fill */
char fill_6[]={32,0,2,0,128,0,8,0};         /*    6% fill */
char fill_12[]={32,2,128,8,32,2,128,8};     /*   12% fill */
char fill_25[]={68,17,68,17,68,17,68,17};   /*   25% fill */
char fill_37[]={170,68,170,17,170,68,170,17};  /* 37% fill */
char fill_50[]={85,170,85,170,85,170,85,170};  /* 50% fill */
char fill_62[]={85,187,85,238,85,187,85,238};  /* 62% fill */
char fill_75[]={187,238,187,238,187,238,187,238};  /* 75% fill */
char fill_87[]={223,253,127,247,223,253,127,247};  /* 87% fill */
char fill_93[]={255,223,255,255,255,253,255,255};  /* 93% fill */
char fill_100[]={255,255,255,255,255,255,255,255};  /* 100% fill */
char hatch_1[]={204,204,204,204,204,204,204,204};  /* hatch fill */
char hatch_2[]={240,240,240,240,240,240,240,240};
char hatch_3[]={255,255,0,0,255,255,0,0};
char hatch_4[]={255,255,255,255,0,0,0,0};
char hatch_5[]={24,48,96,192,129,3,6,12};
char hatch_6[]={24,12,6,3,129,192,96,48};
char hatch_7[]={15,15,15,15,240,240,240,240};
char hatch_8[]={255,1,1,1,255,16,16,16};
char hatch_9[]={0,126,66,66,66,66,126,0};
char hatch_10[]={0,126,126,126,126,126,126,0};
char hatch_11[]={130,68,40,16,40,68,130,1};
char hatch_12[]={129,24,24,126,126,24,24,129};
int p1=0,p2=0;        /* install coords for panning highlight bar */
int px1=0,px2=0,px3=0,px4=0,px5=0,px6=0,px7=0;    /* pan coords */
int py1=0,py2=0,py3=0,py4=0,py5=0,py6=0;       /* scroll coords */
int t2=0;             /* position of scrolling highlight bar */
int t3=0;             /* number of choices in active menu */
int p3=0,p4=0;           /* xy install coords for active menu */
int p5=0,p6=0;       /* xy coords for scrolling highlight bar */
int pbg1=0,pbg2=0;   /* width,depth of bg to save under menu */
int status=0;             /* status of level 1 menus logic */
int choice=0;    /* flag to indicate user-selected core function */
int pb1=0,pb2=0;     /* install coords for scrolling button bar */
int pbx1=0;              /* x coord for button bar */
```

Fig. 8-3.
Continued.

```
int pby1=0,pby2=0,pby3=0,pby4=0,pby5=0,pby6=0,pby7=0;
int pby8=0,pby9=0,pby10=0,pby11=0,pby12=0,pby13=0;    /* y coords */
char far * bitmap0;                    /* storage of hidden page in RAM */
char far * bitmap1;
char far * bitmap2;
char far * bitmap3;
union( struct (unsigned int a1; unsigned int a2;) address;
        char far * faraddress;) u1;
unsigned int seg1,seg2,seg3,seg4,off1,off2,off3,off4;
int mouse_flag=0;                         /* indicates if mouse present */
int mouse_button=0;              /* indicates if mouse button pressed */
int mouse_x=0,mouse_y=0;       /* mouse cursor screen coordinates */
int mouse_minx=0,mouse_maxx=0;            /* mouse horizontal range */
int mouse_miny=0,mouse_maxy=0;            /* mouse vertical range */
char Herc=6;                  /* preparatory value for Hercules mode */
char far *HPtr;                    /* will point to Herc variable */
char * textptr;         /* text to be displayed on graphics screen */
char text1[]="SketchPad ready.";
char text2[]="Input:";
char text3[]="Your Microcomputer SketchPad";
char text4[]="Current File C:\\DRAWINGS\\IMAGE001.DWG";
char text5[]="            ";              /* empty string */
char text6[]="Inactive feature. Consult User's Manual.";
char text7[]="SketchPad ready for your next command.";
char text8[]="Insufficient memory available. Press any key.";
char text9[]="Filename to edit:";
char text10[]="Current filename:";
char text11[]="Mouse or tablet required for drawing and painting.";
char text12[]="Undo completed.";
char text13[]="Press Tab to see next choice, Enter to select.";
char text14[]="Access denied.  Font files not found at start-up.";
char text15[]="Font files not found.  Text menu affected.";
long freemem1=0;                      /* size of free RAM available */
struct SREGS segregs;            /* structure of CPU register values */
unsigned int segment=0;          /* value of data segment register */
unsigned int offset=0;           /* destination offset for movedata */
FILE *image_file;                            /* data stream */
char image_buffer[38400]; /* temporary buffer to store bit plane */
char f1[3]="C:";                                      /* drive */
char f2[9]="DRAWINGS";                           /* directory */
char f3[9]="UNTITLED";                           /* filename */
char f4[5]=".DWG";                               /* extension */
char f5[3]="\\";                            /* backward slash */
char f6[13]="UNTITLED.DWG";         /* filename + extension */
char f7[5]=".BLU";
char f8[5]=".GRN";
char f9[5]=".RED";
char f10[5]=".INT";
char f11[2]="X";                           /* instroke carrier */
char f12[9]="UNTITLED";           /* backup storage for edit undo */
            /* current graphics state variables */
int GS_penx=0,GS_peny=0;                 /* current pen position */
int GS_penclr=0,GS_fillclr=0,GS_boundaryclr=0;/* foreground clrs */
int GS_bgclr=0;                          /* background color */
unsigned char * GS_hatch;                  /* hatch pattern */
unsigned char * GS_shade;                  /* halftone pattern */
int GS_text_st=0;                          /* style of font */
int GS_textavail=0;          /* token indicates if font loaded OK */
int GS_text_ht=0,GS_text_wd=0;        /* height, width of font */
int GS_text_clr=0;                        /* color of font */
int GS_text_x=0,GS_text_y=0;          /* xy position of font */
char GS_text_script[81];      /* current message to be fonted */
int hatch_index=0,shade_index=0;
int penclr_index=0,fillclr_index=0,boundary_index=0;
/*_____

FUNCTION DEFINITIONS  */

main(){                          /* this is the master routine */
```

Fig. 8-3.
Continued.

```
Graphics_Setup();                        /* establishes the graphics mode */
#if GraphicsLibrary==QuickC
  _getvideoconfig(&vc);                   /* initialize QuickC's table */
#endif
SetParameters();              /* defines menu system sizes & colors */
CreateBars();                             /* creates the menu bars */
CreateButton();                           /* creates the pushbutton */
CreateList();                    /* creates text list of functions */
CreateMenus();                   /* creates level 1 pull-down menus */
CreateHiBars();        /* creates panning & scrolling highlight bars */
InitUndo();                      /* initializes hidden page for Undo */
DrawScreen();                         /* creates the sign-on screen */
MouseStartUp();          /* sets mouse_flag to 0 if no mouse found */
/*       use this section of code to test memory while prototyping
  #if Compiler==QuickC
    if (GS_textavail==0){
       freemem1=GetFreeMemory();
       SetTextRowCol(1,20);printf("%lu (%u) bytes free.",
                             freemem1,_memavl());}
  #elif Compiler==TurboC
    if (GS_textavail==0){
       freemem1=GetFreeMemory();
       gotoxy(20,1);printf("%lu bytes free.",freemem1);}
  #endif
*/
GS_penx=20;GS_peny=20;                 /* initialize graphics state */
GS_penclr=C0;GS_fillclr=C0;GS_boundaryclr=C0;GS_bgclr=C7;
GS_hatch=hatch_1;GS_shade=fill_50;
hatch_index=1;shade_index=7;
penclr_index=0;fillclr_index=0;boundary_index=0;
#if GraphicsLibrary==TurboC
  GS_fillclr=C1;fillclr_index=1;
  if (mode_flag==5){
    GS_fillclr=C0;fillclr_index=0;}
#endif
MenuBarLoop();                         /* activate the menu system */
Quit_Pgm();                                     /* boilerplate */
}
/*_____*/

void SetParameters(void){  /* define sizes, colors for interface */
vx1=(alpha_x*18)+6;vy1=(alpha_y*2)+18;vx2=x_res-((alpha_x*3)+2);
vy2=y_res-(alpha_y+18);                       /* canvas coords */
ix1=alpha_x+6;iy1=vy1;ix2=vx1-((alpha_x*2)+12);
iy2=vy2;                                  /* icon panel coords */
shx=12;shy=10;                  /* width, depth of dropshadow */
ox1=4;oy1=alpha_y+3;ox2=4;oy2=3;           /* width, depth of rule */
barclr=C7;bgclr=C1;bgtint=C9;canvasclr=C7;shadowclr=C0;
panelclr=C7;ruleclr=C0;
bx1=100;by1=100;bx2=124;by2=118;          /* coords for pushbutton */
bxo=5;byo=4;                            /* offsets for pushbutton */
buttonclr=C4;buttontint=C12;              /* pushbutton colors */
sx=22;sy=48;                  /* install position for pushbutton */
syoffset=21;                  /* vertical spacing for pushbutton */
ty1=alpha_y;                  /* capture position for text items */
ty2=sy;                       /* install position for text items */
ty3=ty2;                 /* final capture position for text items */
numbuttons=13;buttoncount=13;            /* number of pushbuttons */
  vertspace=(iy2-oy2)-(iy1+oy1)-((buttoncount+1)*3);
  vertsize=vertspace/buttoncount;
  by2=by1+vertsize;     /* device-dependent coord for pushbuttons */
  syoffset=vertsize+3;    /* device-dependent spacing forbuttons */
if (mode_flag==6){              /* device-dependent pan spacing */
  px1=17;px2=89;px3=161;px4=242;px5=332;px6=405;px7=512;}
else {px1=15;px2=79;px3=143;px4=215;px5=295;px6=359;px7=455;}
p1=px1;p2=15;      /* initialize coords for panning highlight bar */
if (mode_flag==6){              /* device-dependent scroll spacing */
  py1=38;py2=52;py3=66;py4=80;py5=94;py6=108;}
else {py1=32;py2=40;py3=48;py4=56;py5=64;py6=72;}
```

Fig. 8-3.
Continued.

```
p4=py1-6;                          /* y coord for level 1 pull-down menus */
pb1=sx;pb2=sy;                     /* install position for button bar */
if (mode_flag==6) pb2=pb2+18;              /* if Hercules adapter */
pbx1=pb1;pby1=pb2;                    /* button bar scroll spacing */
pby2=pby1+syoffset;pby3=pby2+syoffset;pby4=pby3+syoffset;
pby5=pby4+syoffset;pby6=pby5+syoffset;pby7=pby6+syoffset;
pby8=pby7+syoffset;pby9=pby8+syoffset;pby10=pby9+syoffset;
pby11=pby10+syoffset;pby12=pby11+syoffset;pby13=pby12+syoffset;
return;}
/*_____*/

void CreateBars(void){                     /* creates bar arrays */
SetHue(C7);SetFill(fill_100,C7);
BlankPage();
strcpy(text5,"File");PutText(2,3,C7,text5);    /* create menu bar */
strcpy(text5,"Draw");PutText(2,11,C7,text5);
strcpy(text5,"Paint");PutText(2,19,C7,text5);
strcpy(text5,"Modify");PutText(2,28,C7,text5);
strcpy(text5,"Text");PutText(2,38,C7,text5);
strcpy(text5,"Settings");PutText(2,46,C7,text5);
strcpy(text5,"Undo");PutText(2,58,C7,text5);
x1=0;y1=alpha_y-2;                      /* upper left coords */
x2=x_res-1;y2=(alpha_y*2)+1;            /* lower right coords */
menubarBitBlt=MemBlock(x1,y1,x2,y2);         /* allocate memory */
GetBlock(x1,y1,x2,y2,menubarBitBlt);
DrawPanel(x1,y1,x2,y2);
PutXOR(x1,y1,menubarBitBlt);
GetBlock(x1,y1,x2,y2,menubarBitBlt);       /* store menubar graphic */
BlankPage();
strcpy(text5,"<F1=Help>");PutText(4,2,C7,text5);
strcpy(text5,"<F2=Save>");PutText(4,12,C7,text5);
strcpy(text5,"<Esc=Cancel>");PutText(4,22,C7,text5);
strcpy(text5,"<Alt+X=Quit>");PutText(4,35,C7,text5);
PutText(4,52,C7,text3);         /* Your Microcomputer SketchPad */
x1=0;y1=(alpha_y*3)-2;
x2=x_res-1;y2=(alpha_y*4)+1;
helpbarBitBlt=MemBlock(x1,y1,x2,y2);         /* allocate memory */
GetBlock(x1,y1,x2,y2,helpbarBitBlt);
DrawPanel(x1,y1,x2,y2);
PutXOR(x1,y1,helpbarBitBlt);
GetBlock(x1,y1,x2,y2,helpbarBitBlt);       /* store helpbar graphic */
BlankPage();
PutText(5,1,C7,text4);                  /* filename display */
x1=0;y1=alpha_y*4;
x2=alpha_x*38;y2=alpha_y*5;
fileBitBlt=MemBlock(x1,y1,x2,y2);            /* allocate memory */
GetBlock(x1,y1,x2,y2,fileBitBlt);
DrawPanel(x1,y1,x2,y2);
PutXOR(x1,y1,fileBitBlt);
GetBlock(x1,y1,x2,y2,fileBitBlt);          /* store filename graphic */
BlankPage();
strcpy(text5,"Functions");PutText(7,1,C7,text5);
x1=0;y1=alpha_y*6;
x2=alpha_x*9;y2=alpha_y*7;
funcBitBlt=MemBlock(x1,y1,x2,y2);            /* allocate memory */
GetBlock(x1,y1,x2,y2,funcBitBlt);
DrawPanel(x1,y1,x2,y2);
PutXOR(x1,y1,funcBitBlt);
GetBlock(x1,y1,x2,y2,funcBitBlt);        /* store functions graphic */
BlankPage();
return;}
/*_____*/

void CreateButton(void){                /* creates the button array */
SetHue(C15);
if (mode_flag>3) DrawPanel(bx1,by1,bx2,by2);
else DrawBorder(bx1,by1,bx2,by2);        /* draw the button cursor */
ButtonBar=MemBlock(bx1,by1,bx2,by2);     /* allocate memory for it */
GetBlock(bx1,by1,bx2,by2,ButtonBar);     /* ...and save the array */
```

Fig. 8-3.
Continued.

```
BlankPage();                        /* ...now draw the sculpted button... */
SetHue(buttonclr);SetFill(fill_100,buttonclr);              /* shadow */
DrawPanel(bx1,by1,bx2,by2);
SetHue(shadowclr);SetFill(fill_62,shadowclr);
DrawPanel(bx1,by1,bx2,by2);
SetHue(C6);SetFill(fill_100,C6);                        /* highlight */
SetPosition(bx1,by1);DrawLine(bx2,by1);
DrawLine(bx1,by2);DrawLine(bx1,by1);
Fill(bx1+2,by1+2,C6);
SetHue(buttonclr);SetFill(fill_100,buttonclr);
SetPosition(bx1,by1);DrawLine(bx2,by1);
DrawLine(bx1,by2);DrawLine(bx1,by1);
Fill(bx1+2,by1+2,buttonclr);
SetHue(buttontint);SetFill(fill_25,buttontint);
SetPosition(bx1,by1);DrawLine(bx2,by1);
DrawLine(bx1,by2);DrawLine(bx1,by1);
Fill(bx1+2,by1+2,buttontint);
SetHue(shadowclr);                                       /* outline */
SetPosition(bx1,by1);DrawLine(bx2,by1);DrawLine(bx1,by2);
DrawLine(bx1,by1);
SetHue(buttonclr);SetFill(fill_100,buttonclr);     /* top surface */
DrawPanel(bx1+bxo,by1+byo,bx2-bxo,by2-byo);
SetHue(buttontint);SetFill(fill_50,buttontint);
DrawPanel(bx1+bxo,by1+byo,bx2-bxo,by2-byo);
buttonBitBlt=MemBlock(bx1,by1,bx2,by2);          /* allocate memory */
GetBlock(bx1,by1,bx2,by2,buttonBitBlt);
BlankPage();
return;}
/*_____*/

void CreateList(void){ /* creates text list of program functions */
SetHue(C7);
strcpy(text5,"Line");PutText(2,4,C7,text5);
strcpy(text5,"Sketch");PutText(3,4,C7,text5);
strcpy(text5,"Curve");PutText(4,4,C7,text5);
strcpy(text5,"Rectngle");PutText(5,4,C7,text5);
strcpy(text5,"Circle");PutText(6,4,C7,text5);
strcpy(text5,"Ellipse");PutText(7,4,C7,text5);
strcpy(text5,"Eraser");PutText(8,4,C7,text5);
strcpy(text5,"Airbrush");PutText(9,4,C7,text5);
strcpy(text5,"Splatter");PutText(10,4,C7,text5);
strcpy(text5,"Fill");PutText(11,4,C7,text5);
strcpy(text5,"Pattern");PutText(12,4,C7,text5);
strcpy(text5,"Shade");PutText(13,4,C7,text5);
strcpy(text5,"Roller");PutText(14,4,C7,text5);
x2=alpha_x*3;y1=alpha_y;
x2=(alpha_x*11)-1;y2=(alpha_y*2)-1;
itemBitBlt=MemBlock(x1,y1,x2,y2);                /* allocate memory */
for (t1=1;t1<=13;t1++){
  GetBlock(x1,ty1,x2,ty1+(alpha_y-1),itemBitBlt);
  PutPSET(x_res/2,ty2,itemBitBlt);
  ty1=ty1+alpha_y;ty2=ty2+syoffset;}
FreeBlock(itemBitBlt);                    /* deallocate memory block */
ty2=ty2-syoffset;ty2=ty2+(alpha_y-1);
x1=x_res/2;x2=x1+((alpha_x*8)-1);
listBitBlt=MemBlock(x1,ty3,x2,ty2);              /* allocate memory */
GetBlock(x1,ty3,x2,ty2,listBitBlt);
BlankPage();
return;}
/*_____*/

void CreateMenus(void){                 /* creates the pull-down menus */
strcpy(text5,"New");PutText(2,4,C7,text5);
strcpy(text5,"Load...");PutText(3,4,C7,text5);
strcpy(text5,"Save");PutText(4,4,C7,text5);
strcpy(text5,"Save as...");PutText(5,4,C7,text5);
strcpy(text5,"Delete...");PutText(6,4,C7,text5);
strcpy(text5,"Shutdown");PutText(7,4,C7,text5);
x1=alpha_x*2;y1=alpha_y-6;
```

Fig. 8-3.
Continued.

```
x2=x1+((alpha_x*12)-1);y2=y1+((alpha_y*6)+11);
pbg1=x2-x1;pbg2=y2-y1; /* width, depth of bg to save under menus */
FileMenu=MemBlock(x1,y1,x2,y2);                    /* allocate memory */
GetBlock(x1,y1,x2,y2,FileMenu);            /* temporary store of text */
SetHue(C7);SetFill(fill_100,C7);
DrawPanel(x1,y1,x2,y2);                                /* menu panel */
SetHue(C0);DrawBorder(x1+2,y1+2,x2-2,y2-2);             /* rule trim */
DrawBorder(x1,y1,x2,y2);                              /* border trim */
PutXOR(x1,y1,FileMenu);                        /* xor text onto menu */
GetBlock(x1,y1,x2,y2,FileMenu);               /* File Menu is done */
BlankPage();
strcpy(text5,"Copy...");PutText(2,4,C7,text5);
strcpy(text5,"Move...");PutText(3,4,C7,text5);
strcpy(text5,"Cut...");PutText(4,4,C7,text5);
strcpy(text5,"Paste...");PutText(5,4,C7,text5);
y2=y2-(alpha_y*2);
ModifyMenu=MemBlock(x1,y1,x2,y2);                  /* allocate memory */
GetBlock(x1,y1,x2,y2,ModifyMenu);          /* temporary store of text */
SetHue(C7);SetFill(fill_100,C7);
DrawPanel(x1,y1,x2,y2);                                /* menu panel */
SetHue(C0);DrawBorder(x1+2,y1+2,x2-2,y2-2);             /* rule trim */
DrawBorder(x1,y1,x2,y2);                              /* border trim */
PutXOR(x1,y1,ModifyMenu);                      /* xor text onto menu */
GetBlock(x1,y1,x2,y2,ModifyMenu);          /* Modify Menu is done */
BlankPage();
strcpy(text5,"Height...");PutText(2,4,C7,text5);
strcpy(text5,"Width...");PutText(3,4,C7,text5);
strcpy(text5,"Sans serif");PutText(4,4,C7,text5);
strcpy(text5,"Serif");PutText(5,4,C7,text5);
TextMenu=MemBlock(x1,y1,x2,y2);                    /* allocate memory */
GetBlock(x1,y1,x2,y2,TextMenu);            /* temporary store of text */
SetHue(C7);SetFill(fill_100,C7);
DrawPanel(x1,y1,x2,y2);                                /* menu panel */
SetHue(C0);DrawBorder(x1+2,y1+2,x2-2,y2-2);             /* rule trim */
DrawBorder(x1,y1,x2,y2);                              /* border trim */
PutXOR(x1,y1,TextMenu);                        /* xor text onto menu */
GetBlock(x1,y1,x2,y2,TextMenu);               /* Text Menu is done */
BlankPage();
strcpy(text5,"Active clr");PutText(2,4,C7,text5);
strcpy(text5,"Fill clr");PutText(3,4,C7,text5);
strcpy(text5,"Boundary");PutText(4,4,C7,text5);
strcpy(text5,"Pattern");PutText(5,4,C7,text5);
strcpy(text5,"Shade");PutText(6,4,C7,text5);
y2=y2+alpha_y;
SettingsMenu=MemBlock(x1,y1,x2,y2);                /* allocate memory */
GetBlock(x1,y1,x2,y2,SettingsMenu);        /* temporary store of text */
SetHue(C7);SetFill(fill_100,C7);
DrawPanel(x1,y1,x2,y2);                                /* menu panel */
SetHue(C0);DrawBorder(x1+2,y1+2,x2-2,y2-2);             /* rule trim */
DrawBorder(x1,y1,x2,y2);                              /* border trim */
PutXOR(x1,y1,SettingsMenu);                    /* xor text onto menu */
GetBlock(x1,y1,x2,y2,SettingsMenu);        /* Settings Menu is done */
BlankPage();
return;}
/*_____*/

void CreateHiBars(void){       /* creates the menu highlight bars */
SetHue(C7);SetFill(fill_100,C7);
x1=0;y1=0;
x2=(alpha_x*8)-1;y2=alpha_y+1;
DrawPanel(x1,y1,x2,y2);
PanBar=MemBlock(x1,y1,x2,y2);                      /* allocate memory */
GetBlock(x1,y1,x2,y2,PanBar);         /* store panning highlight bar */
x1=0;y1=0;
if (mode_flag==6){x2=(alpha_x*11)+2;}
else {x2=(alpha_x*11)+1;}
y2=alpha_y-1;
DrawPanel(x1,y1,x2,y2);
ScrollBar=MemBlock(x1,y1,x2,y2);                   /* allocate memory */
```

Fig. 8-3.
Continued.

```
GetBlock(x1,y1,x2,y2,ScrollBar);/* store scrolling highlight bar */
DrawPanel(0,0,50,50);
swatchprep=MemBlock(0,0,50,50);
GetBlock(0,0,50,50,swatchprep);                  /* store swatch prep */
swatchbg=MemBlock(0,0,50,50);
GetBlock(0,0,50,50,swatchbg);           /* initialize swatch bg saver */
BlankPage();
return;}
/*_____*/

void DrawScreen(void){                  /* creates the sign-on screen */
SetHue(bgclr);SetFill(fill_100,bgclr);
DrawPanel(4,14,x_res-5,y_res-1);                          /* bg prep */
#if GraphicsLibrary==QuickC
  SetHue(bgtint);SetFill(fill_0,bgtint);       /* optional overlay */
  DrawPanel(4,14,x_res-5,y_res-1);           /* finished backgrnd */
#endif
if (mode_flag>3){              /* if bw mode on CGA, MCGA, or Herc */
  SetHue(C0);SetFill(fill_100,C0);
  DrawPanel(4,14,x_res-5,y_res-1);
  SetHue(bgclr);SetFill(fill_50,bgclr);
  DrawPanel(4,14,x_res-5,y_res-1);}
PutPSET(0,14,menubarBitBlt);                    /* install menu bar */
FreeBlock(menubarBitBlt);             /* deallocate memory block */
if (mode_flag==6){
  PutPSET(0,y_res-18,helpbarBitBlt);}
else {PutPSET(0,y_res-12,helpbarBitBlt);}     /* install help bar */
FreeBlock(helpbarBitBlt);             /* deallocate memory block */
#if GraphicsLibrary==QuickC
  SetHue(bgclr);SetFill(fill_100,bgclr);     /* icon shadow prep */
  DrawPanel(ix1+shx,iy1+shy,ix2+shx,iy2+shy);
  SetHue(shadowclr);SetFill(fill_75,shadowclr);   /* icon shadow */
  DrawPanel(ix1+shx,iy1+shy,ix2+shx,iy2+shy);
#elif GraphicsLibrary==TurboC
  SetHue(bgclr);SetFill(fill_25,bgclr);
  DrawPanel(ix1+shx,iy1+shy,ix2+shx,iy2+shy);      /* icon shadow */
#endif
SetHue(panelclr);SetFill(fill_100,panelclr);        /* icon panel */
DrawPanel(ix1,iy1,ix2,iy2);
SetHue(ruleclr);                                   /* icon panel rule */
DrawBorder(ix1+ox1,iy1+oy1,ix2-ox2,iy2-oy2);
#if GraphicsLibrary==QuickC
  SetHue(bgclr);SetFill(fill_100,bgclr);   /* canvas shadow prep */
  DrawPanel(vx1+shx,vy1+shy,vx2+shx,vy2+shy);
  SetHue(shadowclr);SetFill(fill_75,shadowclr); /* canvas shadow */
  DrawPanel(vx1+shx,vy1+shy,vx2+shx,vy2+shy);
#elif GraphicsLibrary==TurboC
  SetHue(bgclr);SetFill(fill_25,bgclr);
  DrawPanel(vx1+shx,vy1+shy,vx2+shx,vy2+shy);   /* canvas shadow */
#endif
SetHue(canvasclr);SetFill(fill_100,canvasclr);          /* canvas */
DrawPanel(vx1,vy1,vx2,vy2);
SetHue(ruleclr);                                    /* canvas rule */
DrawBorder(vx1+ox1,vy1+oy1,vx2-ox2,vy2-oy2);
PutPSET(32,iy1+2,funcBitBlt);                       /* Function */
FreeBlock(funcBitBlt);                /* deallocate memory block */
PutPSET(238,vy1+2,fileBitBlt);                       /* filename */
SetHue(C7);Notice(x_res-60,1);                      /* copyright */
PutText(1,2,C7,text1);                       /* SketchPad ready. */
PutText(1,57,C7,text2);                                /* Input: */
ty1=sy;                                           /* realign ty1 */
if (mode_flag==6){sy=sy+18;}            /* if Hercules mode */
for (t1=1;t1<=numbuttons;t1++){
  PutPSET(sx,sy,buttonBitBlt);              /* install pushbutton */
  sy=sy+syoffset;}
sx=sx+((bx2-bx1)+4);            /* realign list install coord */
switch (mode_flag){                    /* adjust install coord */
  case 1: ty1=ty1+10;break;            /* 640x480x16 VGA mode */
  case 2: ty1=ty1+5;break;             /* 640x350x16 EGA mode */
```

Fig. 8-3.
Continued.

```
  case 3: break;                                /* 640x200x16 EGA mode */
  case 4: ty1=ty1+5;break;                      /* 640x480x2 MCGA mode */
  case 5: break;                                /* 640x200x2 CGA mode  */
  case 6: ty1=ty1+20;break;                     /* 720x348x2 Herc mode */
  default: break;}
PutXOR(sx,ty1,listBitBlt);                              /* install list */
FreeBlock(listBitBlt);                      /* deallocate memory block */
clipx1=(vx1+ox1)+1;clipy1=(vy1+oy1)+1;      /* set clipping coords */
clipx2=(vx2-ox2)-1;clipy2=(vy2-oy2)-1;      /* set clipping coords */
BackUp();                                /* store backup page for Undo */
#if Compiler==QuickC
  GS_textavail=_registerfonts("TMSRB.FON");    /* init font table */
  if (GS_textavail==-1){             /* if cannot find font file... */
    ClearTextLine();PutText(1,2,C7,text15);goto debug1;}
  GS_textavail=0;
  _setfont("t'tms rmn',h26,w16");      /* pick Times Roman typeface */
  _setcolor(C0);                              /* set color to black */
  _moveto(t1x,t1y);_outgtext("Your Microcomputer SketchPad");
  _setfont("t'tms rmn',h10,w5");
  _setcolor(C0);_moveto(t2x,t2y);_outgtext("TM");
  _setfont("t'tms rmn',h20,w12");
  _moveto(t3x,t3y);_outgtext("here-is-how-it's-done source code");
  _moveto(t4x,t4y);_outgtext("for QuickC and Turbo C programmers");
  _unregisterfonts();                        /* free up font memory */
#elif Compiler==TurboC
  settextstyle(1,HORIZ_DIR,0);                        /* set typeface */
  gettextsettings(&loadquery);
  if(loadquery.font!=1){        /* if font file was not found... */
    GS_textavail=-1;
    settextstyle(DEFAULT_FONT,HORIZ_DIR,1);
    ClearTextLine();PutText(1,2,C7,text15);goto debug1;}
  setcolor(C0);                              /* set type color */
  setusercharsize(55,64,7,8);                        /* set type size */
  moveto(t1x,t1y);outtext("Your Microcomputer SketchPad");
  setusercharsize(1,3,1,3);
  moveto(t2x,t2y);outtext("TM");
  setusercharsize(15,24,8,12);
  moveto(t3x,t3y);outtext("here-is-how-it's-done source code");
  moveto(t4x,t4y);outtext("for QuickC and Turbo C programmers");
  settextstyle(DEFAULT_FONT,HORIZ_DIR,1);/* restore default font */
#endif
debug1:
#if GraphicsLibrary==QuickC
  _setviewport(0,0,x_res-1,y_res-1);          /* clipping viewport */
#elif GraphicsLibrary==TurboC
  setviewport(0,0,x_res-1,y_res-1,1);          /* clipping viewport */
#endif
return;}
/*_____*/

void InitUndo(void){       /* initialize hidden page for Undo */
switch(mode_flag){
  case 1: bitmap0=InitHiddenPage();                /* 640x480x16 */
          u1.faraddress=bitmap0;
          seg1=u1.address.a2;off1=u1.address.a1;
          bitmap1=InitHiddenPage();
          u1.faraddress=bitmap1;
          seg2=u1.address.a2;off2=u1.address.a1;
          bitmap2=InitHiddenPage();
          u1.faraddress=bitmap2;
          seg3=u1.address.a2;off3=u1.address.a1;
          bitmap3=InitHiddenPage();
          u1.faraddress=bitmap3;
          seg4=u1.address.a2;off4=u1.address.a1;break;
  case 2: break;                                   /* 640x350x16 */
  case 3: break;                                   /* 640x200x16 */
  case 4: bitmap0=InitHiddenPage();                /* 640x480x2  */
          u1.faraddress=bitmap0;
          seg1=u1.address.a2;off1=u1.address.a1;break;
```

Fig. 8-3.
Continued.

```
      case 5: bitmap0=InitHiddenPage();                /* 640x200x2  */
              u1.faraddress=bitmap0;
              seg1=u1.address.a2;off1=u1.address.a1;break;
      case 6: break;}                                  /* 720x348x2  */
return;}
/*_____*/

void MouseStartUp(void){        /* initializes a mouse, if present */
mouse_minx=clipx1;mouse_miny=clipy1;        /* set minimum range */
mouse_maxx=clipx2;mouse_maxy=clipy2;        /* set maximum range */
mouse_x=mouse_minx+50;mouse_y=mouse_miny+50; /* set mouse coords */
Mouse_Initialize();             /* attempt to initialize the mouse */
if (mouse_flag==0) return;              /* abort if no mouse found */
Mouse_Setrangeh();Mouse_Setrangev();Mouse_Setposition();
sx=mouse_x;sy=mouse_y;        /* initialize current pen position */
return;}
/*_____*/

void Quit_Pgm(void){                     /* terminates the program */
#if GraphicsLibrary==QuickC                     /* if using QuickC */
  _clearscreen(_GCLEARSCREEN);               /* clear the screen */
  _setvideomode(_DEFAULTMODE);        /* restore the original mode */
#elif GraphicsLibrary==TurboC                    /* if using Turbo C */
  cleardevice();                             /* clear the screen */
  closegraph();        /* shut down graphics, restore original mode */
#endif
exit(0);}                                 /* terminate the program */
/*_____*/

void FreeBlock(char far *blk){       /* deallocate far heap block */
#if GraphicsLibrary==QuickC
  _ffree(blk);
#elif GraphicsLibrary==TurboC
  farfree(blk);
#endif
return;}
/*_____*/

void Graphics_Setup(void){    /* autodetect of graphics hardware */
#if GraphicsLibrary==QuickC
/*  if (_setvideomoderows(_VRES16COLOR,60)!=FAIL) goto VGA_mode; */
  if (_setvideomoderows(_ERESCOLOR,43)!=FAIL) goto EGA_ECD_mode;
  if (_setvideomoderows(_HRES16COLOR,25)!=FAIL) goto EGA_SCD_mode;
  if (_setvideomoderows(_VRES2COLOR,60)!=FAIL) goto MCGA_mode;
  if (_setvideomoderows(_HRESBW,25)!=FAIL) goto CGA_mode;
  if (_setvideomoderows(_HERCMONO,25)!=FAIL) goto Hercules_mode;
#elif GraphicsLibrary==TurboC
  int graphics_adapter,graphics_mode;
  detectgraph(&graphics_adapter,&graphics_mode);
  if (graphics_adapter==VGA){
      graphics_adapter=VGA;graphics_mode=VGAHI;
      initgraph(&graphics_adapter,&graphics_mode,"");
      settextstyle(0,0,1);
      goto VGA_mode;}
  if (graphics_mode==EGAHI){
      graphics_adapter=EGA;graphics_mode=EGAHI;
      initgraph(&graphics_adapter,&graphics_mode,"");
      settextstyle(0,0,1);
      goto EGA_ECD_mode;}
  if (graphics_mode==EGALO){
      graphics_adapter=EGA;graphics_mode=EGALO;
      initgraph(&graphics_adapter,&graphics_mode,"");
      settextstyle(0,0,1);
      goto EGA_SCD_mode;}
  if (graphics_adapter==MCGA){
      graphics_adapter=MCGA;graphics_mode=MCGAHI;
      initgraph(&graphics_adapter,&graphics_mode,"");
      settextstyle(0,0,1);
      goto MCGA_mode;}
```

Fig. 8-3.
Continued.

```
        if (graphics_adapter==CGA){
            graphics_adapter=CGA;graphics_mode=CGAHI;
            initgraph(&graphics_adapter,&graphics_mode,"");
            settextstyle(0,0,1);
            goto CGA_mode;}
        if (graphics_adapter==HERCMONO){
            graphics_adapter=HERCMONO;graphics_mode=HERCMONOHI;
            initgraph(&graphics_adapter,&graphics_mode,"");
            goto Hercules_mode;}
#endif
goto abort_pgm;                     /* if no graphics hardware found */

/* ASSIGN MODE-DEPENDENT VARIABLES AND TEST EGA DISPLAY MEMORY    */
VGA_mode:       /* VGA 640x480x16-color mode, 8x8 character matrix */
x_res=640;y_res=480;mode_flag=1;
t1x=174;t1y=128;t2x=590;t2y=128;t3x=216;t3y=160;t4x=198;t4y=180;
alpha_x=8;alpha_y=8;plane_length=38400;return;
EGA_ECD_mode: /* EGA 640x350x16-color mode, 8x8 character matrix */
#if GraphicsLibrary==QuickC
    if (_setactivepage(1)<0){            /* if no page 1 found... */
        _setvideomoderows(_HRES16COLOR,25);
        goto EGA_SCD_mode;}              /* ...try a different mode */
    _setactivepage(0);               /* else reset active page to 0 */
#endif      /* Turbo C's detectgraph has already confirmed this */
x_res=640;y_res=350;mode_flag=2;
t1x=174;t1y=108;t2x=590;t2y=108;t3x=216;t3y=140;t4x=198;t4y=160;
alpha_x=8;alpha_y=8;plane_length=28000;return;
EGA_SCD_mode: /* EGA 640x200x16-color mode, 8x8 character matrix */
#if GraphicsLibrary==QuickC
    if (_setactivepage(1)<0){            /* if no page 1 found... */
        _setvideomoderows(_HRESBW,25);
        goto CGA_mode;}                  /* ...try a different mode */
    _setactivepage(0);               /* ...else reset active page to 0 */
#endif      /* Turbo C's detectgraph has already confirmed this */
x_res=640;y_res=200;mode_flag=3;
t1x=174;t1y=78;t2x=590;t2y=78;t3x=216;t3y=110;t4x=198;t4y=130;
alpha_x=8;alpha_y=8;plane_length=16000;return;
MCGA_mode:      /* MCGA 640x480x2-color mode, 8x8 character matrix */
x_res=640;y_res=480;mode_flag=4;
C0=0;C1=1;C2=1;C3=1;C4=1;C5=1;C6=1;C7=1;
C8=1;C9=1;C10=1;C11=1;C12=1;C13=1;C14=1;C15=1;
t1x=174;t1y=128;t2x=590;t2y=128;t3x=216;t3y=160;t4x=198;t4y=180;
alpha_x=8;alpha_y=8;plane_length=38400;return;
CGA_mode:       /* CGA 640x200x2-color mode, 8x8 character matrix */
x_res=640;y_res=200;mode_flag=5;
C0=0;C1=1;C2=1;C3=1;C4=1;C5=1;C6=1;C7=1;
C8=1;C9=1;C10=1;C11=1;C12=1;C13=1;C14=1;C15=1;
t1x=174;t1y=78;t2x=590;t2y=78;t3x=216;t3y=110;t4x=198;t4y=130;
alpha_x=8;alpha_y=8;plane_length=16384;return;
Hercules_mode:  /* Hercules 720x348x2-color mode, 9x14 character */
x_res=720;y_res=348;mode_flag=6;
C0=0;C1=1;C2=1;C3=1;C4=1;C5=1;C6=1;C7=1;
C8=1;C9=1;C10=1;C11=1;C12=1;C13=1;C14=1;C15=1;
t1x=216;t1y=108;t2x=634;t2y=108;t3x=263;t3y=140;t4x=244;t4y=160;
alpha_x=9;alpha_y=14;plane_length=32406;return;

abort_pgm:      /* jump to here if no supported graphics hardware */
printf("\n\n\rUnable to proceed.\n\r");
printf("Requires VGA, EGA, CGA, MCGA, or\n\r");
printf("Hercules adapter and appropriate monitor.\n\n\r");
exit(0);
}
/*_____*/

long GetFreeMemory(void){            /* determine size of free RAM */
    int c1=0;unsigned block=0;long totalmem=0;
    char far * vptr;char far * vptrarray[ATTEMPTS];
c1=0;totalmem=0;block=CHUNK;
#if Compiler==QuickC
```

Fig. 8-3.
Continued.

```
    while (block>REMAINDER){
      if((vptr=(char far *)_fmalloc(block))!=NULL){
        vptrarray[c1]=vptr;totalmem=totalmem+block;c1++;}
      else block=block/2;}
    for ( ;c1;c1--){
    _ffree(vptrarray[c1-1]);}
#elif Compiler==TurboC
    while (block>REMAINDER){
      if((vptr=(char far *)farmalloc(block))!=NULL){
        vptrarray[c1]=vptr;totalmem=totalmem+block;c1++;}
      else block=block/2;}
    for ( ;c1;c1--){
      farfree(vptrarray[c1-1]);}
#endif
return totalmem;}
/*_____*/

void Notice(int x,int y){        /* displays the copyright notice */
int copyright[][3]={0x7c00,0x0000,0x0000, /* array of bit styles */
                    0x8279,0x819c,0x645e,
                    0xba4a,0x4252,0x96d0,
                    0xa27a,0x4252,0x955e,
                    0xba0a,0x43d2,0xf442,
                    0x8219,0x825c,0x945e,
                    0x7c00,0x0000,0x0000};
int a,b,c; int t1=0;                     /* local variables */
for (t1=0;t1<=6;t1++){                   /* draw 7 styled lines */
  a=copyright[t1][0];b=copyright[t1][1];c=copyright[t1][2];
  SetLine(a);SetPosition(x,y);DrawLine(x+15,y);
  SetLine(b);SetPosition(x+16,y);DrawLine(x+31,y);
  SetLine(c);SetPosition(x+32,y);DrawLine(x+47,y);y=y+1;);
SetLine(0xFFFF);return;
}
/*_____
```

Module two
begins here

```
End of Module 1 source code.  (This program has 3 modules.) */
/*                    tm
Your Microcomputer SketchPad              Source file: SKETCH2.C

By: Lee Adams    Version: 1.00    Revision: n/a.
Notices: (c) Copyright 1990 Lee Adams.  All rights reserved.
   Your Microcomputer SketchPad is a trademark of
   TAB Books Inc. and is used by permission.
First published: 1990 by Windcrest Books (div. of TAB Books Inc.)

Source notes:  module 2 of 3.  The project list should include
SKETCH1.C, SKETCH2.C, and SKETCH3.C named in QuickC's MAK file
or Turbo C's PRJ file.

Operation:  provides menu system management routines and
core functions for the run-time environment established by module 1.

Compiler:  QuickC or Turbo C integrated programming environment.
Default is QuickC. To use Turbo C change the preprocessor directive
in COMPILER DIRECTIVES (see below).  Compile using the medium
memory model.  Refer to the book for instructions on command-line
compiling and linking.

Graphics library:  QuickC, Turbo C, or third-party add-on library.
Default is QuickC.  To use Turbo C graphics library, change the
preprocessor directive in COMPILER DIRECTIVES (see below).  To use
a third-party graphics library, refer to the book.

License:  As purchaser of the book in which this program is
published, you are granted a non-exclusive royalty-free license
to reproduce and distribute these routines in executable form
as part of your software product, subject to any copyright,
trademark, or patent rights of others, and subject to the limited
```

warranty described in the introduction of the book. All other
rights reserved.

Fig. 8-3.
Continued.

```
COMPILER DIRECTIVES  */

                    /* compilers and graphics libraries */
#define QuickC      1
#define TurboC      2
#define MicrosoftC 3
#define LatticeC    4
#define HALO        7
#define MetaWINDOW 8
#define Essential   9
#define GSS         10

#define Compiler QuickC          /* change to TurboC if required */
#define GraphicsLibrary QuickC   /* change to library being used */

#define EMPTY     0              /* for checking keyboard buffer */
#define ACTIVE    1                      /* menu system status */
#define BACKOUT   2                      /* menu system status */
#define STUB      3                      /* menu system status */
#include <bios.h>             /* supports keyboard functions */
#include <stdio.h>                  /* supports printf function */
#include <string.h>          /* supports string manipulation */
#if Compiler==QuickC
  #include <conio.h>                  /* supports QuickC port IO */
  #include <malloc.h>    /* supports memory allocation for arrays */
#elif Compiler==TurboC
  #include <dos.h>                     /* supports TurboC port IO */
  #include <alloc.h>     /* supports memory allocation for arrays */
#endif
#if GraphicsLibrary==QuickC
  #include <graph.h>                 /* QuickC graphics library */
#elif GraphicsLibrary==TurboC
  #include <graphics.h>              /* Turbo C graphics library */
#endif
#include <process.h>              /* supports the exit function
```

```
FUNCTION PROTOTYPES  */

/* MENU MANAGEMENT ROUTINES IN THIS MODULE */
void MenuBarLoop(void);     /* manages the menu system at runtime */
void CheckForKey(void);             /* checks for user keystrokes */
void KeySwitch1(void);    /* manages keystrokes at menu bar level */
void Panning(void);          /* moves the panning highlight bar */
void Purge(void);                 /* empties the keyboard buffer */
void InstallMenu(void); /* installs a level 1 menu on the screen */
void UninstallMenu(void);/* removes level 1 menu from the screen */
void PanMenu(void);             /* manages inter-menu panning */
void Scrolling(void);        /* manages scrolling highlight bar */
void KeySwitch2(void);    /* manages keystrokes for level 1 menus */
void MenuChoices(void); /* calls pgm functions for level 1 menus */
void StubRoutine(void);     /* do-nothing stub for prototyping */
void MenuBarText(void);      /* back-out stub for prototyping */
void ClearTextLine(void);     /* blanks the dialog text line */
void MakeSound(int,int);             /* generates a sound */
void GetTextCoords(void); /* convert QuickC text to Turbo C text */
void MouseManager(void);            /* mouse polling loop */
void Delayed(void);     /* timing delay for mouse double-hits */
void EditName(void);            /* allows user to edit filename */
void ButtonScroll(void);    /* controls scrolling button cursor */
void EditColor(void);    /* allows user to alter colors, patterns */

/* ROUTINES IN MODULE 3 CALLED BY THIS MODULE */
void SetHue(int);               /* sets the current drawing color */
void SetLine(int);               /* sets the current line style */
```

Fig. 8-3.
Continued.

```
void SetFill(char *, int);              /* sets the area fill style */
void BlankPage(void);              /* blanks the current active page */
void SetPosition(int,int);            /* sets the current xy position */
void DrawLine(int,int);    /* draws line from current xy position */
void DrawBorder(int,int,int,int);              /* draws rectangle */
void DrawPanel(int,int,int,int);           /* draws solid rectangle */
void Fill(int,int,int);                               /* area fill */
char far * MemBlock(int,int,int,int);    /* allocate array memory */
void GetBlock(int,int,int,int,char far *); /* save graphic array */
void PutXOR(int,int,char far *);         /* show XOR graphic array */
void PutPSET(int,int,char far *);       /* show PSET graphic array */
void PutText(int,int,int,char *);                  /* display text */
void SetTextRowCol(int,int);               /* set text position */
char far * InitHiddenPage(void);       /* initialize hidden bitmap */
void BackUp(void);              /* copies page 0 to hidden page */
void Restore(void);             /* copies hidden page to page 0 */
void Mouse_Initialize(void);             /* initializes the mouse */
void Mouse_Show(void);             /* displays the mouse cursor */
void Mouse_Hide(void);               /* hides the mouse cursor */
void Mouse_Setposition(void);     /* resets mouse cursor xy coords */
void Mouse_Status(void); /* checks mouse location, button status */
void Mouse_Setrangeh(void);        /* sets mouse horizontal range */
void Mouse_Setrangev(void);          /* sets mouse vertical range */
void SaveImage(void);                    /* prep for image save */
void LoadImage(void);                    /* prep for image load */
void SaveVGAEGAImage(void);     /* saves VGA or EGA image to disk */
void LoadVGAEGAImage(void);   /* loads VGA or EGA image from disk */
void SaveCGAimage(void);             /* saves CGA image to disk */
void LoadCGAimage(void);           /* loads CGA image from disk */
void SaveHGAimage(void);         /* saves Hercules image to disk */
void LoadHGAimage(void);       /* loads Hercules image from disk */
void SaveMCGAimage(void);            /* saves MCGA image to disk */
void LoadMCGAimage(void);          /* loads MCGA image from disk */
void WindowOpen(int,int,int,int);             /* opens viewport */
void WindowClose(int,int);               /* shut down viewport */
void WindowClear(int);                  /* blanks the viewport */
void GetWindowCoords(int,int);/* convert phys coords to viewport */
void WriteToPage(int);                     /* sets active page */
void DisplayPage(int);                    /* sets visible page */
void DrawDot(int,int);                          /* draws dot */
void DrawCircle(int,int,int);           /* draws outline circle */
void DrawDisk(int,int,int);              /* draws filled circle */
void DrawEllipse(int,int,int,int);      /* draws outline ellipse */
void DrawSolidEllipse(int,int,int,int);  /* draws filled ellipse */
void DrawCurve(int,int,int,int,int,int,int,int);  /* draws curve */

/* ROUTINES IN MODULE 1 CALLED BY THIS MODULE */
void Quit_Pgm(void);             /* ends the program gracefully */
void FreeBlock(char far *);       /* deallocate far heap memory */
/*_____*/

/* DECLARATION OF GLOBAL VARIABLES */
char far *SaveBgd;   /* array to save background under each menu */

/* RE-DECLARATION OF GLOBAL VARIABLES initialized in Module 1,
but also visible to all functions in this source file. */
#if GraphicsLibrary==QuickC
  extern struct vc;
#endif
extern int C0,C1,C2,C3,C4,C5,C6,C7,C8,C9,C10,C11,C12,C13,C14,C15;
/* color codes */
extern int x_res,y_res,mode_flag,alpha_x,alpha_y,x1,y1,x2,y2,t1;
extern int sx,sy,ty1,ty2,ty3,TextRow,TextColumn,TextX,TextY;
extern char keycode,keynum;
extern char far *menubarBitBlt;
extern char far *helpbarBitBlt;
extern char far *fileBitBlt;
extern char far *funcBitBlt;
extern char far *buttonBitBlt;
```

Fig. 8-3.
Continued.

```
extern char far *listBitBlt;
extern char far *itemBitBlt;
extern char far *FileMenu;
extern char far *ModifyMenu;
extern char far *TextMenu;
extern char far *SettingsMenu;
extern char far *PanBar;
extern char far *ScrollBar;
extern char far *ButtonBar;
extern char far *swatchprep;
extern char far *swatchbg;
extern int vx1,vy1,vx2,vy2,clipx1,clipy1,clipx2,clipy2;
extern int ix1,iy1,ix2,iy2,shx,shy,ox1,ox2,oy1,oy2;
extern int bx1,by1,bx2,by2,bxo,byo;
extern int syoffset,numbuttons,buttoncount;
extern int vertspace,vertsize;
extern int barclr,bgclr,bgtint,canvasclr;
extern int shadowclr,panelclr,ruleclr,buttonclr,buttontint;
extern char fill_0[],fill_3[],fill_6[],fill_12[];
extern char fill_25[],fill_37[],fill_50[],fill_62[];
extern char fill_75[],fill_87[],fill_93[],fill_100[];
extern char hatch_1[],hatch_2[],hatch_3[],hatch_4[];
extern char hatch_5[],hatch_6[],hatch_7[],hatch_8[];
extern char hatch_9[],hatch_10[],hatch_11[],hatch_12[];
extern int p1,p2,px1,px2,px3,px4,px5,px6,px7;
extern int py1,py2,py3,py4,py5,py6;
extern int t2,t3,p3,p4,p5,p6,pbg1,pbg2,status,choice;
extern int pb1,pb2,pbx1;
extern int pby1,pby2,pby3,pby4,pby5,pby6,pby7;
extern int pby8,pby9,pby10,pby11,pby12,pby13;
extern unsigned int plane_length;
extern char far * bitmap0;
extern char far * bitmap1;
extern char far * bitmap2;
extern char far * bitmap3;
extern union{ struct {unsigned int a1; unsigned int a2;} address;
        char far * faraddress;} u1;
extern unsigned int seg1,seg2,seg3,seg4,off1,off2,off3,off4;
extern char * textptr;
extern char text1[],text2[],text3[],text4[],text5[];
extern char text6[],text7[],text8[],text9[],text10[];
extern char text11[],text12[],text13[],text14[];
extern int mouse_flag,mouse_button,mouse_x,mouse_y;
extern int mouse_minx,mouse_maxx,mouse_miny,mouse_maxy;
extern char Herc;
extern char far *HPtr;
extern struct SREGS segregs;
extern unsigned int segment;
extern unsigned int offset;
extern FILE *image_file;
extern char image_buffer[];
extern char f1[],f2[],f3[],f4[],f5[],f6[],f7[];
extern char f8[],f9[],f10[],f11[],f12[];
extern int GS_penx,GS_peny,GS_penclr,GS_fillclr,GS_boundaryclr;
extern int GS_bgclr;
extern unsigned char * GS_hatch;
extern unsigned char * GS_shade;
extern int GS_textavail;
extern int GS_text_st,GS_text_ht,GS_text_wd,GS_text_clr;
/* color of font */
extern int GS_text_x,GS_text_y;
extern char GS_text_script[];
extern int hatch_index,shade_index;
extern int penclr_index,fillclr_index,boundary_index;
/*_____

            M E N U    S Y S T E M    M A N A G E R
_____*/
```

Fig. 8-3.
Continued.

```
void MenuBarLoop(void){      /* manages the menu system at runtime */
t1=1;      /* initialize panning highlight bar position indicator */
SaveBgd=MemBlock(16,2,127,61);         /* allocate memory to save bg */
PutXOR(p1,p2,PanBar);           /* install panning hilite bar */
MakeSound(250,6000);                                /* audio cue */
loop0:                                       /* menu bar loop begins */
CheckForKey();                          /* check for user keystroke */
if (keycode!=2) goto Label1;      /* jump if not an extended key */
switch (keynum){
  case 77: t1=t1+1;Panning();Purge();
            ClearTextLine();goto loop0;               /* right arrow */
  case 75: t1=t1-1;Panning();Purge();
            ClearTextLine();goto loop0;}               /* left arrow */
Label1:
if (keycode!=1) goto Label2;    /* jump past if not a normal key */
if (keynum==13){                           /* if <Enter> key... */
  InstallMenu();Purge();
  switch (t1){
    case 1: goto menuloop;                               /* Files */
    case 2: if (mouse_flag==0){      /* deny access if no mouse */
              UninstallMenu();
              PutText(1,2,C11,text11);
              PutXOR(p1,p2,PanBar);
              MakeSound(250,6000);goto loop0;}
            goto menuloop;                          /* Draw icons */
    case 3: if (mouse_flag==0){      /* deny access if no mouse */
              UninstallMenu();
              PutText(1,2,C11,text11);
              PutXOR(p1,p2,PanBar);
              MakeSound(250,6000);goto loop0;}
            goto menuloop;                         /* Paint icons */
    case 4: goto menuloop;                             /* Modify */
    case 5: goto menuloop;                               /* Text */
    case 6: goto menuloop;                           /* Settings */
    case 7: Restore();PutXOR(p1,p2,PanBar);             /* Undo */
            ClearTextLine();PutText(1,2,C7,text12);
            goto loop0;}}
Label2:
if (keycode!=0){                        /* if a key was retrieved */
  KeySwitch1();             /* switcher for system keystrokes */
  Purge();)                  /* empty the keyboard buffer */
goto loop0;                                      /* loop back */

menuloop:                           /* level 1 menus loop begins */
CheckForKey();                       /* check for user keystroke */
if (keycode!=2) goto Label3;      /* jump if not an extended key */
switch (keynum){
  case 80: t2=t2+1;                                  /* down arrow */
            Scrolling();
            Purge();
            ClearTextLine();goto menuloop;
  case 72: t2=t2-1;                                    /* up arrow */
            Scrolling();
            Purge();
            ClearTextLine();goto menuloop;
  case 77: if (t1==2) {MakeSound(400,6000);goto menuloop;}
            if (t1==3) {MakeSound(400,6000);goto menuloop;}
            t1=t1+1;                                /* right arrow */
            if (t1==2) t1=4;               /* bypass position 2 */
            if (t1==3) t1=4;               /* bypass position 3 */
            PanMenu();Purge();
            ClearTextLine();goto menuloop;
  case 75: if (t1==2) {MakeSound(400,6000);goto menuloop;}
            if (t1==3) {MakeSound(400,6000);goto menuloop;}
            t1=t1-1;                                 /* left arrow */
            if (t1==2) t1=1;               /* bypass position 2 */
            if (t1==3) t1=1;               /* bypass position 3 */
            PanMenu();Purge();
            ClearTextLine();goto menuloop;}
```

Fig. 8-3.
Continued.

```
Label3:
if (keycode!=1) goto Label4;      /* jump past if not a normal key */
if (keynum==13){                             /* if <Enter> key... */
   MenuChoices();Purge();goto Label5;} /* call the core function */
if (keynum==27){                               /* if <Esc> key... */
   UninstallMenu();Purge();             /* back out of the menu */
   PutXOR(p1,p2,PanBar);MenuBarText();
   goto loop0;}
Label4:
if (keycode!=0){                         /* if a key was retrieved */
  KeySwitch2();           /* switcher for level 1 menus keystrokes */
  Purge();}                           /* empty the keyboard buffer */
goto menuloop;                                      /* loop back */
Label5:          /* decide re-entrant point after core function */
switch (status){
   case ACTIVE:   switch (choice){
                    case 2:                      /* trap Files menu */
                    case 3:
                    case 4:PutXOR(p1,p2,PanBar);MenuBarText();
                         goto loop0;
                    default: UninstallMenu();
                         PutXOR(p1,p2,PanBar);MenuBarText();
                         goto loop0;}
   case BACKOUT: UninstallMenu();goto loop0;
   case STUB:    goto menuloop;}
return;}                                           /* boilerplate */
/*_____*/

void Panning(void){             /* moves the panning highlight bar */
if (t1>7) t1=1;                          /* wraparound past right */
if (t1<1) t1=7;                           /* wraparound past left */
switch (t1){        /* use t1 to determine where to move cursor */
   case 1: PutXOR(p1,p2,PanBar);p1=px1;              /* File */
           PutXOR(p1,p2,PanBar);break;
   case 2: PutXOR(p1,p2,PanBar);p1=px2;              /* Draw */
           PutXOR(p1,p2,PanBar);break;
   case 3: PutXOR(p1,p2,PanBar);p1=px3;             /* Paint */
           PutXOR(p1,p2,PanBar);break;
   case 4: PutXOR(p1,p2,PanBar);p1=px4;            /* Modify */
           PutXOR(p1,p2,PanBar);break;
   case 5: PutXOR(p1,p2,PanBar);p1=px5;          /* Settings */
           PutXOR(p1,p2,PanBar);break;
   case 6: PutXOR(p1,p2,PanBar);p1=px6;              /* Text */
           PutXOR(p1,p2,PanBar);break;
   case 7: PutXOR(p1,p2,PanBar);p1=px7;              /* Undo */
           PutXOR(p1,p2,PanBar);break;
   default: break;}
return;}
/*_____*/

void InstallMenu(void){         /* install level 1 menu on screen */
t2=1;                            /* reset virtual scroll position */
p6=py1;                          /* reset y coord scroll position */
switch (t1){
   case 1: p3=px1-1;      /* reset x install coord for File menu */
           PutXOR(p1,p2,PanBar);            /* remove panning bar */
           BackUp();      /* store backup page for possible Undo */
           GetBlock(p3,p4,(p3+pbg1),(p4+pbg2),SaveBgd);  /*save */
           PutPSET(p3,p4,FileMenu);             /* install menu */
           p5=px1+2;  /* reset x install coord for scrolling bar */
           PutXOR(p5,p6,ScrollBar);             /* install bar */
           t3=6;              /* reset number of choices in menu */
           break;                      /* get out of switch branch */
   case 2: pb1=pbx1;pb2=pby1;   /* reset cursor install for Draw */
           PutXOR(p1,p2,PanBar);            /* remove panning bar */
           BackUp();      /* store backup page for possible Undo */
           PutXOR(pb1,pb2,ButtonBar);      /* install button bar */
           t3=7;             /* reset number of choices available */
           break;
```

Fig. 8-3.
Continued.

```
        case 3:   pb1=pbx1;pb2=pby8;                        /* Paint icons */
                  PutXOR(p1,p2,PanBar);
                  BackUp();
                  PutXOR(pb1,pb2,ButtonBar);
                  t3=6;
                  break;
        case 4:   p3=px4-1;                                 /* Modify menu */
                  PutXOR(p1,p2,PanBar);
                  BackUp();
                  GetBlock(p3,p4,(p3+pbg1),(p4+pbg2),SaveBgd);
                  PutPSET(p3,p4,ModifyMenu);
                  p5=px4+2;PutXOR(p5,p6,ScrollBar);t3=4;break;
        case 5:   p3=px5-1;                                   /* Text menu */
                  PutXOR(p1,p2,PanBar);
                  BackUp();
                  GetBlock(p3,p4,(p3+pbg1),(p4+pbg2),SaveBgd);
                  PutPSET(p3,p4,TextMenu);
                  p5=px5+2;PutXOR(p5,p6,ScrollBar);t3=4;break;
        case 6:   p3=px6-1;                               /* Settings menu */
                  PutXOR(p1,p2,PanBar);
                  BackUp();
                  GetBlock(p3,p4,(p3+pbg1),(p4+pbg2),SaveBgd);
                  PutPSET(p3,p4,SettingsMenu);
                  p5=px6+2;PutXOR(p5,p6,ScrollBar);t3=5;break;
        case 7:   break;                                         /* Undo */
        default:  break;}
    return;}
    /*_____*/

    void UninstallMenu(void){    /* removes level 1 menu from screen */
    if (t1==2){PutXOR(pb1,pb2,ButtonBar);return;}     /* remove icons */
    if (t1==3){PutXOR(pb1,pb2,ButtonBar);return;}
    PutPSET(p3,p4,SaveBgd);    /* ...else restore previous background */
    return;}
    /*_____*/

    void PanMenu(void){                  /* manages inter-menu panning */
    if (t1>6) t1=1;                      /* wraparound to skip Undo */
    if (t1<1) t1=6;                                  /* wraparound */
    t2=1;                          /* reset virtual scroll position */
    p6=py1;                          /* reset y coord scroll position */
    UninstallMenu();                 /* remove existing level 1 menu */
    switch (t1){
      case 1: p1=px1;              /* reset x coord for panning bar */
              t3=6;                /* reset number of choices on menu */
              p3=px1-1;                    /* reset x coord for menu */
              p5=px1+2;           /* reset x coord for scrolling bar */
              GetBlock(p3,p4,(p3+pbg1),(p4+pbg2),SaveBgd);    /*save */
              PutPSET(p3,p4,FileMenu);            /* install menu */
              PutXOR(p5,p6,ScrollBar);             /* install bar */
              break;                  /* get out of switch branch */
      case 4: p1=px4;t3=4;p3=px4-1;p5=px4+2;
              GetBlock(p3,p4,(p3+pbg1),(p4+pbg2),SaveBgd);
              PutPSET(p3,p4,ModifyMenu);
              PutXOR(p5,p6,ScrollBar);
              break;
      case 5: p1=px5;t3=4;p3=px5-1;p5=px5+2;
              GetBlock(p3,p4,(p3+pbg1),(p4+pbg2),SaveBgd);
              PutPSET(p3,p4,TextMenu);
              PutXOR(p5,p6,ScrollBar);
              break;
      case 6: p1=px6;t3=5;p3=px6-1;p5=px6+2;
              GetBlock(p3,p4,(p3+pbg1),(p4+pbg2),SaveBgd);
              PutPSET(p3,p4,SettingsMenu);
              PutXOR(p5,p6,ScrollBar);
              break;}
    return;}
    /*_____*/
```

```
void Scrolling(void){          /* manages scrolling highlight bar */
if (t1==2){ButtonScroll();return;}
if (t1==3){ButtonScroll();return;}
if (t2>t3) t2=1;  /* handle vertical wraparound of scrolling bar */
if (t2<1) t2=t3;                      /* vertical wraparound */
switch (t2){
  case 1: PutXOR(p5,p6,ScrollBar);                 /* remove former */
          p6=py1;                                  /* reset y coord */
          PutXOR(p5,p6,ScrollBar);                   /* install new */
          break;                          /* get out of switch branch */
  case 2: PutXOR(p5,p6,ScrollBar);p6=py2;
          PutXOR(p5,p6,ScrollBar);break;
  case 3: PutXOR(p5,p6,ScrollBar);p6=py3;
          PutXOR(p5,p6,ScrollBar);break;
  case 4: PutXOR(p5,p6,ScrollBar);p6=py4;
          PutXOR(p5,p6,ScrollBar);break;
  case 5: PutXOR(p5,p6,ScrollBar);p6=py5;
          PutXOR(p5,p6,ScrollBar);break;
  case 6: PutXOR(p5,p6,ScrollBar);p6=py6;
          PutXOR(p5,p6,ScrollBar);break;}
return;}
/*_____*/

void ButtonScroll(void){        /* manages scrolling button cursor */
if (t2>t3) t2=1;  /* handle vertical wraparound of scrolling bar */
if (t2<1) t2=t3;                      /* vertical wraparound */
switch (t2){
  case 1: PutXOR(pb1,pb2,ButtonBar);               /* remove former */
          if (t1==2) pb2=pby1;                     /* reset y coord */
          if (t1==3) pb2=pby8;
          PutXOR(pb1,pb2,ButtonBar);                 /* install new */
          break;                          /* get out of switch branch */
  case 2: PutXOR(pb1,pb2,ButtonBar);
          if (t1==2) pb2=pby2;
          if (t1==3) pb2=pby9;
          PutXOR(pb1,pb2,ButtonBar);break;
  case 3: PutXOR(pb1,pb2,ButtonBar);
          if (t1==2) pb2=pby3;
          if (t1==3) pb2=pby10;
          PutXOR(pb1,pb2,ButtonBar);break;
  case 4: PutXOR(pb1,pb2,ButtonBar);
          if (t1==2) pb2=pby4;
          if (t1==3) pb2=pby11;
          PutXOR(pb1,pb2,ButtonBar);break;
  case 5: PutXOR(pb1,pb2,ButtonBar);
          if (t1==2) pb2=pby5;
          if (t1==3) pb2=pby12;
          PutXOR(pb1,pb2,ButtonBar);break;
  case 6: PutXOR(pb1,pb2,ButtonBar);
          if (t1==2) pb2=pby6;
          if (t1==3) pb2=pby13;
          PutXOR(pb1,pb2,ButtonBar);break;
  case 7: PutXOR(pb1,pb2,ButtonBar);
          pb2=pby7;
          PutXOR(pb1,pb2,ButtonBar);break;}
return;}
/*_____*/

void MenuChoices(void){          /* calls level 1 core functions */
  int x1,x2,y1,y2,xrad,yrad;  /* locals to be passed to routines */
  int x3,y3,x4,y4;
switch (t1){                    /* determine which menu is being used */
  case 1: goto filechoices;
  case 2: goto drawchoices;
  case 3: goto paintchoices;
  case 4: goto modifychoices;
  case 5: goto textchoices;
  case 6: goto settingschoices;}
filechoices:
```

Fig. 8-3.
Continued.

Fig. 8-3.
Continued.

```
switch (t2){                         /* determine which scroll choice */
   case 1: choice=1;status=ACTIVE;                           /* New */
           WindowOpen(clipx1,clipy1,clipx2,clipy2);
           WindowClear(GS_bgclr);
           WindowClose(x_res,y_res);break;
   case 2: choice=2;status=ACTIVE;                        /* Load... */
           Restore();EditName();LoadImage();
           break;
   case 3: choice=3;status=ACTIVE;                          /* Save */
           Restore();SaveImage();
           break;
   case 4: choice=4;status=ACTIVE;                     /* Save as... */
           Restore();EditName();SaveImage();
           break;
   case 5: choice=5;StubRoutine();break;               /* Delete... */
   case 6: choice=6;Quit_Pgm();}                        /* Shutdown */
return;
drawchoices:
switch (t2){
   case 1: choice=7;status=ACTIVE;                          /* line */
           SetHue(GS_penclr);
           MouseManager();                /* poll the mouse or tablet */
           if (mouse_button!=1) break;    /* if right button, stop */
           GetWindowCoords(sx,sy);  /* convert to viewport coords */
           WindowOpen(clipx1,clipy1,clipx2,clipy2);   /* viewport */
           DrawDot(GS_penx,GS_peny);      /* draw the first vertex */
           SetPosition(GS_penx,GS_peny);
           lineloop:                /* enter the line-drawing loop */
           Delayed();
           MouseManager();                /* poll the mouse or tablet */
           if (mouse_button!=1){
              WindowClose(x_res,y_res);break;}  /* if right button */
           GetWindowCoords(sx,sy);  /* convert to viewport coords */
           DrawLine(GS_penx,GS_peny);    /* draw the line segment */
           goto lineloop;          /* loop until right button pressed */
   case 2: choice=8;status=ACTIVE;                        /* sketch */
           SetHue(GS_penclr);
           sketchloop:
           MouseManager();
           if (mouse_button!=1) break;
           GetWindowCoords(sx,sy);
           WindowOpen(clipx1,clipy1,clipx2,clipy2);
           DrawDot(GS_penx,GS_peny);WindowClose(x_res,y_res);
           Delayed();
           goto sketchloop;
   case 3: choice=9;status=ACTIVE;                         /* curve */
           SetHue(GS_penclr);
           curveloop:
           MouseManager();                  /* get starting point */
           if (mouse_button!=1) break;
           GetWindowCoords(sx,sy);x1=GS_penx;y1=GS_peny;
           Delayed();MouseManager();     /* get first magnetic point */
           if (mouse_button!=1) break;
           GetWindowCoords(sx,sy);x2=GS_penx;y2=GS_peny;
           Delayed();MouseManager();    /* get second magnetic point */
           if (mouse_button!=1) break;
           GetWindowCoords(sx,sy);x3=GS_penx;y3=GS_peny;
           Delayed();MouseManager();          /* get ending point */
           if (mouse_button!=1) break;
           GetWindowCoords(sx,sy);x4=GS_penx;y4=GS_peny;
           WindowOpen(clipx1,clipy1,clipx2,clipy2);
           DrawCurve(x1,y1,x2,y2,x3,y3,x4,y4);
           WindowClose(x_res,y_res);
           Delayed();goto curveloop;
   case 4: choice=10;status=ACTIVE;                      /* rectngle */
           SetHue(GS_penclr);
           rectngleloop1:
           MouseManager();              /* get upper left vertex */
           if (mouse_button!=1) break;
```

Fig. 8-3.
Continued.

```
                GetWindowCoords(sx,sy);x1=GS_penx;y1=GS_peny;
                rectngleloop:
                Delayed();
                MouseManager();                  /* get lower right vertex */
                if (mouse_button!=1) break;
                GetWindowCoords(sx,sy);x2=GS_penx;y2=GS_peny;
                if (x2==x1) goto rectngleloop;
                if (y2==y1) goto rectngleloop;
                if (x1>x2){xrad=x1;x1=x2;x2=xrad;}
                xrad=x2-x1;
                if (y1>y2){yrad=y1;y1=y2;y2=yrad;}
                yrad=y2-y1;
                WindowOpen(clipx1,clipy1,clipx2,clipy2);
                DrawBorder(x1,y1,x2,y2);
                WindowClose(x_res,y_res);
                Delayed();
                goto rectngleloop1;
      case 5:   choice=11;status=ACTIVE;                        /* circle */
                SetHue(GS_penclr);
                circleloop1:
                MouseManager();                  /* get center coords */
                if (mouse_button!=1) break;
                GetWindowCoords(sx,sy);x1=GS_penx;y1=GS_peny;
                circleloop:
                Delayed();
                MouseManager();                  /* get radius size */
                if (mouse_button!=1) break;
                GetWindowCoords(sx,sy);x2=GS_penx;
                if (x2==x1) goto circleloop;
                if (x2>x1) xrad=x2-x1;
                if (x1>x2) xrad=x1-x2;
                if (xrad<10) goto circleloop;
                WindowOpen(clipx1,clipy1,clipx2,clipy2);
                DrawCircle(x1,y1,xrad);
                WindowClose(x_res,y_res);
                Delayed();
                goto circleloop1;
      case 6:   choice=12;status=ACTIVE;                        /* ellipse */
                SetHue(GS_penclr);
                ellipseloop1:
                MouseManager();                  /* get center coords */
                if (mouse_button!=1) break;
                GetWindowCoords(sx,sy);x1=GS_penx;y1=GS_peny;
                ellipseloop:
                Delayed();
                MouseManager();                  /* get radius coords */
                if (mouse_button!=1) break;
                GetWindowCoords(sx,sy);x2=GS_penx;y2=GS_peny;
                if (x2==x1) goto ellipseloop;
                if (y2==y1) goto ellipseloop;
                if (x2>x1) xrad=x2-x1;
                if (x1>x2) xrad=x1-x2;
                if (xrad<10) goto ellipseloop;
                if (y2>y1) yrad=y2-y1;
                if (y1>y2) yrad=y1-y2;
                if (yrad<10) goto ellipseloop;
                WindowOpen(clipx1,clipy1,clipx2,clipy2);
                DrawEllipse(x1,y1,xrad,yrad);
                WindowClose(x_res,y_res);
                Delayed();
                goto ellipseloop1;
      case 7:   choice=13;status=ACTIVE;                        /* eraser */
                SetHue(GS_bgclr);SetFill(fill_100,GS_bgclr);
                eraserloop:
                MouseManager();
                if (mouse_button!=1){ SetHue(GS_penclr);break;}
                GetWindowCoords(sx,sy);
                x1=GS_penx;y1=GS_peny;x2=x1+14;y2=y1+8;
                WindowOpen(clipx1,clipy1,clipx2,clipy2);
```

Fig. 8-3.
Continued.

```
                              DrawPanel(x1,y1,x2,y2);
                              WindowClose(x_res,y_res);
                              Delayed();
                              goto eraserloop;
          }
      return;
      paintchoices:
      switch (t2){
        case 1: choice=14;status=ACTIVE;                        /* airbrush */
                SetHue(GS_penclr);
                airbrushloop:
                MouseManager();
                if (mouse_button!=1){ SetHue(GS_penclr);break;}
                GetWindowCoords(sx,sy);
                x1=GS_penx;y1=GS_peny;
                WindowOpen(clipx1,clipy1,clipx2,clipy2);
                DrawDot(x1-1,y1-3);DrawDot(x1+3,y1-2);
                DrawDot(x1-3,y1-1);DrawDot(x1+1,y1);
                DrawDot(x1-1,y1+1);DrawDot(x1+3,y1+2);
                DrawDot(x1-3,y1+3);DrawDot(x1,y1+3);
                DrawDot(x1+2,y1+4);
                WindowClose(x_res,y_res);
                Delayed();
                goto airbrushloop;
        case 2: choice=15;status=ACTIVE;                        /* splatter */
                SetHue(GS_penclr);SetFill(fill_100,GS_penclr);
                xrad=10;
                splatterloop:
                MouseManager();                    /* get center coords */
                if (mouse_button!=1) break;
                GetWindowCoords(sx,sy);x1=GS_penx;y1=GS_peny;
                WindowOpen(clipx1,clipy1,clipx2,clipy2);
                DrawDisk(x1,y1,xrad);
                WindowClose(x_res,y_res);
                Delayed();
                goto splatterloop;
        case 3: choice=16;status=ACTIVE;                        /* fill */
                SetFill(fill_100,GS_fillclr);
                fill_loop:
                MouseManager();
                if (mouse_button!=1){SetHue(GS_penclr);break;}
                GetWindowCoords(sx,sy);
                WindowOpen(clipx1,clipy1,clipx2,clipy2);
                Fill(GS_penx,GS_peny,GS_boundaryclr);
                WindowClose(x_res,y_res);
                goto fill_loop;
                break;
        case 4: choice=17;status=ACTIVE;                        /* pattern */
                SetFill(GS_hatch,GS_fillclr);
                patternloop:
                MouseManager();
                if (mouse_button!=1){SetHue(GS_penclr);break;}
                GetWindowCoords(sx,sy);
                WindowOpen(clipx1,clipy1,clipx2,clipy2);
                Fill(GS_penx,GS_peny,GS_boundaryclr);
                WindowClose(x_res,y_res);
                goto patternloop;
                break;
        case 5: choice=18;status=ACTIVE;                        /* shade */
                SetFill(GS_shade,GS_fillclr);
                shadeloop:
                MouseManager();
                if (mouse_button!=1){SetHue(GS_penclr);break;}
                GetWindowCoords(sx,sy);
                WindowOpen(clipx1,clipy1,clipx2,clipy2);
                Fill(GS_penx,GS_peny,GS_boundaryclr);
                WindowClose(x_res,y_res);
                goto shadeloop;
                break;
```

```
              case 6: choice=19;status=ACTIVE;                          /* roller */
                      SetFill(fill_100,GS_fillclr);
                      rollerloop:
                      MouseManager();
                      if (mouse_button!=1){ SetHue(GS_penclr);break;}
                      GetWindowCoords(sx,sy);
                      x1=GS_penx;y1=GS_peny;x2=x1+16;y2=y1+4;
                      WindowOpen(clipx1,clipy1,clipx2,clipy2);
                      DrawPanel(x1,y1,x2,y2);
                      WindowClose(x_res,y_res);
                      Delayed();
                      goto rollerloop;
              }
          return;
          modifychoices:
          switch (t2){                          /* determine which scroll choice */
            case 1: choice=20;StubRoutine();break;                  /* Copy... */
            case 2: choice=21;StubRoutine();break;                  /* Move... */
            case 3: choice=22;StubRoutine();break;                   /* Cut... */
            case 4: choice=23;StubRoutine();break;}                /* Paste... */
          return;
          textchoices:
          switch (t2){                          /* determine which scroll choice */
            case 1: choice=24;StubRoutine();break;                /* Height... */
            case 2: choice=25;StubRoutine();break;                 /* Width... */
            case 3: choice=26;StubRoutine();break;               /* Sans serif */
            case 4: choice=27;StubRoutine();break;}                  /* Serif */
          return;
          settingschoices:
          ClearTextLine();PutText(1,2,C7,text13);
          switch (t2){                          /* determine which scroll choice */
            case 1: choice=28;status=ACTIVE;                     /* Active clr */
                    EditColor();break;
            case 2: choice=29;status=ACTIVE;                       /* Fill clr */
                    EditColor();break;
            case 3: choice=30;status=ACTIVE;                       /* Boundary */
                    EditColor();break;
            case 4: choice=31;status=ACTIVE;                        /* Pattern */
                    EditColor();break;
            case 5: choice=32;status=ACTIVE;                          /* Shade */
                    EditColor();break;}
          return;}
          /*_____*/

          void StubRoutine(void){               /* do-nothing core function */
          status=STUB;
          if (GS_textavail==-1){                      /* if no font loaded... */
            switch(choice){               /* ...and user wants a text function */
              case 24:
              case 25:
              case 26:
              case 27: ClearTextLine();
                      PutText(1,2,C7,text14);      /* font files not loaded */
                      MakeSound(250,6000);return;
              default: break;}}
          ClearTextLine();PutText(1,2,C7,text6);        /* inactive feature. */
          MakeSound(250,6000);
          return;}
          /*_____*/

          void MenuBarText(void){               /* back-out status dialog text */
          ClearTextLine();
          PutText(1,2,C7,text7); /* SketchPad ready for your next command. */
          return;}
          /*_____*/

          void ClearTextLine(void){             /* blanks the dialog text line */
          SetHue(C0);SetLine(0xffff);SetFill(fill_100,C0);
          #if GraphicsLibrary==TurboC
```

Fig. 8-3.
Continued.

Fig. 8-3.
Continued.

```
    setfillstyle(SOLID_FILL,C0);
#endif
if (mode_flag==6){                          /* if Hercules 9x14 characters */
  DrawPanel(0,0,486,13);}
else {DrawPanel(0,0,431,7);}                     /* if 8x8 characters */
return;}
/*_____*/

void CheckForKey(void){              /* checks for user keystrokes */
union u_type{int a;char b[3];}keystroke; /* define the structure */
char inkey=0;
#if Compiler==QuickC
  if (_bios_keybrd(_KEYBRD_READY)==EMPTY){keycode=0;return;}
  keystroke.a=_bios_keybrd(_KEYBRD_READ);   /* fetch ASCII codes */
#elif Compiler==TurboC
  if (bioskey(1)==EMPTY){keycode=0;return;}
  keystroke.a=bioskey(0);                     /* fetch ASCII codes */
#endif
inkey=keystroke.b[0];                        /* retrieve first code */
if (inkey!=0){                              /* if a normal keystroke... */
  keycode=1;                               /* set flag to normal keystroke */
  keynum=inkey;                      /* and load ASCII code into variable */
  return;}
if (inkey==0){                            /* if an extended keystroke... */
  keycode=2;                              /* set flag to extended keystroke */
  keynum=keystroke.b[1];     /* and load second code into variable */
  return;}
}
/*_____*/

void KeySwitch1(void){     /* switcher for keys at menu bar level */
int tempclr=0;
if (keycode==2) goto ExtendedKeys;     /* if extended key, jump... */
NormalKeys:                       /* ...else use switcher for normal keys */
#if Compiler==QuickC
  _settextposition(1,64);_settextcolor(C7);
switch (keynum){
  case 27:  _outtext("Esc            ");return;
  case 13:  _outtext("Enter          ");return;
  case 9:   _outtext("Tab            ");return;
  default:  _outtext("inactive key   ");
            MakeSound(400,6000);return;}
#elif Compiler==TurboC
  tempclr=getcolor();
  setcolor(C0);setlinestyle(USERBIT_LINE,0xffff,NORM_WIDTH);
  setfillstyle(SOLID_FILL,C0);
  TextRow=1;TextColumn=64;GetTextCoords();
  if (mode_flag==6){                          /* if Hercules 9x14 characters */
    bar(TextX,TextY,TextX+144,TextY+13);}
  else {bar(TextX,TextY,TextX+128,TextY+7);}/* if 8x8 characters */
  setcolor(C7);
switch (keynum){
  case 27:  outtextxy(TextX,TextY,"Esc            ");break;
  case 13:  outtextxy(TextX,TextY,"Enter          ");break;
  case 9:   outtextxy(TextX,TextY,"Tab            ");break;
  default:  outtextxy(TextX,TextY,"inactive key   ");
            MakeSound(400,6000);break;}
  setcolor(tempclr);return;
#endif
ExtendedKeys:                       /* switcher for extended keystrokes */
#if Compiler==QuickC
  _settextposition(1,64);_settextcolor(C7);
switch (keynum){
  case 59:  _outtext("F1             ");return;
  case 60:  _outtext("F2             ");return;
  case 71:  _outtext("Home           ");return;
  case 79:  _outtext("End            ");return;
  case 73:  _outtext("PgUp           ");return;
  case 81:  _outtext("PgDn           ");return;
```

Fig. 8-3.
Continued.

```
    case 75:  _outtext("left arrow key  ");return;
    case 77:  _outtext("right arrow key ");return;
    case 72:  _outtext("up arrow key    ");return;
    case 80:  _outtext("down arrow key  ");return;
    case 45:  _outtext("Alt+X           ");Quit_Pgm();
    default:  _outtext("inactive key    ");
              MakeSound(400,6000);return;}         /* undefined */
#elif Compiler==TurboC
  tempclr=getcolor();
  setcolor(C0);setlinestyle(USERBIT_LINE,0xffff,NORM_WIDTH);
  setfillstyle(SOLID_FILL,C0);
  TextRow=1;TextColumn=64;GetTextCoords();
  if (mode_flag==6){                  /* if Hercules 9x14 characters */
    bar(TextX,TextY,TextX+144,TextY+13);}
  else {bar(TextX,TextY,TextX+128,TextY+7);}/* if 8x8 characters */
  setcolor(C7);
switch (keynum){
    case 59:  outtextxy(TextX,TextY,"F1              ");break;
    case 60:  outtextxy(TextX,TextY,"F2              ");break;
    case 71:  outtextxy(TextX,TextY,"Home            ");break;
    case 79:  outtextxy(TextX,TextY,"End             ");break;
    case 73:  outtextxy(TextX,TextY,"PgUp            ");break;
    case 81:  outtextxy(TextX,TextY,"PgDn            ");break;
    case 75:  outtextxy(TextX,TextY,"left arrow key  ");break;
    case 77:  outtextxy(TextX,TextY,"right arrow key ");break;
    case 72:  outtextxy(TextX,TextY,"up arrow key    ");break;
    case 80:  outtextxy(TextX,TextY,"down arrow key  ");break;
    case 45:  outtextxy(TextX,TextY,"Alt+X           ");Quit_Pgm();
    default:  outtextxy(TextX,TextY,"inactive key    ");
              MakeSound(400,6000);break;}          /* undefined */
setcolor(tempclr);return;
#endif
}
/*_____*/

void KeySwitch2(void){     /* switcher for keys at level 1 menus */
int tempclr=0;
if (keycode==2) goto ExtendedKeys2; /* if extended key, jump... */
NormalKeys2:                /* ...else use switcher for normal keys */
#if Compiler==QuickC
  _settextposition(1,64);_settextcolor(C7);
switch (keynum){
    case 27:  _outtext("Esc             ");return;
    case 13:  _outtext("Enter           ");return;
    case 9:   _outtext("Tab             ");return;
    default:  _outtext("inactive key    ");
              MakeSound(400,6000);return;}
#elif Compiler==TurboC
  tempclr=getcolor();
  setcolor(C0);setlinestyle(USERBIT_LINE,0xffff,NORM_WIDTH);
  setfillstyle(SOLID_FILL,C0);
  TextRow=1;TextColumn=64;GetTextCoords();
  if (mode_flag==6){                  /* if Hercules 9x14 characters */
    bar(TextX,TextY,TextX+144,TextY+13);}
  else {bar(TextX,TextY,TextX+128,TextY+7);}/* if 8x8 characters */
  setcolor(C7);
switch (keynum){
    case 27:  outtextxy(TextX,TextY,"Esc             ");break;
    case 13:  outtextxy(TextX,TextY,"Enter           ");break;
    case 9:   outtextxy(TextX,TextY,"Tab             ");break;
    default:  outtextxy(TextX,TextY,"inactive key    ");
              MakeSound(400,6000);break;}
setcolor(tempclr);return;
#endif
ExtendedKeys2:                  /* switcher for extended keystrokes */
#if Compiler==QuickC
  _settextposition(1,64);_settextcolor(C7);
switch (keynum){
    case 59:  _outtext("F1              ");return;
```

Fig. 8-3.
Continued.

```
    case 60:  _outtext("F2                  ");return;
    case 71:  _outtext("Home                ");return;
    case 79:  _outtext("End                 ");return;
    case 73:  _outtext("PgUp                ");return;
    case 81:  _outtext("PgDn                ");return;
    case 75:  _outtext("left arrow key   ");return;
    case 77:  _outtext("right arrow key  ");return;
    case 72:  _outtext("up arrow key     ");return;
    case 80:  _outtext("down arrow key   ");return;
    case 45:  _outtext("Alt+X            ");Quit_Pgm();
    default:  _outtext("inactive key     ");
              MakeSound(400,6000);return;}         /* undefined */
#elif Compiler==TurboC
  tempclr=getcolor();
  setcolor(C0);setlinestyle(USERBIT_LINE,0xffff,NORM_WIDTH);
  setfillstyle(SOLID_FILL,C0);
  TextRow=1;TextColumn=64;GetTextCoords();
  if (mode_flag==6){                   /* if Hercules 9x14 characters */
    bar(TextX,TextY,TextX+144,TextY+13);}
  else {bar(TextX,TextY,TextX+128,TextY+7);}/* if 8x8 characters */
  setcolor(C7);
switch (keynum){
    case 59:  outtextxy(TextX,TextY,"F1                ");break;
    case 60:  outtextxy(TextX,TextY,"F2                ");break;
    case 71:  outtextxy(TextX,TextY,"Home              ");break;
    case 79:  outtextxy(TextX,TextY,"End               ");break;
    case 73:  outtextxy(TextX,TextY,"PgUp              ");break;
    case 81:  outtextxy(TextX,TextY,"PgDn              ");break;
    case 75:  outtextxy(TextX,TextY,"left arrow key    ");break;
    case 77:  outtextxy(TextX,TextY,"right arrow key ");break;
    case 72:  outtextxy(TextX,TextY,"up arrow key      ");break;
    case 80:  outtextxy(TextX,TextY,"down arrow key    ");break;
    case 45:  outtextxy(TextX,TextY,"Alt+X             ");Quit_Pgm();
    default:  outtextxy(TextX,TextY,"inactive key      ");
              MakeSound(400,6000);break;}         /* undefined */
setcolor(tempclr);return;
#endif
return;}
/*_____*/

void Purge(void){  /* empties kybrd buffer, avoids cursor run-on */
do {CheckForKey();}      /* keep fetching keys from the buffer... */
while (keycode!=0);       /* ...while the keystroke is not NULL */
return;}                              /* then return to caller */
/*_____*/

void EditName(void){          /* allows user to edit the filename */
/* NOTE:  This rudimentary editor operates on the following
    principles:  1. Press legal keys to type in a new filename. The
    Filename must be 8 characters in length.  2. Press Enter to
    accept the currently displayed filename and exit the editor.
    3. Press Esc to restore the previous filename and exit the
    editor.  4. The program issues an audio cue if an illegal key
    is detected. */
  int position;                          /* declare local variable */
  position=0;                            /* reset position index */
  strcpy(f12,f3);      /* store current filename for possible undo */
  ClearTextLine();PutText(1,2,C7,text9);    /* display the prompt */
  PutText(1,20,C3,f3);                 /* display current filename */
editloop1:                               /* loop begins here */
CheckForKey();                           /* check for keystroke */
if (keycode==0) goto editloop1;          /* loop back if no key */
if (keycode==2){                  /* loop back if extended key */
  MakeSound(250,6000);goto editloop1;}
if ((keynum>63)&&(keynum<91)) goto editline;
if ((keynum>96)&&(keynum<123)) goto editline;
if ((keynum>47)&&(keynum<58)) goto editline;
if (keynum==33) goto editline;
if ((keynum>34)&&(keynum<39)) goto editline;
```

Fig. 8-3.
Continued.

```
if (keynum==45) goto editline;
if (keynum==95) goto editline;
if (keynum==13){                              /* if Enter keystroke */
  ClearTextLine();PutText(1,2,C7,text10);
  PutText(1,20,C7,f3);PutText(1,28,C7,f4);
  Purge();return;}
if (keynum==27){                              /* if Esc keystroke */
  strcpy(f3,f12);                      /* reset to former filename */
  ClearTextLine();PutText(1,2,C7,text10);
  PutText(1,20,C7,f3);PutText(1,28,C7,f4);
  Purge();return;}
MakeSound(250,6000);goto editloop1;          /* ...else loop back */
editline:                  /* jump to here if an editable keystroke */
f11[0]=keynum;                    /* load ASCII code into carrier */
if (position>7){        /* if filename edit already at character 8...*/
  MakeSound(250,6000);goto editloop1;}
f3[position]=f11[0];          /* write new character into filename */
position++;                          /* increment character number */
if (position>7) position=8;   /* avoid possible numeric overflow */
ClearTextLine();PutText(1,2,C7,text9);
PutText(1,20,C3,f3);
goto editloop1;                                     /* loop back */
return;}                                           /* boilerplate */
/*_____*/

void EditColor(void){                /* alter colors and patterns */
switch(choice){                /* set appropriate color variables */
  case 28: SetFill(fill_100,GS_penclr);break;
  case 29: SetFill(fill_100,GS_fillclr);break;
  case 30: SetFill(fill_100,GS_boundaryclr);break;
  case 31: SetFill(GS_hatch,GS_fillclr);break;
  case 32: SetFill(GS_shade,GS_fillclr);break;}
GetBlock(clipx1,clipy1,clipx1+50,clipy1+50,swatchbg);/* save bg */
PutPSET(clipx1,clipy1,swatchprep);        /* prep the screen area */
WindowOpen(clipx1,clipy1,clipx2,clipy2);      /* display swatch */
DrawPanel(0,0,50,50);WindowClose(x_res,y_res);

editcolorloop:                                    /* keyboard loop */
CheckForKey();
if (keycode==0) goto editcolorloop;
if (keycode==2){MakeSound(250,6000);goto editcolorloop;}
switch(keynum){
  case 27: PutPSET(clipx1,clipy1,swatchbg);return;        /* Esc */
  case 13: PutPSET(clipx1,clipy1,swatchbg);return;      /* Enter */
  case 9:  goto whichcolor;                               /* Tab */
  default: MakeSound(250,6000);break;}       /* any other key */
goto editcolorloop;                               /* loop back */

whichcolor:                /* jump to here if a new swatch needed */
switch(choice){                /* jump to appropriate swatch generator */
  case 28: goto setpenclr;
  case 29: goto setfillclr;
  case 30: goto setboundaryclr;
  case 31: goto sethatch;
  case 32: goto setshade;}

setpenclr:                           /* display new penclr swatch */
penclr_index=penclr_index+1;
if (penclr_index>15) penclr_index=0;
switch(penclr_index){
  case 0: GS_penclr=C0;break;
  case 1: GS_penclr=C1;break;
  case 2: GS_penclr=C2;break;
  case 3: GS_penclr=C3;break;
  case 4: GS_penclr=C4;break;
  case 5: GS_penclr=C5;break;
  case 6: GS_penclr=C6;break;
  case 7: GS_penclr=C7;break;
  case 8: GS_penclr=C8;break;
```

Fig. 8-3.
Continued.

```
        case 9: GS_penclr=C9;break;
        case 10: GS_penclr=C10;break;
        case 11: GS_penclr=C11;break;
        case 12: GS_penclr=C12;break;
        case 13: GS_penclr=C13;break;
        case 14: GS_penclr=C14;break;
        case 15: GS_penclr=C15;break;}
   SetFill(fill_100,GS_penclr);
   WindowOpen(clipx1,clipy1,clipx2,clipy2);
   DrawPanel(0,0,50,50);WindowClose(x_res,y_res);
   goto editcolorloop;

   setfillclr:                            /* display new fillclr swatch */
   fillclr_index=fillclr_index+1;
   if (fillclr_index>15) fillclr_index=0;
   switch(fillclr_index){
     case 0: GS_fillclr=C0;break;
     case 1: GS_fillclr=C1;break;
     case 2: GS_fillclr=C2;break;
     case 3: GS_fillclr=C3;break;
     case 4: GS_fillclr=C4;break;
     case 5: GS_fillclr=C5;break;
     case 6: GS_fillclr=C6;break;
     case 7: GS_fillclr=C7;break;
     case 8: GS_fillclr=C8;break;
     case 9: GS_fillclr=C9;break;
     case 10: GS_fillclr=C10;break;
     case 11: GS_fillclr=C11;break;
     case 12: GS_fillclr=C12;break;
     case 13: GS_fillclr=C13;break;
     case 14: GS_fillclr=C14;break;
     case 15: GS_fillclr=C15;break;}
   SetFill(fill_100,GS_fillclr);
   WindowOpen(clipx1,clipy1,clipx2,clipy2);
   DrawPanel(0,0,50,50);WindowClose(x_res,y_res);
   goto editcolorloop;

   setboundaryclr:                        /* display new boundaryclr swatch */
   boundary_index=boundary_index+1;
   if (boundary_index>15) boundary_index=0;
   switch(boundary_index){
     case 0: GS_boundaryclr=C0;break;
     case 1: GS_boundaryclr=C1;break;
     case 2: GS_boundaryclr=C2;break;
     case 3: GS_boundaryclr=C3;break;
     case 4: GS_boundaryclr=C4;break;
     case 5: GS_boundaryclr=C5;break;
     case 6: GS_boundaryclr=C6;break;
     case 7: GS_boundaryclr=C7;break;
     case 8: GS_boundaryclr=C8;break;
     case 9: GS_boundaryclr=C9;break;
     case 10: GS_boundaryclr=C10;break;
     case 11: GS_boundaryclr=C11;break;
     case 12: GS_boundaryclr=C12;break;
     case 13: GS_boundaryclr=C13;break;
     case 14: GS_boundaryclr=C14;break;
     case 15: GS_boundaryclr=C15;break;}
   SetFill(fill_100,GS_boundaryclr);
   WindowOpen(clipx1,clipy1,clipx2,clipy2);
   DrawPanel(0,0,50,50);WindowClose(x_res,y_res);
   goto editcolorloop;

   sethatch:                              /* display new hatch swatch */
   hatch_index=hatch_index+1;
   if (hatch_index>12) hatch_index=1;
   switch(hatch_index){
     case 1: GS_hatch=hatch_1;break;
     case 2: GS_hatch=hatch_2;break;
     case 3: GS_hatch=hatch_3;break;
```

Fig. 8-3.
Continued.

```
    case 4: GS_hatch=hatch_4;break;
    case 5: GS_hatch=hatch_5;break;
    case 6: GS_hatch=hatch_6;break;
    case 7: GS_hatch=hatch_7;break;
    case 8: GS_hatch=hatch_8;break;
    case 9: GS_hatch=hatch_9;break;
    case 10: GS_hatch=hatch_10;break;
    case 11: GS_hatch=hatch_11;break;
    case 12: GS_hatch=hatch_12;break;}
SetFill(GS_hatch,GS_fillclr);
PutPSET(clipx1,clipy1,swatchprep);          /* prep the screen area */
WindowOpen(clipx1,clipy1,clipx2,clipy2);
DrawPanel(0,0,50,50);WindowClose(x_res,y_res);
goto editcolorloop;

setshade:                                 /* display new shade swatch */
shade_index=shade_index+1;
if (shade_index>12) shade_index=1;
switch(shade_index){
    case 1: GS_shade=fill_0;break;
    case 2: GS_shade=fill_3;break;
    case 3: GS_shade=fill_6;break;
    case 4: GS_shade=fill_12;break;
    case 5: GS_shade=fill_25;break;
    case 6: GS_shade=fill_37;break;
    case 7: GS_shade=fill_50;break;
    case 8: GS_shade=fill_62;break;
    case 9: GS_shade=fill_75;break;
    case 10: GS_shade=fill_87;break;
    case 11: GS_shade=fill_93;break;
    case 12: GS_shade=fill_100;break;}
SetFill(GS_shade,GS_fillclr);
PutPSET(clipx1,clipy1,swatchprep);          /* prep the screen area */
WindowOpen(clipx1,clipy1,clipx2,clipy2);
DrawPanel(0,0,50,50);WindowClose(x_res,y_res);
goto editcolorloop;
return;}                                        /* boilerplate */
/*_____*/

void MakeSound(int hertz,int duration){      /* generates a sound */
int t1=1,high_byte=0,low_byte=0;
short count=0;unsigned char old_port=0,new_port=0;
if (hertz<40) return;
if (hertz>4660) return;
count=1193180L/hertz;
high_byte=count/256;low_byte=count-(high_byte*256);
#if Compiler==QuickC
    outp(0x43,0xB6);outp(0x42,low_byte);outp(0x42,high_byte);
    old_port=inp(0x61);new_port=(old_port|0x03);outp(0x61,new_port);
    for (t1=1;t1<=duration;t1++);outp(0x61,old_port);
#elif Compiler==TurboC
    outportb(0x43,0xB6);outportb(0x42,low_byte);
    outportb(0x42,high_byte);old_port=inportb(0x61);
    new_port=(old_port | 0x03);outportb(0x61,new_port);
    for (t1=1;t1<=duration;t1++);outportb(0x61,old_port);
#endif
return;}
/*_____*/

void MouseManager(void){                    /* mouse polling loop */
Mouse_Show();                          /* display the mouse cursor */
mousemgr1:                                   /* loop begins here */
Mouse_Status();                        /* check the mouse's status */
if (mouse_button==1){                   /* if left button pressed... */
    sx=mouse_x;sy=mouse_y;          /* update current pen position */
    Mouse_Hide();return;}    /* remove cursor and return to caller. */
if (mouse_button==2){                  /* if right button pressed... */
    Mouse_Hide();return;}    /* remove cursor and return to caller. */
goto mousemgr1;                                /* infinite loop */
```

Fig. 8-3.
Continued.

```
    return;}
    /*_____*/

    void Delayed(void){            /* suppress mouse/tablet double-hits */
      int t1=0;
    do {t1++;} while (t1<20000);
    return;}
    /*_____*/

    void GetTextCoords(void){           /* convert QC row,col to TC xy */
    if (mode_flag==6){                  /* if Hercules 9x14 characters */
      TextX=(TextColumn*9)-9;TextY=(TextRow*14)-14;}
    else {TextX=(TextColumn*8)-8;TextY=(TextRow*8)-8;}       /* if 8x8 */
    return;}
    /*_____
```

Module three
begins here

```
    End of Module 2 source code.  (This program has 3 modules.) */
    /*                      tm
    Your Microcomputer SketchPad              Source file: SKETCH3.C

    By: Lee Adams    Version: 1.00    Revision: n/a.
    Notices: (c) Copyright 1990 Lee Adams.  All rights reserved.
       Your Microcomputer SketchPad is a trademark of
       TAB Books and is used by permission.
    First published: 1990 by Windcrest Books (div. of TAB Books)

    Source notes:  module 3 of 3.  The project list should include
    SKETCH1.C, SKETCH2.C, and SKETCH3.C named in QuickC's MAK file
    or Turbo C's PRJ file.

    Operation:  provides library-independent low-level graphics
    routines, mouse routines, and disk I/O routines for the run-time
    environment established by module 1.

    Compiler:  QuickC or Turbo C integrated programming environment.
    Default is QuickC. To use Turbo C change the preprocessor directive
    in COMPILER DIRECTIVES (see below).  Compile using the medium
    memory model.  Refer to the book for instructions on command-line
    compiling and linking.

    Graphics library:  QuickC, Turbo C, or third-party add-on library.
    Default is QuickC.  To use Turbo C graphics library, change the
    preprocessor directive in COMPILER DIRECTIVES (see below).  To use
    a third-party graphics library, refer to the book.

    License:  As purchaser of the book in which this program is
    published, you are granted a non-exclusive royalty-free license
    to reproduce and distribute these routines in executable form
    as part of your software product, subject to any copyright,
    trademark, or patent rights of others, and subject to the limited
    warranty described in the introduction of the book.  All other
    rights reserved.
    _____

    COMPILER DIRECTIVES   */

                   /* compilers and graphics libraries */
    #define QuickC      1
    #define TurboC      2
    #define MicrosoftC  3
    #define LatticeC    4
    #define HALO        7
    #define MetaWINDOW  8
    #define Essential   9
    #define GSS         10

    #define Compiler QuickC           /* change to TurboC if required */
    #define GraphicsLibrary QuickC    /* change to library being used */
```

```
#define MOUSE      0x33              /* DOS interrupt for mouse driver */

#include <bios.h>                   /* supports keyboard functions */
#include <stdio.h>                  /* supports printf function */
#include <string.h>                 /* supports string manipulation */
#if Compiler==QuickC
    #include <conio.h>              /* supports QuickC port IO */
    #include <malloc.h>  /* supports memory allocation for arrays */
    #include <memory.h>             /* supports QuickC memory moves */
#elif Compiler==TurboC
    #include <dos.h>                /* supports TurboC port IO */
    #include <alloc.h>   /* supports memory allocation for arrays */
    #include <mem.h>                /* supports Turbo C memory moves */
#endif
#if GraphicsLibrary==QuickC
    #include <graph.h>              /* QuickC graphics library */
#elif GraphicsLibrary==TurboC
    #include <graphics.h>           /* Turbo C graphics library */
#endif
#include <process.h>               /* supports the exit function */
#include <dos.h>          /* supports int 33h for mouse routines */
/*_____

FUNCTION PROTOTYPES  */

/* LOW-LEVEL GRAPHICS ROUTINES IN THIS MODULE */
void SetHue(int);               /* sets the current drawing color */
void SetLine(int);                 /* sets the current line style */
void SetFill(char *, int);          /* sets the area fill style */
void BlankPage(void);        /* blanks the current active page */
void SetPosition(int,int);       /* sets the current xy position */
void DrawLine(int,int);    /* draws line from current xy position */
void DrawBorder(int,int,int,int);           /* draws rectangle */
void DrawPanel(int,int,int,int);      /* draws solid rectangle */
void Fill(int,int,int);                        /* area fill */
char far * MemBlock(int,int,int,int);   /* allocate array memory */
void GetBlock(int,int,int,int,char far *); /* save graphic array */
void PutXOR(int,int,char far *);       /* show XOR graphic array */
void PutPSET(int,int,char far *);      /* show PSET graphic array */
void PutText(int,int,int,char *);           /* display text */
void SetTextRowCol(int,int);             /* set text position */
char far * InitHiddenPage(void);     /* initialize hidden bitmap */
void BackUp(void);           /* copies page 0 to hidden page */
void Restore(void);          /* copies hidden page to page 0 */
void Mouse_Initialize(void);         /* initializes the mouse */
void Mouse_Show(void);           /* displays the mouse cursor */
void Mouse_Hide(void);           /* hides the mouse cursor */
void Mouse_Setposition(void);   /* resets mouse cursor xy coords */
void Mouse_Status(void); /* checks mouse location, button status */
void Mouse_Setrangeh(void);      /* sets mouse horizontal range */
void Mouse_Setrangev(void);        /* sets mouse vertical range */
void SaveImage(void);                /* prep for image save */
void LoadImage(void);                /* prep for image load */
void SaveVGAEGAImage(void);   /* saves VGA or EGA image to disk */
void LoadVGAEGAImage(void);  /* loads VGA or EGA image from disk */
void SaveCGAimage(void);         /* saves CGA image to disk */
void LoadCGAimage(void);         /* loads CGA image from disk */
void SaveHGAimage(void);       /* saves Hercules image to disk */
void LoadHGAimage(void);     /* loads Hercules image from disk */
void SaveMCGAimage(void);        /* saves MCGA image to disk */
void LoadMCGAimage(void);        /* loads MCGA image from disk */
void WindowOpen(int,int,int,int);          /* opens viewport */
void WindowClose(int,int);            /* shut down viewport */
void WindowClear(int);             /* blanks the viewport */
void GetWindowCoords(int,int);/* convert phys coords to viewport */
void WriteToPage(int);                   /* sets active page */
void DisplayPage(int);                  /* sets visible page */
void DrawDot(int,int);                         /* draws dot */
void DrawCircle(int,int,int);          /* draws outline circle */
```

Fig. 8-3.
Continued.

Fig. 8-3.
Continued.

```
    void DrawDisk(int,int,int);                    /* draws filled circle */
    void DrawEllipse(int,int,int,int);             /* draws outline ellipse */
    void DrawSolidEllipse(int,int,int,int);  /* draws filled ellipse */
    void DrawCurve(int,int,int,int,int,int,int,int); /* draws curve */
    void GetCurvePoint(int,int,int,int,int,int,      /* point on curve */
                       int,int,float,float,float);

    /* ROUTINES IN MODULE 1 OR 2 CALLED BY THIS MODULE */
    void Quit_Pgm(void);                /* ends the program gracefully */
    void ClearTextLine(void);           /* blanks the dialog text line */
    void CheckForKey(void);             /* checks for user keystrokes */
    /*_____*/

    /* DECLARATION OF GLOBAL VARIABLES */
    #if Compiler==QuickC
      union REGS inregs,outregs;        /* data structure for interrupt */
    #elif Compiler==TurboC
      union REGS regs;                  /* data structure for interrupt */
    #endif

    /* RE-DECLARATION OF GLOBAL VARIABLES initialized in Module 1,
    but also visible to all functions in this source file. */
    #if GraphicsLibrary==QuickC
      extern struct vc;
    #endif
    extern int C0,C1,C2,C3,C4,C5,C6,C7,C8,C9,C10,C11,C12,C13,C14,C15;
    /* color codes */
    extern int x_res,y_res,mode_flag,alpha_x,alpha_y,x1,y1,x2,y2,t1;
    extern int sx,sy,ty1,ty2,ty3,TextRow,TextColumn,TextX,TextY;
    extern char keycode,keynum;
    extern int vx1,vy1,vx2,vy2,clipx1,clipy1,clipx2,clipy2;
    extern int ix1,iy1,ix2,iy2,shx,shy,ox1,ox2,oy1,oy2;
    extern int bx1,by1,bx2,by2,bxo,byo;
    extern char fill_0[],fill_3[],fill_6[],fill_12[];
    extern char fill_25[],fill_37[],fill_50[],fill_62[];
    extern char fill_75[],fill_87[],fill_93[],fill_100[];
    extern char hatch_1[],hatch_2[],hatch_3[],hatch_4[];
    extern char hatch_5[],hatch_6[],hatch_7[],hatch_8[];
    extern char hatch_9[],hatch_10[],hatch_11[],hatch_12[];
    extern int p1,p2,px1,px2,px3,px4,px5,px6,px7;
    extern int py1,py2,py3,py4,py5,py6;
    extern int t2,t3,p3,p4,p5,p6,pbg1,pbg2,status,choice;
    extern unsigned int plane_length;
    extern char far * bitmap0;
    extern char far * bitmap1;
    extern char far * bitmap2;
    extern char far * bitmap3;
    extern union{ struct {unsigned int a1; unsigned int a2;} address;
                  char far * faraddress;} u1;
    extern unsigned int seg1,seg2,seg3,seg4,off1,off2,off3,off4;
    extern char * textptr;
    extern char text1[],text2[],text3[],text4[],text5[];
    extern char text6[],text7[],text8[];
    extern int mouse_flag,mouse_button,mouse_x,mouse_y;
    extern int mouse_minx,mouse_maxx,mouse_miny,mouse_maxy;
    extern char Herc;
    extern char far *HPtr;
    extern struct SREGS segregs;
    extern unsigned int segment;
    extern unsigned int offset;
    extern FILE *image_file;
    extern char image_buffer[];
    extern char f1[],f2[],f3[],f4[],f5[],f6[],f7[],f8[],f9[],f10[],f11[];
    extern int GS_penx,GS_peny,GS_penclr,GS_fillclr,GS_boundaryclr;
    extern int GS_bgclr;
    extern unsigned char * GS_hatch;
    extern unsigned char * GS_shade;
    extern int GS_text_st,GS_text_ht,GS_text_wd,GS_text_clr;
    /* color of font */
```

```
extern int GS_text_x,GS_text_y;
extern char GS_text_script[];

/*_____

                L I B R A R Y - I N D E P E N D E N T
                G R A P H I C S      R O U T I N E S
  _____

This set of library-independent routines is currently able to
map generic calls to the specific syntax of the QuickC graphics
library and the Turbo C graphics library.  By following the
book, it is a straightforward task to add code to support the
syntax of third-party graphics libraries such as HALO 88 (tm),
Essential Graphics (tm), MetaWINDOW (tm), and others.
  _____ */

void WindowOpen(int x1,int y1,int x2,int y2){    /* open viewport */
#if GraphicsLibrary==QuickC
  _setviewport(x1,y1,x2,y2);
#elif GraphicsLibrary==TurboC
  setviewport(x1,y1,x2,y2,1);
#endif
return;}
/*_____ */

void WindowClose(int x_res,int y_res){       /* shut down viewport */
#if GraphicsLibrary==QuickC
  _setviewport(0,0,x_res-1,y_res-1);
#elif GraphicsLibrary==TurboC
  setviewport(0,0,x_res-1,y_res-1,1);
#endif
return;}
/*_____ */

void WindowClear(int bgclr){        /* blanks the drawing viewport */
#if GraphicsLibrary==QuickC
  SetFill(fill_100,bgclr);
  DrawPanel(0,0,(clipx2-clipx1),(clipy2-clipy1));
#elif GraphicsLibrary==TurboC
  setfillstyle(SOLID_FILL,bgclr);
  DrawPanel(0,0,(clipx2-clipx1),(clipy2-clipy1));
#endif
return;}
/*_____ */

void GetWindowCoords(int x,int y){    /* converts physical screen
                    coords return by the mouse to viewport coords
                    relative to the 0,0 viewport origin. */
GS_penx=x-clipx1;GS_peny=y-clipy1;
return;}
/*_____ */

void SetHue(int hueclr){        /* sets the active drawing color */
#if GraphicsLibrary==QuickC
  _setcolor(hueclr);
#elif GraphicsLibrary==TurboC
  setcolor(hueclr);
#endif
return;}
/*_____ */

void SetLine(int style){          /* sets the current line style */
#if GraphicsLibrary==QuickC
  _setlinestyle(style);
#elif GraphicsLibrary==TurboC
  setlinestyle(USERBIT_LINE,style,NORM_WIDTH);
#endif
return;}
```

Fig. 8-3.
Continued.

Fig. 8-3.
Continued.

```
/*_____*/
void SetFill(char *pattern,int hueclr){      /* sets fill pattern */
#if GraphicsLibrary==QuickC
  _setcolor(hueclr);
  _setfillmask(pattern);
#elif GraphicsLibrary==TurboC
  setfillpattern(pattern,hueclr);
  if (pattern==fill_100) setfillstyle(SOLID_FILL,hueclr);
#endif
return;}
/*_____*/
void SetPosition(int x,int y){    /* sets the current xy position */
#if GraphicsLibrary==QuickC
  _moveto(x,y);
#elif GraphicsLibrary==TurboC
  moveto(x,y);
#endif
return;}
/*_____*/
void WriteToPage(int p){                   /* sets the active page */
#if GraphicsLibrary==QuickC
  _setactivepage(p);
#elif GraphicsLibrary==TurboC
  setactivepage(p);
#endif
return;}
/*_____*/
void DisplayPage(int p){                  /* sets the visible page */
#if GraphicsLibrary==QuickC
  _setvisualpage(p);
#elif GraphicsLibraryk==TurboC
  setvisualpage(p);
#endif
return;}
/*_____*/
void BlankPage(void){          /* blanks the current active page */
#if GraphicsLibrary==QuickC
  _clearscreen(_GCLEARSCREEN);
#elif GraphicsLibrary==TurboC
  cleardevice();
#endif
return;}
/*_____*/
void DrawDot(int x,int y){       /* draws dot at current position */
#if GraphicsLibrary==QuickC
  _moveto(x,y);_setpixel(x,y);
#elif GraphicsLibrary==TurboC
  moveto(x,y);putpixel(x,y,GS_penclr);
#endif
return;}
/*_____*/
void DrawLine(int x,int y){   /* draws line from current position */
#if GraphicsLibrary==QuickC
  _lineto(x,y);
#elif GraphicsLibrary==TurboC
  lineto(x,y);
#endif
return;}
/*_____*/
void DrawBorder(int x1,int y1,int x2,int y2){ /* draws rectangle */
#if GraphicsLibrary==QuickC
```

Fig. 8-3.
Continued.

```
  _rectangle(_GBORDER,x1,y1,x2,y2);
#elif GraphicsLibrary==TurboC
  rectangle(x1,y1,x2,y2);
#endif
return;}
/*_____*/

void DrawPanel(int x1,int y1,int x2,int y2){  /* solid rectangle */
#if GraphicsLibrary==QuickC
  _rectangle(_GFILLINTERIOR,x1,y1,x2,y2);
#elif GraphicsLibrary==TurboC
  bar(x1,y1,x2,y2);
#endif
return;}
/*_____*/

void Fill(int x,int y,int edgeclr){              /* fountain fill */
#if GraphicsLibrary==QuickC
  _floodfill(x,y,edgeclr);
#elif GraphicsLibrary==TurboC
  floodfill(x,y,edgeclr);
#endif
return;}
/*_____*/

void DrawCircle(int x,int y,int radius){ /* draws outline circle */
  int xradius;float yradius;
  int x1,y1,x2,y2;
xradius=radius;
switch(mode_flag){        /* use pixel aspect ratio to determine y */
  case 1: yradius=(float)radius;break;
  case 2: yradius=((float)radius)*.729;break;
  case 3: yradius=((float)radius)*.417;break;
  case 4: yradius=(float)radius;break;
  case 5: yradius=((float)radius)*.417;break;
  case 6: yradius=((float)radius)*.64;break;}
#if GraphicsLibrary==QuickC
  x1=x-xradius;y1=y-((int)yradius);
  x2=x+xradius;y2=y+((int)yradius);
  _ellipse(_GBORDER,x1,y1,x2,y2);
#elif GraphicsLibrary==TurboC
  ellipse(x,y,0,360,xradius,(int)yradius);
#endif
return;}
/*_____*/

void DrawDisk(int x,int y,int radius){    /* draws filled circle */
  int xradius;float yradius;
  int x1,y1,x2,y2;
xradius=radius;
switch(mode_flag){        /* use pixel aspect ratio to determine y */
  case 1: yradius=(float)radius;break;
  case 2: yradius=((float)radius)*.729;break;
  case 3: yradius=((float)radius)*.417;break;
  case 4: yradius=(float)radius;break;
  case 5: yradius=((float)radius)*.417;break;
  case 6: yradius=((float)radius)*.64;break;}
#if GraphicsLibrary==QuickC
  x1=x-xradius;y1=y-((int)yradius);
  x2=x+xradius;y2=y+((int)yradius);
  _ellipse(_GFILLINTERIOR,x1,y1,x2,y2);
#elif GraphicsLibrary==TurboC
  fillellipse(x,y,xradius,(int)yradius);
#endif
return;}
/*_____*/

void DrawEllipse(int x,int y,int xrad,int yrad){       /* outline */
  int x1,y1,x2,y2;
```

Fig. 8-3.
Continued.

```
#if GraphicsLibrary==QuickC
  x1=x-xrad;x2=x+xrad;
  y1=y-yrad;y2=y+yrad;
  _ellipse(_GBORDER,x1,y1,x2,y2);
#elif GraphicsLibrary==TurboC
  ellipse(x,y,0,360,xrad,yrad);
#endif
return;}
/*_____*/

void DrawSolidEllipse(int x,int y,int xrad,int yrad){    /* solid */
  int x1,y1,x2,y2;
#if GraphicLibrary==QuickC
  x1=x-xrad;x2=x+xrad;
  y1=y-yrad;y2=y+yrad;
  _ellipse(_GFILLINTERIOR,x1,y1,x2,y2);
#elif GraphicsLibrary==TurboC
  fillellipse(x,y,xrad,yrad);
#endif
return;}
/*_____*/

void DrawCurve(int x1,int y1,int x2,int y2,  /* parametric curve */
               int x3,int y3,int x4,int y4){
  float t,t2,t3;                         /* declare local variables */
t=0.0;t2=t*t;t3=t*t*t;                    /* reset control parameters */
GetCurvePoint(x1,y1,x2,y2,x3,y3,x4,y4,t,t2,t3);   /* start point */
SetPosition(GS_penx,GS_peny);DrawDot(GS_penx,GS_peny);
for (t=0.0;t<=1.01;t+=.05){        /* find all subsequent points */
  t2=t*t;t3=t*t*t;
  GetCurvePoint(x1,y1,x2,y2,x3,y3,x4,y4,t,t2,t3);
  DrawLine(GS_penx,GS_peny);}
return;}
/*_____*/

void GetCurvePoint(int x1,int y1,int x2,int y2, /* get one point */
               int x3,int y3,int x4,int y4,
               float t,float t2,float t3){
  float j1,j2,j3,j4;                     /* declare local variables */
j1=x1*(-t3+3*t2-3*t+1);j2=x2*(3*t3-6*t2+3*t);
j3=x3*(-3*t3+3*t2);j4=x4*t3;
GS_penx=j1+j2+j3+j4;                          /* reset x coordinate */
j1=y1*(-t3+3*t2-3*t+1);j2=y2*(3*t3-6*t2+3*t);
j3=y3*(-3*t3+3*t2);j4=y4*t3;
GS_peny=j1+j2+j3+j4;                          /* reset y coordinate */
return;}
/*_____*/

char far * MemBlock(int x1,int y1,int x2,int y2){
                         /* allocate array block in far heap */
char far *blk;
#if GraphicsLibrary==QuickC
  blk=(char far*)_fmalloc((unsigned int)_imagesize(x1,y1,x2,y2));
#elif GraphicsLibrary==TurboC
  blk=(char far*)farmalloc((unsigned long)imagesize(x1,y1,x2,y2));
#endif
return blk;}
/*_____*/

void GetBlock(int x1,int y1,int x2,int y2,char far *blk){
/* save graphic array in pre-allocated memory block */
#if GraphicsLibrary==QuickC
  _getimage(x1,y1,x2,y2,blk);
#elif GraphicsLibrary==TurboC
  getimage(x1,y1,x2,y2,blk);
#endif
return;}
/*_____*/
```

```
void PutXOR(int x,int y,char far *blk){    /* XOR a graphic array */
#if GraphicsLibrary==QuickC
  _putimage(x,y,blk,_GXOR);
#elif GraphicsLibrary==TurboC
  putimage(x,y,blk,XOR_PUT);
#endif
return;}
/*_____*/

void PutPSET(int x,int y,char far *blk){ /* PSET a graphic array */
#if GraphicsLibrary==QuickC
  _putimage(x,y,blk,_GPSET);
#elif GraphicsLibrary==TurboC
  putimage(x,y,blk,COPY_PUT);
#endif
return;}
/*_____*/

void PutText(int row,int col,int clr,char * tptr){ /* write text */
int TCrow,TCcol,tempclr;
#if GraphicsLibrary==QuickC
  _settextposition(row,col);_settextcolor(clr);_outtext(tptr);
#elif GraphicsLibrary==TurboC
  TCcol=(col*alpha_x)-alpha_x;               /* convert col to x */
  TCrow=(row*alpha_y)-alpha_y;               /* convert row to y */
  tempclr=getcolor();setcolor(clr);    /* save, set active color */
  outtextxy(TCcol,TCrow,tptr);               /* display the text */
  setcolor(tempclr);            /* restore previous active color */
#endif
return;}
/*_____*/

void SetTextRowCol(int row,int col){          /* set text position */
int TCrow,TCcol;
#if GraphicsLibrary==QuickC
  _settextposition(row,col);
#elif GraphicsLibrary==TurboC
  TCcol=(col*alpha_x)-alpha_x;TCrow=(row*alpha_y)-alpha_y;
  moveto(TCcol,TCrow);
#endif
return;}
/*_____*/

char far * InitHiddenPage(void){      /* initialize hidden bitmap */
  char far * vptr;    /* buffer address to be returned to caller */
#if Compiler==QuickC
  vptr=(char far *)_fmalloc(plane_length);
#elif Compiler==TurboC
  vptr=(char far *)farmalloc(plane_length);
#endif
if (vptr==NULL){                      /* if allocation failed... */
  ClearTextLine();                    /* display error message... */
  PutText(1,2,C14,text8);    /* Insufficient memory for Undo. */
  do {CheckForKey();}               /* wait for any keystroke */
    while (keycode==0);
  Quit_Pgm();}                    /* ...then shut down the pgm */
return vptr;}               /* else return buffer address to caller */
/*_____*/

void BackUp(void){                /* copies page 0 to hidden page */
switch(mode_flag){
  case 1:                            /* VGA 640x480x16-color */
          #if Compiler==QuickC
            outp(0x3ce,4);outp(0x3cf,0);
          #elif Compiler==TurboC
            outportb(0x03ce,(unsigned char)4);
            outportb(0x03cf,(unsigned char)0);
          #endif
          movedata(0xa000,0x0000,seg1,off1,plane_length);
```

Fig. 8-3.
Continued.

Fig. 8-3.
Continued.

```
                 #if Compiler==QuickC
                   outp(0x3ce,4);outp(0x3cf,1);
                 #elif Compiler==TurboC
                   outportb(0x03ce,(unsigned char)4);
                   outportb(0x03cf,(unsigned char)1);
                 #endif
                 movedata(0xa000,0x0000,seg2,off2,plane_length);
                 #if Compiler==QuickC
                   outp(0x3ce,4);outp(0x3cf,2);
                 #elif Compiler==TurboC
                   outportb(0x03ce,(unsigned char)4);
                   outportb(0x03cf,(unsigned char)2);
                 #endif
                 movedata(0xa000,0x0000,seg3,off3,plane_length);
                 #if Compiler==QuickC
                   outp(0x3ce,4);outp(0x3cf,3);
                 #elif Compiler==TurboC
                   outportb(0x03ce,(unsigned char)4);
                   outportb(0x03cf,(unsigned char)3);
                 #endif
                 movedata(0xa000,0x0000,seg4,off4,plane_length);
                 #if Compiler==QuickC
                   outp(0x3ce,4);outp(0x3cf,0);
                 #elif Compiler==TurboC
                   outportb(0x03ce,(unsigned char)4);
                   outportb(0x03cf,(unsigned char)0);
                 #endif
                 break;
      case 2:                                    /* EGA 640x350x16-color */
                 #if Compiler==QuickC
                 outp(0x03ce,0x08);outp(0x03cf,0xff);outp(0x03c4,0x02);
                 outp(0x03c5,0x0f);outp(0x03ce,0x05);outp(0x03cf,0x01);
                 movedata(0xa000,0x0000,0xa800,0x0000,plane_length);
                 outp(0x03ce,0x05);outp(0x03cf,0x00);
                 #elif Compiler==TurboC
                 outportb(0x03ce,(unsigned char)4);
                 outportb(0x03cf,(unsigned char)0);
                 outportb(0x03c4,(unsigned char)2);
                 outportb(0x03c5,(unsigned char)1);
                 movedata(0xa000,0x0000,0xa800,0x0000,plane_length);
                 outportb(0x03ce,(unsigned char)4);
                 outportb(0x03cf,(unsigned char)1);
                 outportb(0x03c4,(unsigned char)2);
                 outportb(0x03c5,(unsigned char)2);
                 movedata(0xa000,0x0000,0xa800,0x0000,plane_length);
                 outportb(0x03ce,(unsigned char)4);
                 outportb(0x03cf,(unsigned char)2);
                 outportb(0x03c4,(unsigned char)2);
                 outportb(0x03c5,(unsigned char)4);
                 movedata(0xa000,0x0000,0xa800,0x0000,plane_length);
                 outportb(0x03ce,(unsigned char)4);
                 outportb(0x03cf,(unsigned char)3);
                 outportb(0x03c4,(unsigned char)2);
                 outportb(0x03c5,(unsigned char)8);
                 movedata(0xa000,0x0000,0xa800,0x0000,plane_length);
                 outportb(0x03ce,(unsigned char)4);
                 outportb(0x03cf,(unsigned char)0);
                 outportb(0x03c4,(unsigned char)2);
                 outportb(0x03c5,(unsigned char)15);
                 #endif
                 break;
      case 3:                                    /* EGA 640x200x16-color */
                 #if Compiler==QuickC
                 outp(0x03ce,0x08);outp(0x03cf,0xff);outp(0x03c4,0x02);
                 outp(0x03c5,0x0f);outp(0x03ce,0x05);outp(0x03cf,0x01);
                 movedata(0xa000,0x0000,0xa400,0x0000,plane_length);
                 outp(0x03ce,0x05);outp(0x03cf,0x00);
                 #elif Compiler==TurboC
                 outportb(0x03ce,(unsigned char)4);
```

Fig. 8-3.
Continued.

```
               outportb(0x03cf,(unsigned char)0);
               outportb(0x03c4,(unsigned char)2);
               outportb(0x03c5,(unsigned char)1);
               movedata(0xa000,0x0000,0xa400,0x0000,plane_length);
               outportb(0x03ce,(unsigned char)4);
               outportb(0x03cf,(unsigned char)1);
               outportb(0x03c4,(unsigned char)2);
               outportb(0x03c5,(unsigned char)2);
               movedata(0xa000,0x0000,0xa400,0x0000,plane_length);
               outportb(0x03ce,(unsigned char)4);
               outportb(0x03cf,(unsigned char)2);
               outportb(0x03c4,(unsigned char)2);
               outportb(0x03c5,(unsigned char)4);
               movedata(0xa000,0x0000,0xa400,0x0000,plane_length);
               outportb(0x03ce,(unsigned char)4);
               outportb(0x03cf,(unsigned char)3);
               outportb(0x03c4,(unsigned char)2);
               outportb(0x03c5,(unsigned char)8);
               movedata(0xa000,0x0000,0xa400,0x0000,plane_length);
               outportb(0x03ce,(unsigned char)4);
               outportb(0x03cf,(unsigned char)0);
               outportb(0x03c4,(unsigned char)2);
               outportb(0x03c5,(unsigned char)15);
               #endif
               break;
   case 4: movedata(0xa000,0x0000,seg1,off1,plane_length);
               break;                        /* MCGA 640x480x2-color */
   case 5: movedata(0xb800,0x0000,seg1,off1,plane_length);
               break;                        /* CGA 640x200x2-color */
   case 6: movedata(0xb000,0x0000,0xb800,0x0000,plane_length);
               break;}                       /* Herc 720x348x2-color */
return;}
/*_____*/

void Restore(void){            /* copies hidden page to page 0 */
switch(mode_flag){
   case 1:                              /* VGA 640x480x16-color */
               #if Compiler==QuickC
                 outp(0x3c4,2);outp(0x3c5,1);
               #elif Compiler==TurboC
                 outportb(0x03c4,(unsigned char)2);
                 outportb(0x03c5,(unsigned char)1);
               #endif
               movedata(seg1,off1,0xa000,0x0000,plane_length);
               #if Compiler==QuickC
                 outp(0x3c4,2);outp(0x3c5,2);
               #elif Compiler==TurboC
                 outportb(0x03c4,(unsigned char)2);
                 outportb(0x03c5,(unsigned char)2);
               #endif
               movedata(seg2,off2,0xa000,0x0000,plane_length);
               #if Compiler==QuickC
                 outp(0x3c4,2);outp(0x3c5,4);
               #elif Compiler==TurboC
                 outportb(0x03c4,(unsigned char)2);
                 outportb(0x03c5,(unsigned char)4);
               #endif
               movedata(seg3,off3,0xa000,0x0000,plane_length);
               #if Compiler==QuickC
                 outp(0x3c4,2);outp(0x3c5,8);
               #elif Compiler==TurboC
                 outportb(0x03c4,(unsigned char)2);
                 outportb(0x03c5,(unsigned char)8);
               #endif
               movedata(seg4,off4,0xa000,0x0000,plane_length);
               #if Compiler==QuickC
                 outp(0x3c4,2);outp(0x3c5,0xf);
               #elif Compiler==TurboC
                 outportb(0x03c4,(unsigned char)2);
```

Fig. 8-3.
Continued.

```
                          outportb(0x03c5,(unsigned char)15);
                      #endif
                      break;
case 2:                                        /* 640x350x16-color */
                      #if Compiler==QuickC
                      outp(0x03ce,0x08);outp(0x03cf,0xff);outp(0x03c4,0x02);
                      outp(0x03c5,0x0f);outp(0x03ce,0x05);outp(0x03cf,0x01);
                      movedata(0xa800,0x0000,0xa000,0x0000,plane_length);
                      outp(0x03ce,0x05);outp(0x03cf,0x00);
                      #elif Compiler==TurboC
                      outportb(0x03ce,(unsigned char)4);
                      outportb(0x03cf,(unsigned char)0);
                      outportb(0x03c4,(unsigned char)2);
                      outportb(0x03c5,(unsigned char)1);
                      movedata(0xa800,0x0000,0xa000,0x0000,plane_length);
                      outportb(0x03ce,(unsigned char)4);
                      outportb(0x03cf,(unsigned char)1);
                      outportb(0x03c4,(unsigned char)2);
                      outportb(0x03c5,(unsigned char)2);
                      movedata(0xa800,0x0000,0xa000,0x0000,plane_length);
                      outportb(0x03ce,(unsigned char)4);
                      outportb(0x03cf,(unsigned char)2);
                      outportb(0x03c4,(unsigned char)2);
                      outportb(0x03c5,(unsigned char)4);
                      movedata(0xa800,0x0000,0xa000,0x0000,plane_length);
                      outportb(0x03ce,(unsigned char)4);
                      outportb(0x03cf,(unsigned char)3);
                      outportb(0x03c4,(unsigned char)2);
                      outportb(0x03c5,(unsigned char)8);
                      movedata(0xa800,0x0000,0xa000,0x0000,plane_length);
                      outportb(0x03ce,(unsigned char)4);
                      outportb(0x03cf,(unsigned char)0);
                      outportb(0x03c4,(unsigned char)2);
                      outportb(0x03c5,(unsigned char)15);
                      #endif
                      break;
case 3:                                        /* 640x200x16-color */
                      #if Compiler==QuickC
                      outp(0x03ce,0x08);outp(0x03cf,0xff);outp(0x03c4,0x02);
                      outp(0x03c5,0x0f);outp(0x03ce,0x05);outp(0x03cf,0x01);
                      movedata(0xa400,0x0000,0xa000,0x0000,plane_length);
                      outp(0x03ce,0x05);outp(0x03cf,0x00);
                      #elif Compiler==TurboC
                      outportb(0x03ce,(unsigned char)4);
                      outportb(0x03cf,(unsigned char)0);
                      outportb(0x03c4,(unsigned char)2);
                      outportb(0x03c5,(unsigned char)1);
                      movedata(0xa400,0x0000,0xa000,0x0000,plane_length);
                      outportb(0x03ce,(unsigned char)4);
                      outportb(0x03cf,(unsigned char)1);
                      outportb(0x03c4,(unsigned char)2);
                      outportb(0x03c5,(unsigned char)2);
                      movedata(0xa400,0x0000,0xa000,0x0000,plane_length);
                      outportb(0x03ce,(unsigned char)4);
                      outportb(0x03cf,(unsigned char)2);
                      outportb(0x03c4,(unsigned char)2);
                      outportb(0x03c5,(unsigned char)4);
                      movedata(0xa400,0x0000,0xa000,0x0000,plane_length);
                      outportb(0x03ce,(unsigned char)4);
                      outportb(0x03cf,(unsigned char)3);
                      outportb(0x03c4,(unsigned char)2);
                      outportb(0x03c5,(unsigned char)8);
                      movedata(0xa400,0x0000,0xa000,0x0000,plane_length);
                      outportb(0x03ce,(unsigned char)4);
                      outportb(0x03cf,(unsigned char)0);
                      outportb(0x03c4,(unsigned char)2);
                      outportb(0x03c5,(unsigned char)15);
                      #endif
                      break;
```

Fig. 8-3.
Continued.

```
       case 4: movedata(seg1,off1,0xa000,0x0000,plane_length);
               break;                            /* MCGA 640x480x2-color */
       case 5: movedata(seg1,off1,0xb800,0x0000,plane_length);
               break;                            /* CGA 640x200x2-color */
       case 6: movedata(0xb800,0x0000,0xb000,0x0000,plane_length);
               break;}                           /* Herc 720x348x2-color */
return;}

/*_____

                  M O U S E    R O U T I N E S
_____*/

void Mouse_Initialize(){                /* initializes the mouse */
#if Compiler==QuickC
   inregs.x.ax=0;                               /* mouse function #0 */
   int86(MOUSE,&inregs,&outregs);       /* call interrupt 33 hex */
   mouse_flag=outregs.x.ax;         /* equals 0 if no mouse present */
#elif Compiler==TurboC
   regs.x.ax=0;int86(MOUSE,&regs,&regs);mouse_flag=regs.x.ax;
#endif
return;}                                       /* return to caller */

void Mouse_Show(){                /* displays the mouse cursor */
#if Compiler==QuickC
   inregs.x.ax=1;                               /* mouse function #1 */
   int86(MOUSE,&inregs,&outregs);       /* call interrupt 33 hex */
#elif Compiler==TurboC
   regs.x.ax=1;int86(MOUSE,&regs,&regs);
#endif
return;}                                       /* return to caller */

void Mouse_Hide(){                /* erases the mouse cursor */
#if Compiler==QuickC
   inregs.x.ax=2;                               /* mouse function #2 */
   int86(MOUSE,&inregs,&outregs);       /* call interrupt 33 hex */
#elif Compiler==TurboC
   regs.x.ax=2;int86(MOUSE,&regs,&regs);
#endif
return;}                                       /* return to caller */

void Mouse_Status(){        /* gets cursor location, button status */
#if Compiler==QuickC
   inregs.x.ax=3;                               /* mouse function #3 */
   int86(MOUSE,&inregs,&outregs);       /* call interrupt 33 hex */
   mouse_button=outregs.x.bx; /* 1 (left) or 2 (right) if pressed */
   mouse_x=outregs.x.cx;                        /* get x coordinate */
   mouse_y=outregs.x.dx;                        /* get y coordinate */
#elif Compiler==TurboC
   regs.x.ax=3;int86(MOUSE,&regs,&regs);
   mouse_button=regs.x.bx;
   mouse_x=regs.x.cx;mouse_y=regs.x.dx;
#endif
return;}                                       /* return to caller */

void Mouse_Setposition(){         /* sets mouse cursor location */
#if Compiler==QuickC
   inregs.x.ax=4;                               /* mouse function #4 */
   inregs.x.cx=mouse_x;                    /* set the x coordinate */
   inregs.x.dx=mouse_y;                    /* set the y coordinate */
   int86(MOUSE,&inregs,&outregs);       /* call interrupt 33 hex */
#elif Compiler==TurboC
   regs.x.ax=4;regs.x.cx=mouse_x;regs.x.dx=mouse_y;
   int86(MOUSE,&regs,&regs);
#endif
return;}                                       /* return to caller */

void Mouse_Setrangeh(){         /* sets min max horizontal range */
#if Compiler==QuickC
```

Fig. 8-3.
Continued.

```
      inregs.x.ax=7;                                    /* mouse function #7 */
      inregs.x.cx=mouse_minx;                 /* set the minimum x coord */
      inregs.x.dx=mouse_maxx;                 /* set the maximum x coord */
      int86(MOUSE,&inregs,&outregs);           /* call interrupt 33 hex */
#elif Compiler==TurboC
      regs.x.ax=7;regs.x.cx=mouse_minx;regs.x.dx=mouse_maxx;
      int86(MOUSE,&regs,&regs);
#endif
return;}                                            /* return to caller */

void Mouse_Setrangev(){            /* sets min max vertical range */
#if Compiler==QuickC
      inregs.x.ax=8;                               /* mouse function #8 */
      inregs.x.cx=mouse_miny;                 /* set the minimum y coord */
      inregs.x.dx=mouse_maxy;                 /* set the maximum y coord */
      int86(MOUSE,&inregs,&outregs);           /* call interrupt 33 hex */
#elif Compiler==TurboC
      regs.x.ax=8;regs.x.cx=mouse_miny;regs.x.dx=mouse_maxy;
      int86(MOUSE,&regs,&regs);
#endif
return;}                                            /* return to caller */

/*_____

          D I S K     I N P U T / O U T P U T     R O U T I N E S
  _____*/

void SaveImage(void){            /* device-independent image save */
switch(mode_flag){         /* call appropriate image save function */
   case 1: strcpy(f7,".BL1");strcpy(f8,".GR1");
           strcpy(f9,".RE1");strcpy(f10,".IN1");
           SaveVGAEGAImage();break;   /* VGA 640x480x16-color mode */
   case 2: strcpy(f7,".BL2");strcpy(f8,".GR2");
           strcpy(f9,".RE2");strcpy(f10,".IN2");
           SaveVGAEGAImage();break;   /* EGA 640x350x16-color mode */
   case 3: strcpy(f7,".BL3");strcpy(f8,".GR3");
           strcpy(f9,".RE3");strcpy(f10,".IN3");
           SaveVGAEGAImage();break;   /* EGA 640x200x16-color mode */
   case 4: SaveMCGAimage();break;      /* MCGA 640x480x2-color mode */
   case 5: SaveCGAimage();break;        /* CGA 640x200x2-color mode */
   case 6: SaveHGAimage();break;}/* Hercules 720x348x2-color mode */
return;}
/*_____*/

void LoadImage(void){            /* device-independent image load */
switch(mode_flag){         /* call appropriate image load function */
   case 1: strcpy(f7,".BL1");strcpy(f8,".GR1");
           strcpy(f9,".RE1");strcpy(f10,".IN1");
           LoadVGAEGAImage();break;   /* VGA 640x480x16-color mode */
   case 2: strcpy(f7,".BL2");strcpy(f8,".GR2");
           strcpy(f9,".RE2");strcpy(f10,".IN2");
           LoadVGAEGAImage();break;   /* EGA 640x350x16-color mode */
   case 3: strcpy(f7,".BL3");strcpy(f8,".GR3");
           strcpy(f9,".RE3");strcpy(f10,".IN3");
           LoadVGAEGAImage();break;   /* EGA 640x200x16-color mode */
   case 4: LoadMCGAimage();break;      /* MCGA 640x480x2-color mode */
   case 5: LoadCGAimage();break;        /* CGA 640x200x2-color mode */
   case 6: LoadHGAimage();break;}/* Hercules 720x348x2-color mode */
return;}
/*_____*/

void SaveVGAEGAImage(void){                      /* saves image to disk */
segread(&segregs);segment=segregs.ds; /* determine segment value */
offset=(unsigned int)image_buffer;      /* determine offset value */
strcpy(f6,f3);strcat(f6,f7);            /* initialize the filename */
image_file=fopen(f6,"wb");                     /* open the file */
#if Compiler==QuickC
  outp(0x3ce,4);outp(0x3cf,0);     /* set EGA,VGA to read plane 0 */
#elif Compiler==TurboC
```

Fig. 8-3.
Continued.

```
   outportb(0x3ce,4);outportb(0x3cf,0);
#endif
movedata(0xa000,0x0000,segment,offset,plane_length);
fwrite((char *)image_buffer,1,plane_length,image_file);
fclose(image_file);                           /* close the file */
strcpy(f6,f3);strcat(f6,f8);           /* initialize the filename */
image_file=fopen(f6,"wb");              /* open the file */
#if Compiler==QuickC
   outp(0x3ce,4);outp(0x3cf,1);    /* set EGA,VGA to read plane 1 */
#elif Compiler==TurboC
   outportb(0x3ce,4);outportb(0x3cf,1);
#endif
movedata(0xa000,0x0000,segment,offset,plane_length);
fwrite((char *)image_buffer,1,plane_length,image_file);
fclose(image_file);                           /* close the file */
strcpy(f6,f3);strcat(f6,f9);           /* initialize the filename */
image_file=fopen(f6,"wb");                    /* open the file */
#if Compiler==QuickC
   outp(0x3ce,4);outp(0x3cf,2);    /* set EGA,VGA to read plane 2 */
#elif Compiler==TurboC
   outportb(0x3ce,4);outportb(0x3cf,2);
#endif
movedata(0xa000,0x0000,segment,offset,plane_length);
fwrite((char *)image_buffer,1,plane_length,image_file);
fclose(image_file);                           /* close the file */
strcpy(f6,f3);strcat(f6,f10);          /* initialize the filename */
image_file=fopen(f6,"wb");                    /* open the file */
#if Compiler==QuickC
   outp(0x3ce,4);outp(0x3cf,3);    /* set EGA,VGA to read plane 3 */
#elif Compiler==TurboC
   outportb(0x3ce,4);outportb(0x3cf,3);
#endif
movedata(0xa000,0x0000,segment,offset,plane_length);
fwrite((char *)image_buffer,1,plane_length,image_file);
fclose(image_file);                           /* close the file */
#if Compiler==QuickC
   outp(0x3ce,4);outp(0x3cf,0);       /* restore EGA,VGA registers */
#elif Compiler==TurboC
   outportb(0x3ce,4);outportb(0x3cf,0);
#endif
return;}
/*_____*/

void LoadVGAEGAImage(void){                 /* loads image from disk */
segread(&segregs);segment=segregs.ds;  /* determine segment value */
offset=(unsigned int)image_buffer;      /* determine offset value */
strcpy(f6,f3);strcat(f6,f7);           /* initialize the filename */
image_file=fopen(f6,"rb");                    /* open the file */
#if Compiler==QuickC
   outp(0x3c4,2);outp(0x3c5,1);    /* set EGA,VGA to write plane 0 */
#elif Compiler==TurboC
   outportb(0x3c4,2);outportb(0x3c5,1);
#endif
fread((char *)image_buffer,1,plane_length,image_file);
movedata(segment,offset,0xa000,0x0000,plane_length);
fclose(image_file);                           /* close the file */
strcpy(f6,f3);strcat(f6,f8);           /* initialize the filename */
image_file=fopen(f6,"rb");                    /* open the file */
#if Compiler==QuickC
   outp(0x3c4,2);outp(0x3c5,2);    /* set EGA,VGA to write plane 1 */
#elif Compiler==TurboC
   outportb(0x3c4,2);outportb(0x3c5,2);
#endif
fread((char *)image_buffer,1,plane_length,image_file);
movedata(segment,offset,0xa000,0x0000,plane_length);
fclose(image_file);                           /* close the file */
strcpy(f6,f3);strcat(f6,f9);           /* initialize the filename */
image_file=fopen(f6,"rb");                    /* open the file */
#if Compiler==QuickC
```

Fig. 8-3.
Continued.

```
    outp(0x3c4,2);outp(0x3c5,4);    /* set EGA,VGA to write plane 2 */
#elif Compiler==TurboC
    outportb(0x3c4,2);outportb(0x3c5,4);
#endif
fread((char *)image_buffer,1,plane_length,image_file);
movedata(segment,offset,0xa000,0x0000,plane_length);
fclose(image_file);                               /* close the file */
strcpy(f6,f3);strcat(f6,f10);       /* initialize the filename */
image_file=fopen(f6,"rb");                          /* open the file */
#if Compiler==QuickC
    outp(0x3c4,2);outp(0x3c5,8);    /* set EGA,VGA to write plane 3 */
#elif Compiler==TurboC
    outportb(0x3c4,2);outportb(0x3c5,8);
#endif
fread((char *)image_buffer,1,plane_length,image_file);
movedata(segment,offset,0xa000,0x0000,plane_length);
fclose(image_file);                               /* close the file */
#if Compiler==QuickC
    outp(0x3c4,2);outp(0x3c5,0xF);    /* restore EGA,VGA registers */
#elif Compiler==TurboC
    outportb(0x3c4,2);outportb(0x3c5,0xF);
#endif
return;}
/*_____*/

void SaveCGAimage(void){                     /* saves image to disk */
segread(&segregs);segment=segregs.ds; /* determine segment value */
offset=(unsigned int)image_buffer;       /* determine offset value */
strcpy(f6,f3);strcat(f6,".CGA");     /* initialize the filename */
image_file=fopen(f6,"wb");                          /* open the file */
movedata(0xb800,0x0000,segment,offset,plane_length);
fwrite((char *)image_buffer,1,plane_length,image_file);
fclose(image_file);                               /* close the file */
return;}
/*_____*/

void LoadCGAimage(void){                     /* loads image from disk */
segread(&segregs);segment=segregs.ds; /* determine segment value */
offset=(unsigned int)image_buffer;       /* determine offset value */
strcpy(f6,f3);strcat(f6,".CGA");     /* initialize the filename */
image_file=fopen(f6,"rb");                          /* open the file */
fread((char *)image_buffer,1,plane_length,image_file);
movedata(segment,offset,0xB800,0x0000,plane_length);
fclose(image_file);                               /* close the file */
return;}
/*_____*/

void SaveHGAimage(void){                     /* saves image to disk */
segread(&segregs);segment=segregs.ds; /* determine segment value */
offset=(unsigned int)image_buffer;       /* determine offset value */
strcpy(f6,f3);strcat(f6,".HGA");     /* initialize the filename */
image_file=fopen(f6,"wb");                          /* open the file */
movedata(0xb000,0x0000,segment,offset,plane_length);
fwrite((char *)image_buffer,1,plane_length,image_file);
fclose(image_file);                               /* close the file */
return;}
/*_____*/

void LoadHGAimage(void){                     /* loads image from disk */
segread(&segregs);segment=segregs.ds; /* determine segment value */
offset=(unsigned int)image_buffer;       /* determine offset value */
strcpy(f6,f3);strcat(f6,".HGA");     /* initialize the filename */
image_file=fopen(f6,"rb");                          /* open the file */
fread((char *)image_buffer,1,plane_length,image_file);
movedata(segment,offset,0xb000,0x0000,plane_length);
fclose(image_file);                               /* close the file */
return;}
/*_____*/
```

```
void SaveMCGAimage(void){                          /* saves image to disk */
segread(&segregs);segment=segregs.ds;  /* determine segment value */
offset=(unsigned int)image_buffer;         /* determine offset value */
strcpy(f6,f3);strcat(f6,".MCG");        /* initialize the filename */
image_file=fopen(f6,"wb");                           /* open the file */
movedata(0xa000,0x0000,segment,offset,plane_length);
fwrite((char *)image_buffer,1,plane_length,image_file);
fclose(image_file);                                /* close the file */
return;}
/*_____*/

void LoadMCGAimage(void){                      /* loads image from disk */
segread(&segregs);segment=segregs.ds;  /* determine segment value */
offset=(unsigned int)image_buffer;         /* determine offset value */
strcpy(f6,f3);strcat(f6,".MCG");        /* initialize the filename */
image_file=fopen(f6,"rb");                           /* open the file */
fread((char *)image_buffer,1,plane_length,image_file);
movedata(segment,offset,0xa000,0x0000,plane_length);
fclose(image_file);                                /* close the file */
return;}
/*_____*/

End of Module 3 source code.   (This program has 3 modules.) */
```

Fig. 8-3.
Continued.

COMPILING INSIDE QuickC

To compile and run this demonstration program from within the integrated programming environment of QuickC version 2.00 or newer, follow these instructions.

First, ensure that the three source files, SKETCH1.C, SKETCH2.C, and SKETCH3.C, are in the directory where your C source files are usually found. If you are using the companion disk, copy them from the disk to the directory. If you are not using the companion disk, type them in from the listings in the book.

If you are using the companion disk, be sure to also copy the file named SKETCH.MAK from the disk to the source files directory. If you are not using the companion disk, you will need to create a MAK file. This file tells QuickC which C source files to collect together to make the desired EXE program.

The first step in the compilation process is to tell QuickC the names of the C source files in the project. Select Set Program List from the Make menu. If SKETCH.MAK already exists, select it from the menu display directory. QuickC will automatically load the first module for the project, SKETCH1.C. If SKETCH-.MAK does not yet exist, type its name in. QuickC will ask you if you want to create a new make file. Answer yes. QuickC will present you with a directory of C source files whose names you can place into the MAK file. Select SKETCH1.C, SKETCH2.C, and SKETCH3.C. Select Save to save the newly created MAK file. QuickC will automatically load the first module for the project, SKETCH1.C.

Press F5 to compile, link, and run the program. QuickC will check the contents of SKETCH.MAK to see which C source files to collect together.

If you experience any difficulties during the compilation and linking process, refer to Appendix A for a no-nonsense, quick-and-easy guide to getting the demonstration programs up and running.

For guidance on using the program once it is up and running, refer to the mini User's Guide in Chapter 9.

COMPILING INSIDE TURBO C

To compile and run this demonstration program from within the integrated programming environment of Turbo C version 2.0 or newer, follow these instructions.

First, ensure that the three source files, SKETCH1.C, SKETCH2.C, and SKETCH3.C, are in the directory where your C source files are usually found. If you are using the companion disk, copy them from the disk to the directory. If you are not using the companion disk, type them in from the listings in the book.

If you are using the companion disk, be sure to also copy the file named SKETCH.PRJ from the disk to the source files directory. If you are not using the companion disk, you will need to create a PRJ project file. This file tells Turbo C which C source files to collect together to make the desired EXE program.

The first step in the compilation process is to tell Turbo C the names of the C source files in the project. Select Program Name from the Project menu. Press the Enter key to see a directory listing of available PRJ files. If SKETCH.PRJ already exists, select it from the menu display directory. If SKETCH.PRJ does not yet exist, you must create it. Go to the editor and type in the names of the three C source files SKETCH1.C, SKETCH2.C, SKETCH3.C, each on its own line. Save that file as SKETCH.PRJ. Now go to the Project menu and type in the name SKETCH.PRJ.

Select Run from the Run menu to compile, link, and run the program. Turbo C will check the contents of SKETCH.PRJ to see which C source files to collect together.

If you experience any difficulties during the compilation and linking process, refer to Appendix A for a no-nonsense quick-and-easy guide to getting the demonstration programs up and running.

For guidance on using the program once it is up and running, refer to the mini User's Guide in Chapter 9.

COMPILING WITH THE QuickC COMMAND LINE

First, ensure that the three source files are in the current drive and directory. Second, use the following command line to create SKETCH.EXE:

```
C:\QC2\BIN\QCL /Ox /AM /F 1000 /FeSKETCH /W1 SKETCH1.C SKETCH2.C SKETCH3.C
/link /INF ⟨Enter⟩
```

This command line assumes that the command-line program QCL.EXE is located in the directory named C:\QC2\BIN.

For guidance on using the program once it is up and running, refer to the mini User's Guide in Chapter 9.

COMPILING WITH THE TURBO C COMMAND LINE

First, ensure that the files TCC.EXE and TLINK.EXE are in the current drive and directory.

Second, use the following command line to create SKETCH.EXE:

```
TCC -mm -G -IC:\TC2\INCLUDE -LC:\TC2\LIB -nC:\TC2\SOURCE SKETCH1.C
   SKETCH2.C SKETCH3.C GRAPHICS.LIB (Enter)
```

This command line assumes that the #include files are in the directory named C:\TC2\INCLUDE, that the library files are in the directory named C:\TC2\LIB, and that the three C source files are in the directory named C:\TC2\SOURCE. You can change these directory names on the command line to suit your own needs, if required.

Using the above command line, the resulting EXE file will be written to the directory named C:\TC2\SOURCE. When you run the EXE program, it expects to find the *.BGI graphics driver files in the current directory. It will behave erratically at run-time if the .BGI files were not found.

For guidance on using the program once it is up and running, refer to the mini User's Guide in Chapter 9.

USING THE PROGRAM AS A TOOLKIT

If you intend to use routines from the demonstration program in your own original programs, whether retail, corporate, shareware, or freeware, it is important that you read the licensing arrangements contained in the header of the source code and the full License Agreement contained in the Introduction of the book.

FILENAME CONFLICT WARNINGS

The EXE file produced by these demonstration listings might conflict with other EXE programs in your system. The run-time file for AutoSketch, for example, is also named SKETCH.EXE. This file would be overwritten if it is in the target directory when you are compiling Your Microcomputer SketchPad. In addition, the operating system may load and run the wrong version of SKETCH-.EXE if you are not careful in how you name your directories.

Play it safe. If you have AutoSketch or any of the other commercial software programs that use SKETCH.EXE as a filename on your fixed disk, change the name of the project file if you are compiling from within the integrated programming environment of QuickC or Turbo C. Change the desired name of the EXE file on the command line if you are using the command-line compilation/link process of QuickC or Turbo C.

9

User's Guide:
Your Microcomputer Sketchpad

THIS CHAPTER contains a mini user's guide for Your Microcomputer Sketch-
Pad—a full-length, full-featured paint/draw program. The complete source code
for the program appears in Chapter 8.

If you prefer to dive right into the program without reading this user's guide,
go right ahead. Your Microcomputer SketchPad is a robust piece of software with
an intuitive menu system operated by common-sense keystrokes. (Remember,
however, that disk I/O errors are not trapped—they can lock up your system in
some cases. No harm will be done, however. Simply power off and then reboot
your computer. You must be careful to ensure that there is enough free space on
the current drive to save images. Likewise, you should exercise care not to
misspell a filename during a save or load process. For tips on adding error-
handling routines to the source code, see Appendix C.)

INTRODUCTION

Your Microcomputer SketchPad is a powerful and versatile drawing program
that takes full advantage of the 16-color modes of VGA and EGA graphics
adapters. It will also run on MCGA, CGA, and Hercules adapters in the 2-color
mode. A special autodetect capability ensures that the program starts up in the
best mode for your particular computer system.

Using the program, you can create colorful drawings, realistic or otherwise. A complete kit of drawing tools are provided for you to use, including lines, dots, rectangles, automatic smooth curves, circles, ellipses, and more. Coloring and shading tools like airbrush, splatter, floodfill, pattern fill, and halftone shade fill are available. Specialized features like eraser and roller are also provided.

The easy-to-use, intuitive menu system of Your Microcomputer SketchPad makes you an expert the moment you start up the program, and the software works with virtually any mouse or tablet, so you can use the drawing tool with which you feel most comfortable.

You can customize Your Microcomputer SketchPad to suit your own creative tastes. Through the Settings menu, you can change the drawing color or the fill color to any one of 16 different hues. You can also pick from 16 different patterns, ranging from simple parallel line patterns to checkerboard and simulated brick patterns. Ten different halftone shades, ranging from 0% to 100% are available.

You can save your drawings to disk as image files. You can reload previously-saved image files for additional editing or to create impromptu slideshows.

You can create print-outs of your drawings by using memory-resident third-party utility programs which capture the screen. Many of the line drawings used to illustrate the text in this book were in fact created with Your Microcomputer SketchPad and printed out on an ordinary dot matrix printer.

SYSTEM REQUIREMENTS

Your Microcomputer SketchPad requires an IBM PC, XT, AT, PS/2 or true compatible with either a VGA, EGA, MCGA, CGA, or Hercules graphics adapter and appropriate display monitor.

If you are running Your Microcomputer SketchPad from DOS, the program may need as little as 256K bytes of memory to run, depending upon the graphics adapter you have installed in your system. If you are running Your Microcomputer SketchPad under the control of the QuickC or Turbo C editor, you will likely require 640K bytes of RAM.

Although the program will run when only a keyboard is used, you will need either a mouse or a tablet to actually draw on the screen canvas. Any Microsoft-compatible mouse will do. Be sure to install the memory-resident mouse driver software which comes with your mouse before starting Your Microcomputer SketchPad.

Any Kurta-compatible digitizing tablet can be used with Your Microcomputer SketchPad. Again, be sure to install the memory-resident tablet driver software which comes with your tablet before starting Your Microcomputer SketchPad.

INSTALLATION

Before your start the program, set the current drive and directory to the directory where you want to save your drawings or to where previously-saved drawings are located. If your version of Your Microcomputer SketchPad was compiled using QuickC, then the font file named TMSRB.FON should also be in this directory. If your version of Your Microcomputer SketchPad was compiled using Turbo C, then the font file named TRIPP.CHR should be in this directory. The software needs to be able to read the font file when it starts up.

To start Your Microcomputer SketchPad, simply type

SKETCH 〈Enter〉

at the operating system prompt. If the program file is located in a drive or directory other than the current drive and directory, then you must type the full pathname. For example, if the program was in a directory named C:\DEMOS, you would type:

C:\DEMOS\SKETCH 〈Enter〉

The program will load into memory and will construct the pull-down menus for later use by the menu system. Then it will build the sign-on display. Now it looks for the appropriate font file in the current directory and uses the font to present the name of the program as a title. If the font file is not found, the program will issue a cautionary message and will continue running anyway.

Your Microcomputer SketchPad is now ready to use. Press the Enter key to pull down the File menu. Press the Enter key again to clear the screen. You're now ready to begin to draw!

USING THE PROGRAM

All of SketchPad's powerful features are accessed via its intuitive menu system. Some selections on the main menu bar—such as File, Modify, Text, and Settings—will cause a pull-down menu to appear. Other selections on the main menu bar—like Draw and Paint—will move you to the on-screen pushbuttons situated along the left side of the display. Pressing any of these buttons will pop you right into the drawing canvas. The final selection on the main menu bar—Undo—immediately executes an undo function.

The Dialog Line

The dialog line at the top of the screen is the program's way of talking to you from time to time. It is also where you edit the name of any image file which you are saving or loading. The Input line at the top right corner of the screen displays the identity of any unsupported keys which you might press while the program is running.

The Help Bar

The text line at the bottom of the screen is the help bar. Pressing F1 will display a context-sensitive help message, pertinent to whatever menu selection you are currently using. Pressing F2 will immediately save to disk the current drawing. Pressing the Esc key will back out of the current menu position and return you to the main menu bar. Pressing Alt+X at any time will end the program.

In this implementation of Your Microcomputer SketchPad, the F1 and F2 keys are not activated.

The Canvas Filename

The Current File text, located at the top of the drawing canvas, displays the name of the current drawing. You can change this name by using the File menu.

In this implementation of Your Microcomputer SketchPad, the canvas filename display does not correspond to the actual active filename.

USING THE MENU SYSTEM

The menu system is controlled by the keyboard. Use the Enter key to activate any selection currently highlighted. Use the Esc key to back out of your current position and return to the main menu bar. Use the left-arrow and right-arrow keys to choose selections on the main menu bar.

When you are in a pull-down menu, use the up-arrow and down-arrow keys to make a selection. Using the left-arrow or right-arrow will move you to the next pull-down menu, bypassing the main menu bar.

When you are in the pushbutton area, use the up-arrow or left-arrow key to move to a different pushbutton. Press the Enter key to move to the drawing canvas to use the drawing tool you have selected, or use the Esc key to return to the main menu bar.

At any location in the menu system, you can use Alt+X to end the program. Hold the Alt key down and press X.

THE FILE MENU

The File menu controls the start-up and shutdown of the drawing session, as well as the saving and loading of image files.

Choose New to clear the drawing canvas. If you change your mind and wish to continue working on the drawing which you have just cleared, use Undo on the main menu bar to restore your drawing.

Select Load... if you wish to load a previously-saved image file. The current file name will be displayed on the dialog line. Press the Enter key to load this file, otherwise type in the name of the desired file and press the Enter key. If you make a mistake, press the Esc key to restore the filename to the name which existed before you began typing.

Choose Save to immediately save the current drawing as an image file using the current filename. The default image filename at program start-up is UNTI-TLED.DWG.

Choose Save as... if you want to specify the name of the image file to save before saving it. The current filename appears on the dialog line. Type in the name you want. You can press the Esc key at any time to restore the previously existing filename and save your drawing under that name.

Use Delete to erase a previously-saved image file from disk. This feature is inactive in this implementation of Your Microcomputer SketchPad.

Select Shutdown to end the program and return to the operating system (or to the editor if you are running the program under the control of QuickC or Turbo C). Any drawing that you have not saved to disk will be lost when you select Shutdown.

THE DRAW MENU

The Draw menu is implemented as a series of pushbuttons along the left side of the display screen. Use the up-arrow and down-arrow keys to scroll through the Line, Sketch, Curve, Rectngle, Circle, Ellipse, and Eraser functions. If you are unhappy with a shape you have just created, choose Undo from the main menu bar to remove it before creating any more shapes.

Line

Press the left mouse button or tablet button to set the starting point of the line. Move the cursor to where you want the end of the line to be. Press the button again and the line will be drawn. See FIG. 9-1. You can keep moving the cursor and pressing the button to continue the line, if you wish. Press the right mouse button or tablet button at any time to return to the main menu bar.

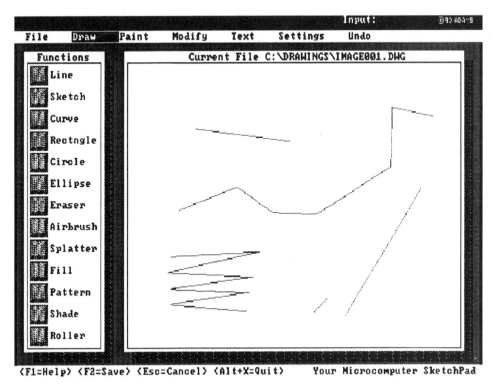

Fig. 9-1. Lines and polylines generated by the demonstration program in Chapter 8.

Sketch

Press the left mouse button or tablet button to draw a single dot on the canvas. Hold the button down while moving the pointing device to create a free-form line of any shape. Press the right mouse button or tablet button at any time to return to the main menu bar.

Curve

The automatic smooth curve function uses four points: two end-points and two magnetic control points. First, press the left button of the mouse or tablet to set the starting point for the curve. Next, move the cursor to an appropriate location and press the button to set the first magnetic control point. Then move and set the second control point. Finally, move to a desired location and press the button to define the end-point. There will be a short pause while the program draws the curve according to the points you have defined. See Fig. 9-2. Then you can begin setting points to draw a second curve, or you can press the right button to return to the main menu bar. You can also press the right button at any time during the point-setting process to abort the procedure and return to the main menu bar.

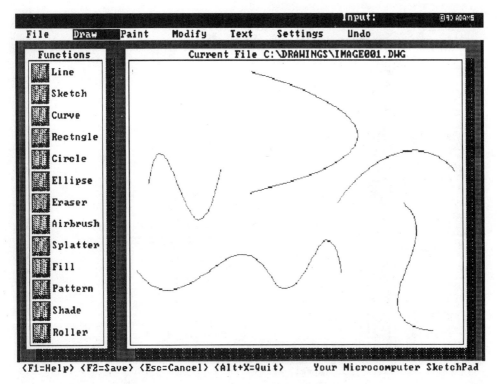

Fig. 9-2. Smooth curves generated by the demonstration program in Chapter 8.

Rectngle

Press the left mouse button or tablet button to set the first corner of the rectangle. Move to an appropriate location and press the button again to set the diagonally-opposite corner. The program will draw the rectangle you have defined. See Fig. 9-3. You can continue to draw other rectangles or you can press the right mouse button or tablet button to return to the main menu bar.

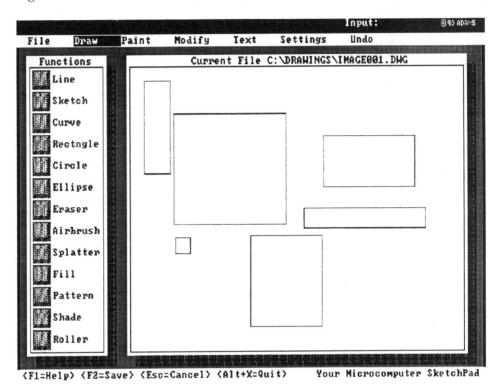

Fig. 9-3. The rectangle function capabilities of the demonstration program in Chapter 8.

Circle

Move the cursor to an appropriate location and press the left mouse button or tablet button to set the center of the circle. Then move the cursor left or right and press the button to set the radius of the circle. The program will then draw the circle you have described. See Fig. 9-4. You can continue to draw more circles, or you can press the right mouse button or tablet button to return to the main menu bar. If your radius request is too small, no circle will be drawn.

Ellipse

Move the cursor to an appropriate location and press the left mouse button or tablet button to set the center of the ellipse. Then move the cursor to a position

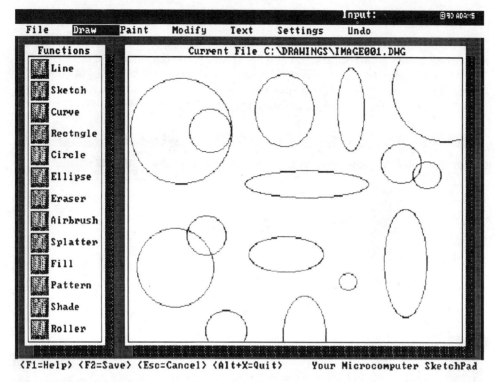

File   Draw   Paint   Modify   Text   Settings   Undo

Functions   Current File C:\DRAWINGS\IMAGE001.DWG

Line
Sketch
Curve
Rectngle
Circle
Ellipse
Eraser
Airbrush
Splatter
Fill
Pattern
Shade
Roller

‹F1=Help› ‹F2=Save› ‹Esc=Cancel› ‹Alt+X=Quit›   Your Microcomputer SketchPad

Fig. 9-4. Circles and ovals generated by the demonstration program in Chapter 8.

which indicates the horizontal radius and the vertical radius you wish. Press the button and the software will draw the ellipse. See FIG. 9-4. You can continue to draw more ellipses, or you can press the right button to return to the main menu bar. If your radius request is too small, no ellipse will be drawn.

Eraser

Press the left mouse button or tablet button to erase a small rectangular portion of the canvas pointed to by the cursor. The eraser actually clears this small rectangle to the same color as the canvas background color. If you wish, hold down the button while moving the cursor to sweep a broad area clean. Press the right mouse button or tablet button to return to the main menu bar. See the entry for Roller and FIG. 9-9 for an example of Eraser.

THE PAINT MENU

The Paint menu is implemented as a series of pushbuttons along the left side of the display screen. Use the up-arrow and down-arrow keys to scroll through the Airbrush, Splatter, Fill, Pattern, Shade, and Roller functions. If you are unhappy with an effect you have just created, choose Undo from the main menu bar to remove it before doing any more coloring.

Airbrush

Press the left mouse button or tablet button to spray a small group of paint droplets onto the canvas in the current drawing color, which can be reset by using the Settings menu. Continue as desired. Press the right button to return to the main menu bar. See the entry for Roller and Fig. 9-9 for an example of Airbrush.

Splatter

Move the cursor to an appropriate location and press the left mouse button or tablet button to splatter a glob of paint onto the canvas in the current drawing color, which can be reset by using the Settings menu. Keep splattering as desired. Press the right mouse button or tablet button to return to the main menu bar. See the entry for Roller and Fig. 9-9 for an example of Splatter.

Fill

Position the cursor inside a closed shape. Press the left mouse button or tablet button to fill the shape with a solid color. The color to be used as a fill can be

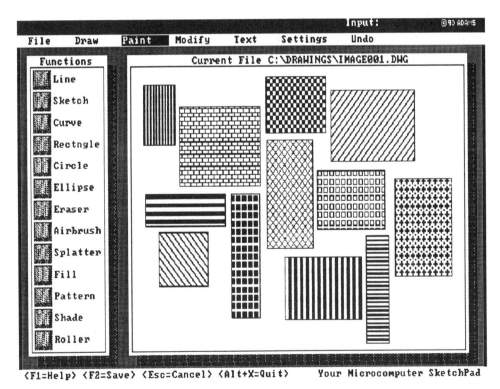

Fig. 9-5. Various area fill patterns provided by the demonstration program in Chapter 8.

set by using the Settings menu. The boundary color (the limits of the fill) can be set by using the Settings menu. Continue filling other shapes as desired or press the right button to return to the main menu bar.

Pattern

Position the cursor inside a closed shape. Press the left mouse button or tablet button to fill the shape with the current pattern in the current fill color. See FIG. 9-5. Both the pattern and the color can be redefined by using the Settings menu. Continue to fill other shapes or press the right mouse button or tablet button to return to the main menu bar. Different patterns in different colors can be overlaid to create an almost infinite variety of fill designs.

Shade

Position the cursor inside a closed shape. Press the left mouse button or tablet button to fill the shape with the current shade in the current fill color. See FIG. 9-6. You can use the Settings menu to reset the shade to a value from 0% shade to 100% shade. Continue to fill other shapes as desired or press the right button to return to the main menu bar.

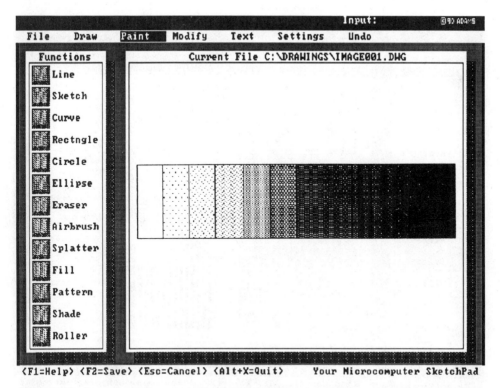

Fig. 9-6. The demonstration program in Chapter 8 provides a range of halftones (dither) shades from 0% to 100%.

Different shade colors can be applied over different background colors to create an almost inexhaustable selection of effects. See FIG. 9-7. Experimentation can yield interesting results. Even simulated optical effects such as transparency and translucency can be created, as shown in FIG. 9-8.

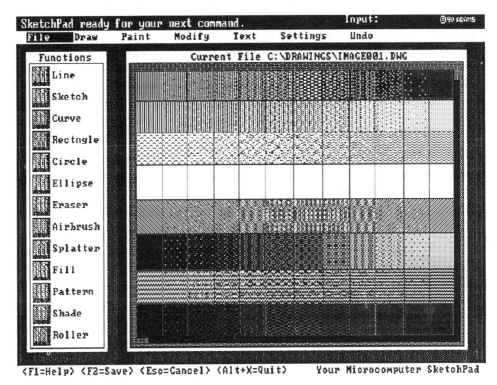

Fig. 9-7. By applying halftone fill (dither) over a colored background, over 2,000 different mixed colors can be produced on a VGA or EGA by the demonstration program in Chapter 8.

Roller

Press the left mouse button or tablet button to activate the paint roller. A small rectangle will be rolled onto the canvas in the current fill color. See FIG. 9-9. Hold the button down while you move the pointing device to roll on the paint. Press the right button at any time to return to the main menu bar.

THE MODIFY MENU

The Modify menu provides cut and paste capabilities for rectangular areas of the drawing canvas. Four functions are available: Copy, Move, Cut, and Paste.

These features are inactive in this implementation of Your Microcomputer SketchPad.

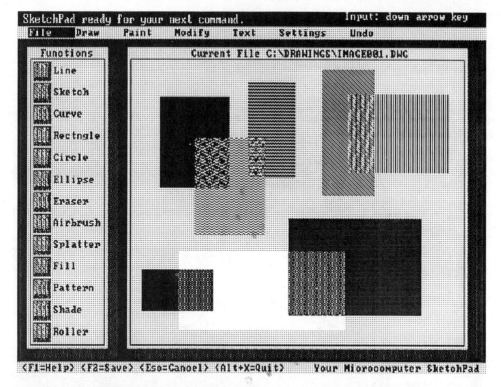

Fig. 9-8. By careful application of principles of radiosity, realistic simulations of transparency can be created by the demonstration program in Chapter 8. (The moiré patterns in this figure were introduced when the graphics were printed.)

THE TEXT MENU

The Text menu provides text display capabilities. Use the menu to pick the desired type style, as well as the desired height and width of the type. Four functions are available: Height, Width, Sans Serif, and Serif.

These features are inactive in this implementation of Your Microcomputer SketchPad.

THE SETTINGS MENU

The Settings menu lets you customize the drawing colors and patterns used by Your Microcomputer SketchPad. Five functions are provided: Active clr, Fill clr, Boundary, Pattern, and Shade.

Active clr

A swatch showing the current active color appears in the upper left corner of the drawing canvas. Press the Tab key to cycle through the available colors. On a VGA or EGA, 16 colors are available. On an MCGA, CGA, or Hercules, only monochrome drawing is supported. Press the Enter key to accept the displayed swatch and to return to the main menu bar. Pressing the Esc key will also return you to the main menu bar. Any lines or geometric shapes that you subsequently draw on the canvas will be drawn in the new color you have selected.

Fill clr

A swatch showing the current fill color appears in the upper left corner of the drawing canvas. This is the color which will be used by any Airbrush, Splatter, Fill, Pattern, Shade, or Roller functions in the Paint menu. Press the Tab key to cycle through the available colors. 16 colors are available on a VGA or EGA, otherwise only one color is available. Press the Enter key to accept the displayed swatch and to return to the main menu bar. Pressing the Esc key will also return you to the main menu bar.

Boundary

A swatch showing the current boundary color appears in the upper left corner of the drawing canvas. This is the boundary color for any fill operations

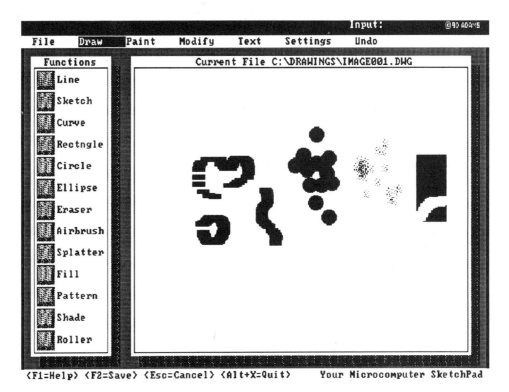

Fig. 9-9. From left: roller, splatter, airbrush, eraser functions from the demonstration program in Chapter 8.

like Fill, Pattern, and Shade. On a VGA or EGA, 16 colors are available. Only monochrome drawing is supported on an MCGA, CGA, or Hercules. Press the Tab key to preview the colors available. Press the Enter key to accept the displayed swatch and to return to the main menu bar. Pressing the Esc key will also return you to the main menu bar.

Pattern

A swatch showing the current fill pattern appears in the upper left corner of the drawing canvas. The swatch appears in the current fill color against a black background. 13 different fill patterns are available. Press the Tab key to see the patterns which are supported. Press the Enter key to accept the displayed swatch and to return to the main menu bar. Pressing the Esc key will also return you to the main menu bar.

Shade

A swatch showing the current shade density appears in the upper left corner of the drawing canvas. The swatch appears in the current fill color against a black background. 12 shades are avaiable, ranging from 0% to 100% halftone. Press the Tab key to preview the different shades. Press the Enter key to accept the displayed shade and to return to the main menu bar. Pressing the Esc key will also return you to the main menu bar.

THE UNDO SELECTION

Choosing Undo on the main menu bar will cause a canvas undo function to be immediately executed by the system. The results of your most recent drawing activity on the canvas will be removed, and the prior image that existed will be restored. If there is nothing to be undone, the drawing will be unchanged.

SAMPLE SESSIONS

Your Microcomputer SketchPad is powerful and versatile, yet surprisingly easy to use. The menu system is very intuitive. The drawing commands flow smoothly and the overall drawing environment is very forgiving. The program encourages creativity. Two sample sessions will serve to illustrate its potential.

Sample Session #1: American Flag

Figure 9-10 depicts the results of a 35-minute session using a mouse in a freehand manner. The image shown is of an EGA 640x350x16-color screen.

Before beginning, the entire canvas was filled with dark gray.

To build the drawing, first the mouse was used in LINE mode to sketch out the shape of the top edge of the flag. The line was drawn in red, in contemplation of future painting. Next, the line where the flag curves out of sight was drawn, also in red.

Fig. 9-10. Sample session 1. Surrealistic rendering of the flag, completed in under 35 minutes using Your Microcomputer SketchPad™, the demonstration program provided in Chapter 8.

The active color was then set to blue. The upper left blue corner of the flag was outlined and then painted in blue.

Next, the active color, fill color, and boundary color was set to white. The five-pointed stars were drawn. There was much experimentation at this stage. Many false starts were abandoned and corrected with the Undo function. After all the stars were finished, each was filled with solid white.

Then the active color, fill color, and boundary color were set to red. The outlines for each of the stripes on the flag were drawn—six panels in all. Each was filled with pure red. The same process was then repeated for the white stripes— four panels and a sliver.

The fill color was then set to intense white. Airbrush mode was selected from the pushbuttons and highlights were applied to each star. This looked rather appealing, so a thin strip of highlight was applied to the curve in the flag. Again, the result seemed appropriate, so the highlight was enlarged and emphasized.

At this stage, the flag looked right, but something was lacking in the drawing. It was the background.

First, the upper corners of the background were airbrushed black, to give a softened effect. Then a series of intense colors were airbrushed over the background. The artist's eye was used to scatter the color in such a manner as to accent the edge of the flag and to give a feeling of fireworks-like celebration of the flag's importance.

Finally, the airbrush color was set to black and a bit of shading was added to the bit of flag just behind the curve.

The entire drawing was done freehand. From start to finish no more than 35 minutes elapsed—and a good portion of that was spent deciding what to do next.

Sample Session #2:
Realistic Illustration of Aircraft

Figure 9-11 depicts the results of a 20 minute session using a digitizing tablet. The image shown is of an EGA 640x350x16-color screen, although the drawing is rendered in black and white.

First, an attractive photograph of an old U.S. military aircraft was placed on the drawing surface of the Kurta digitizing tablet. The four-button handheld cursor was positioned at each end of the photograph and the cursor was checked on the display screen to ensure that the drawing would fit on the canvas. After a bit of tinkering, the photograph was taped into position.

Next, the silhouette outline of the aircraft was drawn in black by tracing the crosshair cursor around the image in the photograph. Some of the details, including the cockpit cowling, ailerons, and rudder, were added.

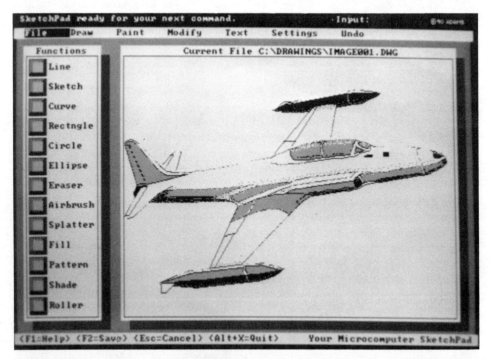

Fig. 9-11. Sample session 2. Realistic illustration of aircraft, completed in two sessions of 20 minutes each using Your Microcomputer SketchPad™, the demonstration program provided in Chapter 8.

Still using the tablet, a few areas were painted with a shade.

The image was then saved to disk. The computer system was shut down and the tablet was disconnected. A mouse was attached and the computer was restarted.

After reloading the image file, the mouse was used freehand to delete some of the black outline, especially at the top of the aircraft, where the light would be brighter. A few cautious experiments turned out pretty well, so the artist became more ambitious and began drawing large segments of the fuselage in white to break up the continuity of the sketch.

Then the drawing color was reset back to black. Using the SKETCH function, the mouse was used to add dots here and there, using a stipling effect to add realism to the drawing.

The artist then acquired a handmirror from the bathroom and inspected the drawing in the mirror in order to obtain a fresh viewpoint on the work in progress. Everything seemed acceptable and the finished drawing was saved as an image file.

After the photograph had been positioned on the tablet, the creative process took only 20 minutes. Half the drawing was done using the crosshair cursor of the digitizing tablet; the other half was performed freehand with the mouse.

TIPS AND TRICKS

Like any creative tool, the trick to producing really outstanding work is to be willing to experiment. Your Microcomputer SketchPad makes this type of tinkering easy, primarily because of its powerful Undo function.

However, to realize the full potential of creative experimentation, you must use an aggressive archiving strategy. As you reach a plateau in your work, save the drawing as an image file. Then, later, if you find you have come to a dead end, you can reload the previous drawing and try a new avenue of experimentation. At each important milestone in your drawing's evolution, save your work under a different filename. Don't ever leave yourself in the position where the only copy of your drawing is the copy on the display screen.

Another important consideration in using the drawing tools effectively is being familiar with what the tools can do. The pattern-fill function and the shade-fill function, in particular, are extremely powerful and versatile. They can be overlaid in a myriad of hyper creative ways.

It is the wise artist who knows their palette. Don't be afraid to take the time to just doodle with the program. Try out each of the pushbuttons and tinker with each drawing command. Change the colors and try different effects. Put circles inside ovals inside rectangles and splash some splatter or airbrush around. The more you experiment, the more ideas you'll get. Later, when you are working on a serious drawing, you'll recall some of these effects and you'll be able to apply them to your drawing. After all, its pretty difficult to use a tool effectively if you don't know its full potential.

ERROR MESSAGE REFERENCE

Two types of errors might be encountered during use of Your Microcomputer SketchPad. The first, run-time errors, are trapped and handled by the program itself. Messages are usually displayed on the dialog line at the top of the screen. The second type of error is associated with the operating system and usually involves the loading of the program and the return to the operating system after program shutdown.

The following run-time errors will be displayed on the dialog line during program execution.

RUN-TIME ERRORS

Font files not found. Text menu affected.

This message is displayed along with the sign-on screen. It means that the program could not find the font file it needed in the current directory. If the program was originally compiled with QuickC, then TMSRB.FON must be available. If Turbo C was used to compile the program, then TRIPP.CHR must be found. Program performance is not affected, except that the title on the canvas at sign-on will not be fonted text. Access to the text menu will be denied later in the program.

Access denied. Font files not found at start-up.

You are not being allowed to enter the Text menu because no font file was available to be loaded into memory at program start-up. See the previous entry in this section.

Inactive feature. Consult User's Manual.

The menu function that you are attempting to use has not been implemented beyond the stub routine stage in this version of Your Microcomputer SketchPad. See the next chapter for some guidance on enhancing the program's source code.

SketchPad ready for your next command.

The program is idling, waiting for your next keyboard input. Press the Enter key to activate the currently highlighted menu bar selection, or press the left-arrow or right-arrow key to reposition the highlight bar along the main menu bar.

Insufficient memory available. Press any key.

During program start-up, the software could not find sufficient memory to establish a hidden buffer to support the Undo function. Before each drawing command, the existing screen image is saved to a hidden buffer, so it is ready to be copied back onto the screen in the event you use the Undo function. This error condition will only occur with a VGA, MCGA, or CGA, because both the EGA and Hercules use a hidden page from the on-board display memory as the hidden buffer. If you are running the program under the control of the QuickC or Turbo

C editor, recompile the program as an EXE file and run from the operating system to free up more memory (see Chapter 2 for more on this).

Mouse or tablet required for drawing and painting.

A mouse or digitizing tablet must be installed in order for you to be able to use the pushbuttons and to draw on the canvas. The hardware must be physically connected to your computer and the mouse/tablet software driver must be loaded and resident in memory before starting Your Microcomputer SketchPad. Even if no mouse or tablet is present, the other menu functions are available.

SYSTEM ERRORS

Memory allocation error.
Cannot load COMMAND, system halted.

This condition occurs with some workalike graphics adapters running in an emulation mode, such as a VGA which is emulating a Hercules adapter. When Your Microcomputer SketchPad is shut down, the operating system cannot regain control because some pointers in low memory have been corrupted. The operating system is unable to find the starting address of COMMAND.COM in high memory and can neither reload COMMAND.COM nor pass control to it. The immediate solution is to reboot your system. The long-term solution is out of your control (unless you are an expert programmer), because of bugs in the driver provided by the manufacturer of the graphics adapter. The error condition does not affect the performance of Your Microcomputer SketchPad, only your ability to cleanly return to the operating system after ending your drawing session.

FATAL: Internal stack failure. System halted.

You held down a key on the keyboard while simultaneously holding down a button on either a mouse or a crosshair cursor.

Drive not ready

You are using a 5.25-inch or 3.5-inch diskdrive and the door is open or the drive is empty. The error message itself might have corrupted the appearance of the display screen.

Condition: system locks up after you attempt to load a file—
As discussed in Chapter 8 and Chapter 10, the source code for Your Microcomputer SketchPad contains no error-handlers for disk I/O. In this error condition, you have asked the program to load an image file that does not exist in the current directory. Because no method has been provided to recover from the file-not-found error, the system hangs.

Condition: garbage appears on the screen after you load a file—
You might have loaded an image into memory that was created while Your Microcomputer SketchPad was running in a different mode. An image created in the 640x350x16-color mode will load into the 640x200x16-color mode, but the result will be nonsense.

Condition: the mouse cursor or tablet cursor appears scattered when running in the Hercules mode—

Many VGA and EGA graphics adapters which claim to provide Hercules emulation actually do a very sloppy job of it. In this instance the mouse/tablet driver software is trying to write its cursor to a four-way-interleaved buffer when the adapter is still operating as a linear buffer. In other instances, Turbo C code has some difficulty recognizing some Hercules clones and VGAs or EGAs running in Hercules-emulation mode. QuickC seems able to recognize most Hercules clones and most other adapters running in the Hercules-emulation mode.

10

Programmer's Reference:
Your Microcomputer Sketchpad

THIS CHAPTER describes how the draw program presented in Chapter 8 works, from a programmer's viewpoint. The general algorithms and processes are described. A sequential discussion of the source code functions is provided. Also noted are program idiosyncracies and potential areas for enhancement.

For the complete source code of Your Microcomputer SketchPad, refer back to Chapter 8. For a mini user's guide, refer back to Chapter 9.

HOW THE PROGRAM WORKS: An Overview

The program is driven by six general states: preparation of the menu system, running the menu system, maintaining the graphics state, producing graphics output, and managing disk I/O.

Some of these runtime states exist concurrently; others only exist for a brief period and then disappear forever.

Preparation of the Menu System

The first task performed by the software is to create the graphical elements to be used by the interactive pull-down menu system. The graphics for the pull-down menus themselves are saved in RAM in graphic arrays, ready for later use. The design for the pushbuttons is also saved as a graphic array, but will be used when the sign-on screen is built. Other collateral components, like the highlight bars, are also created and saved.

All of this frenetic activity takes place in module 1 of the source code (see Chapter 8). Some of the library-independent graphics routines located in module 3 are called during this process. In addition, a module 3 routine which allocates a block of memory in the far heap is called from module 1 in order to set aside memory in RAM for a backup page for the Undo function if a VGA, MCGA, or CGA graphics adapter is being used.

Concomitant with all this activity, module 1 is also responsible for detecting and initializing the best graphics mode for whatever graphics adapter is installed. It will abort the start-up process if a compatible graphics adapter is not found (including an EGA with less than the industry-wide standard 256K of display RAM).

The final task of module 1 is to actually draw the sign-on screen and pass control to module 2. The program will not thereafter return to module 1 until shutdown.

Running the Menu System

When module 2 receives control, the menu system is activated. The main loop controls the interface with the user at the menu bar level. This loop will pass control to the pull-down menu loop or the pushbutton loop when directed to do so by the user's keyboard input. Each of these loops will jump to a switcher at the appropriate time to decide which core routine must be called in order to carry out the wishes of the end-user.

The menu system is a curtain between the end-user and the core functions. The end-user does not call the core routines directly, but rather graphically manipulates cursors and highlight bars around on the display screen. What appears to be happening on the screen, and what is actually happening in the run-time code, are two quite different animals indeed.

In a nutshell, the menu system gives the user control over three core routine processes: maintaining the graphics state, producing graphics output, and managing disk I/O.

Maintaining the Graphics State

The graphics state refers to such parameters as the current drawing color, the current fill pattern or color, the current shade percentage and color, the current viewport dimensions, the current background color, and so on.

Both QuickC and Turbo C maintain a table of global variables which hold these and other arguments. When a graphics routine from either the QuickC graphics library or the Turbo C graphics library is called, the routine uses these global variables to determine what color to draw a line, or where to clip a circle, and so forth.

Your Microcomputer SketchPad provides a higher measure of control by maintaining its own set of global variables. For example, a separate value for drawing color and fill color are maintained.

The user can specify the colors which are to be used by various drawing and painting functions. The core routines themselves are responsible for checking the appropriate variables, and for restoring any variables which they might change.

Producing Graphics Output

The most visible output of the program is its graphics output: the various shapes and colors which are displayed on the canvas portion of the screen. The menu system is resposible for managing a set of switch( ) routines which call the appropriate core function to perform low-level graphics output.

Prior to entering the core routine, any menu artifacts must be removed from the screen. When returning to the menu loops after the core routine is finished, any cursors and highlight bars must be cleanly restored. The invisible curtain between the menu system code and the core routines is impenetrable. The two systems work hand in hand, but they remain two separate systems.

This programming strategy makes it possible to surgically remove the graphics output core functions from the menu system. This means you can readily adapt the menu system routines to act as a front end for other C graphics programs you create. In addition, you can easily use the low-level graphics routines in other programs without being forced to use the same menuing system.

When all is said and done, however, the most important tools provided by the program during its provision of graphics output are the Undo function and the New function. Both tools provide essentially the same power: The ability to restore a previously existing condition. Clearly, New restores the system to a start-up condition: the canvas is blanked. Undo restores only by one increment: the canvas is backed up to its condition prior to the most recent drawing command.

The relationship between the menuing system and the graphics output routines is at its most fragile state during Undo or New. All other run-time conditions tend to move the program forward, but these two conditions are moving the system backwards.

Managing Disk I/O

The final state which is maintained by the program is that of disk input and output. The program uses the current drive and directory for all input and output, but permits the user to edit the names of files used for saving/loading images.

The menu system performs two fundamental services here. During a load, for example, the program must first find the image file and load it into memory. Next, it must move the data up into display memory on the graphics adapter.

ANALYSIS OF THE SOURCE CODE: Module 1

Module 1 of the source code contains the routines which create and save the menu graphics, create the sign-on screen, and handle general start-up protocol.

Compiler Directives

Note the addition of new constants in the Compiler Directives section. New compilers and graphics libraries have been defined in the expectation of possible conversion to these systems. The balance of this section of code is similar to the menu manager presented in Chapter 6.

Function Prototypes

The section of code named Function Prototypes contains declarations for functions that are used by module 1. As the source code indicates, some of these routines are actually present in module 1, while others are present in module 2 or 3 but are called by module 1. Note the significant number of low-level, library-independent graphics routines in module 3 which are used by module 1 during preparation of screen graphics.

Declaration of Global Variables

The section of source code named Global Variables serves to declare and initialize (assign a value to) variables which can be used by all the functions in module 1. Any of these variables that are declared again in the header of module 2 or module 3 can be also used by the routines in those modules, of course.

Many of the variables in this section of code are similar to the source code for the menu manager presented in Chapter 6. Note, however, the series of arrays named char hatch_1[ ] through char hatch_12[ ]. These are the patterns for the pattern fill function. Whereas the airbrush feature of the program uses a dynamic pixel-setting algorithm to create the pattern, as shown in Fig. 10-1, the pattern

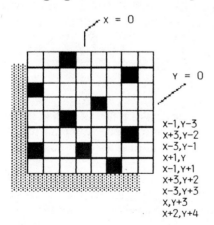

X = 0

Y = 0

x-1,y-3
x+3,y-2
x-3,y-1
x+1,y
x-1,y+1
x+3,y+2
x-3,y+3
x,y+3
x+2,y+4

Fig. 10-1. The airbrush pattern matrix and the corresponding xy offsets.

fill feature uses a predefined matrix. See FIG. 10-2 for a few examples of this matrix.

The numbers in each array are the decimal equivalent of the bits found in an 8x8 matrix which denotes the pattern. The author used a programmer's calculator to convert binary numbers to decimal during the codewriting process.

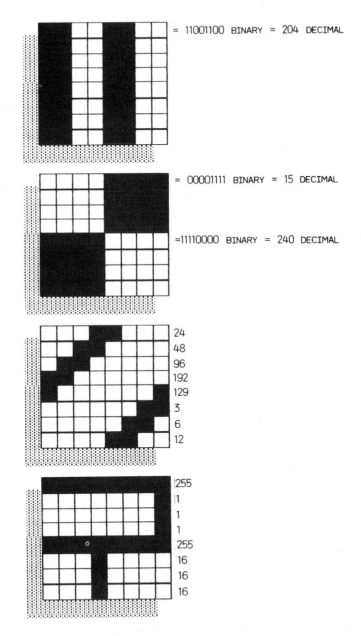

= 11001100 BINARY = 204 DECIMAL

= 00001111 BINARY = 15 DECIMAL

=11110000 BINARY = 240 DECIMAL

24
48
96
192
129
3
6
12

255
1
1
1
255
16
16
16

Fig. 10-2. How some of the fill patterns are derived.

Also of interest in this section of code are the strings named char text1[ ] through char text15[ ]. These contain the various dialog prompts and error messages used by Your Microcomputer SketchPad at run-time.

At the end of this section of code are the graphics state variables, each prefixed by GS_. These are global variables which can be redefined by the user through the menu system. The graphics output routines use these variables as arguments for color, shade percentage, pattern type, boundary color, and so on.

Function Definitions

The remainder of the source code for module 1 is taken up by executable code.

main( )

The main( ) routine calls the functions which perform the preparation work for installation of the menu system. Its first step, however, is to call Graphics _Setup( ) to initialize the best graphics mode for the hardware being used.

Note the section of code which has been disabled with remark tokens. You can remove these tokens and the code will test the amount of available RAM when the program starts up. This piece of source code is very useful for monitoring memory usage during program development.

After main( ) has completed its work, it calls MenuBarLoop( ) in module 2 to manage the menu system.

SetParameters( )

The function named SetParameters( ) assigns values to variables which control the sizes, colors, and position of various elements of the menu system. These values are used during the initial preparation of the menu system graphics.

The positioning of the pushbuttons is mode-dependent, and the code does a few gymnastics here to ensure that the spacing will be correct no matter what graphics adapter is being used.

CreateBars( )

The function named CreateBars( ) creates the main menu bar, the help bar, the current filename bar, and the label which appears above the pushbutton panel.

In each instance, the alphanumerics are first saved in a graphic array. Then the solid rectangle is drawn and the alphanumerics are XOR'd into the bar to produce the finished white-on-color graphic.

Note how the variable named text5 is used to hold a text string which is passed to the low-level text output routine, PutText( ), located in module 3.

CreateButton( )

The function named CreateButton( ) draws a single button and saves it in a graphic array. Note how different shades and colors are used to give the pushbutton a sculpted effect. fill_50, for example, denotes a 50% halftone shade.

CreateList( )

The function named CreateList( ) creates the text labels which accompany the pushbuttons along the left side of the screen. These are saved in a graphic array for later use when the sign-on screen is built.

CreateMenus( )

The function named CreateMenus( ) is responsible for creating each of the pull-down menus.

For each menu, the alphanumeric text is first saved in a graphic array. Then the color and border for the menu is drawn on the screen. The alphanumeric array is then XOR'd into the menu to create the finished image. The final graphic is again saved in a graphic array, ready for use when the user activates the menu system.

CreateHiBars( )

The function named CreateHiBars( ) draws and then saves in a graphic array the panning highlight bar for the menu bar, the scrolling highlight bar for the pull-down menus, and the graphic array which prepares the color swatch for the Settings menu. This routine also initializes a graphic array which will save the background before the color swatch is installed.

DrawScreen( )

The function named DrawScreen( ) is the workhorse of this module. Draw-Screen( ) creates the sign-on screen for Your Microcomputer SketchPad.

First, the background is created (blue in a 16-color mode, a gray shade in a 2-color mode). Note how the source code is specialized for each different graphics adapter.

Then the graphic arrays containing the main menu bar and the help bar are installed at the top and bottom of the screen, respectively.

The dropshadow is then drawn for the pushbutton panel. The panel itself is drawn.

Next, the dropshadow is drawn for the canvas, followed by the canvas, of course.

After a few housekeeping details, a short for( ){ loop installs the pushbuttons down the left side of the screen. The spacing for this was calculated in an earlier routine, remember. Then the alphanumeric labels for the pushbuttons are installed.

Next, DrawScreen calls BackUp( ) to store a copy of the current screen in a hidden buffer, just in case the user's first act is to ask for a New function.

Finally, the code initializes a font and displays the banner for the program in the middle of the canvas area.

The routine's last act is to set up a full-screen viewport and return to its caller.

InitUndo

The InitUndo function calls a routine in module 3 to allocate memory for a hidden page to be used by the Undo function. If not enough RAM is available and a VGA, MCGA, or CGA is being used, the program will abort and a warning message will be issued. Refer to the user's guide in Chapter 8 if you encounter this situation at run-time.

Note how the far address of each bitmap buffer, expressed as a segment address and an offset address, is first stored into the structure named u1. Next, these two values are copied to separate variables named seg and off, which will be used by the movedata( ) statement later when pages are being moved back and forth between the hidden buffer and the screen.

MouseStartUp( )

The function named MouseStartUp( ) tests to see if a mouse or tablet is installed. If so, it initializes the software driver and passes back to the caller a token named mouse_flag to indicate whether or not the program can use a mouse or tablet. The software will still run if no pointing device is installed, but the user will not be able to actually draw any graphics on the canvas area of the display screen.

Note how this function also sets some important parameters for the pointing device, such as the vertical and horizontal range, which is restricted to the canvas area. The low-level routines for the mouse are located in module 3.

QuitPgm( )

The function named Quit_Pgm( ) gracefully terminates the program. This routine can be activated when the user presses the Alt+X combination or when the user selects Shutdown from the Files menu.

FreeBlock( )

The function named FreeBlock( ) deallocates a block of memory from the far heap. This routine is called by DrawScreen( ) to free up memory after the main menu bar has been installed, for example.

GraphicsSetup( )

The function named Graphics_Setup( ) is the already familiar auto-detect routine. You can trace the different variables defined during this function's run by referring back to SetParameters( ) near the beginning of the executable code in module 1.

GetFreeMemory( )

The function named GetFreeMemory( ) is the same algorithm used by the demonstration program presented in Chapter 2 to determine the amount of free memory at run-time. This routine will never be called unless you activate the appropriate section of source code in DrawScreen( ).

Notice( )

The function named Notice( ) places a graphical copyright notice in the upper right corner of the menu sign-on screen.

ANALYSIS OF THE SOURCE CODE: Module 2

Module 2 of the source code contains the routines which manipulate the menu system, as well as the graphics routines which are the core functions of the program.

Function Prototypes

The section of source code named Function Prototypes declares functions that are called from module 2. Some of these functions are actually present in module 2, while others are found in either module 3 or module 1.

Declaration of Global Variables

The section of source code named Global Variables uses the extern keyword to redeclare variables which have been already declared and initialized in module 1. This ensures that these variables can be used by all routines in module 2.

Note the declaration of *SaveBgd, however. This variable is used by routines only in module 2. It is the address of the graphic array which is used to store the background before any pull-down menu is installed on the screen.

MenuBarLoop( )

The function named MenuBarLoop( ) is a loop which manages the main menu bar of the interface. It adheres to the algorithm discussed in Chapter 6.

Note how access to either the Draw menu or the Paint menu is denied if no mouse or tablet is present. To ensure that a pointing device is present, the following statement is used:

```
if (mouse_flag==0){
```

The line label menuloop: indicates the beginning of the loop that manages the pull-down menus. It works its magic by calling a routine named Scrolling( ), which determines whether the menu highlight bar is to be manipulated or whether the pushbuttons are to be manipulated.

Pay particular attention to the final dozen lines of code in this section. The switch( ) function is used to decide where to loop back to in the menu manager code, based upon which menu has been used, or whether or not the Esc key has been pressed and the user is simply backing out of a menu without using any of its functions.

Panning( )

The function named Panning( ) moves the highlight bar along the main menu bar of the menu system, ensuring proper wraparound at the end of the bar.

InstallMenu( )

The function named InstallMenu( ) is responsible for installing either a pull-down menu or a pushbutton cursor.

UninstallMenu( )

The function named UninstallMenu( ) is responsible for tidying up before the user returns to the main menu bar. Note how the routine makes a decision whether to remove a pushbutton cursor or whether to remove a pull-down menu.

PanMenu( )

The function named PanMenu() makes it possible to jump directly from one pull-down menu to another, bypassing any non-menu positions such as Draw, Paint, and Undo.

Scrolling( )

The function named Scrolling( ) controls scrolling of the highlight bar in a pull-down menu.

ButtonScroll( )

The function named ButtonScroll( ) controls scrolling of the pushbutton cursor when the user is selecting from either the Draw or Paint on-screen icons.

MenuChoices( )

The function named MenuChoices( ) is a pivotal point between the menu system and the core graphics functions. Using a series of switch( ) statements, MenuChoices( ) jumps to the appropriate core function and calls low-level, library-independent graphics routines from module 3 as necessary.

Note how the GS_ variables, which maintain the graphics state, are continually accessed and changed during this section of source code.

It is illustrative also to see how the WindowOpen( ) and WindowClose( ) functions are called whenever graphics output is generated. These two functions set up and disable a viewport which has the same dimensions as the drawing canvas, thereby ensuring that all graphics are clipped at the edge of the drawing surface.

Later in this section of source code, StubRoutine( ) is used often as a placeholder for routines which have yet to be written, such as features of the Modify and Text menus.

StubRoutine( )

The function named StubRoutine is called whenever the user asks for a feature which is not implemented semantically in the source code. StubRoutine( ) issues a standard message on the dialog line and then returns to the caller. In a unique case where the user wants to use the Text menu but no font file was found at program start-up, StubRoutine( ) issues a message specific to this situation.

MenuBarText( )

The function named MenuBarText( ) is called whenever the menu system wishes to display the message, "SketchPad ready for your next command."

ClearTextLine( )

The function named ClearTextLine( ) blanks the dialog text line. This routine uses #if and #elif preprocessor directives to determine which section of compiler-dependent code should be compiled. Note also how the code handles the special case of 9x14 characters used by the Hercules graphics adapter.

CheckForKey( )

The function named CheckForKey( ) checks to see if any keystrokes are waiting in the keyboard buffer. If so, CheckForKey( ) sets two variables which tell the caller whether the keystroke is a normal key or an extended key and what the ASCII value of the key is.

KeySwitch1( )

The function named KeySwitch1( ) is a switcher for keystrokes that are received at the menu bar level. In its current implementation, it displays the name of the key received on the upper right corner of the display screen. If <Alt+X> is pressed, you can see how the code will branch to a program shutdown.

KeySwitch2( )

The function named KeySwitch2( ) is a switcher for keystrokes which are received at the pull-down menu or pushbutton panel level.

Purge( )

The function named Purge( ) is used to empty the keyboard buffer. This function is handy to use whenever the user is leaving a menu function, in order to ensure that any unwanted keystrokes are not left in the buffer, where they might cause unwanted effects if read by the main menu bar, for example.

Purge( ) is also useful for preventing highlight bar run-on, also known as cursor run-on. If the user is holding down an arrow key to move a highlight bar, Purge( ) is repeatedly called after each step of the highlight bar. This means the highlight bar will stop moving the same instant that the user lifts their finger from the key.

EditName( )

The function named EditName( ) gives to the user the ability to edit the filename of images during the save or load process.

EditName( ) works by carefully keeping track of which character position is being edited and by copying any legal keystroke into that position with the line:

f3[position] = f11[0]

where f11[0] holds the ASCII value of the keystroke.

Note the use of multiple if statements to ensure that only characters which fall between certain ASCII values are accepted.

You can easily enhance this rudimentary editor to permit a wider range of legal keystrokes and to allow more editing features, such as a moveable highlighted cursor.

In its present implementation, EditName( ) will accept the currently displayed filename if the Enter key is pressed. If the Esc key is pressed, the previous filename is restored and used. Note how the previous filename was stored in a temporary string near the beginning of this section of source code by the line:

strcpy(f12,f3);

EditColor( )

The function named EditColor( ) lets the user alter various colors and patterns used by the Draw and Paint functions of the program.

Note how a switch( ) statement is used to first set the appropriate GS_ graphics state variable. Then the code tests to see if the Tab key has been pressed. If so, control branches to the appropriate section of code to display a color swatch in the upper left corner of the canvas.

This section of code is a good example of code that can be easily further optimized for speed and size. There is a lot of redundancy here, although the redundancy is what makes the source easy to understand.

MakeSound( )

The function named MakeSound( ) generates a sound from the computer's sound chip and speaker.

MouseManager( )

The function named MouseManager( ) is the central switching point for the mouse and tablet pointing devices. MouseManager( ) is an endless loop which keeps reporting the status of the pointing device until a button is pressed.

Because the mouse/tablet cursor is displayed only at the beginning of this routine, and because the cursor is always erased from the screen upon exit from this routine, it is a simple matter to keep track of the cursor to ensure that no graphics output corrupts it. Refer back to Chapter 4 for more information on managing a mouse or a digitizing tablet.

Delayed( )

The function named Delayed( ) is used to pause momentarily after each press of a button on the pointing device. This ensures that the program does not read x,y coordinates from the pointing device more than once while the user presses the button.

This function could be made more robust by making it dependent upon real time, not upon the do/while loop which is a function of microprocessor speed.

You might find it interesting to tinker around with the effects of this routine. Place a return; statement in the first line of this function, thereby rendering it ineffective. Then run the program and try using a function like rectangle or curve—you will immediately see the havoc caused by routines mistakenly reading the pointing device twice during a single button press.

GetTextCoords( )

The function named GetTextCoords( ) converts QuickC's row-column text coordinates to Turbo C's pixel-based x,y text coordinates. Note how the 9x14 character matrix of the Hercules graphics adapter is handled, as opposed to the code for the 8x8 character matrices of all the other IBM-compatible modes.

ANALYSIS OF THE SOURCE CODE: Module 3

Module 3 of the source code contains the low-level, library-independent graphics routines, the mouse/tablet routines, and the disk I/O routines.

Compiler Directives

Note the added constant definition for MOUSE in the section named Compiler Directives. This programming convention serves to make the mouse routines more readable.

Function Prototypes

The section of code named Function Prototypes declares functions called by code in module 3. Most of these routines actually reside in module 3; only three external functions are called by module 3 code.

Declaration of Global Variables

The section of code named Global Variables redeclares variables which were declared and initialized in modules 1 or 2, thereby ensuring that routines in module 3 can also use those variables.

Library-independent Graphics Routines

The section of source code named Library-independent Graphics Routines contains functions for low-level graphics output. Each routine expects to receive the parameters it needs from the caller, except for some graphics state conditions, of course.

Note the heavy use of #if and #elif preprocessor directives in this section to ensure that the code can be compiled with either QuickC or Turbo C. If you are using a third-party graphics library like HALO, Essential Graphics, MetaWIN-DOW, or Lattice C's GFX, you can easily add library-dependent code to this section. Be sure to also set the appropriate constant in the header of each source file to tell the compiler which code to compile.

The DrawCircle( ) routine is interesting in how it compensates for the aspect ratio of the display screen. This aspect ratio has been precalculated from the 4:3 physical ratio and the horizontal-by-vertical resolution of each graphics mode. DrawDisk( ), which draws a filled circle, uses the same approach.

DrawCurve( ) and GetCurvePoint( ) are used to draw a smooth curve from four control points supplied by the user. For a discussion of the mathematics involved here, refer to an earlier book, *High-Performance CAD Graphics in C*, #3059. See the end of the book for further details about related texts by the author.

Mouse Routines

The section of code named Mouse Routines contains the low-level mouse routines that are called by module 1 at program start-up and by the mouse manager in module 2, MouseManager( ).

These routines adhere closely to the industry-wide Microsoft standard and will work with any mouse or digitizing tablet which claims Microsoft compatibility.

If you are writing code which will use a tablet, you should avoid any calls to Mouse_Setposition( ), because the tablet cursor will immediately jump to its real physical position whether or not you have forced the cursor to a new x,y position on the screen.

Refer back to Chapter 4 for further discussion of mouse/tablet control routines.

Disk Input/Output Routines

The section of code named Disk Input/Output Routines contains the functions which save a binary image file to disk and which load a previously-saved binary image file from disk.

These routines use the algorithms introduced earlier in Chapter 5. Remember, this I/O is not error-trapped. Your computer will likely hang if you attempt to load a non-existant file. No feedback will be reported if the routines run out of disk space while saving an image. See Appendix C for helpful tips on writing your own error-handlers.

KNOWN BUGS AND POTENTIAL ENHANCEMENTS

A number of potential enhancements would make Your Microcomputer SketchPad a more powerful drawing tool.

First, you might find it useful to write a keyboard routine to control a cursor on the canvas. Then, if the program does not find a mouse or tablet at start-up, the user could use the arrow keys on the keypad to draw.

Second, you might wish to consider enhancing the capabilities of the filename editor. In its present form, if a typing mistake is made the program will hang the system when the routines attempt to load a non-existant file. In addition, if the user presses the Esc key the previous filename is restored, but the save/load routines are still called. You might wish to modify the code so no save/load is implemented if the Esc key was used in the keyboard editor.

Third, you could easily add many more pattern fill styles. Refer back to FIG. 10-2 to see how this is done. Then simply add more hatch[ ] arrays to module 1 and add more cases to the appropriate switch( ) in EditColor( ) in module 2.

Fourth, in its current implementation, the program offers only a single Undo buffer. You could easily modify the code to initialize and manage three or four buffers, depending upon available memory. This would make it possible for the user to Undo a series of drawing commands, not just one.

Fifth, you might wish to consider adding modules from the PCX Programmer's Toolkit to provide support for .PCX image files. These files can be exported to desktop publishing systems, other drawing programs, and some word processing programs. The Toolkit also provides image library management routines. See Chapter 5 for more discussion about the Toolkit.

Sixth, you might wish to add support for the 256-color mode. QuickC supports the 320x200x256-color mode of the VGA. Turbo C supports the 640x480x256-color mode of the 8514/A graphics adapter.

Part Three

3D Software Skills

11

Making Your Software Competitive:
Features of 3D CAD Programs

LAST YEAR the worldwide market for hardware, software, and consulting for 3D applications grew by 24%. And the explosive growth of this market shows no sign of letting up. 3D is here and it is here now.

Clearly, if you have aspirations of writing 3D software, you are hitching your wagon to a rising star.

AN INTRODUCTION TO 3D MODELING

3D software is used for everything from designing better jogging shoes to building better offices and homes, to planning more efficient space probe trajectories. The leading innovators and researchers in 3D applications are now working on computer-animated 3D humanoids which are nearly indistinguishable from genuine human actors and actresses. The potential for 3D software is as broad as humankind's imagination.

The car you are driving was likely designed with 3D software. The toaster you use probably was too. Ditto the design on your toothpaste tube.

The surgeon who is planning your operation is likely using 3D graphics to plan the tactics in the operating room. The municipal engineer who is laying out a new subdivision in your city is likely using 3D software to route the utilities.

Half of the special effects you see in the movies are created with 3D software. Many of the television program intros and TV news graphics are produced with 3D software—some of it on personal computers!

3D computer software can be divided into two distinct types: B-rep modeling and CSG modeling.

B-REP MODELING

B-rep modeling is an acronym for Boundary-*rep*resentation. See FIG. 11-1. Only the outer skin, or boundary, of the model being drawn is computed by the 3D routines. The surfaces of a B-rep model are usually made up of facets, also called polygons. By collecting together groups of facets intricate shapes, curves, and objects can be created.

B-rep modeling is easy to implement on personal computers. It is fast and produces good-looking images. Hidden surface removal can be accomplished using one of ten or more different algorithms.

Because of the algorithms used to build B-rep models, however, it is difficult to join two models together or to drill a hole into a model, so to speak. The B-rep model algorithm concerns itself only with the boundaries of the object, not with solid volumes or internal composition.

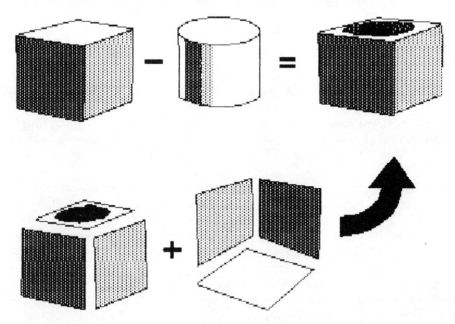

Fig. 11-1. Top: conceptual representation of the CSG (constructive solid geometry) method of 3D modeling. Bottom: conceptual depiction of the B-rep (boundary representation) method of 3D modeling.

───── **RELATED MATERIAL** ─────

A more detailed discussion of 3D modeling on personal computers can be found in another of the author's books, *High-Performance CAD Graphics in C,* book #3059, published March 1989, ISBN 0-8306-9359-9, available through your favorite bookstore or order direct from TAB Books.

CSG MODELING

CSG modeling is an acronym for Constructive Solid Geometry. Each CSG model is made up of 3D solids: cubes, parallelepipeds, cylinders, spheres, and others. See FIG. 11-1. Because each of these sub-objects is a legitimate 3D solid, they can be combined together just as in real life to produce more complex objects; and because CSG is based upon the volumetric structure of an object, the software can drill a hole into a model. As FIG. 11-1 depicts, a cylinder (the intended hole) can be subtracted from the model. This type of 3D logical operation is called a 3D boolean operation.

CSG modeling excels in applications where specific gravity, mass, moment of inertia, density, and other engineering-based calculations must be made. CSG modeling is true solid modeling.

Unlike B-rep modeling, however, CSG is very time-consuming and memory-intensive. CSG software often pushes personal computers to their limits.

USER INPUT

3D software often provides the end-user with an opportunity to control the design of the 3D primitives being used. This input generally falls into two categories: extrusion or sub-objects.

REVOLVE, EXTRUDE, SWEEP

The 3D functions revolve, extrude, and sweep are used to build 3D entities from a 2D outline or silhouette. FIG. 11-2 depicts an object being created by revolve. The end-user first specifies the silhouette shape of the desired entity. Next, the user indicates to the software which direction to revolve the outline and how many degrees to rotate. Finally, the software is responsible for generating the 3D object. Revolve works with both B-rep and CSG based modeling programs.

The extrude function also takes a 2D user-supplied outline and turns it into a 3D object. See FIG. 11-3. In this instance, the end-user specifies how far forward to extrude the shape. Extrude works with both B-rep and CSG based modeling programs.

The sweep function is similar to extrude, except that the extrusion takes place along a curve specified by the user.

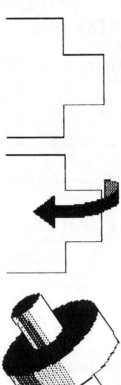

Fig. 11-2. The revolve function, also called revolution. Top: the silhouette or outline is created by the user. Center: the amount of rotation is defined. Bottom: the resulting solid.

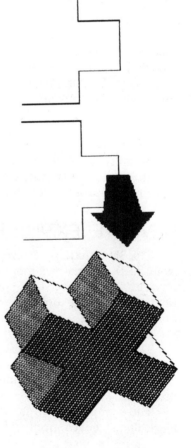

Fig. 11-3. The extrude function. Top: the outline. Center: the distance of extrusion is defined. Bottom: the resulting solid.

SUB-OBJECTS

Whereas revolve, extrude, and sweep require creative input from the end-user, software which provides ready-to-use sub-objects use a 3D toolkit. See FIG. 11-4. Often, the user simply selects a desired sub-object from a menu and then tells the 3D software where to position the entity.

FACT

Sub-objects are used by 3D software packages to provide the end-user with a toolkit of ready-to-use 3D objects.

Typical sub-objects include cylinders, cones, spheres, parallelepipeds, wedges, pyramids, laminas, toruses, and others. The user can alter the scale and ratio of each sub-object.

FLEXI-SURFACES

For randomly curved surfaces, flexi-surfaces are useful. Smoothly curved surfaces can be constructed in either B-rep or CSG modeling systems. See FIG. 11-5.

A ruled surface is based upon the surface created between two roughly parallel curved lines. These two lines are usually parametric curves whose end-points and control points have been specified by the end-user.

A cubic patch surface is based upon the surface created between four independently-curved edges. Each of these lines is usually based upon a user-specified parametric curve.

Ruled surfaces and cubic patch surfaces are useful for designing aircraft, automobiles, and consumer appliances.

REAL WORLD FUNCTIONS

Although many 3D software programs offer a myriad of features to build, combine, and alter 3D shapes, only a few functions are actually required in order to faithfully mimic the real world.

Consider a carpenter, for example. When working with a piece of raw wood, the carpenter's choices are somewhat limited to cutting it or attaching something to it. A cut is called *divide-and-discard* by 3D software. An attachment is called *attach* by 3D software.

Needless to say, however, a divide can take many forms. A 3D entity could be cut into two pieces. Both pieces might be re-arranged, or one of the pieces might be discarded. The cut might take the form of drilling a hole into the entity.

Likewise, an attachment can take many forms. The 3D entity might be replicated and attached to its former self to create a new 3D shape. Two separate 3D entities might be attached together and yet remain nothing more than two attached objects—or they might become a new single solid.

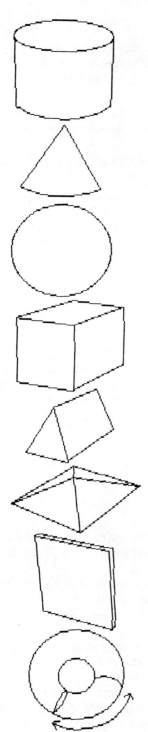

Fig. 11-4. Subobjects for 3D modeling. From top: cylinder, cone, sphere, parallel-epiped, wedge, pyramid, lamina, torus.

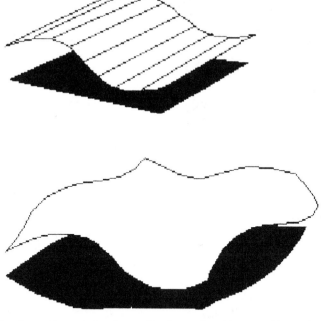

Fig. 11-5. Flexi-surfaces. Top: ruled surface or B-spline surface. Bottom: cubic patch or Coon's surface.

THE BAT vs. THE MOUSE

The keypad at the right side of your computer keyboard is often called a *bat* by 3D software programmers. Whereas a mouse operates in 2D on a flat surface, a bat flies through space, operating in 3D.

See FIG. 11-6. By carefully constructing your 3D program, you can give the user control over three different dimensions by using the arrow keys. The yaw, roll, and pitch planes are the same attitudes which describe an aircraft's

Fig. 11-6. The keypad as bat. The bat can operate in any of three modes, affecting translation, rotation, or extrusion of a three-dimensional model. Shown here in its rotation mode. See also Fig. 12-11 in Chapter 12.

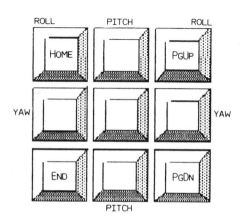

position. *Yaw* is a change in compass direction. *Roll* is a clockwise or counter-clockwise rotation. *Pitch* is leaning forward or backward. Look ahead to FIG. 12-6 in the next chapter for a graphic illustration of this concept.

COORDINATE SYSTEMS

3D software makes heavy use of coordinate systems that use x, y, and z coordinates to describe shapes and environments. The x dimension describes a left-right distance. The y coordinate describes an up-down dimension. The z coordinate describes a near-far relationship. (This is not always entirely true, however, as the next chapter explains.)

_____ **RELATED MATERIAL** _____

A more detailed discussion of 3D animation on personal computers can be found in another of the author's books, *High-Performance Graphics in C: Animation and Simulation*, book #3049, published November 1988, ISBN 0-8306-9349-9, available through your favorite bookstore or order direct from TAB Books.

Object coordinates are the xyz dimensions which describe the shape and nature of an individual 3D entity, model, or sub-object.

World coordinates describe the xyz coordinates which would describe the object if it were placed in a 3D environment (world) at a certain location and rotation.

Camera coordinates describe how the object would appear to an observer at a specified location in the 3D environment. The camera location is the viewpoint.

Image plane coordinates refer to the 2D coordinates that would be present on an image plane placed between the camera and the 3D object.

Screen coordinates are the xy coordinates that can be drawn on the computer display screen, corresponding to the 2D image plane coordinates.

Calculating each set of coordinates in this 3D cycle involves sine and cosine formulas derived from matrix math.

12

Programming Concepts:
Modeling and Rendering in 3D

IN ADDITION to a thorough understanding of standard graphics programming techniques, any programmer wishing to write a 3D graphics program must have at least a rudimentary understanding of 3D programming concepts.

COMMON 3D PROGRAMMING TERMS

A number of terms are used regularly by 3D graphics programmers.

Modeling refers to the drawing of the shape of the 3D object.

Coordinates refers to the xyz representation of a point on the model. *Coordinate system* means the xyz axes of measurement, relating to width, height, and depth: the three dimensions or 3D. A number of contradictory coordinate systems are in use today.

━━━━━ RELATED MATERIAL ━━━━━

For a more thorough discussion of 3D modeling and rendering, refer to the author's previous book, High-Performance Graphics in C, #3059, published March 1989, ISBN 0-8306-9359-9, available at good computer bookstores or order direct through TAB Books. (see listing at end of this book).

Rendering is used to describe the manner in which the 3D model is colored or shaded. Hidden surface removal and visible surface determination refer to techniques of drawing 3D objects so that backside surfaces or surfaces hidden by nearer surfaces are correctly drawn (or not drawn, as the case may be).

Solids modeling refers to 3D algorithms which treat each object as a real solid having properties of mass. Constructive solid geometry (CSG, see previous chapter) uses solids modeling. B-rep modeling refers to 3D algorithms which use facets or polygons to make up the skin (or boundary) of the object.

CREATING AND MANIPULATING 3D MODELS

The backbone of 3D graphics programming is the concept of xyz coordinates, which are used to describe a unique location in 3D space. There are, however, different types of 3D space, and a model must be carefully evolved through each type until it can be displayed on the screen.

Object Coordinates

Object coordinates are the xyz coordinates which describe the fundamental shape of the model. See FIG. 12-1(a). These coordinates describe object space, which for all intents and purposes is in limbo—it is not related to any other environment nor to any other object. Object coordinates comprise a major part of a 3D database: the data used to create a 3D scene.

You can picture this concept as the measurements which describe the shape of a common object like an eraser, for example.

Object coordinates describe object space.

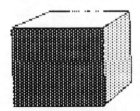

Fig. 12-1(a). Five transformations are used to define, manipulate, and display a 3D model. Shown here is Step One: define the fundamental shape of the object as xyz object coordinates. See also the other four illustrations in Fig. 12-1.

World Coordinates

World coordinates are the xyz coordinates that describe the shape and location of the model in a specific 3D environment (called the *world*). See FIG. 12-1(b).

You can conceive of this concept as the position of an eraser sitting on a table top. The angle of the eraser on the table top—or the angle of the model in the world environment—is called *rotation.* The location of the eraser on the table top—or the location of the model in the world environment—is called *translation.*

World coordinates describe world space. Because the light source is also present in world space, illumination and lighting calculations are usually made using world coordinates.

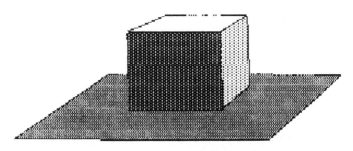

Fig. 12-1(b). Five transformations are used to define, manipulate, and display a 3D model. Shown here is Step Two: place the object into the world scene, describing its position as rotated and translated world coordinates, and performing all lighting illuminations. See also the other four illustrations in Fig. 12-1.

Camera Coordinates

Camera coordinates (also called *view* coordinates) use xyz coordinates to describe how the model would look to a viewer at a particular location (viewpoint) in the 3D world. See FIG. 12-1(c).

Viewing *distance* refers to the distance between the viewpoint and the model. Angular distortion or focal length determines the 3D appearance of the image.

Because the location of the viewpoint often determines which surfaces of a particular model are visible or hidden, hidden surface calculations are often made in camera space.

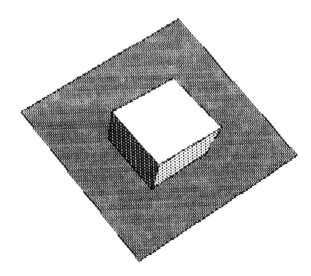

Fig. 12-1(c). Five transformations are used to define, manipulate, and display a 3D model. Shown here is Step Three: move the world scene away from the viewpoint and apply an appropriate rotation. The resulting xyz coordinates are camera (view) coordinates. Perform all hidden surface calculations. See also the other four illustrations in Fig. 12-1.

Normalized Coordinates

If an imaginary plane is placed between the viewer and the model, then geometry can be used to determine how a 2D representation of the 3D model would be drawn. See FIG. 12-1(d).

Normalized coordinates are device-independent. That is, they are not yet scaled to the display screen; they are still scaled to the 3D world environment being used (which is completely arbitrary). Truly normalized coordinates usually range from 0 to 1.0, although this convention is not rigorously followed in the 3D graphics programming community.

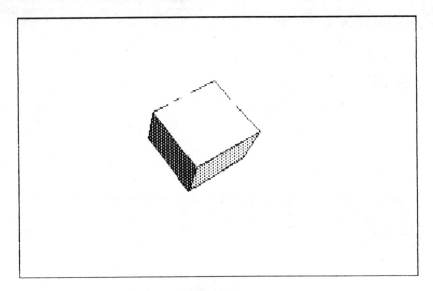

Fig. 12-1(d). Five transformations are used to define, manipulate, and display a 3D model. Shown here is Step Four: place an imaginary image plane between the viewpoint and the world scene. The resulting xy image plane coordinates are device-independent. See also the other four illustrations in Fig. 12-1.

Display Coordinates

Display coordinates (also called raster coordinates) are the xy coordinates which are used to draw the image on the screen. See FIG. 12-1(e). Formulas that calculate ratios are used to scale the image to fit the screen. Clipping formulas are used to clip the image at the screen's boundaries.

Display coordinates are device-dependent. A set of display coordinates that works correctly in one graphics mode might not necessarily produce a legitimate image in a different graphics mode.

The Coordinate Sequence

In most serious 3D CAD programs, any model being created follows a natural evolutionary path. First, object coordinates are used to describe the fundamental

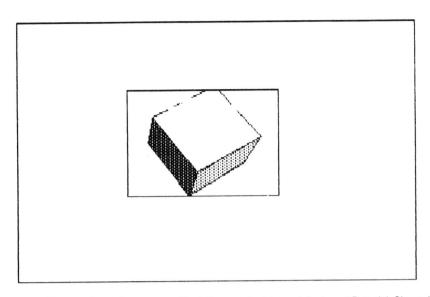

Fig. 12-1(e). Five transformations are used to define, manipulate, and display a 3D model. Shown here is Step Five: scale or clip the image plane coordinates to fit the display screen being used. The xy display coordinates can be directly drawn on the screen. See also the other four illustrations in Fig. 12-1.

shape of the model. Second, world coordinates are used to describe its position (rotation and translation) in the particular 3D environment (world) being considered. Third, camera coordinates are used to describe how the model would appear to a viewer located at a specific viewpoint. Fourth, an imaginary image plane is placed between the viewpoint and the model in order to convert the 3D camera coordinates to a 2D image. This fourth step is somewhat optional and is often bundled into step five in many 3D systems. And, fifth, the 2D image is scaled and clipped to create the display coordinates which are used to actually draw the 3D image on the screen.

XYZ COORDINATES: Two Contradictory Systems

A number of contradictory 3D coordinate systems are in use today. See FIG. 12-2. These systems are usually named according to how they can be visualized by using the human hand.

The standard right-hand coordinate system, as depicted in FIG. 12-2, is the most widely used. Its distinguishing features are the use of positive z as representing nearer, positive y as indicating higher, and positive x as representing right. This xyz juxtaposition is most often used by 3D CAD developers, academia, and researchers. The ground plane is represented by xz coordinates.

The left-hand coordinate system, as depicted in FIG. 12-2, is used by some programmers, most notably Pixar's RenderMan™ rendering interface. Fortunately, simple assignment formulas can be used to convert between databases which use left-hand xyz coordinates to databases which use right-hand xyz coordinates.

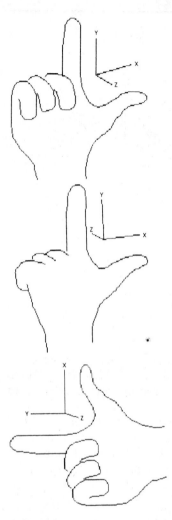

Fig. 12-2. Contradictory 3D coordinate systems. Top: standard right-hand system used by academia, many 3D CAD vendors, and most scientific researchers. Center: standard left-hand system, used most notably by Pixar's RenderMan™ interface. Bottom: Autodesk's rotated right-hand system, which places the plan view in the xy plane in order to maintain backwards compatibility with earlier (2D) versions of AutoCAD™.

The distinguishing features of the left-hand system are the use of negative z as nearer. In other respects, the x and y coordinates mean the same as they do in the right-hand system. The ground plane is represented by xz coordinates.

An interesting twist on these two systems is the coordinate system used by AutoCAD™. In order to maintain backwards compatiblity with their previous 2D CADD drafting programs, AutoDesk Inc. chose to represent the ground plane with xy coordinates. Their 3D coordinate system, shown in FIG. 12-2, is really just a standard right-hand system that has been rotated.

The major demonstration program in this book (a full-featured, interactive 3D modeling and rendering program presented in the next chapter) uses the standard right-hand coordinate system.

STRUCTURAL COMPONENTS OF 3D MODELS

3D models are usually constructed from small four-sided or three-sided polygons called *facets.* See Fig. 12-3. Each side of a facet is called a *halfedge.* Note that halfedges do not exist in the real world. In fact, facets (called *laminas*) do not exist in the real world either. Real objects have three dimensions: width, depth, and height. Facets or laminas have no thickness.

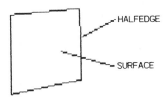

Fig. 12-3. Properties of a one-sided facet, from which more complex 3D models and solids are constructed. One-sided facets have no thickness and do not exist in the real world. A two-sided facet with a nominal thickness is called a lamina.

When a facet shares a halfedge with another facet as part of a genuine 3D solid, the result is called an *edge.* See Fig. 12-4.

A 3D model constructed from individual facets is comprised of certain properties. A *vertex* is a corner where three or more edges meet. An edge is the boundary between two facets. A facet is one small plane on the surface of the model. A *hidden surface* is any facet (or portion of a facet) which is hidden from view, either because it faces away from the viewer or because it is obscured by other nearer facets. A *hidden line* is a part of the image which is obscured from view.

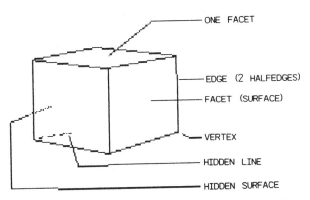

Fig. 12-4. Properties of a 3D model, constructed from halfedge facets.

MODELING FORMULAS

The mathematical formulas which are used to manipulate a 3D model and to yield the appropriate display coordinates are based on matrix math, using sine and cosine in a traditional algebraic formula format.

As you will see in the demonstration program in the next chapter, the rotation formulas can be broken down into their three components: yaw, roll, and pitch. Likewise, the translation formulas can be broken down into their three components: near/far, left/right, and up/down. By selective manipulation of these individual components in the formulas, the position of the model, world, and viewpoint can be all rotated and moved—completely independent of one another. For example, it is not a difficult task to rotate and move a model inside a world scene which is itself rotating and moving while the viewer (viewpoint) is walking around turning their head looking in different directions. The demonstration program in the next chapter permits you to move the 3D environment (the scene) and the 3D model independent of one another.

WHERE TO LOOK

For a more thorough discussion of 3D modeling techniques, including numerous demonstration programs for QuickC and Turbo C, refer to the author's previous book, *High-Performance Graphics in C, #3059*, published March 1989, ISBN 0-8306-9359-9, available at good computer bookstores or order direct through TAB Books (see the listing at the end of this book).

RENDERING METHODS: Wireframe, Solid, Shaded

Three methods of rendering are available to C graphics programmers. See FIG. 12-5.

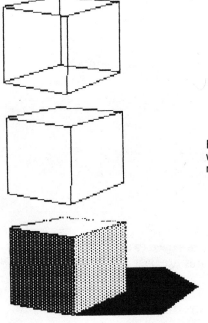

Fig. 12-5. Rendering methods. From top: wire-frame model, solid model, shaded model.

Wire-frame models are 3D objects constructed of edges only. No attempt is made at hidden line removal or at hidden surface removal. If a wire-frame model is constructed of facets, the facets are not shaded, but are left transparent. Wire-frame models are often used for rapid prototyping because they require less time to draw than other types of rendering.

Solid models are 3D objects constructed of opaque facets. See FIG. 12-5. Hidden surfaces are not displayed. The model appears solid, as it would it real life. No attempt is made to shade the model according to lighting conditions, however.

Shaded models are solid models whose surfaces have been shaded to represent the intensity of light falling upon each facet. Using either the 16-color modes or the 2-color modes of IBM-compatible graphics adapters, an acceptable range of colors can be generated using bit tiling (halftoning) techniques. Bit tiling relies upon setting a mixture of pixels in an area. The eye sees the resulting overall pattern, not the individual pixels, so different shades of any particular hue can be simulated.

TECHNIQUES FOR HIDDEN SURFACE REMOVAL

There are at least ten different algorithms available for visible surface detection, also called *hidden surface removal.*

The *radial pre-sort* method requires the programmer to use only coordinates that are visible. The *radial sort* method involves using the program itself to determine which coordinates are visible, and therefore which will be provided as input to the 3D modeling and rendering formulas.

The plane equation method is also called the *backplane removal* method. In any simple 3D solid, such as a cube, facets which face away from the viewer are hidden from view. This algorithm relies upon surface normals (perpendiculars) and vector cross-products.

The *separation plane* method places an imaginary plane between two solid 3D models. Vector math can be used to determine on which side of the plane each model lays. This information can be extrapolated further to identify which is farther from the viewpoint, and thereby hidden from view by the nearer model.

The *depth-sort* method compares the z coordinates of different facets to determine which facets are nearer to the viewer.

The *ray tracing* method uses complicated formulas to trace the path of light rays followed backward from the viewer's eye to various objects in the scene.

Radiosity uses formulas to calculate the distribution of light rays in the scene, independent of the location of the viewer.

The *decomposition* method breaks up the scene into small cubic solids.

The *z-buffer* method maintains a separate database comprised of the z coordinate for each pizel on the display screen. If a new object is drawn, the element in the database is changed only if the object is nearer than the former model. This method uses a lot of memory.

The *minimax* method makes its calculations on the display screen. Two bounding rectangles are used to determine if there is any potential overlap of two images on the screen.

The *scan line* method is similar to the z-buffer method, but it maintains a database comprised of only a single scan line as it works its way down the screen.

THE 3D ENVIRONMENT: Yaw, Roll, Pitch

The 3D environment is typically based upon a spherical coordinate system. The angles represented in such a system are used by the sine and cosine formulas in the 3D modeling and rendering calculations. See FIG. 12-6.

The viewpoint is always located at position 0,0,0 (called the origin) in a spherical coordinate system. Rotation is based upon the yaw, roll, and pitch planes. Translation is achieved by moving various object coordinates and world coordiantes about the coordinate system—the viewpoint is always at 0,0,0.

This book uses x to represent the left/right axis, y to represent the up/down axis, and z to represent the near/far axis.

THE LIGHT SOURCE

The position of the light source in a 3D scene is expressed in world coordinates. See FIG. 12-7. This means that any calculations regarding illumination are made after the object coordinates have been converted to world coordinates.

If the world itself is rotated, the position of the light source remains fixed, relative to the position of the world environment. This means that if your viewpoint changes, the illumination level may appear to change, as you walk around behind an object, for example.

ILLUMINATION

The level of illumination falling upon any one facet is determined by comparing the incoming light vector to the surface perpendicular. See FIG. 12-8. Generally, the smaller the angle, the brighter the surface will appear. If the angle

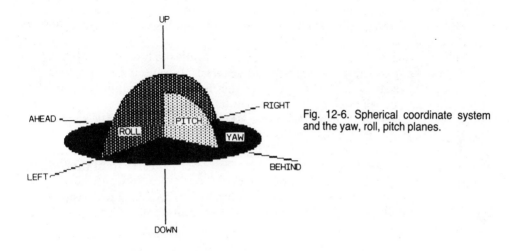

Fig. 12-6. Spherical coordinate system and the yaw, roll, pitch planes.

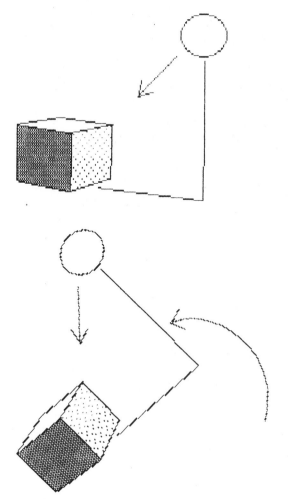

Fig. 12-7. The location of the light source is defined in xyz world coordinates (top). When the scene is rotated and translated to yield camera coordinates (bottom), the location of the light source remains constant relative to the world scene. See also Fig. 12-1.

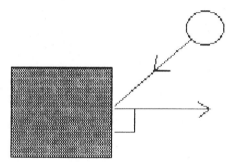

Fig. 12-8. The perceived brightness of a model is primarily determined by its orientation to the light source.

exceeds 90 degrees, then the surface is unlit by the light source and will receive only ambient (bounced or reflected) lighting.

FACET, GOURAUD, PHONG SHADING METHODS

To represent illumination on the screen, a number of different algorithms are commonly used.

Facet shading techniques lend themselves well to the 2-color and 16-color graphics modes. Bit tiling (halftoning) is used to shade each individual facet of the 3D model. See Fig. 12-9. First, a solid model is drawn, using either black or a solid color to fill in the contents of each visible facet. Next, halftoning is used to shade each facet to an appropriate shade and hue. Finally, linestyling is used to draw each edge in a pattern and hue that will camouflage the edges between the facets.

Other, more realistic methods, like Gouraud and Phong shading, operate on a pixel by pixel basis and can represent gradiated tones on the screen. These methods require the 256-color modes, however.

ILLUMINATION FORMULAS

The formulas that calculate illumination are based upon a simple geometric principle. See Fig. 12-10. If the distance between the light source and the facet is expressed as a unit vector (of length 1 unit), then the square of the three dimensions which make up the vector will equal one.

—————— A CLOSER LOOK ——————

Moving the Light Source

Because of the relationship between a unit vector and its three xyz components, it is a relatively straightforward task to move the light source and determine the new components, provided the light source position is expressed in terms of angles of elevation and heading. Consider the following code, which will work with the demonstration program in the next chapter:

```
/*         enter with degrees_elevation and degrees_heading for the light source */
elevation = degrees_elevation*.017453292;              /* convert to radians */
yi = SIN(elevation);                                   /* y component of new vector */
maxrem = SQR(1-(yi*yi);                                /* max range for xi 2 + zi 2 sum */
heading = degrees_heading*.017453292;                  /* convert to radians */
xi = (SIN(heading))*maxrem;                            /* x component of new vector */
zi = (COS(heading))*maxrem*(-1);                       /* z component of new vector */
/*                    exit with xi,yi,zi components of unit vector for the light source */
```

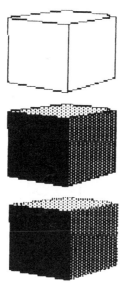

Fig. 12-9. Facet shading of a solid 3D model on personal computers. Top: facets are used to build a solid model, with the backplane removal algorithm being employed to discard hidden surfaces. Center: each facet is shaded (dithered) according to the relationship between its surface normal and the light source. Bottom: line styling (dithering) is used to camouflage the boundaries between each facet (the edges and halfedges).

MOVING THE MODEL: Translation, Rotation, Extrusion

Building a 3D model using interactive input from the end-user usually involves three manipulations: translation, rotation, and extrusion. The keyboard bat (introduced in the previous chapter) can be used for all input.

See FIG. 12-11. Translation is movement along the x axis, y axis, or z axis in the 3D environment. The model is not rotated, but merely moved along these axes.

Rotation changes the yaw, roll, or pitch angle of the model. It is not moved to any new location in the 3D environment, but merely rotated.

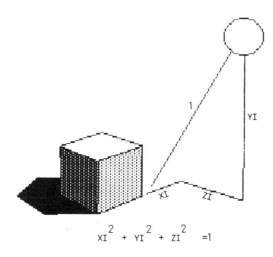

Fig. 12-10. The xyz component of the unit vector which describes the location of a point light source in 3D space.

$$XI^2 + YI^2 + ZI^2 = 1$$

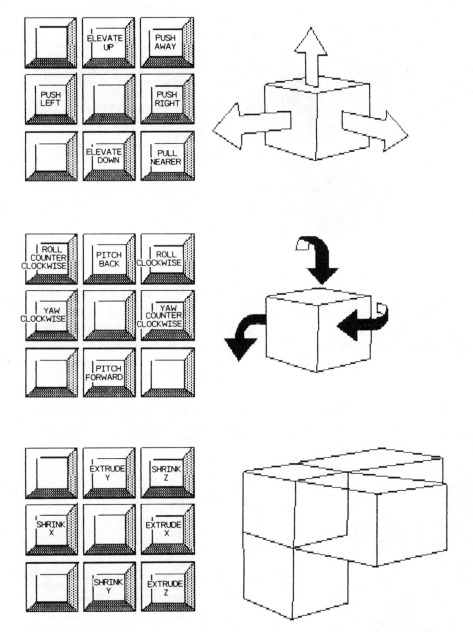

Fig. 12-11. The keypad bat, used for controlling a 3D modeling session. From top: translation, rotation, extrusion. See also Fig. 11-6 in Chapter 11.

Extrusion changes the shape of the model. A facet can be deformed along either the x axis, y axis, or z axis. Other connected facets will also be deformed during this process, of course.

In this input scenario, rotation and translation are performed using world coordinates; extrusion is performed on the object coordinates which describe the fundamental shape of the object.

3D SOLIDS DATABASE: Doubly Linked List

3D CAD programs that deal with solids-based objects often use a database built on the concept of a *doubly linked list*.

Each element in the list contains a pointer which indicates its parent. The parent of a vertex is its facet. The parent of a facet is its sub-object. The parent of a sub-object is its object. The parent of an object is its scene.

Each element in the list also contains a pointer to other connected elements. A vertex will point to the next vertex in the loop of vertices which make up a facet, for example.

Because of C's powerful pointer capabilities, it is an idea language for creating and manipulating doubly linked lists.

In order for such a database to be of value, however, certain rules must be imposed upon the solids which it represents. First, each facet may belong to only one sub-object or primitive. Second, each halfedge must be a part of an edge. Third, each edge must be complete. By using these three constraints, the database can ensure that only legitimate solids are being represented.

The nodes in a doubly linked list database are often comprised of seven levels: scene, solids, primitives, facets, halfedges, edges, and vertices. These are the minimum categories that are required to draw the model, ensure that it is indeed a solid which could exist in the real world, remove any hidden surfaces, and perform illumination calculations.

In 3D modeling programs, whether they use a doubly linked list database or a standard array-based database, it is the database not the bitmap image which is saved. This means the software must have a Regen module which is capable of redrawing the image from the database whenever a new file is loaded from disk, or whenever the user requests a regen.

13

Program Listing:
Your Microcomputer 3D CAD Designer

THIS CHAPTER contains the complete source code for a full-featured, interactive 3D modeling and rendering program entitled "Your Microcomputer 3D CAD Designer." The program listing is comprised of three C source files: DESIGN1.C, DESIGN2.C, and DESIGN3.C.

The image in FIG. 13-1 shows the sign-on screen for Your Microcomputer 3D CAD Designer.

Your Microcomputer 3D CAD Designer will run on VGA, EGA, MCGA, CGA, and Hercules graphics adapters. If you are using a VGA, the program will run in the 640x480x16-color graphics mode using 60 rows of text. If you are using an EGA and enhanced monitor, the program will run in the 640x350x16-color graphics mode using 43 rows of text. If you are using an EGA and standard monitor, the program will run in the 640x200x16-color graphics mode using 25 rows of text. If you are using an MCGA, the program will run in the 640x480x2-color graphics mode using 60 rows of text. If you are using a CGA, the program will run in the 640x200x2-color graphics mode using 25 rows of text. If you are using a Hercules graphics adapter, the program will run in the 720x348x2-color graphics mode using 24 rows of text.

The interactive menu system used by the program is controlled by the keyboard. The 3D modeling features are controlled by the bat on the keypad, giving you access to rotation, translation, and extrusion functions. No mouse or digitizing tablet is required in order to run this full-length program.

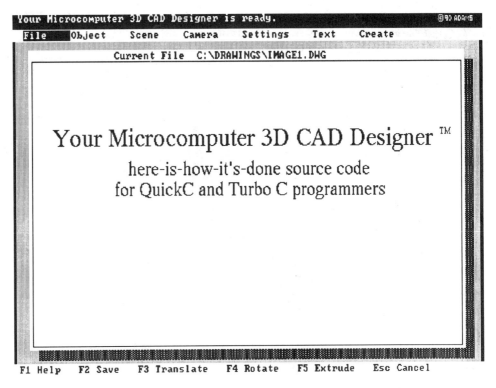

Fig. 13-1. Print of the start-up image produced by the full-length program listing in this chapter.

The image in FIG. 13-2 is an example of the kinds of 3D models that can be created by this powerful, full-featured demonstration program. Objects can be viewed from any angle during construction. The ready-to-use primitive objects provided in the modeling toolkit—cube and sphere—may be rotated and moved independently of the viewing angle for the overall scene. Other examples and tutorial sessions can be found in Chapter 14's mini user's guide.

The complete source code for Your Microcomputer 3D CAD Designer is presented in FIG. 13-3.

HOW TO COMPILE THE PROGRAM

There are two ways to compile, link, and run this demonstration program. You can compile it within the integrated programming environment of QuickC or Turbo C, or you can use the QuickC or Turbo C command-line compilation procedure.

COMPILING INSIDE QuickC

To compile and run this demonstration program from within the integrated programming environment of QuickC version 2.00 or newer, follow these instructions.

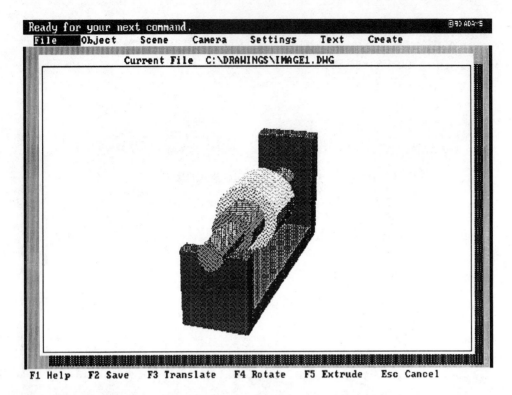

File   Object   Scene   Camera   Settings   Text   Create

Current File   C:\DRAWINGS\IMAGE1.DWG

F1 Help   F2 Save   F3 Translate   F4 Rotate   F5 Extrude   Esc Cancel

Fig. 13-2. Example of 3D modeling output which can be produced by the interactive 3D CAD program presented in this chapter.

Fig. 13-3. Source code for Your Microcomputer 3D CAD Designer℠, a full-featured, interactive, 3D modeling and rendering program which runs on VGA, EGA, MCGA, CGA, and Hercules graphics adapters. Refer to Chapter 14 for the user's guide. See Chapter 15 for the programmer's reference. The three modules for this program, DESIGN1.C, DESIGN2.C, and DESIGN3.C, are ready to compile under QuickC and Turbo C.

```
/*                              tm
Your Microcomputer 3D CAD Designer            Source file: DESIGN1.C

By: Lee Adams    Version: 1.00    Revision: n/a.
Notices: (c) Copyright 1990 Lee Adams.  All rights reserved.
  Your Microcomputer 3D CAD Designer is a trademark of
  TAB Books and is used by permission.
First published: 1990 by Windcrest Books (div. of TAB Books)

SOURCE NOTES:  This is module 1 of 3.  The project list should
include DESIGN1.C, DESIGN2.C, and DESIGN3.C named in QuickC's MAK
file or Turbo C's PRJ file.  At run-time the program expects to
find the appropriate font file in the current directory (TMSRB.FON
if you are using QuickC, TRIP.CHR if you are using Turbo C),
although the program is smart enough to carry on if the font file
is not found.  If you are using Turbo C, the program MUST be able
to find the appropriate *.BGI graphics driver in the current
directory.
```

Fig. 13-3.
Continued.

OPERATION: This program demonstrates how to create full-featured, interactive 3D modeling/shading software with QuickC or Turbo C.

COMPILER: QuickC or Turbo C integrated programming environment. Default is QuickC. To use Turbo C change the preprocessor directive in COMPILER DIRECTIVES (see below). Compile using the medium memory model. If you are using QuickC, you can compile and run the program while in QuickC's integrated programming environment. If you are using Turbo C, compile the program with source debugging turned off (in the Debug menu) to keep the EXE file small enough to co-exist with the Turbo C editor at run-time. Refer to the notes in the book.

GRAPHICS LIBRARY: QuickC, Turbo C, or third-party library. Default is QuickC. To use Turbo C graphics library, change the preprocessor directive in COMPILER DIRECTIVES (see below). To use a third-party graphics library such as MetaWINDOW, HALO 88, Lattice C GFX, Essential Graphics, or others, refer to the book.

MARKETABILITY: will detect and support VGA, EGA, MCGA, CGA, and Hercules graphics adapters; provides fully-shaded solid modeling in color; uses a unique algorithm to ensure correct shading of solid objects when using the bw mode of the CGA, MCGA, or Hercules; will save the user's images to disk for export or later editing. Refer to the book for important information concerning trapping of run-time errors.

LICENSE: As purchaser of the book in which this program is published, you are granted a non-exclusive royalty-free license to reproduce and distribute these routines in executable form as part of your software product, subject to any copyright, trademark, or patent rights of others, and subject to the limited warranty described in the introduction of the book. All other rights reserved.

```
COMPILER DIRECTIVES   */

                /* compilers and graphics libraries */
#define QuickC      1
#define TurboC      2
#define MicrosoftC 3
#define LatticeC    4
#define HALO        7
#define MetaWINDOW 8
#define Essential   9

#define Compiler QuickC          /* change to TurboC if required */
#define GraphicsLibrary QuickC   /* change to library being used */

#define FAIL       0                   /* for graphics auto-detect */
#define CHUNK      32768   /* size of block to attempt to allocate */
#define REMAINDER 255                       /* accuracy limit */
#define ATTEMPTS  40             /* max number of attempts... */

#include <bios.h>              /* supports keyboard functions */
#include <stdio.h>              /* supports printf function */
#include <string.h>           /* supports string manipulation */
#if Compiler==QuickC
  #include <conio.h>                  /* supports QuickC port IO */
  #include <malloc.h>    /* supports memory allocation for arrays */
#elif Compiler==TurboC
  #include <conio.h>                  /* supports text cursor */
  #include <dos.h>                    /* supports TurboC port IO */
  #include <alloc.h>     /* supports memory allocation for arrays */
#endif
#if GraphicsLibrary==QuickC
  #include <graph.h>                  /* QuickC graphics library */
```

Fig. 13-3.
Continued.

```
#elif GraphicsLibrary==TurboC
  #include <graphics.h>                    /* Turbo C graphics library */
#endif
#include <process.h>                       /* supports the exit function
_____

FUNCTION PROTOTYPES  */

/* ROUTINES IN THIS MODULE */
void Quit_Pgm(void);                    /* ends the program gracefully */
void Notice(int,int);                   /* displays the copyright notice */
void Graphics_Setup(void);              /* initializes the graphics mode */
void SetParameters(void); /* defines sizes, colors for interface */
void DrawScreen(void);      /* creates the user interface graphics */
void CreateBars(void);                       /* creates menu bars */
void CreateMenus(void);              /* creates the pull-down menus */
void CreateHiBars(void);             /* creates the highlight bars */
void FreeBlock(char far *);          /* deallocate far heap memory */
void InitUndo(void);          /* initializes hidden page for Undo */
long GetFreeMemory(void);            /* calculate size of free RAM */

/* ROUTINES IN MODULE 2 CALLED BY THIS MODULE */
void MenuBarLoop(void);      /* manages the menu system at runtime */
void ClearTextLine(void);            /* blanks the dialog text line */

/* ROUTINES IN MODULE 3 CALLED BY THIS MODULE */
void SetHue(int);                 /* sets the current drawing color */
void SetLine(int);                   /* sets the current line style */
void SetFill(char *, int);             /* sets the area fill style */
void BlankPage(void);           /* blanks the current active page */
void SetPosition(int,int);           /* sets the current xy position */
void DrawLine(int,int);   /* draws line from current xy position */
void DrawBorder(int,int,int,int);              /* draws rectangle */
void DrawPanel(int,int,int,int);         /* draws solid rectangle */
void Fill(int,int,int);                             /* area fill */
char far * MemBlock(int,int,int,int);   /* allocate array memory */
void GetBlock(int,int,int,int,char far *); /* save graphic array */
void PutXOR(int,int,char far *);       /* show XOR graphic array */
void PutPSET(int,int,char far *);      /* show PSET graphic array */
void PutText(int,int,int,char *);             /* display text */
void SetTextRowCol(int,int);               /* set text position */
char far * InitHiddenPage(void);     /* initialize hidden bitmap */
void BackUp(void);              /* copies page 0 to hidden page */
void InitBwMattes(void);     /* allocate memory for bw key mattes */

/*_____

DECLARATION OF GLOBAL VARIABLES
Visible to all functions in all source files. */

#if GraphicsLibrary==QuickC
  struct videoconfig vc;                  /* QuickC's graphics table */
#endif
#if Compiler==TurboC
  struct textsettingstype loadquery;      /* use to test font load */
  extern unsigned _stklen=4096;           /* set stack to 4096 bytes */
#endif   /* (QuickC uses the Utility/Make menu to set stack size */
int C0=0,C1=1,C2=2,C3=3,C4=4,C5=5,C6=6,C7=7,C8=8,C9=9,C10=10,
C11=11,C12=12,C13=13,C14=14,C15=15;              /* color codes */
int x_res=0,y_res=0;                          /* screen resolution */
int mode_flag=0;  /* indicates which graphics mode is being used */
int alpha_x=0,alpha_y=0;       /* dimensions of character matrix */
unsigned int plane_length=0; /* length of bitmap or one bitplane */
int t1x=0,t1y=0,t2x=0,t2y=0,t3x=0,t3y=0,t4x=0,t4y=0;    /* title */
int x1=0,yf1=0,x2=0,y2=0;       /* coords for graphic array saves */
int t1=1;       /* loop counter & panning bar position indicator */
int sx=0,sy=0;                          /* current pen position */
char keycode=0;  /* flag for NULL, normal, or extended keystroke */
char keynum=0;                  /* ASCII number of keystroke */
```

Fig. 13-3.
Continued.

```
char far *menubarBitBlt;                        /* menu bar graphic array */
char far *helpbarBitBlt;                        /* help bar graphic array */
char far *fileBitBlt;                           /* file name graphic array */
char far *funcBitBlt;                           /* function graphic array */
char far *FileMenu;                                  /* File Menu array */
char far *ObjectMenu;                              /* Object Menu array */
char far *SceneMenu;                                /* Scene Menu array */
char far *CameraMenu;                             /* Camera Menu array */
char far *SettingsMenu;                         /* Settings Menu array */
char far *TextMenu;                                  /* Text Menu array */
char far *CreateMenu;                              /* Create Menu array */
char far *PanBar;                              /* panning highlight bar */
char far *ScrollBar;                         /* scrolling highlight bar */
char far *swatchprep;                     /* preps area for swatch display */
char far *swatchbg;                       /* stores area beneath swatch */
int vx1=0,vy1=0,vx2=0,vy2=0;                          /* canvas coords */
int clipx1=0,clipy1=0,clipx2=0,clipy2=0;          /* clipping coords */
int shx=0,shy=0;                          /* width, depth of dropshadow */
int ox1=0,ox2=0,oy1=0,oy2=0;                  /* width, depth of rule */
int barclr=0,bgclr=0,canvasclr=0;            /* user interface colors */
int shadowclr=0,panelclr=0,ruleclr=0;    /* user interface colors */
char fill_0[]={0,0,0,0,0,0,0,0};                       /*    0% fill */
char fill_3[]={0,32,0,0,2,0,0};                        /*    3% fill */
char fill_6[]={32,0,2,0,128,0,8,0};                    /*    6% fill */
char fill_12[]={32,2,128,8,32,2,128,8};                /*   12% fill */
char fill_25[]={68,17,68,17,68,17,68,17};              /*   25% fill */
char fill_37[]={170,68,170,17,170,68,170,17};          /*   37% fill */
char fill_50[]={85,170,85,170,85,170,85,170};          /*   50% fill */
char fill_62[]={85,187,85,238,85,187,85,238};          /*   62% fill */
char fill_75[]={187,238,187,238,187,238,187,238};      /*   75% fill */
char fill_87[]={223,253,127,247,223,253,127,247};      /*   87% fill */
char fill_93[]={255,223,255,255,255,253,255,255};      /*   93% fill */
char fill_100[]={255,255,255,255,255,255,255,255};  /* 100% fill */
int p1=0,p2=0;          /* install coords for panning highlight bar */
int px1=0,px2=0,px3=0,px4=0,px5=0,px6=0,px7=0;         /* pan coords */
int py1=0,py2=0,py3=0,py4=0,py5=0,py6=0;            /* scroll coords */
int py7=0,py8=0,py9=0,py10=0;
int t2=0;                    /* position of scrolling highlight bar */
int t3=0;                         /* number of choices in active menu */
int p3=0,p4=0;                    /* xy install coords for active menu */
int p5=0,p6=0;                 /* xy coords for scrolling highlight bar */
int pbg1=0,pbg2=0;            /* width,depth of bg to save under menu */
int status=0;                       /* status of level 1 menus logic */
int choice=0;            /* token indicates selected core function */
char far * bitmap0;                    /* storage of hidden page in RAM */
char far * bitmap1;
char far * bitmap2;
char far * bitmap3;
union{ struct {unsigned int a1; unsigned int a2;} address;
       char far * faraddress;} u1;
unsigned int seg1,seg2,seg3,seg4,off1,off2,off3,off4;
char Herc=6;                     /* preparatory value for Hercules mode */
char far *HPtr;                     /* will point to Herc variable */
char * textptr;          /* text to be displayed on graphics screen */
char text1[]="Your Microcomputer 3D CAD Designer is ready.";
char text4[]="Current File  C:\\DRAWINGS\\IMAGE1.DWG";
char text5[]="                    ";        /* empty string */
char text6[]="Inactive feature. Consult User's Manual.";
char text7[]="Ready for your next command.";
char text8[]="Insufficient memory available. Press any key.";
char text9[]="Filename to edit:";
char text10[]="Current filename:";
char text12[]="Undo completed.";
char text13[]="Press Tab to see next choice, Enter to select.";
char text14[]="Access denied.  Font files not found at start-up.";
char text15[]="Font files not found.  Text menu affected.";
char text16[]="Adjust Camera angle with arrow keys.";
char text17[]="Select REGEN to view new Camera parameters.";
```

Fig. 13-3.
Continued.

```
long freemem1=0;                   /* size of free RAM available */
struct SREGS segregs;         /* structure of CPU register values */
unsigned int segment=0;          /* value of data segment register */
unsigned int offset=0;       /* destination offset for movedata */
FILE *image_file;                          /* data stream */
char image_buffer[38400]; /* temporary buffer to store bit plane */
char f3[9]="UNTITLED";                          /* filename */
char f4[5]=".DWG";                             /* extension */
char f6[13]="UNTITLED.DWG";          /* filename + extension */
char f7[5]=".BLU";
char f8[5]=".GRN";
char f9[5]=".RED";
char f10[5]=".INT";
char f11[2]="X";                         /* instroke carrier */
char f12[9]="UNTITLED";      /* backup storage for edit undo */
int GS_bgclr=0;                          /* background color */
int GS_textavail=0;      /* token indicates if font loaded OK */
int fillclr_index=0;
/*_____

FUNCTION DEFINITIONS   */

main(){                        /* this is the master routine */
Graphics_Setup();          /* establishes the graphics mode */
#if GraphicsLibrary==QuickC
  _getvideoconfig(&vc);          /* initialize QuickC's table */
#endif
SetParameters();      /* defines menu system sizes & colors */
CreateBars();                      /* creates the menu bars */
CreateMenus();            /* creates level 1 pull-down menus */
CreateHiBars();    /* creates panning & scrolling highlight bars */
InitUndo();           /* initializes hidden page for Undo */
DrawScreen();                  /* creates the sign-on screen */
InitBwMattes();        /* initializes key mattes for bw modes */
/* #if Compiler==QuickC
  if (GS_textavail==0){
    freemem1=GetFreeMemory();ClearTextLine();SetTextRowCol(1,2);
    printf("%lu (%u) bytes free.",freemem1,_memavl());;}
#elif Compiler==TurboC
  if (GS_textavail==0){
    freemem1=GetFreeMemory();ClearTextLine();
    gotoxy(2,1);printf("%lu bytes free.",freemem1);;}
#endif */
GS_bgclr=C7;
fillclr_index=0;
#if GraphicsLibrary==TurboC
  fillclr_index=1;
  if (mode_flag==5){
    fillclr_index=0;}
#endif
MenuBarLoop();                     /* activate the menu system */

Quit_Pgm();                                  /* boilerplate */
}
/*_____*/

void SetParameters(void){  /* define sizes, colors for interface */
vx1=(alpha_x*2)+6;vy1=(alpha_y*2)+18;            /* canvas UL */
vx2=x_res-((alpha_x*3)+2);vy2=y_res-(alpha_y+18);   /* canvas LR */
shx=12;shy=10;                   /* width, depth of dropshadow */
ox1=4;oy1=alpha_y+3;ox2=4;oy2=3;       /* width, depth of rule */
barclr=C7;bgclr=C6;canvasclr=C7;shadowclr=C0;ruleclr=C0;
if (mode_flag==6){              /* device-dependent pan spacing */
  px1=17;px2=89;px3=179;px4=260;px5=350;px6=459;px7=530;}
else {px1=15;px2=79;px3=159;px4=231;px5=311;px6=407;px7=471;}
p1=px1;p2=15;       /* initialize coords for panning highlight bar */
if (mode_flag==6){              /* device-dependent scroll spacing */
  py1=38;py2=52;py3=66;py4=80;py5=94;py6=108;
  py7=122;py8=136;py9=150;py10=164;}
```

Fig. 13-3.
Continued.

```
else {py1=32;py2=40;py3=48;py4=56;py5=64;py6=72;
  py7=80;py8=88;py9=96;py10=104;}
p4=py1-6;                          /* y coord for level 1 pull-down menus */
return;}
/*_____*/

void CreateBars(void){                          /* creates bar arrays */
SetHue(C7);SetFill(fill_100,C7);
BlankPage();
strcpy(text5,"File");PutText(2,3,C7,text5);     /* create menu bar */
strcpy(text5,"Object");PutText(2,11,C7,text5);
strcpy(text5,"Scene");PutText(2,21,C7,text5);
strcpy(text5,"Camera");PutText(2,30,C7,text5);
strcpy(text5,"Settings");PutText(2,40,C7,text5);
strcpy(text5,"Text");PutText(2,52,C7,text5);
strcpy(text5,"Create");PutText(2,60,C7,text5);
x1=0;yf1=alpha_y-2;                              /* upper left coords */
x2=x_res-1;y2=(alpha_y*2)+1;                     /* lower right coords */
menubarBitBlt=MemBlock(x1,yf1,x2,y2);           /* allocate memory */
GetBlock(x1,yf1,x2,y2,menubarBitBlt);
DrawPanel(x1,yf1,x2,y2);
PutXOR(x1,yf1,menubarBitBlt);
GetBlock(x1,yf1,x2,y2,menubarBitBlt);           /* store menubar graphic */
BlankPage();
strcpy(text5,"F1 Help");PutText(4,2,C7,text5);
strcpy(text5,"F2 Save");PutText(4,12,C7,text5);
strcpy(text5,"F3 Translate");PutText(4,22,C7,text5);
strcpy(text5,"F4 Rotate");PutText(4,37,C7,text5);
strcpy(text5,"F5 Extrude");PutText(4,49,C7,text5);
strcpy(text5,"Esc Cancel");PutText(4,62,C7,text5);
x1=0;yf1=(alpha_y*3)-2;
x2=x_res-1;y2=(alpha_y*4)+1;
helpbarBitBlt=MemBlock(x1,yf1,x2,y2);           /* allocate memory */
GetBlock(x1,yf1,x2,y2,helpbarBitBlt);
DrawPanel(x1,yf1,x2,y2);
PutXOR(x1,yf1,helpbarBitBlt);
GetBlock(x1,yf1,x2,y2,helpbarBitBlt);           /* store helpbar graphic */
BlankPage();
PutText(5,1,C7,text4);                           /* filename display */
x1=0;yf1=alpha_y*4;
x2=alpha_x*36;y2=alpha_y*5;
fileBitBlt=MemBlock(x1,yf1,x2,y2);              /* allocate memory */
GetBlock(x1,yf1,x2,y2,fileBitBlt);
DrawPanel(x1,yf1,x2,y2);
PutXOR(x1,yf1,fileBitBlt);
GetBlock(x1,yf1,x2,y2,fileBitBlt);             /* store filename graphic */
BlankPage();
return;}
/*_____*/

void CreateMenus(void){               /* creates the pull-down menus */
strcpy(text5,"New");PutText(2,4,C7,text5);
strcpy(text5,"Load file");PutText(3,4,C7,text5);
strcpy(text5,"Save file");PutText(4,4,C7,text5);
strcpy(text5,"Load slide");PutText(5,4,C7,text5);
strcpy(text5,"Save slide");PutText(6,4,C7,text5);
strcpy(text5,"Shutdown");PutText(7,4,C7,text5);
x1=alpha_x*2;yf1=alpha_y-6;
x2=x1+((alpha_x*12)-1);y2=yf1+((alpha_y*6)+11);
FileMenu=MemBlock(x1,yf1,x2,y2);                        /* allocate memory */
GetBlock(x1,yf1,x2,y2,FileMenu);             /* temporary store of text */
SetHue(C7);SetFill(fill_100,C7);
DrawPanel(x1,yf1,x2,y2);                                /* menu panel */
SetHue(C0);DrawBorder(x1+2,yf1+2,x2-2,y2-2);          /* rule trim */
DrawBorder(x1,yf1,x2,y2);                              /* border trim */
PutXOR(x1,yf1,FileMenu);                          /* xor text onto menu */
GetBlock(x1,yf1,x2,y2,FileMenu);                     /* File Menu is done */
BlankPage();
strcpy(text5,"Cube");PutText(2,4,C7,text5);
```

Fig. 13-3.
Continued.

```
strcpy(text5,"Cylinder");PutText(3,4,C7,text5);
strcpy(text5,"Cone");PutText(4,4,C7,text5);
strcpy(text5,"Sphere");PutText(5,4,C7,text5);
strcpy(text5,"Polygon");PutText(6,4,C7,text5);
strcpy(text5,"Line");PutText(7,4,C7,text5);
strcpy(text5,"Ruled surf");PutText(8,4,C7,text5);
strcpy(text5,"Mesh");PutText(9,4,C7,text5);
strcpy(text5,"User obj");PutText(10,4,C7,text5);
strcpy(text5,"User obj");PutText(11,4,C7,text5);
y2=y2+(alpha_y*4);
pbg1=x2-x1;pbg2=y2-yf1; /* width, depth of bg to save under menus */
ObjectMenu=MemBlock(x1,yf1,x2,y2);                  /* allocate memory */
GetBlock(x1,yf1,x2,y2,ObjectMenu);         /* temporary store of text */
SetHue(C7);SetFill(fill_100,C7);
DrawPanel(x1,yf1,x2,y2);                                /* menu panel */
SetHue(C0);DrawBorder(x1+2,yf1+2,x2-2,y2-2);             /* rule trim */
DrawBorder(x1,yf1,x2,y2);                              /* border trim */
PutXOR(x1,yf1,ObjectMenu);                    /* xor text onto menu */
GetBlock(x1,yf1,x2,y2,ObjectMenu);         /* Object Menu is done */
BlankPage();
strcpy(text5,"Rotate");PutText(2,4,C7,text5);
strcpy(text5,"Move...");PutText(3,4,C7,text5);
strcpy(text5,"Extrude");PutText(4,4,C7,text5);
strcpy(text5,"REGEN");PutText(5,4,C7,text5);
strcpy(text5,"UNDO");PutText(6,4,C7,text5);
y2=y2-(alpha_y*5);
SceneMenu=MemBlock(x1,yf1,x2,y2);                  /* allocate memory */
GetBlock(x1,yf1,x2,y2,SceneMenu);         /* temporary store of text */
SetHue(C7);SetFill(fill_100,C7);
DrawPanel(x1,yf1,x2,y2);                                /* menu panel */
SetHue(C0);DrawBorder(x1+2,yf1+2,x2-2,y2-2);             /* rule trim */
DrawBorder(x1,yf1,x2,y2);                              /* border trim */
PutXOR(x1,yf1,SceneMenu);                     /* xor text onto menu */
GetBlock(x1,yf1,x2,y2,SceneMenu);          /* Scene Menu is done */
BlankPage();
strcpy(text5,"Distance");PutText(2,4,C7,text5);
strcpy(text5,"Angle");PutText(3,4,C7,text5);
strcpy(text5,"Focal lgth");PutText(4,4,C7,text5);
strcpy(text5,"Light elev");PutText(5,4,C7,text5);
strcpy(text5,"Light dir");PutText(6,4,C7,text5);
strcpy(text5,"DEFAULTS");PutText(7,4,C7,text5);
y2=y2+(alpha_y*1);
CameraMenu=MemBlock(x1,yf1,x2,y2);                 /* allocate memory */
GetBlock(x1,yf1,x2,y2,CameraMenu);        /* temporary store of text */
SetHue(C7);SetFill(fill_100,C7);
DrawPanel(x1,yf1,x2,y2);                                /* menu panel */
SetHue(C0);DrawBorder(x1+2,yf1+2,x2-2,y2-2);             /* rule trim */
DrawBorder(x1,yf1,x2,y2);                              /* border trim */
PutXOR(x1,yf1,CameraMenu);                    /* xor text onto menu */
GetBlock(x1,yf1,x2,y2,CameraMenu);         /* Camera Menu is done */
BlankPage();
strcpy(text5,"Display");PutText(2,4,C7,text5);
strcpy(text5,"Render");PutText(3,4,C7,text5);
strcpy(text5,"Model");PutText(4,4,C7,text5);
strcpy(text5,"Color");PutText(5,4,C7,text5);
strcpy(text5,"Edit mode");PutText(6,4,C7,text5);
strcpy(text5,"Gnomon Y/N");PutText(7,4,C7,text5);
strcpy(text5,"Grid Y/N");PutText(8,4,C7,text5);
y2=y2+(alpha_y*1);
SettingsMenu=MemBlock(x1,yf1,x2,y2);               /* allocate memory */
GetBlock(x1,yf1,x2,y2,SettingsMenu);   /* temporary store of text */
SetHue(C7);SetFill(fill_100,C7);
DrawPanel(x1,yf1,x2,y2);                                /* menu panel */
SetHue(C0);DrawBorder(x1+2,yf1+2,x2-2,y2-2);             /* rule trim */
DrawBorder(x1,yf1,x2,y2);                              /* border trim */
PutXOR(x1,yf1,SettingsMenu);                  /* xor text onto menu */
GetBlock(x1,yf1,x2,y2,SettingsMenu);       /* Settings Menu is done */
BlankPage();
strcpy(text5,"Input...");PutText(2,4,C7,text5);
```

Fig. 13-3.
Continued.

```
strcpy(text5,"Set size");PutText(3,4,C7,text5);
strcpy(text5,"Set color");PutText(4,4,C7,text5);
strcpy(text5,"Setfont");PutText(5,4,C7,text5);
y2=y2-(alpha_y*3);
TextMenu=MemBlock(x1,yf1,x2,y2);                        /* allocate memory */
GetBlock(x1,yf1,x2,y2,TextMenu);            /* temporary store of text */
SetHue(C7);SetFill(fill_100,C7);
DrawPanel(x1,yf1,x2,y2);                                   /* menu panel */
SetHue(C0);DrawBorder(x1+2,yf1+2,x2-2,y2-2);              /* rule trim */
DrawBorder(x1,yf1,x2,y2);                                 /* border trim */
PutXOR(x1,yf1,TextMenu);                        /* xor text onto menu */
GetBlock(x1,yf1,x2,y2,TextMenu);               /* Text Menu is done */
BlankPage();
strcpy(text5,"Outline");PutText(2,4,C7,text5);
strcpy(text5,"Revolve");PutText(3,4,C7,text5);
strcpy(text5,"Extrude");PutText(4,4,C7,text5);
strcpy(text5,"Deform");PutText(5,4,C7,text5);
strcpy(text5,"Sweep");PutText(6,4,C7,text5);
strcpy(text5,"REGEN");PutText(7,4,C7,text5);
strcpy(text5,"UNDO");PutText(8,4,C7,text5);
strcpy(text5,"STORE");PutText(9,4,C7,text5);
y2=y2+(alpha_y*4);
CreateMenu=MemBlock(x1,yf1,x2,y2);                      /* allocate memory */
GetBlock(x1,yf1,x2,y2,CreateMenu);         /* temporary store of text */
SetHue(C7);SetFill(fill_100,C7);
DrawPanel(x1,yf1,x2,y2);                                   /* menu panel */
SetHue(C0);DrawBorder(x1+2,yf1+2,x2-2,y2-2);              /* rule trim */
DrawBorder(x1,yf1,x2,y2);                                 /* border trim */
PutXOR(x1,yf1,CreateMenu);                      /* xor text onto menu */
GetBlock(x1,yf1,x2,y2,CreateMenu);             /* Create Menu is done */
BlankPage();
return;}
/*_____*/

void CreateHiBars(void){       /* creates the menu highlight bars */
SetHue(C7);SetFill(fill_100,C7);
x1=0;yf1=0;
x2=(alpha_x*8)-1;y2=alpha_y+1;
DrawPanel(x1,yf1,x2,y2);
PanBar=MemBlock(x1,yf1,x2,y2);                       /* allocate memory */
GetBlock(x1,yf1,x2,y2,PanBar);      /* store panning highlight bar */
x1=0;yf1=0;
if (mode_flag==6){x2=(alpha_x*11)+2;}
else {x2=(alpha_x*11)+1;}
y2=alpha_y-1;
DrawPanel(x1,yf1,x2,y2);
ScrollBar=MemBlock(x1,yf1,x2,y2);                   /* allocate memory */
GetBlock(x1,yf1,x2,y2,ScrollBar);/* store scrolling highlight bar */
DrawPanel(0,0,50,50);
swatchprep=MemBlock(0,0,50,50);
GetBlock(0,0,50,50,swatchprep);                    /* store swatch prep */
swatchbg=MemBlock(0,0,50,50);
GetBlock(0,0,50,50,swatchbg);           /* initialize swatch bg saver */
BlankPage();return;}
/*_____*/

void DrawScreen(void){              /* creates the sign-on screen */
SetHue(bgclr);SetFill(fill_100,bgclr);
DrawPanel(4,14,x_res-5,y_res-1);                          /* bg prep */
if (mode_flag>3){          /* if bw mode on CGA, MCGA, or Herc */
  SetHue(C0);SetFill(fill_100,C0);
  DrawPanel(4,14,x_res-5,y_res-1);
  SetHue(bgclr);SetFill(fill_50,bgclr);
  DrawPanel(4,14,x_res-5,y_res-1);}
PutPSET(0,14,menubarBitBlt);                       /* install menu bar */
FreeBlock(menubarBitBlt);                /* deallocate memory block */
if (mode_flag==6){
  PutPSET(0,y_res-18,helpbarBitBlt);}
else {PutPSET(0,y_res-12,helpbarBitBlt);}    /* install help bar */
```

```
FreeBlock(helpbarBitBlt);                    /* deallocate memory block */
#if GraphicsLibrary==QuickC
  SetHue(bgclr);SetFill(fill_100,bgclr);     /* canvas shadow prep */
  DrawPanel(vx1+shx,vy1+shy,vx2+shx,vy2+shy);
  SetHue(shadowclr);SetFill(fill_75,shadowclr); /* canvas shadow */
  DrawPanel(vx1+shx,vy1+shy,vx2+shx,vy2+shy);
#elif GraphicsLibrary==TurboC
  SetHue(bgclr);SetFill(fill_25,bgclr);
  DrawPanel(vx1+shx,vy1+shy,vx2+shx,vy2+shy);   /* canvas shadow */
#endif
SetHue(canvasclr);SetFill(fill_100,canvasclr);         /* canvas */
DrawPanel(vx1,vy1,vx2,vy2);
SetHue(ruleclr);                                       /* canvas rule */
DrawBorder(vx1+ox1,vy1+oy1,vx2-ox2,vy2-oy2);
PutPSET(138,vy1+2,fileBitBlt);                     /* filename */
SetHue(C7);Notice(x_res-60,1);                     /* copyright */
PutText(1,2,C7,text1);                       /* 3D Designer ready. */
clipx1=(vx1+ox1)+1;clipy1=(vy1+oy1)+1;       /* set clipping coords */
clipx2=(vx2-ox2)-1;clipy2=(vy2-oy2)-1;       /* set clipping coords */
#if Compiler==QuickC
  GS_textavail=_registerfonts("TMSRB.FON");  /* init font table */
  if (GS_textavail==-1){           /* if cannot find font file... */
    ClearTextLine();PutText(1,2,C7,text15);goto debug1;}
  GS_textavail=0;
  _setfont("t'tms rmn',h26,w16");    /* pick Times Roman typeface */
  _setcolor(C0);                          /* set color to black */
  _moveto(t1x,t1y);_outgtext("Your Microcomputer 3D CAD Designer");
  _setfont("t'tms rmn',h10,w5");
  _setcolor(C0);_moveto(t2x,t2y);_outgtext("TM");
  _setfont("t'tms rmn',h20,w12");
  _moveto(t3x,t3y);_outgtext("here-is-how-it's-done source code");
  _moveto(t4x,t4y);_outgtext("for QuickC and Turbo C programmers");
  _unregisterfonts();                     /* free up font memory */
#elif Compiler==TurboC
  settextstyle(1,HORIZ_DIR,0);                   /* set typeface */
  gettextsettings(&loadquery);
  if(loadquery.font!=1){          /* if font file was not found... */
    GS_textavail=-1;
    settextstyle(DEFAULT_FONT,HORIZ_DIR,1);
    ClearTextLine();PutText(1,2,C7,text15);goto debug1;}
  setcolor(C0);                               /* set type color */
  setusercharsize(55,64,7,8);t1x=t1x+20;      /* set type size */
  moveto(t1x,t1y);outtext("Your Microcomputer 3D CAD Designer");
  setusercharsize(1,3,1,3);
  moveto(t2x,t2y);outtext("TM");
  setusercharsize(15,24,8,12);
  moveto(t3x,t3y);outtext("here-is-how-it's-done source code");
  moveto(t4x,t4y);outtext("for QuickC and Turbo C programmers");
  settextstyle(DEFAULT_FONT,HORIZ_DIR,1);/* restore default font */
#endif
debug1:
BackUp();                          /* store backup page for Undo */
#if GraphicsLibrary==QuickC
  _setviewport(0,0,x_res-1,y_res-1);         /* clipping viewport */
#elif GraphicsLibrary==TurboC
  setviewport(0,0,x_res-1,y_res-1,1);        /* clipping viewport */
#endif
return;}
/*_____*/

void InitUndo(void){            /* initialize hidden page for Undo */
switch(mode_flag){
  case 1: bitmap0=InitHiddenPage();                 /* 640x480x16 */
          ul.faraddress=bitmap0;
          seg1=ul.address.a2;off1=ul.address.a1;
          bitmap1=InitHiddenPage();
          ul.faraddress=bitmap1;
          seg2=ul.address.a2;off2=ul.address.a1;
          bitmap2=InitHiddenPage();
```

Fig. 13-3.
Continued.

Fig. 13-3.
Continued.

```
                          u1.faraddress=bitmap2;
                          seg3=u1.address.a2;off3=u1.address.a1;
                          bitmap3=InitHiddenPage();
                          u1.faraddress=bitmap3;
                          seg4=u1.address.a2;off4=u1.address.a1;break;
        case 2: break;                                  /* 640x350x16 */
        case 3: break;                                  /* 640x200x16 */
        case 4: bitmap0=InitHiddenPage();               /* 640x480x2  */
                u1.faraddress=bitmap0;
                seg1=u1.address.a2;off1=u1.address.a1;break;
        case 5: bitmap0=InitHiddenPage();               /* 640x200x2  */
                u1.faraddress=bitmap0;
                seg1=u1.address.a2;off1=u1.address.a1;break;
        case 6: break;}                                 /* 720x348x2  */
return;}
/*_____*/

void Quit_Pgm(void){                       /* terminates the program */
#if GraphicsLibrary==QuickC                       /* if using QuickC */
  _clearscreen(_GCLEARSCREEN);                    /* clear the screen */
  _setvideomode(_DEFAULTMODE);          /* restore the original mode */
#elif GraphicsLibrary==TurboC                    /* if using Turbo C */
  cleardevice();                                 /* clear the screen */
  closegraph();        /* shut down graphics, restore original mode */
#endif
exit(0);}                                  /* terminate the program */
/*_____*/

void FreeBlock(char far *blk){       /* deallocate far heap block */
#if GraphicsLibrary==QuickC
  _ffree(blk);
#elif GraphicsLibrary==TurboC
  farfree(blk);
#endif
return;}
/*_____*/


void Graphics_Setup(void){      /* autodetect of graphics hardware */
#if GraphicsLibrary==QuickC
/*  if (_setvideomoderows(_VRES16COLOR,60)!=FAIL) goto VGA_mode; */
  if (_setvideomoderows(_ERESCOLOR,43)!=FAIL) goto EGA_ECD_mode;
  if (_setvideomoderows(_HRES16COLOR,25)!=FAIL) goto EGA_SCD_mode;
  if (_setvideomoderows(_VRES2COLOR,60)!=FAIL) goto MCGA_mode;
  if (_setvideomoderows(_HRESBW,25)!=FAIL) goto CGA_mode;
  if (_setvideomoderows(_HERCMONO,25)!=FAIL) goto Hercules_mode;
#elif GraphicsLibrary==TurboC
  int graphics_adapter,graphics_mode;
  detectgraph(&graphics_adapter,&graphics_mode);
  if (graphics_adapter==VGA){
     graphics_adapter=VGA;graphics_mode=VGAHI;
     initgraph(&graphics_adapter,&graphics_mode,"");
     settextstyle(0,0,1);
     goto VGA_mode;}
  if (graphics_mode==EGAHI){
     graphics_adapter=EGA;graphics_mode=EGAHI;
     initgraph(&graphics_adapter,&graphics_mode,"");
     settextstyle(0,0,1);
     goto EGA_ECD_mode;}
  if (graphics_mode==EGALO){
     graphics_adapter=EGA;graphics_mode=EGALO;
     initgraph(&graphics_adapter,&graphics_mode,"");
     settextstyle(0,0,1);
     goto EGA_SCD_mode;}
  if (graphics_adapter==MCGA){
     graphics_adapter=MCGA;graphics_mode=MCGAHI;
     initgraph(&graphics_adapter,&graphics_mode,"");
     settextstyle(0,0,1);
     goto MCGA_mode;}
```

Fig. 13-3.
Continued.

```c
  if (graphics_adapter==CGA){
     graphics_adapter=CGA;graphics_mode=CGAHI;
     initgraph(&graphics_adapter,&graphics_mode,"");
     settextstyle(0,0,1);
     goto CGA_mode;}
  if (graphics_adapter==HERCMONO){
     graphics_adapter=HERCMONO;graphics_mode=HERCMONOHI;
     initgraph(&graphics_adapter,&graphics_mode,"");
     goto Hercules_mode;}
#endif
goto abort_pgm;                         /* if no graphics hardware found */

/* ASSIGN MODE-DEPENDENT VARIABLES AND TEST EGA DISPLAY MEMORY     */

VGA_mode:       /* VGA 640x480x16-color mode, 8x8 character matrix */
x_res=640;y_res=480;mode_flag=1;
t1x=54;t1y=128;t2x=580;t2y=128;t3x=156;t3y=160;t4x=138;t4y=180;
alpha_x=8;alpha_y=8;plane_length=38400;return;

EGA_ECD_mode: /* EGA 640x350x16-color mode, 8x8 character matrix */
#if GraphicsLibrary==QuickC
  if (_setactivepage(1)<0){               /* if no page 1 found... */
    _setvideomoderows(_HRES16COLOR,25);
    goto EGA_SCD_mode;}                  /* ...try a different mode */
  _setactivepage(0);                /* else reset active page to 0 */
#endif      /* Turbo C's detectgraph has already confirmed this */
x_res=640;y_res=350;mode_flag=2;
t1x=54;t1y=108;t2x=580;t2y=108;t3x=156;t3y=140;t4x=138;t4y=160;
alpha_x=8;alpha_y=8;plane_length=28000;return;

EGA_SCD_mode: /* EGA 640x200x16-color mode, 8x8 character matrix */
#if GraphicsLibrary==QuickC
  if (_setactivepage(1)<0){               /* if no page 1 found... */
    _setvideomoderows(_HRESBW,25);
    goto CGA_mode;}                       /* ...try a different mode */
  _setactivepage(0);             /* ...else reset active page to 0 */
#endif      /* Turbo C's detectgraph has already confirmed this */
x_res=640;y_res=200;mode_flag=3;
t1x=54;t1y=78;t2x=580;t2y=78;t3x=156;t3y=110;t4x=138;t4y=130;
alpha_x=8;alpha_y=8;plane_length=16000;return;

MCGA_mode:      /* MCGA 640x480x2-color mode, 8x8 character matrix */
x_res=640;y_res=480;mode_flag=4;
C0=0;C1=1;C2=1;C3=1;C4=1;C5=1;C6=1;C7=1;
C8=1;C9=1;C10=1;C11=1;C12=1;C13=1;C14=1;C15=1;
t1x=54;t1y=128;t2x=580;t2y=128;t3x=156;t3y=160;t4x=138;t4y=180;
alpha_x=8;alpha_y=8;plane_length=38400;return;

CGA_mode:       /* CGA 640x200x2-color mode, 8x8 character matrix */
x_res=640;y_res=200;mode_flag=5;
C0=0;C1=1;C2=1;C3=1;C4=1;C5=1;C6=1;C7=1;
C8=1;C9=1;C10=1;C11=1;C12=1;C13=1;C14=1;C15=1;
t1x=54;t1y=78;t2x=580;t2y=78;t3x=156;t3y=110;t4x=138;t4y=130;
alpha_x=8;alpha_y=8;plane_length=16384;return;

Hercules_mode:  /* Hercules 720x348x2-color mode, 9x14 character */
x_res=720;y_res=348;mode_flag=6;
C0=0;C1=1;C2=1;C3=1;C4=1;C5=1;C6=1;C7=1;
C8=1;C9=1;C10=1;C11=1;C12=1;C13=1;C14=1;C15=1;
t1x=96;t1y=108;t2x=624;t2y=108;t3x=203;t3y=140;t4x=176;t4y=160;
alpha_x=9;alpha_y=14;plane_length=32406;return;

abort_pgm:      /* jump to here if no supported graphics hardware */
printf("\n\n\rUnable to proceed.\n\r");
printf("Requires VGA, EGA, CGA, MCGA, or\n\r");
printf("Hercules adapter and appropriate monitor.\n\n\r");
exit(0);
}
/*_____*/
```

Fig. 13-3.
Continued.

```
long GetFreeMemory(void){              /* determine size of free RAM */
  int c1=0;unsigned block=0;long totalmem=0;
  char far * vptr;char far * vptrarray[ATTEMPTS];
c1=0;totalmem=0;block=CHUNK;
#if Compiler==QuickC
  while (block>REMAINDER){
    if((vptr=(char far *)_fmalloc(block))!=NULL){
      vptrarray[c1]=vptr;totalmem=totalmem+block;c1++;}
    else block=block/2;}
  for ( ;c1;c1--){
    _ffree(vptrarray[c1-1]);}
#elif Compiler==TurboC
  while (block>REMAINDER){
    if((vptr=(char far *)farmalloc(block))!=NULL){
      vptrarray[c1]=vptr;totalmem=totalmem+block;c1++;}
    else block=block/2;}
  for ( ;c1;c1--){
    farfree(vptrarray[c1-1]);}
#endif
return totalmem;}
/*_____*/

void Notice(int x,int y){        /* displays the copyright notice */
int copyright[][3]={0x7c00,0x0000,0x0000, /* array of bit styles */
                    0x8279,0x819c,0x645e,
                    0xba4a,0x4252,0x96d0,
                    0xa27a,0x4252,0x955e,
                    0xba0a,0x43d2,0xf442,
                    0x8219,0x825c,0x945e,
                    0x7c00,0x0000,0x0000};
int a,b,c; int t1=0;                          /* local variables */
for (t1=0;t1<=6;t1++){                     /* draw 7 styled lines */
  a=copyright[t1][0];b=copyright[t1][1];c=copyright[t1][2];
  SetLine(a);SetPosition(x,y);DrawLine(x+15,y);
  SetLine(b);SetPosition(x+16,y);DrawLine(x+31,y);
  SetLine(c);SetPosition(x+32,y);DrawLine(x+47,y);y=y+1;};
SetLine(0xFFFF);return;
}
/*_____
```

```
End of Module 1 source code.  (This program has 3 modules.) */
/*                          tm
Your Microcomputer 3D CAD Designer            Source file: DESIGN2.C

By: Lee Adams     Version: 1.00     Revision: n/a.
Notices: (c) Copyright 1990 Lee Adams.  All rights reserved.
  Your Microcomputer 3D CAD Designer is a trademark of
  TAB Books Inc. and is used by permission.
First published: 1990 by Windcrest Books (div. of TAB Books Inc.)

SOURCE NOTES:  This is module 2 of 3.  The project list should
include DESIGN1.C, DESIGN2.C, and DESIGN3.C named in QuickC's MAK
file or Turbo C's PRJ file.

OPERATION:  provides menu system management routines and core
functions for the user interface established by module 1.

LICENSE:  As purchaser of the book in which this program is
published, you are granted a non-exclusive royalty-free license
to reproduce and distribute these routines in executable form
as part of your software product, subject to any copyright,
trademark, or patent rights of others, and subject to the limited
warranty described in the introduction of the book.  All other
rights reserved.
_____

COMPILER DIRECTIVES   */

              /* compilers and graphics libraries */
```

Fig. 13-3.
Continued.

```
#define QuickC        1
#define TurboC        2
#define MicrosoftC 3
#define LatticeC    4
#define HALO          7
#define MetaWINDOW 8
#define Essential   9

#define Compiler QuickC          /* change to TurboC if required */
#define GraphicsLibrary QuickC   /* change to library being used */

#define EMPTY      0          /* for checking keyboard buffer */
#define ACTIVE     1                    /* menu system status */
#define BACKOUT    2                    /* menu system status */
#define STUB       3                    /* menu system status */
#define YES'       1              /* decision-making token */
#define NO         0                            /* ibid */

#include <bios.h>              /* supports keyboard functions */
#include <stdio.h>               /* supports printf function */
#include <string.h>          /* supports string manipulation */
#include <math.h>               /* supports sine and cosine */
#if Compiler==QuickC
  #include <conio.h>               /* supports QuickC port IO */
  #include <malloc.h>   /* supports memory allocation for arrays */
#elif Compiler==TurboC
  #include <dos.h>                 /* supports TurboC port IO */
  #include <alloc.h>    /* supports memory allocation for arrays */
#endif
#if GraphicsLibrary==QuickC
  #include <graph.h>               /* QuickC graphics library */
#elif GraphicsLibrary==TurboC
  #include <graphics.h>            /* Turbo C graphics library */
#endif
#include <process.h>         /* supports the exit function
```

```
FUNCTION PROTOTYPES   */

/* MENU MANAGEMENT ROUTINES IN THIS MODULE */
void MenuBarLoop(void);     /* manages the menu system at runtime */
void CheckForKey(void);              /* checks for user keystrokes */
void KeySwitch1(void);     /* manages keystrokes at menu bar level */
void Panning(void);           /* moves the panning highlight bar */
void Purge(void);               /* empties the keyboard buffer */
void InstallMenu(void); /* installs a level 1 menu on the screen */
void UninstallMenu(void);/* removes level 1 menu from the screen */
void PanMenu(void);              /* manages inter-menu panning */
void Scrolling(void);       /* manages scrolling highlight bar */
void KeySwitch2(void);     /* manages keystrokes for level 1 menus */
void MenuChoices(void); /* calls pgm functions for level 1 menus */
void StubRoutine(void);      /* do-nothing stub for prototyping */
void MenuBarText(void);       /* back-out stub for prototyping */
void ClearTextLine(void);     /* blanks the dialog text line */
void MakeSound(int,int);              /* generates a sound */
void EditName(void);              /* user can edit filename */
void EditColor(void);         /* user can change shading hue */
void CursorManager(void);    /* user can rotate, move 3D cursor */
void CamAngleMgr(void);        /* user can alter Camera angle */
void GetCubeCoords(void);   /* camera coords & display coords */
void DrawCube(void);                      /* draw 3D cube */
void DrawCylinder(void);               /* draw 3D cylinder */
void GetCylObjCoords(void);  /* calculate cylinder obj coords */
void DrawCylFacet(void);         /* draw a facet on cylinder */
void DrawCylNearEnd(void);           /* draw cylinder end */
void DrawCylFarEnd(void);            /* draw cylinder end */

/* ROUTINES IN MODULE 3 CALLED BY THIS MODULE */
void SetHue(int);              /* sets the current drawing color */
```

Fig. 13-3.
Continued.

```
void SetLine(int);                         /* sets the current line style */
void SetFill(char *, int);                  /* sets the area fill style */
void BlankPage(void);                   /* blanks the current active page */
void SetPosition(int,int);              /* sets the current xy position */
void DrawLine(int,int);      /* draws line from current xy position */
void DrawBorder(int,int,int,int);              /* draws rectangle */
void DrawPanel(int,int,int,int);          /* draws solid rectangle */
void Fill(int,int,int);                            /* area fill */
char far * MemBlock(int,int,int,int);    /* allocate array memory */
void GetBlock(int,int,int,int,char far *); /* save graphic array */
void PutXOR(int,int,char far *);         /* show XOR graphic array */
void PutPSET(int,int,char far *);        /* show PSET graphic array */
void PutText(int,int,int,char *);               /* display text */
void SetTextRowCol(int,int);                 /* set text position */
char far * InitHiddenPage(void);     /* initialize hidden bitmap */
void BackUp(void);                 /* copies page 0 to hidden page */
void Restore(void);                /* copies hidden page to page 0 */
void SaveImage(void);                       /* prep for image save */
void LoadImage(void);                       /* prep for image load */
void SaveVGAEGAImage(void);      /* saves VGA or EGA image to disk */
void LoadVGAEGAImage(void);      /* loads VGA or EGA image from disk */
void SaveCGAimage(void);               /* saves CGA image to disk */
void LoadCGAimage(void);              /* loads CGA image from disk */
void SaveHGAimage(void);          /* saves Hercules image to disk */
void LoadHGAimage(void);         /* loads Hercules image from disk */
void SaveMCGAimage(void);             /* saves MCGA image to disk */
void LoadMCGAimage(void);            /* loads MCGA image from disk */
void WindowOpen(int,int,int,int);             /* opens viewport */
void WindowClose(int,int);                 /* shut down viewport */
void WindowClear(int);                   /* blanks the viewport */
void SetRatios(void);        /* set aspect ratio, viewport ratio */
void Init3D(void);                 /* initialize all 3D parameters */
void DrawCursor(void);                        /* draws 3D cursor */
void DrawGrndPlane(void);                 /* draws 3D groundplane */
void GetNewObjParams(void);     /* object rotation, translation */
void GetWorldCoords(void);           /* object to world coords */
void GetCameraCoords(void);          /* world to camera coords */
void GetImageCoords(void);     /* camera to image plane coords */
void GetScreenCoords(void);   /* image plane to display coords */
void SetCamAngle(void);            /* gets sine, cosine factors */

/* ROUTINES IN MODULE 1 CALLED BY THIS MODULE */
void Quit_Pgm(void);              /* ends the program gracefully */
void FreeBlock(char far *);       /* deallocate far heap memory */
/*_____*/


/* DECLARATION OF GLOBAL VARIABLES */
char far *SaveBgd;     /* array to save background under each menu */
int Continue=1;              /* used to hold decision-making token */
float cubeObj[][3]={ /* array of cube vertices xyz object coords */
      10,-10,10,    10,10,10,    -10,10,10,    -10,-10,10,
      10,10,-10,    -10,10,-10,    -10,-10,-10,    10,-10,-10};
float cubeWorld[8][3];  /* xw1,yw1,zw1 vertext world coordinates */
float camcoords[8][3];  /* xc1,yc1,zc1 vertex camera coordinates */
float displaycoords[8][2];       /* sx1,sy1 vertex display coords */
int pitchheading=360,yawheading=0;    /* camera angle in degrees */
int viewchg=2;          /* degrees to change camera angle */
double yawdelta=0,pitchdelta=0;      /* current absolute change */
float signmx=1,signmy=-1,signmz=-1;      /* coord system tweaking */
int WhichObj=0;            /* token indicates user-selected object */
float cylradius=0,cyldepth=0;            /* cylinder radius, depth */
float CylWorldNear[18][3];  /* 18 sets of world coords, near end */
float CylWorldFar[18][3];   /* 18 sets of world coords, far end */
float CylCamNear[18][3];   /* 18 sets of camera coords, near end */
float CylCamFar[18][3];    /* 18 sets of camera coords, far end */
float CylDisplayNear[18][2]; /* 18 sets display coords, near end */
float CylDisplayFar[18][2];  /* 18 sets display coords, far end */
double sr4=0.0,cr4=0.0,sr5=0.0,cr5=0.0;     /* rotation factors */
```

```
double r4=6.28319,r5=6.28319;      /* spherical coordinate angles */
int q=0,q1=0,q2=0;                 /* cylinder surface & vertex counters */

/* RE-DECLARATION OF GLOBAL VARIABLES initialized in Module 1,
   but also visible to all functions in this source file. */
#if GraphicsLibrary==QuickC
  extern struct vc;
#endif
extern int C0,C1,C2,C3,C4,C5,C6,C7,C8,C9,C10,C11,C12,C13,C14,C15;
extern int x_res,y_res,mode_flag,alpha_x,alpha_y,x1,yf1,x2,y2,t1;
extern int sx,sy;
extern char keycode,keynum;
extern char far *menubarBitBlt;extern char far *helpbarBitBlt;
extern char far *fileBitBlt;extern char far *funcBitBlt;
extern char far *FileMenu;extern char far *ObjectMenu;
extern char far *SceneMenu;extern char far *CameraMenu;
extern char far *SettingsMenu;extern char far *TextMenu;
extern char far *CreateMenu;extern char far *PanBar;
extern char far *ScrollBar;extern char far *swatchprep;
extern char far *swatchbg;
extern int clipx1,clipy1,clipx2,clipy2;
extern int barclr,bgclr,canvasclr;
extern int shadowclr,panelclr,ruleclr;
extern char fill_0[],fill_3[],fill_6[],fill_12[];
extern char fill_25[],fill_37[],fill_50[],fill_62[];
extern char fill_75[],fill_87[],fill_93[],fill_100[];
extern int p1,p2,px1,px2,px3,px4,px5,px6,px7;
extern int py1,py2,py3,py4,py5,py6,py7,py8,py9,py10;
extern int t2,t3,p3,p4,p5,p6,pbg1,pbg2,status,choice;
extern unsigned int plane_length;
extern char far * bitmap0;
extern char far * bitmap1;
extern char far * bitmap2;
extern char far * bitmap3;
extern union{ struct {unsigned int a1; unsigned int a2;} address;
        char far * faraddress;} u1;
extern unsigned int seg1,seg2,seg3,seg4,off1,off2,off3,off4;
extern char * textptr;
extern char text1[],text4[],text5[];
extern char text6[],text7[],text8[],text9[],text10[];
extern char text12[],text13[],text14[],text15[],text16[];
extern char text17[];
extern char Herc;
extern char far *HPtr;
extern struct SREGS segregs;
extern unsigned int segment;
extern unsigned int offset;
extern FILE *image_file;
extern char image_buffer[];
extern char f3[],f4[],f6[],f7[];
extern char f8[],f9[],f10[],f11[],f12[];
extern int GS_bgclr;
extern int GS_textavail;
extern int fillclr_index;

/* RE-DECLARATION OF GLOBAL VARIABLES initialized in Module 3,
   but also visible to all functions in this source file. */
extern int NormHue,IntHue,KeyMatte,EdgeClr,SolidClr;
extern int DitherPrep,DitherStyle,DitherClr;
extern double ObjYawChg,ObjRollChg,ObjPitchChg;
extern float xObjChg,yObjChg,zObjChg;
extern float cursorx,cursory,cursorz;
extern float cursorxchg,cursorychg,cursorzchg;
extern float x,y,z,sx3D,sy3D,visible;
extern float xc1,xc2,xc3,xc4,xc5,xc6,xc7,yc1,yc2,yc3,yc4,yc5,yc6,
             yc7,zc1,zc2,zc3,zc4,zc5,zc6,zc7;
extern float sx1,sx2,sx3,sx4,sx5,sy1,sy2,sy3,sy4,sy5;
extern float yawdist,dist;
extern double CamPitch,CamYaw,sCPitch,cCPitch;
```

Fig. 13-3.
Continued.

Fig. 13-3.
Continued.

```
extern float xCam,yCam,zCam;
extern float xw1,xw2,xw3,yw1,yw2,yw3,zw1,zw2,zw3;
extern int minx,miny,maxx,maxy;
extern char far *matteA;extern char far *matteB;

/*_____


          M E N U    S Y S T E M    M A N A G E R
_____ */

void MenuBarLoop(void){      /* manages the menu system at runtime */
SetRatios();Init3D();              /* initialize the 3D parameters */
t1=1;      /* initialize panning highlight bar position indicator */
SaveBgd=MemBlock(16,2,127,61);       /* allocate memory to save bg */
PutXOR(p1,p2,PanBar);                /* install panning hilite bar */
MakeSound(250,6000);                            /* audio cue */
loop0:                               /* menu bar loop begins */
CheckForKey();                       /* check for user keystroke */
if (keycode!=2) goto Label1;      /* jump if not an extended key */
switch (keynum){
  case 77: t1=t1+1;Panning();Purge();
            ClearTextLine();goto loop0;          /* right arrow */
  case 75: t1=t1-1;Panning();Purge();
            ClearTextLine();goto loop0;}          /* left arrow */
Label1:
if (keycode!=1) goto Label2;      /* jump past if not a normal key */
if (keynum==13){                          /* if <Enter> key... */
  InstallMenu();Purge();
  switch (t1){
    case 1: goto menuloop;                          /* File */
    case 2: goto menuloop;                        /* Object */
    case 3: goto menuloop;                         /* Scene */
    case 4: goto menuloop;                        /* Camera */
    case 5: goto menuloop;                      /* Settings */
    case 6: goto menuloop;                          /* Text */
    case 7: goto menuloop;}}                      /* Create */
Label2:
if (keycode!=0){                         /* if a key was retrieved */
  KeySwitch1();                   /* switcher for system keystrokes */
  Purge();}                        /* empty the keyboard buffer */
goto loop0;                                      /* loop back */
menuloop:                           /* level 1 menus loop begins */
CheckForKey();                      /* check for user keystroke */
if (keycode!=2) goto Label3;      /* jump if not an extended key */
switch (keynum){
  case 80: t2=t2+1;                                /* down arrow */
          Scrolling();
          Purge();
          ClearTextLine();goto menuloop;
  case 72: t2=t2-1;                                  /* up arrow */
          Scrolling();
          Purge();
          ClearTextLine();goto menuloop;
  case 77: t1=t1+1;                               /* right arrow */
          PanMenu();Purge();
          ClearTextLine();goto menuloop;
  case 75: t1=t1-1;                                /* left arrow */
          PanMenu();Purge();
          ClearTextLine();goto menuloop;}
Label3:
if (keycode!=1) goto Label4;      /* jump past if not a normal key */
if (keynum==13){                          /* if <Enter> key... */
  MenuChoices();Purge();goto Label5;} /* call the core function */
if (keynum==27){                          /* if <Esc> key... */
  UninstallMenu();Purge();              /* back out of the menu */
  PutXOR(p1,p2,PanBar);MenuBarText();
  goto loop0;}
Label4:
if (keycode!=0){                         /* if a key was retrieved */
```

Fig. 13-3.
Continued.

```
        KeySwitch2();              /* switcher for level 1 menus keystrokes */
        Purge();)}                         /* empty the keyboard buffer */
goto menuloop;                                        /* loop back */
Label5:              /* decide re-entrant point after core function */
switch (status){
   case ACTIVE:   PutXOR(p1,p2,PanBar);goto loop0;
   case BACKOUT: UninstallMenu();goto loop0;
   case STUB:     goto menuloop;}
return;}                                              /* boilerplate */
/*_____*/

void Panning(void){            /* moves the panning highlight bar */
if (t1>7) t1=1;                            /* wraparound past right */
if (t1<1) t1=7;                             /* wraparound past left */
switch (t1){           /* use t1 to determine where to move cursor */
   case 1: PutXOR(p1,p2,PanBar);p1=px1;
           PutXOR(p1,p2,PanBar);break;
   case 2: PutXOR(p1,p2,PanBar);p1=px2;
           PutXOR(p1,p2,PanBar);break;
   case 3: PutXOR(p1,p2,PanBar);p1=px3;
           PutXOR(p1,p2,PanBar);break;
   case 4: PutXOR(p1,p2,PanBar);p1=px4;
           PutXOR(p1,p2,PanBar);break;
   case 5: PutXOR(p1,p2,PanBar);p1=px5;
           PutXOR(p1,p2,PanBar);break;
   case 6: PutXOR(p1,p2,PanBar);p1=px6;
           PutXOR(p1,p2,PanBar);break;
   case 7: PutXOR(p1,p2,PanBar);p1=px7;
           PutXOR(p1,p2,PanBar);break;
   default: break;}
return;}
/*_____*/

void InstallMenu(void){        /* install level 1 menu on screen */
t2=1;                          /* reset virtual scroll position */
p6=py1;                        /* reset y coord scroll position */
switch (t1){
   case 1:  p3=px1-1;                                /* File menu */
            PutXOR(p1,p2,PanBar);           /* remove panning bar */
            BackUp();        /* store backup page for possible Undo */
            GetBlock(p3,p4,(p3+pbg1),(p4+pbg2),SaveBgd);   /*save */
            PutPSET(p3,p4,FileMenu);            /* install menu */
            p5=px1+2;  /* reset x install coord for scrolling bar */
            PutXOR(p5,p6,ScrollBar);            /* install bar */
            t3=6;              /* reset number of choices in menu */
            break;
   case 2:  p3=px2-1;                              /* Object menu */
            PutXOR(p1,p2,PanBar);
            BackUp();
            GetBlock(p3,p4,(p3+pbg1),(p4+pbg2),SaveBgd);
            PutPSET(p3,p4,ObjectMenu);
            p5=px2+2;PutXOR(p5,p6,ScrollBar);t3=10;break;
   case 3:  p3=px3-1;                               /* Scene menu */
            PutXOR(p1,p2,PanBar);
            GetBlock(p3,p4,(p3+pbg1),(p4+pbg2),SaveBgd);
            PutPSET(p3,p4,SceneMenu);
            p5=px3+2;PutXOR(p5,p6,ScrollBar);t3=5;break;
   case 4:  p3=px4-1;                              /* Camera menu */
            PutXOR(p1,p2,PanBar);
            BackUp();
            GetBlock(p3,p4,(p3+pbg1),(p4+pbg2),SaveBgd);
            PutPSET(p3,p4,CameraMenu);
            p5=px4+2;PutXOR(p5,p6,ScrollBar);t3=6;break;
   case 5:  p3=px5-1;                            /* Settings menu */
            PutXOR(p1,p2,PanBar);
            BackUp();
            GetBlock(p3,p4,(p3+pbg1),(p4+pbg2),SaveBgd);
            PutPSET(p3,p4,SettingsMenu);
            p5=px5+2;PutXOR(p5,p6,ScrollBar);t3=7;break;
```

Fig. 13-3.
Continued.

```
        case 6:  p3=px6-1;                              /* Text menu */
                 PutXOR(p1,p2,PanBar);
                 BackUp();
                 GetBlock(p3,p4,(p3+pbg1),(p4+pbg2),SaveBgd);
                 PutPSET(p3,p4,TextMenu);
                 p5=px6+2;PutXOR(p5,p6,ScrollBar);t3=4;break;
        case 7:  p3=px7-1;                              /* Create menu */
                 PutXOR(p1,p2,PanBar);
                 BackUp();
                 GetBlock(p3,p4,(p3+pbg1),(p4+pbg2),SaveBgd);
                 PutPSET(p3,p4,CreateMenu);
                 p5=px7+2;PutXOR(p5,p6,ScrollBar);t3=8;break;
      default:  break;}
    return;}
/*_____*/

void UninstallMenu(void){    /* removes level 1 menu from screen */
PutPSET(p3,p4,SaveBgd);return;}
/*_____*/


void PanMenu(void){                    /* manages inter-menu panning */
if (t1>7) t1=1;                        /* wraparound to skip Undo */
if (t1<1) t1=7;                                   /* wraparound */
t2=1;                               /* reset virtual scroll position */
p6=py1;                             /* reset y coord scroll position */
UninstallMenu();                    /* remove existing level 1 menu */
switch (t1){
  case 1: p1=px1;                    /* reset x coord for panning bar */
          t3=6;                /* reset number of choices on menu */
          p3=px1-1;                      /* reset x coord for menu */
          p5=px1+2;              /* reset x coord for scrolling bar */
          GetBlock(p3,p4,(p3+pbg1),(p4+pbg2),SaveBgd);    /*save */
          PutPSET(p3,p4,FileMenu);                /* install menu */
          PutXOR(p5,p6,ScrollBar);                 /* install bar */
          break;                        /* get out of switch branch */
  case 2: p1=px2;t3=10;p3=px2-1;p5=px2+2;
          GetBlock(p3,p4,(p3+pbg1),(p4+pbg2),SaveBgd);
          PutPSET(p3,p4,ObjectMenu);
          PutXOR(p5,p6,ScrollBar);
          break;
  case 3: p1=px3;t3=5;p3=px3-1;p5=px3+2;
          GetBlock(p3,p4,(p3+pbg1),(p4+pbg2),SaveBgd);
          PutPSET(p3,p4,SceneMenu);
          PutXOR(p5,p6,ScrollBar);
          break;
  case 4: p1=px4;t3=6;p3=px4-1;p5=px4+2;
          GetBlock(p3,p4,(p3+pbg1),(p4+pbg2),SaveBgd);
          PutPSET(p3,p4,CameraMenu);
          PutXOR(p5,p6,ScrollBar);
          break;
  case 5: p1=px5;t3=7;p3=px5-1;p5=px5+2;
          GetBlock(p3,p4,(p3+pbg1),(p4+pbg2),SaveBgd);
          PutPSET(p3,p4,SettingsMenu);
          PutXOR(p5,p6,ScrollBar);
          break;
  case 6: p1=px6;t3=4;p3=px6-1;p5=px6+2;
          GetBlock(p3,p4,(p3+pbg1),(p4+pbg2),SaveBgd);
          PutPSET(p3,p4,TextMenu);
          PutXOR(p5,p6,ScrollBar);
          break;
  case 7: p1=px7;t3=8;p3=px7-1;p5=px7+2;
          GetBlock(p3,p4,(p3+pbg1),(p4+pbg2),SaveBgd);
          PutPSET(p3,p4,CreateMenu);
          PutXOR(p5,p6,ScrollBar);
          break;}
    return;}
/*_____*/
```

Fig. 13-3.
Continued.

```
void Scrolling(void){           /* manages scrolling highlight bar */
if (t2>t3) t2=1;   /* handle vertical wraparound of scrolling bar */
if (t2<1) t2=t3;                        /* vertical wraparound */
switch (t2){
  case 1: PutXOR(p5,p6,ScrollBar);                  /* remove former */
          p6=py1;                                   /* reset y coord */
          PutXOR(p5,p6,ScrollBar);                    /* install new */
          break;                       /* get out of switch branch */
  case 2:  PutXOR(p5,p6,ScrollBar);p6=py2;
           PutXOR(p5,p6,ScrollBar);break;
  case 3:  PutXOR(p5,p6,ScrollBar);p6=py3;
           PutXOR(p5,p6,ScrollBar);break;
  case 4:  PutXOR(p5,p6,ScrollBar);p6=py4;
           PutXOR(p5,p6,ScrollBar);break;
  case 5:  PutXOR(p5,p6,ScrollBar);p6=py5;
           PutXOR(p5,p6,ScrollBar);break;
  case 6:  PutXOR(p5,p6,ScrollBar);p6=py6;
           PutXOR(p5,p6,ScrollBar);break;
  case 7:  PutXOR(p5,p6,ScrollBar);p6=py7;
           PutXOR(p5,p6,ScrollBar);break;
  case 8:  PutXOR(p5,p6,ScrollBar);p6=py8;
           PutXOR(p5,p6,ScrollBar);break;
  case 9:  PutXOR(p5,p6,ScrollBar);p6=py9;
           PutXOR(p5,p6,ScrollBar);break;
  case 10: PutXOR(p5,p6,ScrollBar);p6=py10;
           PutXOR(p5,p6,ScrollBar);break;}
return;}
/*_____*/


void MenuChoices(void){          /* calls level 1 core functions */
switch (t1){             /* determine which menu is being used */
  case 1: goto filechoices;
  case 2: goto objectchoices;
  case 3: goto scenechoices;
  case 4: goto camerachoices;
  case 5: goto settingschoices;
  case 6: goto textchoices;
  case 7: goto createchoices;}
filechoices:
switch (t2){                     /* determine which scroll choice */
  case 1: choice=1;status=ACTIVE;                       /* New */
          ClearTextLine();UninstallMenu();
          WindowOpen(clipx1,clipy1,clipx2,clipy2);
          WindowClear(GS_bgclr);WindowClose(x_res,y_res);Init3D();
          break;
  case 2: choice=2;StubRoutine();break;            /* Load file */
  case 3: choice=3;StubRoutine();break;            /* Save file */
  case 4: choice=4;status=ACTIVE;Restore();       /* Load slide */
          EditName();
          if (Continue==YES) LoadImage();
          break;
  case 5: choice=5;status=ACTIVE;Restore();        /* Save slide */
          EditName();
          if (Continue==YES) SaveImage();
          break;
  case 6: choice=6;Quit_Pgm();}                     /* Shutdown */
if (status!=STUB) {ClearTextLine();PutText(1,2,C7,text7);}
return;
objectchoices:
switch (t2){
  case 1: choice=7;status=ACTIVE;WhichObj=7;              /* cube */
          MakeSound(200,6000);UninstallMenu();break;
  case 2: choice=8;status=ACTIVE;WhichObj=8;          /* cylinder */
          MakeSound(200,6000);UninstallMenu();break;
  case 3: choice=9;status=ACTIVE;WhichObj=9;             /* cone */
          MakeSound(200,6000);UninstallMenu();break;
  case 4: choice=10;status=ACTIVE;WhichObj=10;         /* sphere */
          MakeSound(200,6000);UninstallMenu();break;
```

Fig. 13-3.
Continued.

```
      case 5: choice=11;status=ACTIVE;WhichObj=11;          /* polygon */
              MakeSound(200,6000);UninstallMenu();break;
      case 6: choice=12;status=ACTIVE;WhichObj=12;          /* line */
              MakeSound(200,6000);UninstallMenu();break;
      case 7: choice=13;StubRoutine();break;            /* ruled surface */
      case 8: choice=14;StubRoutine();break;               /* mesh */
      case 9: choice=15;StubRoutine();break;            /* user object */
      case 10: choice=16;StubRoutine();break;}          /* user object */
  if (status!=STUB) {ClearTextLine();PutText(1,2,C7,text7);}
  return;
  scenechoices:
  switch (t2){
      case 1: choice=17;status=ACTIVE;                      /* rotate */
              UninstallMenu();BackUp();
              WindowOpen(clipx1,clipy1,clipx2,clipy2);
              CursorManager();WindowClose(x_res,y_res);break;
      case 2: choice=18;status=ACTIVE;                      /* move */
              UninstallMenu();BackUp();
              WindowOpen(clipx1,clipy1,clipx2,clipy2);
              CursorManager();WindowClose(x_res,y_res);break;
      case 3: choice=19;status=ACTIVE;                      /* extrude */
              UninstallMenu();BackUp();
              WindowOpen(clipx1,clipy1,clipx2,clipy2);
              CursorManager();WindowClose(x_res,y_res);break;
      case 4: choice=20;StubRoutine();break;
      case 5: choice=21;status=ACTIVE;                      /* undo */
              Restore();break;}
  if (status!=STUB) {ClearTextLine();PutText(1,2,C7,text7);}
  return;
  camerachoices:
  switch (t2){                       /* determine which scroll choice */
    case 1: choice=22;StubRoutine();break;
    case 2: choice=23;status=ACTIVE;                        /* Angle */
            UninstallMenu();ClearTextLine();PutText(1,2,C7,text16);
            WindowOpen(clipx1,clipy1,clipx2,clipy2);
            CamAngleMgr();WindowClose(x_res,y_res);break;
    case 3: choice=24;StubRoutine();break;
    case 4: choice=25;StubRoutine();break;
    case 5: choice=26;StubRoutine();break;
    case 6: choice=27;StubRoutine();break;}
  if (status!=STUB) {ClearTextLine();PutText(1,2,C7,text17);}
  return;
  settingschoices:
  switch (t2){                       /* determine which scroll choice */
    case 1: choice=28;StubRoutine();break;
    case 2: choice=29;StubRoutine();break;
    case 3: choice=30;StubRoutine();break;
    case 4: choice=31;status=ACTIVE;                        /* color */
            ClearTextLine();PutText(1,2,C7,text13);
            EditColor();UninstallMenu();
            break;
    case 5: choice=32;StubRoutine();break;
    case 6: choice=33;StubRoutine();break;
    case 7: choice=34;StubRoutine();break;}
  if (status!=STUB) {ClearTextLine();PutText(1,2,C7,text7);}
  return;
  textchoices:
  switch (t2){                       /* determine which scroll choice */
    case 1: choice=35;StubRoutine();break;
    case 2: choice=36;StubRoutine();break;
    case 3: choice=37;StubRoutine();break;
      case 4: choice=38;StubRoutine();break;}
  if (status!=STUB) {ClearTextLine();PutText(1,2,C7,text7);}
  return;
  createchoices:
  switch (t2){                       /* determine which scroll choice */
    case 1: choice=39;StubRoutine();break;
    case 2: choice=40;StubRoutine();break;
    case 3: choice=41;StubRoutine();break;
```

Fig. 13-3.
Continued.

```
      case 4: choice=42;StubRoutine();break;
      case 5: choice=43;StubRoutine();break;
      case 6: choice=44;StubRoutine();break;
      case 7: choice=45;StubRoutine();break;
      case 8: choice=46;StubRoutine();break;}
if (status!=STUB) {ClearTextLine();PutText(1,2,C7,text7);}
return;}
/*_____*/

void StubRoutine(void){              /* do-nothing core function */
status=STUB;
if (GS_textavail==-1){                     /* if no font loaded... */
  switch(choice){               /* ...and user wants a text function */
    case 35:
    case 36:
    case 37:
    case 38: ClearTextLine();
             PutText(1,2,C7,text14);     /* font files not loaded */
             MakeSound(250,6000);return;
    default: break;}}
ClearTextLine();PutText(1,2,C7,text6);       /* inactive feature. */
MakeSound(250,6000);
return;}
/*_____*/

void MenuBarText(void){              /* back-out status dialog text */
ClearTextLine();
PutText(1,2,C7,text7);               /* ready for your next command. */
return;}
/*_____*/

void ClearTextLine(void){            /* blanks the dialog text line */
SetHue(C0);SetLine(0xffff);SetFill(fill_100,C0);
if (mode_flag==6){                   /* if Hercules 9x14 characters */
  DrawPanel(0,0,486,13);}
else {DrawPanel(0,0,431,7);}               /* if 8x8 characters */
return;}
/*_____*/

void CheckForKey(void){              /* checks for user keystrokes */
union u_type{int a;char b[3];}keystroke; /* define the structure */
char inkey=0;
#if Compiler==QuickC
  if (_bios_keybrd(_KEYBRD_READY)==EMPTY){keycode=0;return;}
  keystroke.a=_bios_keybrd(_KEYBRD_READ);    /* fetch ASCII codes */
#elif Compiler==TurboC
  if (bioskey(1)==EMPTY){keycode=0;return;}
  keystroke.a=bioskey(0);                    /* fetch ASCII codes */
#endif
inkey=keystroke.b[0];                        /* retrieve first code */
if (inkey!=0){                         /* if a normal keystroke... */
  keycode=1;                      /* set flag to normal keystroke */
  keynum=inkey;             /* and load ASCII code into variable */
  return;}
if (inkey==0){                    /* if an extended keystroke... */
  keycode=2;                    /* set flag to extended keystroke */
  keynum=keystroke.b[1];   /* and load second code into variable */
  return;}
}
/*_____*/

void KeySwitch1(void){     /* switcher for keys at menu bar level */
if (keycode==2) goto ExtendedKeys;     /* if extended key, jump... */
NormalKeys:                      /* ...else use switcher for normal keys */
switch (keynum){
  case 27: return;         /* Esc */
  case 13: return;         /* Enter */
  case 9:  return;         /* Tab */
  default: MakeSound(400,6000);return;}
```

Fig. 13-3.
Continued.

```
ExtendedKeys:                      /* switcher for extended keystrokes */
switch (keynum){
  case 59:  return;      /* F1 */
  case 60:  return;      /* F2 */
  case 71:  return;      /* Home */
  case 79:  return;      /* End */
  case 73:  return;      /* PgUp */
  case 81:  return;      /* PgDn */
  case 75:  return;      /* left arrow */
  case 77:  return;      /* right arrow */
  case 72:  return;      /* up arrow */
  case 80:  return;      /* down arrow */
  case 45:  Quit_Pgm(); /* Alt+X */
  default:  MakeSound(400,6000);return;}
return;}
/*_____*/

void KeySwitch2(void){      /* switcher for keys at level 1 menus */
if (keycode==2) goto ExtendedKeys2;  /* if extended key, jump... */
NormalKeys2:                   /* ...else use switcher for normal keys */
switch (keynum){
  case 27:  return;   /* Esc */
  case 13:  return;   /* Enter */
  case 9:   return;   /* Tab */
  default:  MakeSound(400,6000);return;}
ExtendedKeys2:                      /* switcher for extended keystrokes */
switch (keynum){
  case 59:  return;   /* F1 */
  case 60:  return;   /* F2 */
  case 71:  return;   /* Home */
  case 79:  return;   /* End */
  case 73:  return;   /* PgUp */
  case 81:  return;   /* PgDn */
  case 75:  return;   /* left arrow */
  case 77:  return;   /* right arrow */
  case 72:  return;   /* up arrow */
  case 80:  return;   /* down arrow */
  case 45:  Quit_Pgm();   /* Alt+X */
  default:  MakeSound(400,6000);return;}
return;}
/*_____*/

void Purge(void){   /* empties kybrd buffer, avoids cursor run-on */
do {CheckForKey();}      /* keep fetching keys from the buffer... */
while (keycode!=0);         /* ...while the keystroke is not NULL */
return;}                              /* then return to caller */
/*_____*/

void EditName(void){           /* allows user to edit the filename */
/* NOTE:  This barebones editor operates by the following rules:
    1. Press legal keys to type in a new filename. The filename
       must be 8 characters in length.
    2. Press Enter to accept the currently displayed filename,
       exit the editor, and save/load the named file.
    3. Press Esc to restore the previous filename and exit the
       editor (without saving/loading the named file).
    4. Audio cue is issued if an illegal key is detected.       */
int position;                            /* declare local variable */
position=0;                              /* reset position index */
strcpy(f12,f3);         /* store current filename for possible undo */
ClearTextLine();PutText(1,2,C7,text9);      /* display the prompt */
PutText(1,20,C3,f3);                  /* display current filename */
editloop1:                               /* loop begins here */
CheckForKey();                           /* check for keystroke */
if (keycode==0) goto editloop1;          /* loop back if no key */
if (keycode==2){                    /* loop back if extended key */
  MakeSound(250,6000);goto editloop1;}
if ((keynum>63)&&(keynum<91)) goto editline;
```

Fig. 13-3.
Continued.

```
if ((keynum>96)&&(keynum<123)) goto editline;
if ((keynum>47)&&(keynum<58)) goto editline;
if (keynum==33) goto editline;
if ((keynum>34)&&(keynum<39)) goto editline;
if (keynum==45) goto editline;
if (keynum==95) goto editline;
if (keynum==13){                           /* if Enter keystroke */
  ClearTextLine();PutText(1,2,C7,text10);
  PutText(1,20,C7,f3);PutText(1,28,C7,f4);
  Purge();Continue=YES;return;}
if (keynum==27){                           /* if Esc keystroke */
  strcpy(f3,f12);                   /* reset to former filename */
  ClearTextLine();PutText(1,2,C7,text10);
  PutText(1,20,C7,f3);PutText(1,28,C7,f4);
  Purge();Continue=NO;return;}
MakeSound(250,6000);goto editloop1;      /* ...else loop back */
editline:                 /* jump to here if an editable keystroke */
f11[0]=keynum;                   /* load ASCII code into carrier */
if (position>7){    /* if filename edit already at character 8...*/
  MakeSound(250,6000);goto editloop1;}
f3[position]=f11[0];          /* write new character into filename */
position++;                       /* increment character number */
if (position>7) position=8;    /* avoid possible numeric overflow */
ClearTextLine();PutText(1,2,C7,text9);
PutText(1,20,C3,f3);
goto editloop1;                              /* loop back */
return;}                                  /* boilerplate */
/*_____*/

void EditColor(void){   /* allows user to change the object color */
SetFill(fill_100,IntHue);
GetBlock(clipx1,clipy1,clipx1+50,clipy1+50,swatchbg);
PutPSET(clipx1,clipy1,swatchprep);
WindowOpen(clipx1,clipy1,clipx2,clipy2);
DrawPanel(0,0,50,50);WindowClose(x_res,y_res);
editcolorloop:
CheckForKey();
if (keycode==0) goto editcolorloop;
if (keycode==2) {MakeSound(250,6000);goto editcolorloop;}
switch(keynum){
  case 27: PutPSET(clipx1,clipy1,swatchbg);return;       /* Esc */
  case 13: PutPSET(clipx1,clipy1,swatchbg);return;     /* Enter */
  case 9:  goto whichcolor;                             /* Tab */
  default: MakeSound(250,6000);break;}
goto editcolorloop;
whichcolor:
fillclr_index=fillclr_index+1;
if (fillclr_index>5) fillclr_index=0;
switch(fillclr_index){
  case 0:  NormHue=C7;IntHue=C15;break;
  case 1:  NormHue=C1;IntHue=C9;break;
  case 2:  NormHue=C2;IntHue=C10;break;
  case 3:  NormHue=C3;IntHue=C11;break;
  case 4:  NormHue=C4;IntHue=C12;break;
  case 5:  NormHue=C5;IntHue=C13;break;}
SetFill(fill_100,IntHue);
WindowOpen(clipx1,clipy1,clipx2,clipy2);
DrawPanel(0,0,50,50);WindowClose(x_res,y_res);
goto editcolorloop;
return;}
/*_____*/

void MakeSound(int hertz,int duration){      /* generates a sound */
int t1=1,high_byte=0,low_byte=0;
short count=0;unsigned char old_port=0,new_port=0;
if (hertz<40) return;
if (hertz>4660) return;
count=1193180L/hertz;
high_byte=count/256;low_byte=count-(high_byte*256);
```

Fig. 13-3.
Continued.

```
#if Compiler==QuickC
  outp(0x43,0xB6);outp(0x42,low_byte);outp(0x42,high_byte);
  old_port=inp(0x61);new_port=(old_port|0x03);outp(0x61,new_port);
  for (t1=1;t1<=duration;t1++);outp(0x61,old_port);
#elif Compiler==TurboC
  outportb(0x43,0xB6);outportb(0x42,low_byte);
  outportb(0x42,high_byte);old_port=inportb(0x61);
  new_port=(old_port | 0x03);outportb(0x61,new_port);
  for (t1=1;t1<=duration;t1++);outportb(0x61,old_port);
#endif
return;}


/*_____

              3 D     E X E C U T I V E S
_____

    These routines call the low-level 3D graphics routines in
    module 3.
_____ */

void CursorManager(void){           /* dynamic control of 3D cursor */
Purge();                                   /* reset keyboard buffer */
BackUp();                                  /* store existing screen */
DrawCursor();                                    /* install cursor */
cursormgrloop:                               /* start of polling loop */
ObjYawChg=0;ObjRollChg=0;ObjPitchChg=0; /* reset rotation change */
xObjChg=0;yObjChg=0;zObjChg=0;        /* reset translation change */
cursorxchg=0;cursorychg=0;cursorzchg=0;/* reset extrusion change */
CheckForKey();                               /* check for keystroke */
if (keycode==2) goto ExtendedKeys3;  /* if extended key, jump... */
if (keycode==0) goto cursormgrloop;          /* if no key */
NormalKeys3:                    /* ...else use switcher for normal keys */
switch (keynum){
  case 27:  Restore();return;                          /* Esc */
  case 13:  Restore();                               /* Enter */
            switch (WhichObj){   /* decide which object to draw */
                case 7: GetCubeCoords();DrawCube();break;
                case 8: DrawCylinder();break;
                case 9:
                case 10:
                case 11:
                case 12:
                default: GetCubeCoords();DrawCube();}
            return;
  default:  MakeSound(400,6000);}           /* unsupported key */
goto cursormgrloop;
ExtendedKeys3:
if (choice==17) goto rotation3;            /* if rotation keypad */
if (choice==18) goto translation3;       /* if translation keypad */
if (choice==19) goto extrude3;             /* if extrude keypad */
MakeSound(400,6000);Restore();return;          /* boilerplate */
rotation3:                                 /* rotation switcher */
  switch (keynum){
    case 71:  ObjRollChg=-.087267;break;             /* Home */
    case 73:  ObjRollChg=.087267;break;              /* PgUp */
    case 75:  ObjYawChg=.087267;break;           /* left arrow */
    case 77:  ObjYawChg=-.087267;break;          /* right arrow */
    case 72:  ObjPitchChg=.087267;break;           /* up arrow */
    case 80:  ObjPitchChg=-.087267;break;          /* down arrow */
    case 45:  Quit_Pgm();  /* Alt+X */      /* instant shutdown */
    default:  MakeSound(400,6000);
              goto cursormgrloop;}
  goto drawcursor3;              /* jump to cursor-drawing code */
translation3:                            /* translation switcher */
  switch (keynum){
    case 80:  yObjChg=2;break;                     /* down arrow */
    case 72:  yObjChg=-2;break;                      /* up arrow */
    case 75:  xObjChg=2;break;                     /* left arrow */
```

```
        case 77:   xObjChg=-2;break;                          /* right arrow */
        case 73:   zObjChg=2;break;                                 /* PgDn */
        case 81:   zObjChg=-2;break;                            /* down arrow */
        case 45:   Quit_Pgm();   /* Alt+X */          /* instant shutdown */
        default:   MakeSound(400,6000);
                   goto cursormgrloop;)              /* unsupported key */
     goto drawcursor3;                    /* jump to cursor-drawing code */
extrude3:                                        /* extrusion switcher */
  switch (keynum){
     case 80:   cursorychg=-2;break;                       /* down arrow */
     case 72:   cursorychg=2;break;                           /* up arrow */
     case 75:   cursorxchg=-2;break;                         /* left arrow */
     case 77:   cursorxchg=2;break;                          /* right arrow */
     case 73:   cursorzchg=-2;break;                               /* PgUp */
     case 81:   cursorzchg=2;break;                                /* PgDn */
     case 45:   Quit_Pgm();   /* Alt+X */            /* instant shutdown */
     default:   MakeSound(400,6000);
                goto cursormgrloop;)              /* unsupported key */
     goto drawcursor3;                    /* jump to cursor-drawing code */
drawcursor3:                          /* jump to here after calculations */
  GetNewObjParams();        /* calculate new instancing parameters */
  DrawCursor();                                  /* install new cursor */
  Purge();
  goto cursormgrloop;                              /* and loop back */
return;)                                            /* boilerplate */
/*_____*/

void CamAngleMgr(void){          /* dynamic control of Camera angle */
Purge();BackUp();DrawGrndPlane();
camangleloop:                                /* start of polling loop */
CheckForKey();                             /* check for keystroke */
if (keycode==2) goto ExtendedKeys4;  /* if extended key, jump... */
if (keycode==0) goto camangleloop;                  /* if no key */
NormalKeys4:            /* ...else use switcher for normal keys */
switch (keynum){
   case 27:   Restore();return;                               /* Esc */
   case 13:   Restore();return;                             /* Enter */
   default:   MakeSound(400,6000);)
goto camangleloop;
ExtendedKeys4:
switch (keynum){
     case 75:   yawheading=yawheading+viewchg;          /* left arrow */
                if (yawheading>360) yawheading=yawheading-360;
                goto calccamyaw;
     case 77:   yawheading=yawheading-viewchg;          /* right arrow */
                if (yawheading<0) yawheading=yawheading+360;
                goto calccamyaw;
     case 80:   pitchheading=pitchheading+viewchg;     /* down arrow */
                if (pitchheading>360)     /* keep above groundlevel */
                   {pitchheading=360;MakeSound(400,6000);)
                goto calccampitch;
     case 72:   pitchheading=pitchheading-viewchg;       /* up arrow */
                if (pitchheading<270)     /* do not exceed vertical */
                   {pitchheading=270;MakeSound(400,6000);)
                goto calccampitch;
     case 45:   Quit_Pgm();   /* Alt+X */          /* instant shutdown */
     default:   MakeSound(400,6000);goto camangleloop;)
calccampitch:                       /* jump to here if pitch change */
  CamPitch=((double)pitchheading)*.0174533;/* convert to radians */
  if (pitchheading==360) CamPitch=6.28319;
  if (pitchheading==0) CamPitch=0.0;
  SetCamAngle();
  pitchdelta=6.28319-CamPitch; /* change in pitch from start-up */
  yCam=sin(pitchdelta)*dist*signmy;  /* new y Camera translation */
  yawdist=sqrt((dist*dist)-(yCam*yCam));       /* find hypotenuse */
  xCam=sin(yawdelta)*yawdist*signmx; /* new x Camera translation */
  zCam=sqrt((yawdist*yawdist)-(xCam*xCam))*signmz;/* new z trans */
  DrawGrndPlane();Purge();        /* show new world orientation */
  goto camangleloop;                                /* loop back */
```

Fig. 13-3.
Continued.

Fig. 13-3.
Continued.

```
calccamyaw:                                /* jump to here if yaw change */
  CamYaw=((double)yawheading)*.0175433;
  if (yawheading==360) CamYaw=6.28319;
  if (yawheading==0) CamYaw=0.0;
  SetCamAngle();
  if ((CamYaw>=4.71239)&&(CamYaw<=6.28319)){
    signmx=-1;signmz=-1;yawdelta=6.28319-CamYaw;goto calccamyaw1;}
  if ((CamYaw>=0)&&(CamYaw<1.57079)){
    signmx=1;signmz=-1;yawdelta=CamYaw;goto calccamyaw1;}
  if ((CamYaw>=1.57079)&&(CamYaw<3.14159)){
    signmx=1;signmz=1;yawdelta=3.14159-CamYaw;goto calccamyaw1;}
  if ((CamYaw>=3.14159)&&(CamYaw<4.71239)){
    signmx=-1;signmz=1;yawdelta=CamYaw-3.14159;goto calccamyaw1;}
  calccamyaw1:
  xCam=sin(yawdelta)*yawdist*signmx;
  zCam=cos(yawdelta)*yawdist*signmz;
  DrawGrndPlane();Purge();
  goto camangleloop;
return;}
/*_____*/


void GetCubeCoords(void){  /* get camera coords & display coords */
    int t=0;
    float negx,negy,negz;
  /* step one: load array with the current extrusion parameters    */
  negx=(-1)*cursorx;negy=(-1)*cursory;negz=(-1)*cursorz;
  cubeObj[0][0]=cursorx;cubeObj[0][1]=negy;cubeObj[0][2]=cursorz;
  cubeObj[1][0]=cursorx;cubeObj[1][1]=cursory;cubeObj[1][2]=cursorz;
  cubeObj[2][0]=negx;cubeObj[2][1]=cursory;cubeObj[2][2]=cursorz;
  cubeObj[3][0]=negx;cubeObj[3][1]=negy;cubeObj[3][2]=cursorz;
  cubeObj[4][0]=cursorx;cubeObj[4][1]=cursory;cubeObj[4][2]=negz;
  cubeObj[5][0]=negx;cubeObj[5][1]=cursory;cubeObj[5][2]=negz;
  cubeObj[6][0]=negx;cubeObj[6][1]=negy;cubeObj[6][2]=negz;
  cubeObj[7][0]=cursorx;cubeObj[7][1]=negy;cubeObj[7][2]=negz;
  /* step two: calculate the world, camera, and display coords    */
  for (t=0;t<=7;t++){
    x=cubeObj[t][0];y=cubeObj[t][1];z=cubeObj[t][2];
    GetWorldCoords();
    cubeWorld[t][0]=x;cubeWorld[t][1]=y;cubeWorld[t][2]=z;
    GetCameraCoords();
    camcoords[t][0]=x;camcoords[t][1]=y;camcoords[t][2]=z;
    GetImageCoords();GetScreenCoords();
    displaycoords[t][0]=sx3D;displaycoords[t][1]=sy3D;};
  return;}
/*_____*/


void DrawCube(void){          /* draw 3D cube at 3D cursor position */
surface0:
  xc1=camcoords[7][0];yc1=camcoords[7][1];zc1=camcoords[7][2];
  xc2=camcoords[0][0];yc2=camcoords[0][1];zc2=camcoords[0][2];
  xc3=camcoords[3][0];yc3=camcoords[3][1];zc3=camcoords[3][2];
  xc4=camcoords[6][0];yc4=camcoords[6][1];zc4=camcoords[6][2];
  VisibilityTest();if (visible>-150) goto surface1;
  sx1=displaycoords[7][0];sy1=displaycoords[7][1];
  sx2=displaycoords[0][0];sy2=displaycoords[0][1];
  sx3=displaycoords[3][0];sy3=displaycoords[3][1];
  sx4=displaycoords[6][0];sy4=displaycoords[6][1];
  xw3=cubeWorld[7][0];yw3=cubeWorld[7][1];zw3=cubeWorld[7][2];
  xw2=cubeWorld[0][0];yw2=cubeWorld[0][1];zw2=cubeWorld[0][2];
  xw1=cubeWorld[3][0];yw1=cubeWorld[3][1];zw1=cubeWorld[3][2];
  FindCenter();DrawFacet();
  GetBrightness();SetShading();DitherFacet();
surface1:
  xc1=camcoords[6][0];yc1=camcoords[6][1];zc1=camcoords[6][2];
  xc2=camcoords[5][0];yc2=camcoords[5][1];zc2=camcoords[5][2];
  xc3=camcoords[4][0];yc3=camcoords[4][1];zc3=camcoords[4][2];
  xc4=camcoords[7][0];yc4=camcoords[7][1];zc4=camcoords[7][2];
  VisibilityTest();if (visible>-150) goto surface2;
```

Fig. 13-3.
Continued.

```
    sx1=displaycoords[6][0];sy1=displaycoords[6][1];
    sx2=displaycoords[5][0];sy2=displaycoords[5][1];
    sx3=displaycoords[4][0];sy3=displaycoords[4][1];
    sx4=displaycoords[7][0];sy4=displaycoords[7][1];
    xw3=cubeWorld[6][0];yw3=cubeWorld[6][1];zw3=cubeWorld[6][2];
    xw2=cubeWorld[5][0];yw2=cubeWorld[5][1];zw2=cubeWorld[5][2];
    xw1=cubeWorld[4][0];yw1=cubeWorld[4][1];zw1=cubeWorld[4][2];
    FindCenter();DrawFacet();
    GetBrightness();SetShading();DitherFacet();
surface2:
    xc1=camcoords[3][0];yc1=camcoords[3][1];zc1=camcoords[3][2];
    xc2=camcoords[2][0];yc2=camcoords[2][1];zc2=camcoords[2][2];
    xc3=camcoords[5][0];yc3=camcoords[5][1];zc3=camcoords[5][2];
    xc4=camcoords[6][0];yc4=camcoords[6][1];zc4=camcoords[6][2];
    VisibilityTest();if (visible>-150) goto surface3;
    sx1=displaycoords[3][0];sy1=displaycoords[3][1];
    sx2=displaycoords[2][0];sy2=displaycoords[2][1];
    sx3=displaycoords[5][0];sy3=displaycoords[5][1];
    sx4=displaycoords[6][0];sy4=displaycoords[6][1];
    xw3=cubeWorld[3][0];yw3=cubeWorld[3][1];zw3=cubeWorld[3][2];
    xw2=cubeWorld[2][0];yw2=cubeWorld[2][1];zw2=cubeWorld[2][2];
    xw1=cubeWorld[5][0];yw1=cubeWorld[5][1];zw1=cubeWorld[5][2];
    FindCenter();DrawFacet();
    GetBrightness();SetShading();DitherFacet();
surface3:
    xc1=camcoords[0][0];yc1=camcoords[0][1];zc1=camcoords[0][2];
    xc2=camcoords[1][0];yc2=camcoords[1][1];zc2=camcoords[1][2];
    xc3=camcoords[2][0];yc3=camcoords[2][1];zc3=camcoords[2][2];
    xc4=camcoords[3][0];yc4=camcoords[3][1];zc4=camcoords[3][2];
    VisibilityTest();if (visible>-150) goto surface4;
    sx1=displaycoords[0][0];sy1=displaycoords[0][1];
    sx2=displaycoords[1][0];sy2=displaycoords[1][1];
    sx3=displaycoords[2][0];sy3=displaycoords[2][1];
    sx4=displaycoords[3][0];sy4=displaycoords[3][1];
    xw3=cubeWorld[0][0];yw3=cubeWorld[0][1];zw3=cubeWorld[0][2];
    xw2=cubeWorld[1][0];yw2=cubeWorld[1][1];zw2=cubeWorld[1][2];
    xw1=cubeWorld[2][0];yw1=cubeWorld[2][1];zw1=cubeWorld[2][2];
    FindCenter();DrawFacet();
    GetBrightness();SetShading();DitherFacet();
surface4:
    xc1=camcoords[7][0];yc1=camcoords[7][1];zc1=camcoords[7][2];
    xc2=camcoords[4][0];yc2=camcoords[4][1];zc2=camcoords[4][2];
    xc3=camcoords[1][0];yc3=camcoords[1][1];zc3=camcoords[1][2];
    xc4=camcoords[0][0];yc4=camcoords[0][1];zc4=camcoords[0][2];
    VisibilityTest();if (visible>-150) goto surface5;
    sx1=displaycoords[7][0];sy1=displaycoords[7][1];
    sx2=displaycoords[4][0];sy2=displaycoords[4][1];
    sx3=displaycoords[1][0];sy3=displaycoords[1][1];
    sx4=displaycoords[0][0];sy4=displaycoords[0][1];
    xw3=cubeWorld[7][0];yw3=cubeWorld[7][1];zw3=cubeWorld[7][2];
    xw2=cubeWorld[4][0];yw2=cubeWorld[4][1];zw2=cubeWorld[4][2];
    xw1=cubeWorld[1][0];yw1=cubeWorld[1][1];zw1=cubeWorld[1][2];
    FindCenter();DrawFacet();
    GetBrightness();SetShading();DitherFacet();
surface5:
    xc1=camcoords[1][0];yc1=camcoords[1][1];zc1=camcoords[1][2];
    xc2=camcoords[4][0];yc2=camcoords[4][1];zc2=camcoords[4][2];
    xc3=camcoords[5][0];yc3=camcoords[5][1];zc3=camcoords[5][2];
    xc4=camcoords[2][0];yc4=camcoords[2][1];zc4=camcoords[2][2];
    VisibilityTest();if (visible>-150) goto surfaces_done;
    sx1=displaycoords[1][0];sy1=displaycoords[1][1];
    sx2=displaycoords[4][0];sy2=displaycoords[4][1];
    sx3=displaycoords[5][0];sy3=displaycoords[5][1];
    sx4=displaycoords[2][0];sy4=displaycoords[2][1];
    xw3=cubeWorld[1][0];yw3=cubeWorld[1][1];zw3=cubeWorld[1][2];
    xw2=cubeWorld[4][0];yw2=cubeWorld[4][1];zw2=cubeWorld[4][2];
    xw1=cubeWorld[5][0];yw1=cubeWorld[5][1];zw1=cubeWorld[5][2];
    FindCenter();DrawFacet();
    GetBrightness();SetShading();DitherFacet();
```

Fig. 13-3.
Continued.

```
surfaces_done:
return;}
/*_____*/

void DrawCylinder(void){  /* draws 3D cylinder at cursor position */
  int t=0;                                      /* loop counter */
cyldepth=cursorz;                         /* set depth of cylinder */
if(cursory>cursorx) cylradius=cursory; /* set radius of cylinder */
  else cylradius=cursorx;
r4=0;r5=0;
for (t=0;t<=17;t++){              /* calculate coords for near end */
  x=cylradius;GetCylObjCoords();z=z+cyldepth;
  GetWorldCoords();
  CylWorldNear[t][0]=x;CylWorldNear[t][1]=y;CylWorldNear[t][2]=z;
  GetCameraCoords();
  CylCamNear[t][0]=x;CylCamNear[t][1]=y;CylCamNear[t][2]=z;
  GetImageCoords();GetScreenCoords();
  CylDisplayNear[t][0]=sx3D;CylDisplayNear[t][1]=sy3D;
  r5=r5+.34907;}                     /* increment r5 by 20 degrees */
r4=0;r5=0;
for (t=0;t<=17;t++){               /* calculate coords for far end */
  x=cylradius;GetCylObjCoords();z=z-cyldepth;
  GetWorldCoords();
  CylWorldFar[t][0]=x;CylWorldFar[t][1]=y;CylWorldFar[t][2]=z;
  GetCameraCoords();
  CylCamFar[t][0]=x;CylCamFar[t][1]=y;CylCamFar[t][2]=z;
  GetImageCoords();GetScreenCoords();
  CylDisplayFar[t][0]=sx3D;CylDisplayFar[t][1]=sy3D;
  r5=r5+.34907;}                     /* increment r5 by 20 degrees */
for (q1=0;q1<=17;q1++){                  /* draw body of cylinder */
  q2=q1+1;if (q2>17) q2=0;DrawCylFacet();}
DrawCylNearEnd();                    /* draw near end if visible */
DrawCylFarEnd();                      /* draw far end if visible */
return;}
/*_____*/

void GetCylObjCoords(void){  /* calculate cylinder object coords */
  float xtemp;
sr4=sin(r4);cr4=cos(r4);
sr5=sin(r5);cr5=cos(r5);
xtemp=sr5*x;
y=cr5*x;x=cr4*xtemp;z=sr4*x1;
return;}
/*_____*/

void DrawCylFacet(void){              /* draws one facet on cylinder */
xc1=CylCamNear[q1][0];yc1=CylCamNear[q1][1];zc1=CylCamNear[q1][2];
xc2=CylCamNear[q2][0];yc2=CylCamNear[q2][1];zc2=CylCamNear[q2][2];
xc3=CylCamFar[q2][0];yc3=CylCamFar[q2][1];zc3=CylCamFar[q2][2];
xc4=CylCamFar[q1][0];yc4=CylCamFar[q1][1];zc4=CylCamFar[q1][2];
VisibilityTest();if (visible>-150) return;
sx1=CylDisplayNear[q1][0];sy1=CylDisplayNear[q1][1];
sx2=CylDisplayNear[q2][0];sy2=CylDisplayNear[q2][1];
sx3=CylDisplayFar[q2][0];sy3=CylDisplayFar[q2][1];
sx4=CylDisplayFar[q1][0];sy4=CylDisplayFar[q1][1];
xw3=CylWorldNear[q1][0];yw3=CylWorldNear[q1][1];zw3=CylWorldNear[q1][2];
xw2=CylWorldNear[q2][0];yw2=CylWorldNear[q2][1];zw2=CylWorldNear[q2][2];
xw1=CylWorldFar[q2][0];yw1=CylWorldFar[q2][1];zw1=CylWorldFar[q2][2];
FindCenter();DrawFacet();
GetBrightness();SetShading();DitherFacet();
return;}
/*_____*/

void DrawCylNearEnd(void){           /* draws near end of cylinder */
  float tminx,tminy,tmaxx,tmaxy;        /* temporary variables */
xc1=CylCamNear[0][0];yc1=CylCamNear[0][1];zc1=CylCamNear[0][2];
xc2=CylCamNear[12][0];yc2=CylCamNear[12][1];zc2=CylCamNear[12][2];
xc3=CylCamNear[6][0];yc3=CylCamNear[6][1];zc3=CylCamNear[6][2];
xw3=CylWorldNear[0][0];yw3=CylWorldNear[0][1];zw3=CylWorldNear[0][2];
```

Fig. 13-3.
Continued.

```
xw2=CylWorldNear[12][0];yw2=CylWorldNear[12][1];zw2=CylWorldNear[12][2];
xw1=CylWorldNear[6][0];yw1=CylWorldNear[6][1];zw1=CylWorldNear[6][2];
VisibilityTest();if (visible>-150) return;
if (mode_flag>3) goto bwnearversion;
SetHue(KeyMatte);SetFill(fill_100,KeyMatte);SetLine(0xFFFF);
for (q1=0;q1<=17;q1++){                         /* draw key matte */
  q2=q1+1;if (q2>17) q2=0;
  sx1=CylDisplayNear[q1][0];sy1=CylDisplayNear[q1][1];
  sx2=CylDisplayNear[q2][0];sy2=CylDisplayNear[q2][1];
  SetPosition(sx1,sy1);DrawLine(sx2,sy2);}
x=0.0;y=0.0;z=cyldepth;                          /* fill point */
GetWorldCoords();GetCameraCoords();
GetImageCoords();GetScreenCoords();sx5=sx3D;sy5=sy3D;
Fill(sx5,sy5,KeyMatte);
SetHue(EdgeClr);
for (q1=0;q1<=17;q1++){            /* draw 18 vertices of polyline */
  q2=q1+1;if (q2>17) q2=0;
  sx1=CylDisplayNear[q1][0];sy1=CylDisplayNear[q1][1];
  sx2=CylDisplayNear[q2][0];sy2=CylDisplayNear[q2][1];
  SetPosition(sx1,sy1);DrawLine(sx2,sy2);}
SetFill(fill_100,SolidClr);Fill(sx5,sy5,EdgeClr);
goto nearshading;                         /* jump past bw code */
bwnearversion:                       /* jump to here if a bw mode */
for (q1=0;q1<=17;q1++){                       /* make key matte */
  q2=q1+1;if (q2>17) q2=0;
  sx1=CylDisplayNear[q1][0];sy1=CylDisplayNear[q1][1];
  sx2=CylDisplayNear[q2][0];sy2=CylDisplayNear[q2][1];
  if (q1==0){
    if (sx1<sx2){tminx=sx1;tmaxx=sx2;} else {tminx=sx2;tmaxx=sx1;}
    if (sy1<sy2){tminy=sy1;tmaxy=sy2;} else {tminy=sy2;tmaxy=sy1;}}
  if (sx1<tminx) tminx=sx1;
  if (sx2<tminx) tminx=sx2;
  if (sx1>tmaxx) tmaxx=sx1;
  if (sx2>tmaxx) tmaxx=sx2;
  if (sy1<tminy) tminy=sy1;
  if (sy2<tminy) tminy=sy2;
  if (sy1>tmaxy) tmaxy=sy1;
  if (sy2>tmaxy) tmaxy=sy2;}
minx=(int)tminx + clipx1;      /* because viewport will be off... */
maxx=(int)tmaxx + clipx1;          /* ...while manipulating arrays */
miny=(int)tminy + clipy1;
maxy=(int)tmaxy + clipy1;
x=0.0;y=0.0;z=cyldepth;                       /* find fill point */
GetWorldCoords();GetCameraCoords();
GetImageCoords();GetScreenCoords();sx5=sx3D;sy5=sy3D;
WindowClose(x_res,y_res);     /* disable viewport for array work */
GetBlock(minx,miny,maxx,maxy,matteA);      /* save existing bg */
SetHue(C1);SetLine(0xFFFF);
SetFill(fill_100,C1);DrawPanel(minx,miny,maxx,maxy);
SetHue(C0);
WindowOpen(clipx1,clipy1,clipx2,clipy2);       /* enable viewport */
for (q1=0;q1<=17;q1++){
  q2=q1+1;if (q2>17) q2=0;
  sx1=CylDisplayNear[q1][0];sy1=CylDisplayNear[q1][1];
  sx2=CylDisplayNear[q2][0];sy2=CylDisplayNear[q2][1];
  SetPosition(sx1,sy1);DrawLine(sx2,sy2);}
SetFill(fill_100,C0);Fill(sx5,sy5,C0);
WindowClose(x_res,y_res);                  /* disable viewport */
GetBlock(minx,miny,maxx,maxy,matteB);      /* save reverse matte */
PutPSET(minx,miny,matteA);                     /* restore bg */
PutAND(minx,miny,matteB);      /* install write-ready key matte */
WindowOpen(clipx1,clipy1,clipx2,clipy2);       /* enable viewport */
SetHue(C1);SetLine(0xffff);
for (q1=0;q1<=17;q1++){            /* draw 18 vertices of polyline */
  q2=q1+1;if (q2>17) q2=0;
  sx1=CylDisplayNear[q1][0];sy1=CylDisplayNear[q1][1];
  sx2=CylDisplayNear[q2][0];sy2=CylDisplayNear[q2][1];
  SetPosition(sx1,sy1);DrawLine(sx2,sy2);}
nearshading:
```

Fig. 13-3.
Continued.

```
GetBrightness();SetShading();
for (q1=0;q1<=17;q1++){                          /* line dithering */
  q2=q1+1;if (q2>17) q2=0;
  sx1=CylDisplayNear[q1][0];sy1=CylDisplayNear[q1][1];
  sx2=CylDisplayNear[q2][0];sy2=CylDisplayNear[q2][1];
  SetLine(0xFFFF);SetHue(DitherPrep);
  SetPosition(sx1,sy1);DrawLine(sx2,sy2);
  SetLine(DitherStyle);SetHue(DitherClr);
  SetPosition(sx1,sy1);DrawLine(sx2,sy2);}
return;
}
/*_____*/


void DrawCylFarEnd(void){              /* draws far end of cylinder */
  float tminx,tminy,tmaxx,tmaxy;            /* temporary variables */
xc1=CylCamFar[6][0];yc1=CylCamFar[6][1];zc1=CylCamFar[6][2];
xc2=CylCamFar[12][0];yc2=CylCamFar[12][1];zc2=CylCamFar[12][2];
xc3=CylCamFar[0][0];yc3=CylCamFar[0][1];zc3=CylCamFar[0][2];
xw3=CylWorldFar[6][0];yw3=CylWorldFar[6][1];zw3=CylWorldFar[6][2];
xw2=CylWorldFar[12][0];yw2=CylWorldFar[12][1];zw2=CylWorldFar[12][2];
xw1=CylWorldFar[0][0];yw1=CylWorldFar[0][1];zw1=CylWorldFar[0][2];
VisibilityTest();if (visible>-150) return;
if (mode_flag>3) goto bwfarversion;
SetHue(KeyMatte);SetFill(fill_100,KeyMatte);SetLine(0xFFFF);
for (q1=0;q1<=17;q1++){                          /* draw key matte */
  q2=q1+1;if (q2>17) q2=0;
  sx1=CylDisplayFar[q1][0];sy1=CylDisplayFar[q1][1];
  sx2=CylDisplayFar[q2][0];sy2=CylDisplayFar[q2][1];
  SetPosition(sx1,sy1);DrawLine(sx2,sy2);}
x=0.0;y=0.0;z=(-1)*cyldepth;                          /* fill point */
GetWorldCoords();GetCameraCoords();
GetImageCoords();GetScreenCoords();sx5=sx3D;sy5=sy3D;
Fill(sx5,sy5,KeyMatte);
SetHue(EdgeClr);
for (q1=0;q1<=17;q1++){                /* draw 18 vertices of polyline */
  q2=q1+1;if (q2>17) q2=0;
  sx1=CylDisplayFar[q1][0];sy1=CylDisplayFar[q1][1];
  sx2=CylDisplayFar[q2][0];sy2=CylDisplayFar[q2][1];
  SetPosition(sx1,sy1);DrawLine(sx2,sy2);}
SetFill(fill_100,SolidClr);Fill(sx5,sy5,EdgeClr);
goto farshading;                            /* jump past bw code */
bwfarversion:                            /* jump to here if a bw mode */
for (q1=0;q1<=17;q1++){                          /* make key matte */
  q2=q1+1;if (q2>17) q2=0;
  sx1=CylDisplayFar[q1][0];sy1=CylDisplayFar[q1][1];
  sx2=CylDisplayFar[q2][0];sy2=CylDisplayFar[q2][1];
  if (q1==0){
    if (sx1<sx2){tminx=sx1;tmaxx=sx2;} else {tminx=sx2;tmaxx=sx1;}
    if (sy1<sy2){tminy=sy1;tmaxy=sy2;} else {tminy=sy2;tmaxy=sy1;}
  }
  if (sx1<tminx) tminx=sx1;
  if (sx2<tminx) tminx=sx2;
  if (sx1>tmaxx) tmaxx=sx1;
  if (sx2>tmaxx) tmaxx=sx2;
  if (sy1<tminy) tminy=sy1;
  if (sy2<tminy) tminy=sy2;
  if (sy1>tmaxy) tmaxy=sy1;
  if (sy2>tmaxy) tmaxy=sy2;
}
minx=(int)tminx + clipx1;      /* because viewport will be off... */
maxx=(int)tmaxx + clipx1;          /* ...while manipulating arrays */
miny=(int)tminy + clipy1;
maxy=(int)tmaxy + clipy1;
x=0.0;y=0.0;z=(-1)*cyldepth;                      /* find fill point */
GetWorldCoords();GetCameraCoords();
GetImageCoords();GetScreenCoords();sx5=sx3D;sy5=sy3D;
WindowClose(x_res,y_res);      /* disable viewport for array work */
GetBlock(minx,miny,maxx,maxy,matteA);            /* save existing bg */
```

Fig. 13-3.
Continued.

```
SetHue(C1);SetLine(0xFFFF);
SetFill(fill_100,C1);DrawPanel(minx,miny,maxx,maxy);
SetHue(C0);
WindowOpen(clipx1,clipy1,clipx2,clipy2);        /* enable viewport */
for (q1=0;q1<=17;q1++){
  q2=q1+1;if (q2>17) q2=0;
  sx1=CylDisplayFar[q1][0];sy1=CylDisplayFar[q1][1];
  sx2=CylDisplayFar[q2][0];sy2=CylDisplayFar[q2][1];
  SetPosition(sx1,sy1);DrawLine(sx2,sy2);}
SetFill(fill_100,C0);Fill(sx5,sy5,C0);
WindowClose(x_res,y_res);                        /* disable viewport */
GetBlock(minx,miny,maxx,maxy,matteB);      /* save reverse matte */
PutPSET(minx,miny,matteA);                       /* restore bg */
PutAND(minx,miny,matteB);        /* install write-ready key matte */
WindowOpen(clipx1,clipy1,clipx2,clipy2);        /* enable viewport */
SetHue(C1);SetLine(0xffff);
for (q1=0;q1<=17;q1++){          /* draw 18 vertices of polyline */
  q2=q1+1;if (q2>17) q2=0;
  sx1=CylDisplayFar[q1][0];sy1=CylDisplayFar[q1][1];
  sx2=CylDisplayFar[q2][0];sy2=CylDisplayFar[q2][1];
  SetPosition(sx1,sy1);DrawLine(sx2,sy2);}
farshading:
GetBrightness();SetShading();
for (q1=0;q1<=17;q1++){                           /* line dithering */
  q2=q1+1;if (q2>17) q2=0;
  sx1=CylDisplayFar[q1][0];sy1=CylDisplayFar[q1][1];
  sx2=CylDisplayFar[q2][0];sy2=CylDisplayFar[q2][1];
  SetLine(0xFFFF);SetHue(DitherPrep);
  SetPosition(sx1,sy1);DrawLine(sx2,sy2);
  SetLine(DitherStyle);SetHue(DitherClr);
  SetPosition(sx1,sy1);DrawLine(sx2,sy2);}
return;
}
/*_____

End of Module 2 source code.  (This program has 3 modules.)     */
/*                              tm
Your Microcomputer 3D CAD Designer            Source file: DESIGN3.C

By: Lee Adams     Version: 1.00     Revision: n/a.
Notices: (c) Copyright 1990 Lee Adams.  All rights reserved.
   Your Microcomputer 3D CAD Designer is a trademark of
   TAB Books Inc. and is used by permission.
First published: 1990 by Windcrest Books (div. of TAB Books Inc.)

SOURCE NOTES:  This is module 3 of 3.  The project list should
include DESIGN1.C, DESIGN2.C, and DESIGN3.C named in QuickC's MAK
file or Turbo C's PRJ file.

OPERATION:  provides library-independent low-level graphics
routines, disk I/O routines, and low-level 3D graphics routines
for the run-time environment of module 1.

LICENSE:  As purchaser of the book in which this program is
published, you are granted a non-exclusive royalty-free license
to reproduce and distribute these routines in executable form
as part of your software product, subject to any copyright,
trademark, or patent rights of others, and subject to the limited
warranty described in the introduction of the book.  All other
rights reserved.

_____

COMPILER DIRECTIVES   */

                /* compilers and graphics libraries */
#define QuickC      1
#define TurboC      2
#define MicrosoftC 3
#define LatticeC    4
```

Module three
begins here

Fig. 13-3.
Continued.

```
#define HALO      7
#define MetaWINDOW 8
#define Essential  9

#define Compiler QuickC          /* change to TurboC if required */
#define GraphicsLibrary QuickC   /* change to library being used */

#include <bios.h>                /* supports keyboard functions */
#include <stdio.h>                /* supports printf function */
#include <string.h>             /* supports string manipulation */
#include <math.h>                /* supports sine and cosine */
#if Compiler==QuickC
   #include <conio.h>                   /* supports QuickC port IO */
   #include <malloc.h>   /* supports memory allocation for arrays */
   #include <memory.h>            /* supports QuickC memory moves */
#elif Compiler==TurboC
   #include <dos.h>                     /* supports TurboC port IO */
   #include <alloc.h>    /* supports memory allocation for arrays */
   #include <mem.h>              /* supports Turbo C memory moves */
#endif
#if GraphicsLibrary==QuickC
   #include <graph.h>                  /* QuickC graphics library */
#elif GraphicsLibrary==TurboC
   #include <graphics.h>               /* Turbo C graphics library */
#endif
#include <process.h>             /* supports the exit function */
/*_____


FUNCTION PROTOTYPES  */

/* LOW-LEVEL GRAPHICS ROUTINES IN THIS MODULE */
void SetHue(int);                /* sets the current drawing color */
void SetLine(int);                 /* sets the current line style */
void SetFill(char *, int);        /* sets the area fill style */
void BlankPage(void);         /* blanks the current active page */
void SetPosition(int,int);       /* sets the current xy position */
void DrawLine(int,int);    /* draws line from current xy position */
void DrawBorder(int,int,int,int);              /* draws rectangle */
void DrawPanel(int,int,int,int);         /* draws solid rectangle */
void Fill(int,int,int);                           /* area fill */
char far * MemBlock(int,int,int,int);    /* allocate array memory */
void GetBlock(int,int,int,int,char far *); /* save graphic array */
void PutXOR(int,int,char far *);        /* show XOR graphic array */
void PutPSET(int,int,char far *);      /* show PSET graphic array */
void PutAND(int,int,char far *);        /* show AND graphic array */
void PutText(int,int,int,char *);              /* display text */
void SetTextRowCol(int,int);             /* set text position */
char far * InitHiddenPage(void);       /* initialize hidden bitmap */
void BackUp(void);             /* copies page 0 to hidden page */
void Restore(void);            /* copies hidden page to page 0 */
void SaveImage(void);                    /* prep for image save */
void LoadImage(void);                    /* prep for image load */
void SaveVGAEGAImage(void);    /* saves VGA or EGA image to disk */
void LoadVGAEGAImage(void);   /* loads VGA or EGA image from disk */
void SaveCGAimage(void);             /* saves CGA image to disk */
void LoadCGAimage(void);            /* loads CGA image from disk */
void SaveHGAimage(void);        /* saves Hercules image to disk */
void LoadHGAimage(void);       /* loads Hercules image from disk */
void SaveMCGAimage(void);           /* saves MCGA image to disk */
void LoadMCGAimage(void);          /* loads MCGA image from disk */
void WindowOpen(int,int,int,int);           /* opens viewport */
void WindowClose(int,int);              /* shuts down viewport */
void WindowClear(int);                   /* blanks the viewport */

/* LOW-LEVEL 3D ROUTINES IN THIS MODULE */
void Init3D(void);              /* initializes all 3D parameters */
void SetRatios(void);         /* values used by GetScreenCoords() */
void SetObjAngle(void);         /* sine, cosine rotation factors */
```

Fig. 13-3.
Continued.

```
void SetCamAngle(void);           /* sine, cosine rotation factors */
void PutObjToScreen(void);     /* obj to world to image to screen */
void PutWorldToScreen(void);       /* world to image to screen */
void GetWorldCoords(void);      /* object coords to world coords */
void GetCameraCoords(void);     /* world coords to camera coords */
void GetImageCoords(void);      /* camera coords to image coords */
void GetScreenCoords(void); /* maps image plane coords to screen */
void DrawFacet(void);                              /* draws facet */
void DitherFacet(void);                          /* dithers facet */
void VisibilityTest(void);      /* tests for back-plane visibility */
void GetBrightness(void);        /* finds brightness of a facet */
void SetShading(void);       /* sets halftone & dithering values */
void SetLowVal(void);              /* sets QuickC low values */
void PrepHi(void);          /* preps facet for QC high values */
void SetHiVal(void);              /* sets QuickC high values */
void FindCenter(void);             /* finds center of facet */
void DrawCursor(void);                       /* draws 3D cursor */
void DrawGrndPlane(void);          /* draws 3D xz ground plane */
void GetNewObjParams(void);      /* new object instancing params */
void PolyMiniMax(void); /* find bounding rectangle of 2D polygon */
void MakeBwMatte(void);     /* failsafe key matte for bw modes */
void InitBwMattes(void);    /* allocate memory for bw key mattes */

/* ROUTINES IN MODULE 1 OR 2 CALLED BY THIS MODULE */
void Quit_Pgm(void);             /* ends the program gracefully */
void ClearTextLine(void);        /* blanks the dialog text line */
void CheckForKey(void);          /* checks for user keystrokes */
void FreeBlock(char far *);      /* deallocate far heap memory */
/*_____*/

/* DECLARATION OF GLOBAL VARIABLES */
#if Compiler==QuickC
  union REGS inregs,outregs;     /* data structure for interrupt */
#elif Compiler==TurboC
  union REGS regs;               /* data structure for interrupt */
#endif

/*             VARIABLES FOR 3D MODELING
   These variables are visible to all functions in this
   sourcefile, but not to the other two sourcefiles.            */
float x_database=0.0,y_database=0.0,z_database=0.0;  /* database */
float x=0.0,y=0.0,z=0.0;   /* world coords in, camera coords out */
float xc1=0.0,xc2=0.0,xc3=0.0,xc4=0.0,xc5=0.0,xc6=0.0,xc7=0.0,
   yc1=0.0,yc2=0.0,yc3=0.0,yc4=0.0,yc5=0.0,yc6=0.0,yc7=0.0,
   zc1=0.0,zc2=0.0,zc3=0.0,
   zc4=0.0,zc5=0.0,zc6=0.0,zc7=0.0;       /* camera coords of facet */
float sx1=0.0,sx2=0.0,sx3=0.0,sx4=0.0,sx5=0.0,
   sy1=0.0,sy2=0.0,sy3=0.0,
   sy4=0.0,sy5=0.0;                   /* display coords of facet */
float xw1=0,xw2=0,xw3=0,yw1=0,yw2=0,yw3=0,
   zw1=0,zw2=0,zw3=0;       /* raw world coords for brightness */
float xa=0.0,ya=0.0,za=0.0;         /* temporary in 3D formulas */
float sx3D=0.0,sy3D=0.0;            /* output of 3D formulas */
float focal_length=1200.0;      /* angular perspective factor */
double ObjYaw=6.28319,ObjRoll=6.28319,
   ObjPitch=6.28319;             /* object rotation angles */
double sOYaw=0.0,cOYaw=0.0;
double sORoll=0.0,cORoll=0.0;
double sOPitch=0.0,cOPitch=0.0;
float xObj=0.0,yObj=0.0,zObj=0.0;  /* object translation values */
double ObjYawChg=0.0,ObjRollChg=0.0,
   ObjPitchChg=0.0;             /* instancing rotation change */
float xObjChg=0.0,yObjChg=0.0,
   zObjChg=0.0;                 /* instancing translation change */
double CamYaw=6.28319,CamRoll=6.28319,CamPitch=6.28319;/* camera */
double sCYaw=0.0,sCRoll=0.0,sCPitch=0.0;
double cCYaw=0.0,cCRoll=0.0,cCPitch=0.0;
float xCam=0.0,yCam=0.0,zCam=-360.0; /* world translation values */
float rx=0.0,ry=0.0;                /* ratios used in windowing */
```

Fig. 13-3.
Continued.

```
float hcenter=0.0,vcenter=0.0;                    /* center of viewport */
float viewheight=0;              /* viewer's height 0 ft above ground */
float dist=360;                  /* viewer's virtual distance from scene */
float yawdist=360;               /* viewer's actual distance from scene */
float cursorx=40,cursory=40,cursorz=40;    /* volume of 3D cursor */
float planex=100,planey=0,planez=100;    /* volume of groundplane */
int CursorClr1=0,CursorClr2=0;                /* color of 3D cursor */
int PlaneClr1=0,PlaneClr2;                    /* color of groundplane */
float cursorxchg=0,cursorychg=0,
      cursorzchg=0;                   /* extrude cursor and object */

/*        VARIABLES FOR RENDERING AND HIDDEN SURFACE REMOVAL
          These variables are visible to all functions in this
          sourcefile, but not to the other two sourcefiles.          */
int KeyMatte=6;                               /* key matte color */
int EdgeClr=7;                                /* modeling color */
int SolidClr=0;                               /* solid fill color */
float visible=0.0;                            /* visibility factor */
float sp1=0.0,sp2=0.0,sp3=0.0;                /* temp values of sp */
int PrepClr=0,NormHue=0,IntHue=0;             /* halftoning colors */
int DitherPrep=0;                       /* dithering underlay color */
int DitherClr=0;                        /* dithering overlay color */
unsigned short DitherStyle=0xffff;            /* dithering pattern */
float xLight=-.1294089,yLight=.8660256,zLight=.4829627;
float normalized_illum=0.0;          /* illum factor 0 to 1 range */
int expanded_illum=0;                /* illum factor base 1 range */
float illum_range=22;            /* VGA and EGA illum range 0 to 22 */
int temp_illum=0;                  /* temp variable for illum range */
float xu=0.0,yu=0.0,zu=0.0;        /* vector, vertex 1 to vertex 2 */
float xv=0.0,yv=0.0,zv=0.0;        /* vector, vertex 1 to vertex 3 */
float x_surf_normal=0.0,y_surf_normal=0.0,z_surf_normal=0.0;
float v1=0.0,v2=0.0;          /* length, surface perpendicular vector */
float v3=0.0;                      /* ratio, surf perp to unit vector */
float x_unit_vector=0.0,y_unit_vector=0.0,z_unit_vector=0.0;
int minx=0,maxx=0,miny=0,maxy=0;            /* bounding rectangle */
char far *matteA;    /* array to store existing bg for bw modes */
char far *matteB;    /* array to create key matte for bw modes */

/* RE-DECLARATION OF GLOBAL VARIABLES initialized in Module 1,
   but also visible to all functions in this source file.          */
#if GraphicsLibrary==QuickC
  extern struct vc;
#endif
extern int C0,C1,C2,C3,C4,C5,C6,C7,C8,C9,C10,C11,C12,C13,C14,C15;
extern int x_res,y_res,mode_flag,alpha_x,alpha_y,x1,yf1,x2,y2,t1;
extern int sx,sy;
extern char keycode,keynum;
extern int clipx1,clipy1,clipx2,clipy2;
extern char fill_0[],fill_3[],fill_6[],fill_12[];
extern char fill_25[],fill_37[],fill_50[],fill_62[];
extern char fill_75[],fill_87[],fill_93[],fill_100[];
extern int p1,p2,px1,px2,px3,px4,px5,px6,px7;
extern int py1,py2,py3,py4,py5,py6;
extern int t2,t3,p3,p4,p5,p6,pbg1,pbg2,status,choice;
extern unsigned int plane_length;
extern char far * bitmap0;extern char far * bitmap1;
extern char far * bitmap2;extern char far * bitmap3;
extern union{ struct {unsigned int a1; unsigned int a2;} address;
      char far * faraddress;} u1;
extern unsigned int seg1,seg2,seg3,seg4,off1,off2,off3,off4;
extern char * textptr;
extern char text1[],text4[],text5[];
extern char text6[],text7[],text8[];
extern char Herc;extern char far *HPtr;
extern struct SREGS segregs;
extern unsigned int segment;extern unsigned int offset;
extern FILE *image_file;extern char image_buffer[];
extern char f3[],f4[],f6[],f7[],f8[],f9[],f10[],f11[];
extern int fillclr_index;
```

Fig. 13-3.
Continued.

```
/* RE-DECLARATION OF GLOBAL VARIABLES initialized in Module 2,
   but also visible to all functions in this source file.        */
extern int pitchheading,yawheading,viewchg;
extern double yawdelta,pitchdelta;

/*_____

                3 D    R O U T I N E S
   _____
```

These 3D modeling and rendering routines provide the capability to create fully-shaded 3D objects with automatic hidden surface removal and a movable light source. Each object can be independently rotated inside the world scene, which itself can be rotated independently. The routines call the library-independent low-level graphics routines in this module.
```
   _____ */

void Init3D(void){              /* initializes all 3D parameters */
focal_length=1200.0;viewheight=0;dist=360;
xLight=-.21131;yLight=.86603;zLight=.45315;
#if GraphicsLibrary==QuickC
   illum_range=22;          /* QC uses non-destructive overlay tiling */
   if (mode_flag>3) illum_range=11;              /* bw mode version */
#elif GraphicsLibrary==TurboC
   illum_range=11;          /* TC uses destructive overwrite tiling */
#endif
CamYaw=0.0;CamRoll=0.0;CamPitch=6.28319;/* head-on view of world */
pitchheading=360;yawheading=0;viewchg=2;
yawdelta=0,pitchdelta=0;
SetCamAngle();
xCam=0.0;yCam=0.0;zCam=-360.0;      /* 0,0,0 pushed back 360 units */
ObjYaw=0.0;ObjRoll=0.0;ObjPitch=0.0;SetObjAngle();
xObj=0.0;yObj=0.0;zObj=0.0;
ObjYawChg=0;ObjRollChg=0;ObjPitchChg=0;
xObjChg=0;yObjChg=0;zObjChg=0;
cursorx=10;cursory=10;cursorz=10;CursorClr1=C14;CursorClr2=C14;
planex=80;planey=0;planez=60;PlaneClr1=C0;PlaneClr2=C15;
if (mode_flag>3) {
   CursorClr1=C0;CursorClr2=C0;PlaneClr2=C0;}   /* bw mode version */
KeyMatte=C6;EdgeClr=C8;SolidClr=C0;
fillclr_index=1;NormHue=C1;IntHue=C9;
PrepClr=C0;DitherPrep=C1;DitherClr=C9;
return;}
/*_____ */

void SetRatios(void){      /*
     Enter with resolution of current graphics mode and
     constants for range of raw world data (800x600).
     Exit with rx,ry scaling factors and center of viewport.     */
rx=((float)x_res)/799;ry=((float)y_res)/599;
hcenter=((float)(clipx2-clipx1))/2;
vcenter=((float)(clipy2-clipy1))/2;
return;}
/*_____ */

void DrawCursor(void){                     /* draws 3D cursor */
   int cx1,cy1,cx2,cy2,cx3,cy3,cx4,cy4,
       cx5,cy5,cx6,cy6,cx7,cy7,cx8,cy8;
x=(-1)*cursorx;y=(-1)*cursory;z=(-1)*cursorz;
PutObjToScreen();cx1=(int)sx3D;cy1=(int)sy3D;
x=cursorx;y=(-1)*cursory;z=(-1)*cursorz;
PutObjToScreen();cx2=(int)sx3D;cy2=(int)sy3D;
x=cursorx;y=(-1)*cursory;z=cursorz;
PutObjToScreen();cx3=(int)sx3D;cy3=(int)sy3D;
x=(-1)*cursorx;y=(-1)*cursory;z=cursorz;
PutObjToScreen();cx4=(int)sx3D;cy4=(int)sy3D;
x=(-1)*cursorx;y=cursory;z=cursorz;
PutObjToScreen();cx5=(int)sx3D;cy5=(int)sy3D;
```

Fig. 13-3.
Continued.

```
x=(-1)*cursorx;y=cursory;z=(-1)*cursorz;
PutObjToScreen();cx6=(int)sx3D;cy6=(int)sy3D;
x=cursorx;y=cursory;z=(-1)*cursorz;
PutObjToScreen();cx7=(int)sx3D;cy7=(int)sy3D;
x=cursorx;y=cursory;z=cursorz;
PutObjToScreen();cx8=(int)sx3D;cy8=(int)sy3D;
SetHue(CursorClr1);SetLine(0x2222);
Restore();                           /* remove the former cursor */
SetPosition(cx6,cy6);         /* and install the new cursor... */
DrawLine(cx1,cy1);DrawLine(cx4,cy4);
SetPosition(cx1,cy1);DrawLine(cx2,cy2);
SetHue(CursorClr2);SetLine(0xFFFF);
SetPosition(cx5,cy5);
DrawLine(cx6,cy6);DrawLine(cx7,cy7);DrawLine(cx8,cy8);
SetPosition(cx3,cy3);
DrawLine(cx8,cy8);DrawLine(cx5,cy5);DrawLine(cx4,cy4);
DrawLine(cx3,cy3);DrawLine(cx2,cy2);DrawLine(cx7,cy7);
return;}
/*_____*/

void DrawGrndPlane(void){                    /* draws 3D groundplane */
   int cx1,cy1,cx2,cy2,cx3,cy3,cx4,cy4;
x=planex;y=planey;z=planez;
PutWorldToScreen();cx1=(int)sx3D;cy1=(int)sy3D;
x=planex;y=planey;z=(-1)*planez;
PutWorldToScreen();cx2=(int)sx3D;cy2=(int)sy3D;
x=(-1)*planex;y=planey;z=(-1)*planez;
PutWorldToScreen();cx3=(int)sx3D;cy3=(int)sy3D;
x=(-1)*planex;y=planey;z=planez;
PutWorldToScreen();cx4=(int)sx3D;cy4=(int)sy3D;
SetHue(PlaneClr1);SetLine(0xFFFF);
Restore();                        /* remove the former groundplane */
SetPosition(cx1,cy1);      /* and install the new groundplane... */
DrawLine(cx2,cy2);DrawLine(cx3,cy3);
DrawLine(cx4,cy4);
SetHue(PlaneClr2);DrawLine(cx1,cy1);
return;}
/*_____*/

void VisibilityTest(void){        /*
     Enter with 3 vertices as camera coords.
     Exit with visibility token.                                  */
sp1=xc1*(yc2*zc3-yc3*zc2);sp1=(-1)*sp1;
sp2=xc2*(yc3*zc1-yc1*zc3);sp3=xc3*(yc1*zc2-yc2*zc1);
visible=sp1-sp2-sp3;return;}
/*_____*/

void GetNewObjParams(void){        /*
     Enter with the desired change in instancing rotation and
     translation.  Exit with the new object yaw, roll, pitch,
     and translation parameters.                                  */
ObjYaw=ObjYaw+ObjYawChg;                          /* new object yaw */
if (ObjYaw<=0) ObjYaw=ObjYaw+6.28319;
if (ObjYaw>6.28319) ObjYaw=ObjYaw-6.28319;
ObjRoll=ObjRoll+ObjRollChg;                       /* new object roll */
if (ObjRoll<=0) ObjRoll=ObjRoll+6.28319;
if (ObjRoll>6.28319) ObjRoll=ObjRoll-6.28319;
ObjPitch=ObjPitch+ObjPitchChg;                    /* new object pitch */
if (ObjPitch<=0) ObjPitch=ObjPitch+6.28319;
if (ObjPitch>6.28319) ObjPitch=ObjPitch-6.28319;
SetObjAngle();  /* get new object sine, cosine rotation factors */
xObj=xObj-xObjChg;               /* new object left-right position */
yObj=yObj-yObjChg;               /* new object high-low position */
zObj=zObj-zObjChg;               /* new object near-far position */
cursorx=cursorx+cursorxchg;             /* new extrusion width */
if (cursorx<2) cursorx=2;
cursory=cursory+cursorychg;             /* new extrusion height */
if (cursory<2) cursory=2;
cursorz=cursorz+cursorzchg;             /* new extrusion depth */
```

Fig. 13-3.
Continued.

```
if (cursorz<2) cursorz=2;
return;}
/*_____*/

void SetObjAngle(void){       /*
     Enter with ObjYaw,ObjRoll,ObjPitch object rotation angles.
     Exit with sine, cosine object rotation factors.         */
sOYaw=sin(ObjYaw);cOYaw=cos(ObjYaw);
sORoll=sin(ObjRoll);cORoll=cos(ObjRoll);
sOPitch=sin(ObjPitch);cOPitch=cos(ObjPitch);
return;}
/*_____*/

void SetCamAngle(void){       /*
     Enter with Yaw,Roll,Pitch world rotation angles.
     Exit with sine, cosine world rotation factors.          */
sCYaw=sin(CamYaw);sCRoll=sin(CamRoll);sCPitch=sin(CamPitch);
cCYaw=cos(CamYaw);cCRoll=cos(CamRoll);cCPitch=cos(CamPitch);
return;}
/*_____*/

void PutObjToScreen(void){       /*
     Enter with xyz object coordinates.  This routine transforms
     the obj coords to world coords to image plane coords to
     sx3D,sy3D physical screen coords.                        */
GetWorldCoords();GetCameraCoords();GetImageCoords();
GetScreenCoords();return;}
/*_____*/

void PutWorldToScreen(void){       /*
     Enter with xyz world coordinates.  This routine transforms
     the world coords to image plane coords to sx3D,sy3D physical
     screen coords.                                           */
GetCameraCoords();GetImageCoords();GetScreenCoords();return;}

/*_____*/

void GetWorldCoords(void){       /*
     Enter with xyz unclipped object coordinates.
     Exit with unclipped xyz world coordinates.              */
xa=cORoll*x+sORoll*y;ya=cORoll*y-sORoll*x;        /* roll rotate */
x=cOYaw*xa-sOYaw*z;za=sOYaw*xa+cOYaw*z;           /* yaw rotate */
z=cOPitch*za-sOPitch*ya;y=sOPitch*za+cOPitch*ya; /* pitch rotate */
x=x+xObj;y=y+yObj;z=z+zObj;                       /* lateral movement */
return;}
/*_____*/

void GetCameraCoords(void){       /*
     Enter with unclipped xyz world coordinates.
     Exit with unclipped xyz camera coordinates.             */
x=(-1)*x;                /* adjust for cartesian coords of 2D screen */
y=y-viewheight;          /* adjust world coords to height of viewer */
x=x-xCam;y=y+yCam;z=z+zCam;                 /* lateral movement */
xa=cCYaw*x-sCYaw*z;za=sCYaw*x+cCYaw*z;           /* yaw rotate */
z=cCPitch*za-sCPitch*y;ya=sCPitch*za+cCPitch*y;  /* pitch rotate */
x=cCRoll*xa+sCRoll*ya;y=cCRoll*ya-sCRoll*xa;     /* roll rotate */
return;}
/*_____*/

void GetImageCoords(void){       /*
     Enter with clipped xyz camera coordinates.
     Exit with unclipped sx3D,sy3D display coordinates.      */
sx3D=focal_length*(x/z);
sy3D=focal_length*(y/z);
return;}
/*_____*/

void GetScreenCoords(void){       /*
     Enter with unclipped sx3D,sy3D display coordinates.
```

Fig. 13-3.
Continued.

```
        Exit with sx3D,sy3D device-dependent display coordinates
        scaled to the world range with correct aspect ratio.        */
sx3D=sx3D*rx;sy3D=sy3D*ry;
sx3D=sx3D+hcenter;sy3D=sy3D+vcenter;
return;}
/*_____*/

void DrawFacet(void){   /* draw 4-sided polygon on display screen */
if (mode_flag<4){                           /* if a 16-color mode */
  SetLine(0xffff);SetFill(fill_100,KeyMatte);SetHue(KeyMatte);
  SetPosition(sx1,sy1);DrawLine(sx2,sy2);DrawLine(sx3,sy3);
  DrawLine(sx4,sy4);DrawLine(sx1,sy1);Fill(sx5,sy5,KeyMatte);
  SetHue(EdgeClr);SetPosition(sx1,sy1);DrawLine(sx2,sy2);
  DrawLine(sx3,sy3);DrawLine(sx4,sy4);DrawLine(sx1,sy1);
  SetHue(SolidClr);Fill(sx5,sy5,EdgeClr);return;}
PolyMiniMax();MakeBwMatte();       /* else if a black-and-white mode */
SetHue(C1);SetLine(0xffff);
SetPosition(sx1,sy1);DrawLine(sx2,sy2);
DrawLine(sx3,sy3);DrawLine(sx4,sy4);DrawLine(sx1,sy1);
return;}
/*_____*/

void FindCenter(void){      /* find center of polygon view coords */
xc6=xc2+.5*(xc1-xc2);yc6=yc2+.5*(yc1-yc2);
zc6=zc2+.5*(zc1-zc2);
xc7=xc3+.5*(xc4-xc3);yc7=yc3+.5*(yc4-yc3);zc7=zc3+.5*(zc4-zc3);
x=xc7+.5*(xc6-xc7);y=yc7+.5*(yc6-yc7);z=zc7+.5*(zc6-zc7);
sx3D=focal_length*x/z;sy3D=focal_length*y/z;
GetScreenCoords();sx5=sx3D;sy5=sy3D;
return;}
/*_____*/

void GetBrightness(void){        /* calculate illumination level
        Enter with facet world coordinates.
        Exit with illumination level token.                        */
xu=xw2-xw1;yu=yw2-yw1;zu=zw2-zw1; /* vector vertex 1 to vertex 2 */
xv=xw3-xw1;yv=yw3-yw1;zv=zw3-zw1; /* vector vertex 1 to vertex 3 */
x_surf_normal=(yu*zv)-(zu*yv);
y_surf_normal=(zu*xv)-(xu*zv);
z_surf_normal=(xu*yv)-(yu*xv);
y_surf_normal=y_surf_normal*(-1);
z_surf_normal=z_surf_normal*(-1); /* convert to cartesian system */
v1=(x_surf_normal*x_surf_normal)+(y_surf_normal*y_surf_normal)
   +(z_surf_normal*z_surf_normal);
v2=sqrt(v1);       /* magnitude of surface perpendicular vector */
v3=1/v2;        /* ratio of magnitude to length of unit vector */
x_unit_vector=v3*x_surf_normal;
y_unit_vector=v3*y_surf_normal;
z_unit_vector=v3*z_surf_normal;/* surf perpendicular unit vector */
normalized_illum=(x_unit_vector*xLight)+(y_unit_vector*yLight)
   +(z_unit_vector*zLight);        /* illumination factor 0 to 1 */
normalized_illum=normalized_illum*illum_range;          /* expand */
temp_illum=(int)normalized_illum;           /* convert to integer */
expanded_illum=temp_illum+1;   /* illumination range from base 1 */
return;}
/*_____*/

void SetShading(void){                      /* brightness matrix */
switch (expanded_illum){
case 1:  SetFill(fill_6,NormHue);DitherStyle=0x1010;
         SetLowVal();return;
case 2:  SetFill(fill_6,NormHue);DitherStyle=0x1010;
         SetLowVal();return;
case 3:  SetFill(fill_6,NormHue);DitherStyle=0x1010;
         SetLowVal();return;
case 4:  SetFill(fill_12,NormHue);DitherStyle=0x2020;
         SetLowVal();return;
case 5:  SetFill(fill_25,NormHue);DitherStyle=0x2222;
         SetLowVal();return;
```

Fig. 13-3.
Continued.

```
case 6:   SetFill(fill_37,NormHue);DitherStyle=0xaaaa;
          SetLowVal();return;
case 7:   SetFill(fill_50,NormHue);DitherStyle=0xaaaa;
          SetLowVal();return;
case 8:   SetFill(fill_62,NormHue);DitherStyle=0xaaaa;
          SetLowVal();return;
case 9:   SetFill(fill_75,NormHue);DitherStyle=0xbbbb;
          SetLowVal();return;
case 10:  SetFill(fill_87,NormHue);DitherStyle=0xdddd;
          SetLowVal();return;
case 11:  SetFill(fill_93,NormHue);DitherStyle=0xefef;
          SetLowVal();return;
case 12:  SetFill(fill_100,NormHue);DitherStyle=0xffff;
          SetLowVal();return;
case 13:  PrepHi();SetFill(fill_3,IntHue);
          DitherStyle=0x1010;SetHiVal();return;
case 14:  PrepHi();SetFill(fill_6,IntHue);
          DitherStyle=0x1010;SetHiVal();return;
case 15:  PrepHi();SetFill(fill_12,IntHue);
          DitherStyle=0x2020;SetHiVal();return;
case 16:  PrepHi();SetFill(fill_25,IntHue);
          DitherStyle=0x2222;SetHiVal();return;
case 17:  PrepHi();SetFill(fill_37,IntHue);
          DitherStyle=0xaaaa;SetHiVal();return;
case 18:  PrepHi();SetFill(fill_50,IntHue);
          DitherStyle=0xaaaa;SetHiVal();return;
case 19:  PrepHi();SetFill(fill_62,IntHue);
          DitherStyle=0xaaaa;SetHiVal();return;
case 20:  PrepHi();SetFill(fill_75,IntHue);
          DitherStyle=0xbbbb;SetHiVal();return;
case 21:  PrepHi();SetFill(fill_87,IntHue);
          DitherStyle=0xdddd;SetHiVal();return;
case 22:  PrepHi();SetFill(fill_93,IntHue);
          DitherStyle=0xefef;SetHiVal();return;
case 23:  PrepHi();SetFill(fill_100,IntHue);
          DitherStyle=0xffff;SetHiVal();return;
default:  SetFill(fill_6,NormHue);DitherStyle=0x1010;
          SetLowVal();return;}
return;}

void SetLowVal(void){        /* set low shade values (QC and TC) */
Fill(sx5,sy5,EdgeClr);
DitherPrep=PrepClr;DitherClr=NormHue;return;}

void SetHiVal(void){         /* set high shade values (QC only ) */
Fill(sx5,sy5,EdgeClr);
DitherPrep=NormHue;DitherClr=IntHue;return;}

void PrepHi(void){  /* prep target for high shade fill (QC only) */
SetFill(fill_100,NormHue);
Fill(sx5,sy5,EdgeClr);return;}
/*_____*/

void DitherFacet(void){                  /* apply dithering to facet */
SetLine(0xffff);SetHue(DitherPrep);SetPosition(sx1,sy1);
DrawLine(sx2,sy2);DrawLine(sx3,sy3);DrawLine(sx4,sy4);
DrawLine(sx1,sy1);SetLine(DitherStyle);SetHue(DitherClr);
SetPosition(sx1,sy1);DrawLine(sx2,sy2);DrawLine(sx3,sy3);
DrawLine(sx4,sy4);DrawLine(sx1,sy1);return;}
/*_____*/

void PolyMiniMax(void){  /* find bounding rectangle for bw modes */
  float tminx,tmaxx,tminy,tmaxy;          /* temporary variables */
if (sx1<sx2) tminx=sx1; else tminx=sx2;      /* find leftmost x */
if (sx3<tminx) tminx=sx3;
if (sx4<tminx) tminx=sx4;
if (sx1>sx2) tmaxx=sx1; else tmaxx=sx2;      /* find rightmost x */
if (sx3>tmaxx) tmaxx=sx3;
if (sx4>tmaxx) tmaxx=sx4;
```

Fig. 13-3.
Continued.

```
if (sy1<sy2) tminy=sy1; else tminy=sy2;        /* find uppermost y */
if (sy3<tminy) tminy=sy3;
if (sy4<tminy) tminy=sy4;
if (sy1>sy2) tmaxy=sy1; else tmaxy=sy2;        /* find lowermost y */
if (sy3>tmaxy) tmaxy=sy3;
if (sy4>tmaxy) tmaxy=sy4;
minx=(int)tminx + clipx1;          /* because viewport will be off... */
maxx=(int)tmaxx + clipx1;          /* ...while manipulating arrays */
miny=(int)tminy + clipy1;
maxy=(int)tmaxy + clipy1;
return;}
/*_____*/

void MakeBwMatte(void){       /* make a key matte for bw rendering */
WindowClose(x_res,y_res);           /* disable viewport for array work */
GetBlock(minx,miny,maxx,maxy,matteA);          /* save existing bg */
SetHue(C1);SetLine(0xFFFF);
SetFill(fill_100,C1);DrawPanel(minx,miny,maxx,maxy);
SetHue(C0);
WindowOpen(clipx1,clipy1,clipx2,clipy2);        /* enable viewport */
SetPosition(sx1,sy1);DrawLine(sx2,sy2);DrawLine(sx3,sy3);
DrawLine(sx4,sy4);DrawLine(sx1,sy1);
SetFill(fill_100,C0);Fill(sx5,sy5,C0);
WindowClose(x_res,y_res);                       /* disable viewport */
GetBlock(minx,miny,maxx,maxy,matteB);           /* save reverse matte */
PutPSET(minx,miny,matteA);                      /* restore bg */
PutAND(minx,miny,matteB);          /* install write-ready key matte */
WindowOpen(clipx1,clipy1,clipx2,clipy2);        /* enable viewport */
return;}
/*_____*/

void InitBwMattes(void){       /* initialize key matte for bw modes */
if (mode_flag<4) return;                        /* if a color mode */
matteA=MemBlock(clipx1,clipy1,clipx2,clipy2);
matteB=MemBlock(clipx1,clipy1,clipx2,clipy2);
return;}
/*_____
```

```
                    L I B R A R Y - I N D E P E N D E N T
                     G R A P H I C S    R O U T I N E S
```

This set of library-independent routines is currently able to
map generic calls to the specific syntax of the QuickC graphics
library and the Turbo C graphics library. By following the
book, it is a straightforward task to add code to support the
syntax of third-party graphics libraries such as HALO 88,
Essential Graphics, MetaWINDOW, Lattice C GFX Library, GSS,
and others.

This set of routines is used by module 1 to create the user
interface and menu system, by module 2 to manage the runtime
environment and disk I/O, and by the 3D routines in this module.

```
                                                                   */

void WindowOpen(int x1,int yf1,int x2,int y2){  /* open viewport */
#if GraphicsLibrary==QuickC
  _setviewport(x1,yf1,x2,y2);
#elif GraphicsLibrary==TurboC
  setviewport(x1,yf1,x2,y2,1);
#endif
return;}
/*_____*/

void WindowClose(int x_res,int y_res){       /* shut down viewport */
#if GraphicsLibrary==QuickC
  _setviewport(0,0,x_res-1,y_res-1);
#elif GraphicsLibrary==TurboC
  setviewport(0,0,x_res-1,y_res-1,1);
```

Fig. 13-3.
Continued.

```
#endif
return;}
/*_____*/

void WindowClear(int bgclr){        /* blanks the drawing viewport */
#if GraphicsLibrary==QuickC
  SetFill(fill_100,bgclr);
  DrawPanel(0,0,(clipx2-clipx1),(clipy2-clipy1));
#elif GraphicsLibrary==TurboC
  setfillstyle(SOLID_FILL,bgclr);
  DrawPanel(0,0,(clipx2-clipx1),(clipy2-clipy1));
#endif
return;}
/*_____*/

void SetHue(int hueclr){        /* sets the active drawing color */
#if GraphicsLibrary==QuickC
  _setcolor(hueclr);
#elif GraphicsLibrary==TurboC
  setcolor(hueclr);
#endif
return;}
/*_____*/

void SetLine(int style){        /* sets the current line style */
#if GraphicsLibrary==QuickC
  _setlinestyle(style);
#elif GraphicsLibrary==TurboC
  setlinestyle(USERBIT_LINE,style,NORM_WIDTH);
#endif
return;}
/*_____*/

void SetFill(char *pattern,int hueclr){        /* sets fill pattern */
#if GraphicsLibrary==QuickC
  _setcolor(hueclr);
  _setfillmask(pattern);
#elif GraphicsLibrary==TurboC
  setfillpattern(pattern,hueclr);
  if (pattern==fill_100) setfillstyle(SOLID_FILL,hueclr);
#endif
return;}
/*_____*/

void SetPosition(int x,int y){    /* sets the current xy position */
#if GraphicsLibrary==QuickC
  _moveto(x,y);
#elif GraphicsLibrary==TurboC
  moveto(x,y);
#endif
return;}
/*_____*/

void BlankPage(void){        /* blanks the current active page */
#if GraphicsLibrary==QuickC
  _clearscreen(_GCLEARSCREEN);
#elif GraphicsLibrary==TurboC
  cleardevice();
#endif
return;}
/*_____*/

void DrawLine(int x,int y){  /* draws line from current position */
#if GraphicsLibrary==QuickC
  _lineto(x,y);
#elif GraphicsLibrary==TurboC
  lineto(x,y);
#endif
```

Fig. 13-3.
Continued.

```
return;}
/*_____*/

void DrawBorder(int x1,int yf1,int x2,int y2){  /* draws rectangle */
#if GraphicsLibrary==QuickC
  _rectangle(_GBORDER,x1,yf1,x2,y2);
#elif GraphicsLibrary==TurboC
  rectangle(x1,yf1,x2,y2);
#endif
return;}
/*_____*/

void DrawPanel(int x1,int yf1,int x2,int y2){   /* solid rectangle */
#if GraphicsLibrary==QuickC
  _rectangle(_GFILLINTERIOR,x1,yf1,x2,y2);
#elif GraphicsLibrary==TurboC
  bar(x1,yf1,x2,y2);
#endif
return;}
/*_____*/

void Fill(int x,int y,int edgeclr){              /* fountain fill */
#if GraphicsLibrary==QuickC
  _floodfill(x,y,edgeclr);
#elif GraphicsLibrary==TurboC
  floodfill(x,y,edgeclr);
#endif
return;}
/*_____*/

char far * MemBlock(int x1,int yf1,int x2,int y2){
                        /* allocate array block in far heap */
char far *blk;
#if GraphicsLibrary==QuickC
  blk=(char far*)_fmalloc((unsigned int)_imagesize(x1,yf1,x2,y2));
#elif GraphicsLibrary==TurboC
  blk=(char far*)farmalloc((unsigned long)imagesize(x1,yf1,x2,y2));
#endif
return blk;}
/*_____*/

void GetBlock(int x1,int yf1,int x2,int y2,char far *blk){
/* save graphic array in pre-allocated memory block */
#if GraphicsLibrary==QuickC
  _getimage(x1,yf1,x2,y2,blk);
#elif GraphicsLibrary==TurboC
  getimage(x1,yf1,x2,y2,blk);
#endif
return;}
/*_____*/

void PutXOR(int x,int y,char far *blk){    /* XOR a graphic array */
#if GraphicsLibrary==QuickC
  _putimage(x,y,blk,_GXOR);
#elif GraphicsLibrary==TurboC
  putimage(x,y,blk,XOR_PUT);
#endif
return;}
/*_____*/

void PutPSET(int x,int y,char far *blk){ /* PSET a graphic array */
#if GraphicsLibrary==QuickC
  _putimage(x,y,blk,_GPSET);
#elif GraphicsLibrary==TurboC
  putimage(x,y,blk,COPY_PUT);
#endif
return;}
/*_____*/
```

```
void PutAND(int x,int y,char far *blk){      /* AND a graphic array */
#if GraphicsLibrary==QuickC
  _putimage(x,y,blk,_GAND);
#elif GraphicsLibrary==TurboC
  putimage(x,y,blk,AND_PUT);
#endif
return;}
/*_____*/

void PutText(int row,int col,int clr,char * tptr){ /* write text */
int TCrow,TCcol,tempclr;
#if GraphicsLibrary==QuickC
  _settextposition(row,col);_settextcolor(clr);_outtext(tptr);
#elif GraphicsLibrary==TurboC
  TCCol=(col*alpha_x)-alpha_x;               /* convert col to x */
  TCrow=(row*alpha_y)-alpha_y;               /* convert row to y */
  tempclr=getcolor();setcolor(clr);      /* save, set active color */
  outtextxy(TCcol,TCrow,tptr);               /* display the text */
  setcolor(tempclr);            /* restore previous active color */
#endif
return;}
/*_____*/

void SetTextRowCol(int row,int col){          /* set text position */
int TCrow,TCcol;
#if GraphicsLibrary==QuickC
  _settextposition(row,col);
#elif GraphicsLibrary==TurboC
  TCCol=(col*alpha_x)-alpha_x;TCrow=(row*alpha_y)-alpha_y;
  moveto(TCcol,TCrow);
#endif
return;}
/*_____*/

char far * InitHiddenPage(void){      /* initialize hidden bitmap */
  char far * vptr;     /* buffer address to be returned to caller */
#if Compiler==QuickC
  vptr=(char far *)_fmalloc(plane_length);
#elif Compiler==TurboC
  vptr=(char far *)farmalloc(plane_length);
#endif
if (vptr==NULL){                        /* if allocation failed... */
  ClearTextLine();                    /* display error message... */
  PutText(1,2,C14,text8);      /* Insufficient memory for Undo. */
  do {CheckForKey();}                   /* wait for any keystroke */
    while (keycode==0);
  Quit_Pgm();}}                    /* ...then shut down the pgm */
return vptr;}                /* else return buffer address to caller */
/*_____*/

void BackUp(void){               /* copies page 0 to hidden page */
switch(mode_flag){
  case 1:                             /* VGA 640x480x16-color */
          #if Compiler==QuickC
            outp(0x3ce,4);outp(0x3cf,0);
          #elif Compiler==TurboC
            outportb(0x03ce,(unsigned char)4);
            outportb(0x03cf,(unsigned char)0);
          #endif
          movedata(0xa000,0x0000,seg1,off1,plane_length);
          #if Compiler==QuickC
            outp(0x3ce,4);outp(0x3cf,1);
          #elif Compiler==TurboC
            outportb(0x03ce,(unsigned char)4);
            outportb(0x03cf,(unsigned char)1);
          #endif
          movedata(0xa000,0x0000,seg2,off2,plane_length);
          #if Compiler==QuickC
```

Fig. 13-3.
Continued.

Fig. 13-3.
Continued.

```
                        outp(0x3ce,4);outp(0x3cf,2);
                #elif Compiler==TurboC
                  outportb(0x03ce,(unsigned char)4);
                  outportb(0x03cf,(unsigned char)2);
                #endif
                movedata(0xa000,0x0000,seg3,off3,plane_length);
                #if Compiler==QuickC
                  outp(0x3ce,4);outp(0x3cf,3);
                #elif Compiler==TurboC
                  outportb(0x03ce,(unsigned char)4);
                  outportb(0x03cf,(unsigned char)3);
                #endif
                movedata(0xa000,0x0000,seg4,off4,plane_length);
                #if Compiler==QuickC
                  outp(0x3ce,4);outp(0x3cf,0);
                #elif Compiler==TurboC
                  outportb(0x03ce,(unsigned char)4);
                  outportb(0x03cf,(unsigned char)0);
                #endif
                break;
        case 2:                                 /* EGA 640x350x16-color */
                #if Compiler==QuickC
                outp(0x03ce,0x08);outp(0x03cf,0xff);outp(0x03c4,0x02);
                outp(0x03c5,0x0f);outp(0x03ce,0x05);outp(0x03cf,0x01);
                movedata(0xa000,0x0000,0xa800,0x0000,plane_length);
                outp(0x03ce,0x05);outp(0x03cf,0x00);
                #elif Compiler==TurboC
                outportb(0x03ce,(unsigned char)4);
                outportb(0x03cf,(unsigned char)0);
                outportb(0x03c4,(unsigned char)2);
                outportb(0x03c5,(unsigned char)1);
                movedata(0xa000,0x0000,0xa800,0x0000,plane_length);
                outportb(0x03ce,(unsigned char)4);
                outportb(0x03cf,(unsigned char)1);
                outportb(0x03c4,(unsigned char)2);
                outportb(0x03c5,(unsigned char)2);
                movedata(0xa000,0x0000,0xa800,0x0000,plane_length);
                outportb(0x03ce,(unsigned char)4);
                outportb(0x03cf,(unsigned char)2);
                outportb(0x03c4,(unsigned char)2);
                outportb(0x03c5,(unsigned char)4);
                movedata(0xa000,0x0000,0xa800,0x0000,plane_length);
                outportb(0x03ce,(unsigned char)4);
                outportb(0x03cf,(unsigned char)3);
                outportb(0x03c4,(unsigned char)2);
                outportb(0x03c5,(unsigned char)8);
                movedata(0xa000,0x0000,0xa800,0x0000,plane_length);
                outportb(0x03ce,(unsigned char)4);
                outportb(0x03cf,(unsigned char)0);
                outportb(0x03c4,(unsigned char)2);
                outportb(0x03c5,(unsigned char)15);
                #endif
                break;
        case 3:                                 /* EGA 640x200x16-color */
                #if Compiler==QuickC
                outp(0x03ce,0x08);outp(0x03cf,0xff);outp(0x03c4,0x02);
                outp(0x03c5,0x0f);outp(0x03ce,0x05);outp(0x03cf,0x01);
                movedata(0xa000,0x0000,0xa400,0x0000,plane_length);
                outp(0x03ce,0x05);outp(0x03cf,0x00);
                #elif Compiler==TurboC
                outportb(0x03ce,(unsigned char)4);
                outportb(0x03cf,(unsigned char)0);
                outportb(0x03c4,(unsigned char)2);
                outportb(0x03c5,(unsigned char)1);
                movedata(0xa000,0x0000,0xa400,0x0000,plane_length);
                outportb(0x03ce,(unsigned char)4);
                outportb(0x03cf,(unsigned char)1);
                outportb(0x03c4,(unsigned char)2);
```

Fig. 13-3.
Continued.

```
            outportb(0x03c5,(unsigned char)2);
            movedata(0xa000,0x0000,0xa400,0x0000,plane_length);
            outportb(0x03ce,(unsigned char)4);
            outportb(0x03cf,(unsigned char)2);
            outportb(0x03c4,(unsigned char)2);
            outportb(0x03c5,(unsigned char)4);
            movedata(0xa000,0x0000,0xa400,0x0000,plane_length);
            outportb(0x03ce,(unsigned char)4);

            outportb(0x03cf,(unsigned char)3);
            outportb(0x03c4,(unsigned char)2);
            outportb(0x03c5,(unsigned char)8);
            movedata(0xa000,0x0000,0xa400,0x0000,plane_length);
            outportb(0x03ce,(unsigned char)4);
            outportb(0x03cf,(unsigned char)0);
            outportb(0x03c4,(unsigned char)2);
            outportb(0x03c5,(unsigned char)15);
            #endif
            break;
  case 4: movedata(0xa000,0x0000,seg1,off1,plane_length);
          break;                          /* MCGA 640x480x2-color */
  case 5: movedata(0xb800,0x0000,seg1,off1,plane_length);
          break;                          /* CGA  640x200x2-color */
  case 6: movedata(0xb000,0x0000,0xb800,0x0000,plane_length);
          break;}                         /* Herc 720x348x2-color */
return;}
/*_____*/

void Restore(void){                 /* copies hidden page to page 0 */
switch(mode_flag){
  case 1:                                 /* VGA 640x480x16-color */
            #if Compiler==QuickC
              outp(0x3c4,2);outp(0x3c5,1);
            #elif Compiler==TurboC
              outportb(0x03c4,(unsigned char)2);
              outportb(0x03c5,(unsigned char)1);
            #endif
            movedata(seg1,off1,0xa000,0x0000,plane_length);
            #if Compiler==QuickC
              outp(0x3c4,2);outp(0x3c5,2);
            #elif Compiler==TurboC
              outportb(0x03c4,(unsigned char)2);
              outportb(0x03c5,(unsigned char)2);
            #endif
            movedata(seg2,off2,0xa000,0x0000,plane_length);
            #if Compiler==QuickC
              outp(0x3c4,2);outp(0x3c5,4);
            #elif Compiler==TurboC
              outportb(0x03c4,(unsigned char)2);
              outportb(0x03c5,(unsigned char)4);
            #endif
            movedata(seg3,off3,0xa000,0x0000,plane_length);
            #if Compiler==QuickC
              outp(0x3c4,2);outp(0x3c5,8);
            #elif Compiler==TurboC
              outportb(0x03c4,(unsigned char)2);
              outportb(0x03c5,(unsigned char)8);
            #endif
            movedata(seg4,off4,0xa000,0x0000,plane_length);
            #if Compiler==QuickC
              outp(0x3c4,2);outp(0x3c5,0xf);
            #elif Compiler==TurboC
              outportb(0x03c4,(unsigned char)2);
              outportb(0x03c5,(unsigned char)15);
            #endif
            break;
  case 2:                                 /* 640x350x16-color */
            #if Compiler==QuickC
            outp(0x03ce,0x08);outp(0x03cf,0xff);outp(0x03c4,0x02);
            outp(0x03c5,0x0f);outp(0x03ce,0x05);outp(0x03cf,0x01);
```

Fig. 13-3.
Continued.

```
                        movedata(0xa800,0x0000,0xa000,0x0000,plane_length);
                        outp(0x03ce,0x05);outp(0x03cf,0x00);
                        #elif Compiler==TurboC
                        outportb(0x03ce,(unsigned char)4);
                        outportb(0x03cf,(unsigned char)0);
                        outportb(0x03c4,(unsigned char)2);
                        outportb(0x03c5,(unsigned char)1);
                        movedata(0xa800,0x0000,0xa000,0x0000,plane_length);
                        outportb(0x03ce,(unsigned char)4);
                        outportb(0x03cf,(unsigned char)1);
                        outportb(0x03c4,(unsigned char)2);
                        outportb(0x03c5,(unsigned char)2);
                        movedata(0xa800,0x0000,0xa000,0x0000,plane_length);
                        outportb(0x03ce,(unsigned char)4);
                        outportb(0x03cf,(unsigned char)2);
                        outportb(0x03c4,(unsigned char)2);
                        outportb(0x03c5,(unsigned char)4);
                        movedata(0xa800,0x0000,0xa000,0x0000,plane_length);
                        outportb(0x03ce,(unsigned char)4);
                        outportb(0x03cf,(unsigned char)3);
                        outportb(0x03c4,(unsigned char)2);
                        outportb(0x03c5,(unsigned char)8);
                        movedata(0xa800,0x0000,0xa000,0x0000,plane_length);
                        outportb(0x03ce,(unsigned char)4);
                        outportb(0x03cf,(unsigned char)0);
                        outportb(0x03c4,(unsigned char)2);
                        outportb(0x03c5,(unsigned char)15);
                        #endif
                        break;
            case 3:                                      /* 640x200x16-color */
                        #if Compiler==QuickC
                        outp(0x03ce,0x08);outp(0x03cf,0xff);outp(0x03c4,0x02);
                        outp(0x03c5,0x0f);outp(0x03ce,0x05);outp(0x03cf,0x01);
                        movedata(0xa400,0x0000,0xa000,0x0000,plane_length);
                        outp(0x03ce,0x05);outp(0x03cf,0x00);
                        #elif Compiler==TurboC
                        outportb(0x03ce,(unsigned char)4);
                        outportb(0x03cf,(unsigned char)0);
                        outportb(0x03c4,(unsigned char)2);
                        outportb(0x03c5,(unsigned char)1);
                        movedata(0xa400,0x0000,0xa000,0x0000,plane_length);
                        outportb(0x03ce,(unsigned char)4);
                        outportb(0x03cf,(unsigned char)1);
                        outportb(0x03c4,(unsigned char)2);
                        outportb(0x03c5,(unsigned char)2);
                        movedata(0xa400,0x0000,0xa000,0x0000,plane_length);
                        outportb(0x03ce,(unsigned char)4);
                        outportb(0x03cf,(unsigned char)2);
                        outportb(0x03c4,(unsigned char)2);
                        outportb(0x03c5,(unsigned char)4);
                        movedata(0xa400,0x0000,0xa000,0x0000,plane_length);
                        outportb(0x03ce,(unsigned char)4);
                        outportb(0x03cf,(unsigned char)3);
                        outportb(0x03c4,(unsigned char)2);
                        outportb(0x03c5,(unsigned char)8);
                        movedata(0xa400,0x0000,0xa000,0x0000,plane_length);
                        outportb(0x03ce,(unsigned char)4);
                        outportb(0x03cf,(unsigned char)0);
                        outportb(0x03c4,(unsigned char)2);
                        outportb(0x03c5,(unsigned char)15);
                        #endif
                        break;
         case 4: movedata(seg1,off1,0xa000,0x0000,plane_length);
                 break;                               /* MCGA 640x480x2-color */
         case 5: movedata(seg1,off1,0xb800,0x0000,plane_length);
                 break;                               /* CGA 640x200x2-color */
         case 6: movedata(0xb800,0x0000,0xb000,0x0000,plane_length);
                 break;}                              /* Herc 720x348x2-color */
      return;}
```

Fig. 13-3.
Continued.

```
/*_____

        D I S K   I N P U T / O U T P U T   R O U T I N E S
_____*/

void SaveImage(void){              /* device-independent image save */
switch(mode_flag){         /* call appropriate image save function */
  case 1: strcpy(f7,".BL1");strcpy(f8,".GR1");
          strcpy(f9,".RE1");strcpy(f10,".IN1");
          SaveVGAEGAImage();break;   /* VGA 640x480x16-color mode */
  case 2: strcpy(f7,".BL2");strcpy(f8,".GR2");
          strcpy(f9,".RE2");strcpy(f10,".IN2");
          SaveVGAEGAImage();break;   /* EGA 640x350x16-color mode */
  case 3: strcpy(f7,".BL3");strcpy(f8,".GR3");
          strcpy(f9,".RE3");strcpy(f10,".IN3");
          SaveVGAEGAImage();break;   /* EGA 640x200x16-color mode */
  case 4: SaveMCGAimage();break;     /* MCGA 640x480x2-color mode */
  case 5: SaveCGAimage();break;       /* CGA 640x200x2-color mode */
  case 6: SaveHGAimage();break;}/* Hercules 720x348x2-color mode */
return;}
/*_____*/

void LoadImage(void){              /* device-independent image load */
switch(mode_flag){         /* call appropriate image load function */
  case 1: strcpy(f7,".BL1");strcpy(f8,".GR1");
          strcpy(f9,".RE1");strcpy(f10,".IN1");
          LoadVGAEGAImage();break;   /* VGA 640x480x16-color mode */
  case 2: strcpy(f7,".BL2");strcpy(f8,".GR2");
          strcpy(f9,".RE2");strcpy(f10,".IN2");
          LoadVGAEGAImage();break;   /* EGA 640x350x16-color mode */
  case 3: strcpy(f7,".BL3");strcpy(f8,".GR3");
          strcpy(f9,".RE3");strcpy(f10,".IN3");
          LoadVGAEGAImage();break;   /* EGA 640x200x16-color mode */
  case 4: LoadMCGAimage();break;     /* MCGA 640x480x2-color mode */
  case 5: LoadCGAimage();break;       /* CGA 640x200x2-color mode */
  case 6: LoadHGAimage();break;}/* Hercules 720x348x2-color mode */
return;}
/*_____*/

void SaveVGAEGAImage(void){                  /* saves image to disk */
segread(&segregs);segment=segregs.ds; /* determine segment value */
offset=(unsigned int)image_buffer;      /* determine offset value */
strcpy(f6,f3);strcat(f6,f7);          /* initialize the filename */
image_file=fopen(f6,"wb");                      /* open the file */
#if Compiler==QuickC
  outp(0x3ce,4);outp(0x3cf,0);      /* set EGA,VGA to read plane 0 */
#elif Compiler==TurboC
  outportb(0x3ce,4);outportb(0x3cf,0);
#endif
movedata(0xa000,0x0000,segment,offset,plane_length);
fwrite((char *)image_buffer,1,plane_length,image_file);
fclose(image_file);                          /* close the file */
strcpy(f6,f3);strcat(f6,f8);          /* initialize the filename */
image_file=fopen(f6,"wb");            /* open the file */
#if Compiler==QuickC
  outp(0x3ce,4);outp(0x3cf,1);      /* set EGA,VGA to read plane 1 */
#elif Compiler==TurboC
  outportb(0x3ce,4);outportb(0x3cf,1);
#endif
movedata(0xa000,0x0000,segment,offset,plane_length);
fwrite((char *)image_buffer,1,plane_length,image_file);
fclose(image_file);                          /* close the file */
strcpy(f6,f3);strcat(f6,f9);          /* initialize the filename */
image_file=fopen(f6,"wb");                      /* open the file */
#if Compiler==QuickC
  outp(0x3ce,4);outp(0x3cf,2);      /* set EGA,VGA to read plane 2 */
#elif Compiler==TurboC
  outportb(0x3ce,4);outportb(0x3cf,2);
#endif
```

Fig. 13-3.
Continued.

```
movedata(0xa000,0x0000,segment,offset,plane_length);
fwrite((char *)image_buffer,1,plane_length,image_file);
fclose(image_file);                        /* close the file */
strcpy(f6,f3);strcat(f6,f10);        /* initialize the filename */
image_file=fopen(f6,"wb");                  /* open the file */
#if Compiler==QuickC
  outp(0x3ce,4);outp(0x3cf,3);    /* set EGA,VGA to read plane 3 */
#elif Compiler==TurboC
  outportb(0x3ce,4);outportb(0x3cf,3);
#endif
movedata(0xa000,0x0000,segment,offset,plane_length);
fwrite((char *)image_buffer,1,plane_length,image_file);
fclose(image_file);                        /* close the file */
#if Compiler==QuickC
  outp(0x3ce,4);outp(0x3cf,0);        /* restore EGA,VGA registers */
#elif Compiler==TurboC
  outportb(0x3ce,4);outportb(0x3cf,0);
#endif
return;}
/*_____*/


void LoadVGAEGAImage(void){              /* loads image from disk */
segread(&segregs);segment=segregs.ds; /* determine segment value */
offset=(unsigned int)image_buffer;      /* determine offset value */
strcpy(f6,f3);strcat(f6,f7);         /* initialize the filename */
image_file=fopen(f6,"rb");                  /* open the file */
#if Compiler==QuickC
  outp(0x3c4,2);outp(0x3c5,1);    /* set EGA,VGA to write plane 0 */
#elif Compiler==TurboC
  outportb(0x3c4,2);outportb(0x3c5,1);
#endif
fread((char *)image_buffer,1,plane_length,image_file);
movedata(segment,offset,0xa000,0x0000,plane_length);
fclose(image_file);                        /* close the file */
strcpy(f6,f3);strcat(f6,f8);         /* initialize the filename */
image_file=fopen(f6,"rb");                  /* open the file */
#if Compiler==QuickC
  outp(0x3c4,2);outp(0x3c5,2);    /* set EGA,VGA to write plane 1 */
#elif Compiler==TurboC
  outportb(0x3c4,2);outportb(0x3c5,2);
#endif
fread((char *)image_buffer,1,plane_length,image_file);
movedata(segment,offset,0xa000,0x0000,plane_length);
fclose(image_file);                        /* close the file */
strcpy(f6,f3);strcat(f6,f9);         /* initialize the filename */
image_file=fopen(f6,"rb");                  /* open the file */
#if Compiler==QuickC
  outp(0x3c4,2);outp(0x3c5,4);    /* set EGA,VGA to write plane 2 */
#elif Compiler==TurboC
  outportb(0x3c4,2);outportb(0x3c5,4);
#endif
fread((char *)image_buffer,1,plane_length,image_file);
movedata(segment,offset,0xa000,0x0000,plane_length);
fclose(image_file);                        /* close the file */
strcpy(f6,f3);strcat(f6,f10);        /* initialize the filename */
image_file=fopen(f6,"rb");                  /* open the file */
#if Compiler==QuickC
  outp(0x3c4,2);outp(0x3c5,8);    /* set EGA,VGA to write plane 3 */
#elif Compiler==TurboC
  outportb(0x3c4,2);outportb(0x3c5,8);
#endif
fread((char *)image_buffer,1,plane_length,image_file);
movedata(segment,offset,0xa000,0x0000,plane_length);
fclose(image_file);                        /* close the file */
#if Compiler==QuickC
  outp(0x3c4,2);outp(0x3c5,0xF);    /* restore EGA,VGA registers */
#elif Compiler==TurboC
  outportb(0x3c4,2);outportb(0x3c5,0xF);
```

Fig. 13-3.
Continued.

```
#endif
return;}
/*_____*/

void SaveCGAimage(void){                      /* saves image to disk */
segread(&segregs);segment=segregs.ds; /* determine segment value */
offset=(unsigned int)image_buffer;       /* determine offset value */
strcpy(f6,f3);strcat(f6,".CGA");         /* initialize the filename */
image_file=fopen(f6,"wb");                        /* open the file */
movedata(0xb800,0x0000,segment,offset,plane_length);
fwrite((char *)image_buffer,1,plane_length,image_file);
fclose(image_file);                              /* close the file */
return;}
/*_____*/

void LoadCGAimage(void){                    /* loads image from disk */
segread(&segregs);segment=segregs.ds; /* determine segment value */
offset=(unsigned int)image_buffer;       /* determine offset value */
strcpy(f6,f3);strcat(f6,".CGA");         /* initialize the filename */
image_file=fopen(f6,"rb");                        /* open the file */
fread((char *)image_buffer,1,plane_length,image_file);
movedata(segment,offset,0xB800,0x0000,plane_length);
fclose(image_file);                              /* close the file */
return;}
/*_____*/

void SaveHGAimage(void){                      /* saves image to disk */
segread(&segregs);segment=segregs.ds; /* determine segment value */
offset=(unsigned int)image_buffer;       /* determine offset value */
strcpy(f6,f3);strcat(f6,".HGA");         /* initialize the filename */
image_file=fopen(f6,"wb");                        /* open the file */
movedata(0xb000,0x0000,segment,offset,plane_length);
fwrite((char *)image_buffer,1,plane_length,image_file);
fclose(image_file);                              /* close the file */
return;}
/*_____*/

void LoadHGAimage(void){                    /* loads image from disk */
segread(&segregs);segment=segregs.ds; /* determine segment value */
offset=(unsigned int)image_buffer;       /* determine offset value */
strcpy(f6,f3);strcat(f6,".HGA");         /* initialize the filename */
image_file=fopen(f6,"rb");                        /* open the file */
fread((char *)image_buffer,1,plane_length,image_file);
movedata(segment,offset,0xb000,0x0000,plane_length);
fclose(image_file);                              /* close the file */
return;}
/*_____*/

void SaveMCGAimage(void){                     /* saves image to disk */
segread(&segregs);segment=segregs.ds; /* determine segment value */
offset=(unsigned int)image_buffer;       /* determine offset value */
strcpy(f6,f3);strcat(f6,".MCG");         /* initialize the filename */
image_file=fopen(f6,"wb");                        /* open the file */
movedata(0xa000,0x0000,segment,offset,plane_length);
fwrite((char *)image_buffer,1,plane_length,image_file);
fclose(image_file);                              /* close the file */
return;}
/*_____*/

void LoadMCGAimage(void){                   /* loads image from disk */
segread(&segregs);segment=segregs.ds; /* determine segment value */
offset=(unsigned int)image_buffer;       /* determine offset value */
strcpy(f6,f3);strcat(f6,".MCG");         /* initialize the filename */
image_file=fopen(f6,"rb");                        /* open the file */
fread((char *)image_buffer,1,plane_length,image_file);
movedata(segment,offset,0xa000,0x0000,plane_length);
```

Fig. 13-3.
Continued.

```
      fclose(image_file);                    /* close the file */
      return;}
/*_____

End of Module 3 source code.  (This program has 3 modules.) */
```

First, ensure that the three source files, DESIGN1.C, DESIGN2.C, and DESIGN3.C, are in the directory where your C source files are usually found. If you are using the companion disk, copy them from the disk to the directory. If you are not using the companion disk, type them in from the listings in the book.

If you are using the companion disk, be sure to also copy the file named DESIGN.MAK from the disk to the source files directory. If you are not using the companion disk, you will need to create a MAK file. This file tells QuickC which C source files to collect together to make the desired EXE program.

The first step in the compilation process is to tell QuickC the names of the C source files in the project. Select Set Program List from the Make menu. If DESIGN.MAK already exists, select it from the menu display directory. QuickC will automatically load the first module for the project: DESIGN1.C. If DESIGN .MAK does not yet exist, type its name in. QuickC will ask you if you want to create a new make file. Answer yes. QuickC will present you with a directory of C source files whose names you can place into the MAK file. Select DESIGN1.C, DESIGN2.C, and DESIGN3.C. Select Save to save the newly created MAK file. QuickC will automatically load the first module for the project, DESIGN1.C.

Press F5 to compile, link, and run the program. QuickC will check the contents of DESIGN.MAK to see which C source files to collect together.

If you experience any difficulties during the compilation and linking process, refer to Appendix A for a no-nonsense quick-and-easy guide to getting the demonstration programs up and running.

For guidance on using the program once it is up and running, refer to the mini user's guide in Chapter 14.

COMPILING INSIDE TURBO C

To compile and run this demonstration program from within the integrated programming environment of Turbo C version 2.0 or newer, follow these instructions.

Because of the size of this demonstration program, you should use Turbo C's menu system to turn off the debugging code which is normally embedded in the resultant EXE file. This will make the EXE file small enough to co-exist in RAM with the Turbo C editor.

Select the Debug menu from the main menu bar and turn off Source Debugging.

First, ensure that the three source files, DESIGN1.C, DESIGN2.C, and DESIGN3.C, are in the directory where your C source files arc usually found. If you arc using the companion disk, copy them from the disk to the directory. If you are not using the companion disk, type them in from the listings in the book.

TRAP

When you are running an EXE program under the control of the Turbo C editor, you must be mindful that both Turbo C and the EXE program exist in RAM at the same time. The demonstration program in this chapter will produce an EXE program that is larger than remaining memory when both DOS and Turbo C are present in 640K of RAM. However, the integrated programming environment of Turbo C places a lot of debugging code into any program which it compiles. This increases the size of the resulting executable file. By turning off Source Debugging in the Debug menu of Turbo C, you can produce an EXE file that is 60% the size of a file containing debugging hooks. To compile the interactive 3D modeling and rendering program in this chapter using the Turbo C editor, turn off the debugging code. If you are using command-line compilation and linking, no changes are required. See Chapter 2 for more on this.

If you are using the companion disk, be sure to also copy the file named DESIGN.PRJ from the disk to the source files directory. If you are not using the companion disk, you will need to create a PRJ project file. This file tells Turbo C which C source files to collect together to make the desired EXE program.

The first step in the compilation process is to tell Turbo C the names of the C source files in the project. Select Program Name from the Project menu. Press the Enter key to see a directory listing of available PRJ files. If DESIGN.PRJ already exists, select it from the menu display directory. If DESIGN.PRJ does not yet exist, you must create it. Go to the editor and type in the names of the three C source files, DESIGN1.C, DESIGN2.C, DESIGN3.C, each on its own line. Save that file as DESIGN.PRJ. Now go to the Project menu and type in the name DESIGN.PRJ.

Select Run from the Run menu to compile, link, and run the program. Turbo C will check the contents of DESIGN.PRJ to see which C source files to collect together.

If you experience any difficulties during the compilation and linking process, refer to Appendix A for a no-nonsense quick-and-easy guide to getting the demonstration programs up and running. If you get an out-of-memory error report from Turbo C during compilation or linking, then you should remove any memory-resident programs that you might be using. The program will compile on a computer with 640K RAM when only DOS and Turbo C 2.0 are loaded. If the program still will not compile, use the command-line version of Turbo C to produce the EXE file.

For guidance on using the program once it is up and running, refer to the mini user's guide in Chapter 14.

COMPILING WITH THE QuickC COMMAND LINE

First, ensure that the three source files are in the current drive and directory. Second, use the following command line to create DESIGN.EXE:

```
C:\QC2\BIN\QCL /Ox /AM /F 1000 /FeDESIGN /W1 DESIGN1.C DESIGN2.C DESIGN3.C
/link /INF (Enter)
```

This command line assumes that the command-line program QCL.EXE is located in the directory named C:\QC2\BIN.

For guidance on using the program once it is up and running, refer to the mini user's guide in Chapter 14.

COMPILING WITH THE TURBO C COMMAND LINE

First, ensure that the files TCC.EXE and TLINK.EXE are in the current drive and directory.

Second, use the following command line to create DESIGN.EXE:

```
TCC -mm -G -IC:\TC2\INCLUDE -LC:\TC2\LIB -nC:\TC2\SOURCE DESIGN1.C
DESIGN2.C DESIGN3.C GRAPHICS.LIB (Enter)
```

This command line assumes that the #include files are in the directory named C:\TC2\INCLUDE, that the library files are in the directory named C:\TC2\LIB, and that the three C source files are in the directory named C:\TC2\SOURCE. You can change these directory names on the command line to suit your own needs, if required.

Using the above command line, the resulting EXE file will be written to the directory named C:\TC2\SOURCE. When you run the EXE program, it expects to find the *.BGI graphics driver files in the current directory. It will behave erratically at run-time if the .BGI files were not found.

For guidance on using the program once it is up and running, refer to the mini user's guide in Chapter 14.

USING THE PROGRAM AS A TOOLKIT

If you intend to use routines from the demonstration program in your own original programs—whether retail, corporate, shareware, or freeware—it is important that you read the licensing arrangements contained in the header of the source code and the full License Agreement contained in the Introduction of this book.

FILENAME CONFLICT WARNINGS

The EXE file produced by these demonstration listings might conflict with other EXE programs in your system.

Play it safe. If you have any commercial software program that uses DESIGN .EXE as a filename on your fixed disk, change the name of the project file if you are compiling from within the integrated programming environment of QuickC or Turbo C. Also change the desired name of the EXE file on the command line if you are using the command-line compilation/link process of QuickC or Turbo C.

14

User's Guide:
Your Microcomputer 3D CAD Designer

THIS CHAPTER contains a mini user's guide for Your Microcomputer 3D CAD Designer, a full-length, interactive 3D modeling and rendering program. The complete source code for the program appears in Chapter 13.

If you prefer to begin using the program without reading the user's guide, go right ahead. Your Microcomputer 3D CAD Designer is a sturdy program with an intuitive menu system operated by common-sense keystrokes.

Be forewarned that disk I/O errors are not trapped and can lock up your system in some cases. No harm will be done, though; simply power-off and then reboot your computer. You must be careful to ensure that there is enough free space on the current drive to save images. Likewise, be careful not to misspell a filename during a save or load process. For tips on adding error-handling routines to the source code, see Appendix C.

INTRODUCTION

Your Microcomputer 3D CAD Designer is a powerful and versatile program that takes full advantage of the 16-color modes of VGA and EGA graphics adapters. It will also run on MCGA, CGA, and Hercules adapters in the 2-color mode. A special autodetect capability ensures that the program starts up in the best mode for your particular computer system.

Using the program you can create shaded 3D models with all backplane facets automatically hidden. A kit of sub-object primitives like boxes and cylinders makes it easy to assemble complex models. You can choose which color a primitive will exhibit; the automatic shading routines will calculate the illumination intensity for each facet of the sub-object and will shade it in your preferred hue.

The easy-to-use, intuitive menu system of Your Microcomputer 3D CAD Designer makes you an expert the moment you start up the program. The software is completely keyboard-driven, including the powerful keypad bat features which allow you to translate, rotate, and extrude any of the 3D primitives in 3D space in real time.

You can customize Your Microcomputer 3D CAD Designer to suit your own creative tastes. Through the Settings menu, you can change the shading color to any one of 6 different hues if you are using a VGA or EGA.

You can save your drawings to disk as image files. You can reload previously-saved image files for additional editing or to create dynamic slideshow presentations.

You can create print-outs of your drawings by using memory-resident third-party utility programs which capture the screen. Some of the drawings used to illustrate the text in this book were created with Your Microcomputer 3D CAD Designer and printed on a standard dot matrix printer.

SYSTEM REQUIREMENTS

Your Microcomputer 3D CAD Designer requires an IBM PC, XT, AT, PS/2 or true compatible with either a VGA, EGA, MCGA, CGA, or Hercules graphics adapter and appropriate display monitor.

If you are running Your Microcomputer 3D CAD Designer from DOS, the program might need as little as 256K bytes of memory to run, depending upon the graphics adapter you have installed in your system. If you are running Your Microcomputer 3D CAD Designer under the control of the QuickC or Turbo C editor, you will require a full 640K bytes of RAM. If you are using Turbo C, see the previous chapter for compilation tips.

INSTALLATION

This installation guide assumes you are running the software from the operating system prompt.

Before your start the program, set the current drive and directory to the directory where you want to save your images or to where previously saved images are located.

If your version of Your Microcomputer 3D CAD Designer was compiled using QuickC, then the font file named TMSRB.FON should also be in this directory. If your version of Your Microcomputer 3D CAD Designer was compiled using Turbo C, then the font file named TRIPP.CHR should be in this directory. The software needs to be able to read the font file when it starts up.

To start Your Microcomputer 3D CAD Designer, simply type

DESIGN ⟨Enter⟩

at the operating system prompt. If the program file is located in a drive or directory other than the current drive and directory, then you must type the full pathname. For example, if the program was in a directory named C:\DEMOS. you would type:

C:\DEMOS\DESIGN ⟨Enter⟩

The program will load into memory and will construct the pull-down menus for later use by the menu system. Then it will build the sign-on display. Now it looks for the appropriate font file in the current directory and uses the font to present the name of the program as a title. If the font file is not found, the program will issue a cautionary message and will continue running.

Your Microcomputer 3D CAD Designer is now ready to use. Press the Enter key to pull down the File menu. Press the Enter key again to clear the 3D window. You are now ready to begin to build your first 3D model.

USING THE PROGRAM

All of the software's powerful features are accessed via its intuitive menu system. Each selection on the main menu bar will cause a pull-down menu to appear. If you ever make a mistake during a modeling function, simply select Undo from the Scene menu and your previous condition will be instantly restored.

The Dialog Line

The dialog line at the top of the screen is the program's way of talking to you. It is also where you edit the name of any image file which you are saving or loading.

The Help Bar

The text line at the bottom of the screen is the help bar. Pressing F1 will display a context-sensitive help message, pertinent to whatever menu selection you are currently using. Pressing F2 will immediately save to disk the current drawing. Pressing F3 will put you into the translation mode so you can move the currently selected primitive in 3D space. Pressing F4 puts you into the rotate mode. Pressing F5 sets you into the Extrude mode. Pressing the Esc key will back out of the current menu position and return you to the main menu bar. Pressing Alt+X at any time will end the program.

In this implementation of Your Microcomputer 3D CAD Designer, function keys F1 through F5 are not activated. See Chapter 3 for guidance on managing the keyboard.

The Session Filename

The Current File text, located at the top of the 3D window, displays the name of the current drawing. You can change this name by using the File menu.

In this implementation of Your Microcomputer 3D CAD Designer, the 3D window filename display does not correspond to the actual current filename which is used whenever the program reads or writes to or from disk.

USING THE MENU SYSTEM

The menu system is controlled by the keyboard. Use the Enter key to activate any selection currently highlighted. Use the Esc key to back out of your current position and return to the main menu bar. Use the left-arrow and right-arrow keys to choose selections on the main menu bar.

When you are in a pull-down menu, use the up-arrow and down-arrow keys to make a selection. Using the left-arrow or right-arrow will move you to the next pull-down menu, bypassing the main menu bar.

At any location in the menu system, you can use Alt+X to end the program. Hold the Alt key down and press X.

THE FILE MENU

The File menu controls the start-up and shutdown of the modeling session, as well as the saving and loading of database files and image files.

Choose New to clear the 3D window. If you change your mind and wish to continue working on the scene which you have just cleared, use Undo from the Scene menu to restore your drawing.

Choose Load File to load a previously-created database file into memory. This feature is inactive in this version of Your Microcomputer 3D CAD Designer.

Choose Save File to save the current database to disk. This feature is inactive in this version of Your Microcomputer 3D CAD Designer.

Select Load Slide if you wish to load a previously-saved image file. Press the Enter key to load this file, otherwise type in the name of the desired file and press the Enter key. If you make a mistake, press the Esc key to restore the filename to the name which existed before you began typing.

Choose Save Slide to save the current drawing as an image file using the current filename. The default image filename at program start-up is UNTITLED .DWG.

Select Shutdown to end the program and return to the operating system or to the editor if you are running the program under the control of QuickC or Turbo C. Any image or database which you have not saved to disk will be lost when you select Shutdown.

THE OBJECT MENU

The Object menu lets you select the sub-object or primitive which you can manipulate in the 3D window. Whichever primitive you select, the 3D cursor is always a box, however.

The available selections are Cube, Cylinder, Cone, Sphere, Polygon, Line, Ruled surf, Mesh, and two user-defined primitives.

Only Cube and Cylinder are semantically implemented in this version of Your Microcomputer 3D CAD Designer.

THE SCENE MENU

The Scene menu gives you the ability to manipulate the 3D cursor in 3D space in real time, as displayed in the 3D window on the screen. Five functions are available: Rotate, Move, Extrude, Regen, and Undo.

Note: you should adjust the camera rotation by using the Camera menu before you use any of the Scene menu functions.

Figure 14-1 illustrates the position of the 3D scene phantom cursor at program start-up. Figure 14-2 depicts the scene after being pitched forward. Figure 14-3 shows the 3D scene space after being rotated in the yaw plane. Figure 14-4 shows the 3D cursor, which represents the shape, location, and orientation of the 3D sub-object which will be drawn in that position.

Rotate

Select Rotate if you wish to rotate the primitive in either the yaw, roll, or pitch plane.

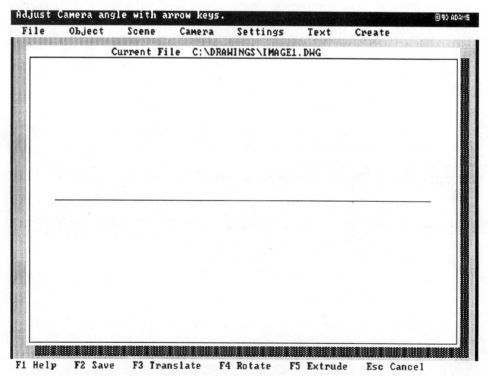

Fig. 14-1. The head-on view of the groundplane cursor at program start-up.

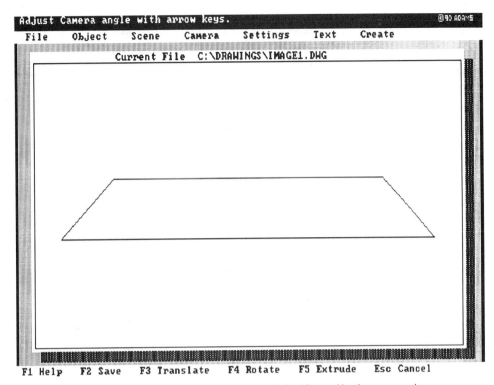

File   Object   Scene   Camera   Settings   Text   Create

Current File   C:\DRAWINGS\IMAGE1.DWG

F1 Help   F2 Save   F3 Translate   F4 Rotate   F5 Extrude   Esc Cancel

Fig. 14-2. The groundplane cursor has been pitched forward by the up-arrow key.

See FIG. 14-5. When the 3D cursor appears in the 3D window, use the left-arrow and right-arrow keys to rotate the box in the yaw plane. Use the up-arrow and down-arrow keys to rotate the 3D cursor in the pitch plane. Use the PgUp and Home keys to rotate the sub-object in the roll plane.

When the 3D cursor is in the desired position, press the Enter key to instruct the software to draw the shaded sub-object at that orientation. Otherwise, simply press the Esc key to return to the main menu bar without drawing the primitive.

Extrude

Select Extrude if you wish to alter the size of the sub-object along either the x axis, the y axis, or the z axis.

See FIG. 14-6. When the box appears in the 3D window, use the left-arrow and right-arrow keys to stretch or shrink the object left and right (along the x axis). Use the up-arrow and down-arrow keys to stretch or shrink the object taller or shorter (along the y axis). Use the PgUp and PgDn keys to stretch or shrink the object fatter or thinner (along the z axis).

When the model is in the desired shape and size, press the Enter key to draw the shaded object in that configuration. Press the Esc key to return to the main menu bar without drawing anything.

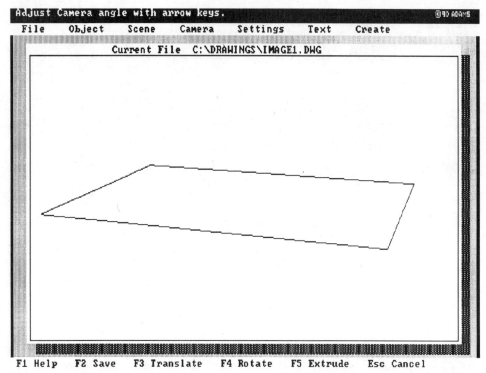

Fig. 14-3. Using the right-arrow key rotates the pitched groundplane cursor to a comfortable viewing angle.

Move...

Select Move if you wish to translate the primitive along either the x axis, the y axis, or the z axis.

See FIG. 14-7. When the 3D cursor appears in the 3D window, use the left-arrow and right-arrow keys to move the cursor left and right (or along the x axis). Use the PgUp and PgDn keys to move the box near and farther away (along the z axis). Use the up-arrow and down-arrow keys to move the 3D cursor up or down (along the y axis).

When the shape is in the desired location, select the Enter key to draw the shaded model at that position. Press the Esc key to return to the main menu bar without drawing the sub-object.

Regen

Select Regen to force the program to redraw all objects in the 3D window. Regen is not implemented in this version of Your Microcomputer 3D CAD Designer, because no 3D doubly linked database is maintained internally.

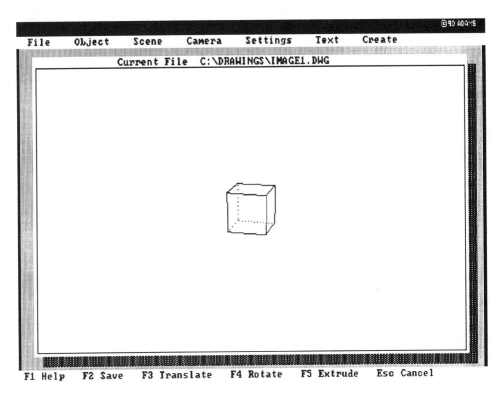

File   Object   Scene   Camera   Settings   Text   Create

Current File   C:\DRAWINGS\IMAGE1.DWG

F1 Help   F2 Save   F3 Translate   F4 Rotate   F5 Extrude   Esc Cancel

Fig. 14-4. The default 3D cursor.

Undo

Select Undo to undo the effects of your most recent activity in the Scene menu. Your previous image will be restored. In the current implementation of Your Microcomputer 3D CAD Designer, Undo uses a bitmap-based algorithm; the database is unaffected.

THE CAMERA MENU

The Camera menu gives you control over the viewpoint. In effect, it moves the entire 3D environment into which you will later install various sub-objects. Using the Camera menu you can move the viewpoint closer to the scene or farther away; you can rotate the entire 3D environment to different viewing angles; you can alter the focal length of the camera from a telephoto lens effect to a wide-angle lens effect; you can change the elevation and compass heading of the light source.

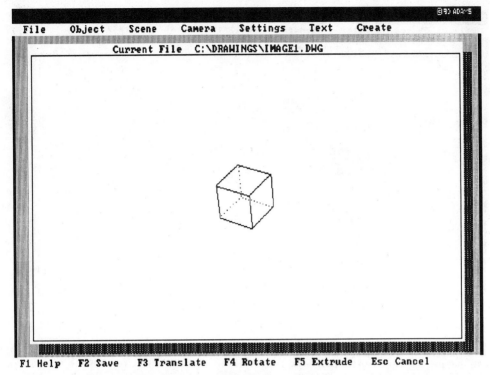

File   Object   Scene   Camera   Settings   Text   Create

Current File   C:\DRAWINGS\IMAGE1.DWG

F1 Help   F2 Save   F3 Translate   F4 Rotate   F5 Extrude   Esc Cancel

Fig. 14-5. The 3D cursor can be rotated in each of the yaw, roll, and pitch planes, independent of the world viewpoint. See also Fig. 14-4.

Distance

Select Distance to change the distance of the viewpoint from the scene. Press up-arrow to move closer to the scene. Press down-arrow to move farther away from the scene.

Distance is not implemented in this version of Your Microcomputer 3D CAD Designer.

Angle

Select Angle to rotate the scene to a pleasing viewpoint. Press left-arrow or right-arrow to rotate the scene in the yaw plane as depicted in FIG. 14-3. Press up-arrow or down-arrow to rotate the scene in the pitch plane as shown in FIG. 14-2. Press Home or PgUp to rotate the scene in the roll plane.

A phantom scene cursor will appear on the screen when you select this function. It is suggested that you press the up-arrow key six times, then the right-arrow key eight times, to create a pleasing scene angle when you first being your session.

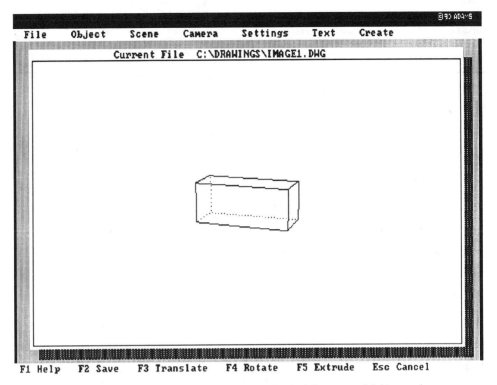

| File | Object | Scene | Camera | Settings | Text | Create |

Current File   C:\DRAWINGS\IMAGE1.DWG

F1 Help   F2 Save   F3 Translate   F4 Rotate   F5 Extrude   Esc Cancel

Fig. 14-6. The effect of an x extrusion, controlled by the left-arrow and right-arrow keys.

The roll rotation function is not implemented in this version of Your Microcomputer 3D CAD Designer.

Focal lgth

Choose this selection to adjust the angular distortion of the displayed 3D models. Press the up-arrow key to make the images appear as if viewed through a wide-angle lens. Press the down-arrow key to make the images flatter, as if viewed through a telephoto lens.

The Focal lgth function is not implemented in this version of Your Microcomputer 3D CAD Designer.

Light elev

Select Light elev to adjust the elevation of the point light source. This feature is not implemented in this version of Your Microcomputer 3D CAD Designer. (See Chapter 13 for source code that will do the job, however.)

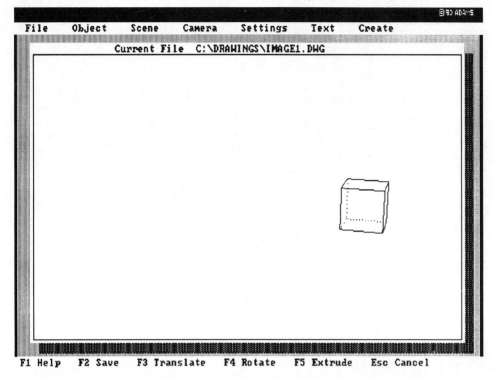

File	Object	Scene	Camera	Settings	Text	Create

Current File   C:\DRAWINGS\IMAGE1.DWG

F1 Help   F2 Save   F3 Translate   F4 Rotate   F5 Extrude   Esc Cancel

Fig. 14-7. The 3D cursor can be moved (translated) to different locations in the world scene.

Light dir

Choose Light dir to change the direction from which the light is coming. This feature is not implemented in this version of Your Microcomputer 3D CAD Designer. (See the sidebar in the previous chapter for C source code that can be used to activate this feature.)

Defaults

Select Defaults to restore the Scene menu parameters to their start-up settings. This feature is not implemented in this version of Your Microcomputer 3D CAD Designer. If you select New from the Files menu, all default settings for Scene will be reset.

THE SETTINGS MENU

The Settings menu gives you control over the session environment.

Display

Select Display to toggle between the 3D window and the 2D/3D window, which splits the screen into four viewports showing front, side, top, and 3D views.

This feature is not implemented in this version of Your Microcomputer 3D CAD Designer. The display is always in the 3D window mode.

Render

Choose Render to toggle computer-controlled shading on or off. In this version of Your Microcomputer 3D CAD Designer, the shaded mode is always in effect, as shown in FIG. 14-8. The essential source code is already in place, however, to implement this feature. Refer to Chapter 15 for comments on upgrading the source code.

Model

Choose Model to toggle between wire-frame or solid modeling. When wire-frame is in effect, no shading can be performed. In this version of Your Microcomputer 3D CAD Designer, solid modeling is always in effect.

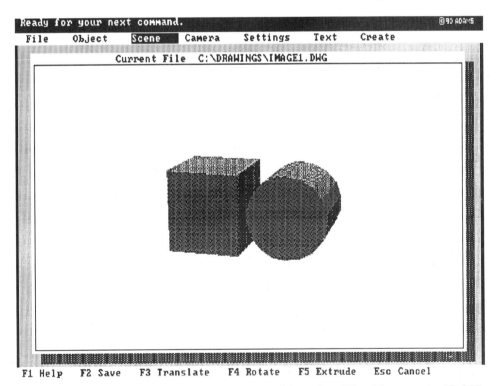

Fig. 14-8. The two fundamental subobjects provided by this version of Your Microcomputer 3D CAD Designer™: the cube and the cylinder, from which other complex models may be created.

Color

Select Color to change the color in which shaded models will be constructed by the software. A swatch showing the current color is displayed in the upper left corner of the 3D window. Use the Tab key to cycle through the colors supported by your graphics adapter. Six hues are available on VGA and EGA adapters. Only shades of white are available on 2-color adapters like MCGA, CGA, and Hercules. Press the Enter key to accept the currently-displayed swatch, or press the Esc key to return to the main menu bar.

Edit Mode

Select Edit Mode to switch the software into the user-defined object creation mode. In this mode, you are using revolve, sweep, and extrude to create your own sub-objects which you can later select from the Object menu to manipulate in the scene.

In this implementation of Your Microcomputer 3D CAD Designer this feature is not active.

Gnomon Y/N

Select this feature to toggle the 3D axis display on or off. This function is not implemented in this version of Your Microcomputer 3D CAD Designer.

Grid Y/N

Select Grid Y/N to toggle a grid display on each of the 3D planes. This function is inactive in this implementation of Your Microcomputer 3D CAD Designer.

THE TEXT MENU

The Text menu uses the built-in font features of either QuickC or Turbo C to permit you to write text labels on the screen. Although this feature has not been implemented in this version of Your Microcomputer 3D CAD Designer, the assorted variables and start-up code is in place.

THE CREATE MENU

The Create menu lets you design your own 3D primitives by using revolve, extrude, and sweep. See the discussion in Chapter 12 for further information about this modeling concept. The primitives which you create in this menu are later selectable from the user-defined choices available in the Object menu.

This menu is not implemented in this version of Your Microcomputer 3D CAD Designer.

SAMPLE SESSIONS

Your Microcomputer 3D CAD Designer is powerful and versatile, yet surprisingly easy to use. The menu system is very intuitive. The modeling environment is very forgiving. The program encourages creativity. Three sample sessions will serve to illustrate its capabilities.

Sample Session #1: Industrial Widget

The image depicted in FIG. 14-9 was created in less than 15 minutes using Your Microcomputer 3D CAD Designer.

First, the ground plane of the 3D scene was pitched forward and rotated in the yaw plane to provide a pleasing viewpoint.

Next, the Object menu was used to select the Cube primitive. Then, using the Rotate, Move, and Extrude functions of the Scene menu, the rectangular support for the widget was drawn.

The Object menu was then used to select the Cylinder primitive. The Settings menu was used to change the shading color. The Scene menu was activated, and Rotate, Move, and Extrude were used to build the cylindrical features of the widget. Each component was built using the farthest-to-nearest concept, thereby ensuring that nearer sub-objects would conveniently cover the appropriate facets of farther sub-objects.

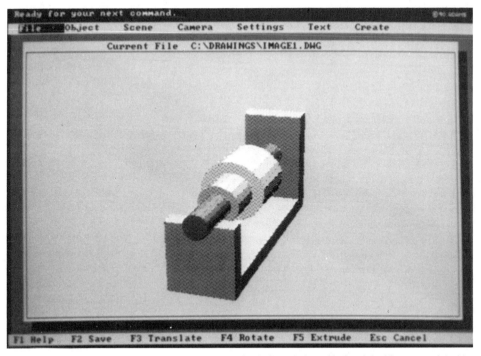

Fig. 14-9. Sample session 1. Three-dimensional, shaded rendering of industrial widget, completed in less than 15 minutes using Your Microcomputer 3D CAD Designer™, the demonstration program provided in Chapter 13.

During the drawing session, a pen and notepad were used to keep track of various elevations and distances in order to ensure that the diameters of the widget permitted it to rest on the surface of the rectangular support.

Sample Session #2: 3D Business Chart

The image shown in FIG. 14-10 was created in under 20 minutes using Your Microcomputer 3D CAD Designer.

The Settings menu was used to change the current shading color at appropriate times during the session.

Most of the work was done with the Scene menu. Extrusion was used to change the size of the 3D cursor box during the construction. Move was used to locate the various elements of the image.

The trick, again, is the concept of nearest-to-farthest. First, the base was drawn. Next, the two side walls were drawn. Note how these are actually constructed of three parallelepipeds each.

Finally, the size of the risers was set. From here on, only the height of the riser would be adjusted using the extrude function. The risers were installed back to front, thereby ensuring that near risers hide portions of far risers.

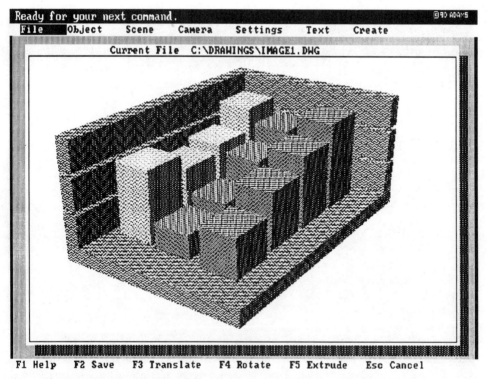

Fig. 14-10. Sample session 2. Three-dimensional business chart, completed in under 20 minutes using Your Microcomputer 3D CAD Designer™, the demonstration program presented in Chapter 13.

Sample Session #3: 3D Solid Text

The image in FIG. 14-11 was created in 25 minutes using Your Microcomputer 3D CAD Designer. Note how a simple parallelepiped is repeatedly drawn in order to create these three-dimension characters.

The first character was drawn from outside-in. In particular, the top and bottom horizontal features were drawn first in order to ensure bilateral equality. Then the character was redrawn from bottom to top to ensure that near boxes covered far boxes.

The same approach was used for the second character. The final redrawing started at the lower left corner of the character, went up the side of the letter, then restarted from the lower left and proceeded counterclockwise around the character until the letter was complete.

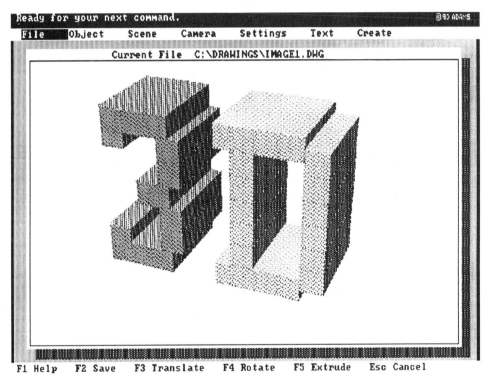

Fig. 14-11. Sample session 3. Three-dimensional solid text, completed in 25 minutes using Your Microcomputer 3D CAD Designer™, the demonstration program presented in Chapter 13.

TIPS AND TRICKS

You can increase your productivity with Your Microcomputer 3D CAD Designer by organizing your work before you start the program. Know what shape you want to draw. Picture in your mind's eye the viewpoint that will make it most understandable.

When you first start up Your Microcomputer 3D CAD Designer, use the Rotate selection in the Camera menu to adjust the viewpoint. Then, as you begin installing various sub-objects on the screen in various sizes, shapes, colors, and orientations, be sure to save the image regularly to disk. If you make an error which cannot be corrected by the Undo function in the Scene menu, you can always backtrack by reloading your most recent backup from disk.

ERROR MESSAGE REFERENCE

Two types of errors might be encountered during use of Your Microcomputer 3D CAD Designer. The first, run-time errors, are usually trapped and handled by the program itself. Messages are usually displayed on the dialog line at the top of the screen. The second type of error is associated with the operating system and usually involves the loading of the program and the return to the operating system after program shutdown.

The following run-time errors might be displayed on the dialog line during program execution.

RUN-TIME ERRORS

Font files not found. Text menu affected.

This message is displayed along with the sign-on screen. It means that the program could not find the font file it needed in the current directory. If the program was originally compiled with QuickC, then TMSRB.FON must be available. If Turbo C was used to compile the program, then TRIPP.CHR must be found. Program performance is not affected, except that the title on the canvas at sign-on will not be fonted text. Access to the text menu will be denied later in the program.

Access denied. Font files not found at start-up.

You are not being allowed to enter the Text menu because no font file was available to be loaded into memory at program start-up. See the previous entry in this section.

Inactive feature. Consult User's Manual.

The menu function which you are attempting to use has not been implemented beyond the stub routine stage in this version of Your Microcomputer 3D CAD Designer. See the next chapter for some guidance on enhancing the program's source code.

3D CAD Designer ready for your next command.

The program is idling, waiting for your next keyboard input. Press the Enter key to activate the currently highlighted menu bar selection, or press the left-arrow or right-arrow key to reposition the highlight bar along the main menu bar.

Insufficient memory available. Press any key.

During program start-up, the software could not find sufficient memory to establish a hidden buffer to support the Undo function. Before each drawing command, the existing screen image is saved to a hidden buffer, so it is ready to be copied back onto the screen in the event you use the Undo function. This error condition will only occur with a VGA, MCGA, or CGA, because both the EGA and Hercules use a hidden page from the on-board display memory as the hidden buffer. If you are running the program under the control of the QuickC or Turbo C editor, recompile the program as an EXE file and run from the operating system to free up more memory (see Chapter 2 for more on this).

Observable Condition: the shading seems to spill out of the facet being shaded and corrupts the entire 3D window.

This error is caused by the algorithm used to find the seed point to begin filling the facet. The algorithm uses geometry to find the center of the polygon on the screen, but two factors can work to make this seed point actually fall outside of the polygon on the 2D screen. First, rounding errors in the floating point library of the compiler can make the resulting integer coordinates miss when a facet which is barely visible is being considered. Second, the aliasing (stepping) of an oblique line on the display screen can cause the seed point to be drawn just outside the line, rather than right on it when a barely visible facet surface is encountered. Developers and serious programmers may contact the author directly to obtain work around source code to suppress this bug.

SYSTEM ERRORS

DOS Error Message: Memory allocation error. Cannot load COMMAND, system halted.

This condition occurs with some workalike graphics adapters running in an emulation mode, such as a VGA which is emulating a Hercules adapter. When Your Microcomputer 3D CAD Designer is shut down, the operating system cannot regain control because some pointers in low memory have been corrupted. The operating system is unable to find the starting address of COMMAND.COM in high memory, and can neither reload COMMAND.COM nor pass control to it. The immediate solution is to reboot your system. The long-term solution is out of your control because of bugs in the driver provided by the manufacturer of the graphics adapter. The error condition does not affect the performance of Your Microcomputer 3D CAD Designer, only your ability to cleanly return to the operating system after ending your drawing session.

DOS Error Message: FATAL: Internal stack failure. System Halted.

On some digitizing tablets, you can cause DOS's stack to become corrupted by holding down a keyboard key while simultaneously pressing a button on the crosshair cursor.

DOS Error Message: Drive not ready

You are using a 5.25-inch or 3.5-inch diskdrive and the door is open or the drive is empty. The error message itself might have corrupted the appearance of the display screen.

DOS Run-time Condition: your entire system locks up after you attempt to load a file

As discussed in Chapter 13 and Chapter 15, the source code for Your Microcomputer 3D CAD Designer contains no error-handlers for disk I/O. In this error condition, you have asked the program to load an image file which does not exist in the current directory. Because no method has been provided to recover from the file-not-found error, the system hangs.

DOS Run-time Condition: garbage appears on the screen after you load a file

You might have loaded an image into memory which was created while Your Microcomputer 3D CAD Designer was running in a different mode. An image created in the 640x350x16-color mode will load into the 640x200x16-color mode, but the result will be nonsense.

15

Programmer's Reference:
Your Microcomputer 3D CAD Designer

THIS CHAPTER describes how the 3D modeling and rendering program presented in Chapter 13 works from a programmer's point of view. The general algorithms and processes are described, and a module-by-module discussion of the source code functions is provided. Program idiosyncracies and potential areas for enhancement are discussed.

For the complete source code of Your Microcomputer 3D CAD Designer, refer back to Chapter 13. For a mini user's guide, refer back to Chapter 14.

HOW THE PROGRAM WORKS: An Overview

The program is driven by five general states: preparation of the menu system, running the menu system, maintaining the 3D state, producing graphics output, and managing disk I/O.

Preparation of the Menu System

The first task performed by the software is to create the graphical elements to be used by the interactive pull-down menu system. The graphics for the pull-down menus themselves are saved in RAM in graphic arrays, ready for later use. Other components, like the highlight bars, are also created and saved.

This activity takes place in module 1 of the source code (see Chapter 13). Some of the library-independent graphics routines located in module 3 are called during this process. In addition, a module 3 routine which allocates a block of memory in the far heap is called from module 1 in order to set aside memory in RAM for a backup page for the Undo function if a VGA, MCGA, or CGA graphics adapter is being used.

Module 1 is also responsible for detecting and initializing the best graphics mode for whatever graphics adapter is installed. It will abort the start-up process if a compatible graphics adapter is not found, such as an EGA with less than the industry-wide standard 256K of display RAM.

The final task of module 1 is to draw the sign-on screen and pass control to module 2. The program will not return again to module 1 until the session ends.

Running the Menu System

When module 2 receives control, the menu system is activated. The main loop controls the interface with the user at the menu bar level. This loop will pass control to the pull-down menu loop or the pushbutton loop when directed to do so by the user's keyboard input. Each of these loops will jump to a switcher at the appropriate time to decide which core routine must be called in order to carry out the wishes of the end-user.

The menu system is a curtain between the end-user and the core functions. The end-user does not call the core routines directly, but rather graphically manipulates cursors and highlight bars around on the display screen. What appears to be happening on the screen, and what is actually happening in the run-time code, are two quite different situations.

The menu system gives the user control over three core routine processes: maintaining the 3D state, producing graphics output, and managing disk I/O.

Maintaining the 3D State

The current shading color, the current yaw rotation of the scene, the current translation position of the sub-object—these are just a few of the conditions which describe the current 3D state.

The software behind the menu system keeps track of these variables and alters them as required to support keyboard input from the user. When the user presses the right-arrow key, for example, the software must increment the variable which describes the yaw rotation of the sub-object.

In addition to the 3D state, the menu system must also keep track of the graphics state, similar to the way the draw program presented in Chapter 8 does. This lower level state supports the higher level 3D state, of course.

Producing Graphics Output

The result of the user's work is graphical output: the contents of the 3D window. The menu system is responsible for passing control to the core 3D routines in such a way as to ensure that they can draw in the 3D window without worrying about drawing over a pull-down menu. The menu system does a smoke and mirrors act in jumping from its own graphics (the graphic arrays which are the menus) and the 3D graphics—and back again. It must also carefully manage a hidden graphics page, which is used to support the Undo function in the Scene menu.

Managing Disk I/O

The final state which is maintained by the program is that of disk input and output. The program uses the current drive and directory for all input and output, but permits the user to edit the names of files used for saving and loading images.

The menu system performs two fundamental services here. During a load, for example, the program must first find the image file and load it into memory. Next, it must move the data up into display memory on the graphics adapter.

ANALYSIS OF THE SOURCE CODE: Module 1

Module 1 of the source code contains the routines which create and save the menu graphics, create the sign-on screen, and handle general start-up overhead.

Compiler Directives

Note the constants in the Compiler Directives section. New compilers and graphics libraries have been defined in the expectation of possible conversion to these systems. The balance of this section of code is similar to the menu manager presented in Chapter 6 and the draw program presented in Chapter 8.

Function Prototypes

The section of code named "Function Prototypes" contains declarations for functions which are used by module 1. As the source code indicates, some of these routines are actually present in module 1, while others are present in module 2 or 3 but are called by module 1. Note the significant number of low-level, library-independent graphics routines in module 3 which are used by module 1 during preparation of screen graphics. All of the 3D routines are found in module 3, but are only called from module 2 (the menu system).

Declaration of Global Variables

The section of source code named "Global Variables" serves to declare and initialize variables that can be used by all the functions in module 1. Any of these variables that are declared again in the header of module 2 or module 3 can be also used by the routines in those modules, of course.

Many of the variables in this section of code are similar to the source code for the menu manager presented in Chapter 6 and the draw program presented in Chapter 8.

Also of interest in this section of code are the strings named char text1[ ] through char text15[ ]. These contain the various dialog prompts and error messages used by Your Microcomputer 3D CAD Designer at run-time.

Function Definitions

The remainder of the source code for module 1 is taken up by executable code.

main( )

The main( ) routine calls the functions which perform the preparation work for installation of the menu system. Its first step, however, is to call Graphics _Setup( ) to initialize the best graphics mode for the hardware being used.

Note the section of code which has been disabled with remark tokens. You can remove these tokens and the code will test the amount of available RAM when the program starts up. This piece of source code is very useful for monitoring memory usage during program development.

After main( ) has completed its work, it calls MenuBarLoop( ) in module 2 to manage the menu system.

SetParameters( )

The function named SetParameters( ) assigns values to variables which control the sizes, colors, and position of various elements of the menu system. These values are used during the initial preparation of the menu system graphics.

CreateBars( )

The function named CreateBars( ) creates the main menu bar, the help bar, and the current filename bar.

In each instance, the alphanumerics are first saved in a graphic array. Then the solid rectangle is drawn and the alphanumerics are XOR'd into the bar to produce the finished white-on-color graphic.

Note how the variable named text5 is used to hold a text string which is passed to the low-level text output routine, PutText( ), located in module 3.

CreateMenus( )

The function named CreateMenus( ) is responsible for creating each of the pull-down menus.

For each menu, the alphanumeric text is first saved in a graphic array. Then the color and border for the menu are drawn on the screen. The alphanumeric array is then XOR'd into the menu to create the finished image. The final graphic is again saved in a graphic array, ready for use when the user activates the menu system.

CreateHiBars( )

The function named CreateHiBars( ) draws and then saves in a graphic array the panning highlight bar for the menu bar, the scrolling highlight bar for the pull-down menus, and the graphic array which prepares the color swatch for the Settings menu. This routine also initializes a graphic array that will save the background before the color swatch is installed.

DrawScreen( )

The function named DrawScreen( ) is the workhorse of this module. Draw-Screen( ) creates the sign-on screen for Your Microcomputer 3D CAD Designer.

First, the background is created (brown in a 16-color mode, a gray shade in a 2-color mode). Note how the source code is specialized for each different graphics adapter.

Then the graphic arrays containing the main menu bar and the help bar are installed at the top and bottom of the screen, respectively.

Next, the dropshadow is drawn for the 3D window, followed by the window itself, of course.

DrawScreen then calls BackUp( ) to store a copy of the current screen in a hidden buffer, just in case the user's first act is to ask for a New function.

Finally, the code initializes a font and displays the banner for the program in the middle of the canvas area.

The routine's last act is to set up a full-screen viewport and return to its caller.

InitUndo

The InitUndo function calls a routine in module 3 to allocate memory for a hidden page to be used by the Undo function. If not enough RAM is available and a VGA, MCGA, or CGA is being used, the program will abort and a warning message will be issued. Refer to the user's guide in Chapter 14 if you encounter this situation at run-time.

Note how the far address of each bitmap buffer, expressed as a segment address and an offset address, is first stored into the structure named u1. Next, these two values are copied to separate variables named seg and off, which will be used by the movedata( ) statement later when pages are being moved back and forth between the hidden buffer and the screen.

Quit_Pgm( )

The function named Quit_Pgm( ) gracefully terminates the program. This routine can be activated when the user presses the Alt+X combination or when the user selects Shutdown from the Files menu.

FreeBlock( )

The function named FreeBlock( ) deallocates a block of memory from the far heap. This routine is called by DrawScreen( ) to free up memory after the main menu bar has been installed, for example.

Graphics_Setup( )

The function named Graphics_Setup( ) is the familiar auto-detect routine. You can trace the different variables defined during this function's run by referring back to SetParameters( ) near the beginning of the executable code in module 1.

GetFreeMemory( )

The function named GetFreeMemory( ) is the same algorithm used by the demonstration program presented in Chapter 2 and by the draw program presented in Chapter 8 to determine the amount of free memory at run-time. This routine will never be called unless you activate the appropriate section of remarked-out source code in DrawScreen( ).

Notice( )

The function named Notice( ) places a graphical copyright notice in the upper right corner of the menu sign-on screen.

ANALYSIS OF THE SOURCE CODE: Module 2

Module 2 of the source code contains the routines which manipulate the menu system, as well as the graphics routines which are the core functions of the program.

Function Prototypes

The section of source code named "Function Prototypes" declares functions which are called from module 2. Some of these functions are actually present in module 2, while others are found in either module 3 or module 1.

Declaration of Global Variables

The section of source code named "Global Variables" defines the variables which control the 3D state of the software. The remarks explain the purpose of each variable.

This section also uses the extern keyword to redeclare variables that have been already declared and initialized in module 1. This ensures that these variables can be used by all routines in module 2.

MenuBarLoop( )

The function named MenuBarLoop( ) is a loop which manages the main menu bar of the interface. It follows the algorithm introduced in Chapter 6.

The line label menuloop: indicates the beginning of the loop that manages the pull-down menus. It works by calling a routine named Scrolling( ).

Pay particular attention to the final dozen lines of code in this section. The switch( ) function is used to decide where to loop back to in the menu manager code, based upon which menu has been used, or whether or not the Esc key has been pressed and the user is simply backing out of a menu without using any of its functions.

Panning( )

The function named Panning( ) moves the highlight bar along the main menu bar of the menu system, ensuring proper wraparound at the end of the bar.

InstallMenu( )

The function named InstallMenu( ) is responsible for installing each of the pull-down menus.

UninstallMenu( )

The function named UninstallMenu( ) is responsible for tidying up before the user returns to the main menu bar.

PanMenu( )

The function named PanMenu( ) makes it possible to jump directly from one pull-down menu to another.

Scrolling( )

The function named Scrolling( ) controls scrolling of the highlight bar in any of the pull-down menus.

MenuChoices( )

The function named MenuChoices( ) is the latch between the menu system and the core graphics functions. Using a series of switch( ) statements, Menu-Choices( ) jumps to the appropriate core functions and calls 3D routines and low-level, library-independent graphics routines from module 3 as necessary.

It is illustrative also to see how the WindowOpen( ) and WindowClose( ) functions are called whenever graphics output is generated. These two functions set up and disable a viewport which has the same dimensions as the drawing canvas, thereby ensuring that all graphics are clipped at the edge of the drawing surface.

Later in this section of source code, StubRoutine( ) is used often as a place-holder for routines which have yet to be written, such as features of the Text and Create menus.

StubRoutine( )

The function named StubRoutine is called whenever the user asks for a feature which is not implemented semantically in the source code. StubRoutine( ) issues a standard message on the dialog line and then returns to the caller. In a unique case where the user wants to use the Text menu but no font file was found at program start-up, StubRoutine( ) issues a message specific to this situation.

MenuBarText( )

The function named MenuBarText( ) is called whenever the menu system wishes to display the message, "3D Designer ready."

ClearTextLine( )

The function named ClearTextLine( ) blanks the dialog text line. This routine uses #if and #elif preprocessor directives to determine which section of compiler-dependent code should be compiled. Note also how the code handles the special case of 9x14 characters used by the Hercules graphics adapter.

CheckForKey( )

The function named CheckForKey( ) checks to see if any keystrokes are waiting in the keyboard buffer. If so, CheckForKey( ) sets two variables which tell the caller whether the keystroke is a normal key or an extended key and what the ASCII value of the key is.

KeySwitch1( )

The function named KeySwitch1( ) is a switcher for keystrokes which are received at the menu bar level. In its current implementation, it displays the name of the key received on the upper right corner of the display screen. If Alt+X is pressed, you can see how the code will branch to a program shutdown.

KeySwitch2( )

The function named KeySwitch2( ) is a switcher for keystrokes that are received at the pull-down menu or pushbutton panel level.

Purge( )

The function named Purge( ) is used to empty the keyboard buffer. This function is handy to use whenever the user is leaving a menu function, in order to ensure that any unwanted keystrokes are not left in the buffer, where they might cause unwanted effects if read by the main menu bar, for example.

Purge( ) is also useful for preventing highlight bar run-on, also known as cursor run-on. If the user is holding down an arrow key to move a highlight bar, Purge( ) is repeatedly called after each step of the highlight bar. This means the highlight bar will stop moving the same instant that the user lifts their finger from the key.

EditName( )

The function named EditName( ) gives to the user the ability to edit the filename of images during the save or load process.

EditName( ) works by carefully keeping track of which character position is being edited and by copying any legal keystroke into that position with the line:

f3[position] = f1 1[0]

where f1 1[0] holds the ASCII value of the keystroke.

Note the use of multiple if statements to ensure that only characters which fall between certain ASCII values are accepted.

You can easily enhance this rudimentary editor to permit a wider range of legal keystrokes and to allow more editing features, such as a moveable highlighted cursor.

In its present implementation, EditName( ) will accept the currently-displayed filename if the Enter key is pressed. If the Esc key is pressed, the previous filename is restored and used. Note how the previous filename was stored in a temporary string near the beginning of this section of source code by the line:

strcpy(f12,f3);

EditColor( )

The function named EditColor( ) lets the user change the current shading color. This is basically a stripped-down version of the routine named EditColor( ) in Your Microcomputer SketchPad, presented in Chapter 8.

MakeSound( )

The function named MakeSound( ) generates a sound.

3D Executives

The section of source code titled "3D Executives" contains high-level 3D graphics routines which manage the 3D cursor, draw a fully-shaded cube or cylinder at any position and any size, change the camera angle, and so on. The low-level 3D formulas and 3D drawing routines are located in module 3.

CursorManager( )

The function named CursorManager( ) provides run-time control of the 3D cursor. It calls other routines to draw a new cursor as the user presses keys on the bat. It calls other routines to draw the fully-shaded box or cylinder at the appropriate position if the user presses the Enter key. It manages the 3D state by incrementing or decrementing the various sub-object rotation and translation factors, the various scene rotation and translation factors, and the various sub-object extrusion factors.

By examining the source code you can see that CursorManager( ) uses algorithms similar to the menu manager.

CamAngleMgr( )

The function named CamAngleMgr( ) provides run-time control of the viewing angle. As described in Chapter 14, the 3D environment can be pitched forward or back by the up-arrow and down-arrow keys, and can be yawed left or right by the left-arrow and right-arrow keys.

CamAngleMgr( ) keeps track of a viewchg variable and either adds it to or subtracts it from the appropriate heading variable. Note also how if statements are used to keep the scene from exceeding the vertical, although the yaw heading is permitted to rotate through a full 360-degree circle if the user so desires.

GetCubeCoords( )

The function GetCubeCoords( ) is the first stage in any session that draws the box in the 3D window. The function first retrieves the object coordinates which describe the current size of the box (extrusion). Next, GetCubeCoords( ) calls routines in module 3 to compute the world coordinates, the camera coordinates, and finally the display coordinates. Refer back to Chapter 12 for a discussion of these.

DrawCube( )

The function named DrawCube( ) actually draws the 3D parallelepiped at the current position of the 3D cursor in the 3D window. Note how it handles each of six different surfaces (facets) which make up the box.

For each facet it first uses camera coordinates to test to see if the surface is hidden or visible. If hidden, it aborts and jumps to the next surface. Next, the display coordinates and world coordinates are loaded into global variables which will be used by subsequent routines called by DrawCube( ).

DrawCube( ) then calls FindCenter( ) to determine the geometric 3D center of the facet being drawn. This will be used as a seed point for later floodfills. Then DrawFacet( ) is called to draw a solid facet.

The appropriate level of illumination is then calculated by calling GetBrightness( ) in module 3. SetShading( ) uses bit tiling to fill the facet to the appropriate shade. Finally, a call to DitherFacet( ) will redraw the edges of the facet using a line style which will camouflage the border of the surface.

RELATED MATERIAL

A thorough discussion of 3D modeling and rendering techniques for QuickC and Turbo C may be found in another of the author's books, *High-Performance CAD Graphics in C*, book #3059, published March 1989, ISBN 0-8306-9359-9, available through stores that sell good computer books or order direct from TAB Books by referring to listings at the end of this book.

DrawCylinder( )

The function named DrawCylinder( ) works similarly to DrawCube( ) described earlier, except that it draws a 3D cylinder.

Because a cylinder is much more complicated to construct than a parallelepiped, DrawCylinder( ) calls four functions to get the job done: GetCylObjCoords( ), DrawCylFacet( ), DrawCylNearEnd( ), and DrawCylFarEnd( ).

ANALYSIS OF THE SOURCE CODE: Module 3

Module 3 of the source code contains the low-level device-independent 3D routines, the low-level library-independent graphics routines, and the disk I/O routines.

Function Prototypes

The section of code named "Function Prototypes" declares functions called by code in module 3. Most of these routines actually reside in module 3; only four external functions are called by module 3 code.

Declaration of Global Variables

The section of code named "Global Variables" redeclares variables that were declared and initializes in modules 1 or 2, thereby ensuring that routines in module 3 can also use those variables.

3D Routines

The section of code named "3D Routines" contains device-independent 3D graphics routines that will operate correctly in any screen mode.

Init3D( )

The function named Init3D( ) initializes the parameters used by the 3D state. These parameters control the location of the light source, the rotation and translation of the scene, and the rotation and translation of each sub-object, among other things.

SetRatios( )

The function named SetRatios( ) is called once at program start-up to calculate some scaling parameters which are used to map the 800x600 3D world to the resolution of whatever screen mode is being used.

DrawCursor( )

The function named DrawCursor( ) physically draws the 3D cursor on the screen. It makes frequent calls to the low-level, library-independent graphics routines.

DrawGrndPlane( )

The function named DrawGrndPlane( ) physically draws the 3D phantom scene cursor which is on the screen while the user is adjusting the viewpoint.

VisibilityTest( )

The function named VisibilityTest( ) uses vector math to determine which side of a facet is facing the viewpoint. The result is returned to the caller in a variable named visible.

GetNewObjParams( )

The function named GetNewObjParams( ) calculates the angles and distances which other routines will use to draw a sub-object in the 3D environment. This function is called each time the 3D cursor is moved. Each new occurence of the cursor is called an *instance*.

SetObjAngle( )

The function named SetObjAngle( ) calculates the new sine and cosine values for a new instance of a sub-object. These values are used by the 3D formulas.

SetCamAngle( )

The function named SetCamAngle( ) calculates the new sine and cosine values for a new viewpoint. These values are used by the 3D formulas.

PutObjToScreen( )

The function named PutObjToScreen( ) is actually a macro which calls other lower level 3D routines to take a set of coordinates through the evolution from object coordinates, world coordinates, camera coordinates, image plane coordinates, and display coordinates. See Chapter 12 for more on this.

PutWorldToScreen( )

The function named PutWorldToScreen( ) is also a macro. It takes a set of coordinates from the world and puts them on the display.

GetWorldCoords( )

The function named GetWorldCoords( ) converts object coordinates to world coordinates.

GetCameraCoords( )

The function named GetCameraCoords( ) converts world coordinates to camera coordinates.

GetImageCoords( )

The function named GetImageCoords( ) converts camera coordinates to image plane coordinates. These coordinates are 2D but they are not yet ready to be plotted on the screen.

GetScreenCoords( )

The function named GetScreenCoords( ) converts image plane coordinates to display coordinates, scaled and clipped to fit the screen.

DrawFacet( )

The function named DrawFacet( ) draws a four-sided polygon. Note how the routine first fills the area in a unique color in order to ensure that the background is always overwritten during any subsequent floodfill. If a black-and-white mode is in effect, the routine calls MakeBwMatte( ) to perform this feat with bitblt manipulations and a bounding rectangle.

FindCenter( )

The function named FindCenter( ) uses diagonal geometry to find the center of a four-sided polygon, expressed in camera coordinates.

GetBrightness( )

The function named GetBrightness( ) uses the cross product of two vectors to determine the amount of illumination falling upon a vector whose three camera coordinates have been provided to the routine.

SetShading( )

The function named SetShading( ) uses the results from GetBrightness( ) to set the appropriate fill pattern and line style for the facet. The facet is filled at this point.

DitherFacet( )

The function named DitherFacet( ) uses the line style set by SetShading( ) to redraw the outline of the polygon, thereby ensuring that the outline matches the filled interior.

PolyMiniMax( )

The function named PolyMiniMax( ) calculates the coordinates of a bounding rectangle for a four-sided facet when a black-and-white mode is being used. This bounding rectangle will be manipulated as a graphic array to set up a matte so the floodfill will correctly fill any subsequent facet drawn in this region. This routine is not used if a VGA or EGA is present.

MakeBwMatte( )

The function named MakeBwMatte( ) makes a matte for the facet to be drawn. By using consecutive saves and writes of graphic arrays using boolean logic, a hole in the background is punched out, ready to receive the new polygon. This ensures that the floodfill for the shading will not be defeated by pre-existing background lines inside the facet.

InitBwMattes( )

The function named InitBwMattes( ) allocates memory in the far heap for the two graphic arrays that are used to create a matte when a black-and-white mode is being used.

LIBRARY-INDEPENDENT GRAPHICS ROUTINES

The section of source code named "Library-Independent Graphics Routines" contains functions for low-level graphics output. Each routine expects to receive the parameters it needs from the caller, except for some graphics state conditions, of course.

Note the heavy use of #if and #elif preprocessor directives in this section to ensure that the code can be compiled with either QuickC or Turbo C. If you are using a third-party graphics library like HALO, Essential Graphics, MetaWINDOW, or Lattice C's GFX, you can easily add library-dependent code to this section. Be sure to also set the appropriate constant in the header of each source file to tell the compiler which code to compile.

Disk Input/Output Routines

The section of code named "Disk Input/Output Routines" contains the functions which save a binary image file to disk and which load a previously-saved binary image file from disk.

These routines use the algorithms introduced earlier in Chapter 5. Remember, this I/O is not error-trapped. Your computer will likely hang if you attempt to load a non-existant file. No feedback will be reported if the routines run out of disk space while saving an image. See Appendix C for helpful tips on writing your own error-handlers.

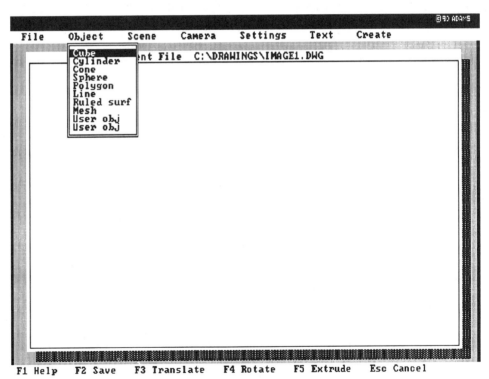

Fig. 15-1. Expandable capabilities of the Object menu.

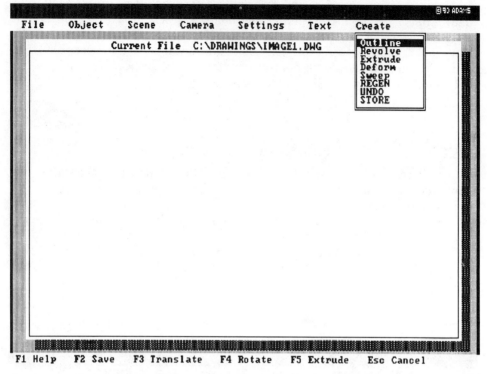

Fig. 15-2. User creation of original 3D solids by revolve, extrusion, sweep, and other deformations can be programmed into the interface provided by the Create menu.

KNOWN BUGS AND POTENTIAL ENHANCEMENTS

A number of potential enhancements would make Your Microcomputer 3D CAD Designer a more powerful drawing tool.

First, you might wish to expand the capabilities of the Object menu. See FIG. 15-1. Adding functions to support sub-objects like a sphere, polygon, line, ruled surface, and mesh are not difficult if the existing source code structure is expanded along its existing lines. Refer to the books mentioned in the sidebars throughout this text for additional information about 3D programming.

Second, you might wish to give the user the ability to create customized sub-objects or primitives. See FIG. 15-2. The Create menu suggests how this might be done. The user first selects Outline to create the silhouette to be revolved, extruded, or deformed (swept). Next, the resulting primitive is stored in a database by selecting Store from the Create menu.

Third, you might wish to add a simple internal database to this program. See FIG. 15-3. By storing appropriate coordinates and a token to indicate the type of primitive being drawn, you can readily retrieve these variables and redraw the object if the user selects Regen from the Scene menu. Regen is, after all, simply a section of source code which draws the object in the same manner as the core graphics code which created the object on the screen in the first place.

Fourth, in its current implementation, the program offers only a single Undo buffer. You could easily modify the code to initialize and manage three or four buffers, depending upon available memory. This would make it possible for the user to Undo a series of drawing commands, not just one.

Fifth, you might wish to consider adding modules from the PCX Programmer's Toolkit to provide support for .PCX image files. These files can be exported to desktop publishing systems, other drawing programs, and some word processing programs. The Toolkit also provides image library management routines. See Chapter 5 for more discussion about the Toolkit.

Sixth, you might wish to add support for the 256-color mode. QuickC supports the 320x200x256-color mode of the VGA. Turbo C supports the 640x480x256-color mode of the 8514/A graphics adapter.

Seventh, you might decide to alter the algorithm which determines the seed point for filling each facet. As described in Chapter 14, idiosyncracies in rounding of floating-point variables and aliasing (stair-stepping) of diagonal lines can cause a seed point which should lie on or near a boundary to be placed just outside the facet by the math routines. This, of course, causes the floodfill to corrupt the entire screen. You can test this bug by drawing the cylinder in a number of angles. Turbo C offers a fill routine which considers the array of vertices and which would overcome this problem. Many of the third-party graphics libraries discussed in Appendix B offer similar fill algorithms.

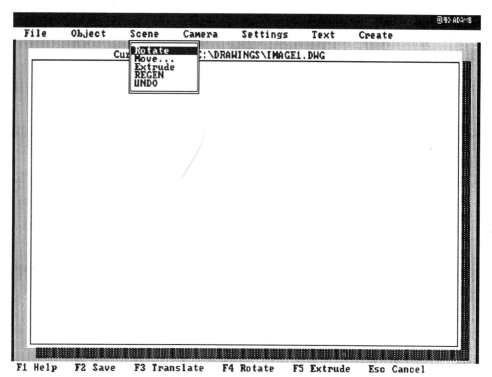

Fig. 15-3. Only the REGEN core function requires enhancement in the Scene menu.

Appendices

A

For the Beginner:
How to Start the Demonstration Programs

FOR THE TYRO—the inexperienced beginner—QuickC and Turbo C can be intimidating and confusing. If you have no C programming experience, or if you have never used QuickC or Turbo C, this appendix gives you the guidance you need to get the demonstration programs up and running.

If you are using QuickC, read the section entitled "Using Your QuickC Compiler."

If you are using Turbo C, read the section entitled "Using Your Turbo C Compiler."

NO-HASSLE GUIDE

This appendix assumes only one precondition: that you have been able to install either QuickC or Turbo C on your computer system. Be certain that you are using version 2.00 of QuickC or version 2.0 of Turbo C. Although most of the demonstration programs in this book will run on earlier versions, some will refuse to compile because they rely upon features found in the newer versions of QuickC and Turbo C.

Both the QuickC and Turbo C installation processes usually get the job done with a minimum of fuss, but if you are still experiencing difficulties, there are a number of things you can do.

First, contact the software dealer where you purchased your compiler and ask for help.

Second, ask a friend, associate, or coworker who has computer experience to help you. Even users (non-programmers) with substantive computing experience can handle the duties involved in following QuickC's and Turbo C's installation process.

Third, if you are a member of a user's group—or even if you are not—you can usually get help fast by getting in touch with a group in your area.

Fourth, if you are really stuck, telephone the support line provided in the documentation for QuickC and Turbo C.

USING YOUR QuickC COMPILER

You should be using a fixed disk (also called a hard drive). Although Microsoft implies that QuickC 2.00 can be used with a dual floppy disk drive system, such an arrangement is like going to sea in a dinghy—without lifejackets; and it is not Charlie Tuna out there, it is Jaws.

Before you start—If you are using a Hercules graphics adapter, you must load a special graphics driver before you start QuickC. This driver, called MSHERC-.COM, is supplied on the QuickC product disks. You can load the driver by typing MSHERC at the operating system prompt. It is a memory-resident graphics driver. If you are using a VGA, EGA, MCGA, or CGA graphics adapter, you do not need to perform this preparatory step.

Step One—If you are using the companion disk to this book, copy the C source file, DETECT.C, to the appropriate directory on your fixed disk. This directory is likely to be C:\QC2\SOURCE if you followed QuickC's installation process. If you are not using the companion disk, you will be typing in the listing later.

Step Two—From the operating system prompt, set the current directory to the directory where the C source file is stored.

Step Three—Start the QuickC editor by typing in the full pathname plus QC and pressing the Enter key. If you are typing in the listing from the book, do so now. Then press the Alt key to activate the menu bar, choose the File menu and save the source file.

Step Four—Choose the Options menu from the main menu bar. Select Full Menus.

Step Five—Choose the Options menu from the main menu bar. Select Make. Use the left-arrow key to choose Debug. Use the Tab key to choose Compiler Flags. Activate the following tokens: medium memory model, level 1 warnings, MS extensions, line numbers only, pointer check, incremental compile, full optimizations, and stack check.

Step Six—Choose the Options menu from the main menu bar. Select Make. Use the Tab key to choose Linker Flags. Activate the following tokens: extended dictionary, stack size 4096, CodeView info, and incremental link.

Step Seven—Choose the Options menu from the main menu bar. Select Display. Set the Tab stops to 2.

Step Eight—Choose the File menu from the main menu bar. Choose Open... and select DETECT.C. If you do not see a listing for DETECT.C, then you should return to the operating system and copy the DETECT.C file to the directory that will be current while the QuickC editor is running.

Step Nine—When the actual source code appears on the screen, press F5 to command the compiler to compile, link, and run the program. You will be required to wait a short time while the compiler prepares the program to be executed. If any problems arise during the compilation and linking process, the compiler will advise you.

Step Ten—If the compiler warns you that it cannot find the #include files or library files, choose the Options menu from the main menu bar. Select Environment and type in the name of the appropriate directories.

Step Eleven: Success!—You should now be looking at the output of the DETECT.C demonstration program. You can use the above steps to run any of the other single-module program listings. If you wish to run one of the multiple-module demonstration programs, you must create a .MAK file that tells QuickC which modules to collect together to create the finished executable program. See Chapter 2 and Chapter 6 for more about this.

USING YOUR Turbo C COMPILER

You should be using a fixed disk (also called a hard drive), although Turbo C 2.00 can be run from a dual floppy disk drive system. The following steps assume a fixed disk is being used. Simply change the disk drive assignments if you wish to run from floppy disks.

Step One—If you are using the companion disk to this book, copy the C source file, DETECT.C, to the appropriate directory on your fixed disk. This directory is likely to be C:\TC2\BIN if you followed Turbo C's installation process. If you are not using the companion disk, you will be typing in the listing later.

Step Two—From the operating system prompt, set the current directory to the directory where you want Turbo C to store the resulting EXE programs that you create.

Step Three—Start the Turbo C editor by typing in the full pathname plus TC and pressing the Enter key. If you are typing in the listing from the book, do so now. Then press F10 to activate the menu bar, choose the File menu, choose Write To, and save the source file.

Step Four—Press F10 to activate the main menu bar. Choose the Options menu. Choose Compiler and set the model to medium. (Remember, during the original installation process, you chose the medium memory model. If you did not choose the medium model, then the appropriate runtime libraries will not be available on your fixed disk.)

Step Five—Choose the Options menu on the main menu bar. Choose Linker and turn on the following tokens: graphics library, stack warning, and case-sensitive link.

Step Six—Choose the Options menu on the main menu bar. Choose Environment and set Tab size to 2.

Step Seven—Choose the Options menu on the main menu bar. Choose Directories and set the first four entries as follows: C:\TC2\INCLUDE, C:\TC2\LIB, C:\TC2\SOURCE, and C:\TC2\BIN.

Step Eight—Choose the File menu on the main menu bar. Select Load and then press the Enter key twice to see a directory listing containing the DETECT.C source file. If it is not there, go back to Step One. Select DETECT.C and load the file.

Step Nine—Use the Turbo C editor to move to line 34 of the source code. Change "#define Compiler QuickC" to "#define Compiler TurboC". (Do not type in the " quote marks.)

Step Ten—Choose the Run menu from the main menu bar. Select Run and press the Enter key to command the compiler to compile, link, and run the program. If any problems arise during compilation and linking, Turbo C will alert you.

Step Eleven—If the compiler warns you that it cannot find the #include files or library files, choose the Options menu from the main menu bar, go to the Directories option and type in the name of the directories required.

A CLOSER LOOK

Your finished program will appear to load correctly but will do nothing at runtime if the system cannot find the appropriate graphics driver when the program starts up. The system must be able to find EGAVGA.BGI if you are using a VGA or EGA. It must find CGA.BGI if you are using a CGA, or HERC.BGI if you are using a Hercules graphics adapter.

Step Twelve—If the program does nothing on the screen at runtime, it probably couldn't find the appropriate .BGI graphics driver at start-up. Ensure that the appropriate graphics driver for your graphics adapter is in the C:\TC2\SOURCE directory where Turbo C can find it. Use EGAVGA.BGI if you are using a VGA or EGA; use CGA.BGI if you are using a CGA; use HERC.BGI if you are using a Hercules graphics adapter.

Step Thirteen: Success!—You should now be looking at the output of the DETECT.C demonstration program. You can use the above steps to run any of the other single-module programs. Do not forget to change the "#define Compiler TurboC" line in the COMPILER DIRECTIVES section of each C source file. If you wish to run one of the multiple-module programs, you must create a .PRJ file that tells Turbo C which modules to collect together to create the finished executable program. See Chapter 2 and Chapter 6 for more about this.

B

Using a Graphics Library:
MetaWINDOW, QuickWINDOW/C, TurboWINDOW/C, HALO 88, Essential Graphics, Lattice CGFX

GRAPHICS LIBRARIES are like word processors: users love to hate them; but it is also a love-hate relationship—and every C graphics programmer has a favorite graphics library. If you earned your graphics wings using the built-in graphics library of QuickC or Turbo C, chances are that you are happy with the powerful, versatile, and reliable features of that library; but many C programmers' first taste of graphics was via a third-party library like MetaWINDOW, HALO, Essential Graphics, Lattice C GFX, or others.

FACT

It matters not which graphics library you use, but how you use the graphics library you have. As the proverb goes, it is the poor craftsperson who blames the tool.

If you prefer to use a third-party library, this appendix gives you the information you need to painlessly convert the program listings in the main body of the book.

Alternatively, if your programming experience is centered around the built-in libraries of QuickC or Turbo C, this appendix will expose to you some of the highly specialized features of third-party libraries. Perhaps your interest will be aroused enough to try one of these exciting third-party libraries for yourself—perhaps not.

THE CHOICES

Although not a comprehensive list, the graphics libraries (or graphics toolkits) discussed in this appendix are: MetaWINDOW 3.4b, QuickWINDOW/C 3.4b, TurboWINDOW/C 3.4b—all from Metagraphics Software Corporation, HALO 88 1.00.04 from Media Cybernetics, Inc., Essential Graphics 3.0 from South Mountain Software Inc., and the built-in GFX graphics library of Lattice C 6.0 from Lattice, Incorporated.

Each graphics library has a few specialties at which it shines—and the decision to buy often revolves around these finely tuned specialties. Essential Graphics, for example, excels at business graphics, charts, and diagrams. Lattice C's bragging rights revolve around practicality, ease of use, reliability, and a no-nonsense syntax. HALO 88's superb support for a gamut of graphics adapters, dot matrix printers, laser printers—in addition to its very polished selection of flashy functions, including scanner support—makes it a strong contender for use in applications that must be portable. MetaWINDOW's well thought-out approach to windows and viewports (they call them ports, bitmaps, and images), its good documentation, and its support for a broad array of different graphics adapters (and modes) makes it a library difficult to ignore.

WHICH IS BEST?

This author is often asked which graphics library is best. The right answer, of course, is easily arrived at. If the programmer asking the question already has a favorite toolkit, then that is the one the author recommends. As the old saw goes, it matters not so much what you've got, but how well you use it; and there is a lot to be said in favor of a graphics library with which you are already familiar. The sweat equity that you have built up as you learned the undocumented idiosyncracies of your favorite graphics library is a valuable asset in your toolbox of programming skills.

On the other hand, if the programmer has no clear favorite, then the best choice is the graphics library which offers the strongest features in areas most important to the application program being developed—and which does not suffer from any major deficiencies in areas critical to the project. In this context, the author has recommended at one time or another each one of the libraries discussed in this appendix, including the built-in libraries of QuickC and Turbo C.

COMPATIBILITY

You might be surprised to learn that there are many fundamental similarities in the libraries discussed here. As Table B-1 shows, all of the generic, library-independent graphics routines used in the source code for Your Microcomputer SketchPad (Chapter 8) and Your Microcomputer 3D CAD Designer (Chapter 13) can be easily mapped to the routines provided by third-party graphics libraries. In some cases the only significant difference between the six libraries shown in Table B-1 is the name of the function. In other cases, some libraries outshine their competitors.

The generic routine SetHue( ) is a good example. This function maps directly to _setcolor( ) in QuickC and to setcolor( ) in Turbo C. MetaWINDOW, Quick-WINDOW/C, and TurboWINDOW/C implement the function as PenColor( ). HALO 88 implements the same function as setcolor( ). Lattice C 6.0 and Essential Graphics 3.0 do not have an explicit function to change the current pen color, opting instead to set the color dynamically when other graphics output routines are called.

All of the libraries provide the cornerstone graphics functions such as DrawLine( ), SetFill( ), DrawCircle( ), WriteToPage( ), and others. There are some pleasant surprises, however. HALO 88 and Lattice C offer built-in functions to copy a graphics page from one buffer to another. HALO 88 even offers a built-in function to initialize a buffer in RAM to store a graphics page.

Comparison of Graphics Library Syntax

Demo programs	QuickC 2.00	Turbo C 2.0	MetaWINDOW 3.4b	HALO 88 1.00,04	Lattice C 3.4 & 6.0	Essential 3.0
Graphics_Setup();	_setvideomode-rows();	initgraph();	InitGrafix();	initgraphics();	init_gfx_struct(); screen();	initgraf();
SetHue();	_setcolor();	setcolor();	PenColor();	setcolor();	[dynamic]	[dynamic]
SetLine();	_setlinestyle();	setlinestyle();	DefineDash();	deflnstyle(); setlnstyle();	[dynamic]	set_line_style();
SetFill();	_setfillmask();	setfillstyle(); setfillpattern();	DefinePattern();	defhatchstyle(); sethatchstyle();	[dynamic]	htdefind(); htdefst();
SetPosition();	_moveto();	moveto();	MoveTo();	movabs();	—	set_base();
DrawDot();	_setpixel();	putpixel();	SetPixel();	ptabs();	pset();	eg_dot();
DrawLine();	_lineto();	lineto();	LineTo();	lnabs();	line();	eg_line(); eg_line2();
DrawBorder();	_rectangle();	rectangle();	FrameRect();	box();	line();	eg_rectangle();
DrawPanel();	_rectangle();	bar();	PaintRect();	bar();	line();	eg_rectangle();
DrawCircle();	_ellipse();	circle();	FrameOval();	cir();	circle();	eg_circle();

Table B-1. Comparison of syntax used by popular graphics libraries. (Not all vendors' products are described here. Some syntax is version-specific and may change in newer versions.)

Demo programs	QuickC 2.00	Turbo C 2.0	MetaWINDOW 3.4b	HALO 88 1.00,04	Lattice C 3.4 & 6.0	Essential 3.0
DrawDisk();	_ellipse();	circle(); floodfill();	PaintOval();	fcir();	circle(); fastfill();	eg_circle(); sfill();
DrawEllipse();	_ellipse();	ellipse();	FrameOval();	ellipse();	ellipse();	eg_ellipse();
DrawCurve();	—	—	—	polycrel();	—	—
Fill();	_floodfill();	floodfill();	FillPoly(); PaintPoly();	flood2(); fill();	fastfill(); paint();	sfill();
BlankPage();	_clearscreen();	cleardevice();	EraseRect();	clr(); fclr();	cls();	clearscr();
MemBlock();	_fmalloc(); _imagesize();	farmalloc(); imagesize();	ImageSize();	inqpflen();	get_pic();	calcbyts();
FreeBlock();	_ffree();	farfree();	HardCopy();	[compiler]	free_pic();	[compiler]
GetBlock();	_getimage();	getimage();	ReadImage();	movefrom();	get_pic();	get();
PutXOR();	_putimage();	putimage();	WriteImage();	moveto();	put_pic();	put();
PutPSET();	_putimage();	putimage();	WriteImage();	moveto();	put_pic();	put();
PutAND();	_putimage();	putimage();	WriteImage();	moveto();	put_pic();	put();
PutText();	_outtext();	outtextxy();	DrawString();	ftext();	puts_font();	fhatsay();
SetTextRowCol();	_settext- position();	moveto();	MoveTo();	ftlocate();	locate();	fcurloc();
InitHiddenPage();	_fmalloc();	farmalloc();	HardCopy();	buf32(); buf128();	—	[compiler]
BackUp();	movedata();	movedata();	HardCopy();	insave();	copy_video_pages();	copypage() copyfmem()
Restore();	movedata();	movedata();	HardCopy();	imrest();	copy_video_pages();	copypage() copytmem()
WindowOpen();	_setviewport();	setviewport();	MovePortTo(); PortSize();	setviewport();	open_view();	setview();
WindowClose();	_setviewport();	setviewport();	MovePortTo(); PortSize();	setviewport();	close_view();	setview();
SaveImage();	[compiler]	[compiler]	HardCopy();	gwrite();	get_fpic();	scrtodsk();
LoadImage();	[compiler]	[compiler]	HardCopy();	gread();	put_fpic();	dsktoscr();
WriteToPage();	_setactivepage();	setactivepage();	SetBitmap();	setscreen();	set_video_pages();	grefpag();
DisplayPage();	_setvisualpage();	setvisualpage();	SetDisplay();	display();	set_video_pages();	gdisppag();
DumpToPrinter();	[compiler]	[compiler]	HardCopy();	gprint();	[compiler]	devcdump();

HOW TO ADAPT THE PROGRAM LISTINGS

If you are converting the program listings in this book to your favorite third-party graphics library, you may well find that Table B-1 is the only reference you need—along with the technical manuals for your graphics library, of course.

If you are converting a program listing that uses generic, library-independent graphics routines, then you can focus your attention on the first column in Table B-1 and on the column for your particular library. Program listings that use library-independent graphics routines are: the menu manager shell from Chapter 6, the full-length paint program from Chapter 8, and the full-length 3D CAD program from Chapter 13.

_____ CAUTION _____

Adapt one of the shorter program listings to run with your graphics library before you tackle a major program.

If you are converting a program listing that uses #if and #elif directives to switch between QuickC graphics and Turbo C graphics, then you can focus your attention on either the QuickC column or the Turbo C column and on the column for your particular library. You might find it prudent to adapt one of the shorter demonstration programs before you tackle Your Microcomputer SketchPad or Your Microcomputer 3D CAD Designer.

Take care to replace the appropriate #include statements at the start of the program to ensure that the correct header files for your particular graphics library are used. Clearly, you will not be needing QuickC's GRAPH.H file or Turbo C's GRAPHICS.H file. In fact, some of the constants defined in the QuickC and Turbo C header file might conflict with constants or variables used by the third-party graphics library, although this is unlikely.

Essential Graphics, HALO 88, and Lattice C each provide built-in functions to save a screen image to disk in standard file formats. Functions are also provided to load in an image from disk, of course.

Essential Graphics even offers a function to dump a screen image to a dot matrix printer, while HALO 88 offers a built-in driver for scanners.

Clearly, a careful review of Table B-1 is a requisite for any C programmer considering acquisition of a third-party graphics library. As a prudent purchaser, you would also scrutinize the sales literature (features list) available from each software publisher before you make your final decision. Word of mouth referrals from satisfied (or dissatisfied) users are also helpful. And don't forget to consider the royalty arrangements—or lack thereof—payable to each publisher, keeping in mind that royalties are not necessarily such a bad thing if the library offers built-in features that save you weeks, perhaps months, of programming effort.

MetaWINDOW, QuickWINDOW/C, TurboWINDOW/C

Here are some of the major points to consider when converting the program listings in the book to run with MetaWINDOW 3.4b or newer. This discussion applies also to QuickWINDOW/C and TurboWINDOW/C.

The documentation for MetaWINDOW (see FIG. B-1) is very well presented. If you are already familiar with the library, the only reference you will likely need while adapting the program listings is Table B-1.

Initializing the Graphics Mode

MetaWINDOW offers a broader array—and a more explicitly defined selection—of supported graphics adapters. The InitGrafix( ) function, for example, permits initialization of the standard VGA, EGA, MCGA, CGA, and Hercules modes supported by QuickC and Turbo C, as well as manufacturer-dependent modes such as the 720x352x2-color mode of the Tecmar Graphics Master, the 710x410x16-color mode of the Video-7 VEGA Deluxe, the 736x1008x2-color mode of the MDS Genius Adaptor, the 360x350x4-color mode of the IBM PC-3270 adapter, and many more.

The InitGrafix( ) function returns 0 if successful, a negative value if unsuccessful, so you can employ the same autodetect algorithm used in the program listings in this book to support an impressive range of graphics hardware.

Line Drawing

MetaWINDOW uses the MoveTo( ) function to reposition the current drawing position. This corresponds to the generic graphics routine SetPosition( ) in the program listings. QuickC uses _moveto( ), while Turbo C uses moveto( ).

Fig. B-1. MetaWINDOW 3.4b programming reference guide.

MetaWINDOW's LineTo( ) function operates the same as the generic graphics routine DrawLine( ). This maps to QuickC's _lineto( ) function, and to Turbo C's lineto( ) procedure.

The color of the line must be set in advance by a call to MetaWINDOW's PenColor( ) function. The line will be drawn in a style defined by the DefineDash( ) function and activated by the PenDash( ) procedure. Refer to the user's manual for a listing of seven built-in line styles available to the PenDash( ) function. You use DefineDash( ) to redefine one of these default styles to a pattern of your own design.

Advanced Line Drawing

A major advantage offered by MetaWINDOW is its ability to draw lines (and other entities) using boolean logic. Rather than merely drawing a line, you can change the graphics state by a call to RasterOp( ) and tell MetaWINDOW to exclusive-or, replace, or invert the pixels being written. Clearly, this has significant performance advantages for managing your own cursors in both 2D and 3D applications.

Creating Fill Patterns

MetaWINDOW offers 32 built-in fill patterns, illustrated in appendix B of the user's manual. The first eight patterns (0 through 7) are reserved for the library, but the remaining 24 styles can be redefined by the programmer by calling the procedure, DefinePattern( ). Like QuickC and Turbo C, patterns are defined via an 8x8 matrix, although MetaWINDOW offers a few more bells and whistles for the advanced C programmer.

The area fill routines provided in the MetaWINDOW toolkit are non-destructive, like QuickC. This means that you can layer colors and patterns on top of each other to create interesting cumulative effects.

Area Fill

The two fill functions offered by MetaWINDOW are FillPoly( ) and PaintPoly( ). They use an array of polygon vertices to control the filling operation. Although this algorithm means faster fill operations with fewer runtime errors, it is not compatible with the fill routines of QuickC and Turbo C used in the program listings in this book. You will have to maintain an array of the vertices which define the area to be filled. You can disregard the seed points in the program listings, of course.

Blanking the Screen

Although other methods are available, the function which provides the most precise control is EraseRect( ). This corresponds roughly to the _clearscreen( ) function in QuickC and the cleardevice( ) procedure in Turbo C.

Bitblt Operations: Manipulating Arrays

MetaWINDOW's array manipulators are well designed and do not pose any difficulties. ReadImage( ) and WriteImage( ) are used to save a portion of the screen to an array and to write an array to the screen, respectively. The arguments to WriteImage( ) control the boolean logic during the write process. Like QuickC and Turbo C, MetaWINDOW offers an ImageSize( ) function to calculate the size of the array required to store the rectangular image being stored, although you are still responsible for using your compiler to explicity initialize the memory block to hold the array data.

Hidden Page Operations

The routines used in the program listings in the book will work with MetaWINDOW. The movedata( ) function of QuickC and Turbo C is still the method to be used.

Image Save/Load Operations

The routines provided in the program listings in the book will work with MetaWINDOW. The movedata( ) function of QuickC and Turbo C gets the job done.

Active Page Operations

To set the active, written-to graphics page, use MetaWINDOW's SetBitmap( ) function. To set the displayable page, use the SetDisplay( ) procedure. It is important to note that MetaWINDOW supports up to two graphics pages, defined by the arguments GrafPg0 and GrafPg1.

Viewports

MetaWINDOW possesses advanced viewport and windowing operations, far surpassing the routines used in the demonstration programs in this book. A familiarity with the advanced features offered by MetaWINDOW's MovePortTo( ), PortSize( ), and other procedures will give your original programs real pizazz. At a basic level, however, MetaWINDOW's MovePortTo( ) and PortSize( ) roughly correspond to the generic graphics routines WindowOpen( ) and WindowClose( ) used in the program listings in this book.

Vector Fonts

MetaWINDOW's stroked font capabilities are indeed impressive. In addition, a separately available option called MetaFONTS can be purchased for even more versatility and power. SetFont( ) is used to select the active text style. TextFace( ) chooses normal, bold, italic, underline, strikeout, proportional spacing, and other flashy parameters. TextMode( ) sets the boolean operation to control the writing operation, including replace, overlay, invert, and erase. TextPath( ) controls the writing direction: left to right, right to left, up to down, or down to up.

Text is actually placed on the screen by the DrawString( ) function and the DrawChar( ) procedure.

The Working Environment

MetaWINDOW, QuickWINDOW/C, and TurboWINDOW/C are memory-resident libraries that are accessed by an interrupt. The driver is loaded by your application program at start-up. This means that all the graphics routines are loaded, no matter how many or how few are called by your program.

Metagraphics Software Corporation provides purchasers of their libraries with the royalty-free right to distribute the driver with the programmer's application program, provided that the library's copright notice is displayed at start-up. If you prefer to actually link the graphics library routines into your finished EXE file, then you might wish to purchase the MetaWINDOW/Plus graphics library, which involves distribution royalties, however.

Other Noteworthy features

Two additional MetaWINDOW features are worthy of mention. First, MetaWINDOW provides an impressive selection of zoombit procedures. This gives you the ability to enlarge portions of the screen, just like you have seen in commercial paint programs. Second, MetaWINDOW provides object selection and object proximity capabilities, whereby your program can tell if a point is near a certain already-drawn entity, for example, just like you have seen in commercial CADD drafting programs.

Clearly, if your programming project requires these capabilities, MetaWINDOW can save you weeks of programming effort.

ESSENTIAL GRAPHICS

Here are some of the major points to consider when converting the program listings in the book to run with Essential Graphics 2.0 or newer. If you are already familiar with the library (see FIG. B-2), the only additional reference you will likely need while adapting the program listings is Table B-1.

Initializing the Graphics Mode

Essential Graphics uses the initgraf( ) function to set up the graphics environment. In addition to the standard VGA, EGA, MCGA, CGA, and Hercules modes supported by QuickC and Turbo C, Essential Graphics supports the 640x 480x256-color mode of the IBM PGA, the 640x480x16-color mode of the Quadram QuadEGA ProSync, the 640x400x16-color mode of the ATT DEB adapter, and many others.

Fig. B-2. Essential Graphics 3.0 programming reference guide.

Although the Essential Graphics initgraf( ) procedure does not return any value, it is still possible to use the autodetect algorithm presented in the program listings throughout this book. After a call to initgraf( ) to attempt to set up a particular graphics mode, simply make a call to clearscr( ) to attempt to blank the graphics screen to a particular color. The clearscr( ) procedure returns a value of 0 if successful, a value of −1 if not in a valid graphics mode.

It is important to realize that you must explicitly load the low-level graphics drivers by calls to setvga( ), setega( ), and so on, when using the Essential Graphics toolkit. The advantage of this approach is that you load only what you need.

Line Drawing

The generic graphics routine DrawLine( ) can be mapped to Essential Graphics' eg_lineto( ) procedure, which draws a line from the current position. All coordinates maybe expressed as absolute or relative coordinates. This function corresponds to QuickC's _lineto( ) function and to Turbo C's lineto( ) function. To set the current graphics position, use the set_base( ) procedure of Essential Graphics. This corresponds to the generic graphics routine, SetPosition( ).

It is important to note that the eg_lineto( ) function of Essential Graphics expects to receive a color as one of its arguments. Of the graphics libraries discussed in this appendix, only Essential Graphics and Lattice C use dynamic color setting for line drawing output. The eg_lineto( ) draws a solid line. Use set_line_style( ) to define a dithered line and use set_line_width( ) to define the width of a line.

Advanced Line Drawing

Essential Graphics provides the powerful typedot( ) procedure, which determines the subsequent output of all line, circle, box, and arc calls. The typedot( ) function can be used to XOR any future graphics write operations. This capability can offer strong advantages if you are managing a graphics cursor in your program.

Creating Fill Patterns

To define a fill pattern (called a hatch style by Essential Graphics), use the htdefstl( ) function. You can use htdefstl( ) to define up to ten patterns. To create the pixel-by-pixel pattern matrices used throughout this book, you must also call htdefind( ) to define the color and width combinations used by htdefstl( ). To alter the hue being filled, a call to htdefind( ) is required. This differs from QuickC and Turbo C, where a call to _setcolor( ) or setcolor( ) is used to change the current color.

Refer to the "Getting Started" section of the Essential Graphics user's manual for an illustration of the ten default fill patterns.

Area Fill

The _floodfill( ) function of QuickC and the floodfill( ) function of TurboC are matched by the sfill( ) procedure provided by Essential Graphics. The sfill( ) function will fill in either solid or hatched patterns.

Alternatively, you can use the high-speed polyfill( ) function of Essential Graphics to fill a convex polygon by passing the vertices along with the call, although this algorithm is not compatible with the methods used in the program listings in this book.

Blanking the Screen

The clearscr( ) function provided by Essential Graphics can be used instead of the _clearscreen( ) function of QuickC or the cleardevice( ) function of Turbo C. These map to the BlankPage( ) library-independent routine used in the major program listings in the book.

Bitblt Operations: Manipulating Arrays

The Essential Graphics library contains a good set of functions to handle graphic arrays. The calcbyts( ) procedure can be used to calculate the size of the array needed to store a portion of the screen, similar to QuickC's _imagesize( ) function and Turbo C's imagesize( ) function. Essential Graphics uses the get( ) function to capture an image to an array, and uses the put( ) function to write an array to the screen. Boolean operations are available with the put( ) procedure, of course.

Hidden Page Operations

Essential Graphics offers a powerful copypage( ) function to copy the contents of one graphics page to another. This can be used in place of the routines provided in the program listings if a VGA, EGA, or Hercules adapter is being used. In the case of an MCGA or CGA adapter, the copytmem( ) and copyfmem( ) functions should be used to copy the screen to and from RAM.

Image Save/Load Operations

Essential Graphics provides a versatile set of built-in image manipulators. The scrtodsk( ) function will save a screen image to disk as a binary image file, while the scrtopcx( ) will save a screen image in a standard PCX file format. The dsktoscr( ) procedure will load a binary image file from disk; the pcx_load( ) function will load a PCX image from disk.

These built-in procedures can be used instead of the C routines provided in the program listings in this book.

Active Page Operations

Essential Graphics supports the full range of addressable graphics pages in any particular mode. The grefpag( ) procedure corresponds to the _setactivepage( ) function of QuickC and the setactivepage( ) function of Turbo C. These map to the WriteToPage( ) generic graphics routine used in the program listings. Using Essential Graphics, the gdisppag( ) function sets the page to be displayed. This corresponds to the generic graphics routine, DisplayPage( ), and operates similar to the QuickC and Turbo C functions, _setvisualpage( ) and setvisualpage( ).

Viewports

The setview( ) procedure provided by Essential Graphics provides the same capabilities as QuickC's _setviewport( ) function and Turbo C's setviewport( ) function.

Bitmapped Fonts

Essential Graphics offers 12 bitmapped and 10 stroked fonts, which can be rotated before display. (See Chapter 7 for a discussion of the difference between bitmapped fonts and vector fonts.) The fonts are licensed by South Mountain Software from PROSOFT, the publisher of FONTASY. The PROSOFT copyright notice must be displayed on any application program which uses the Essential Graphics font routines.

The Working Environment

The routines from the Essential Graphics library are linked into your program as needed. South Mountain Software provides you with a royalty-free right to distribute programs containing these linked-in graphics routines, as well as any font material which is provided with the Essential Graphics toolkit.

Other Noteworthy Features

Essential Graphics supports some flashy features, including rubberband lines, plotter output, PCX image file capabilities, numerous ways to draw and fill boxes, arcs, and circles, exploded pie charts, 30 graphs, direct control over a mouse and scanner, and screen dumps to a dot matrix printer. These impressive features, when combined with the built-in graphics page copying functions and availability of source code (at extra cost) make Essential Graphics a package to be seriously considered.

HALO 88

Here are some of the major points to consider when converting the program listings in the book to run with HALO 88 1.00.04 or newer. If you are already familiar with HALO's excellent documentation (see FIG. B-3), the only additional reference you will likely need while adapting the program listings is Table B-1.

Initializing the Graphics Mode

HALO's initgraphics( ) function is used to set up the graphics mode, much like QuickC's _setvideomoderows( ) and Turbo C's initgraph( ). It is important to realize, however, that you must explicitly load the graphics driver for the particular adapter and mode you are using by calling the setdev( ) procedure.

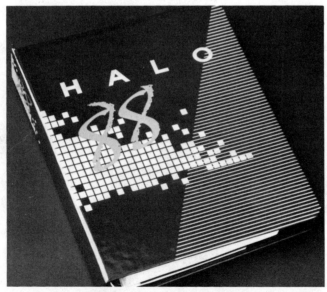

Fig. B-3. HALO 88 1.00.24 programming reference guide.

Use the inqerr( ) function to see if the initgraphics( ) procedure has been successful or not. A return value of 0 indicates success; any other value means the function failed.

Line Drawing

HALO's lnabs( ) function draws a line from the current position to a set of absolute xy coordinates using the current line attributes. This function is comparable to QuickC's _lineto( ) function and Turbo C's lineto( ) function. The color of the line is set via the setcolor( ) function. The line style is defined by calling setlinestyle( ) and deflnstyle( ). The SetPosition( ) generic library-independent routine used in the program listings in this book correlates to HALO's movabs( ) function.

Advanced Line Drawing

Most graphics drawn with HALO can be either overwritten or XOR'd onto the screen by a prior call to the setxor( ) function. In addition, a specialized rubber-banding algorithm can be used with lines, boxes, circles, and a built-in crosshair cursor.

Creating Fill Patterns

HALO's defhatchstyle( ) function is used to define a fill pattern. Five patterns can be defined. Another five default patterns are provided by the library. A call to sethatchstyle( ) makes a particular pattern current. HALO's algorithms permit you to vary the size of the pattern matrix, unlike QuickC's and Turbo C's 8x8 matrix size.

Area Fill

HALO offers a number of functions to provide area fill capabilities. HALO's flood2( ) function and fill( ) function operate similarly to the floodfill functions of QuickC and Turbo C. Patterns, including user-defined patterns, are supported. HALO's algorithm uses a non-destructive approach similar to QuickC's, meaning that different colors and patterns can be overlaid to produce an almost infinite variety of shades.

Blanking the Screen

The BlankPage( ) generic function used in the major program listings can be mapped to HALO's clr( ) and fclr( ) procedures. You should note that clr( ) will blank only the current viewport, while fclr( ) will always blank the entire screen.

Bitblt Operations: Manipulating Arrays

Versatile routines to capture and display graphic arrays are provided by HALO 88. To store a portion of the display screen in an array, use the movefrom( )

function. To display a previously saved graphic array, use the moveto( ) procedure. The moveto( ) function provides boolean logic capabilities, similar to the capabilities of QuickC's _putimage( ) and Turbo C's putimage( ).

HALO's inqpflen( ) function is useful for determining how much memory is required to store a graphic array. This corresponds to QuickC's _imagesize( ) routine and Turbo C's imagesize( ) routine.

Hidden Page Operations

The BackUp( ) library-independent routine used in the major program listings in this book can be replaced by HALO's imsave( ) function, which will move a graphics page to a specified address in RAM. The Restore( ) library-independent routine used in the program listings can be replaced by HALO's imrest( ) function. These two powerful routines can take the place of the movedata( ) functions necessary when QuickC and Turbo C are being used.

Image Save/Load Operations

HALO offers a good set of image save and load routines. The gwrite( ) function can be used to save an image to disk. The gread( ) procedure will load a previously saved image from disk. These two functions will always save/load the entire screen. The files written or read are binary images, which are device-dependent.

Active Page Operations

The WriteToPage( ) library-independent routine used in the program listings is mirrored by HALO's setscreen( ) function. This is the same as the _setactivepage( ) function in QuickC and the setactivepage( ) function in Turbo C. The DisplayPage( ) generic routine used in the program listing can be mapped to HALO's display( ) procedure. This is similar to QuickC's _setvisualpage( ) function and Turbo C's setvisualpage( ) function.

Viewports

HALO's setviewport( ) function is similar to QuickC's _setviewport( ) function and Turbo C's setviewport( ) function. This single function can be used to match the WindowOpen( ) and WindowClose( ) generic routines used in the program listings throughout this book.

Vector Fonts

In addition to normal and fast bitmapped fonts, HALO offers vector font capabilities. HALO's vector font output includes scaling, proportional spacing, rotating, slant, and more. The .FNT font files included with the library include standard-sized bitmapped fonts (called small dot text by HALO), oversized bitmapped fonts (called large dot text by HALO), and vector fonts (called stroke text by HALO).

Vector fonts displayed by HALO use the current line style and line width settings.

The Working Environment

Routines from the HALO graphics toolkit are linked into your applications program during the compile/link process. It is interesting to note that Media Cybernetics also provides a memory-resident version of their library, which is intended to be used with the GW-BASIC interpreter and the IBM BASICA interpreter.

Unlike the other graphics libraries discussed in this appendix, HALO routines expect to receive the address—not a copy of the value—of any arguments being passed by the caller, and only 2-byte integer values and 4-byte single-precision real numbers are allowed.

The single-site license provided to you when you purchase the HALO 88 graphics toolkit gives you the right to use the HALO routines on a single computer. You may contact Media Cybernetics to arrange an additional license for distribution of the routines as part of your finished graphics programs. This licensing policy reflects HALO's unparalleled support for different hardware input and output devices.

Other Noteworthy Features

HALO's superb list of specialized features includes support for scanners, plotters, and printers, as well as a comprehensive list of supported graphics adapters, including high end graphics boards like the AT&T Image Capture Board, TARGA boards, the Number Nine Revolution boards and Pepper boards, the IBM Professional Graphics Adapter, and others. The HALO library also supports all the standard VGA, EGA, MCGA, CGA, and Hercules graphics modes supported by QuickC and Turbo C.

HALO provides an impressive array of procedures to move graphics data, including a memcom( ) routine which compresses graphics data and a memexp( ) function to restore previously compressed data. Mouse control routines are also supplied.

HALO 88 will also save an image to disk as a binary image, and will load a previously saved image from disk. A screen image can also be printed on a dot matrix printer.

LATTICE C GRAPHICS AND GFX GRAPHICS

Here are some of the major points to consider when converting the program listings in the book to run with the Lattice C 3.4 and 6.0 Graphics Library or GFX graphics library. If you are already familiar with Lattice C's excellent documentation (see FIG. B-4), the only additional reference you will likely need while adapting the program listings is Table B-1.

Fig. B-4. Lattice C 6.0 GFX graphics library programming reference guide.

The Lattice C Graphics Library is a licensed edition of the GFX Library graphics library of CSource, Inc. No further differentiation will be made between the two libraries.

C programmers who have a lot of experience with GW-BASIC, IBM BASICA, QuickBASIC, or Turbo BASIC graphics libraries will be immediately comfortable with the syntax and environment used by Lattice C's Graphics Library. Many of the mnemonics are the same as those used in BASIC graphics, and the policy of assigning colors and styles as a dynamic part of graphics output is reminiscent of the BASIC regime. The Lattice C GFX library far surpasses anything that the BASIC libraries can produce, however.

Initializing the Graphics Mode

The Graphics_Setup( ) library-independent routine used in the program listings throughout this book can be compared to Lattice's init_gfx_struct( ) and screen( ) functions. You can use Lattice's _gfx_get_card_type( ) function to determine which graphics adapter and monitor are installed at start-up. Alternatively, you can use the value returned by screen( ) to implement the autodetect algorithm used throughout the programs in this book. A returned value of 0 indicates that screen( ) failed in its attempt to set up a particular graphics mode. The _gfx.err-_number variable will be set to BAD_VIDEO in this instance.

It is important to realize that Lattice's screen( ) procedure will use the highest graphics mode supported by the hardware unless you use the FORCE_ prefix on the argument to force a lower resolution supported by the adapter. Lattice's GFX graphics library supports the standard VGA, EGA, MCGA, CGA, and Hercules modes supported by QuickC and Turbo C for up to 16 colors. Lattice's set_extend-ed_ega_mode( ) function can be used to support some of the super EGA clone modes for up to 16 colors.

Line Drawing

The DrawLine( ) library-independent routine used in the major program listings can be mapped to Lattice's line( ) function, which takes a number of arguments, including color, type, and style. You can OR the internal variables PAT and XOR_PEL with the color for special effects. Lattice's line( ) function approximates the _lineto( ) function of QuickC and the lineto( ) function of Turbo C, except that the arguments must include both the starting vertex and the ending vertex.

Advanced Line Drawing

Lines can be XOR'd over existing graphics by using the XOR_PEL argument to Lattice's line( ) procedure. Line styles can be customized by using a 16-bit pattern in line( )'s argument list, similar to the methodology used by QuickC and Turbo C.

Creating Fill Patterns

Lattice C offers a very versatile and powerful algorithm for creating user-defined fill patterns. The fill_pattern argument of Lattice's fastfill( ) function is actually a char pointer to an array. The array's first element defines the number of bytes per row of the pattern. The second element defines the number of rows in the pattern. The remaining elements describe a two-dimensional array bitmap: if a bit is on, the pixel is written; if a bit is not on, the screen pixel is left untouched. This algorithm means that you can define fill patterns of variable-sized matrices, unlike QuickC and Turbo C, which are limited to an 8x8 matrix. It also means that Lattice C uses a non-destructive overlay algorithm similar to QuickC's, whereby you can create new shades and patterns by laying one or more patterns over existing hues.

Area Fill

Lattice's fastfill( ) function is a floodfill routine that will fill in either a solid color or a pattern. Lattice's paint( ) procedure fills in a solid color. These two functions compare to QuickC's _floodfill( ) function and Turbo C's floodfill( ) function as used in the library-independent routine, Fill( ). Unlike the QuickC and Turbo C functions, however, Lattice's fill functions expect to receive the fill color dynamically as one of the passed arguments. Lattice's fastfill( ) function operates upon simple figures—islands and peninsulas can cause it to thrash. Its paint( ) function handles even the most complex shapes.

Blanking the Screen

Use the cls( ) function to blank the screen. This corresponds to QuickC's _clearscreen( ) function and Turbo C's cleardevice( ) function. When using Lattice C, if a viewport is active, then cls( ) will clear only the active viewport.

Bitblt Operations: Manipulating Arrays

Lattice C automatically handles the allocation of memory required to store an array. The get_pic( ) function calculates how much memory is required, initializes the block, and stores the appropriate portion of the screen in the array. All graphic arrays are stored in the default data segment. The put_pic( ) function corresponds to QuickC's _putimage( ) function and Turbo C's putimage( ) function. Boolean operations like OR, AND, XOR are provided. Images can be swapped to and from disk when memory is sparse.

Hidden Page Operations

The BackUp( ) and Restore( ) functions used to support the Undo functions in the major program listings in this book can be replaced by Lattice's powerful copy_video_pages( ) function. The copy_video_pages( ) function will work with VGA, EGA, and Hercules modes that have more than one graphics page. If you are using an adapter or a mode that has only one page, then you should retain the movedata( ) routines used by QuickC and Turbo C in the program listings throughout this book.

Image Save/Load Operations

The routines in the demonstration programs which save an image to disk and which load an image from disk can be replaced by Lattice's get_fpic( ) and put_fpic( ) functions. These two functions can be used to read/write an entire screen image, or any rectangular portion of the screen. As an added feature, the put_fpic( ) function which loads an image from disk can use boolean operations such as bitwise AND, bitwise XOR, and so on. The image files created by Lattice are binary images and are device-dependent.

Active Page Operations

Lattice's set_video_pages( ) function provides the results given by the library-independent routines, WriteToPage( ) and DisplayPage( ), found in the program listings. The set_video_pages( ) procedure takes two arguments: the first parameter sets the displayed page, the second argument defines the written-to, active page.

Viewports

Lattice C's GFX graphics library endorses a philosophy of root viewports. The open_view( ) procedure corresponds to QuickC's _setviewport( ) function and Turbo C's setviewport( ) function. The close_view( ) function is used by Lattice C to shut down an open viewport. The switch_view( ) function is used to switch between different previously opened viewports.

Bitmapped Fonts

Lattice's putsfont( ) procedure writes a text string to the screen at any legal xy coordinate position and in the color which you provide as an argument to putsfont( ). The standard 8x8 ROM bitmapped font is used.

The put_font( ) function can be used to write either 8x8 or 8x14 bitmapped ROM fonts after a call to set_font( ) to select the desired font.

See Chapter 7 for more discussion about the difference between bitmapped fonts and vector fonts.

The Working Environment

The graphic routines of the GFX library are linked into your EXE program during Lattice's compile\link process. Only the functions called by your program are linked in, keeping RAM requirements reasonable.

Other Noteworthy Features

The Lattice C Graphics Library is noteworthy for its no-nonsense, practical approach to graphics programming. All the fundamentals are present, along with some bells and whistles, in a syntax that is intuitive. The dynamic nature of setting colors and styles used by Lattice C is not compatible with the current-graphics-state approach used by QuickC and Turbo C, but the jury is still out on which approach is better, of course. Probably the most important feature of the GFX graphics library is this: it has been thoroughly pretested as a built-in graphics library with Lattice C 3.4, 6.0 and newer. There are no surprises for the graphics programmer using the Lattice C compiler and the built-in GFX graphics. Using a third-party graphics library with any C compiler sometimes involves some surprises and compromises between such things as conflicting header files and constants. The GFX graphics library works as seamlessly with Lattice C as the built-in libraries of QuickC and Turbo C work with their compilers—and it compares very favorably with those libraries.

The user's manual for the Lattice C Graphics Library is second to none—it is thorough and consistent throughout: a very professional piece of work.

C

Handling Runtime Errors:
5 Strategies

THE PROGRAM listings in this book lack the robustness necessary in commercial software to gracefully recover from runtime errors like open diskdrive doors, attempting to write to a non-existant directory, math overflow, and others. Although a thorough treatment of techniques useful for implementing a bullet-proof error-trapping algorithm could easily fill an entire book, the discussion in this appendix will serve to introduce the topic.

And it is a topic that should receive the serious attention of every C graphics programmer. End-users, after all, expect software to be smart enough to handle typical mistakes like open diskdrive doors without locking up the user's system. If you do not provide that level of sophistication in your graphics programs, then you can rest assured that your competitors will.

EXCEPTION HANDLING

Error trapping is exception handling. An exception is a runtime condition which does not fit the expected or the norm. A proper exception-handling algorithm follows a two-step process: detection and recovery.

Detection

A number of different detection procedures are applicable, including both built-in compiler features and user-implemented trapping routines.

Recovery

The number of recovery algorithms is limited only by the imagination of the programmer writing the program. Anything from complete shutdown to ignoring the problem can be (and has been) coded by C graphics programmers.

TEST SUITE

Like any other algorithm, you must thoroughly test your error-trapping routines before you begin to distribute your program. Most C graphics programs will be well-protected if your error handler can deal gracefully with the following seven conditions:

1) division by zero,
2) math overflow,
3) disk drive door open,
4) insufficient space on disk,
5) file not found,
6) illegal drive letter or non-existant directory,
7) mouse or tablet not found.

As you develop your error handlers, you should force your program to encounter each of these seven conditions. Only by exercising every possible runtime condition in a controlled environment can you be sure that your error handler is up to the task—and even then you can expect some unforseen conditions to cause you grief when you beta-test your program.

FIVE METHODS FOR DETECTING RUNTIME ERRORS

Clearly, before you can successfully handle a runtime error, you must be able to detect that an error has occurred in the first place. This is not as easy at it seems at first glance, and the detection algorithm must often be modified to be able to detect different classes of runtime errors: user mistakes, math errors, disk and file errors, I/O hardware errors, and logic errors.

There are five fundamental approaches available to the C graphics programmer seeking to protect an application program from runtime errors. A program that is bulletproof to runtime errors will likely use all five algorithms.

Method One

Use the value returned by the function to determine if an error has occurred or not.

This is essentially the same algorithm used by the autodetect routine used in each demonstration program in this book. Applied to disk input/output operations, you can check if a file exists or not by using the following QuickC syntax:

```
if((access("filename.ext",0)) = = -1){ /* if file does not exist */
  _settextposition(2,1);
  _outtext("File does not exist!");}
```

The Turbo C syntax is:

```
if((access("filename.ext",0))= =-1){
 moveto(0,7);
 outtext("File does not exist!");)}
```

In addition, you could check to see if a directory was successfully deleted by using the following QuickC syntax:

```
if((rmdir("C:\\DIRNAME")= =-1) {/* if cannot delete directory */
 _settextposition(2,1);
 _outtext("Unable to delete that subdirectory...");}
```

Although this method provides a powerful tool for detecting and handling runtime errors, it has limitations. It cannot trap hardware I/O errors such as an open disk drive door, or attempting to write a write-protected disk, a seek error, or a bad FAT (file allocation table).

Method Two

Use QuickC's _harderr( ) function or Turbo C's harderr( ) function to detect the error and to branch to a programmer-defined error-handler. This method will detect and trap many of the hardware errors that may slip past Method One. Once inside your error-handler, a call to QuickC's _hardretn( ) or Turbo C's hardretn( ) will return to the program at the instruction following the one which caused the error.

If you are using QuickC, your error-handling routine can detect what type of hardware error caused the _harderr( ) function to activate your routine by inspecting the global system variable named errcode. Refer to the QuickC Run-Time Library Reference entry for _harderr( ), _hardresume( ), and _hardretn( ) for a listing of the possible values of errcode and their meanings. A global system variable named deverr is used for some disk errors.

If you are using Turbo C, you can inspect the global system variable named errno which is passed to your error-handler. Refer to the Turbo C Reference Guide for a list of the mnemonics and their meanings.

Although there are a number of different ways to exit your error-handling routine, the safest is to do so via QuickC's _hardretn( ) function or Turbo C's hardretn( ) function, which forces a return to the instruction immediately following the one which caused the error. Other methods of exiting your error-handler, including _hardresume( ) and return( ), will simply branch back to the operating system, where still further arrangements must be made to enable a graceful recovery.

Method Three

Use the value returned by the function and the error code stored in the global system variable, errno. Table A.1 in the QuickC Run-Time Library Reference gives a list of the errno values and their meanings. Chapter 1 in the Turbo C Reference Guide provides a similar listing.

You could check if a disk is full by using the following QuickC syntax after an attempted write operation returns a value of -1:

```
if(errno = = ENOSPC){                                    /* if disk is full */
                                          } /* put desired action here */
```

You could check if a path was found by using the following Turbo C syntax after an attempted write operation returns a value of -1:

```
if(errno = = ENOPATH){                    /* if not found */ }/* put desired action here */
```

This method will detect conditions ranging from out-of-memory, to no-such-file-or-directory, to invalid-argument, to permission-denied, and others. It will even detect arguments for math functions that are outside the range that can be handled by the math function (but it will not detect errors resulting from the execution of the math function).

Method Four

Use the matherr( ) function to detect and identify different types of math errors at runtime. This method can be used to recover gracefully from math overflow, math underflow, and other conditions. The different values returned by matherr( ) are described in Appendix A.3 of the QuickC Run-Time Library Reference.

The matherr( ) function is called automatically by the compiler's math routines whenever an error condition is encountered. Various information concerning the error is stored in an exception type structure described in the QuickC Run-Time Library Reference for matherr( ) and in the Turbo C Reference Guide. By inspecting this structure, you can decide upon an appropriate response.

The following QuickC and Turbo C syntax will check if a negative value had been passed to the sqrt( ) function:

```
int matherr(x)
struct exception *x;
if(x→type = = DOMAIN){                   /* if argument not in legal domain */
                    }                                 /* ... then do this */
```

Method Five

Use assert( ) to test for a specific logic condition and to abort the program if the result is false.

This method is useful for debugging your C graphics programs during development. As an added bonus, you can insert the preprocessor directive #define NDEBUG at the beginning of your source code when you are ready to compile the corrected code and the QuickC or Turbo C preprocessor will automatically remove all assert( ) calls from the source file.

Suppose, for example, that you wish to ensure that a particular variable never equals zero at runtime. The following QuickC and Turbo C syntax will trap the condition and stop the program:

```
assert(variable = = 0);                              /* variable must not be zero */
```

A BLACK ART

There is a lot of art and intuition involved in writing good error-handling algorithms for any major program. It is a field pitted with snares for the unwary—and even experienced professional programmers sometimes blunder.

If you are writing an error-handler, you are tackling one of the toughest challenges any C graphics programmer can face—but also one of the most essential components of a professional-caliber program.

D

Faster is Better:
Using Performance Analyzers

THIRD-PARTY performance analyzers can be useful in helping you to determine if your C graphics program would benefit from optimization. The analyzers can show you where the bottlenecks are located in your program and which routines in your program are doing the most work. A performance analyzer can make you more efficient by showing you where to concentrate your optimization efforts. Optimization can include simply improving the algorithm you are using, or can be as intensive as replacing sections of C code with inline assembly routines.

Case Study: STOPWATCH

STOPWATCH is a performance analyzer from Custom Real-Time Software. See FIG. D-1. It is a software program that can be used to time specific events in your program.

STOPWATCH begins timing when it is activated by a trigger and stops timing when it encounters a terminator. A summary report is produced which shows time spent in BIOS calls, calls to the operating system, disk access, program duties, and total time. Because three different types of triggers will start the timing sequence, STOPWATCH can be used in a number of modes.

While an EXE program is running, you can activate the timing process by entering Ctrl + M at the keyboard. STOPWATCH will begin its timing run and will continue until a specific character is output to the display through the BIOS, or until the end of the program. This mode does not require any access to the source

Fig. D-1. Programmer's reference guide for STOPWATCH performance analyzer software.

code, nor any modifications to the source code, and it can produce an interesting report detailing the amount of time spend performing various chores. It is useful for locating bottlenecks and often-used routines.

Alternatively, you can insert an INT 65H in your source code as a trigger and an INT 66H as a terminator. When you run the resulting EXE program, STOP-WATCH will begin its timing run as the INT 65H is executed and will conclude the timing when the INT 66H is encountered. This mode allows you precise control over which sections of your code will be timed. It is useful for comparing the performance of different algorithms that you might be experimenting with in your source code.

Timing can also be performed while you are using a debugger. During the moment of transition from the debugger to the program, STOPWATCH will interpret that shift as a trigger and will begin its timing run. The timing run will stop when a breakpoint is encountered (remember, the program is being run under debugger control).

STOPWATCH offers two important advantages to a C graphics programmer: first, it is easy to use; second, it is language-independent.

Case Study: INSIDE!

More detailed information concerning your program's execution profile can be provided by INSIDE!, from Paradigm Systems Incorporated. (The exclamation mark is a part of the program's title, but will be omitted hereafter in the interests of keeping the text legible.) See Fig. D-2. INSIDE is available in a version specifically for QuickC and a version specifically for Turbo C.

Fig. D-2. Programmer's reference guide for INSIDE! performance analyzer software.

INSIDE can be configured to time a function, or a specific line in the source code, or an arbitrary event, or other parts of your C graphics program. It supports run-time overlays and inline assembly language routines.

The reports generated by INSIDE can be very detailed. An analysis of a function's performance, for example, might include the number of executions of the function, the minimum execution time, the maximum execution time, the total time spent executing that particular function, and the percentage of time spent in that function compared to the entire process being timed. Other useful information like program load time, program elapsed time, and program stack requirements is also reported.

The same level of detail is generated in a report where individual lines of source code are being timed.

INSIDE is cleverly designed to plug into the debugging atmosphere of QuickC, and to work in harmony alongside the debugging capabilities of Turbo C. When you are using INSIDE with either compiler, it seems as if INSIDE is just a natural extension of the compiler's built-in debugging capabilities. In point of fact, INSIDE installs itself in front of your application, trapping events such as function entry points. When working with QuickC, for example, you simply activate CodeView Info and Optimizations Full in the Options menu, while disabling the incremental linker. By adding INSIDE as a menu item in the Utilities menu, you can activate INSIDE through a hot key without ever leaving the QuickC interactive programming environment.

Because the trigger and terminate points used by INSIDE are direct references to the source code—and because this performance analyzer works so well alongside Quick and Turbo C—it is very helpful during prototyping and during program development.

WHICH PERFORMANCE ANALYZER IS BETTER?

If you want a quick and general idea of where the bottlenecks are in your program—and if you do not want to spend a lot of time setting up and using a performance analyzer—then your best choice is probably STOPWATCH.

If you demand a more detailed accounting of what each routine or individual line is doing—and if you want a performance analyzer that can be used as an integral part of your QuickC or Turbo C interactive programming session—then your best choice is probably INSIDE!.

E

Playing for Keeps:
Adding Copy Protection

CLEARLY, for any C graphics program, copy protection is a nuisance—but, like a padlock on a common garden shed, it might be a necessary evil. Without the padlock in place, the neighborhood children may get into mischief with your tools and gardening supplies, or—even worse—vandals or thieves may loot your unprotected goods.

The garden shed analogy is not trivial. Just like copy protection, the padlock is an ongoing nuisance to the end-user, in this instance the gardener, who needs access to the garden shed on a regular basis; but, just like copy protection, the padlock protects the property of the owner.

A MEASURED RESPONSE

If you have only a few old rakes, shovels—and perhaps a beat-up lawn mower—you might not bother with any padlock on the garden shed. If you have a $150 lawn mower and a set of new rakes, hoes, spades, and other tools, you might decide to invest in a $10 padlock; but if you have a $2000 riding mower, a $400 electric posthole auger, and other expensive tools, you might decide to apply a $75 top-of-the-line padlock—some individuals might even install an alarm system on the shed.

The same measured response might be applicable to graphics software.

Mass Market Software

It does not make sense for a software product priced in the $69 to $199 range to be copy protected. From a marketing viewpoint, it is better to use subtler protection in the form of a thick user's manual which—in addition to being awkward and expensive to copy—contains information essential to the operation of your graphics program. Without access to your documentation, the user will find it difficult to take advantage of the many features of your program, and it can easily cost $50 or more to photocopy a set of manuals.

As the retail price of a software package increases, however, some individuals might find it more attractive to pirate a copy than to incur the expense of purchasing a legitimate copy. If you have a substantive investment of time and money in your software project, each stolen copy inflicts damage to your business. Each lost sale reduces your return-on-investment. You are losing cash out of your pocket. It is natural for you to want to protect yourself against the actions of dishonest—or unthinking—users who pirate your software product.

Expensive Software

A software package in the $249 to $799 range is a candidate for copy protection of moderate sophistication. In addition to protecting against a simple DOS COPY function, you might also want protection against experienced hackers—or against users who have purchased a $50 so-called copy-buster program. This appendix will introduce a number of third-party software protection schemes that provide such protection.

High-end Software

A high-end graphics software package, priced anywhere from a thousand dollars to many thousands of dollars on the retail market, is a prime candidate for copy protection of advanced sophistication. In addition to protecting against the threats discussed above, you might wish to protect your investment against professional pirates. This appendix will discuss a number of third-party protection schemes that can provide that level of copy protection.

TYPES OF COPY PROTECTION

There are four major types of software copy protection available to you as a serious C graphics programmer. They are:

1) software-based shell key,
2) hardware-based shell key,
3) algorithm-based hardware key, and
4) programmable hardware key.

Each type of copy protection offers a different level of protection. Some copy protection methods require minimal effort by the programmer to apply the protection to the distribution disks; other methods require a serious investment in programming effort and substantive modification of your program's source code.

A discussion of each method follows. It is important for you to realize that the actual procedures used by each copy protection scheme are actually more complex and involve algorithms not discussed in full here in order to protect the trade secrets of the manufacturers—and to protect the programmers who have already used these methods to protect their investment in their software products.

Good: The Software-based Shell Key Method

The software-based shell key method requires very little effort on the programmer's part. The copy protection program appends a routine to the beginning of your finished EXE program and places an additional special hidden file on your distribution disk. The disk is now ready to be distributed. The copy-protection program has placed a protective shell around your finished EXE program. The key that allows the shell to be opened is the hidden file, of course.

When the end-user starts your program, the first task your program performs is to call the copy-protection routine. This routine checks for the existence of the hidden file and other information. If the file is not found, a polite message is displayed and control is returned to the operating system. If the hidden file is found, your program is permitted to run.

A number of tokens can be placed in the hidden file, including a meter count which is useful for controlling the number of times a demo program can execute.

Case Study: The EVERLOCK Software Protection System from AzTech Software, Inc., uses the software-based shell key approach. See Fig. E-1. You are

Fig. E-1. The EVERLOCK programmer's reference guide, a software-based copy protection system.

not required to display any additional copyright notice on any program which you have protected with EVERLOCK, nor do you have to pay any royalties on each copy sold of your program.

The main advantage of the EVERLOCK system is that you do not need to modify your source code. EVERLOCK attaches itself to your finished EXE program. However, if you prefer, you can optionally modify your source code to read the internal data structure used by EVERLOCK at run-time. This would allow you to add additional protection to your program by inserting attempted reads of the structure at numerous points in your program, making it even more difficult for a skilled hacker to use a debugger to locate and nullify the copy protection routines (called software locks by the copy protection companies).

EVERLOCK offers a number of options during the protection process. You can designate how many installs or de-installs will be permitted to a fixed disk, for example. You can define whether or not LAN operation of your software will be permitted. You can instruct the EVERLOCK system to add a serialized number to each distribution disk you protect, and you can implement a meter-count to control how many times a demo disk can be run.

In the event that the copy protection routines discover that an unauthorized copy of your software is being used, EVERLOCK will either simply return to the operating system, or display a programmer-defined message and return to the operating system, or display a programmer-defined message and hang the system. You choose which approach will be used during the protection process.

The EVERLOCK documentation provides a thorough explanation of how the system works, in addition to useful examples of source code showing how to implement the copy protection scheme. A starter's kit allowing for protection of 100 disks is available at moderate cost. A professional kit which allows protection of an unlimited number of disks is also available. A program protected with the EVERLOCK system is approximately 7K larger than an unprotected program.

Better: The Hardware-based Shell Key Method

The hardware-based shell key method is similar to the software-based shell key method, but with a few important differences. The copy protection system places a shell around your finished EXE program just like the software-based method does, but at start-up your program will check for the existence of a hardware key attached to the parallel port of the user's computer.

To make the copy protection even more formidable, some manufacturers encrypt your EXE program during the protection process. When the end-user attempts to start your program, the shell refuses to decrypt the program unless the hardware key is found.

The advantages of this system are ease of use during the protection process (no access to the source code is needed) and the double protection of a hardware key and encrypted code.

Case Study: The hardware-based shell key method is used by the SentinelShell hardware key from Rainbow Technologies, Inc. See FIG. E-2. As an added feature, SentinelShell checks for the presence of the hardware key at random times during the execution of your software, ensuring that the hardware key has

Fig. E-2. The SentinelShell hardware-based copy protection system.

not been removed and perhaps transferred to another computer after program start-up. A program protected by the SentinelShell system is approximately 20K larger than an unprotected program.

Every copy of the protected program requires its own unique hardware key, because each SentinelShell hardware key contains an algorithm to encrypt and decrypt your program. Because thousands of different algorithms are available, each hardware key is unique. A program protected with one hardware key cannot be run with another key, although Rainbow Technologies will, by special arrangement, provide a batch of similar keys to you if you are making many protected copies of the same program.

The hardware-based shell key method provides stronger protection than the software-based approach, primarily because the inner workings of a hardware key are subject to patent. Patent laws are much stricter and easier to enforce than copyright laws. In addition, the pirate simply has no easy way to access the proprietary code stored inside the hardware key.

Best: The Algorithm-based Hardware Key Method

An even more sophisticated level of copy protection is offered by the algorithm-based hardware key method. This increased protection comes at a price in your time and effort, however. In a typical protection system, the programmer adds a number of query routines to the source code. These query routines take advantage of a specific algorithm built into the hardware key. It is typical for your program to pass a string of ASCII characters to the hardware key, which then uses an algorithm to transform the string into a numeric value. The numeric value is passed back to your program for evaluation or analysis. Different input strings will result in different returned values.

The possibilities for variety are endless. You can simply compare the returned value to an expected value. You could store the returned value in a global variable and not use the variable until much later in the program, making it very difficult for a hacker to modify your code. You could perform mathematical operations on the returned value and then use it in your code somewhere else. Or, best of all, you could use the returned value as executable code.

By mixing these approaches and by using multiple random queries of the hardware key during program execution, you can make your program nearly impervious to unauthorized copying.

Case Study: The algorithm-based hardware key method is used by the SentinelPro system from Rainbow Technologies, Inc. (which also manufactures the SentinelShell system discussed earlier). The documentation which accompanies SentinelPro is excellent, offering a wealth of ideas and tips for the programmer new to copy protection. Because you are in full control of when and how to query the hardware key, you can make your copy protection as bulletproof as you want. The more effort you put into your protection scheme, the more resistant it will be to hackers and pirates.

You can purchase batches of SentinelPro hardware keys which are useful for protecting many copies of the same software program. SentinelPro also offers an option which uses the serial number of the disk label in conjunction with the hardware key to provide additional protection and auditing capabilities. A programmable model with non-volatile memory is available to developers who want to store customer-dependent information on the hardware key.

Best: The Programmable Hardware Key Method

The highest level of copy protection sophistication is provided by the programmable hardware key method. A set of fully programmable registers built into the hardware key can be manipulated by your program at run-time and used to create an infinite number of queries and responses. Although this approach requires the most effort on your part, it can also offer an extremely robust level of protection.

Case Study: The Activator hardware key from Software Security Inc. uses the programmable hardware key method. See FIG. E-3. The Activator is comprised of seven 6-bit programmable registers: three counters and four selectors. The interaction between these registers is clever and can be further manipulated by the programmer who is creating the protection routines.

The documentation for the Activator system is designed for the experienced programmer. Some low-level work is required during the creation of the routines that will actually read and manipulate the Activator hardware key, but the security of the resulting protection is impressive. The documentation provides a number of sample code fragments to get you up and running, but Software Security strongly encourages you to develop your own algorithms in order to increase the level of protection.

Fig. E-3. The Activator hardware-based copy protection system.

WHICH METHOD IS BEST?

Only you can decide which of the copy protection methods described in this appendix is best for your particular software project. You must weight the size of your investment in your project, the retail price of your software, the cost of adding copy protection, the cost of the nuisance to the end-user, and the amount of time and effort required of you to actually add the copy protection to your distribution disks.

If you do decide, however, that one of the systems described in this appendix is for you, you will probably sleep better at night because of your decision. After all, even the subtle protection of the thick user's manual approach is better than no protection at all.

Glossary

acronym—a pronounceable abbreviation for a group of words.

active page—the graphics page to which the microprocessor is currently writing, also called the written-to page. The active page is not necessarily the same as the page being displayed.

Ada—a compiled, high level, real-time language used by the U.S. military. The term Ada is a registered trademark of the U.S. Government.

additive operators—the + operator and the - operator, which are addition and subtraction.

addressable—the ability to be addressed directly by a command from the keyboard or by an instruction in a program.

aggregate type—a C array, structure, or union.

ALGOL—a compiled, high level language used for general numeric analysis in scientific computing.

algorithm—a method for solving a problem. See heuristic.

alias—one of several names which refer to the same memory location (ie variable). See union. Also refers to the jagged effect (jaggies) produced by diagonal or curved lines on monitors with coarse resolution.

all-points-addressable—the ability of the microprocessor to read and write each separate pixel on the display monitor. Also called APA.

alphanumeric—a set of characters containing both letters and numbers.

analog—a signal or readout that varies continuously. A digital signal is either fully on or fully off.

analog monitor—a computer monitor which is capable of displaying colors based upon the infinitely varying intensity of the red, green, and blue guns of the cathode ray tube. A digital monitor, on the other hand, typically offers only three intensities: off, normal intensity, and high intensity.

animation—the quick display of separate graphic images in order to deceive the human eye into perceiving motion.

ANSI—an acronym for the American National Standards Institute, which is responsible for defining C language standards in order to assist in program portability between different computer systems.

anti-aliasing—software routines which reduce the visual impact of jagged lines on a display monitor.

APA—an acronym for all-points-addressable, which refers to the ability of every pixel on the display monitor to be written to or read by the microprocessor.

APL—an interpreted, high level language used for data processing.

application—another way of saying software or program.

area fill—to fill a specified region of the display screen with a specified color or pattern. The attribute surrounding the region to be filled is generally called the boundary. Efficient area fill routines employ a double-ended FIFO queue methodology.

argument—a value passed to a C function by the caller.

argument-type list—the listing of arguments found in a C function prototype.

arithmetic operator—a mathematical operator such as addition (+), multiplication (*), and others.

array—a set of data elements of similar type grouped together under a single name, usually arranged in rows and columns. Similar in concept to a collection of smaller groups. An array can be scalar (consisting of numeric or string data) or it can be graphic (consisting of pixel attributes).

assembler—a program that converts assembly language source code into native machine code. Sometimes called MASM. An assembler that works with syntax other than assembly language is usually called a compiler.

assembly language—a low level language whose mnemonics and syntax closely reflect the internal workings of the microprocessor's registers.

assignment—to assign a value to a variable. The C assignment operator is = . Avoid confusion with the C equality operator = = . In C, an arithmetic operation can be performed during the assignment process using the + = addition assignment operator, the - = subtraction assignment operator, the * = multiplication assignment operator, the / = division assignment operator, and the % = remainder assignment operator. Other assignment variations include the << = left-shift assignment operator, the >> = right-shift assignment operator, the & = bitwise-AND assignment operator, and the ^ = bitwise-XOR assignment operator.

background color—the screen color upon which all graphics are drawn. The background is usually black or white.

back-up—a duplicate copy of software or data intended to protect the user from loss of the original.

banner—the sign-on message of an application program. The copyright notice usually appears in the banner message.

BASIC—a high level, general purpose programming language, often used as a prototype development tool, available in both interpreter and compiler versions.

binary file—a file stored in binary format, as opposed to ASCII character (text) format. See image file.

binary operator—a C operator used in binary expressions. Binary operators include multiplicative operators (*,/), additive operators (+ ,-), shift operators (<<,>>), relational operators (<,>,<=,>=,==,!=,), bitwise operators (&,|,^), logical operators (&&,||), and the sequential-evaluation operator (,).

BIOS—assembly language subroutines stored as native machine code in ROM which provide basic input/output services for DOS and for applications programs. Also called ROM BIOS.

bit array—a graphic array.

bitblt—an acronym for bit boundary block transfer. Also called block graphics and graphic array.

bitblt animation—graphic array animation.

bit boundary block transfer—see bitblt.

bit map—an arrangement of bytes in display memory whose bits correspond to the pixels on the display screen. Sometimes used to mean memory-mapped video. The bit map of the VGA and EGA is organized in a linear format distributed over four bit-planes. The bit map of the Color/Graphics Adapter is organized into two banks, one comprised of even-numbered rows, the other containing odd-numbered rows.

bit plane—one of four separate buffers which are sandwiched together by the VGA and EGA hardware in order to drive the video output. Also called a color plane. On the EGA, plane 0 affects the blue attribute; plane 1 affects the green attribute; plane 2 affects the red attribute; and plane 3 affects the intensity attribute.

bit tiling—mixing pixels of different colors to create patterns or shades. Also called halftone, halftoning, patterns, and patterning.

bitwise operators—&, |, and^, which compare bits to check for true and false conditions. C's bitwise operators are AND (&), OR (|), and XOR (^). Contrast with C's logical operators AND (&&), OR (||), and NOT (!).

block—a cohesive sequence of C statements, instructions, declarations, or definitions which are enclosed within braces. { }

block graphics—same as graphic array. See bitblt.

braces—the { } tokens which enclose a block in a C program. See also parentheses and brackets.

brackets—the [ ] tokens which are used to initialize and access the elements of arrays.

B-rep—boundary representation, a method of creating images of 3D models by using planes, polygons, and facets. The boundary envelope of the object is used to portray the solidity of the model. See CSG.

buffer—an area of memory used for temporary storage.

bug—a programming oversight in the source code, usually an error in algorithmic logic.

byte—a group of eight adjacent bits.

C—a compiled, high level programming language originally developed for systems programming (writing compilers, operating systems, text editors). C is useful for high-performance graphics because of its low level capabilities.

CAD—an acronym for computer-aided design and computer-assisted design. CAD is to images what word processing is to words and what electronic spreadsheets are to numbers.

CADD—an acronym for computer-aided design and drafting.

CAE—an acronym for computer-aided engineering.

CAL—an acronym for computer-aided learning.

call—a program instruction which transfers control to a routine, whether a function in C, a subroutine in BASIC, a procedure in MASM, a subprogram in QuickBASIC and Turbo BASIC, or to another program.

CAM—an acronym for computer-aided manufacturing.

camera coordinates—the result of translating and rotating world coordinates in a 3D program. See view coordinates.

CAP—an acronym for computer-aided publishing, sometimes called desktop publishing but more accurately called page composition.

CAS—an acronym for computer-aided styling.

CDF file—comma delimited file. In graphics applications, used for storage of graphics primitives attributes. See data file.

char—a C variable stored in one byte of memory, capable of representing values from -128 to +127. An unsigned char can represent values from 0 to 255. By default, char is signed. A char type is often used to store the integer value of a member of the ASCII alphanumeric character set.

CGA—an acronym for Color/Graphics Adapter. A CGA which conforms to the IBM standard can display a 320x200 4-color graphics mode and a 640x200 2-color graphics mode. Also called a C/GA, a Color/Graphics Card, a color graphics board, and a color card.

CGM—the ANSI computer graphics metafile format for exchanging images between application programs or between computer systems.

CMY—the cyan-magenta-yellow color model.

COBOL—a compiled, high level language used for business applications.

clipping—see line clipping.

Color/Graphics Adapter—see CGA.

color cycling—producing animation by swapping palette values.

command menu—a set of on-screen icons which represent the commands available to the user of a CAD or draw program.

compact memory model—the allocation of RAM for a C program whereby the size of executable code is limited to 64K but data is limited only by available memory.

compatible—usually intended to mean a personal computer which adheres closely to the hardware standards established by IBM. Compatibility can occur at the hardware (register) level, at the BIOS level, at the operating system level (DOS or OS/2).

compiler—a program that translates an entire file of source code into native machine code prior to execution.

configure—to determine how the various parts of a personal computer system are to be physically arranged, or to determine at run-time how the operating system, memory, and peripherals of a personal computer are to be logically arranged.

constant—a value in a program which does not change during execution.

constructive solid geometry—see CSG

contour drawing—a wire-frame drawing that represents the surface of an object.

coordinate system—the arrangement of x,y axes in a 2D display or the arrangement of x,y,z axes in a 3D display. A number of incompatible coordinate systems are in use.

copyright—the right to copy an intellectual property such as a book, manuscript, software program, painting, photograph, et cetera.

core library—the functions which are built into an interactive C compiler such as QuickC and Turbo C, and which are resident in RAM while the user is working with the compiler.

corporate programmer—an employee of a corporation or business enterprise whose assignment is to create and maintain software for in-house use.

cosine—the cosine of an angle in a right-angle triangle defines the relationship between the hypotenuse and the adjacent side.

CPU—an acronym for central processing unit, the part of a microcomputer which actually does the computing. Also called the microprocessor.

crash—a program failure which causes control to return to the operating system or to the interactive C compiler. See also hang and lock-up.

crosshatch—see hatch.

CRT—cathode ray tube: the displaying hardware of computer monitors and of television sets.

CSG—constructive solid geometry, a method of creating images of 3D models by using primitives such as cubes, cylinders, spheres, and cones. Contrast with B-rep.

cubic parametric curve—a formula-generated smooth curve created by providing two end points and two control points as parameters for the formula. Also called a fitted curve.

cursor—the user-controlled symbol that identifies the active location on the display screen.

data file—in graphics programming, a CDF (comma delimited) file used to store attributes of graphics primitives.

debug—the detection and correction of errors in a program.

declaration—the statements that define the name and attributes of a C variable, function, or structure.

decrement—to decrease by a specified amount.

definition—the actual instructions which comprise a function. See also prototype.

delete—to remove.

demon—a user-defined function, usually associated with graphics programming.

depth cuing—the use of colored lines or linestyles to assist the viewer in interpreting depth in the image.

digital—a method of representing data whereby the individual components are either fully on or fully off. See analog.

dimension—the alphanumeric description of the size of an entity in a CAD drafting program.

dimension line—the line and arrows which describe the entity to which a dimension refers in a CAD drafting program.

display coordinates—refers primarily to the converted view coordinates of a 3D modeling program. Display coordinates consist of x and y screen coordinate values. See also view coordinates and world coordinates in this glossary. Also refer to the author's books High-Performance Graphics In C: Animation and Simulation (Windcrest book #3049) and High-Performance CAD Graphics In C (Windcrest book #3059).

distribution disk—the finished program disk containing the command program, which is distributed through marketing channels as commercial software, shareware, or freeware, or which is distributed through a corporation as in-house software.

dither—used in computer rendering. To dither a line is to modify a line (line styling) to match the adjacent shading pattern. Also refer to the author's books High-Performance Graphics In C: Animation and Simulation (Windcrest book #3049) and High-Performance CAD Graphics In C (Windcrest book #3059).

do-nothing routine—a subroutine which merely returns control to the caller. Do-nothing routines are used during preliminary program development and debugging. Also called a stub.

DOS—disk operating system. IBM DOS is often called PC-DOS. Microsoft DOS is often called MS-DOS. Both operating systems are almost but not exactly identical.

double-buffer animation—another name for real-time animation, dynamic page flipping animation, and ping-pong animation. Also refer to the author's books High-Performance Graphics In C: Animation and Simulation (Windcrest book #3049) and High-Performance CAD Graphics In C (Windcrest book #3059).

drafting program—an interactive graphics program which performs many of the drawing functions a draftsperson would perform while creating a technical drawing.

dynamic page flipping animation—also called real-time animation: a technique involving display of a completed image while the microprocessor is drawing the next image on a hidden page. When the next image is complete, the graphics pages are flipped and the procedure is continued. Also refer to the author's book High-Performance Graphics In C: Animation and Simulation (Windcrest book #3049).

ECD—an acronym for enhanced color display. An ECD is a digital display capable of displaying the EGA's 640x350 16-color graphics mode, in addition to all lesser modes.

editor—generally refers to the interface which allows the user to create and modify text data. A graphics editor is the interface which permits the user to create and modify graphics.

EGA—an acronym for enhanced graphics adapter. An EGA which adheres to the IBM standard can display the following graphics modes: 640x350 16-color (out of 64 possible colors), 640x350 2-color, 640x200 16-color, 320x200 16-color, 640x200 2-color, and 320x200 4-color.

elegant—see optimize.

emulation—simulation of unavailable hardware by available hardware/software.

The mathematical routines in QuickC and in Turbo C provide emulation of a math coprocessor even when the coprocessor is not present in the microcomputer.

enhanced graphics adapter—same as EGA.

entity—in computer graphics, a cohesive graphical shape such as a rectangle, circle, or subassembly (as found in a technical drawing).

ergonomics—refers to machine compatibility with human psychology and physiology.

error trapping—using a programmer-defined subroutine to respond to program flow errors which occur during run-time.

expression—a combination of operators acting upon variables.

extrusion—the act of converting a 2D graphic into a 3D model.

facet—usually intended to mean a polygonal surface used to create a solid 3D model constructed by the B-rep method.

file pointer—a variable that indicates the current position of read and write operations on a file. See stream.

fillet—the round corner function in CAD drafting programs.

firmware—software which is stored in ROM. See BIOS.

fitted curve—see cubic parametric curve.

floating point number—generally, a number which contains a decimal point; specifically, a number expressed in scientific notation (which allows the decimal point to float). A floating point number in C (of type float) is stored in four bytes of memory and can range from 3.4E-38 to 3.4E+38 (which is 340,000,000,000,000,000,000,000,000,000,000,000,000—large enough for most applications!). A type float value is accurate to six digits. A floating point value defined as type double occupies eight bytes of memory and can express values ranging from 1.7E-308 to 1.7E+308.

FORTH—a general-purpose language used mainly for robotics and graphics.

formatting—the general layout of a program listing, including tabs, spaces, indentations, and margins.

FORTRAN—a compiled, high level programming language used for scientific and engineering applications. FORTRAN is an acronym for FORmula TRANslator.

fps—an acronym for frames per second, used to measure the display rate of animation programs. Also refer to the author's books High-Performance Graphics In C: Animation and Simulation (Windcrest book #3049) and High-Performance CAD Graphics In C (Windcrest book #3059).

frame—a single image in an animation sequence, usually intended to mean a full screen image.

frame animation—the rapid sequential display of previously-saved graphics pages for the purpose of producing animation.

frame grab—the act of capturing a graphic image and storing it in a buffer or on disk. The graphic image can be one which has been generated by the microcomputer itself or it can be a signal from a video camera, scanner, videocassette player, or television set.

frames per second—the rate of animation, expressed as new images per second. Also called fps.

function declaration—statements which define the name, return type, storage class, and parameter list of a C function. See declaration.

function definition—statements which define the name, return type, storage class, parameter list, and the executable instructions of a C function. See definition.

geometric model—a mathematical defintion of an object.

geometry—a branch of mathematics concerned with the relationship between shapes, angles and distances.

global variable—a variable in a program which is available to all portions and subroutines of the program. A local variable is available only to the function in which it is declared. A variable which is declared outside of any function is global by default.

gnomon—a visual representation of the x,y,z axis system in a 3D CAD program.

graphic array—a rectangular portion of the display buffer which has been saved in RAM as a bit array for later retrieval.

graphic array animation—placing one or more graphic arrays on the display screen (ie into the display buffer) in order to produce animation. Also called software sprite animation, bitblt animation, and block animation. Also refer to the author's book High-Performance Graphics In C: Animation and Simulation (Windcrest book #3049).

graphics driver—a module (usually written in assembly language) designed to interact with the graphics hardware, thereby creating graphics in a particular screen mode.

graphics editor—the interface which allows the user to create and modify computer graphics. CAD, CADD, and draw programs can be considered to be graphics editors.

graphics programmer—an individual capable of creating, testing, debugging, maintaining, improving, and running graphics programs.

graphics page—an area of RAM containing the data to fill the display screen with graphics. The graphics page may or may not be the same as the screen buffer, which is the page being currently displayed.

GW-BASIC—a BASIC interpreter, often used to create prototype programs. GW-BASIC is manufactured by Microsoft Corporation and is licensed to various microcomputer manufacturers. According to programmers' folklore GW is an acronym for "gee whiz".

hacker—a person who is dedicated to high quality programming, especially programming performed for its own sake. By definition, good hackers are good programmers. In recent years the term has come to be associated with persons who attempt to unlawfully penetrate computer security systems.

halftoning—mixing pixels of different colors to simulate varying shades of a color. Also called bit tiling. Also refer to the author's book High-Performance CAD Graphics In C (Windcrest book #3059).

hang—a program failure resulting in an unwanted endless loop.

hardware—the physical and mechanical parts of a microcomputer system.

hatch—the area fill pattern used by CAD software to simulate the ink shading techniques used by many draftspersons.

heap—an area in RAM where data is stored. Also called the default data segment.

The far heap is free high memory often unused by the program, but also available for data storage.

hertz—one cycle per second.

heuristic—the use of trial and error, intuition, or experience to solve a programming problem.

hexadecimal—the base 16 numbering system. The decimal system uses base 10. The base is also called the radix.

hex—same as hexadecimal. A hexadecimal value is prefixed by the 0x symbol in C, by the &H symbol in BASIC, and is followed by the H symbol in assembly language.

hidden line—in graphics programming, a line which should be hidden by another graphic. Also refer to the author's books *High-Performance Graphics In C: Animation and Simulation* (Windcrest book #3049) and High-Performance CAD Graphics In C (Windcrest book #3059).

hidden page—a graphics page which is not currently being displayed.

hidden surface—in graphics modeling, a polygonal plane surface which is hidden by other surfaces.

hidden surface removal—the algorithmic process of removing from the 3D model all surfaces which should be hidden from view. Visible surface algorithms falls into two broad categories: image-space methods and object-space methods. A detailed discussion appears in the author's book *High-Performance CAD Graphics In C* (Windcrest book #3059).

high-performance graphics—refers to graphics applications which stress speed, color, complexity, or fidelity.

HSV—the hue-saturation-value color model.

image file—a binary file on diskette, hard disk, or virtual disk, which contains a graphic image or the algorithm for recreating the image. Common standards include the TIFF, PCX, and CGM formats.

include file—a text file which is logically (but not physically) merged into the user's source code at compile time. An include file is usually a file which contains declarations and definitions, called a header file.

increment—to increase by a specified amount.

indirection—generally, the act of addressing a variable in memory, but specifically the indirection operator (*) which is used in C to declare a pointer. See pointer.

inline code—a section of computer code which does not jump to any functions or subroutines to assist it in completing its assigned tasks. Inline code generally executes quicker than modular code.

instance—an occurrence of a graphical entity in a drawing.

instancing—creating a complex 2D or 3D model by multiple occurrences of the same entity at different locations in the drawing.

integer—a whole number with no fractional parts or decimal point. An integer is normally considered to require two bytes of storage. C signed integers (int) range from -32,768 to 32,767. C unsigned integers (unsigned) range from 0 to 65,535. A signed long integer (long) ranges from -2,147,483,648 to +2,147,483,647. An unsigned long integer (unsigned long) can represent values from 0 to 4,294,967,295.

interactive—accepting input from, and returning feedback to, the user of the computer.

interactive graphics—relating to a computer program which creates or modifies a graphical display in response to user input.

interpreter—a program that executes another program one line at a time. IBM BASICA and GW-BASIC are examples of interpreters.

iterative—repetitive.

keyword—see token.

lamina—a plane which can be viewed from either side.

library—the file that contains modules of object code which comprise the functions available for use by the programmer's C program.

license—the right to use an intellectual property such as a book, software program, musical recording, painting, et cetera. Copyright is the right to copy an intellectual property, which is rarely included in software licenses.

light pen—a pencil-shaped pointing device, through which the microprocessor reads a pixel location for use by the applications program.

line clipping—deletion of a part of a line or graphic which exceeds the physical range of the display screen or viewport.

line styling—using a series of pixel attributes to generate dotted or dashed lines. Also refers to dithering.

LISP—a high level programming language used in artificial intelligence applications. LISP is an acronym for list processing language. LISP works on symbols rather than numbers.

local variable—same as static variable. See also global variable.

logical operators—&& and ||, which perform logical operations on bytes being compared. The && token is used to AND two bytes (the resulting bit will be on only if both the bits being evaluated were on). The || token is used to OR two bytes (the resulting bit will be on if either of the bits being evaluated were on).

LOGO—a high level language used for educational purposes, especially the teaching of geometry and logical thinking.

loop—the iteration or repetition of a group of program instructions.

MASM—an acronym for macro assembler: an assembly language compiler capable of including separately created modules into the finished program. IBM Macro Assembler and Microsoft Macro Assembler are the industry standards.

MCGA—an acronym for multicolor graphics array, which is the proprietary graphics adapter used in the IBM Personal System/2 8086-based personal computer.

medium memory model—an arrangement of RAM for a C program whereby data is limited to 64K but the size of executable code is limited only by available memory.

memory-mapped video—an arrangement whereby the bit contents of an area of RAM correspond directly to the pixels on the display screen. Sometimes used to mean bit map.

memory model—one of the arrangements which C uses to set up memory space for executable code and data.

menu—a series of options presented on the display screen from which the user is to choose.

menu bar—the horizontal graphic from which pull-down menus are positioned.

merge—to combine two or more disk files, programs, or graphic images. See overlay.

microcomputer—see PC.

mode—an operating condition, form, format, or technique. A graphics mode refers to the pixel resolution and availability of colors in a hardware operating condition.

modeling—creating a geometric shape which represents a 3D object on the display screen. Also refer to the author's books *High-Performance Graphics In C: Animation and Simulation* (Windcrest book #3049) and *High-Performance CAD Graphics In C* (Windcrest book #3059).

MODULA-2—a compiled language useful for systems programming and real-time programming.

modular—comprised of individual modules, subroutines, functions, subprograms, or components. See module.

modular programming—the design and creation of programs which use independent modules of code to accomplish specific tasks, thereby completing the overall task.

module—a subroutine in a program. Also called a function by C, a subroutine by BASIC, a subprogram by QuickBASIC and Turbo BASIC, and a procedure by assembly language.

mouse—a hand-held device designed to be rolled across a desktop in order to cause movement of cursors or graphics on the display screen. Called a pointing device by IBM.

mtbf—an acronym for mean time between failures, which is the average length of time that hardware or software will operate before failing.

multi-buffer animation—sometimes used as another name for dynamic page flipping animation, but more often employed to mean frame animation. Also refer to the author's books *High-Performance Graphics In C: Animation and Simulation* (Windcrest book #3049) and *High-Performance CAD Graphics In C* (Windcrest book #3059).

multiplicative operators—* and /, which are multiplication and division.

native code—executable code which is machine-specific (CPU-specific). See also op code.

nested loop—a program loop contained within a larger loop.

90/10 rule—according to programmers' folklore 10% of the program code usually performs 90% of the computing during run-time.

non-disclosure agreement—a contractual undertaking not to disclose proprietary information.

null pointer—a pointer to nothing. See pointer.

object code—machine code. A compiler or assembler takes source code (which can be understood by the programmer) and produces object code (which can be understood by the microprocessor). Raw object code must normally be linked to other modules or library routines before it can be run.

object file—a file containing relocatable object code, which usually must be linked to other modules before it can be executed.

OEM—original equipment manufacturer.

online help—a context-sensitive database of text statements which is available to the user of a program while the program is running. The F1 key is usually used as a hot key to activate the online help.

OOP—object-oriented programming, whereby each independent module contains both executable code and the data upon which it operates. Procedural-oriented programming usually involves modules which contain only executable code and which operate upon a common database of data (ie the default data segment).

op code—an acronym for operational code, which is comprised of the instructions recognized by the central processing unit (CPU). See also native code.

operand—a constant or a variable that is operated upon by operators in an expression.

optimize—to improve a program's speed of execution, while at the same time reducing the amount of memory it requires. A cleverly optimized program is often called elegant.

OS/2—the multitasking operating system developed by IBM and Microsoft.

overlay—a section of program code which is loaded at run-time from disk into RAM over an existing section of code, thereby replacing the previous code.

page flipping—quickly putting a different graphics page on display for the purpose of creating animation or simulation. Page flipping is used in frame animation and in real-time animation. Also refer to the author's books *High-Performance Graphics In C: Animation and Simulation* (Windcrest book #3049) and *High-Performance CAD Graphics In C* (Windcrest book #3059).

paintbrush program—an interactive graphics program which emphasizes artistic creativity of design and color in the resultant image. Also called a draw program.

painter's algorithm—a method of hidden object removal. See z-buffer method. Also refer to the author's book *High-Performance CAD Graphics In C* (Windcrest book #3059).

pan—to move an image to the left or to the right.

parameter—a value which a function expects to receive when it is called. Also called an argument, although Microsoft makes a distinction between the two.

PASCAL—a compiled, high level programming language used mainly for business applications. PASCAL is noted for its highly structured programs and its ability to teach programming skills. TURBO PASCAL has created a large user base for this language on personal computers.

PC—an acronym for personal computer. A personal computer is powerful enough for serious business, scientific, engineering, and graphics applications, yet inexpensive enough to permit individuals to purchase it. PC can mean a PC, an XT, an AT, a PS/2, or any personal computer compatible with these models. Personal computer is synonymous with microcomputer.

pel—IBM 's acronym for picture element, called a pixel by nearly everyone else. A pixel is the smallest addressable graphic or dot on a display screen. See pixel.

personal computer—see PC.

PIC—the picture interchange format standard used for saving and transferring computer images.

ping-pong animation—another name for real-time animation (dynamic page flipping animation). Also refer to the author's book *High-Performance Graphics In C: Animation and Simulation* (Windcrest book #3049).

pixel—an acronym for picture element, called a pel by IBM. A pixel is the smallest addressable graphic on a display screen. A pixel is comprised of a red dot, a green dot, and a blue dot, each of which is excited by the electron guns of the cathode ray tube.

plane equation—a vector formula which describes the qualities of a plane surface, including the location of a given point relative to the surface of the plane. Plane equations are useful for hidden surface removal. Also refer to the author's book *High-Performance CAD Graphics In C* (Windcrest book #3059).

pointer—a variable that contains the address of another variable. See null pointer.

polygon—usually intended to mean a plane surface used to create a 3D solid model constructed by the B-rep method. Also used to describe a multi-sided, closed geometric shape.

pop-up menu—a menu which is created as an island on the screen, unconnected to any other graphics.

PROLOG—an interpreted, high level language used for artificial intelligence applications and database management systems. Japan has formally adopted PROLOG as its official language for nationwide development of AI applications.

prototype—the initial declaration of a function in a C program, usually containing the return type and argument list of the function. The C compiler uses the prototype information to ensure that proper arguments are being used to call the function.

pull-down menu—a menu which is appended to a menu bar, as if it were being pulled down from the menu bar.

radian—a length of arc based upon the relationship between elements of a unit circle.

radiosity—an algorithm which considers the radiant characteristics of light in order to calculate the brightness or darkness of different surfaces in a 3D scene.

radix—the base of a numbering system. The radix of the hexadecimal numbering system is 16, of the decimal system is 10.

RAM—an acronym for random access memory, also called user memory, user RAM, and volatile memory. It is the memory available for use by programs and graphics. When the microcomputer's power is shut off, the contents of RAM are obliterated.

RAM disk—a virtual disk which exists only in RAM memory. See virtual disk.

ray tracing—an algorithm which calculates the illumination level of a model by tracing a ray of light back from the eye to the model and eventually to the light source(s).

real-time—used to describe a program which must respond to events in the real world as the events occur.

real-time animation—also called double-buffer page-flipping animation and ping-pong animation. The microprocessor displays a completed image while constructing the next image on a hidden page. The pages are flipped and the procedure continues.

redundancy—unneeded duplication of software or hardware, usually for the sake of protection against unexpected failures.

refresh buffer—the display buffer. The display hardware uses the display buffer to refresh the display monitor.

regen—regeneration of a graphic entity, also called redraw. The term is used primarily in conjunction with CAD and CADD programs.

relational operators—$<$, $>$, $<=$, $>=$, $==$, and $!=$, which in C mean less-than, greater-than, less-than-or-equal-to, greater-than-or-equal-to, equal-to, and not-equal-to. A relational operator compares the relationship between two values. Relational operators are often used as decision-making tools.

relocatable—OBJ code which does not contain absolute (hard-coded) addresses and which must yet be linked to other OBJ modules or library routines to produce EXE code. Prior to run-time, the operating system assigns memory offset values for the addresses referenced in the EXE code.

rendering—adding illumination, shading, and color to a 3D model. Personal computers using a CGA, an EGA, or a VGA can produce fully-shaded 3D solid models by using an illumination matrix and vector math. Also refer to the author's books *High-Performance Graphics In C: Animation and Simulation* (Windcrest book #3049) and *High-Performance CAD Graphics In C* (Windcrest book #3059).

replay mode—regeneration of a sequence of interactive events, especially in games programming and simulation programming. Many replay algorithms work by storing the user's keystrokes in a buffer for later retrieval when a replay is requested.

ROM—an acronym for read-only memory, which cannot be changed by the user. Turning off the power supply has no effect on ROM, which uses magnetic technology instead of electric technology to store data.

ROM BIOS—same as BIOS.

run-time—the time during which the program is executing.

run-time library—the file containing C routines which a program requires during execution.

scalar—a mathematical quantity that has quantity but not direction. A vector has quantity and direction.

SCD—an acronym for standard color display. An SCD is a digital monitor capable of displaying 16 colors at a maximum resolution of 640x200 pixels. See also analog and ECD.

screen buffer—the area of memory which is being displayed on the screen, usually located at address B8000 hex on the CGA and at address A0000 hex on the EGA and VGA. The location of the screen buffer can be changed on the VGA and EGA by selecting a different graphics page.

scroll—to move a graphic or alphanumeric character upwards or downwards on the display screen.

segment—a block of computer memory whose length is 64K or less.

semantics—the study of the meanings of signs, symbols, and tokens. See semiotics.

semiotics—the study of the function of signs, symbols, and tokens in natural languages, artificial languages, and computer languages. See also syntactics.

sequential-evaluation operator—in C the sequential-evaluation operator (,) is used to separate a series of sequentially evaluated expressions.

SFX—sound effect(s).

shading—adding the effects of illumination, shadow, and color to a 3D model. Sometimes called rendering. Also refer to the author's books *High-Performance CAD Graphics In C* (Windcrest book #3059).

shift operators—<< and >>, which shift the bits in a byte to the left or to the right.

SIMULA—a compiled, high level language used for simulations. SIMULA is an acronym for SIMULAtion language.

simulation—a programming attempt to imitate a real-world event.

simulator—a program that imitates a real-world event.

sine—the sine of an angle in a right-angle triangle defines the relationship between the hypotenuse and the side opposite.

small memory model—an arrangement of RAM for a C program whereby the code and data are limited to one segment each.

SMALLTALK—a compiled, high level language used for simulation and the teaching of thinking skills.

snap—the size of movement of a crosshair cursor in a CAD program. Often used to describe the cursor's ability to skip to the nearest existing entity or line on the screen.

SNOBOL—a high level language used for manipulating non-numerical characters.

software sprite—see graphic array and bitblt.

software sprite animation—see graphic array animation and bitblt.

solid model—a 3D model with hidden surfaces removed. It can be constructed by either the CSG (constructive solid geometry) method or the B-rep (boundary representation) method.

source code—program instructions written in the original programming language. A program listing is a human-readable version on paper of the program source code.

stack—a single-ended queue in memory, where values are stored and retrieved on a first-in, last-out basis (FILO).

statement—an instruction in the program source code. Sometimes called an expression.

static variable—a variable which is available to only the function in which it has been declared. Also called a local variable. See also global variable.

stream—the flow of data to or from a file or other output device.

structure—a set of items grouped under a single name. The elements may be of different types. In an array, the elements must be of similar type.

stub—see do-nothing routine.

subroutine—a subordinate, self-contained portion (or module) of a program designed to perform a specific task. A subroutine is called a function in C, a procedure in assembly language, a subprogram in QuickBASIC and Turbo BASIC, and a module in Modula-2.

surface normal—a line which is perpendicular to the surface of a plane in a 3D environment. The illumination level of a surface can be derived by comparing the surface normal to the angle of incidence of incoming light rays. Also refer to the author's book *High-Performance CAD Graphics In C* (Windcrest book #3059).

syntactics—the study of the relationship between signs, symbols, and tokens and the people who use them.

syntax—the grammar to be used with a programming language.

system overhead—the amount of time the microcomputer allocates to general housekeeping functions instead of executing programs or generating graphics.

3D—three-dimensional graphics, consisting of width, depth, and height. In microcomputer graphics, 3D images are usually described by x,y,z coordinates.

2D—two-dimensional graphics, consisting of width and height. In microcomputer graphics, 2D images are usually defined by x,y coordinates.

TIFF—the device-independent tag image file format, a method of encoding image information so image files can be transferred between different application programs or between different computer systems.

toggle—to change from one possible state to another.

token—a group of characters which is the basic element recognized by a C compiler. Also called a keyword.

touch-screen—a display screen which is made sensitive to finger touch by means of an electronic matrix.

touring—see walkthrough.

trackball—a pointing device similar to a mouse, except the ball is located on the top surface of the device, meant to be activated by moving the palm of the hand over the ball.

trigonometry—a branch of mathematics concerned with the relationship of two sides opposite a specific angle in a right-angle triangle. Sine and cosine are particularly useful for 3D microcomputer graphics.

turnkey system—a computer system consisting of hardware, software, user's guides, system documentation, installation, support, service, and training. Often used to describe high-performance graphics workstations.

type—attribute. For example, an integer variable is of type int.

type cast—the conversion of a value from one type to another type.

unary operator—an operator that manipulates a single variable. C provides the following unary operators: logical NOT (!), bitwise compliment (~), arithmetic negation (-), indirection (*), address-of (&), and unary plus (or arithmetic increment) (+).

union—a C structure which allocates the same memory space to different variables. The variables are often of different types.

user-servile—describes a program which has been designed to serve the needs of the user, as opposed to programs which require the user to adapt in order to use the program.

utility program—a program used as a tool, designed to perform a utilitarian task or system housekeeping type of function. For example, a program which dumps the contents of a screen buffer to a printer is a utility program.

variable—a quantity whose value can change during program execution.

vector—a mathematical value that has quantity and direction. A scalar value has only quantity.

VGA—the propriety graphics adapter in the IBM Personal System/2 series of 80286 and 80386-based microcomputers. The VGA provides CGA, MCGA, and EGA graphics modes, in addition to its enhanced modes of 640x480 16-color and 320x200 256-color. VGA graphics are supported by QuickC and by Turbo C. Also refers to third-party workalite graphics adapters.

view coordinates—the x,y,z coordinates which describe how a 3D model will appear to a hypothetical viewer after rotation and translation. The view coordinates must be converted to display coordinates prior to being displayed on the monitor. Also refer to the author's book *High-Performance CAD Graphics In C* (Windcrest book #3059).

viewport—a rectangular portion of the display screen which becomes a mini-screen within the larger area of the whole display screen. A viewport is a subset of the display screen.

virtual disk—a simulated disk which exists only in RAM memory. Also called a RAM disk. Because no physical disk drives are involved, reads and writes to the disk are much faster. All data contained in a virtual disk is obliterated when the microcomputer is turned off.

virtual screen—a written-to graphics buffer which is not the display buffer. A written-to, hidden graphics page is a virtual screen, although the term is usually reserved for buffers which are much larger than the screen buffer. Panning and scrolling of graphics can be achieved by sending carefully selected portions of the virtual screen to the screen buffer.

visibility—describes whether or not a function or a variable can be used by other parts of a C program.

visible page—the graphics page currently being displayed.

void—in C, used to mean undefined.

walk-through—frame animation of a 3D architectural model which simulates a walk-through by the viewer. Called touring by some 3D CAD programs.

window—a viewport of the display screen. Often used to describe the logical relationship between the display screen and the world coordinates in 3D graphics programming.

wire-frame drawing—a skeletal drawing of an object created by drawing only the edges of surfaces, not the surfaces themselves. The object is depicted as transparent. No effort is made to conceal surfaces or lines which should be hidden.

witness lines—lines which connect a graphic entity to the dimension lines which describe it (in a CAD drafting program).

world coordinates—the raw x,y,z coordinates which describe the shape of an object in a scene context. World coordinates are rotated and translated to produce view coordinates, which describe how a 3D model will appear to a hypothetical viewer. View coordinates are converted to 2D display coordinates before being displayed on the monitor. Also refer to the author's book *High-Performance CAD Graphics In C* (Windcrest book #3059).

written-to page—the graphics page to which the microprocessor is currently writing, also called the active page.

z-buffer—the plane which represents near/far in the 3D environment, often used as the criterion for the correct drawing sequence of multiple models, where nearer objects must obscure farther objects.

z-buffer method—a method of hidden surface removal. See z-buffer. The z-buffer method is also known as the painter's algorithm.

Index

Index

About the
Author

The author, Lee Adams is, internationally known for his series of graphics teaching books, published and distributed worldwide by Windcrest, a division of TAB BOOKS.

Lee Adams is an acknowledged personal computer graphics expert and bestselling author. His books about graphics programming on personal computers are read by programmers in the United States, Canada, Great Britain, and Europe. He creates graphics software in QuickC, Turbo C, Lattice C, MASM, and Quick-BASIC. His books can be found in the private libraries of many software publishers, graphics hardware manufacturers, and professional programmers—as well as beginning and intermediate C programmers.

Mr. Adams is a member of the National Computer Graphics Association and the Authors' Guild. He has 18 years of experience in visual communication, including television animation. He has taught classes in 3D perspective drawing, graphic design, and advertising illustration. His other interests include hiking, environmental issues, animal rights, current affairs, psychology, and history.

Lee Adams is the author of five other bestselling books about graphics programming published by Windcrest, a division of TAB Books, including:

High-Performance Graphics in C: Animation and Simulation
High-Performance CAD Graphics in C
Supercharged Graphics: A Programmer's Source Code Toolbox

High Performance Interactive Graphics: Modeling, Rendering, and Animating
  for IBM PCs and Compatibles
High-Speed Animation and Simulation for Microcomputers

OTHER BOOKS BY THE AUTHOR

Windcrest Books is pleased to offer five related books in the high-performance graphics series by the same author.

High-Performance CAD Graphics in C (#3059, published March 1989, ISBN 0-8306-9359-9)—provides guidance in producing realistic 3D images on your personal computer, including automatic hidden surface removal and illumination-based shading techniques. Over 6,000 lines of source code for QuickC and Turbo C. Compatible with VGA, EGA, MCGA, CGA graphics adapters. $29.95. This popular reference is already in its second printing. Companion disks for QuickC and Turbo C are available.

High-Performance Graphics in C: Animation and Simulation (#3049, published November 1988, ISBN 0-8306-9349-1)—demonstrates high-speed techniques for frame animation, real-time animation, and bitblt animation of 2D and 3D objects. Over 5,000 lines of source code for QuickC and Turbo C useful for creating animated educational, presentation, business, realistic, video game, and 3D modeling graphics. Compatible with VGA, EGA, MCGA, CGA graphics adapters. $29.95. This programmers' favorite is already in its third printing. Companion disks for QuickC and Turbo C are available.

Supercharged Graphics: A Programmer's Source Code Toolbox (#2959, published May 1988, ISBN 0-8306-2959-9)—provides ready-to-run examples of full-featured, interactive graphics programs for QuickBASIC, Turbo BASIC, GW-BASIC, and BASICA programmers. Included is source code for three full-length programs: a drawing program, a multi-layered drafting program, and a 3D modeling & rendering program. Compatible with EGA, CGA, and PCjr graphics adapters. $29.95. This standard reference for BASIC programmers is now in its second printing. A companion disk is available.

High Performance Interactive Graphics: Modeling, Rendering and Animating for IBM PCs and Compatibles (#2879, published November 1987, ISBN 0-8306-2879-7)—teaches programming techniques for producing fully-shaded, realistic 3D images on your personal computer using QuickBASIC, Turbo BASIC, GW-BASIC, and BASICA. The programs support EGA, CGA, and PCjr graphics adapters. Now in its fourth printing. A companion disk is available.

High-Speed Animation and Simulation for Microcomputers (#2859, published January 1987, ISBN 0-8306-0459-6)—is still the classic reference for animation techniques on personal computers. Over 4,000 lines of source code in BASICA and GW-BASIC, combined with superb text and illustrations, provides the interested reader with tools for animating on the CGA and PCjr, with conversion guidelines for the EGA—and the programming principles apply to the VGA and MCGA, too. $29.95. This collector's edition is in its fourth printing. A companion disk is available.

Books may be ordered direct from Windcrest Books (Division of TAB BOOks), Blue Ridge Summit, PA USA 17294-0850, or from The Computer Book Club, or through good computer bookstores in the United States, Canada, Great Britain, and Europe.

SUPERCHARGED C GRAPHICS:
A Programmer's Source Code Toolbox